Survival Communications
in Indiana: North Region

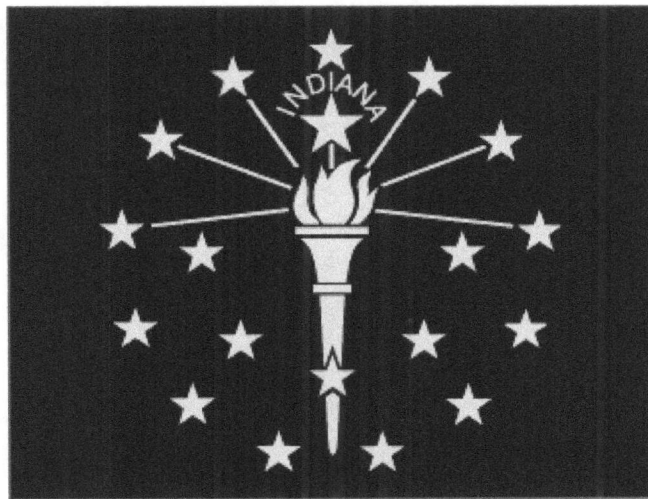

John E. Parnell, KK4HWX

13 ISBN 978-1-62512-008-3

Cover design by:
Lynda Colón
FREELANCE GRAPHIC DESIGN &
MARKETING COMMUNICATIONS
www.hirelynda.webs.com

I do wish to acknowledge the hard work of **Angie Shirley** in putting together the database required for this book. Without her efforts, this book could not have been done.

Titles available in this series:

Survival Communications in Alabama
Survival Communications in Alaska
Survival Communications in Arizona
Survival Communications in Arkansas
Survival Communications in California
Survival Communications in Colorado
Survival Communications in Connecticut
Survival Communications in Delaware
Survival Communications in Florida
Survival Communications in Georgia
Survival Communications in Hawaii
Survival Communications in Idaho
Survival Communications in Illinois
Survival Communications in Indiana
Survival Communications in Iowa
Survival Communications in Kansas
Survival Communications in Kentucky
Survival Communications in Louisiana
Survival Communications in Maine
Survival Communications in Maryland
Survival Communications in Massachusetts
Survival Communications in Michigan
Survival Communications in Minnesota
Survival Communications in Mississippi
Survival Communications in Missouri

Survival Communications in Montana
Survival Communications in Nebraska
Survival Communications in Nevada
Survival Communications in New Hampshire
Survival Communications in New Jersey
Survival Communications in New Mexico
Survival Communications in New York
Survival Communications in North Carolina
Survival Communications in North Dakota
Survival Communications in Ohio
Survival Communications in Oklahoma
Survival Communications in Oregon
Survival Communications in Pennsylvania
Survival Communications in Rhode Island
Survival Communications in South Carolina
Survival Communications in South Dakota
Survival Communications in Tennessee
Survival Communications in Texas
Survival Communications in Utah
Survival Communications in Vermont
Survival Communications in Virginia
Survival Communications in Washington
Survival Communications in West Virginia
Survival Communications in Wisconsin
Survival Communications in Wyoming

The above titles are available from your favorite online or brick-and-mortar bookstore or directly from the publisher at Tutor Turtle Press LLC, 1027 S. Pendleton St. – Suite B-10, Easley, SC 29642.

TABLE OF CONTENTS

Appendix A – Indiana Ham Radio Clubs

ARRL Affiliated Amateur and Ham Radio Clubs – By City

Appendix B – Indiana: North Region Ham Licensees by City

Survival Communications in Indiana

Perhaps you have prepared for WTSHTF or TEOTWAWKI with respect to food, water, self-defense and shelter. But what about communication?

Whenever there is a disaster (hurricane, earthquake, economic collapse, nuclear war, EMF, solar eruption, etc.), the normal means of communication that we're all reliant upon (cell phone, land line phone, the Internet, etc.) will probably be, at best, sporadic and at worst, non-existent.

As this author sees it, short of smoke signals and mirrors, there are three options for communication in "trying times": (1) GMRS or FRS radios; (2) CB radios; and (3) ham or amateur radio. Let's consider each of these options to come up with the most acceptable one.

GMRS (General Mobile Radio Service) / FRS (Family Radio Service)

GMRS (General Mobile Radio Service) / FRS (Family Radio Service) radios work optimally over short distances where there is minimal interference. Originally designed to be used as pagers, particularly inside a building or other such confined area, these radios are low-cost and convenient to carry. Unfortunately their small size and light weight comes with a trade-off – short range and short battery life. These radios are supposed to be able to communicate for up to 25-30 miles. Right. That's on level terrain, without buildings or trees getting in the way. While battery life technology is constantly improving, you will need spare batteries to keep communicating or someway of recharging the ones in the radio. In this author's opinion, GMRS/FRS radios are not first choice when concerned with medium or long range communication.

CB (Citizens Band)

CB (Citizens Band) radios operate in a frequency range originally reserved for ham or amateur radio operation. Because of the overwhelming number of people wishing quick, low-cost, regulation-free communication, the FCC (Federal Communication Commission) split off a portion of the frequency spectrum and allowed anyone to purchase a CB radio and start communicating. No test. No license. Just personal/business communication. Today, CB radios are readily available in such outlets as eBay and Craigslist. This author has seen them at yard/garage/tag sales and at flea markets.

CB radios come in a variety of "flavors." Fixed units, sometimes referred to as base units are intended for home use. For the most part, they derive their power from the utility company. In the event of loss of electricity, most base units can also be connected to a 12-volt battery, like that in your car/truck. If you choose to obtain a fixed unit, make sure you know how to connect the unit to the battery – ahead of time. Trying to figure this out when you're under extra stress is not a good situation.

A second type of CB radio is designed to be mobile, that is, installed in your car/truck. It gets its power from the vehicle's battery. You can either attach an antenna permanently to the vehicle or have a removable, magnetic type antenna.

The third type of CB radio is designed for handheld use. They are small and light. Most weigh less than a pound and operate on batteries. Yes, using batteries in a CB poses the same limitations as those by the GMRS/FRS radios, but have the added advantage that most handheld units come with a cigarette lighter adapter. Comes in handy when you are on the move and wish to be able to communicate both from a vehicle and also when you have to abandon it.

While they have a greater range than GMRS/FRS radios, CB radios are, legally, limited to operate on 40 channels, with a power rating of four (4) watts or less. Yes, it is possible to alter CB radios to get around these limitations, but not legally,

Ham/Amateur Radio

Ham/Amateur radio is very appealing. With a ham radio, you are not limited to less than 50 miles, but can communicate with anyone in the world (who also has access to a ham radio, of course).

Standardized Amateur Radio Prepper Communications Plan

In the event of a nationwide catastrophic disaster, the nationwide network of Amateur Radio licensed preppers will need a set of standardized meeting frequencies to share information and coordinate activities between various prepper groups. This Standardized Amateur Radio Communications Plan establishes a set of frequencies on the 80 meter, 40 meter, 20 meter, and 2 meter Amateur Radio bands for use during these types of catastrophic disasters.

Routine nets will not be held on all of these frequencies, but preppers are encouraged to use them when coordinating with other preppers on a routine basis. Routine nets may be conducted by The American Preparedness Radio Net (TAPRN) on these or other frequencies as they see fit. However, TAPRN will promote the use of these standardized frequencies by all Amateur Radio licensed preppers during times of catastrophic disaster. The promotion of this Standardized Amateur Radio Communications Plan is encouraged by all means within the prepper community, including via Amateur Radio, Twitter, Facebook, and various blogs.

Standardized Frequencies and Modes
80 Meters – 3.818 MHz LSB (TAPRN Net: Sundays at 9 PM ET)   40 Meters – 7.242 MHz LSB   40 Meters Morse Code / Digital – 7.073 MHz USB (TAPRN: Sundays at 7:30 PM ET on CONTESTIA 4/250)   20 Meters – 14.242 MHz USB   2 Meters – 146.420 MHz FM

Nets and Network Etiquette

In times of nationwide catastrophic disaster, the ability of any one prepper to initiate and sustain themselves as a net control may be limited by the availability of power and other resource shortages. However, all licensed preppers are encouraged to maintain a listening watch on these frequencies as often as possible during a catastrophic disaster. Preppers may routinely announce themselves in the following manner:

• This is [Your Callsign Phonetically] in [Your State], maintaining a listening watch on [Standard Frequency] for any preppers on frequency seeking information or looking to provide information. Please call [Your Callsign Phonetically]. Preppers exchanging information that may require follow up should agree upon a designated time to return to the frequency and provide further information. If other stations are utilizing the frequency at the designated time you return, maintain watch and proceed with your communications when those stations are finished. If your communications are urgent and the stations on frequency are not passing information of a critical nature, interrupt with the word "Break" and request use of the frequency.

For More Information

Catastrophe Network: http://www.catastrophenetwork.org or @CatastropheNet on Twitter The American Preparedness Radio Network: http://www.taprn.com or @TAPRN on Twitter

© 2011 Catastrophe Network, Please Distribute Freely

In order to use a ham radio, legally, one must be licensed to do so by the FCC (other countries have analogous governmental bodies to regulate ham radio). To obtain a license is quite easy – take a test and pay your license fee. There are currently three classes of license – Technician, General, and Amateur Extra. With each of these licenses come specific abilities.

Technician class is the beginning level. The exam consists of 35 multiple choice questions randomly drawn from a pool of 395 questions. The question pool is readily available online for free downloading (http://www.ncvec.org/downloads/Revised%20Element%202.Pdf) or in such publications at *Ham Radio License Manual Revised 2nd Edition* (ISBN 978-0-87259-097-7). The current Technician pool of questions is to be used from July 1, 2010 to June 30, 2014. Be sure the question pool you are studying from is current. You will need to score at least 26 correct to pass. (Do not worry, Morse Code is no longer on the test, although many ham operators use it anyway.) You do not need to take a formal class in order to qualify to take the exam. You can learn the material on your own. Most people spend 10-15 hours studying and then successfully take the exam. The cost of taking the exam is under $20. The exam is given in MANY locations throughout the US. Usually the exam is given by area ham clubs. You do not have to belong to the club to take the exam. Check Appendix A for a listing of clubs in Indiana.

Topics for the Technician License in Amateur Radio

The Technician license exam covers such topics as basic regulations, operating practices, and electronic theory, with a focus on VHF and UHF applications. Below is the syllabus for the Technician Class.

Subelement T1 – FCC Rules, descriptions and definitions for the amateur radio service, operator and station license responsibilities

[6 Exam Questions – 6 Groups]

T1A – Amateur Radio services; purpose of the amateur service, amateur-satellite service, operator/primary station license grant, where FCC rules are codified, basis and purpose of FCC rules, meanings of basic terms used in FCC rules

T1B – Authorized frequencies; frequency allocations, ITU regions, emission type, restricted sub-bands, spectrum sharing, transmissions near band edges

T1C – Operator classes and station call signs; operator classes, sequential, special event, and vanity call sign systems, international communications, reciprocal operation, station license licensee, places where the amateur service is regulated by the FCC, name and address on ULS, license term, renewal, grace period

T1D – Authorized and prohibited transmissions

T1E – Control operator and control types; control operator required, eligibility, designation of control operator, privileges and duties, control point, local, automatic and remote control, location of control operator

T1F – Station identification and operation standards; special operations for repeaters and auxiliary stations, third party communications, club stations, station security, FCC inspection

---

Subelement T2 – Operating Procedures

[3 Exam Questions – 3 Groups]

T2A – Station operation; choosing an operating frequency, calling another station, test transmissions, use of minimum power, frequency use, band plans

T2B – VHF/UHF operating practices; SSB phone, FM repeater, simplex, frequency offsets, splits and shifts, CTCSS, DTMF, tone squelch, carrier squelch, phonetics

T2C – Public service; emergency and non-emergency operations, message traffic handling

---

Subelement T3 – Radio wave characteristics, radio and electromagnetic properties, propagation modes

[3 Exam Questions – 3 Groups]

T3A – Radio wave characteristics; how a radio signal travels; distinctions of HF, VHF and UHF; fading, multipath; wavelength vs. penetration; antenna orientation

T3B – Radio and electromagnetic wave properties; the electromagnetic spectrum, wavelength vs. frequency, velocity of electromagnetic waves

T3C – Propagation modes; line of sight, sporadic E, meteor, aurora scatter, tropospheric ducting, F layer skip, radio horizon

Subelement T4 - Amateur radio practices and station setup

[2 Exam Questions – 2 Groups]

T4A – Station setup; microphone, speaker, headphones, filters, power source, connecting a computer, RF grounding

T4B – Operating controls; tuning, use of filters, squelch, AGC, repeater offset, memory channels

Subelement T5 – Electrical principles, math for electronics, electronic principles, Ohm's Law

[4 Exam Questions – 4 Groups]

T5A – Electrical principles; current and voltage, conductors and insulators, alternating and direct current

T5B – Math for electronics; decibels, electronic units and the metric system

T5C – Electronic principles; capacitance, inductance, current flow in circuits, alternating current, definition of RF, power calculations

T5D – Ohm's Law

Subelement T6 – Electrical components, semiconductors, circuit diagrams, component functions

[4 Exam Groups – 4 Questions]

T6A – Electrical components; fixed and variable resistors, capacitors, and inductors; fuses, switches, batteries

T6B – Semiconductors; basic principles of diodes and transistors

T6C – Circuit diagrams; schematic symbols

T6D – Component functions

Subelement T7 – Station equipment, common transmitter and receiver problems, antenna measurements and troubleshooting, basic repair and testing

[4 Exam Questions – 4 Groups]

T7A – Station radios; receivers, transmitters, transceivers

T7B – Common transmitter and receiver problems; symptoms of overload and overdrive, distortion, interference, over and under modulation, RF feedback, off frequency signals; fading and noise; problems with digital communications interfaces

T7C – Antenna measurements and troubleshooting; measuring SWR, dummy loads, feedline failure modes

T7D – Basic repair and testing; soldering, use of a voltmeter, ammeter, and ohmmeter

Subelement T8 – Modulation modes, amateur satellite operation, operating activities, non-voice communications

[4 Exam Questions – 4 Groups]

T8A – Modulation modes; bandwidth of various signals

T8B – Amateur satellite operation; Doppler shift, basic orbits, operating protocols

T8C – Operating activities; radio direction finding, radio control, contests, special event stations, basic linking over Internet

T8D – Non-voice communications; image data, digital modes, CW, packet, PSK31

Subelement T9 – Antennas, feedlines

[2 Exam Groups – 2 Questions]

T9A – Antennas; vertical and horizontal, concept of gain, common portable and mobile antennas, relationships between antenna length and frequency

T9B – Feedlines; types, losses vs. frequency, SWR concepts, matching, weather protection, connectors

Subelement T0 – AC power circuits, antenna installation, RF hazards

[3 Exam Questions – 3 Groups]

T0A – AC power circuits; hazardous voltages, fuses and circuit breakers, grounding, lightning protection, battery safety, electrical code compliance

T0B – Antenna installation; tower safety, overhead power lines

T0C – RF hazards; radiation exposure, proximity to antennas, recognized safe power levels, exposure to others

Once your name and call sign are available in the FCC database, you have the privilege of operating on all VHF (2 m) and UHF (70 cm) frequencies above 30 megahertz (MHz) and HF frequencies 80, 40, and 15 meter, and on the 10 meter band using Morse code (CW), voice, and digital mode. For a Technician license in Indiana, your call sign will consist of a two-letter prefix beginning with K or W, the number nine (9), and a three-letter suffix. The single digit number in the call sign is determined according to which area of the US you obtain your first license. Even though you may move to another state, you keep this number in your call sign. This is also true should you upgrade to a higher license and get a new call sign. The numeral portion of your call sign stays the same.

Call Sign Numbers

Below is a chart showing the various numbers and the state(s) in which you would obtain the number.

Call Sign Number	State(s)
0	CO, IA, KS, MN, MO, NE, ND, SD
1	CT, ME, MA, NH, RI, VT
2	NJ, NY
3	DE, DC, MD, PA
4	AL, FL, GA, KY, NC, SC, TN, VA
5	AR, LA, MS, NM, OK, TX
6	CA
7	AZ, ID, MT, NV, OR, WA, UT, WY
8	MI, OH, WV
9	IL, IN, WI

Residents of Alaska may have any of the following call sign prefixes assigned to them: AL0-7, KL0-7, NL0-7, or WL0-7. Likewise, residents of Hawaii may have the prefix AH6-7, KH6-7, NH6-7, or WH6-7 assigned.

Once you obtain your Technician license, do not stop there. Go and get your General license.

General is the second of three ham license classes. Like the Technician license, to get a General license, you merely have to take a 35-question multiple choice exam and pay your license fee. Passing is still at least 26 correct answers and the fee is the same (less than $20). Again the question pool is available for free online (http://www.ncvec.org/page.php?id=358). It is also available in such print publications as *The ARRL General Class License Manual 7th Edition* (ISBN 978-0-87259-811-9). The current General pool of questions is to be used from July 1, 2011 to June 30, 2015. Be sure the question pool you are using is current. Being a bit more comprehensive than the Technician license, the General license usually requires 15-20 hours of study to learn the material. Check Appendix A for a listing of clubs in Indiana where you might take your exam. Once your name and NEW call sign is listed in the FCC database, you're good to go. For a General license in Indiana, your call sign will consist of a one-letter prefix beginning with K, N or W, the number nine (9), and a three-letter suffix.

Topics for the General License in Amateur Radio

The General license exam covers regulations, operating practices and electronic theory. Below is the syllabus for the General Class.

Subelement G1 – Commission's Rules
(5 Exam Questions – 5 Groups)
G1A – General Class control operator frequency privileges; primary and secondary allocations
G1B – Antenna structure limitations; good engineering and good amateur practice, beacon operation; restricted operation; retransmitting radio signals
G1C – Transmitter power regulations; data emission standards
G1D – Volunteer Examiners and Volunteer Examiner Coordinators; temporary identification
G1E – Control categories; repeater regulations; harmful interference; third party rules; ITU regions

Subelement G2 – Operating procedures
(5 Exam Questions – 5 Groups)
G2A – Phone operating procedures; USB/LSB utilization conventions; procedural signals; breaking into a OSO in progress; VOX operation
G2B – Operating courtesy; band plans, emergencies, including drills and emergency communications
G2C – CW operating procedures and procedural signals; Q signals and common abbreviations; full break in
G2D – Amateur Auxiliary; minimizing interference; HF operations

G2E – Digital operating; procedures, procedural signals and common abbreviations

Subelement G3 – Radio wave propagation

(3 Exam Questions – 3 Groups)

G3A – Sunspots and solar radiation; ionospheric disturbances; propagation forecasting and indices

G3B – Maximum Usable Frequency; Lowest Usable Frequency; propagation

G3C – Ionospheric layers; critical angle and frequency; HF scatter; Near Vertical Incidence Sky waves

Subelement G4 – Amateur radio practices

(5 Exam Questions – 5 Groups)

G4A – Station Operation and setup

G4B – Test and monitoring equipment; two-tone test

G4C – Interference with consumer electronics; grounding; DSP

G4D – Speech processors; S meters; sideband operation near band edges

G4E – HF mobile radio installations; emergency and battery powered operation

Subelement G5 – Electrical principles

(3 Exam Questions – 3 Groups)

G5A – Reactance; inductance; capacitance; impedance; impedance matching

G5B – The Decibel; current and voltage dividers; electrical power calculations; sine wave root-mean-square (RMS) values; PEP calculations

G5C – Resistors; capacitors and inductors in series and parallel; transformers

Subelement G6 – Circuit components

(3 Exam Questions – 3 Groups)

G6A – Resistors; capacitors; inductors

G6B – Rectifiers; solid state diodes and transistors; vacuum tubes; batteries

G6C – Analog and digital integrated circuits (ICs); microprocessors; memory; I/O devices; microwave ICs (MMICs); display devices

Subelement G7 – Practical circuits

(3 Exam Questions – 3 Groups)

G7A – Power supplies; schematic symbols

G7B – Digital circuits; amplifiers and oscillators

G7C – Receivers and transmitters; filters, oscillators

Subelement G8 – Signals and emissions

(2 Exam Questions – 2 Groups)

G8A – Carriers and modulation; AM; FM; single and double sideband; modulation envelope; overmodulation

G8B – Frequency mixing; multiplication; HF data communications; bandwidths of various modes; deviation

Subelement G9 – Antennas and feed lines

(4 Exam Questions – 4 Groups)

G9A – Antenna feed lines; characteristic impedance and attenuation; SWR calculation, measurement and effects; matching networks

G9B – Basic antennas

G9C – Directional antennas

G9D – Specialized antennas

Subelement G0 – Electrical and RF safety

(2 Exam Questions – 2 Groups)

G0A – RF safety principles, rules and guidelines; routine station elevation

G0B – Safety in the ham shack; electrical shock and treatment, safety grounding, fusing, interlocks, wiring, antenna and tower safety

With a General license, you can use all VHF and UHF frequencies and most of the HF frequencies. You would have access to the 160, 30, 17, 12, and 10 meter bands and access to major parts of the 80, 40, 20, and 15 meter bands. Of course, this is in addition to all bands available to Technician license holders.

Amateur Extra is the third of three ham license classes. Like the Technician and General classes, you merely have to pass a test and pay your fee to get your Amateur Extra license. This class of license is more comprehensive than the lower license classes. The exam is longer – 50 questions – and the minimum passing score is higher – 37. However, once you get your Amateur Extra license, all ham frequencies, VHF, UHF and HF are available for your enjoyment. The Extra exam covers regulations, specialized operating practices, advanced electronics theory, and radio equipment design.

Like for the other license classes, the question pool for the Amateur Extra license is available online for downloading (http://www.ncvec.org/downloads/REVISED%202012-2016%20Extra%20Class%20Pool.doc). It is also available in print form in such publications as *The ARRL Extra Class License Manual Revised 9th Edition* (ISBN 978-0-87259-887-4).

Topics for the Extra License in Amateur Radio

Below is the syllabus for the Amateur Extra Class for July 1, 2012 to June 30, 2016.

Subelement E1 – Commission's Rules

[6 Exam Questions – 6 Groups]

E1A – Operating Standards: frequency privileges; emission standards; automatic message forwarding; frequency sharing; stations aboard ships or aircraft

E1B – Station restrictions and special operations: restrictions on station location; general operating restrictions, spurious emissions, control operator reimbursement; antenna structure restrictions; RACES operations

E1C – Station control: definitions and restrictions pertaining to local, automatic and remote control operation; control operator responsibilities for remote and automatically controlled stations

E1D – Amateur Satellite service: definitions and purpose; license requirements for space stations; available frequencies and bands; telecommand and telemetry operations; restrictions, and special provisions; notification requirements

E1E – Volunteer examiner program: definitions, qualifications, preparation and administration of exams; accreditation; question pools; documentation requirements

E1F – Miscellaneous rules: external RF power amplifiers; national quiet zone; business communications; compensated communications; spread spectrum; auxiliary stations; reciprocal operating privileges; IARP and CEPT licenses; third party communications with foreign countries; special temporary authority

Subelement E2 – Operating procedures

[5 Exam Questions – 5 Groups]

E2A – Amateur radio in space: amateur satellites; orbital mechanics; frequencies and modes; satellite hardware; satellite operations

E2B – Television practices: fast scan television standards and techniques; slow scan television standards and techniques

E2C – Operating methods: contest and DX operating; spread-spectrum transmissions; selecting an operating frequency

E2D – Operating methods: VHF and UHF digital modes; APRS

E2E – Operating methods: operating HF digital modes; error correction

Subelement E3 – Radio wave propagation

[3 Exam Questions – 3 Groups]

E3A – Propagation and technique, Earth-Moon-Earth communications; meteor scatter

E3B – Propagation and technique, trans-equatorial; long path; gray-line; multi-path propagation

E3C – Propagation and technique, Aurora propagation; selective fading; radio-path horizon; take-off angle over flat or sloping terrain; effects of ground on propagation; less common propagation modes

Subelement E4 – Amateur practices

[5 Exam Questions – 5 Groups]

E4A – Test equipment: analog and digital instruments; spectrum and network analyzers, antenna analyzers; oscilloscopes; testing transistors; RF measurements

E4B – Measurement technique and limitations: instrument accuracy and performance limitations; probes; techniques to minimize errors; measurement of "Q"; instrument calibration

E4C – Receiver performance characteristics, phase noise, capture effect, noise floor, image rejection, MDS, signal-to-noise-ratio; selectivity

E4D – Receiver performance characteristics, blocking dynamic range, intermodulation and cross-modulation interference; 3rd order intercept; desensitization; preselection

E4E – Noise suppression: system noise; electrical appliance noise; line noise; locating noise sources; DSP noise reduction; noise blankers

Subelement E5 – Electrical principles

[4 Exam Questions – 4 Groups]

E5A – Resonance and Q: characteristics of resonant circuits: series and parallel resonance; Q; half-power bandwidth; phase relationships in reactive circuits

E5B – Time constants and phase relationships: RLC time constants: definition; time constants in RL and RC circuits; phase angle between voltage and current; phase angles of series and parallel circuits

E5C – Impedance plots and coordinate systems: plotting impedances in polar coordinates; rectangular coordinates

E5D – AC and RF energy in real circuits: skin effect; electrostatic and electromagnetic fields; reactive power; power factor; coordinate systems

Subelement E6 – Circuit components

[6 Exam Questions – 6 Groups]

E6A – Semiconductor materials and devices: semiconductor materials germanium, silicon, P-type, N-type; transistor types: NPN, PNP, junction, field-effect transistors: enhancement mode; depletion mode; MOS; CMOS; N-channel; P-channel

E6B – Semiconductor diodes

E6C – Integrated circuits: TTL digital integrated circuits; CMOS digital integrated circuits; gates

E6D – Optical devices and toroids: cathode-ray tube devices; charge-coupled devices (CCDs); liquid crystal displays (LCDs); toroids: permeability, core material, selecting, winding

E6E – Piezoelectric crystals and MMICs: quartz crystals; crystal oscillators and filters; monolithic amplifiers

E6F – Optical components and power systems: photoconductive principles and effects, photovoltaic systems, optical couplers, optical sensors, and optoisolators

Subelement E7 – Practical circuits

[8 Exam Questions – 8 Groups]

E7A – Digital circuits: digital circuit principles and logic circuits: classes of logic elements; positive and negative logic; frequency dividers; truth tables

E7B – Amplifiers: Class of operation; vacuum tube and solid-state circuits; distortion and intermodulation; spurious and parasitic suppression; microwave amplifiers

E7C – Filters and matching networks: filters and impedance matching networks: types of networks; types of filters; filter applications; filter characteristics; impedance matching; DSP filtering

E7D – Power supplies and voltage regulators

E7E – Modulation and demodulation: reactance, phase and balanced modulators; detectors; mixer stages; DSP modulation and demodulation; software defined radio systems

E7F – Frequency markers and counters: frequency divider circuits; frequency marker generators; frequency counters

E7G – Active filters and op-amps: active audio filters; characteristics; basic circuit design; operational amplifiers

E7H – Oscillators and signal sources: types of oscillators; synthesizers and phase-locked loops; direct digital synthesizers

Subelement E8 – Signals and emissions

[4 Exam Questions – 4 Groups]

E8A – AC waveforms: sine, square, sawtooth and irregular waveforms; AC measurements; average and PEP of RF signals; pulse and digital signal waveforms

E8B – Modulation and demodulation: modulation methods; modulation index and deviation ratio; pulse modulation; frequency and time division multiplexing

E8C – Digital signals: digital communications modes; CW; information rate vs. bandwidth; spread-spectrum communications; modulation methods

E8D – Waves, measurements, and RF grounding: peak-to-peak values, polarization; RF grounding

Subelement E9 – Antennas and transmission lines

[8 Exam Questions – 8 Groups]

E9A – Isotropic and gain antennas: definition; used as a standard for comparison; radiation pattern; basic antenna parameters: radiation resistance and reactance, gain, beamwidth, efficiency

E9B – Antenna patterns: E and H plane patterns; gain as a function of pattern; antenna design; Yagi antennas

E9C – Wire and phased vertical antennas: beverage antennas; terminated and resonant rhombic antennas; elevation above real ground; ground effects as related to polarization; take-off angles

E9D – Directional antennas: gain; satellite antennas; antenna beamwidth; losses; SWR bandwidth; antenna efficiency; shortened and mobile antennas; grounding

E9E – Matching: matching antennas to feed lines; power dividers

E9F – Transmission lines: characteristics of open and shorted feed lines: 1/8 wavelength; 1/4 wavelength; 1/2 wavelength; feed lines: coax versus open-wire; velocity factor; electrical length; transformation characteristics of line terminated in impedance not equal to characteristic impedance

E9G – The Smith chart

E9H – Effective radiated power; system gains and losses; radio direction finding antennas

Subelement E0 – Safety

[1 exam question – 1 group]

E0A – Safety: amateur radio safety practices; RF radiation hazards; hazardous materials

Once your new call sign is listed in the FCC database, you are good to go. For an Amateur Extra license in Indiana, your call sign will consist of a prefix of K, N or W, the number nine (9), and a two-letter suffix, or a two-letter prefix beginning with A, N, K or W, the number nine (9), and a one-letter suffix, or a two-letter prefix beginning with A, the number nine (9), and a two-letter suffix.

Ham radio equipment can be expensive or you can do it "on the cheap." The cost will run from a couple hundred dollars to well in the thousands, depending on what you have available. eBay, and Craigslist are good places to start looking. Most ham clubs do some sort of hamfest annually wherein club members or others are willing to part with older equipment. See Appendix A for a list of clubs in Indiana.

Another excellent source of equipment, as well as advice on setting the equipment up and how to use it properly, is current ham operators. In Appendix B, the author has listed all the FCC licensed ham operators in Indiana, listed by city, and then sorted by street and house number on the street. Who knows, maybe someone who lives close to you is a ham operator. Be a good neighbor, stop by and have a chat with him/her.

Like CB radios, ham radios come in three formats – base, mobile, and handheld. They can use the electric company for power, or operate off a car battery. In the opinion of this author, in spite of the slightly higher cost of the equipment and having to take a test to legally use the equipment, ham radio is the way to go when concerned about communication during times of crisis.

Canadian Call Sign Prefixes

Because of our proximity to Canada, many times ham contact is made with our northern neighbors. Below is a chart showing the origin of Canadian call sign prefixes.

Call Sign Prefix	Provence or Territory
CY0	Sable Island
CY9	St. Paul Island
VA1, VE1	New Brunswick, Nova Scotia
VA2, VE2	Quebec
VA3, VE3	Ontario
VA4, VE4	Manitoba
VA5, VE5	Saskatchewan
VA6, VE6	Alberta
VA7, VE7	British Columbia
VE8	North West Territories
VE9	New Brunswick
VO1	Newfoundland
VO2	Labrador
VY0	Nunavut
VY1	Yukon
VY2	Prince Edward Island

Common Radio Bands in the United States

Certain radio bands are more popular with ham radio enthusiasts than others. Below is a chart showing these bands and when they are most popular.

	Band (meter)	Frequency (MHz)	Use
HF	160	1.8 – 2.0	Night
	80	3.5 – 4.0	Night and Local Day
	40	7.0 – 7.3	Night and Local Day
	30	10.1 – 10.15	CW and Digital
	20	14.0 – 14.350	World Wide Day and Night
	17	18.068 – 18.168	World Wide Day and Night
	15	21.0 – 21.450	Primarily Daytime
	12	24.890 – 24.990	Primarily Daytime
	10	28.0 – 29.70	Daytime during Sunspot highs
VHF	6	50 – 54	Local to World Wide
	2	144 – 148	Local to Medium Distance
UHF	70 cm	430 – 440	Local

Common Amateur Radio Bands in Canada

160 Meter Band - Maximum bandwidth 6 kHz
1.800 - 1.820 MHz - CW
1.820 - 1.830 MHz - Digital Modes
1 830 - 1.840 MHz - DX Window
1.840 - 2.000 MHz - SSB and other wide band modes

80 Meter Band - Maximum bandwidth 6 kHz
3.500 - 3.580 MHz - CW
3.580 - 3.620 MHz - Digital Modes
3.620 - 3.635 MHz - Packet/Digital Secondary
3.635 - 3.725 MHz - CW
3.725 - 3.790 MHz - SSB and other side band modes*
3.790 - 3.800 MHz - SSB DX Window
3.800 - 4.000 MHz - SSB and other wide band modes

40 Meter Band - Maximum bandwidth 6 kHz
7.000 - 7.035 MHz - CW
7.035 - 7.050 MHz - Digital Modes
7.040 - 7.050 MHz - International packet
7.050 - 7.100 MHz - SSB
7.100 - 7.120 MHz - Packet within Region 2
7.120 - 7.150 MHz - CW
7.150 - 7.300 MHz - SSB and other wide band modes

30 Meter Band - Maximum bandwidth 1 kHz

10.100 - 10.130 MHz - CW only
10.130 - 10.140 MHz - Digital Modes
10.140 - 10.150 MHz - Packet

20 Meter Band - Maximum bandwidth 6 kHz

14.000 - 14.070 MHz - CW only
14.070 - 14.095 MHz - Digital Mode
14.095 - 14.099 MHz - Packet
14.100 MHz - Beacons
14.101 - 14.112 MHz - CW, SSB, packet shared
14.112 - 14.350 MHz - SSB
14.225 - 14.235 MHz - SSTV

17 Meter Band - Maximum bandwidth 6 kHz

18.068 - 18.100 MHz - CW
18.100 - 18.105 MHz - Digital Modes
18.105 - 18.110 MHz - Packet
18.110 - 18.168 MHz - SSB and other wide band modes

15 Meter Band - maximum bandwidth 6 kHz

21.000 - 21.070 MHz - CW
21.070 - 21.090 MHz - Digital Modes
21.090 - 21.125 MHz - Packet
21.100 - 21.150 MHz - CW and SSB
21.150 - 21.335 MHz - SSB and other wide band modes
21.335 - 21.345 MHz - SSTV
21.345 - 21.450 MHz - SSB and other wide band modes

12 Meter Band - Maximum bandwidth 6 kHz

24.890 - 24.930 MHz - CW
24.920 - 24.925 MHz - Digital Modes
24.925 - 24.930 MHz - Packet
24.930 - 24.990 MHz - SSB and other wide band modes

10 Meter Band - Maximum band width 20 kHz

28.000 - 28.200 MHz - CW
28.070 - 28.120 MHz - Digital Modes
28.120 - 28.190 MHz - Packet
28.190 - 28.200 MHz - Beacons
28.200 - 29.300 MHz - SSB and other wide band modes
29.300 - 29.510 MHz - Satellite
29.510 - 29.700 MHz - SSB, FM and repeaters

160 Meters (1.8-2.0 MHz)

1.800 - 2.000 CW
1.800 - 1.810 Digital Modes
1.810 CW QRP
1.843-2.000 SSB, SSTV and other wideband modes
1.910 SSB QRP
1.995 - 2.000 Experimental
1.999 - 2.000 Beacons

80 Meters (3.5-4.0 MHz)

3.590 RTTY/Data DX
3.570-3.600 RTTY/Data
3.790-3.800 DX window
3.845 SSTV
3.885 AM calling frequency

40 Meters (7.0-7.3 MHz)

7.040 RTTY/Data DX
7.080-7.125 RTTY/Data
7.171 SSTV
7.290 AM calling frequency

30 Meters (10.1-10.15 MHz)

10.130-10.140 RTTY
10.140-10.150 Packet

20 Meters (14.0-14.35 MHz)

14.070-14.095 RTTY
14.095-14.0995 Packet
14.100 NCDXF Beacons
14.1005-14.112 Packet
14.230 SSTV
14.286 AM calling frequency

17 Meters (18.068-18.168 MHz)

18.100-18.105 RTTY
18.105-18.110 Packet

15 Meters (21.0-21.45 MHz)

21.070-21.110 RTTY/Data
21.340 SSTV

12 Meters (24.89-24.99 MHz)

24.920-24.925 RTTY
24.925-24.930 Packet

10 Meters (28-29.7 MHz)

28.000-28.070 CW
28.070-28.150 RTTY
28.150-28.190 CW
28.200-28.300 Beacons
28.300-29.300 Phone
28.680 SSTV
29.000-29.200 AM
29.300-29.510 Satellite Downlinks
29.520-29.590 Repeater Inputs
29.600 FM Simplex
29.610-29.700 Repeater Outputs

6 Meters (50-54 MHz)

50.0-50.1 CW, beacons
50.060-50.080 beacon subband
50.1-50.3 SSB, CW
50.10-50.125 DX window
50.125 SSB calling
50.3-50.6 All modes
50.6-50.8 Nonvoice communications
50.62 Digital (packet) calling
50.8-51.0 Radio remote control (20-kHz channels)
51.0-51.1 Pacific DX window
51.12-51.48 Repeater inputs (19 channels)
51.12-51.18 Digital repeater inputs
51.5-51.6 Simplex (six channels)
51.62-51.98 Repeater outputs (19 channels)
51.62-51.68 Digital repeater outputs
52.0-52.48 Repeater inputs (except as noted; 23 channels)
52.02, 52.04 FM simplex
52.2 TEST PAIR (input)
52.5-52.98 Repeater output (except as noted; 23 channels)
52.525 Primary FM simplex
52.54 Secondary FM simplex
52.7 TEST PAIR (output)
53.0-53.48 Repeater inputs (except as noted; 19 channels)
53.0 Remote base FM simplex
53.02 Simplex
53.1, 53.2, 53.3, 53.4 Radio remote control
53.5-53.98 Repeater outputs (except as noted; 19 channels)
53.5, 53.6, 53.7, 53.8 Radio remote control
53.52, 53.9 Simplex

2 Meters (144-148 MHz)

144.00-144.05 EME (CW)
144.05-144.10 General CW and weak signals
144.10-144.20 EME and weak-signal SSB
144.200 National calling frequency
144.200-144.275 General SSB operation
144.275-144.300 Propagation beacons
144.30-144.50 New OSCAR subband
144.50-144.60 Linear translator inputs
144.60-144.90 FM repeater inputs
144.90-145.10 Weak signal and FM simplex (145.01,03,05,07,09 are widely used for packet)
145.10-145.20 Linear translator outputs
145.20-145.50 FM repeater outputs
145.50-145.80 Miscellaneous and experimental modes
145.80-146.00 OSCAR subband
146.01-146.37 Repeater inputs
146.40-146.58 Simplex
146.52 National Simplex Calling Frequency
146.61-146.97 Repeater outputs
147.00-147.39 Repeater outputs
147.42-147.57 Simplex
147.60-147.99 Repeater inputs

1.25 Meters (222-225 MHz)

222.0-222.150 Weak-signal modes
222.0-222.025 EME
222.05-222.06 Propagation beacons
222.1 SSB & CW calling frequency
222.10-222.15 Weak-signal CW & SSB
222.15-222.25 Local coordinator's option; weak signal, ACSB, repeater inputs, control
222.25-223.38 FM repeater inputs only
223.40-223.52 FM simplex
223.52-223.64 Digital, packet
223.64-223.70 Links, control
223.71-223.85 Local coordinator's option; FM simplex, packet, repeater outputs
223.85-224.98 Repeater outputs only

70 Centimeters (420-450 MHz)

420.00-426.00 ATV repeater or simplex with 421.25 MHz video carrier control links and experimental
426.00-432.00 ATV simplex with 427.250-MHz video carrier frequency
432.00-432.07 EME (Earth-Moon-Earth)
432.07-432.10 Weak-signal CW
432.10 70-cm calling frequency

432.10-432.30 Mixed-mode and weak-signal work
432.30-432.40 Propagation beacons
432.40-433.00 Mixed-mode and weak-signal work
433.00-435.00 Auxiliary/repeater links
435.00-438.00 Satellite only (internationally)
438.00-444.00 ATV repeater input with 439.250-MHz video carrier frequency and repeater links
442.00-445.00 Repeater inputs and outputs (local option)
445.00-447.00 Shared by auxiliary and control links, repeaters and simplex (local option)
446.00 National simplex frequency
447.00-450.00 Repeater inputs and outputs (local option)

33 Centimeters (902-928 MHz)

902.0-903.0 Narrow-bandwidth, weak-signal communications
902.0-902.8 SSTV, FAX, ACSSB, experimental
902.1 Weak-signal calling frequency
902.8-903.0 Reserved for EME, CW expansion
903.1 Alternate calling frequency
903.0-906.0 Digital communications
906-909 FM repeater inputs
909-915 ATV
915-918 Digital communications
918-921 FM repeater outputs
921-927 ATV
927-928 FM simplex and links

23 Centimeters (1240-1300 MHz)

1240-1246 ATV #1
1246-1248 Narrow-bandwidth FM point-to-point links and digital, duplex with 1258-1260.
1248-1258 Digital Communications
1252-1258 ATV #2
1258-1260 Narrow-bandwidth FM point-to-point links digital, duplexed with 1246-1252
1260-1270 Satellite uplinks, reference WARC '79
1260-1270 Wide-bandwidth experimental, simplex ATV
1270-1276 Repeater inputs, FM and linear, paired with 1282-1288, 239 pairs every 25 kHz, e.g. 1270.025, .050, etc.
1271-1283 Non-coordinated test pair
1276-1282 ATV #3
1282-1288 Repeater outputs, paired with 1270-1276
1288-1294 Wide-bandwidth experimental, simplex ATV
1294-1295 Narrow-bandwidth FM simplex services, 25-kHz channels
1294.5 National FM simplex calling frequency
1295-1297 Narrow bandwidth weak-signal communications (no FM)
1295.0-1295.8 SSTV, FAX, ACSSB, experimental
1295.8-1296.0 Reserved for EME, CW expansion

1296.00-1296.05 EME-exclusive
1296.07-1296.08 CW beacons
1296.1 CW, SSB calling frequency
1296.4-1296.6 Crossband linear translator input
1296.6-1296.8 Crossband linear translator output
1296.8-1297.0 Experimental beacons (exclusive)
1297-1300 Digital Communications

2300-2310 and 2390-2450 MHz
2300.0-2303.0 High-rate data
2303.0-2303.5 Packet
2303.5-2303.8 TTY packet
2303.9-2303.9 Packet, TTY, CW, EME
2303.9-2304.1 CW, EME
2304.1 Calling frequency
2304.1-2304.2 CW, EME, SSB
2304.2-2304.3 SSB, SSTV, FAX, Packet AM, Amtor
2304.30-2304.32 Propagation beacon network
2304.32-2304.40 General propagation beacons
2304.4-2304.5 SSB, SSTV, ACSSB, FAX, Packet AM, Amtor experimental
2304.5-2304.7 Crossband linear translator input
2304.7-2304.9 Crossband linear translator output
2304.9-2305.0 Experimental beacons
2305.0-2305.2 FM simplex (25 kHz spacing)
2305.20 FM simplex calling frequency
2305.2-2306.0 FM simplex (25 kHz spacing)
2306.0-2309.0 FM Repeaters (25 kHz) input
2309.0-2310.0 Control and auxiliary links
2390.0-2396.0 Fast-scan TV
2396.0-2399.0 High-rate data
2399.0-2399.5 Packet
2399.5-2400.0 Control and auxiliary links
2400.0-2403.0 Satellite
2403.0-2408.0 Satellite high-rate data
2408.0-2410.0 Satellite
2410.0-2413.0 FM repeaters (25 kHz) output
2413.0-2418.0 High-rate data
2418.0-2430.0 Fast-scan TV
2430.0-2433.0 Satellite
2433.0-2438.0 Satellite high-rate data
2438.0-2450.0 WB FM, FSTV, FMTV, SS experimental

3300-3500 MHz
3456.3-3456.4 Propagation beacons

5650-5925 MHz
5760.3-5760.4 Propagation beacons

10.00-10.50 GHz
10.368 Narrow band calling frequency 10.3683-10.3684 Propagation beacons
10.3640 Calling frequency

Now that you have your license (you do, don't you?), and your equipment, you are ready to go live. Below is a suggested start.

1) Assuming you have the HT set up to the appropriate frequency, and offset, press the mic button on the HT and say, "KK4HWX listening." Replace the KK4HWX with your own call sign, the one assigned to you by the FCC (it's the law). If no one responds to your call, you may wish to try again. Hopefully someone will respond to your call.

2) Once you get a response, it will be in the form of something like, "KK4HWX this is ??1??? in Eastport returning. My name is Florence. Back to you. ??1???" then a tone. Let us examine the response more closely. She first acknowledged your call sign (KK4HWX), then identified hers (??1???). From the 1 in her call sign, you know that she first got her license in Region 1, meaning she got it while a resident of CT, ME, MA, NH, RI, or VT. She then told you where she's transmitting from (Eastport). The term "returning" means that she is returning your call. Her name is Florence. The phrase, "Back to you" indicates that she is turning over the conversation to you. She then repeats her call sign. The tone indicates to you that it is okay to proceed with your response. BTW if she had used the term "Over" instead of "Back to you," it would mean the same thing, just fewer words.

3) At this point, press the mic button and continue with the conversation. You should restate your call sign often during the conversation (perhaps every 10 minutes or less and whenever you begin transmitting). Don't forget to say, "Over" or "Back to you" whenever you are giving Florence control of the conversation again.

4) When you are ready to stop the conversation, you should say goodbye or use the phrase "73", meaning "best wishes." Your conversation would end something like, "??1??? 73, this is KK4HWX clear and monitoring." The "clear and monitoring" indicates that you are going to continue to monitor the frequency. If you are not going to continue monitoring, you may wish to end the conversation with Florence with, "clear and QRT" instead. The QRT means that you are stopping transmissions.

Call Sign Phonics

Because of different accents of various people, sometimes it is difficult to understand call sign letters when spoken. For this reason, most ham operators verbalize their call sign using phonics. Below is a table listing the accepted phonics for letters and numbers.

A = ALFA
B = BRAVO
C = CHARLIE
D = DELTA
E = ECHO
F = FOXTROT
G = GOLF
H = HOTEL
I = INDIA
J = JULIETT
K = KILO
L = LIMA
M = MIKE
N = NOVEMBER
O = OSCAR
P = PAPA (PA-PA')
Q = QUEBEC (KAY-BEK')
R = ROMEO

S = SIERRA
T = TANGO
U = UNIFORM
V = VICTOR
W = WHISKEY
X = X-RAY
Y = YANKEE
Z = ZULU (ZED)
1 = ONE
2 = TWO
3 = THREE (TREE)
4 = FOUR
5 = FIVE (FIFE)
6 = SIX
7 = SEVEN
8 = EIGHT
9 = NINE (NINER)
0 = ZERO

The words in parentheses are the pronunciation or the alternate pronunciations for the words or numbers, but you will hear both used. With the letter Z, (ZED) is by far the most commonly used. With the number 9, NINER is the most common and easiest to understand ON THE AIR.

If you wish to use Morse code (CW) instead of voice communication, the "conversation" would follow the same steps, with a few modifications. To type out each word would require a lot of typing and translating. If you are like this author, more means more, i.e., more typing means more typos are likely. To help with this situation, CW enthusiasts have developed a language all their own – they use abbreviations for common phrases. Below is a chart showing some of these abbreviations.

Abbreviation	Use
AR	Over
de	From or "this is"
ES	And
GM	Good Morning
K	Go
KN	Go only
NM	Name
QTH	Location
RPT	Report
R	Roger
SK	Clear
tnx	Thanks
UR	Your, you are
73	Best Wishes

Morse Code and Amateur Radio

If you wish to use CW, but are concerned about accuracy, you might consider purchasing a Morse code translator. This is an electronic device that you place in front of your speakers. It takes the CW sounds and translates them into English and displays the transmission on an LCD display. For the reverse, you can pick up a CW keyboard. With the keyboard, you type in your message and it converts the text to Morse code. The translator does not need to be attached to your ham equipment, whereas the keyboard would.

For your convenience, below is a table showing the Morse code signals and their meaning.

Character	Code
A	· —
B	— · · ·
C	— · — ·
D	— · ·
E	·
F	· · — ·
G	— — ·
H	· · · ·
I	· ·
J	· — — —
K	— · —
L	· — · ·
M	— —
N	— ·
O	— — —
P	· — — ·
Q	— — · —
R	· — ·
S	· · ·
T	—
U	· · —
V	· · · —
W	· — —
X	— · · —
Y	— · — —
Z	— — · ·
0	— — — — —
1	· — — — —
2	· · — — —
3	· · · — —
4	· · · · —
5	· · · · ·

6	— · · · ·
7	— — · · ·
8	— — — · ·
9	— — — — ·
Ampersand [&], Wait	· — · · ·
Apostrophe [']	· — — — — ·
At sign [@]	· — — · — ·
Colon [:]	— — — · · ·
Comma [,]	— — · · — —
Dollar sign [$]	· · · — · · —
Double dash [=]	— · · · —
Exclamation mark [!]	— · — · — —
Hyphen, Minus [-]	— · · · · —
Parenthesis closed [)]	— · — — · —
Parenthesis open [(]	— · — — ·
Period [.]	· — · — · —
Plus [+]	· — · — ·
Question mark [?]	· · — — · ·
Quotation mark ["]	· — · · — ·
Semicolon [;]	— · — · — ·
Slash [/], Fraction bar	— · · — ·
Underscore [_]	· · — — · —

An advantage of using Morse Code is that when broadcasting CW, you are using reduced power, thereby saving your battery. Your battery is used only while actually transmitting or receiving.

International Call Sign Prefixes

As was stated earlier, all ham radio call signs begin with letters (or numbers) taken from blocks assigned to each country of the world by the *ITU - International Telecommunications Union*, a body controlled by the United Nations. The following chart indicates which call sign series are allocated to which countries.

Call Sign Series	Allocated to
AAA-ALZ	**United States of America**
AMA-AOZ	Spain
APA-ASZ	Pakistan (Islamic Republic of)
ATA-AWZ	India (Republic of)
AXA-AXZ	Australia
AYA-AZZ	Argentine Republic
A2A-A2Z	Botswana (Republic of)
A3A-A3Z	Tonga (Kingdom of)
A4A-A4Z	Oman (Sultanate of)
A5A-A5Z	Bhutan (Kingdom of)

A6A-A6Z	United Arab Emirates
A7A-A7Z	Qatar (State of)
A8A-A8Z	Liberia (Republic of)
A9A-A9Z	Bahrain (State of)
BAA-BZZ	China (People's Republic of)
CAA-CEZ	Chile
CFA-CKZ	Canada
CLA-CMZ	Cuba
CNA-CNZ	Morocco (Kingdom of)
COA-COZ	Cuba
CPA-CPZ	Bolivia (Republic of)
CQA-CUZ	Portugal
CVA-CXZ	Uruguay (Eastern Republic of)
CYA-CZZ	Canada
C2A-C2Z	Nauru (Republic of)
C3A-C3Z	Andorra (Principality of)
C4A-C4Z	Cyprus (Republic of)
C5A-C5Z	Gambia (Republic of the)
C6A-C6Z	Bahamas (Commonwealth of the)
C7A-C7Z	World Meteorological Organization
C8A-C9Z	Mozambique (Republic of)
DAA-DRZ	Germany (Federal Republic of)
DSA-DTZ	Korea (Republic of)
DUA-DZZ	Philippines (Republic of the)
D2A-D3Z	Angola (Republic of)
D4A-D4Z	Cape Verde (Republic of)
D5A-D5Z	Liberia (Republic of)
D6A-D6Z	Comoros (Islamic Federal Republic of the)
D7A-D9Z	Korea (Republic of)
EAA-EHZ	Spain
EIA-EJZ	Ireland
EKA-EKZ	Armenia (Republic of)
ELA-ELZ	Liberia (Republic of)
EMA-EOZ	Ukraine
EPA-EQZ	Iran (Islamic Republic of)
ERA-ERZ	Moldova (Republic of)
ESA-ESZ	Estonia (Republic of)
ETA-ETZ	Ethiopia (Federal Democratic Republic of)
EUA-EWZ	Belarus (Republic of)
EXA-EXZ	Kyrgyz Republic
EYA-EYZ	Tajikistan (Republic of)
EZA-EZZ	Turkmenistan
E2A-E2Z	Thailand
E3A-E3Z	Eritrea
E4A-E4Z	Palestinian Authority

E5A-E5Z	New Zealand - Cook Islands (WRC-07)
E7A-E7Z	Bosnia and Herzegovina (Republic of) (WRC-07)
FAA-FZZ	France
GAA-GZZ	United Kingdom of Great Britain and Northern Ireland
HAA-HAZ	Hungary (Republic of)
HBA-HBZ	Switzerland (Confederation of)
HCA-HDZ	Ecuador
HEA-HEZ	Switzerland (Confederation of)
HFA-HFZ	Poland (Republic of)
HGA-HGZ	Hungary (Republic of)
HHA-HHZ	Haiti (Republic of)
HIA-HIZ	Dominican Republic
HJA-HKZ	Colombia (Republic of)
HLA-HLZ	Korea (Republic of)
HMA-HMZ	Democratic People's Republic of Korea
HNA-HNZ	Iraq (Republic of)
HOA-HPZ	Panama (Republic of)
HQA-HRZ	Honduras (Republic of)
HSA-HSZ	Thailand
HTA-HTZ	Nicaragua
HUA-HUZ	El Salvador (Republic of)
HVA-HVZ	Vatican City State
HWA-HYZ	France
HZA-HZZ	Saudi Arabia (Kingdom of)
H2A-H2Z	Cyprus (Republic of)
H3A-H3Z	Panama (Republic of)
H4A-H4Z	Solomon Islands
H6A-H7Z	Nicaragua
H8A-H9Z	Panama (Republic of)
IAA-IZZ	Italy
JAA-JSZ	Japan
JTA-JVZ	Mongolia
JWA-JXZ	Norway
JYA-JYZ	Jordan (Hashemite Kingdom of)
JZA-JZZ	Indonesia (Republic of)
J2A-J2Z	Djibouti (Republic of)
J3A-J3Z	Grenada
J4A-J4Z	Greece
J5A-J5Z	Guinea-Bissau (Republic of)
J6A-J6Z	Saint Lucia
J7A-J7Z	Dominica (Commonwealth of)
J8A-J8Z	Saint Vincent and the Grenadines
KAA-KZZ	**United States of America**
LAA-LNZ	Norway
LOA-LWZ	Argentine Republic

LXA-LXZ	Luxembourg
LYA-LYZ	Lithuania (Republic of)
LZA-LZZ	Bulgaria (Republic of)
L2A-L9Z	Argentine Republic
MAA-MZZ	United Kingdom of Great Britain and Northern Ireland
NAA-NZZ	**United States of America**
OAA-OCZ	Peru
ODA-ODZ	Lebanon
OEA-OEZ	Austria
OFA-OJZ	Finland
OKA-OLZ	Czech Republic
OMA-OMZ	Slovak Republic
ONA-OTZ	Belgium
OUA-OZZ	Denmark
PAA-PIZ	Netherlands (Kingdom of the)
PJA-PJZ	Netherlands (Kingdom of the) - Netherlands Antilles
PKA-POZ	Indonesia (Republic of)
PPA-PYZ	Brazil (Federative Republic of)
PZA-PZZ	Suriname (Republic of)
P2A-P2Z	Papua New Guinea
P3A-P3Z	Cyprus (Republic of)
P4A-P4Z	Netherlands (Kingdom of the) - Aruba
P5A-P9Z	Democratic People's Republic of Korea
RAA-RZZ	Russian Federation
SAA-SMZ	Sweden
SNA-SRZ	Poland (Republic of)
SSA-SSM	Egypt (Arab Republic of)
SSN-STZ	Sudan (Republic of the)
SUA-SUZ	Egypt (Arab Republic of)
SVA-SZZ	Greece
S2A-S3Z	Bangladesh (People's Republic of)
S5A-S5Z	Slovenia (Republic of)
S6A-S6Z	Singapore (Republic of)
S7A-S7Z	Seychelles (Republic of)
S8A-S8Z	South Africa (Republic of)
S9A-S9Z	Sao Tome and Principe (Democratic Republic of)
TAA-TCZ	Turkey
TDA-TDZ	Guatemala (Republic of)
TEA-TEZ	Costa Rica
TFA-TFZ	Iceland
TGA-TGZ	Guatemala (Republic of)
THA-THZ	France
TIA-TIZ	Costa Rica
TJA-TJZ	Cameroon (Republic of)
TKA-TKZ	France

TLA-TLZ	Central African Republic
TMA-TMZ	France
TNA-TNZ	Congo (Republic of the)
TOA-TQZ	France
TRA-TRZ	Gabonese Republic
TSA-TSZ	Tunisia
TTA-TTZ	Chad (Republic of)
TUA-TUZ	Côte d'Ivoire (Republic of)
TVA-TXZ	France
TYA-TYZ	Benin (Republic of)
TZA-TZZ	Mali (Republic of)
T2A-T2Z	Tuvalu
T3A-T3Z	Kiribati (Republic of)
T4A-T4Z	Cuba
T5A-T5Z	Somali Democratic Republic
T6A-T6Z	Afghanistan (Islamic State of)
T7A-T7Z	San Marino (Republic of)
T8A-T8Z	Palau (Republic of)
UAA-UIZ	Russian Federation
UJA-UMZ	Uzbekistan (Republic of)
UNA-UQZ	Kazakhstan (Republic of)
URA-UZZ	Ukraine
VAA-VGZ	Canada
VHA-VNZ	Australia
VOA-VOZ	Canada
VPA-VQZ	United Kingdom of Great Britain and Northern Ireland
VRA-VRZ	China (People's Republic of) - Hong Kong
VSA-VSZ	United Kingdom of Great Britain and Northern Ireland
VTA-VWZ	India (Republic of)
VXA-VYZ	Canada
VZA-VZZ	Australia
V2A-V2Z	Antigua and Barbuda
V3A-V3Z	Belize
V4A-V4Z	Saint Kitts and Nevis
V5A-V5Z	Namibia (Republic of)
V6A-V6Z	Micronesia (Federated States of)
V7A-V7Z	Marshall Islands (Republic of the)
V8A-V8Z	Brunei Darussalam
WAA-WZZ	**United States of America**
XAA-XIZ	Mexico
XJA-XOZ	Canada
XPA-XPZ	Denmark
XQA-XRZ	Chile
XSA-XSZ	China (People's Republic of)
XTA-XTZ	Burkina Faso

XUA-XUZ	Cambodia (Kingdom of)
XVA-XVZ	Viet Nam (Socialist Republic of)
XWA-XWZ	Lao People's Democratic Republic
XXA-XXZ	China (People's Republic of) - Macao (WRC-07)
XYA-XZZ	Myanmar (Union of)
YAA-YAZ	Afghanistan (Islamic State of)
YBA-YHZ	Indonesia (Republic of)
YIA-YIZ	Iraq (Republic of)
YJA-YJZ	Vanuatu (Republic of)
YKA-YKZ	Syrian Arab Republic
YLA-YLZ	Latvia (Republic of)
YMA-YMZ	Turkey
YNA-YNZ	Nicaragua
YOA-YRZ	Romania
YSA-YSZ	El Salvador (Republic of)
YTA-YUZ	Serbia (Republic of) (WRC-07)
YVA-YYZ	Venezuela (Republic of)
Y2A-Y9Z	Germany (Federal Republic of)
ZAA-ZAZ	Albania (Republic of)
ZBA-ZJZ	United Kingdom of Great Britain and Northern Ireland
ZKA-ZMZ	New Zealand
ZNA-ZOZ	United Kingdom of Great Britain and Northern Ireland
ZPA-ZPZ	Paraguay (Republic of)
ZQA-ZQZ	United Kingdom of Great Britain and Northern Ireland
ZRA-ZUZ	South Africa (Republic of)
ZVA-ZZZ	Brazil (Federative Republic of)
Z2A-Z2Z	Zimbabwe (Republic of)
Z3A-Z3Z	The Former Yugoslav Republic of Macedonia
2AA-2ZZ	United Kingdom of Great Britain and Northern Ireland
3AA-3AZ	Monaco (Principality of)
3BA-3BZ	Mauritius (Republic of)
3CA-3CZ	Equatorial Guinea (Republic of)
3DA-3DM	Swaziland (Kingdom of)
3DN-3DZ	Fiji (Republic of)
3EA-3FZ	Panama (Republic of)
3GA-3GZ	Chile
3HA-3UZ	China (People's Republic of)
3VA-3VZ	Tunisia
3WA-3WZ	Viet Nam (Socialist Republic of)
3XA-3XZ	Guinea (Republic of)
3YA-3YZ	Norway
3ZA-3ZZ	Poland (Republic of)
4AA-4CZ	Mexico
4DA-4IZ	Philippines (Republic of the)
4JA-4KZ	Azerbaijani Republic

4LA-4LZ	Georgia (Republic of)
4MA-4MZ	Venezuela (Republic of)
4OA-4OZ	Montenegro (Republic of) (WRC-07)
4PA-4SZ	Sri Lanka (Democratic Socialist Republic of)
4TA-4TZ	Peru
4UA-4UZ	United Nations
4VA-4VZ	Haiti (Republic of)
4WA-4WZ	Democratic Republic of Timor-Leste (WRC-03)
4XA-4XZ	Israel (State of)
4YA-4YZ	International Civil Aviation Organization
4ZA-4ZZ	Israel (State of)
5AA-5AZ	Libya (Socialist People's Libyan Arab Jamahiriya)
5BA-5BZ	Cyprus (Republic of)
5CA-5GZ	Morocco (Kingdom of)
5HA-5IZ	Tanzania (United Republic of)
5JA-5KZ	Colombia (Republic of)
5LA-5MZ	Liberia (Republic of)
5NA-5OZ	Nigeria (Federal Republic of)
5PA-5QZ	Denmark
5RA-5SZ	Madagascar (Republic of)
5TA-5TZ	Mauritania (Islamic Republic of)
5UA-5UZ	Niger (Republic of the)
5VA-5VZ	Togolese Republic
5WA-5WZ	Samoa (Independent State of)
5XA-5XZ	Uganda (Republic of)
5YA-5ZZ	Kenya (Republic of)
6AA-6BZ	Egypt (Arab Republic of)
6CA-6CZ	Syrian Arab Republic
6DA-6JZ	Mexico
6KA-6NZ	Korea (Republic of)
6OA-6OZ	Somali Democratic Republic
6PA-6SZ	Pakistan (Islamic Republic of)
6TA-6UZ	Sudan (Republic of the)
6VA-6WZ	Senegal (Republic of)
6XA-6XZ	Madagascar (Republic of)
6YA-6YZ	Jamaica
6ZA-6ZZ	Liberia (Republic of)
7AA-7IZ	Indonesia (Republic of)
7JA-7NZ	Japan
7OA-7OZ	Yemen (Republic of)
7PA-7PZ	Lesotho (Kingdom of)
7QA-7QZ	Malawi
7RA-7RZ	Algeria (People's Democratic Republic of)
7SA-7SZ	Sweden
7TA-7YZ	Algeria (People's Democratic Republic of)

7ZA-7ZZ	Saudi Arabia (Kingdom of)
8AA-8IZ	Indonesia (Republic of)
8JA-8NZ	Japan
8OA-8OZ	Botswana (Republic of)
8PA-8PZ	Barbados
8QA-8QZ	Maldives (Republic of)
8RA-8RZ	Guyana
8SA-8SZ	Sweden
8TA-8YZ	India (Republic of)
8ZA-8ZZ	Saudi Arabia (Kingdom of)
9AA-9AZ	Croatia (Republic of)
9BA-9DZ	Iran (Islamic Republic of)
9EA-9FZ	Ethiopia (Federal Democratic Republic of)
9GA-9GZ	Ghana
9HA-9HZ	Malta
9IA-9JZ	Zambia (Republic of)
9KA-9KZ	Kuwait (State of)
9LA-9LZ	Sierra Leone
9MA-9MZ	Malaysia
9NA-9NZ	Nepal
9OA-9TZ	Democratic Republic of the Congo
9UA-9UZ	Burundi (Republic of)
9VA-9VZ	Singapore (Republic of)
9WA-9WZ	Malaysia
9XA-9XZ	Rwandese Republic
9YA-9ZZ	Trinidad and Tobago

Third-Party Communications and Amateur Radio

If all of this information about ham radios is somewhat intimidating, do not despair. "You" can still use ham radios for communications without being a licensed operator. Yes, you do have to have a ham license in order to legally transmit by ham equipment (or be under the direct supervision of someone else who is licensed), but there is an alternative – third-party communication.

Third-party communications occur when a licensed operator sends either written or verbal messages on behalf of unlicensed persons or organizations. There are two "controls" on third-party communication.

First, the communication must be noncommercial and of a personal nature. Asking a ham operator to contact another ham operator located in an area just hit by tornados and, because of being without power, phones do not work in Grandma Sally's city so you can check up on her, is okay. Asking a ham to send a message out that you have an old Chevy for sale would not be okay.

Second, the message must be going to a permitted area. Transmitting from a US location to another US location is okay, but transmitting from the US to another country may not. Because third-party communications bypass a country's normal telephone and postal systems, many foreign governments forbid such communications. In order to transmit from one country to another, the other country must have signed a third-party agreement with the US. What follows is a list of those countries that do have third-party a communications agreement with the US.

V2	Antigua / Barbuda
LU	Argentina
VK	Australia
V3	Belize
CP	Bolivia
T9	Bosnia-Herzegovina
PY	Brazil
VE	Canada
CE	Chile
HK	Colombia
D6	Comoros (Federal Islamic Republic of)
TI	Costa Rica
CO	Cuba
HI	Dominican Republic
J7	Dominica
HC	Ecuador
YS	El Salvador
C5	Gambia, The
9G	Ghana
J3	Grenada
TG	Guatemala
8R	Guyana
HH	Haiti
HR	Honduras
4X	Israel
6Y	Jamaica
JY	Jordan
EL	Liberia
V7	Marshall Islands
XE	Mexico
V6	Micronesia, Federated States of
YN	Nicaragua
HP	Panama
ZP	Paraguay
OA	Peru
DU	Philippines
VR6	Pitcairn Island

V4	St. Christopher / Nevis
J6	St. Lucia
J8	St. Vincent and the Grenadines
9L	Sierra Leone
ZS	South Africa
3DA	Swaziland
9Y	Trinidad / Tobago
TA	Turkey
GB	United Kingdom
CX	Uruguay
YV	Venezuela
4U1ITUITU	Geneva
4U1VICVIC	Vienna

Remember, before TSHTF, keep your pantry well stocked, your powder dry, and your batteries fully charged. 73

APPENDIX A

American Radio Relay League

Affiliated Amateur Radio Clubs in

Indiana

ARRL Affiliated Club:	Madison Co Amateur Radio Club Inc.
City:	Alexandria, IN
Call Sign:	W9VCF
Section:	IN
Links:	www.w9vcf.org

ARRL Affiliated Club	Chief Anderson Amateur Radio Club
City:	Anderson, IN
Call Sign:	WA9EOC
Section:	IN

ARRL Affiliated Club:	Anderson Repeater Club, Inc.
City:	Anderson, IN
Call Sign:	KA9SYP/R
Section:	IN
Links:	www.andersonrepeaterclub.org

ARRL Affiliated Club:	Land of Lakes Amateur Radio Club
City:	Angola, IN
Call Sign:	K9HD
Section:	IN
Links:	llarc.tripod.com

ARRL Affiliated Club:	Northeastern Indiana Amateur Radio Club
City:	Auburn, IN
Call Sign:	W9OU
Section:	IN
Links:	w9ou.org/

ARRL Affiliated Club:	Hendricks Co. Amateur Radio Society
City:	Avon, IN
Call Sign:	N9HC
Section:	IN
Links:	HCARS.org

ARRL Affiliated Club:	Putnam County Amateur Radio Club
City:	Bainbridge, IN
Call Sign:	W9BJJ
Section:	IN

ARRL Affiliated Club:	EARS Electric Application Radio Service
City:	Bloomington, IN
Call Sign:	W9EAR
Section:	IN
Links:	w9ear.org

ARRL Affiliated Club: EARS Electric Application Radio Service
City: Bloomington, IN
Call Sign: W9EAR
Section: IN
Links: w9ear.org

ARRL Affiliated Club: Northwest Indiana Skywarn
City: Chesterton, IN
Call Sign: K9NWI
Section: IN
Links: www.geocities.com/kb9zvt73/

ARRL Affiliated Club: Whitley County Amateur Radio Club Inc.
City: Columbia City, IN
Call Sign: WC9AR
Section: IN

ARRL Affiliated Club: Lake County Amateur Radio Club
City: Crown Point, IN
Call Sign: W9LJ
Section: IN
Links: www.lakenetnwi.net/member/lcarc/index.html

ARRL Affiliated Club: Elkhart County Radio Assn. Inc.
City: Elkhart, IN
Call Sign: AA9DG
Section: IN
Links: www.ecra.us

ARRL Affiliated Club: Tri-State Amateur Radio Society-TARS
City: Evansville, IN
Call Sign: W9OG
Section: IN
Links: www.w9og.net

ARRL Affiliated Club: Fort Wayne Radio Club Inc.
City: Fort Wayne, IN
Call Sign: W9TE
Section: IN
Links: www.fwrc.info/

ARRL Affiliated Club: Ivy Tech Northeast Amateur Radio Club
City: Fort Wayne, IN
Call Sign: KU9I
Section: IN

ARRL Affiliated Club:	Zion Lutheran Academy Radio Society
City:	Fort Wayne, IN
Call Sign:	KC9LAR
Section:	IN
Links:	www.zionluthac.org

ARRL Affiliated Club:	Ivy Tech Northeast Amateur Radio Club
City:	Fort Wayne, IN
Call Sign:	KU9I
Section:	IN

ARRL Affiliated Club:	Fort Wayne Radio Club Inc.
City:	Fort Wayne, IN
Call Sign:	W9TE
Section:	IN
Links:	www.fwrc.info/

ARRL Affiliated Club:	Clinton County Amateur Radio Club
City:	Frankfort, IN
Section:	IN
Links:	www.qsl.net/n9sez/ccarc.htm

ARRL Affiliated Club:	Mid-State Amateur Radio Club
City:	Franklin, IN
Call Sign:	WA9RDF
Section:	IN
Links:	www.midstatehams.org/

ARRL Affiliated Club:	Goshen Amateur Radio Club
City:	Goshen, IN
Call Sign:	K9TSM
Section:	IN
Links:	www.goshenarc.org

ARRL Affiliated Club:	Depauw University Amateur Radio Club
City:	Greencastle, IN
Call Sign:	W9YJ
Section:	IN

ARRL Affiliated Club:	Hancock Amateur Radio Club
City:	Greenfield, IN
Call Sign:	W9ATG
Section:	IN
Links:	www.w9atg.org

ARRL Affiliated Club: Purdue Calumet Amateur Radio Society
City: Hammond, IN
Call Sign: W9PUC
Section: IN

ARRL Affiliated Club: Blackford Amateur Radio Club
City: Hartford City, IN
Section: IN
Links: www.blackfordarc.org

ARRL Affiliated Club: RCA Amateur Radio Club
City: Indianapolis, IN
Call Sign: W9RCA
Section: IN
Links: www.W9RCA.org

ARRL Affiliated Club: Hoosier DX & Contest Club
City: Indianapolis, IN
Call Sign: KJ9D
Section: IN
Links: www.HDXCC.org

ARRL Affiliated Club: Indianapolis Radio Club
City: Indianapolis, IN
Call Sign: W9JP
Section: IN
Links: www.indyradioclub.org

ARRL Affiliated Club: Clark County Amateur Radio Club, Inc.
City: Jeffersonville, IN
Call Sign: W9WWI
Section: IN
Links: www.qsl.net/w9wwi/

ARRL Affiliated Club: 807 Club of Kokomo
City: Kokomo, IN
Section: IN

ARRL Affiliated Club: Kokomo Amateur Radio Club
City: Kokomo, IN
Call Sign: W9GO
Section: IN
Links: www.kokomohams.org

ARRL Affiliated Club:	Tippecanoe Amateur Radio Assoc.
City:	Lafayette, IN
Call Sign:	W9REG
Section:	IN
Links:	www.w9reg.org

ARRL Affiliated Club:	Boone County Amateur Radio
City:	Lebanon, IN
Section:	IN
Links:	www.hamsnet.net/BCARC/

ARRL Affiliated Club:	Cass County Amateur Radio Club
City:	Logansport, IN
Call Sign:	W9VMW
Section:	IN
Links:	www.w9vmw.org

ARRL Affiliated Club:	Randolph Amateur Radio Club Inc.
City:	Lynn, IN
Call Sign:	WD9EXZ
Section:	IN
Links:	wd9exz.com

ARRL Affiliated Club:	Calumet Amateur Radio Enthusiasts
City:	Marion, IN
Call Sign:	K9IX
Section:	IN

ARRL Affiliated Club:	Grant County Amateur Radio Club
City:	Marion, IN
Call Sign:	W9EBN
Section:	IN
Links:	www.GrantARC.com

ARRL Affiliated Club	Tri County HF Society
City:	Metamora, IN
Call Sign:	KK9TC
Section:	IN
Links:	www.kk9tc.com

ARRL Affiliated Club:	Henry County Amateur Radio Club
City:	Middletown, IN
Section:	IN
Links:	www.w9ob.org, www.hcarc.org

ARRL Affiliated Club:	White County Amateur Radio Society
City:	Monticello, IN
Call Sign:	KC9PQA
Section:	IN
Links:	www.kc9pqa.net

ARRL Affiliated Club:	Muncie Area Amateur Radio Club
City:	Muncie, IN
Call Sign:	WB9HXG
Section:	IN
Links:	www.wb9hxg.net

ARRL Affiliated Club:	Starke County Amateur Radio Club
City:	North Judson, IN
Call Sign:	W9JOZ
Section:	IN
Links:	www.w9joz.org

ARRL Affiliated Club:	Jennings County Amateur Radio Club
City:	North Vernon, IN
Call Sign:	KC9TME
Section:	IN

ARRL Affiliated Club:	Amateur Radio Club of Notre Dame
City:	Notre Dame, IN
Call Sign:	ND1U
Section:	IN
Links:	www.nd.edu/~arcnd/

ARRL Affiliated Club:	Owen County Amateur Radio Association
City:	Poland, IN
Call Sign:	KB9MZZ
Section:	IN

ARRL Affiliated Club:	Whitewater Valley Amateur Radio Club
City:	Richmond, IN
Call Sign:	N9JM
Section:	IN
Links:	www.wvarc.org

ARRL Affiliated Club:	South Central Indiana Radio League
City:	Seymour, IN
Call Sign:	KC9GKF
Section:	IN

ARRL Affiliated Club: Jackson County Amateur Radio Technical Society
City: Seymour, IN
Call Sign: KC9LVC
Section: IN
Links: Jacksoncountyarts.kickme.to/

ARRL Special Service Club   Michiana Amateur Radio Club
City: South Bend, IN
Call Sign: W9AB
Section: IN
Links: community.michiana.org/marcsite/

ARRL Affiliated Club: Michiana Amateur Radio Club Inc.
City: South Bend, IN
Section: IN

ARRL Affiliated Club: Wabash Valley Amateur Radio Association Inc.
City: Terre Haute, IN
Call Sign: W9UUU
Section: IN
Links: www.w9uuu.org

ARRL Affiliated Club: Illiana Radio Club Inc.
City: Terre Haute, IN
Call Sign: W9IRC
Section: IN
Links: www.w9irc.org

ARRL Affiliated Club: Porter County Amateur Radio Club
City: Valparaiso, IN
Call Sign: K9PC
Section: IN
Links: www.pc-arc.net/

ARRL Affiliated Club: Ripley County Repeater Assoc.
City: Versailles, IN
Call Sign: KC9MBX
Section: IN
Links: rcra.web.officelive.com

ARRL Affiliated Club: Hoosier Lakes Radio Club
City: Warsaw, IN
Call Sign: K9CWD
Section: IN
Links: www.k9cwd.org

ARRL Affiliated Club: Purdue University Amateur Radio Club
City: West Lafayette, IN
Call Sign: W9YB
Section: IN
Links: www.w9yb.org/

ARRL Affiliated Club: Jasper County Skywarn
City: Wheatfield, IN
Call Sign: KC9HUS
Section: IN

ARRL Affiliated Club: Delaware Amateur Radio Association
City: Yorktown, IN
Call Sign: W9DUK
Section: IN

ARRL Affiliated Club: Emcomm ECI
City: Yorktown, IN
Call Sign: W9YFD
Section: IN
Links: www.w9yfd.org

APPENDIX B

Amateur Radio License Holders

in

**Indiana: North Region
(by City)**

FCC Amateur Radio Licenses in Akron

Call Sign: KC9ELI
Carol J Andrews
7405 E 200 N
Akron IN 469109428

Call Sign: N9KAG
Debra A Murphy
7414 E SR 14
Akron IN 46910

Call Sign: KB9TOQ
Kyle B Robinson
411 Orchard St
Akron IN 46910

Call Sign: KB9ORW
George Strohschein
8847 S 1200 W
Akron IN 461109357

Call Sign: KC9RRR
Aaron M Bolinger
3426 S 1300 E
Akron IN 46910

Call Sign: KB9TRO
Heath Bj Kelley
315 S Cherry St
Akron IN 46910

Call Sign: KC9TAW
Heath Bj Kelley
315 S Cherry St
Akron IN 46910

Call Sign: N9NOT
Heath Bj Kelley
315 S Cherry St
Akron IN 46910

FCC Amateur Radio Licenses in Albion

Call Sign: KD9OR
Jack B Kammer
90W
Albion IN 46701

Call Sign: W9AWP
Paul A Clem
Box 435
Albion IN 46701

Call Sign: KB9DGK
William S Hose Jr
Box 577
Albion IN 46701

Call Sign: N9VI
Kendallville Contesters
Club Ars
618 Circle Dr
Albion IN 46701

Call Sign: KC8KXK
Carrie J Ryman
618 Circle Dr
Albion IN 46701

Call Sign: K8IAT
Timothy S Ryman
618 Circle Dr
Albion IN 46701

Call Sign: KB9YNU
Russell L Coe
3800 E 300 S
Albion IN 46701

Call Sign: WA9VKV
Juanita M Leitch
946 E 550 N
Albion IN 46701

Call Sign: WA9UGP
Paul M Leitch
946 E 550 N

Albion IN 46701

Call Sign: N9GLF
Kathy L Becker
800 E Hazel St
Albion IN 46701

Call Sign: KC9SXU
David A Leatherman
1012 E Main St
Albion IN 46701

Call Sign: AB9XF
David A Leatherman
1012 E Main St
Albion IN 46701

Call Sign: KC9AZE
Clifford W Woods
1003 E Seneca St
Albion IN 46701

Call Sign: KA2HDX
Eric V Fasoldt
410 E South St Lot 4
Albion IN 467011277

Call Sign: KA9UYL
Warren E Becker
800 East St
Albion IN 46701

Call Sign: KA0OAC
Leslie G Arthur
3223 N Arthur Dr
Albion IN 46701

Call Sign: WA9UGQ
Nikki M Marker
3454 N Skinner Lk W Dr
Albion IN 46701

Call Sign: KF9LK
Donald D Hoover
311 N York St

Albion IN 46701

Call Sign: N9GOX
Mark A Easterday
609 N York St
Albion IN 46701

Call Sign: N9OBP
Mark L Stangland
4720 S 100 W
Albion IN 46701

Call Sign: K9AIN
Philip C Dunn
2180 S 300 E
Albion IN 46701

Call Sign: KB9ZHB
Lisa A Guyermelli
3758 S 300 W
Albion IN 46701

Call Sign: KB9MDU
Aaron B Rex
3758 S 300 W
Albion IN 46701

Call Sign: WA2EMT
Aaron B Rex
3758 S 300 W
Albion IN 46701

Call Sign: K2NJD
Lisa A Guyermelli
3758 S 300 W
Albion IN 46701

Call Sign: KA9GLX
Harlen A Miller
3207 S 450 W
Albion IN 46701

Call Sign: N9OXO
Amie N Collins
3777 S 475 W

Albion IN 46701

Call Sign: KV4GC
Sara J Wagar
3777 S 475W
Albion IN 46701

Call Sign: W9GRL
Sara J Wagar
3777 S 475W
Albion IN 46701

Call Sign: K9ITC
Sara J Wagar
3777 S 475W
Albion IN 46701

Call Sign: KA9FFV
Stephen M Novell
84 S Willow Haven Dr
Albion IN 46701

Call Sign: WC9I
David K Gaerte
1496 W 400 S
Albion IN 46701

Call Sign: N9NAA
Joshua D Gaerte
1496 W 400 S
Albion IN 46701

Call Sign: KB9SLQ
Billie J Feasel
4111 W 500 S
Albion IN 46701

Call Sign: KB9YHQ
Jason R Shepherd
5899 W Lewis St
Albion IN 46701

Call Sign: KA9GPN
Leonard L Leatherman
Albion IN 46701

Call Sign: N9XRZ
Lowell W Graber
Box 117B
Amboy IN 46911

Call Sign: AA9FV
Donnavon R Graber
3194 E 1000 S
Amboy IN 46911

Call Sign: KF9NT
Marvin Beachy
2386 E 1100 S
Amboy IN 469119480

Call Sign: N9TEK
Ronald E Graber
3164 E 9505
Amboy IN 46911

Call Sign: NZ9R
Kyle E Hobbs
301 N Main St
Amboy IN 46911

Call Sign: N9MBV
Micheal Cantrell
8758 S Bond Cemetery Rd
Amboy IN 46911

Call Sign: KB9WKO
Joseph C Scrivner
5546 Vine St
Amboy IN 46911

Call Sign: KA9HHM
James N Melton
Amboy IN 46911

Call Sign: N9IEM
Danny J Wyatt
600W
Andrews IN 46702

Call Sign: KC9KK
James E Rosen
825W
Andrews IN 46702

Call Sign: KB9WVA
Gerald W Wilcox
7063 E 350N
Andrews IN 46702

Call Sign: KC9DZ
Raymond R Tackett
420 Market St
Andrews IN 46702

Call Sign: N9NNZ
Larry D Oliver
718 Market St
Andrews IN 46702

Call Sign: KB9EHZ
Heath A Newsome
2295 S 950 W
Andrews IN 46702

Call Sign: KB9EIA
Lois E Newsome
2295 S 950 W
Andrews IN 46702

Call Sign: KB9CGA
Worlie Newsome Jr
2295 S 950 W
Andrews IN 46702

Call Sign: NU9C
Kenneth D Baker
6801 W 100 S
Andrews IN 46702

Call Sign: N9WV
Heath A Pressler
8142 W 600 S
Andrews IN 46702

Call Sign: KC9GNJ
Huntington County 440
Repeater Group
Andrews IN 46702

Call Sign: K9DKB
Huntington County 440
Repeater Group
Andrews IN 46702

FCC Amateur Radio
Licenses in Angola

Call Sign: W9KVN
George D Ireland
100N
Angola IN 46703

Call Sign: N9DWS
Harvey J Cowell
275N
Angola IN 467039565

Call Sign: WB9YAB
Jack E Bledsoe
340N
Angola IN 467038032

Call Sign: WD9ENS
Lynn A Blue
80W
Angola IN 46703

Call Sign: KB9NNS
Jerry A Pettit
1206 Apollo Dr
Angola IN 46703

Call Sign: W9YCB
Lloyd G Hanson
Box 265
Angola IN 46703

Call Sign: WB9GPD
De Burl Smith
Box 30 965N 827
Angola IN 46703

Call Sign: WV9E
Jon E Sills
Box 367
Angola IN 46703

Call Sign: KA6VVU
Frankie L Noragon
993 E 300 N Lot 9
Angola IN 46703

Call Sign: KC9CXY
Robert W Neumann
240 E 400 N
Angola IN 46703

Call Sign: KC9LVK
Michael D Hicks
113 E Broad St
Angola IN 46703

Call Sign: W9BBX
Dwight H Donaldson
400 E Felicity St
Angola IN 46703

Call Sign: KC9BEV
Fred L Kissinger
411 E Gilmore St
Angola IN 46703

Call Sign: KC9BEU
Judith K Eaton
411 E Gilmore St
Angola IN 46703

Call Sign: KC9QCB
Nikki P Coleman
409 E Maumee
Angola IN 46703

Call Sign: WB9VES
Schuyler D Seavey
405 E Maumee St
Angola IN 46703

Call Sign: KC9QCC
Shannon D Coleman
409 E Maumee St
Angola IN 46703

Call Sign: KA9EUU
Lu A Dennis
515 E Maumee St
Angola IN 46703

Call Sign: N9UUW
Ronald D Maugherman
313 E Randolph St
Angola IN 46703

Call Sign: KC9UKQ
Sean M Carroll
509 Ettinger St
Angola IN 46703

Call Sign: N9BXZ
Della M Peel
301 Fieldcrest Dr
Angola IN 46703

Call Sign: KB1FQV
James W Yahne
160 Ln 101Fa Jimmerson Lake
Angola IN 467037094

Call Sign: W9CXP
Lester W Nidlinger
2360 Ln 105 Lake James

Angola IN 467037528

Call Sign: KC9LVS
William W Bryan
480 Ln 150 A Lake James
Angola IN 46703

Call Sign: W9LAK
William W Bryan
480 Ln 150 A Lake James
Angola IN 46703

Call Sign: KB9MK
King D Oberlin
60 Ln 165 Jimmerson Lake
Angola IN 46703

Call Sign: KB9KMO
Bruce M Carter
360 Ln 175 Lime Lk
Angola IN 46703

Call Sign: K8HLQ
Bert W Schulz
215 Ln 200A Lake James
Angola IN 46703

Call Sign: N9UZL
Dennis R Martin
75 Ln 201 Crooked Lake
Angola IN 46703

Call Sign: W9DRM
Dennis R Martin
75 Ln 201 Crooked Lake
Angola IN 46703

Call Sign: AA9MU
Mark B Hansbarger
1000 Ln 440 Lake James
Angola IN 46703

Call Sign: KB9TUH
Michael D Hansbarger
1000 Ln 440 Lk James
Angola IN 46703

Call Sign: WB9YRG
Kent E Bledsoe
1445 N 160 W
Angola IN 467039481

Call Sign: W9VCC
David L Syler
1410 N 200 E
Angola IN 467031731

Call Sign: KC9TIK
David Jones
3735 N 425 W
Angola IN 46703

Call Sign: N9ZOA
Patrick G McDonald
850 N 700 E
Angola IN 46703

Call Sign: WB9GPC
Dorris J Smith
965 N 827
Angola IN 46703

Call Sign: WB9AEI
Dale L Smith
965 N 827
Angola IN 46703

Call Sign: W9LKI
Dale L Smith
965 N 827
Angola IN 46703

Call Sign: N9UUX
Richard A Staul
120 N 900 W
Angola IN 46703

Call Sign: KB9CWD
Larry K Ball
127 N Kinney
Angola IN 46703

Call Sign: KC9UKP
Andrea M Mitofsky
606 N Washington St Apt
7
Angola IN 46703

Call Sign: KA9NZR
Mary Ann Burlew
817 N Williams St
Angola IN 46703

Call Sign: N9QYS
Edwin S Munger
315 Oak St Lot 9
Angola IN 46703

Call Sign: KC9LVM
Carl W Renner
405 Pokagon Trl
Angola IN 46703

Call Sign: W9GPJ
Oral R Evans
704 Redding Rd
Angola IN 46703

Call Sign: KB9YJH
Andrew L Sprow
1128 S 450 W
Angola IN 46703

Call Sign: KC8PSI
Sarah E Sprow
1128 S 450 W
Angola IN 46703

Call Sign: KC9EDG
Christopher C Clark
852 S 600 W
Angola IN 46703

Call Sign: KC9GDE
Steven D Cleverly
2572 S 800 E
Angola IN 46703

Call Sign: N9YK
Steven D Cleverly
2572 S 800 E
Angola IN 46703

Call Sign: K9HD
Land Of Lakes ARC
2572 S 800 E
Angola IN 46703

Call Sign: KC9BEQ
James H Harris
1007 S Darling St
Angola IN 467031859

Call Sign: N9DFJ
John E Walker
121 S Kinney
Angola IN 46703

Call Sign: KC9SWK
Steuben County Races
Ares Emergency
Communications Group
205 S Martha St Rm 104
Angola IN 46703

Call Sign: W9ECG
Steuben County Races
Ares Emergency
Communications Group
205 S Martha St Rm 104
Angola IN 46703

Call Sign: KC9GDF
Richard K Limestahl
3355 S Old 27 Lot 28
Angola IN 46703

Call Sign: KA8IUB
David R Finley
631 S Superior St
Angola IN 46703

Call Sign: KG9AB
Stephen L Woodworth
708 S Washington S
Angola IN 46703

Call Sign: WB9VCC
David L Syler
712 Saginaw
Angola IN 46703

Call Sign: KB9VJE
David L Syler
712 Saginaw
Angola IN 467031731

Call Sign: KC9BET
Kenneth D Lowden
1509 Shadow Lake Dr
Angola IN 467036928

Call Sign: K9JKF
Kenneth D Lowden
1509 Shadow Lake Dr
Angola IN 467036928

Call Sign: WB9DGD
Harlan W Kriete
807 Steven St
Angola IN 46703

Call Sign: N9IYE
Donna S Kriete
807 Stevens
Angola IN 46703

Call Sign: N9UZJ
Lama H Chandrasena
305 Unit E
Angola IN 46703

Call Sign: N9HUD
Lainie K Smith
815 Village Green Dr
Angola IN 46703

Call Sign: N5SLL
John H Reinoehl
1112 Village Green Dr
Angola IN 46703

Call Sign: N9BGX
William D Eberhart
3095 W 100 N
Angola IN 46703

Call Sign: KC9EDC
Christopher J Stewart
6680 W 200 N
Angola IN 46703

Call Sign: KB9QQN
Michael J Eckerle
6775 W 300 N
Angola IN 46703

Call Sign: KC9JJZ
Stephanie A Eckerle
6775 W 300 N
Angola IN 46703

Call Sign: KA9RVH
Charles L Parker
1180 W 350 N
Angola IN 46703

Call Sign: KB9YTR
William D White
4760 W 95 S
Angola IN 46703

Call Sign: KC9RDX
Richard C Wirt
4760 W 95 S
Angola IN 46703

Call Sign: N9IJN
John M Bell
214.5 W Broad St
Angola IN 46703

Call Sign: KB9TGE
Jerry L Clark
1102 W Broad St
Angola IN 46703

Call Sign: KC9PJQ
Leslie A Wooster
1975 W Fox Lake Rd
Angola IN 46703

Call Sign: N9FAK
Becky L Hill
2485 W Hwy 20
Angola IN 46703

Call Sign: KD9GK
Jack G Hill
2485 W Hwy 20
Angola IN 46703

Call Sign: KB9KMN
Kenneth L Adams
3735 W Landis Rd
Angola IN 46703

Call Sign: KB9KMM
Ryan S Adams
3735 W Landis Rd
Angola IN 46703

Call Sign: KC9IAM
Christopher L Drake
780 W Mill St
Angola IN 46703

Call Sign: KB9VGJ
Ken K Maier
4065 W Orland Rd
Angola IN 46703

Call Sign: KC9HTG
James P White II
7920 W Orland Rd
Angola IN 46703

Call Sign: N9CVS
Emmett C McCoskey
3121 W Shadyside Rd
Angola IN 46703

Call Sign: KC9EDH
Arthur L Mumma
201 W South St
Angola IN 46703

Call Sign: KB9TLT
Janice E Lamott
2615 W Sycamore Beach
Rd
Angola IN 46703

Call Sign: KB9RRB
Thomas N Lamott
2645 W Sycamore Beach
Rd
Angola IN 46703

Call Sign: NZ9S
Lewis E Hartzler
4305 W US Hwy 20 Lot
16
Angola IN 467031606

Call Sign: KC9UKG
Kent A Alwood
502 Williamson Cir
Angola IN 46703

Call Sign: K9ENT
Kent A Alwood
502 Williamson Cir
Angola IN 46703

**FCC Amateur Radio
Licenses in Arcola**

Call Sign: KC9SYE
James M Skora
10907 Arcola Rd
Arcola IN 46704

Call Sign: W9JMJ
James M Skora
10907 Arcola Rd
Arcola IN 46704

Call Sign: WD9GJI
Todd A Lehman
Arcola IN 46704

FCC Amateur Radio Licenses in Argos

Call Sign: KC9IXL
William A Strong III
316 Center St
Argos IN 46501

Call Sign: KB9PTQ
Daniel J Vialard
10273 E 12th Rd
Argos IN 46501

Call Sign: KB9NGY
Michael A Shoemaker
17638 Hickory Rd
Argos IN 46501

Call Sign: N8ACS
Jimmy L Smiley
17519 Juniper Rd
Argos IN 465019590

Call Sign: K9DE
Robert J Nellans
20737 Linden
Argos IN 465019536

Call Sign: AK9DE
De K9 ARC

20737 Linden Rd
Argos IN 465019536

Call Sign: N9ECC
Dorthy I Nellans
20737 Linden Rd
Argos IN 465019536

Call Sign: WA9OHZ
Howard S Wilhelm
124 Logan St
Argos IN 46501

Call Sign: NE9F
David A Speegle
311 S West St
Argos IN 46501

Call Sign: N9ISU
James W Burroughs
10448 SR 10
Argos IN 46501

Call Sign: N9XTO
Ronald D Sherer
12734 W SR 10
Argos IN 46501

Call Sign: KC9CMI
James W Burroughs
120 Westview Ct
Argos IN 46501

FCC Amateur Radio Licenses in Ashley

Call Sign: KB9SYL
Harold A Scherf
477 CR 15
Ashley IN 46705

Call Sign: KC9GDG
Kyle E Schwyn
525 CR 17
Ashley IN 46705

Call Sign: KB9UKK
Tony J Robertson
1449 CR 2
Ashley IN 46705

Call Sign: KC9APP
Brian T Clark
7547 S 400 W
Ashley IN 46705

Call Sign: N9XYH
Herbert G Grate
201 S Gonser St Box 203
Ashley IN 46705

Call Sign: KB9JVK
Shirley A Miller
309 S Wabash
Ashley IN 46705

Call Sign: KC9LVL
Kelly A Alwood
1760 W 765 S
Ashley IN 46705

Call Sign: K9SOF
Kelly A Alwood
1760 W 765 S
Ashley IN 46705

Call Sign: KC9RDW
Thomas A Overmyer
Ashley IN 46705

FCC Amateur Radio Licenses in Atwood

Call Sign: KB9ORU
David E Melton
116 E South St
Atwood IN 46502

Call Sign: WB9OST
Loren L Melton

Atwood IN 46502

FCC Amateur Radio Licenses in Auburn

Call Sign: KC9IMV
Timothy A Stayner
1511 Adam Ave
Auburn IN 46706

Call Sign: KB9FL
Kenneth D Cool
1302 Ashwood Dr
Auburn IN 46706

Call Sign: KC9APS
Roy E Watson
2015 Bradford Dr
Auburn IN 467061051

Call Sign: N9WOZ
David M Dalton
1008 Bryan Ave
Auburn IN 46706

Call Sign: N9XEQ
Ronald W Grant
1503 Bryan Ave
Auburn IN 46706

Call Sign: KA9LRE
John K Ober
109 Center St
Auburn IN 46706

Call Sign: KF4OTG
Jack W Bortner
1410 Cherry Ln
Auburn IN 46706

Call Sign: N9YR
Jack W Bortner
1410 Cherry Ln
Auburn IN 46706

Call Sign: KC9IPO
Donna M Stayner
1113 Cindy St
Auburn IN 46706

Call Sign: KB9MDY
Sidney B Meyer
5422 CR 11A
Auburn IN 46706

Call Sign: N9MYJ
Karl E Mavis Sr
5499 CR 11A Box 282
Auburn IN 46706

Call Sign: WD9CVX
Leonard Shaffer
3402 CR 19
Auburn IN 46706

Call Sign: WB9RWD
Shirley D Wagner
3741 CR 27
Auburn IN 46706

Call Sign: WA9KWO
Harold W Adams
3896 CR 27
Auburn IN 46706

Call Sign: KF5JSH
Dorothy E Thomas
5365 CR 31
Auburn IN 46706

Call Sign: N9TPO
Jon A Hoard
5587 CR 31
Auburn IN 46706

Call Sign: KB9JAM
Bryan L Dickman
4391 CR 35
Auburn IN 46706

Call Sign: N9XYK
Gregory L Dickman
4391 CR 35
Auburn IN 46706

Call Sign: KC9LNE
John M Fribley
3190 CR 36
Auburn IN 467069450

Call Sign: KB9SAQ
Jay A Oberholtzer
2434 CR 38
Auburn IN 46706

Call Sign: KC9OFQ
Kenneth E Fike
899 CR 40
Auburn IN 46706

Call Sign: KC9JXB
Kenneth H Olson
3208 CR 40
Auburn IN 46706

Call Sign: KC9OWI
Sam O Comfort
3945 CR 427
Auburn IN 46706

Call Sign: KC9AZF
John L Zimmerman
5908 CR 427
Auburn IN 467069510

Call Sign: KC9KLH
Stacey B Cuautle
4318 CR 49
Auburn IN 46706

Call Sign: KB9OZB
Kurt B Grimm
4315 CR 50
Auburn IN 46706

Call Sign: N9VUL
Sherrill L Miles
5149 CR 52
Auburn IN 46706

Call Sign: KC7EXJ
Nathan D Sherman
4488 CR 68
Auburn IN 46706

Call Sign: KA9WRV
Ann M Thomas
7900 Garman Rd
Auburn IN 46706

Call Sign: KA9ODT
William G Miles
5149 CR 52
Auburn IN 46706

Call Sign: N9EHK
Bradley L Witte
3503 CR 72
Auburn IN 467069669

Call Sign: KD9SW
James L Heller
107 Gates Cove
Auburn IN 46706

Call Sign: KB9HPY
Richard L Hill
4488 CR 64
Auburn IN 46706

Call Sign: KC9LSD
Johnathon W Burns
1512 Dallas St
Auburn IN 46706

Call Sign: KC9OAW
Richard L Debolt
2122 Glen Hollow Dr
Auburn IN 46706

Call Sign: KB9HPX
Susan A Hill
4488 CR 64
Auburn IN 46706

Call Sign: WD9GOO
John E Chalmers
1400 Davidson Ct
Auburn IN 46706

Call Sign: KC9MRY
James F Jackson
2124 Glen Hollow Dr
Auburn IN 46706

Call Sign: W9LTN
John E Klein
4128 CR 68
Auburn IN 46706

Call Sign: W9GOO
John E Chalmers
1400 Davidson Ct
Auburn IN 46706

Call Sign: NC9H
James A Roberts
410 Hawthorne Pl
Auburn IN 46706

Call Sign: KC9DHZ
Jack L Hoard
4276 CR 68
Auburn IN 46706

Call Sign: KB9VBW
Stephanie R Bender
605 E 9th St
Auburn IN 467062423

Call Sign: W9OWO
Jack Dold
1201 Hideaway Dr
Auburn IN 46706

Call Sign: KB7LLB
Darla J Sherman
4488 CR 68
Auburn IN 46706

Call Sign: WD9CUJ
Steve F Ulm Sr
121 E Madison St
Auburn IN 46706

Call Sign: KA9RVJ
Paul A Brewer
209 Iwo St
Auburn IN 46706

Call Sign: N7NGO
Douglas W Sherman
4488 CR 68
Auburn IN 46706

Call Sign: KC9CFH
Gina M Teixeira
312 Ensley Ave
Auburn IN 46706

Call Sign: N9JXY
Dennis L Payton
1305 Kiblinger Pl
Auburn IN 46706

Call Sign: KC7UTE
Valerie M Sherman
4488 CR 68
Auburn IN 46706

Call Sign: WD9CVV
Thomas M Culler
2019 Fairview Dr
Auburn IN 46706

Call Sign: N9SCI
Donn E Bly
104 Maxwell Pl
Auburn IN 46706

Call Sign: K9BBZ
Willard R Cupka
916 Midway Dr
Auburn IN 467061330

Call Sign: K9CFJ
Cyrus F Johnson
1121 Packard Pl
Auburn IN 467061340

Call Sign: AB9XT
Jonathan W Decker
617 S Indiana Ave
Auburn IN 46706

Call Sign: N9VXV
Wayne R Pinckney
606 N Cedar St
Auburn IN 46706

Call Sign: N9NYO
Mark B Middaugh
809 Park Pl
Auburn IN 46706

Call Sign: KC9UVS
Michael L Johnson
617 S Indiana Ave
Auburn IN 46706

Call Sign: KB9MYX
Patrick J Barrett
805 N Indiana Ave
Auburn IN 467061105

Call Sign: KC9KNT
Matthew P Boger
902 S Cedar St
Auburn IN 46706

Call Sign: KB9MSA
Joshua M Bowsman
617 S Indiana Ave
Auburn IN 467062846

Call Sign: W9VKW
Albert H Gengnagel
742 N Main St
Auburn IN 46706

Call Sign: KC9TPE
Robert T Gass Jr
1001 S Cedar St
Auburn IN 46706

Call Sign: NJ9M
Steven W Grogg
304 S Iwo St
Auburn IN 46706

Call Sign: WD9CUI
Dorothy J Eckhart
508 N Van Buren St
Auburn IN 46706

Call Sign: KC9JXA
William E Kruse
217 S Cleveland St
Auburn IN 46706

Call Sign: N9YCC
Donald E Dickman
2222 S Wayne St
Auburn IN 46706

Call Sign: WD9CVW
Robert L Eckhart
508 N Van Buren St
Auburn IN 46706

Call Sign: KD8AZN
Charles E Decker IV
601 S Indiana Ave
Auburn IN 46706

Call Sign: KA9HPY
Clarence W Distelrath Jr
3588 SR 327
Auburn IN 46706

Call Sign: WB9VDK
Richard A Toy
801 N Van Buren St
Auburn IN 46706

Call Sign: WD9CJV
William H Sink
615 S Indiana Ave
Auburn IN 46706

Call Sign: WB9SGX
Estil E Taylor
1036 Steve St
Auburn IN 46706

Call Sign: WB9RWF
Paul E Freeburn
1100 Naomi
Auburn IN 46706

Call Sign: KC9NNQ
Jonathan W Decker
617 S Indiana Ave
Auburn IN 46706

Call Sign: N9XYL
Tom E Greenwell
1038 Steve St
Auburn IN 46706

Call Sign: KC9JZR
Cyrus F Johnson
1121 Packard Pl
Auburn IN 467061340

Call Sign: KT1GER
Jonathan W Decker
617 S Indiana Ave
Auburn IN 46706

Call Sign: KB9MHR
Bret B Hall
1210 Superior Dr
Auburn IN 46706

Call Sign: K9HTJ
Clarence L Eley Sr
1104 Superior St
Auburn IN 46706

Call Sign: KC9RVK
Steven W Hayward
707 Tecumseh Ct
Auburn IN 46706

Call Sign: N8LXV
Steven W Hayward
707 Tecumseh Ct
Auburn IN 46706

Call Sign: KC9HSL
Laura J Long
1221 Turnberry Ln
Auburn IN 467069487

Call Sign: KG9NN
Robert F Long
1221 Turnberry Ln
Auburn IN 467069487

Call Sign: KB9BIQ
Wesley D Warstler II
1533 Urban Ave
Auburn IN 46706

Call Sign: N9YCE
Berlin G Slone
1608 Urban Ave
Auburn IN 46706

Call Sign: KG9QU
Martin G Simmonds
1212 Virginia Ln
Auburn IN 46706

Call Sign: KK4PI
Martin G Simmonds
1212 Virginia Ln
Auburn IN 46706

Call Sign: KC9DOY
Christopher S Mays
1300 Virginia Ln
Auburn IN 467063800

Call Sign: KB9MAZ
Christopher S Mays
1300 Virginia Ln
Auburn IN 467063800

Call Sign: KB9YTS
Karen L Scott
414 W 15th St
Auburn IN 46706

Call Sign: N2BMT
Stephen K Kummernuss
107 W 2nd St
Auburn IN 467061719

Call Sign: KB9OPG
Jeremy T Woods
503 W Ensley Ave
Auburn IN 46706

Call Sign: KA9NVZ
Patricia A Stemen
112 Zona Dr
Auburn IN 46706

Call Sign: KC9RSC
Jeffrey Freese
113 Zona Dr
Auburn IN 46706

Call Sign: N9VHD
Lorna S Mavis
Auburn IN 46706

Call Sign: W9JIN
Arthur G Olds
Auburn IN 46706

Call Sign: KC9YY
David L Southern

Auburn IN 46706

Call Sign: N9XYJ
David P Todd
Auburn IN 46706

Call Sign: KB9OZA
John M Haecker
Auburn IN 46706

Call Sign: K9VR
John M Haecker
Auburn IN 46706

Call Sign: KA9TVG
Sharon K Parker
Auburn IN 46706

Call Sign: W9OU
North Eastern Indiana
ARC
Auburn IN 46706

FCC Amateur Radio Licenses in Avilla

Call Sign: KC9EZS
Jason L Gurden
900 Autumn Hills Dr Lot
45
Avilla IN 46710

Call Sign: KC9OZM
Ryan A Duncan
312 Dominic
Avilla IN 46710

Call Sign: W7KRW
James E Groll
217 Dominic St
Avilla IN 476109765

Call Sign: KC9OZN
Halferty Sonne
7189 E 100 N

Avilla IN 46710

Call Sign: KC9OWH
Jeffrey P Sonne
7189 E 100 N
Avilla IN 46710

Call Sign: KA9KOG
Bennie L Grimm
10294 E 100 S
Avilla IN 46710

Call Sign: N9VHI
Russell J Carteaux
539 E Albion St
Avilla IN 46710

Call Sign: KC9OWF
Danin E Fluke
128 E Weimer Rd
Avilla IN 46710

Call Sign: WB9GCU
Robert D Leatherman
1729 E Weimer Rd
Avilla IN 46710

Call Sign: N9OLL
David G Cordray
313 Lewis St
Avilla IN 46710

Call Sign: KC9VCW
Charles M Crager
906 Miner Rd
Avilla IN 46710

Call Sign: KC9KLG
Tyler L Grimm
1489 Old SR 3
Avilla IN 46710

Call Sign: KC9KNU
Duane C Squire
544 S 1100 E

Avilla IN 46710

Call Sign: N9VXN
Keith Bohnenberger
534 S 500 E
Avilla IN 46710

Call Sign: KA9NWJ
James D Culler
1014 S 600 E
Avilla IN 46710

Call Sign: KC9FJD
Marek J Dragan
Avilla IN 46710

FCC Amateur Radio Licenses in Berne

Call Sign: KB9BCP
Jonathan W Vanator
423 Bryan St
Berne IN 46711

Call Sign: N9KBD
Ricky R Lechlitner
366 Clark St
Berne IN 46711

Call Sign: KC9PRM
Norman J Amstutz
880 E 3505
Berne IN 46711

Call Sign: N9QNV
Patrick K Young
406 E Franklin St
Berne IN 46711

Call Sign: KC9TZ
Donald K Van Zuilen
605 E Main
Berne IN 46711

Call Sign: KA9YGY

Randall F Culver
2572 E SR 218
Berne IN 46711

Call Sign: KC9NHT
Landon K Patterson
724 Hendricks St
Berne IN 46711

Call Sign: KC9PRN
Mark R Chaffins
1426 Hendricks St
Berne IN 46711

Call Sign: KB9IAU
Jo E Nevsimal
366 Lane St
Berne IN 46711

Call Sign: KC9UOV
Tyler D Pyle
765 Lehman St
Berne IN 46711

Call Sign: KC9OBL
Cary J Raesner
406 N Jefferson St
Berne IN 46711

Call Sign: KC9OBM
Dennis Raesner
406 N Jefferson St
Berne IN 46711

Call Sign: N9KXY
Randal R Jones
417 N Jefferson St
Berne IN 46711

Call Sign: KC9UT
Stephen W Burry
1525 Old Colonial Dr
Berne IN 46711

Call Sign: AB9RA

Stephen W Burry
1525 Old Colonial Dr
Berne IN 46711

Call Sign: KB9P
Stephen W Burry
1525 Old Colonial Dr
Berne IN 46711

Call Sign: KC9SYI
Andrew W Brotherton
4320 S 000 Rd
Berne IN 46711

Call Sign: KC9PRL
Jenifer L Hirschy
7370 S 000 Rd
Berne IN 46711

Call Sign: KA9FQG
Mark D Hirschy
7370 S 000 Rd
Berne IN 46711

Call Sign: N5VQA
Cy A Schaadt
5595 S 300 E
Berne IN 46711

Call Sign: WB9KQO
Nelson T Clark
3523 S 500 W
Berne IN 46711

Call Sign: KC9GVG
James T Hortenberry Jr
3755 S 500 W
Berne IN 46711

Call Sign: KC9VDD
Jackie W Earl
107 S Portland
Berne IN 46711

Call Sign: WD9EVC

Charles E Circle
305 W Compromise St
Berne IN 46711

Call Sign: KC9NHS
Carla D Steury
817 W Main
Berne IN 46711

Call Sign: N9EGT
Wayne F Steury
817 W Main
Berne IN 46711

Call Sign: KB9KYM
Adams County ARC
817 W Main
Berne IN 46711

Call Sign: WA9QMY
Harry Mazelin
366 W Parr Rd
Berne IN 46711

Call Sign: WB0KZC
Martin B Blocki
666 W Van Buren
Berne IN 46711

Call Sign: N9GXA
Paul B Kahlert
805 W Van Buren St
Berne IN 46711

Call Sign: N9JMZ
Mitchel W Sprunger
518 W Water St
Berne IN 46711

Call Sign: KC9NHX
Gregory A Hagen
867 W Water St
Berne IN 46711

Call Sign: KB9BCQ

Arthur J Lipina
306 Wabash St
Berne IN 467112130

FCC Amateur Radio Licenses in Beverly Shores

Call Sign: WB9CWY
William T Taylor
10 S Palmer Ave
Beverly Shores IN 463010344

Call Sign: KC9NZK
Robert C Elliott
102 Wells Rd
Beverly Shores IN 46301

Call Sign: K9ISS
Robert C Elliott
102 Wells Rd
Beverly Shores IN 46301

Call Sign: KC9FWX
Michael Pavel
Beverly Shores IN 46301

Call Sign: N9YIC
Richard A Rikoski
Beverly Shores IN 46301

Call Sign: W9ZD
Richard A Rikoski
Beverly Shores IN 46301

FCC Amateur Radio Licenses in Bippus

Call Sign: N9MPH
Paul G Deal
Bippus IN 46713

FCC Amateur Radio Licenses in Bluffton

Call Sign: KC9GLJ
David R Shepherd
20 Capri Ct Apt B
Bluffton IN 467141331

Call Sign: KC9CGJ
Matthew K Hartman
1104 Hollyhock Ln
Bluffton IN 46714

Call Sign: N9CIS
Michael Gerwig
703 S Main St
Bluffton IN 46714

Call Sign: W9SFE
Paul I Sell
3244 E 400 N
Bluffton IN 467149213

Call Sign: N9DMX
Robert W Deihl
1296 Lakeview Ct
Bluffton IN 46714

Call Sign: KC9VKP
Ben J Osborn
3011 S Meridian Rd
Bluffton IN 46714

Call Sign: KC9CTW
Kenneth E Moody
1242 E 500 S
Bluffton IN 46714

Call Sign: WB9YPH
Bernard L Osborn
120 Lindenwood Dr
Bluffton IN 46714

Call Sign: KC9JNW
Ronald K Bowman
806 S Oak St
Bluffton IN 46714

Call Sign: KC9CYS
Kenneth E Moody
1242 E 500 S
Bluffton IN 46714

Call Sign: KA9JCV
Carolyn A Osborn
120 Lindenwood Dr
Bluffton IN 46714

Call Sign: WD9JKQ
Herman R Zeps
319 S Williams St
Bluffton IN 46714

Call Sign: K8PKW
Kenneth E Moody
1242 E 500 S
Bluffton IN 46714

Call Sign: N9AHO
Max R Dawson
203 Lindenwood Dr
Bluffton IN 46714

Call Sign: KC9SYJ
Dewey M Jacks
1015 S Williams St
Bluffton IN 467143523

Call Sign: KB9AVE
David C Clark
522 E Townley St
Bluffton IN 46714

Call Sign: WD9FAI
Lawrence W Clifford
201 N Oak St Ext
Bluffton IN 46714

Call Sign: N9ZI
Terry R Hammons
4199 SE SR 116
Bluffton IN 46714

Call Sign: N9FNN
Randy D Meyer
428 E Washington St
Bluffton IN 46714

Call Sign: KB9LYB
Jon C Smith Sr
847 Pkwy Dr
Bluffton IN 46714

Call Sign: KB9QIU
Jeffrey G Eltzroth
23 Sunrise Way
Bluffton IN 467141225

Call Sign: N9CEW
Kenneth L Baker
19 Garden Ln
Bluffton IN 46714

Call Sign: W6JOL
Thomas B Stogdill
820 River Rd
Bluffton IN 46714

Call Sign: KD9XK
Barry E King
80 Sunset Dr Lot 1
Bluffton IN 46714

Call Sign: KC8NUO
Larry E Collins
233 Hickory Knoll Dr
Bluffton IN 46714

Call Sign: KA9YWV
Angela C Streater
420 S 500 E
Bluffton IN 46714

Call Sign: KG9AJ
Michael R Heaton
80 Sunset Dr Lot 17
Bluffton IN 46714

Call Sign: N9VXT
Scott C Moss
5636 SW SR 116 1
Bluffton IN 46714

Call Sign: K9MKN
John O Cowens
207 Toll Cir
Bluffton IN 46714

Call Sign: WD9IZY
Sylvia L Wann
302 Toll Cir
Bluffton IN 467141153

Call Sign: KA9HIY
Thomas W Wann
302 Toll Cir
Bluffton IN 467141153

Call Sign: KB9SAB
Michael J Severini
310 W Central Ave
Bluffton IN 46714

Call Sign: N9GPL
George C Johnson
909 W Cherry St
Bluffton IN 46714

Call Sign: KC9UOU
Gary A Deckard
917 W Lancaster St
Bluffton IN 46714

Call Sign: K9SLQ
Darrell W Grove
1025 W Lancaster St
Bluffton IN 46714

Call Sign: K9WWJ
Harold A Shaft
1014 W Wabash St
Bluffton IN 46714

FCC Amateur Radio Licenses in Boone Grove

Call Sign: KB9QH
Brian R Roeske
Boone Grove IN 46302

FCC Amateur Radio Licenses in Boswell

Call Sign: N9VAI
Richard D Eberhardt
311 N Clinton St
Boswell IN 47921

Call Sign: KC9OZY
W B Alter
Boswell IN 47921

Call Sign: AA5WB
W B Alter
Boswell IN 47921

FCC Amateur Radio Licenses in Bourbon

Call Sign: KB9MED
Scott A Ellinger
1786 12B Rd
Bourbon IN 46504

Call Sign: KC9QAK
Lenny D Berkey
2926 13th Trl
Bourbon IN 46504

Call Sign: KC9RRF
Scott A Haines
1599 E 13th Trl
Bourbon IN 46504

Call Sign: KC9RRA
Ryan F Schori

302 N Harris St
Bourbon IN 46504

Call Sign: WB9JUP
Glenn A Ames
801 N Washington St
Bourbon IN 465041445

Call Sign: KC9RRI
Preston M Brandon
535 S Main
Bourbon IN 46504

Call Sign: KC9RRJ
Kurt R Brandon
535 S Main St
Bourbon IN 46504

Call Sign: KC9QGZ
John J Gomola
402 S Thompson St
Bourbon IN 46504

Call Sign: W9JJG
John J Gomola
402 S Thompson St
Bourbon IN 46504

Call Sign: N9FOS
Calvin E Yoder
108 W Florence
Bourbon IN 46504

Call Sign: KC9AEM
Carl O Lucas
200 W Florence St Apt
17
Bourbon IN 46504

FCC Amateur Radio Licenses in Bremen

Call Sign: KC9NAG
Anthony N Truex
2455 3B Rd

Bremen IN 46506

Bremen IN 46506

Bremen IN 46506

Call Sign: KB9KBY
Robert B Kling
4090 3rd Rd
Bremen IN 46506

Call Sign: KB9ESX
Jeremy P Walter
304 E Plymouth St
Bremen IN 46506

Call Sign: KB9RXX
John L Ott
68906 Miami Rd
Bremen IN 46506

Call Sign: K9BCI
James E Brown
5294 3rd Rd
Bremen IN 46506

Call Sign: N9NCC
Joshua A Walter
304 E Plymouth St
Bremen IN 46506

Call Sign: KB9JHE
Orville O Kling Jr
214 N Bowen Ave
Bremen IN 46506

Call Sign: KC9IWO
Jason L Hanson
1025 Alex Patrick Dr
Bremen IN 46506

Call Sign: N9MGU
Patty L Walter
304 E Plymouth St
Bremen IN 46506

Call Sign: N9YGV
Pamela J Ernsberger
511 N Center
Bremen IN 46506

Call Sign: KC9VKD
Leslie R Turner
404 Burket Ln
Bremen IN 46506

Call Sign: N9FCO
Paul A Walter
304 E Plymouth St
Bremen IN 46506

Call Sign: N9UFA
Michelle M Walter
122 N East St
Bremen IN 46506

Call Sign: W9LRT
Leslie R Turner
404 Burket Ln
Bremen IN 46506

Call Sign: KB9JTF
Robert D Roye Jr
68008 Elm Rd
Bremen IN 46506

Call Sign: N9MFM
Randy J Walter
122 N East St
Bremen IN 46506

Call Sign: N9QFG
Leslie A Graham
8483 Chicago St
Bremen IN 46506

Call Sign: KC9PKA
Michael D Czajkowski III
6984 Filbert Rd
Bremen IN 46506

Call Sign: KA9PBM
Philip S Leman
221 N Maryland St
Bremen IN 46506

Call Sign: KB9YAA
John A Baxter
8410 Clark St
Bremen IN 46506

Call Sign: WB9ODX
Robert L Densmore
4180 Grape Rd
Bremen IN 46506

Call Sign: WA9IWV
Melvere D Sheley
6861 Plymouth Goshen
Trl
Bremen IN 46506

Call Sign: KB9YIK
James E Brown
5294 E 3rd Rd
Bremen IN 46506

Call Sign: KC0BZM
Leighann M Kimble
545 Hope Blvd
Bremen IN 46506

Call Sign: W9MEL
Melvere D Sheley
6861 Plymouth Goshen
Trl
Bremen IN 46506

Call Sign: KA9AIR
Walter A Lynch
436 E North St

Call Sign: KA9SIX
Norman W Rowe
141 Meadowlark Ln

Call Sign: AA9AB

Thaddeus M Jones
19451 Quinn Rd
Bremen IN 46506

Call Sign: N9FX
James R Ernsberger III
2950 Redwood Ct
Bremen IN 46506

Call Sign: KC9HXF
Robert L Locke
550 S Birkey St
Bremen IN 46506

Call Sign: KB9IHR
Tom F Dettbrenner
213 S Bowen Ave
Bremen IN 46506

Call Sign: WB9ZHV
Jeff R Dietrich
514 S Bowen Ave
Bremen IN 46506

Call Sign: KA9RPN
Ralph P Karstedt
348 S Collier St
Bremen IN 46506

Call Sign: N9NAC
Joseph E Radican
421 S East St
Bremen IN 46506

Call Sign: KC9NAK
James L Brown
427 S Liberty Dr
Bremen IN 46506

Call Sign: K9HUM
James L Brown
427 S Liberty Dr
Bremen IN 46506

Call Sign: KC9NAE

Lisa M Brown
427 S Liberty Dr
Bremen IN 46506

Call Sign: KC9LYJ
Richard J Webster
428 S Liberty Dr
Bremen IN 465061975

Call Sign: KC9PJR
Rollo M Stoneburner
227 S Stewart St
Bremen IN 46506

Call Sign: KA9ZSG
Laurene J Gunterman
307 S Whitlock St
Bremen IN 46506

Call Sign: KB9HYC
Sarah E Gumz
4825 SR 331 S
Bremen IN 46506

Call Sign: KD9AO
Allen Stoneburner Sr
3386 US 6
Bremen IN 46506

Call Sign: WD9ECU
Rickey E Leiter
3280 US 6 E
Bremen IN 46506

Call Sign: KA9IYH
James N Anderson
10137 US 6 W
Bremen IN 46506

Call Sign: N9QFF
Harold D Rexstrew Jr
1630 W Grant St
Bremen IN 46506

Call Sign: KB9KFW

Lisa A Wheatbrook
117.5 W Plymouth St
Bremen IN 46506

Call Sign: N9EWN
Thomas W Griffin
4273 W Shore Dr
Bremen IN 46506

Call Sign: WD9EKF
John W Richards
4344 W Shore Dr
Bremen IN 46506

FCC Amateur Radio Licenses in Bringhurst

Call Sign: KB9ISB
Mark B McCracken
2 1st St
Bringhurst IN 46913

Call Sign: N9PWL
Ricky R Durham
Box 86A
Bringhurst IN 46913

Call Sign: W9WX
Joseph W Dinger
7054 E 300 S
Bringhurst IN 46913

Call Sign: K8TEP
Bruce A Hardyniec
5615 E Woodland Way
Bringhurst IN 469139734

Call Sign: W9VP
William V Pickart
4510 S 95 E
Bringhurst IN 46913

FCC Amateur Radio Licenses in Bristol

Call Sign: KC9UMQ
Nico F Valentijn
53560 Baywater Pl
Bristol IN 46507

Call Sign: N9ICO
Nico F Valentijn
53560 Baywater Pl
Bristol IN 46507

Call Sign: KB9ZJR
Karen M Leiby
53615 Bridgewood Dr
Bristol IN 46507

Call Sign: KB9YRA
Scott L Leiby
53615 Bridgewood Dr
Bristol IN 46507

Call Sign: KC9GOK
Keith C Hoover
53536 CR 17
Bristol IN 46507

Call Sign: KB9ZJT
Denny R Overholser
56691 CR 19
Bristol IN 46507

Call Sign: KX4W
Matthew S Gull
50813 CR 23
Bristol IN 46507

Call Sign: KB9QYC
Larry K Byrd
51545 CR 25
Bristol IN 46507

Call Sign: KA9ORN
Cecil T Rust
55238 CR 31
Bristol IN 46507

Call Sign: N9GRO
Burton A Clemens
51374 CR 35
Bristol IN 46507

Call Sign: KC9PNP
Edward Harris
105 Fairway Ave
Bristol IN 46507

Call Sign: KB9NNC
Michael J Newton
53801 Hyde Park Dr
Bristol IN 46507

Call Sign: KC9DZM
Samuel L Borrelli
55503 Lacey Ln
Bristol IN 46507

Call Sign: KC4TIO
Joseph J Covello
53303 Monticola Ln
Bristol IN 46507

Call Sign: KC9ICL
Thomas D Szymanski
14311 SR 120
Bristol IN 46507

Call Sign: KC6TDD
Ric M Butterfield
16675 SR 120
Bristol IN 46507

Call Sign: KA9CZT
Linda I Crusie
56603 SR 15
Bristol IN 46507

Call Sign: KB9MOR
Michelle D Crusie
56603 SR 15
Bristol IN 46507

Call Sign: KA9QVM
Bernard E Crusie Jr
56603 SR 15
Bristol IN 46507

Call Sign: KA9GRS
James R Kaufman
20399 SR 120
Bristol IN 46507

Call Sign: KL7TW
Timohty E King
53150 Sylvan Ct
Bristol IN 46507

Call Sign: KB9VAC
Paula G Coody
19670 US 20
Bristol IN 46526

Call Sign: KC9TSA
Brent Zook Memorial
Group
18582 US Hwy 20
Bristol IN 46507

Call Sign: N9HZ
Brent Zook Memorial
Group
18582 US Hwy 20
Bristol IN 46507

Call Sign: KA9HRD
John T White
Bristol IN 46507

**FCC Amateur Radio
Licenses in Brook**

Call Sign: WA9WWW
Paul G Vandervort
5289 S 150 E
Brook IN 47922

Call Sign: KC9COR

Kyle D Conrad
Brook IN 47922

FCC Amateur Radio Licenses in Brookston

Call Sign: N9VCO
Charles M McDonald
300E
Brookston IN 47923

Call Sign: KC9VHR
Ryan M Maxson
505 E 8th St Apt B
Brookston IN 47923

Call Sign: WB9OFG
John A Rodenbarger Jr
N Prairie
Brookston IN 47923

Call Sign: KA9KCD
William A Szabela
11020 S 200 E
Brookston IN 47923

Call Sign: KB9LKE
Jeannette M Schwartz
8622 S 300 E
Brookston IN 47923

Call Sign: WA9CWC
James M Beavers
700 S Mills St
Brookston IN 47923

Call Sign: W9ARS
James M Beavers
700 S Mills St
Brookston IN 47923

Call Sign: KC9BPE
John A Coy
2877 W 800 S
Brookston IN 47923

Call Sign: KG9J
Charles W Foley
11432 W Horseshoe
Bend Rd
Brookston IN 47923

Call Sign: KC9ETA
Joel S Mahoney
11873 W Tecumseh Bend
Rd
Brookston IN 47923

Call Sign: WS9K
George N Burkhart Jr
Brookston IN 47923

Call Sign: WB9SOY
Paul O Bailey
Brookston IN 479230222

FCC Amateur Radio Licenses in Bryant

Call Sign: WA9QDD
Meredith L Garlinger
405 E Main St
Bryant IN 47326

Call Sign: KC9RIX
Michael E Kimmel
6665 E SR 67
Bryant IN 47326

Call Sign: KB9YKR
Nancy M Armstrong
3418 W 650 N
Bryant IN 47326

FCC Amateur Radio Licenses in Buffalo

Call Sign: KB9PLL
Michael A Pope
9795 Valley Ct

Buffalo IN 47925

Call Sign: W9BOX
Michael A Pope
9795 Valley Ct
Buffalo IN 47925

Call Sign: KC9CDR
David L Roberts
Buffalo IN 47925

FCC Amateur Radio Licenses in Bunker Hill

Call Sign: KB9GGH
Ginny M Quick
223 Center St
Bunker Hill IN 46914

Call Sign: N9WRC
Benjamin Graber
2530 E 900 S
Bunker Hill IN 46914

Call Sign: KB9QNX
Deanna M Perez
651 S Clinton
Bunker Hill IN 46914

Call Sign: N9SOI
Tina M Hollenback
959 W 900 S
Bunker Hill IN 46914

Call Sign: N9LBU
Howard L Twining
2383 W Broadway
Bunker Hill IN 46914

Call Sign: KC9JFT
Jon A Zipperian
2383 W Broadway
Bunker Hill IN 46914

Call Sign: N9LNO

Jon A Zipperian
2383 W Broadway
Bunker Hill IN 46914

Call Sign: KA9FHB
Richard L Jarvis
Bunker Hill IN 46914

Call Sign: W9OKU
Charles E Shrock
Bunker Hill IN 46914

Call Sign: KC9EQX
Bradford C Gallatin
Bunker Hill IN 46914

Call Sign: KC9EEV
David C Gallatin
Bunker Hill IN 46914

Call Sign: KB9QCU
Michael T McAvoy
Bunker Hill IN 46914

Call Sign: KC9ANY
Leroy W Morris III
Bunkar Hill IN 46914

Call Sign: N9TQZ
Rex D Grismore
Bunker Hill IN 46914

FCC Amateur Radio Licenses in Burlington

Call Sign: WA2KVX
Arthur J Dance
Burlington IN 46915

FCC Amateur Radio Licenses in Burnettsville

Call Sign: KC9CRP
Mark A Babb
301 Main St

Burnettsville IN 47926

Call Sign: N9OJB
Gregory D Spence
407 West St
Burnettsville IN 47926

FCC Amateur Radio Licenses in Burns Harbor

Call Sign: KA9BQD
Donald K Carpenter
1188 N Salt Creek Rd
Burns Harbor IN 46304

Call Sign: WA9Q
James C Vokorokos
1171 Rak Rd
Burns Harbor IN 46304

FCC Amateur Radio Licenses in Burrows

Call Sign: KA9UOI
Joseph P Martin
Burrows IN 46916

FCC Amateur Radio Licenses in Butler

Call Sign: KC9GVJ
Dennis E Gauger II
Box 6073
Butler IN 46721

Call Sign: KC9NDK
Donald L Crowl
5761 CR 12
Butler IN 46721

Call Sign: KA8UDY
Mary L Stickan
8155 CR 18
Butler IN 46721

Call Sign: N8GAZ
Christian A Stickan
8155 CR 18
Butler IN 46721

Call Sign: N9OBY
Alva W Crabill
3652 CR 47
Butler IN 46721

Call Sign: KC9HOZ
David S Hepworth
3763 CR 49
Butler IN 46721

Call Sign: KB9WVV
Matthew Peckhart
2220 CR 79
Butler IN 46721

Call Sign: KC9QCA
Billy J Albertson
2060 CR 81
Butler IN 46721

Call Sign: N9DMC
Harold A Seltenright Sr
310 E Green St
Butler IN 46721

Call Sign: KB9AKV
Helen L Seltenright
310 E Green St
Butler IN 46721

Call Sign: KB9IBY
Larry D McCann
209 N Ivy
Butler IN 46721

Call Sign: KK4PI
Martin G Simmonds
19 Northcrest Tr Ct
Butler IN 46721

Call Sign: KB9OXM
Donald H Dilley
240 Park Ln
Butler IN 46721

Call Sign: K9GRX
Katherine E Arnett
4928 SR 1
Butler IN 46721

Call Sign: KB9UQI
Doris A Kray
6660 SR 8
Butler IN 46721

Call Sign: K9DFC
Gerald L Kray
6660 SR 8
Butler IN 46721

Call Sign: KB9UTO
Jon E Wilcox
6942 SR 8
Butler IN 46721

Call Sign: KC9DPB
Marian D Wilcox
6942 SR 8
Butler IN 46721

Call Sign: KA8WFA
Christine L Taylor
7049 SR 8
Butler IN 46721

Call Sign: KA9LAA
Philip H Taylor
7049 SR 8
Butler IN 46721

Call Sign: KB9RCW
Pamela Z Schlosser
320 W Main St
Butler IN 467211326

Call Sign: WB9URM
David A Tupps
130 W Oak
Butler IN 46721

Call Sign: KB9UFM
Max E Deam
319 Walnut
Butler IN 46721

FCC Amateur Radio Licenses in Camden

Call Sign: WD9BIG
Judith K Skiles
Box 132C
Camden IN 46917

Call Sign: WD9BIH
Larry L Skiles
Box 132C
Camden IN 46917

Call Sign: W9WTP
Jean V Pickart
Box 166
Camden IN 46917

Call Sign: KB9SDZ
Michael A Shoemaker
2485 E 750 N
Camden IN 46917

Call Sign: WA9NLO
Otis A Beamer Jr
193 Main St
Camden IN 469170196

Call Sign: K9DDF
Jimpsie F Doyel
684 N Water St
Camden IN 469179551

FCC Amateur Radio Licenses in Cedar Lake

Call Sign: KB9ONQ
Kenneth A Oliver
11630 Belmont Pl
Cedar Lake IN 46303

Call Sign: N9RAK
Dawn L Dunavin
13850 Butternut St
Cedar Lake IN 46303

Call Sign: KB9YJL
Todd A Hunt
13926 Butternut St
Cedar Lake IN 46303

Call Sign: WB9VYW
John R Van Zyl
Carey St
Cedar Lake IN 46303

Call Sign: K9JVZ
John R Van Zyl
Carey St
Cedar Lake IN 46303

Call Sign: KC9EAP
James S Reynhout
12601 Havenwood Pass
Cedar Lake IN
463038651

Call Sign: KA9TAP
Jack A Olthoff
12604 Havenwood Pass
Cedar Lake IN 46303

Call Sign: WB9EWF
David M Heuer
15238 Hawthorne
Cedar Lake IN 46303

Call Sign: N9YEP

Nathanael P Greene
15233 Hawthorne Ct
Cedar Lake IN 46303

Call Sign: KB9CEB
Edward A Fetting Sr
8300 Lake Shore Dr
Cedar Lake IN 46303

Call Sign: KC9LHP
Joseph D Oparka
8510 Lake Shore Dr
Cedar Lake IN 46303

Call Sign: KC9LQF
Stacy M O'Parka
8510 Lakeshore Dr
Cedar Lake IN 46303

Call Sign: KC9ACU
Daniel W Wells
13909 Lauerman St
Cedar Lake IN 46303

Call Sign: KB9PIX
Donald S Kwiatkowski Jr
12736 Parrish Ave
Cedar Lake IN 46303

Call Sign: N1KBR
Bert M Pepowski
12915 Parrish St
Cedar Lake IN 46303

Call Sign: KA9LEM
Lillie M Jukovich
9780 W 113th Ave
Cedar Lake IN 46303

Call Sign: WB9TTI
Lillie M Jukovich
9780 W 113th Ave
Cedar Lake IN 46303

Call Sign: WB9TTI

Vladimir Jukovich
9780 W 113th Ave
Cedar Lake IN 46303

Call Sign: W9VJU
Vladimir Jukovich
9780 W 113th Ave
Cedar Lake IN 46303

Call Sign: K9ADK
Richard G Domazet
9800 W 113th Ave
Cedar Lake IN 46303

Call Sign: AC9D
Steve P Zambo Jr
11624 W 117th Ave
Cedar Lake IN 46303

Call Sign: KB9GTB
Mark A Bradley
13083 W 118th Pl
Cedar Lake IN 46303

Call Sign: KA9LZP
Rennie E Armstrong
11405 W 126th Ave
Cedar Lake IN 46303

Call Sign: KB9ZYJ
David W Carlson
7120 W 128th Ln
Cedar Lake IN 46303

Call Sign: KA9DGR
E Martin
14221 W 135th Ave
Cedar Lake IN 46303

Call Sign: N9TES
Richard A Wheeler
8613 W 139th Pl
Cedar Lake IN 46303

Call Sign: KG9A

William H Campbell
7001 W 140th Ave
Cedar Lake IN 46303

Call Sign: KB9SFQ
Timothy P Burns
7316 W 140th Pl
Cedar Lake IN 46303

Call Sign: KC9HMY
Linda L Bates
7101 W 148 Ave
Cedar Lake IN 46303

Call Sign: W9YGH
Linda L Bates
7101 W 148 Ave
Cedar Lake IN
463039141

Call Sign: WB9VRG
Richard N Bates
7101 W 148th Ave
Cedar Lake IN 46303

Call Sign: N9PCU
Joseph A Kucken
Cedar Lake IN 46303

Call Sign: WZ9T
Kristian K Kortokrax
Cedar Lake IN 46303

Call Sign: KB9MYY
Anthony F Janik
Cedar Lake IN 46303

Call Sign: KB9NSD
Kenneth P Kilroy
Cedar Lake IN 46303

Call Sign: KC9HOA
Michael A Marine
Cedar Lake IN 46303

Call Sign: KB9TAT
Steve Nemeth
Cedar Lake IN 46303

Call Sign: KC9OUP
Michael Marcussen
202 E Earl St
Chalmers IN 47929

Call Sign: KC9WM
Michael Marcussen
202 E Earl St
Chalmers IN 47929

Call Sign: N9TPG
Paul J Bodie
656 4th St
Chesterton IN 46304

Call Sign: KC9AII
David C Lange
274 Arbor Dr
Chesterton IN 46304

Call Sign: WA9TDO
Reginald A Mabin
110 Beverly Dr
Chesterton IN 46304

Call Sign: KB9LHJ
Jim W Ton
321 Bowser
Chesterton IN 46304

Call Sign: W9JOJ
Burton L Cleaveland Sr
531 Brummitt Park Dr
Chesterton IN 463041611

Call Sign: KC9IBO
Elizabeth C Lowry
388 Burdick Rd
Chesterton IN 46304

Call Sign: KC9MCR
Paul M Lowry
388 Burdick Rd
Chesterton IN 46304

Call Sign: KB9TUB
Jovo I Manojlovic
1904 Catkin Cir
Chesterton IN 46304

Call Sign: KC9PXM
Jordan S Hoover
1035 Chestnut Blvd
Chesterton IN 46304

Call Sign: KC9SCL
Terry A Hoover
1035 Chestnut Blvd
Chesterton IN 46304

Call Sign: N9EBX
Joe F Adams Sr
1734 Crocker St
Chesterton IN 46304

Call Sign: NG9B
John R Bowman
2402 Dakota
Chesterton IN 46304

Call Sign: WA9MSD
Joseph Grossbauer Jr
217 Dogwood Dr
Chesterton IN 46304

Call Sign: N9ZDT
Joseph J Jastreboski
1221 Dogwood Dr
Chesterton IN 46304

Call Sign: N9ESS
Lila M Hallberg
80 E 1050 N
Chesterton IN 46304

Call Sign: KD9KH
Carl J Hallberg
80 E 1050 N
Chesterton IN 463049107

Call Sign: W9CJH
Carl J Hallberg
80 E 1050 N
Chesterton IN 463049107

Call Sign: N9MFJ
Eric S Martin
363 E 1050 N
Chesterton IN 46304

Call Sign: N9IRR
Louis S Martin
363 E 1050 N
Chesterton IN 46304

Call Sign: KC9AVL
Robin M Brunder
401 E 1300 N
Chesterton IN 46304

Call Sign: N9BMJ
Richard E Hill
91 E CR 900 N
Chesterton IN 46304

Call Sign: N9UST
Greta L Gordon
66 E Oak Hill Rd
Chesterton IN 46304

Call Sign: N9USU
Patrick R Gordon
66 E Oak Hill Rd
Chesterton IN 46304

Call Sign: KB6ION
James L Freeman
269 E Paul Revere Dr
Chesterton IN 46304

Call Sign: N9CTP
Juliette C Long
511 E Porter Ave
Chesterton IN 46304

Call Sign: N9RBP
Robert F Oberle
906 Fox Pt Dr
Chesterton IN 46304

Call Sign: WD9HDE
Danny W Scheetz
750 Graham Dr
Chesterton IN 46304

Call Sign: W9DWS
Danny W Scheetz
750 Graham Dr
Chesterton IN 46304

Call Sign: W9SAL
All States Radio Club
750 Graham Dr
Chesterton IN 463041620

Call Sign: N9ZWA
Thomas W Magill
1625 Green Meadow Ln
Chesterton IN 46304

Call Sign: KB9PFI
Jerame J Simpson
2027 Hawthorne Ln
Chesterton IN 46304

Call Sign: KC9AXS
Elizabeth N Kozlik
1531 Hogan Ave
Chesterton IN 46304

Call Sign: N9PYD
James A Kieklak
1541 Hogan Ave
Chesterton IN 46304

Call Sign: KC9ATU
Michael L Gawronski
1304 Jefferson Ave
Chesterton IN 46304

Call Sign: K9QKE
Gordon W Kohler
1030 Jefferson St
Chesterton IN 46304

Call Sign: KA9PZP
John W Koelm
5302 La Hayne Rd
Chesterton IN 46304

Call Sign: KC9DJK
Bruce A Resteau
1311 Lake Dr
Chesterton IN 463041655

Call Sign: KB9LHM
Karl J Galamback II
661 Long Bridge Dr
Chesterton IN 46304

Call Sign: KC9MCT
Douglas S Moore
971 Michael Dr
Chesterton IN 46304

Call Sign: KC9FWY
Dan J Watt
1263 Morningside Dr
Chesterton IN 46304

Call Sign: KC9EKC
Northwest Indiana
Skywarn
951 N 100 W
Chesterton IN 46304

Call Sign: K9NWI
Northwest Indiana
Skywarn
951 N 100 W
Chesterton IN 46304

Call Sign: WA9TSQ
Bernard S Gawronski
951 N 100 W
Chesterton IN 46304

Call Sign: KB9JRY
Mary A Gawronski
951 N 100 W
Chesterton IN 46304

Call Sign: KC9DAY
Tom M Green
1210 N 345 E
Chesterton IN 46304

Call Sign: N9FTS
Reginald J Lenard
1115 N 350 E
Chesterton IN 46304

Call Sign: KB9FRM
Richard L Webb
1411 N CR 200 E
Chesterton IN 46304

Call Sign: KB9SVH
Philip J Lacorte III
1096 N CR 475 E
Chesterton IN 463049528

Call Sign: WD9DCO
James P Martin
1603 Old Farm Ln
Chesterton IN 46304

Call Sign: KF9XR
Lowell G Black
2670 Pinehurst Ave

Chesterton IN 46304

Call Sign: KC9TWU
James M Newman
709 Plaza Dr 217 Ste 2
Chesterton IN 46304

Call Sign: KC9KYD
John M Carrigan
709 Plaza Dr Ste 2
Chesterton IN 46304

Call Sign: KB9NLC
Kenneth L Graham
210 Rainbow Dr 14
Chesterton IN 46304

Call Sign: N9EDN
Arthur M Swanson
1185 Rak Rd Burns
Harbor
Chesterton IN 46304

Call Sign: K9LTG
Robert A Jaroll
1251 Redbud Dr
Chesterton IN 463042653

Call Sign: W9VAY
Dallas B Summers
127 S 15th St
Chesterton IN 463042021

Call Sign: KC9HQS
Collin W Koch
314 S 18th St
Chesterton IN 463042042

Call Sign: N9ZYS
Dru J Wilke
321 S 18th St
Chesterton IN 46304

Call Sign: KB9RWU
James D Bane

162 S 19th St
Chesterton IN 46304

Call Sign: WB9YHH
John W Cripliver
801 S 20th St
Chesterton IN 46304

Call Sign: KC9CZE
Cecilia C Houde
317 S 22nd St
Chesterton IN 46304

Call Sign: KB9YOH
Stephen T Early
426 S 3rd St
Chesterton IN 46304

Call Sign: W9KFW
Donald A Wozniak
950 S 5th St
Chesterton IN 46304

Call Sign: KB9YRK
Brandon G Allmon
205 S 8th St
Chesterton IN 46304

Call Sign: N9XIB
Weldon J Slater Jr
318 S 8th St
Chesterton IN 46304

Call Sign: KA9FAU
Virgil J Gassoway
605 S Calumet Ave
Chesterton IN 46304

Call Sign: K9CA
Carrol E Gustafson
706 S Jackson Blvd
Chesterton IN 46304

Call Sign: N3AYU
Charles J Affelder

1081 Sandpiper Dr
Chesterton IN 46304

Call Sign: KC9IUV
Jim R Merryman
501 Shannon Dr
Chesterton IN 46304

Call Sign: W3UPM
Judith A Betts
507 Shannon Dr
Chesterton IN 46304

Call Sign: W3UP
Robert L Betts
507 Shannon Dr
Chesterton IN 46304

Call Sign: KC9VFR
Christopher P Mcnamara
366 Spring View Ct
Chesterton IN 46304

Call Sign: WA9ALW
Robert S Kollar
502 Starwood Dr
Chesterton IN 46304

Call Sign: KC9QPC
George F Cairns
2115 Texas St
Chesterton IN 46304

Call Sign: K9GBB
Julie A Hewitt
512 W 1100 N Apt 1D
Chesterton IN 46304

Call Sign: KC9GUH
Kevin M Wesley
72 W 900 N
Chesterton IN 46304

Call Sign: KB9RXU

Chesterton High School
ARC
651 W Morgan Ave
Chesterton IN 46304

Call Sign: NW9C
John V Swanson
136 W Porter Ave
Chesterton IN 46304

Call Sign: WB9HCI
Robert C Stahl
251 Water Tower Dr
Chesterton IN 463042632

Call Sign: KB9VCU
Joe P Neal
537 Windridge Dr
Chesterton IN 46304

Call Sign: N9TOY
Keith A Saulsgiver
Chesterton IN 46304

**FCC Amateur Radio
Licenses in Churubusco**

Call Sign: KB9UHH
Daniel Ostroinski
418 Charlotte Ave
Churubusco IN 46723

Call Sign: WD9HRP
Paul T Schram
8620 E 300 N
Churubusco IN 46723

Call Sign: KC9BKM
Darrell L Resler
2705 E 500 S 57
Churubusco IN 46723

Call Sign: KC9SKG
Barbara A Ward
3150 E 550 S

Churubusco IN 46723

Call Sign: W9WOZ
Barbara A Ward
3150 E 550 S
Churubusco IN 46723

Call Sign: KC9PJP
Daniel N Ward
3150 E 550 S 57
Churubusco IN 46723

Call Sign: N9WLW
Daniel N Ward
3150 E 550 S 57
Churubusco IN 46723

Call Sign: KB9DUK
Anthony W Carter
4960 E 600 N
Churubusco IN 46723

Call Sign: K9DUK
Anthony W Carter
4960 E 600 N
Churubusco IN 46723

Call Sign: WZ9C
James J Smith
4960 E 600 N
Churubusco IN 46723

Call Sign: AB9UY
Paul R Queitsch
3023 E 600 S 57
Churubusco IN 46723

Call Sign: WQ5I
Paul R Queitsch
3023 E 600 S 57
Churubusco IN 46723

Call Sign: WD8PSW
John A Smith
6699 E McGuire Rd

Churubusco IN 46723

Call Sign: KB9YWX
S Charles Morgan
8616 E SR 205
Churubusco IN 46723

Call Sign: N9XKN
Robert L Plant
McDuffee Rd
Churubusco IN 46723

Call Sign: KC9QVS
Dennis J Gering
6560 N 650 E Lot 42
Churubusco IN 46723

Call Sign: WB9FPK
William R Schane
2785 N 675 E
Churubusco IN
467239513

Call Sign: N9KAQ
Tracy S Gienger
5300 N 700 E Lot 16
Churubusco IN 46723

Call Sign: N9DCA
Michael E Murphy Sr
5405 N Blue Lake Rd
Churubusco IN 46723

Call Sign: KB9JFA
Madalyn B Sade
515 N Mulberry
Churubusco IN 46723

Call Sign: WB1EVZ
Scott A Garner
4679 N Sheldon Rd
Churubusco IN
467239788

Call Sign: KB9JFC

Nick A Shiriaer
7160 N US 30
Churubusco IN 46723

Call Sign: N9YNK
Sharon L Anders
5655 S 100 E 57
Churubusco IN 46723

Call Sign: W9SA
Charles W Anders
5655 S 100 E 57
Churubusco IN 46723

Call Sign: KC9CVB
David L Resler
4719 S 300 E
Churubusco IN 46723

Call Sign: N9VSR
Clarence L Resler
4742 S 300 E 57
Churubusco IN 46723

Call Sign: N9ZTF
Ruth E Resler
4742 S 300 E 57
Churubusco IN 46723

Call Sign: KB8UWG
Douglas A Geese
11610 SR 205
Churubusco IN 46723

Call Sign: K9FQN
John R McKinney
16024 Wappes Rd
Churubusco IN 46723

Call Sign: K9INM
Margaret A McKinney
16024 Wappes Rd
Churubusco IN 46723

Call Sign: K9OMA

James H Pliett
16702 Wappes Rd
Churubusco IN 46723

Call Sign: KA9YYI
Muriel A Pliett
16702 Wappes Rd
Churubusco IN 46723

Call Sign: KF6KMA
Robert J Adams
10109 Watterson Rd
Churubusco IN 46723

Call Sign: WD9HJB
John A Blad
11507 Watterson Rd
Churubusco IN 46723

Call Sign: KE9ND
Paul R Queitsch
Churubusco IN 46723

FCC Amateur Radio Licenses in Claypool

Call Sign: KC9UAE
Edwin P Ksiezopolski
1473 E 700 S
Claypool IN 46510

Call Sign: KC9RRK
William D Sherwin Sr
11530 S 400 E
Claypool IN 46510

Call Sign: KC9BSB
Georg C Langheld
S 400 W
Claypool IN 46510

Call Sign: KC9TRK
David P Miller
4219 S 450 W
Claypool IN 46510

Call Sign: KC9RQO
Elizabeth A Miller
4219 S 450 W
Claypool IN 46510

Call Sign: KC9RQR
Teresa J Miller
4219 S 450 W
Claypool IN 46510

Call Sign: KC9RQQ
Dathan L Reed
4219 S 450 W
Claypool IN 46510

Call Sign: KB9IDB
Howard H Patrick
6206 S Packerton Rd
Claypool IN 46510

FCC Amateur Radio Licenses in Columbia City

Call Sign: N9EDE
Tim H Roberts
500W 57
Columbia City IN 46725

Call Sign: KB9GXU
Graham L Kleespie
5 Blue River Dr
Columbia City IN 46725

Call Sign: KC9QGF
Amanda F Jackson
705 Camden Dr
Columbia City IN 46725

Call Sign: KC9QGG
David M Jackson
705 Camden Dr
Columbia City IN 46725

Call Sign: WB9LAF
David M Jackson
705 Camden Dr
Columbia City IN 46725

Call Sign: KA9HLE
David M Jackson
705 Camden Dr
Columbia City IN 46725

Call Sign: W9SMQ
Lewis W Brown
417 Columbia Dr
Columbia City IN 46725

Call Sign: KA9FDK
Stephen M O
Shaughnessy
CR 700 S
Columbia City IN 46725

Call Sign: N9QCL
Roger L McEntarfer
717 E 400 N
Columbia City IN 46725

Call Sign: KC9ANF
Whitley County Ema
Radio Club
717 E 400 N
Columbia City IN 46725

Call Sign: WB8ORR
Catherine L Evilsizor
250 E 500 N
Columbia City IN
467258993

Call Sign: KA9QWC
Donald L Evilsizor
250 E 500 N
Columbia City IN
467258993

Call Sign: KC9APQ

John W Sebring
335 E 600 N
Columbia City IN 46725

Call Sign: W9YEL
Paul E Brower
690 E 600 N
Columbia City IN
467258909

Call Sign: K9KFR
Robert A Johnson
3580 E 600 N
Columbia City IN 46725

Call Sign: WB9SPY
Herman L Smith Jr
2495 E 800 S
Columbia City IN 46725

Call Sign: K9RWO
Ewing M Potts
5494 E 800 S
Columbia City IN 46725

Call Sign: K9PCX
Robert M Zinn
3542 E Arabian Dr
Columbia City IN
467259228

Call Sign: WB9UDS
Charl R Bandelier
3543 E Arabian Dr
Columbia City IN 46725

Call Sign: KB9YLL
Desiree M Douglas
1915 E Bair Rd
Columbia City IN 46725

Call Sign: N9RJB
Becky J Spencer
1915 E Bair Rd

Columbia City IN
467258941

Call Sign: KF9LZ
Raymond D Spencer
1915 E Bair Rd
Columbia City IN
467258941

Call Sign: K9VU
Raymond D Spencer
1915 E Bair Rd
Columbia City IN
467258941

Call Sign: WB9TBF
Patricia L Giessler
1977 E Bair Rd 8
Columbia City IN 46725

Call Sign: WE9G
Max A Kimble
7006 E Chapine Rd
Columbia City IN 46725

Call Sign: W9NNH
Melanie M Dahms
1320 E Greenbriar Dr
Columbia City IN 46725

Call Sign: N9WNH
Dan M Dahms
1320 E Greenbriar Dr
Columbia City IN 46725

Call Sign: N9RJ
Russell D Johnson
1840 E Inverness Cir
Columbia City IN 46725

Call Sign: N9NXT
Gregory M Hippensteel
207 E Jackson St
Columbia City IN 46725

Call Sign: N9JRY
Gregory S Walls
409 E Jefferson St
Columbia City IN 46725

Call Sign: KB9VNN
Susan M Schane
6625 E Johnson Rd
Columbia City IN 46725

Call Sign: KC9RPR
Ryan D Swangin
5430 E Lincolnway
Columbia City IN 46725

Call Sign: N9KXL
Glenn W Willson
6671 E Lincolnway
Columbia City IN 46725

Call Sign: N9BQG
Louis E Wuellner
1900 E Linker Rd
Columbia City IN 46725

Call Sign: W9JBD
Gene V Williams
2184 E Linker Rd
Columbia City IN
467258927

Call Sign: KB9FZY
Annette I Welling
212 E Market St
Columbia City IN 46725

Call Sign: KB9FWX
Albert E Andreas Jr
2948 E Muncie Dr
Columbia City IN 46725

Call Sign: N9EYO
Gregory S White
2725 E Muncie Rd
Columbia City IN 46725

Call Sign: KC9FBA
John M Butcher
4614 E Old Trl Rd Lot 6
Columbia City IN 46725

Call Sign: KA9IPB
Lowell H Klinefelter
3083 E S Shore Dr
Columbia City IN
467259365

Call Sign: KA9MWK
Robert J Tennant
1861 E Schug Rd
Columbia City IN 46725

Call Sign: N9NNU
Debra K Smith
4477 E SR 14
Columbia City IN 46725

Call Sign: N9FGN
James E Smith
4477 E SR 14
Columbia City IN 46725

Call Sign: KC9LNF
Joshua T Smith
4477 E SR 14
Columbia City IN 46725

Call Sign: N9DOQ
Albert L Volz
4753 E SR 14
Columbia City IN
467259236

Call Sign: KB9IHS
Michael D Macino
5620 E SR 205
Columbia City IN 46725

Call Sign: W9LZ
James A Macino

5620 E SR 205
Columbia City IN 46725

Call Sign: W0GJB
Gregory J Bateman
2903 E Stalf Rd
Columbia City IN 46725

Call Sign: W9GJB
Gregory J Bateman
2903 E Stalf Rd
Columbia City IN 46725

Call Sign: KC9NQU
Edward J Scott
407 E Van Buren St
Columbia City IN 46725

Call Sign: AA9KB
John P Wasmuth Jr
2215 E Whispering Trl
Columbia City IN
467257586

Call Sign: W9WT
Theodore N Tahmisian Jr
1166 E Wildwood Dr
Columbia City IN 46725

Call Sign: KO9E
Gene L Kinney
1661 E Wildwood Dr
Columbia City IN
467258620

Call Sign: KB9VMP
Matthew S White
5461 Fish Hatchery Rd
Columbia City IN 46725

Call Sign: N3QKF
Stanley J Hartzler
724 Graber Ct
Columbia City IN 46725

Call Sign: KB9YOW
Christopher N Harper
24 Jeffrey Dr
Columbia City IN 46725

Call Sign: KA9DFU
William Berry
126 Lake Shore Dr Big
Lake Rr 8
Columbia City IN 46725

Call Sign: N9STR
Kerry A Schultz
3399 Lincolnway W
Columbia City IN 46725

Call Sign: N9NUU
Gregory B Jackson
6828 N 350 W
Columbia City IN 46725

Call Sign: KE6FXO
James T Clark
2262 N 650 W
Columbia City IN
467259147

Call Sign: N9WNI
Matthew R Minier
5892 N Ashford Dr
Columbia City IN
467257755

Call Sign: N9NAB
Donald L Clark
341 N Indian Hills
Columbia City IN 46725

Call Sign: N8SAS
Rebecca J Douglas
2363 N Indiana St
Columbia City IN 46725

Call Sign: N8SAQ
Douglas L Douglas

2363 N Indiana St
Columbia City IN
467259000

Call Sign: WB8LQU
Robert L Rafferty
1540 N Lincolnway
Columbia City IN
467259168

Call Sign: W9EOJ
Robert L Rafferty
1540 N Lincolnway
Columbia City IN
467259168

Call Sign: KA9VBS
Lois A O Neil
6486 N Lynn St
Columbia City IN 46725

Call Sign: NG9M
Raymond C O Neil
6486 N Lynn St
Columbia City IN 46725

Call Sign: KB9UBR
Robert J Mosher
315 N Main St
Columbia City IN 46725

Call Sign: KB9UBS
Robert G Mosher
315 N Main St
Columbia City IN 46725

Call Sign: W9MBK
Charles Q Callahan
480 N Ruckman Rd
Columbia City IN 46725

Call Sign: KA9JJB
Mary R Callahan
480 N Ruckman Rd
Columbia City IN 46725

Call Sign: KC9KTA
Sergey V Zinovyev
1305 N SR 109
Columbia City IN 46725

Call Sign: W9EEE
Richard J Leo
1305 N SR 109
Columbia City IN 46725

Call Sign: WB9DLC
Michael J Barrell
1530 N SR 109
Columbia City IN 46725

Call Sign: KB9WTX
Adam A Chamberlain
4141 N SR 109
Columbia City IN 46725

Call Sign: KT9K
James L Sheehan
6950 N Valley Ave
Columbia City IN 46725

Call Sign: KB9CQO
Henry R Mackey
333 N Walnut St
Columbia City IN 46725

Call Sign: N9HM
Henry R Mackey
333 N Walnut St
Columbia City IN 46725

Call Sign: WD9ITQ
Robert H Geiger
511 N Walnut St
Columbia City IN 46725

Call Sign: KA9FNG
John W Phillips
309 N Washington
Columbia City IN 46725

Call Sign: N9VTF
David A Byers
5546 N Willow Ave
Columbia City IN 46725

Call Sign: N9XXM
Jeannie L Byers
5546 N Willow Ave
Columbia City IN 46725

Call Sign: K9EJS
Edward J Scott
824 Plantation Dr
Columbia City IN 46725

Call Sign: N9PEM
Jon A Shew II
376 River Bluff Dr
Columbia City IN 46725

Call Sign: KB9HLO
Stephanie D Halsey
115 Rolling Hills Ave
Columbia City IN 46725

Call Sign: N8QCR
Timothy-Gene G Wagner
3085 S 150 E
Columbia City IN 46725

Call Sign: KC9DCP
Justin L Whaley
611 S 300 E
Columbia City IN 46725

Call Sign: W9ESK
Herbert R Weaver
3104 S 300 W
Columbia City IN 46725

Call Sign: W9CCX
Charles R Shultz
6978 S 500 E
Columbia City IN 46725

Call Sign: W9WN
John A Coleman
4046 S 600 E
Columbia City IN 46725

Call Sign: W9PMT
Lois A Coleman
4046 S 600 E
Columbia City IN 46725

Call Sign: KC9CDT
Lee B Simmonds
5520 S 600 W 57
Columbia City IN 46725

Call Sign: WB9DAE
Clarence W Hessler
108 S Chauncey St Apt
104
Columbia City IN 46725

Call Sign: N9SBE
Gary W Willson
2040 S Lone Pine Rd
Columbia City IN 46725

Call Sign: N9SBS
Sally A Willson
2040 S Lone Pine Rd
Columbia City IN 46725

Call Sign: N9MFO
James R Weldon
4937 S Northshore Dr 57
Columbia City IN
467259451

Call Sign: N9FNV
Eugene F Morr
4665 S SR 9
Columbia City IN
467259664

Call Sign: KB9YWU

Michael E Waldeck
103 S Walnut St
Columbia City IN 46725

Call Sign: N9STQ
Randy E Waldeck
103 S Walnut St
Columbia City IN 46725

Call Sign: KA9GPM
Terry L Marker
8036 S Washington Rd
Columbia City IN 46725

Call Sign: N9OOS
John E Wainwright
9875 S Washington Rd
Columbia City IN 46725

Call Sign: KC9VAQ
David J Connewell
1161 S Wolf Rd
Columbia City IN 46725

Call Sign: KC9STB
Brandon L Barnes
474 W 200 N
Columbia City IN 46725

Call Sign: KC9FDB
Jon F Weirick
4975 W 200 S
Columbia City IN 46725

Call Sign: KC9ORT
Nathan R Gregory
8538 W 400 S 57
Columbia City IN 46725

Call Sign: KK5PG
Luke J Hollmann
2940 W 450 N
Columbia City IN 46725

Call Sign: K9EBZ

John G Smith
1140 W 500 N
Columbia City IN 46725

Call Sign: N9VSO
Nancy S Beltz
1749 W 600 N
Columbia City IN 46725

Call Sign: KB9MDM
Christina D Chappel
4029 W Camp Whitley
Rd
Columbia City IN 46725

Call Sign: N9UZV
Steven M Chappel
4029 W Camp Whitley
Rd
Columbia City IN 46725

Call Sign: N9ZNN
Teresa D Chappel
4029 W Camp Whitley
Rd
Columbia City IN 46725

Call Sign: N9STS
Michael A Neidigh
3444 W Circle Dr 57
Columbia City IN 46725

Call Sign: WB9FZO
Charles R Longardner
3577 W Circle Dr 57
Columbia City IN 46725

Call Sign: WB9UNL
David E Keiser
310 W Ellsworth St
Columbia City IN 46725

Call Sign: KB9PPX
Whitley County
Emergency Radio Club

310 W Ellsworth St
Columbia City IN 46725

Call Sign: N9EBK
Doris L Smith
3882 W Lakeshore Dr 57
Columbia City IN 46725

Call Sign: K9JS
James V Smith
3882 W Lakeshore Dr 57
Columbia City IN 46725

Call Sign: KB9OFE
David A Cotterman
2520 W Lincoln Way
Columbia City IN 46725

Call Sign: N9REB
Michael A Cotterman
2520 W Lincoln Way
Columbia City IN 46725

Call Sign: KB9NCF
Sally A Cotterman
2520 W Lincoln Way
Columbia City IN 46725

Call Sign: KB9OFD
Stacey R Cotterman
2520 W Lincoln Way
Columbia City IN 46725

Call Sign: N9AWD
Frank J Chance Jr
3384 W Old Lake Rd
Columbia City IN 46725

Call Sign: KC9TIH
Robert W Abbott
2955 W SR 14
Columbia City IN 46725

Call Sign: N9UYG
Gregory W Willson

1354 W Stoneridge Dr
Columbia City IN 46725

Call Sign: KC9QAF
Blueline Users Group
3065 W US Hwy 30
Columbia City IN 46725

Call Sign: K9BLU
Blueline Users Group
3065 W US Hwy 30
Columbia City IN 46725

Call Sign: K9KOP
Joshua R Church
3065 W US Hwy 30
Columbia City IN 46725

Call Sign: WX9RUB
William D Lower
3065 W US Hwy 30
Columbia City IN 46725

Call Sign: N9DWU
John Tripcony
506 W Van Buren St
Columbia City IN 46725

Call Sign: KB9OQP
Scott L Miller
316.5 W Van Buren St
Apt 2
Columbia City IN
467252057

Call Sign: N9FPD
Max E Bennett
3743 W Wilt St 57
Columbia City IN 46725

Call Sign: N9RYM
Joseph D Doyle Jr
2052 Wilcken Rd
Columbia City IN 46725

Call Sign: KB0ON
Donald T Ruf
Columbia City IN 46725

Call Sign: N9BAE
June A Geiger
Columbia City IN 46725

Call Sign: WC9AR
Whitley County ARC
Columbia City IN 46725

Call Sign: KB9KWX
Whitley County ARC
Columbia City IN 46725

Call Sign: KC9AEP
Santa Fe Trail Club
Columbia City IN
467250717

Call Sign: KC9GKE
Ronald L Bowland
1000E
Converse IN 46919

Call Sign: WB9YHF
Beecher A Waters
Box 462
Converse IN 46919

Call Sign: KC9MUY
Roger D Couch
10113 E 1300 S
Converse IN 46919

Call Sign: WD9EIO
George D Chunn
521 N 800 W 27
Converse IN 46919

Call Sign: WD9GRX

Charles S Bailor
806 N Jefferson St
Converse IN 46919

Call Sign: N9QES
Richard A Alexander
7250 W 300 N 27
Converse IN 46919

Call Sign: KA9EDA
Ronald D Jones
8282 W Delphi Pike 27
Converse IN 46919

Call Sign: WD9EOJ
Robert S Hart
7691 W Mier Rd 27
Converse IN 46919

Call Sign: KA9VWO
Mary E Miller
Converse IN 46919

Call Sign: KD7JXJ
Robert H Foltz
1322 CR 20
Corunna IN 467309737

Call Sign: KC9CYA
Michelle R Baumgartner
1021 CR 8
Corunna IN 46730

Call Sign: N9ZUA
Jay A Baumgartner
1021 CR 8
Corunna IN 46730

Call Sign: KB9OZC
Bruce J Flint
104 Heenan St
Corunna IN 46730

Call Sign: KB9HIG
Robin U Nessel
3360 SR 327
Corunna IN 46730

Call Sign: K9JHG
James H Graves
2392 N West St
Craigville IN 46731

Call Sign: AJ9J
James H Graves
2392 N West St
Craigville IN 46731

Call Sign: KA9GZN
Emerson Bushong
Box 23
Cromwell IN 46732

Call Sign: KA9WCJ
Debra J Fulk
Box 559
Cromwell IN 46732

Call Sign: W9BQS
Ben L Gregorowicz
9174 E Cinderella Dr
Cromwell IN 46732

Call Sign: KC9LLX
Sean M Anderson
9169 E Lilac Ln
Cromwell IN 46732

Call Sign: KC9QXU
Sean M Anderson
9169 E Lilac Ln

Cromwell IN 46732

Call Sign: KB8BGQ
John C Sherman
9867 E Starry Eyed Ln
Cromwell IN 46732

Call Sign: KB8CRO
Grace L Sherman
9867 E Starry Eyed Ln
Cromwell IN 46732

Call Sign: KB8CRN
Phillip M Sherman
9867 E Starry Eyed Ln
Cromwell IN 46732

Call Sign: KB9JWJ
John M Rich
3757 N 900 W 95
Cromwell IN 46732

Call Sign: KC9FDA
Brandon D Jamerson
3757 N 900 W Lot 4
Cromwell IN 46732

Call Sign: KC9ATJ
Joel A Pelz
11218 N Honeycomb Ln
Cromwell IN 46732

Call Sign: N9NBM
Mark A Campbell Sr
11994 N Morris Rd
Cromwell IN 46732

Call Sign: KA9JTI
Ted V Hughes
11900 N Rumpelstiltzkin
Dr
Cromwell IN 46732

Call Sign: AA9IH
Tamara S Pence

1058 S Bause Lake Dr W
Cromwell IN 467329787

Call Sign: N9DVP
Marjorie R Bushong
85 S SR 5
Cromwell IN 467329785

Call Sign: KC9BKJ
Bobby L Jacobs
8223 W 100 N
Cromwell IN 46732

Call Sign: N9BCP
Jack W Fulk
10199 W 200 N
Cromwell IN 467329758

Call Sign: KC9RCX
Glade N Rogers
11236 W 75 N
Cromwell IN 46732

Call Sign: N9DVO
Joann K Fulk
Cromwell IN 46732

FCC Amateur Radio Licenses in Crown Point

Call Sign: KC9TEW
Jeff S Kohn
2775 Autumn Dr
Crown Point IN 46307

Call Sign: KD9DP
Daryl E Fraley Jr
1715 Beech Dr
Crown Point IN 46307

Call Sign: KB9ORH
Kerry F Orze
8571 Bell St
Crown Point IN 46307

Call Sign: KC9IUU
Nicholas A Crnokrak
10656 Bell St
Crown Point IN 46307

Call Sign: W9CEY
Earl H Morin Jr
1249 Brandywine Rd
Crown Point IN 46307

Call Sign: NW9F
Steve Vukusic
3905 Brookside Dr
Crown Point IN 46307

Call Sign: NR9D
Steve Vukusic
3905 Brookside Dr
Crown Point IN 46307

Call Sign: KQ7E
Steve Vukusic
3905 Brookside Dr
Crown Point IN 46307

Call Sign: N5OQE
Major B Norman Jr
9571 Bryan Pl
Crown Point IN 46307

Call Sign: KB9KFV
Lawrence J Ryan
12676 Buchanan Ln
Crown Point IN 46307

Call Sign: KC9SQH
Dennis J Hilburger
2935 Burge Dr
Crown Point IN 46307

Call Sign: KA9CHH
William R Aimutis Sr
4043 Burningtree Ct Lofs
Crown Point IN 46307

Call Sign: W9SNF
Neil G Barry
8522 Burr St
Crown Point IN 46307

Call Sign: KE9TC
Kenneth H Brown
918 Chippewa Dr
Crown Point IN 46307

Call Sign: W9EMA
Lake County Emergency
Mgt Comm Group
918 Chippewa Dr
Crown Point IN 46307

Call Sign: KC9PPS
Travis L Clarke
9017 Clark Pl
Crown Point IN 46307

Call Sign: KB9TPW
Mark A Brewer
9419 Clay St
Crown Point IN
463078811

Call Sign: KC9LQQ
Bill Panagiotidis
14861 Clay St
Crown Point IN 46307

Call Sign: N9XWY
Jason M Byars
9111 Cline Ave
Crown Point IN 46307

Call Sign: KB9HSC
Bill A Johnson
11910 Cline Ave
Crown Point IN 46307

Call Sign: KA9TDT
Delton L Nack
1071 Concordia Ln

Crown Point IN 46307

Call Sign: N9RRR
Scott A Sowards
13112 County Line Rd
Crown Point IN 46307

Call Sign: N9WGQ
Elsie J McCarty
771 Courtney Dr
Crown Point IN 46307

Call Sign: KC9CNJ
Hugo O Gomez
771 Courtney Dr
Crown Point IN 46307

Call Sign: W9IFN
John E McCarty
771 Courtney Dr
Crown Point IN
463074365

Call Sign: WA9ICR
Frank A Remes
11520 Delaware St
Crown Point IN
463079792

Call Sign: K9VXI
Philip B Butler
8521 Dewey St
Crown Point IN 46307

Call Sign: KC9THY
Angelo C Lamantia
940 Doe Path Ln
Crown Point IN 46307

Call Sign: KE5LCZ
Avram O Suson
8585 Doubletree Dr S
Crown Point IN 46307

Call Sign: KE5LDA

Daniel J Suson
8585 Doubletree Dr S
Crown Point IN 46307

Call Sign: KC9ACQ
Sidney W Neeley
1215 Driftwood Trl
Crown Point IN 46307

Call Sign: N3LOK
John A Anelli
1525 E 112th Ave
Crown Point IN 46307

Call Sign: W9CNY
Lewis B Coe
115 E 113th Ave
Crown Point IN 46307

Call Sign: WB9QVP
Michael D Gulliver
550 E 115th Pl
Crown Point IN 46307

Call Sign: N9ICK
Dan P Buche
388 E 137th Ave
Crown Point IN 46307

Call Sign: KB9SON
Anova C Frasure
703 E Goldsboro St
Crown Point IN 46307

Call Sign: WD9FMP
Luzviminda G Nelms
728 E Monitor
Crown Point IN 46307

Call Sign: WD9FNY
Robert E Nelms
728 E Monitor St
Crown Point IN
463073415

Call Sign: N9ROJ
Michael D Dault
10240 E New Hampshire
St
Crown Point IN 46307

Call Sign: KB9ZKD
Robert J Valenta
217.5 E North St
Crown Point IN 46307

Call Sign: KF9OM
David L Pierce
813 E South St Apt 32
Crown Point IN
463074649

Call Sign: KB9ZXH
James M Le Beau
11692 Edison St
Crown Point IN 46307

Call Sign: W9FZM
George O Litzkow
1799 Forest Ln
Crown Point IN
463079319

Call Sign: KB9RQP
Duane E Wagner
13805 Grand Blvd
Crown Point IN 46307

Call Sign: KB9ONU
Aco Kaleski
1439 Grandview Ct
Crown Point IN 46307

Call Sign: KC9VPV
Robert G Boyles
7550 Hamlin St
Crown Point IN 46307

Call Sign: N9CA
Timothy H McGillen

8755 Hanley Ln
Crown Point IN 46307

Call Sign: KB9IPD
Nickolas R Jurich
246 Harrington Ave
Crown Point IN 46307

Call Sign: N9NER
Brett D Slager
208 Harrington Ave
Crown Point IN 46307

Call Sign: KC9LXO
Thomas D Breymeyer
2706 Harvest Dr
Crown Point IN 46307

Call Sign: AB9RY
Thomas D Breymeyer
2706 Harvest Dr
Crown Point IN 46307

Call Sign: N9FTW
Scott B Reel
915 Heritage Ct Apt 202
Crown Point IN 46307

Call Sign: KA9JXX
Terrence L McConnell
905 Heritage Ct Apt 203
Crown Point IN 46307

Call Sign: KB9HQN
Marco J Di Anni
323 Holton Ridge
Crown Point IN 46307

Call Sign: N9LUA
Melvin G Solon
9525 Johnson St
Crown Point IN 46307

Call Sign: WD9HET
John E Soltis

12207 Kingfisher Rd
Crown Point IN 46307

Call Sign: NM9W
Stephen Gayda
440 Lake St
Crown Point IN 46307

Call Sign: N9FNB
Neil J Simstad
11471 Lakewood St
Crown Point IN 46307

Call Sign: NI9G
Thomas N Simstad
11471 Lakewood St
Crown Point IN 46307

Call Sign: WB9VUI
Henry P White
117 Las Olas Dr
Crown Point IN 46307

Call Sign: KF9WK
Glyn R Jewart
121 Las Olas Dr
Crown Point IN 46307

Call Sign: W9IBZ
John F Zimmerman
1150 Luther Dr Apt 120
Crown Point IN 46307

Call Sign: N9TEX
John D McConnell Jr
318 Maple St
Crown Point IN 46307

Call Sign: N9YV
Charles E Myers
406 Martin Dr
Crown Point IN 46307

Call Sign: KB9RG
Robert L Wheeler

808 Mary Ellen Dr
Crown Point IN 46307

Call Sign: KB9IEX
Gregory J Engelien
8684 Mathews Ln
Crown Point IN 46307

Call Sign: N9UIL
William C Unwin
926 Maxwell Ct
Crown Point IN 46307

Call Sign: KB9VDB
Thomas L O Brien
9524 McKinley
Crown Point IN 46307

Call Sign: WB9OPP
Arthur O Gumm
9360 McKinley St
Crown Point IN 46307

Call Sign: WD9IJS
James R Smith
2414 Morninglory Ct
Crown Point IN 46307

Call Sign: WA3PRJ
Richard S Morvay
2644 Morningside Dr
Crown Point IN
463079688

Call Sign: KB9VJH
Carl J Kaminsky
2933 Morningside Dr
Crown Point IN 46307

Call Sign: W9IO
Carl J Kaminsky
2933 Morningside Dr
Crown Point IN 46307

Call Sign: KB9UJI

David J Stevens
3 N Court St B241
Crown Point IN 46307

Call Sign: KA9RDH
Leslie A Clites
708 N Grant St
Crown Point IN 46307

Call Sign: N9UVK
Donald F Peters
119 N Ridge St
Crown Point IN 46307

Call Sign: KC9MTP
William A Johnson
312 N West St
Crown Point IN 46307

Call Sign: KB6WNL
Kelly M Rehlander
801 North Ct St
Crown Point IN
463073147

Call Sign: KB7BPV
Raskel E Braund
142 NW St
Crown Point IN
426301555

Call Sign: N0QLC
Henry L Cox
4164 Oakmont Ct
Crown Point IN 46307

Call Sign: N9NKD
Kenneth A Ryan
12592 Pennsylvania Pl
Crown Point IN
463077555

Call Sign: NM9Q
Albert L Roberts
12401 Pennsylvania Pl

Crown Point IN 46307

Call Sign: WB9GXD
Harold W Maresko
10732 Pike St
Crown Point IN 46307

Call Sign: KC9SNS
Elmer R Simpson
9558 Polk St
Crown Point IN 46307

Call Sign: N9OXP
Raymond B Berry
8178 Ralston Ct
Crown Point IN 46307

Call Sign: N7RLY
David H Folker
8427 Randolph St
Crown Point IN
463078818

Call Sign: KC9ASO
Jonathon K Parry
9383 Roosevelt St
Crown Point IN 46307

Call Sign: WD9FZS
Thomas K Parry
9383 Roosevelt St
Crown Point IN 46307

Call Sign: KH6JNY
Thomas K Parry
9383 Roosevelt St
Crown Point IN 46307

Call Sign: N9YRN
Paul A Hohos
3196 Rustic Ln
Crown Point IN 46307

Call Sign: KC9EAO
Kevin W Olson

3288 Rustic Ln
Crown Point IN 46307

Call Sign: KE9CU
Vallan M Reynolds
3945 S Lake Shore Dr
Crown Point IN 46307

Call Sign: KA9SVS
Richard A Gilles
156 S Ridge St
Crown Point IN 46307

Call Sign: KC9OYD
Debra A Bergander
2003 Silver Hawk Dr
Crown Point IN 46307

Call Sign: KB9INZ
Charles A Norrman Sr
1608 Sunny Slope Dr
Crown Point IN 46307

Call Sign: N9DDB
Walter R Sala
1617 Sunnyslope Dr
Crown Point IN 46307

Call Sign: KE9LH
Eugene M Hall
1623 Sunnyslope Dr
Crown Point IN 46307

Call Sign: KC9QQI
Joseph E Antczak
620 Thomas St
Crown Point IN 46307

Call Sign: N9HIO
Pamela J Harrison
3139 Tremont Ln
Crown Point IN 46307

Call Sign: KC9FCO
Thomas H Booth

785 W 100 S
Crown Point IN 46307

Call Sign: KD9QX
Denis Tokarz
4105 W 107th Ave
Crown Point IN 46307

Call Sign: W9LC
Denis Tokarz
4105 W 107th Ave
Crown Point IN 46307

Call Sign: WD9JFT
George E Cadle
4203 W 107th Ave
Crown Point IN 46307

Call Sign: WA9GEP
Kelly J Scuderi
4400 W 109th St
Crown Point IN 46307

Call Sign: WA9GNI
Vincent M Scuderi
4400 W 109th St
Crown Point IN 46307

Call Sign: KC9HIJ
Jeffrey A Jamrosz
6480 W 117th
Crown Point IN 46307

Call Sign: K9PYO
L Franklin Duvall Jr
7206 W 117th Ave
Crown Point IN 46307

Call Sign: KF9NS
Dale A Newlin
5140 W 125th Ave
Crown Point IN 46307

Call Sign: KB9FO
Henry B Ruh

5317 W 133 Ave
Crown Point IN 46307

Call Sign: KC9FZB
Amateur Television
Network - Indiana
5317 W 133 Ave
Crown Point IN 46307

Call Sign: K9ATN
Amateur Television
Network - Indiana
5317 W 133 Ave
Crown Point IN 46307

Call Sign: AA9XW
Henry B Ruhwiedel
5317 W 133 St
Crown Point IN 46307

Call Sign: AB9TP
Christian M Thorne
4106 W 133rd Ave
Crown Point IN 46307

Call Sign: W9BQ
Christian M Thorne
4106 W 133rd Ave
Crown Point IN 46307

Call Sign: WA9FGC
John J Gielniak
785 W 275 S
Crown Point IN 46307

Call Sign: N9QX
Leo Jendraszkiewicz
5459 W 83 Pl
Crown Point IN
463071408

Call Sign: KB9ZDE
David M Isom
6760 W 85th Ave
Crown Point IN 46307

Call Sign: KC9JGY
Matthew D Frysztak
7190 W 86th Pl
Crown Point IN 46307

Call Sign: KB9TXT
David L Stroud
5052 W 88 Ct
Crown Point IN 46307

Call Sign: N9FRA
Mike Blaskovich
5921 W 91st Ave
Crown Point IN 46307

Call Sign: N9YZQ
William A Dittmann II
7401 W 92nd Ln
Crown Point IN 46307

Call Sign: KE5IUV
Patrick M Ohaver
1751 W 98th Pl
Crown Point IN 46307

Call Sign: KB9JWB
Patricia A Jarrard
1932 W 99th Pl
Crown Point IN 46307

Call Sign: K9AZG
Guy W Slaughter
753 W Elizabeth Dr
Crown Point IN 46307

Call Sign: KC9QPQ
William R Willette III
3573 W Lakeshore Dr
Crown Point IN 46307

Call Sign: K9WRW
William R Willette III
3573 W Lakeshore Dr
Crown Point IN 46307

Call Sign: W9NXV
Vernon J Richards Jr
3576 W Lakeshore Dr
Crown Point IN 46307

Call Sign: K9VJR
Vernon J Richards Jr
3576 W Lakeshore Dr
Crown Point IN 46307

Call Sign: WA9VMW
Edward T Czaja
347 W South St Apt 2
Crown Point IN 46307

Call Sign: W9LJ
Lake County Amat Rad
Clb
Crown Point IN 46308

FCC Amateur Radio Licenses in Culver

Call Sign: K9VCM
Roland W Crider
1000E
Culver IN 465119045

Call Sign: N9MFY
M T Schmidt
17591 15B Rd
Culver IN 465110000

Call Sign: KF9LN
Travis W Dexter
16705 16C Rd
Culver IN 46511

Call Sign: W9JWI
Winfield W Behmer
909 Academy Rd
Culver IN 46511

Call Sign: KB9NDZ

Lynn Jordan
Box 61C
Culver IN 46511

Call Sign: KA9PSQ
Joseph S Werner
Box 65
Culver IN 46511

Call Sign: KA9PJL
Steven E Werner
Box 65
Culver IN 46511

Call Sign: KB9WXQ
Chad A Gard
6738 E 750 N
Culver IN 46511

Call Sign: W9PAD
Pete A Dutcher
114 E Mill St
Culver IN 46511

Call Sign: N9SPG
Peter A Dutcher
114 E Mill St
Culver IN 46511

Call Sign: KB9GZC
Stuart J Short
11340 E SR 8
Culver IN 46511

Call Sign: KE9QL
David R Koss
606 Houghton St
Culver IN 46511

Call Sign: N9HLM
Robert E Breyfogle
310 Lake Shore Dr
Culver IN 46511

Call Sign: N9HLN

Scott R Breyfogle
310 Lake Shore Dr
Culver IN 46511

Call Sign: K9ILU
Richard J Basham
515 Liberty
Culver IN 46511

Call Sign: KC9PM
Benita A Basham
515 N Liberty St
Culver IN 46511

Call Sign: WB9AHF
Edward L Easterday
409 N Slate St
Culver IN 46511

Call Sign: KC9KYK
Ronald C Armstead
8925 S 1175 E
Culver IN 46511

Call Sign: N9HEG
James J Kachelmeier
110 S Ohio
Culver IN 46511

Call Sign: KC9ABI
Carl R Boyd
1095 S Shore Dr
Culver IN 465119725

Call Sign: KA9BCP
N Margaret Washburn
446 School St
Culver IN 46511

Call Sign: KB9AIF
Joshua L Richey
16963 Thorn Rd
Culver IN 46511

Call Sign: KC9HMK

Millie L Sytsma
16963 Thorn Rd
Culver IN 46511

Call Sign: N9GPY
Richard A Sytsma
16963 Thorn Rd
Culver IN 46511

Call Sign: KC9VOI
Aaron L McAnally
17642 W 14 B Rd
Culver IN 46511

Call Sign: N9LEB
Jon E Schmidt
17591 W 15B Rd
Culver IN 46511

Call Sign: KC9IXK
Charles A Dilts
212 W Cass St
Culver IN 46511

Call Sign: KD5RFE
Ruth L Dilts
212 W Cass St
Culver IN 46511

Call Sign: WA9HAL
Bernard G Busart
322 W Madison St
Culver IN 46511

Call Sign: WA9ESE
Richard W Hendrix
Rr 1
Cutler IN 46920

**FCC Amateur Radio
Licenses in Decatur**

Call Sign: KC9NHY
Patrick L Norton
1424 N US 33

Decatar IN 46733

Call Sign: WB9GIK
John E Brown Jr
500N
Decatur IN 46733

Call Sign: WA9TNI
James R Miller
900N
Decatur IN 46733

Call Sign: K9PQQ
Gordon A Watts
621 Adams St
Decatur IN 46733

Call Sign: KC9PRP
Terry L Debolt
110 Bellmont Blvd
Decatur IN 46733

Call Sign: WD9GGX
Edward A Gage
615 Bollman St
Decatur IN 46733

Call Sign: KB9PCE
Jack W Robbins
1109 Bollman St Apt 55
Decatur IN 46733

Call Sign: W9DRS
Gerald O Cole
1127 Bollman St Apt 8
Decatur IN 46733

Call Sign: WC9AAT
Adams Co C D Races Net
Box 322
Decatur IN 46733

Call Sign: W9IGE
Kenneth E Gase
115 Briarwood Tr

Decatur IN 46733

Call Sign: K9KKD
Harold E Hunt
1209 Canterbury Dr
Decatur IN 46733

Call Sign: KA9NJT
Frederick J Eyanson
1538 Cherry Ln
Decatur IN 46733

Call Sign: WB9GAX
Kenneth R Lichtle
219 E 900 N
Decatur IN 46733

Call Sign: K9OMW
Robert L Hakes
2939 E 900 N
Decatur IN 46733

Call Sign: KB9FWS
Virginia E Garcia
425 Elm St
Decatur IN 46733

Call Sign: KB9OMW
Robert L Hakes
821 Everhart Dr
Decatur IN 46733

Call Sign: W9CSL
Terry R Hammons
1716 Fairway Dr
Decatur IN 46733

Call Sign: KB9EQV
Libby K Christner
116 Fremont Ln
Decatur IN 46733

Call Sign: WD9HQJ
John S Sheets
404 Gage Ave

Decatur IN 467332222

Call Sign: N9WPF
Tamara S Dull
930 Harrison St
Decatur IN 46733

Call Sign: W9HLY
Vernon D Seitz
45 Homestead
Decatur IN 46733

Call Sign: KC9PRO
James M Blanton
610 Kekionga St
Decatur IN 46733

Call Sign: KA9LTP
Lester R Lee
1043 Lewis Dr
Decatur IN 46733

Call Sign: WA9ZTD
Fr Dave W Voors
414 Madison St
Decatur IN 46733

Call Sign: KB9IXG
Timothy P I Lee
610 Madison St
Decatur IN 46733

Call Sign: KC9NHU
Richard Elzey
1140 Madison St
Decatur IN 46733

Call Sign: WA9KYL
John V Ginter
1412 Madison St
Decatur IN 46733

Call Sign: W9ZQY
William P Schrock Jr
Mercer

Decatur IN 46733

Call Sign: KE9IF
Edgar B Dyer Jr
332 Mercer Ave
Decatur IN 467332033

Call Sign: KD9OP
John W Stauffer
1300 Mercer Ave 308
Woodcrest Garden Apt
Decatur IN 46733

Call Sign: KB9BDM
Wayne L Atkinson
1025 Mix Ave
Decatur IN 46733

Call Sign: KA9EBS
John V Plattner
7921 N 200 E
Decatur IN 46733

Call Sign: WA9NMO
William H Hutker
7939 N 200 W
Decatur IN 46733

Call Sign: W9UZW
Ronald J Kiess
7788 N 250 W
Decatur IN 46733

Call Sign: W9PT
Ronald J Kiess
7788 N 250 W
Decatur IN 46733

Call Sign: N9RYN
Derek C Augsburger
6440 N 400 W
Decatur IN 46733

Call Sign: W9RYN
Derek C Augsburger

6440 N 400 W
Decatur IN 46733

Call Sign: AB9SO
Derek C Augsburger
6440 N 400 W
Decatur IN 46733

Call Sign: KC9QZV
Tina M Augsburger
6440 N 400 W
Decatur IN 46733

Call Sign: WA9LQE
Playtime Ares Radio
Club
6440 N 400 W
Decatur IN 467337805

Call Sign: KC9SYH
Shane L Rekeweg
6043 N 500 W
Decatur IN 46733

Call Sign: KC9PRR
Jacob E Plas
216 N 5th St
Decatur IN 46733

Call Sign: KF9VI
Kenneth G Ward
116 N 6th St
Decatur IN 46733

Call Sign: N9VWW
Michael R Reynolds
2329 N 700 W
Decatur IN 46733

Call Sign: KF9OU
William J Gage
104 N 9th St
Decatur IN 46733

Call Sign: KE9VR

Samuel D Blythe
3616 N Hickory Rd
Decatur IN 46733

Call Sign: WB9WUT
Dorman L Hughes
8211 N Piqua Rd
Decatur IN 46733

Call Sign: KA9HEM
Robert A Mann
8255 N Piqua Rd
Decatur IN 46733

Call Sign: K9TH
Richard T Hoehn
55853 N Piqua Rd
Decatur IN 46733

Call Sign: KF4YD
Allan F Hill
3355 N Salem Rd
Decatur IN 467338054

Call Sign: KB9NKM
Michael J Hakes Jr
1821 N SR 101
Decatur IN 46733

Call Sign: KA9AQK
Charles M Drake
8355 N Th Prqua Rd
Decatur IN 46733

Call Sign: W9ZPT
Franklin M Hobrock
9895 N US Hwy 27
Decatur IN 46733

Call Sign: WB9CNS
Robert G Nave
2375 N US Hwy 33
Decatur IN 46733

Call Sign: W9ADT

Robert G Nave
2375 N US Hwy 33
Decatur IN 46733

Call Sign: KC9NHW
John C August
8255 NW Winchester Rd
Decatur IN 46733

Call Sign: K9UR
Jack L May
5860 Piqua Rd
Decatur IN 46733

Call Sign: WB9SJZ
George C Womack II
1028 S 13th St
Decatur IN 46733

Call Sign: KC9UOW
Cynthia A Moorman
1190 S 14th St
Decatur IN 46733

Call Sign: N9IYI
John E Schnieders
208 S 5th St
Decatur IN 46733

Call Sign: KC9PRQ
Don G Hess
323 S 5th St
Decatur IN 46733

Call Sign: N9VKX
Gary M Pinney
116 Selkirk Ln
Decatur IN 46733

Call Sign: K9HA
Harold E Blythe
221 Stratton Way
Decatur IN 46733

Call Sign: W9YFI

David A Langston
503 Stratton Way
Decatur IN 46733

Call Sign: KB9HVX
Kandra C Griem
US 27 City
Decatur IN 46733

Call Sign: N9ZTH
Donald J Heimann
520 W 200 N
Decatur IN 46733

Call Sign: W9DDF
Carl L Robinson
80 W Honey Suckle Ln
Decatur IN 46733

Call Sign: KC9CGG
Michael W Sweney
2865 W Hwy 224
Decatur IN 46733

Call Sign: KB9HN
Richard D Davidson
910 W Monroe St
Decatur IN 46733

Call Sign: KB9RTC
Eric A Cavanaugh
1411 W Monroe St
Decatur IN 467331403

Call Sign: W9HNG
Edward L Summers
921 Walnut St
Decatur IN 46733

Call Sign: W9FRU
Robert V Blaney
127 Westlawn Dr
Decatur IN 467333017

Call Sign: KC9BKI

Kevin L Emenhiser
904 Woodland Ct
Decatur IN 46733

Call Sign: KB9KWC
Paul W Merrills
1136 Woodridge Dr
Decatur IN 46733

Call Sign: N9KE
Kevin L Emenhiser
Decatur IN 46733

**FCC Amateur Radio
Licenses in Delphi**

Call Sign: KF9QS
David L Kessler
550S
Delphi IN 46923

Call Sign: WB9VQK
Rodney L Rishel
580 W
Delphi IN 46923

Call Sign: N9ARG
Terry L Dill
950N
Delphi IN 46923

Call Sign: W9LZP
Thomas C McCain
Box 1
Delphi IN 46923

Call Sign: WD9HED
Julian E Phillips
Box 336
Delphi IN 46923

Call Sign: N9MXG
Anthony W Smith Sr
3729 S US 421
Delphi IN 46923

Call Sign: N9RND
John K Buchanan Sr
9239 W 310 N
Delphi IN 46923

Call Sign: N9XHG
John K Buchanan Jr
9239 W 310 N
Delphi IN 46923

Call Sign: KB9GTX
James P Pickett
7801 W 950 N
Delphi IN 47960

Call Sign: KC9OZW
Todd M Milburn
6355 W Division Line Rd
Delphi IN 46923

Call Sign: KB9THW
Sara J Clark
Delphi IN 46923

**FCC Amateur Radio
Licenses in DeMotte**

Call Sign: N9IIX
Eric A Liss
524 10th St SW
DeMotte IN 46310

Call Sign: KY9U
William L Liss
524 10th St SW
DeMotte IN 46310

Call Sign: KB9AXK
Kevin M Silverthorne
601 4th Ave NW
DeMotte IN 46310

Call Sign: K9YMY
Edward P Hempen

9621 Bayberry Ct
DeMotte IN 46310

10878 Edgewood Dr
DeMotte IN 46310

11551 N 900 W
DeMotte IN 46310

Call Sign: WB9UQF
Casimir J Pekala
628 Begonia St SE B
DeMotte IN 463108898

Call Sign: K9UOK
John M Oezer
8973 Luann Dr
DeMotte IN 46310

Call Sign: KA9PJQ
Donald J Saberniak Jr
11571 N 900 W
DeMotte IN 46310

Call Sign: KB9HO
Russell K McComb Jr
345 Birch St NW
DeMotte IN 46310

Call Sign: N9IWX
Charles E Shear
10237 Maumee Dr
DeMotte IN 46310

Call Sign: WN9DJS
Donald J Saberniak Jr
11571 N 900 W
DeMotte IN 463108235

Call Sign: WD9HYI
John E Hylemon
4848 E 1047 N
DeMotte IN 463108928

Call Sign: KB9MKR
Tim J Wolotka
10440 N 1100 W
DeMotte IN 46310

Call Sign: KB9WTS
Irwin I Kleinman
9787 N 950 W
DeMotte IN 463108446

Call Sign: KB9VDC
David M Stamper
2925 E 1053 N
DeMotte IN 46310

Call Sign: KB9UUP
Sandra L Hickey
11603 N 200 E
DeMotte IN 46310

Call Sign: KA9QGA
Patricia I Barker
3050 Newport Dr
DeMotte IN 46310

Call Sign: WB9WPJ
Allen T Orzechowicz
5875 E 1156 N
DeMotte IN 46310

Call Sign: KC9EKZ
Ronnie L Perkins
11851 N 457 E
DeMotte IN 46310

Call Sign: WD9CRY
Travis W Barker
3050 Newport Dr
DeMotte IN 46310

Call Sign: KB9OE
Erah M Croft
5955 E 1156 N
DeMotte IN 46310

Call Sign: KB9HLT
Bradford J Allen
11342 N 500 E
DeMotte IN 46310

Call Sign: WB9FBL
Chris E Purdy
10923 Potomac Dr
DeMotte IN 46310

Call Sign: KB9OD
Otis L Croft
5955 E 1156 N
DeMotte IN 46310

Call Sign: KC9THZ
Steven P Guinn
11192 N 600 E
DeMotte IN 46310

Call Sign: N9LFK
Joseph D Anoman
9815 Rustic Dr
DeMotte IN 46310

Call Sign: NB9I
Kenneth R Berkebile
10878 Edgewood Dr
DeMotte IN 46310

Call Sign: KC9BSU
Michael G Mcmahon
13371 N 700 W
DeMotte IN 46310

Call Sign: W9FBR
Robert A Cheever
535 S Halleck St
DeMotte IN 46310

Call Sign: N9HVD
Paul K Berkebile

Call Sign: KB9NDT
Joshua P Holevinsky

Call Sign: KB9LHL
James A Reimer

8924 S Lilac
DeMotte IN 46310

Call Sign: KC9JAL
Todd P Adamczyk
11535 Sandhill Trl
DeMotte IN 46310

Call Sign: W9MDF
Reneta J Banaszak
6111 W 1100 N
DeMotte IN 46310

Call Sign: W9FB
Ronald S Banaszak
6111 W 1100 N
DeMotte IN 46310

Call Sign: N9ULC
David J Saulsgiver
11198 W 1100 N
DeMotte IN 46310

Call Sign: KC9HGT
Kenneth J Bobby
11520 W 1100 N
DeMotte IN 46310

Call Sign: W9CMB
James C Harsin
7840 W 1400 E
DeMotte IN 46310

Call Sign: KD9MI
Gysbertus A Boon
7771 W 1400 N
DeMotte IN 46310

Call Sign: WA9PGP
Homer V Taulbee Jr
409 W Division
DeMotte IN 46310

Call Sign: KB9ZQW
Jason A Blankinship

10553 W Whispering
Woods Dr
DeMotte IN 46310

Call Sign: N9IVV
David E Horvath
DeMotte IN 46310

Call Sign: WA9TEY
Earl D Walton
DeMotte IN 46310

FCC Amateur Radio Licenses in Denver

Call Sign: WB9VGG
Peggy J Wellsand
7642 N 100 E
Denver IN 46926

Call Sign: K9LVL
William D Wellsand
7642 N 100 E
Denver IN 46926

Call Sign: N9WGF
Jeffrey P King
6368 N Eel River Rd
Denver IN 46926

Call Sign: KC9FVH
Jesse R Cowles
8976 N SR 19
Denver IN 46926

FCC Amateur Radio Licenses in Dunkirk

Call Sign: N9LLH
H Katherine Sebastian
136 Barbier St
Dunkirk IN 47336

Call Sign: WB9JBD
Doris C Triplett

Box 281Aa
Dunkirk IN 47336

Call Sign: KA9VHP
John R Skeoch
Box 331A
Dunkirk IN 47336

Call Sign: KB9PPL
Christopher L McCarter
9501 E 1200 N
Dunkirk IN 47336

Call Sign: KB9PPG
Paul L Weaver
9501 E 1200 N
Dunkirk IN 47336

Call Sign: KC9CQW
Kent Smith
273 E Commerce
Dunkirk IN 47336

Call Sign: KB9DKW
Dixie D Mumbower
270 E Commerce St
Dunkirk IN 47336

Call Sign: KA9ENX
Vicki D Holloway
13411 E CR 1100 N
Dunkirk IN 47336

Call Sign: N9AID
Jack L Mitch Sr
12665 E Eaton Albany
Pike
Dunkirk IN 47336

Call Sign: N9GKC
Jerry C Armstrong
422 E High St
Dunkirk IN 47336

Call Sign: KC9KHN

Richard E Buckner
125 Harold Ave
Dunkirk IN 47336

Call Sign: KB9PPJ
Nathen L Hutchinson
413 N CR 1100 W
Dunkirk IN 47336

Call Sign: N9OYH
Joyce A Blakely
15605 N SR 167 N
Dunkirk IN 47336

Call Sign: AA9MV
Ronald L Blakely
15605 N SR 167N
Dunkirk IN 47336

Call Sign: KB9DMB
Betty M Phillips
17000 N St R 167N
Dunkirk IN 47336

Call Sign: KG4BCD
Randall E Mansfield
436 S Knox Rd
Dunkirk IN 47336

Call Sign: N9IYX
Charles R Eltzroth
524 S Main St
Dunkirk IN 47336

Call Sign: WA9KBT
Tommy D Phillips
17000 SR 167 N
Dunkirk IN 47336

Call Sign: N9FGC
Jacob W Ludwick
129 W Oak St
Dunkirk IN 47336

**FCC Amateur Radio
Licenses in Dyer**

Call Sign: WB9VXM
Joseph A Marino
15959 113th Ave
Dyer IN 46311

Call Sign: KC9SCS
Patric D Murphy
648 206th St
Dyer IN 46311

Call Sign: W9EHH
Michael Hrindak
539 213th Pl
Dyer IN 46311

Call Sign: KB9USU
Sean R Feavel
942 213th St
Dyer IN 46311

Call Sign: N9IDB
David H Eichensehr
13504 78th Ct
Dyer IN 46311

Call Sign: N9ZDQ
James A Bathurst
9194 Beall St
Dyer IN 46311

Call Sign: KC9EYD
Ralph Rogers
808 Briarwood Dr
Dyer IN 46311

Call Sign: KC9DX
Robert W Riley
116 Carnation Dr
Dyer IN 46311

Call Sign: W5ESE
Robert W Riley

116 Carnation Dr
Dyer IN 463111540

Call Sign: KC9DX
Robert W Riley
116 Carnation Dr
Dyer IN 463111540

Call Sign: N9XQN
Timothy P Polaskey
1494 Carriage Oaks Ct
Dyer IN 46311

Call Sign: KE9YL
Gerald A Dekker Jr
446 Cherry Hill Rd
Dyer IN 46311

Call Sign: W9FSC
Frank S Carlberg
126 Concord Ct
Dyer IN 463111306

Call Sign: W9JOB
William G Panassow
2700 Edgewood Dr
Dyer IN 46311

Call Sign: N9QXF
John A Clark
9935 Gettler St
Dyer IN 46311

Call Sign: W9CP
John R Miller
Great Lakes Dr
Dyer IN 46311

Call Sign: WS9D
Kirby L Strickland
942 Harrison Ave
Dyer IN 46311

Call Sign: N9VBG
Corey A Schontube

1118 Harrison Ave Apt
7B
Dyer IN 46311

Call Sign: KB9LMS
Jai P Agrawal
925 Harrison Pl
Dyer IN 46311

Call Sign: N9ODM
Michael G O Day
2143 Hart St
Dyer IN 46311

Call Sign: K9EAK
Stanley Jurczuk
121 Harvest Dr
Dyer IN 46311

Call Sign: KE9IV
Gary A Genovese
8900 Henry St
Dyer IN 46311

Call Sign: K9OE
Gary A Genovese
8900 Henry St
Dyer IN 46311

Call Sign: KA9YQV
Judith A Genovese
8900 Henry St
Dyer IN 46311

Call Sign: K9QCK
Phillip D Blanchette
615 Hillside Dr
Dyer IN 46311

Call Sign: KC9GGM
Jason Pajak
2816 Howard Castle
Dyer IN 46311

Call Sign: AB9GV

Michael A Masleid
104 Ivy Ln
Dyer IN 46311

Call Sign: N9QBY
Brian T Stofko
924 Jackson Pl
Dyer IN 46311

Call Sign: WD9EDP
Karen S Charbonneau
645 Laurel Dr
Dyer IN 46311

Call Sign: AE9V
William M Charbonneau
645 Laurel Dr
Dyer IN 46311

Call Sign: N9WVN
Daniel E Mishler
43 Lilac Dr
Dyer IN 46311

Call Sign: K9GSD
Larry W Sidor
1107 Madison Ave
Dyer IN 46311

Call Sign: KB9CUO
Warren B Barton
1305 Madison St
Dyer IN 46311

Call Sign: KB9NYT
Richard A Bukvich
1450 Meadow Ln
Dyer IN 46311

Call Sign: N9POM
Barry S Kekelik
45 Monticello Dr
Dyer IN 46311

Call Sign: KB9NYU

Christine A Canty
Osage Dr
Dyer IN 46311

Call Sign: KB9TKK
Kenneth W Cook
45 Park Manor Dr
Dyer IN 46311

Call Sign: N9YSN
Colette M Paganelli
8109 Patterson 4
Dyer IN 46311

Call Sign: AA3P
Stanley C Houk
2343 Peach Tree Ln
Dyer IN 46311

Call Sign: K9OOG
Thomas P Brokop
126 Potomac Dr
Dyer IN 46311

Call Sign: W9RWN
William W Reed Jr
7980 Rhode Ct
Dyer IN 46311

Call Sign: W9PKG
Paul J Reed
8060 Rhode Ct
Dyer IN 46311

Call Sign: WB9LRK
Larry J Hau
1515 Rokosz Ln
Dyer IN 46311

Call Sign: KI4CFH
John S Litton
665 Rose Bush Ln
Dyer IN 46311

Call Sign: WB9HQR

Hughston T MacConnell
1629 Schaller Ln
Dyer IN 46311

Call Sign: W9HQR
Hughston T MacConnell
1629 Schaller Ln
Dyer IN 46311

Call Sign: W9MOC
Charles E Mitchell
8325 Sheffield Ave
Dyer IN 463112752

Call Sign: KB9QIA
Robert D Trebs
8617 Sheffield Ave
Dyer IN 46311

Call Sign: W9VVA
Paul Pokrifcak
2635 Squire Dr
Dyer IN 46311

Call Sign: WB9TMP
Vincent M Pokrifcak
2635 Squire Dr
Dyer IN 46311

Call Sign: N9DRV
Richard A Dobda
1518 Sunnybrook Ave
Dyer IN 46311

Call Sign: WA9JDP
Clarence Verbeek
2427 Sycamore Dr
Dyer IN 46311

Call Sign: WB9MPK
Richard A Marshall
8545 Towle St
Dyer IN 46311

Call Sign: N9SFQ

Daniel B Neal
12005 W 79th Pl
Dyer IN 46311

Call Sign: K9DQV
Larry L Pasztor
14903 W 82nd St
Dyer IN 46311

Call Sign: N9HFU
James P Wittgren
10203 White Oak
Dyer IN 46311

Call Sign: KA9UBH
Charles E Kurtz
Dyer IN 46311

FCC Amateur Radio Licenses in East Chicago

Call Sign: NK9F
Francisco Osorio
4422 Baring Ave
East Chicago IN 46312

Call Sign: KB9UJJ
Adolfo Velez Jr
5615 Baring Ave
East Chicago IN 46312

Call Sign: KD9WV
Alojzy Moricz
4723 Carey St
East Chicago IN 46312

Call Sign: N9QBL
Joseph M Bajo
4831 Drummond St
East Chicago IN 46312

Call Sign: KB9ONW
Carlos Flores
3826 Elm

East Chicago IN 46321

Call Sign: KC9OMH
Cortney J Murray
3607 Hemlock St
East Chicago IN 46312

Call Sign: K9IMZ
Albert L Furman
4947 Indianapolis Blvd
East Chicago IN 46312

Call Sign: NJ9J
Robert D Du Fon
4114 Northcote Ave
East Chicago IN 46312

Call Sign: WA9EMT
Joseph J Payer Sr
4241 Northcote Ave
East Chicago IN 46312

Call Sign: KC9LLW
Augustin Acevedo
3934 Parrish Ave
East Chicago IN 46312

Call Sign: N9ZDS
Konrad J Werner
1302 W 148th St
East Chicago IN 46312

FCC Amateur Radio Licenses in Elkhart

Call Sign: WV6D
David L Russell
2830 17th St
Elkhart IN 46517

Call Sign: WA9TMZ
John P Bachman
25234 Aqua Dr
Elkhart IN 46514

Call Sign: KA9JZS
James R Kinkaide
51154 Aqua Dr
Elkhart IN 46514

Call Sign: N9DVA
John E Johnson
311 Bank St
Elkhart IN 46514

Call Sign: N9OOH
David W Michaels
23789 Briarwood Dr
Elkhart IN 46514

Call Sign: N9PCM
James H Monroe
224 Arcade Ave
Elkhart IN 46514

Call Sign: K9MSP
Marshall A Craig
2313 Benham Ave
Elkhart IN 46517

Call Sign: WA4MTP
Andrew L McCaskey Jr
2337 Brookwood Dr
Elkhart IN 46514

Call Sign: KB9GTE
David R Eppich
24654 Aric Way
Elkhart IN 46517

Call Sign: KC9FZW
David E Gooding
3519 Bent Oak Trl
Elkhart IN 46517

Call Sign: N4FZX
Teresa H McCaskey
2337 Brookwood Dr
Elkhart IN 46514

Call Sign: N9WGA
Gregory S Sutter
53749 Arrowwood Dr
Elkhart IN 465149156

Call Sign: W9DEG
David E Gooding
3519 Bent Oak Trl
Elkhart IN 46517

Call Sign: KC0WS
Theodore C Miller
56909 Burbank St
Elkhart IN 46516

Call Sign: KC9NYF
Lisa K Brown
2644 Ashton Pines Dr 9N
Elkhart IN 46517

Call Sign: N9PDN
Matthew D Hamilton
56712 Bishop Ct
Elkhart IN 46516

Call Sign: KA9VTL
Dennis D Byrket
2616 By Pass Rd
Elkhart IN 46514

Call Sign: KC9BQF
Andrew S Kozak
2135 Autumn Ridge Ln
Elkhart IN 46514

Call Sign: N9QIA
Kimberley L Maynard
1425 Bower St
Elkhart IN 46514

Call Sign: KB9TGM
David A Pedzinski II
29704 Cardinal Ave
Elkhart IN 46516

Call Sign: K9UVF
William H Peffley
54150 B Dr
Elkhart IN 46514

Call Sign: N9GEZ
Michael D De Metz
54768 Bradley
Elkhart IN 46514

Call Sign: KB9OKQ
Daniel J Miller
23617 Cedar Knoll Cir
Elkhart IN 46516

Call Sign: WD9EZF
Edward D Drudge
54260 Baldwin Ct
Elkhart IN 46514

Call Sign: W9LMX
Donald R Walters
1211 Brentwood Ave
Elkhart IN 46514

Call Sign: N9DOP
Daniel J Miller
23617 Cedar Knoll Cir
Elkhart IN 46516

Call Sign: KC9ENV
Brad E Hocking
1735 Baltic Ave
Elkhart IN 46514

Call Sign: KA4TOC
Thomas D Sutula
1116 Bresseau St
Elkhart IN 46514

Call Sign: KB9GTF
Jeffrey D Miller
23617 Cedar Knoll Cir
Elkhart IN 46516

Call Sign: N9EGH
Jeannette G Yoder
55413 Cedar Ridge Rd
Elkhart IN 46514

Call Sign: KJ4NJ
Daniel K Anderson
1427 Cedar St
Elkhart IN 46514

Call Sign: KC9AVS
Mark L Rushing
27431 Cherry Ln
Elkhart IN 465179710

Call Sign: W9MQR
William P Bradish
30264 Chevy Chase Dr
Elkhart IN 465148779

Call Sign: WD9IIB
Robert L Beacham Sr
1240 Christiana St
Elkhart IN 465142857

Call Sign: WT9U
James A Walter
60112 Circle R Ln
Elkhart IN 46517

Call Sign: WA9WSW
Emil Pozwilka Jr
53795 Cleveland Trls Dr
Elkhart IN 46514

Call Sign: WD9GNP
Richard G Erdmann Jr
1642 Cobblestone Blvd
Elkhart IN 46514

Call Sign: N9RYL
Susan W Erdmann
1642 Cobblestone Blvd
Elkhart IN 46514

Call Sign: K2GFK
Richard G Erdmann
1650 Cobblestone Blvd
Elkhart IN 46514

Call Sign: W9QF
Milton C Koeppen
30084 Cobus Lake Dr
Elkhart IN 465149204

Call Sign: KB9NDY
Thomas L Vanhuffel
1057 Cone St
Elkhart IN 46514

Call Sign: KB8GPS
Clinton M Herron
25780 Coolidge Ave
Elkhart IN 46517

Call Sign: N9QIB
Richard J Rushlow
150 Cottage Ct
Elkhart IN 46514

Call Sign: KA9IJA
James V Wood
54793 Country Manor Pl
Elkhart IN 46514

Call Sign: KC9GTT
Anthony M Meller
50870 Coventry Ct
Elkhart IN 465146078

Call Sign: KC9TSN
Larry L Todt
57709 CR 1
Elkhart IN 46517

Call Sign: KC9PRK
Guy L Shepherd
58387 CR 1
Elkhart IN 46517

Call Sign: KC9NIT
Gaylene Shepherd
58387 CR 1
Elkhart IN 46517

Call Sign: AA9JC
Jeff A Benedict
57826 CR 1 S
Elkhart IN 46517

Call Sign: WD9GCG
Fred D Whitmer
57936 CR 1 S
Elkhart IN 46517

Call Sign: KC9OHB
Melvin E Baltimore
27921 CR 10 W
Elkhart IN 46514

Call Sign: KC9RFV
David M Hartman
30208 CR 108
Elkhart IN 46514

Call Sign: N9MZX
James C Woodard
53815 CR 11 N Lot 180
Elkhart IN 46514

Call Sign: N9UKG
Cwyn D Weldy
59160 CR 11 S
Elkhart IN 46517

Call Sign: KA9RQF
Willis H Simons
58581 CR 111 S R 4
Elkhart IN 46517

Call Sign: KC9AYQ
Rob L Wilsey
59578 CR 113
Elkhart IN 46517

Call Sign: WA9SPD
Dennis M Chiddister
59843 CR 113 S
Elkhart IN 46517

Call Sign: KA9OZK
Wayne A Moore
29376 CR 118
Elkhart IN 46517

Call Sign: KC9HBS
Darrell J Robinson
57844 CR 13
Elkhart IN 46516

Call Sign: KC9IIA
Timothy C Sommers
58073 CR 13
Elkhart IN 46516

Call Sign: N9QID
David M Fair
52361 CR 13 N
Elkhart IN 46514

Call Sign: KC9FVI
Joseph A Fair
52361 CR 13 N
Elkhart IN 46514

Call Sign: N9QIE
Joseph A Fair
52361 CR 13 N
Elkhart IN 46514

Call Sign: KC9QQV
Rex L Mellinger
50992 CR 15
Elkhart IN 46514

Call Sign: KC9SX
Bernard E Crusie Sr
51174 CR 15 N
Elkhart IN 46514

Call Sign: WL7NY
Helen M Le Fever
30204 CR 16
Elkhart IN 465161034

Call Sign: WL7BQ
William L Le Fever Sr
30204 CR 16
Elkhart IN 465161034

Call Sign: K9UYU
Robert L Smith
30295 CR 16 W
Elkhart IN 46516

Call Sign: WA1OSK
Michael L Forgues
30639 CR 16 W
Elkhart IN 46516

Call Sign: KC9DSD
Brent M Forgues
30639 CR 16 W
Elkhart IN 46516

Call Sign: N9KKL
Stephen G Pickrell
30625 CR 16W
Elkhart IN 46516

Call Sign: W9KWX
Stephen G Pickrell
30625 CR 16W
Elkhart IN 46516

Call Sign: K9WYU
Stephen G Pickrell
30625 CR 16W
Elkhart IN 46516

Call Sign: N9KKL
Stephen G Pickrell
30625 CR 16W
Elkhart IN 46516

Call Sign: N9UFB
Jeffrey T Moser Sr
29371 CR 18
Elkhart IN 46517

Call Sign: W8LCJ
Irvin C Palmer
54686 CR 19 405
Elkhart IN 46507

Call Sign: KB9DMS
Dylan Schott
57826 CR 1S
Elkhart IN 46517

Call Sign: WB9CVC
Robert D Jones
24643 CR 20 E
Elkhart IN 46517

Call Sign: WB9AGJ
Donald R Florea
25434 CR 24
Elkhart IN 46517

Call Sign: KC9AZH
Andrew D Hoff
25635 CR 24
Elkhart IN 465179122

Call Sign: KC9NYJ
Mark A Mcguire
25903 CR 24
Elkhart IN 46517

Call Sign: KB9RZT
Joyce G Mcguire
25903 CR 24
Elkhart IN 46517

Call Sign: KB0DMB
Larry A Mcguire
25903 CR 24
Elkhart IN 46517

Call Sign: KC9BQE
Earl B Hoff
25741 CR 24 W
Elkhart IN 46517

Call Sign: N9AOA
Lawrence W Dorman
28070 CR 24 W
Elkhart IN 46517

Call Sign: K9DGW
John L Hartzler
24460 CR 24E
Elkhart IN 46517

Call Sign: KC9ALY
Elkhart County Ema
26861 CR 26
Elkhart IN 46517

Call Sign: KB9BTH
Jerald E Winings Sr
58744 CR 3
Elkhart IN 46517

Call Sign: WA9PQN
Albert J Sindell
56541 CR 3 S
Elkhart IN 46516

Call Sign: KC9RDN
Arie M Voskuil Jr
26115 CR 4
Elkhart IN 46514

Call Sign: KB9AKB
Theodore P Huff
29088 CR 4
Elkhart IN 46514

Call Sign: N9VPM
John N Gard
23893 CR 45
Elkhart IN 46516

Call Sign: KB9SYW
Marcia K Gard
23893 CR 45
Elkhart IN 46516

Call Sign: N9QAB
Jeffery R Farrough
51527 CR 5 N
Elkhart IN 46514

Call Sign: KC9OP
Riley P Grieb
51584 CR 7 N
Elkhart IN 46514

Call Sign: KB9EIX
Alan R Wyne
52365 CR 7 N
Elkhart IN 46514

Call Sign: N9WDF
John E Mann
58942 CR 7 S
Elkhart IN 46517

Call Sign: KB9OY
Randy D Wilson
59725 CR 9 S
Elkhart IN 46517

Call Sign: KB9GKB
Rachel V Benedict
57826 CR One S
Elkhart IN 46517

Call Sign: N9JMG
Gregory R Ostrom
23428 Crest Ct
Elkhart IN 46514

Call Sign: KB9TUL
Benjamin A O Bryant
53144 Crystal Pond Dr
Elkhart IN 46514

Call Sign: K9DDR
Robert E Gallatin
29640 Ct Rd 20
Elkhart IN 46517

Call Sign: KA9WNO
Gerald L Bradshaw
50675 Darlene St
Elkhart IN 46514

Call Sign: KB9PZG
Charles Greathouse
23611 Decamp Blvd
Elkhart IN 46516

Call Sign: K9FPD
James H Robinson
57081 Decamp Blvd
Elkhart IN 46516

Call Sign: N9THY
Ronald S Morgan
52161 Del Rue
Elkhart IN 46514

Call Sign: KA9UOF
Karin G Mann
52088 Del Rue Dr
Elkhart IN 46514

Call Sign: KA9UOG
Wayne L Mann
52088 Del Rue Dr
Elkhart IN 46514

Call Sign: N8AES
Brad E Hocking Jr
1501 Dogwood Dr
Elkhart IN 46514

Call Sign: N9SEX
Billy W Moore Jr
50545 Donna St
Elkhart IN 46514

Call Sign: KB9DZN
Brian E Manges
24570 Dover Ct
Elkhart IN 46516

Call Sign: N9JTZ
Glenn A Yoder
52148 Dover Trace Dr
Elkhart IN 46514

Call Sign: N9TJD
Daryl Bartlett
1307 E Beardsley
Elkhart IN 46514

Call Sign: W9YX
William F Martin
921 E Beardsley Ave
Elkhart IN 46514

Call Sign: KC5EGX
Mark D Price
1853 E Beardsley Ave
Elkhart IN 46514

Call Sign: W1OSK
Michael L Forgues
2100 E Bristol St
Elkhart IN 46514

Call Sign: KA5KMH
Robert W Bunner
3600 E Bristol St Apt 01
Elkhart IN 46514

Call Sign: KA9GRT
Richard G Geiger
2100 E Bristol St L145
Elkhart IN 46514

Call Sign: KC9FNQ
Anthony J Hunt
1111 E Jackson Blvd
Elkhart IN 46516

Call Sign: KC9TL
Richard M Myers
1425 E Jackson Blvd
Elkhart IN 46516

Call Sign: KB9ZAN
Brett A Shaske
855 E Mishawaka Rd 18
Elkhart IN 46517

Call Sign: N9MLO
Judy M Shaske
855 E Mishawaka Rd 18
Elkhart IN 46517

Call Sign: N9QQZ
John C Dickerhoff
3433 Eastlake Dr N Apt
B
Elkhart IN 46514

Call Sign: KC9PFD
Thomas L Stafford
56712 Elm Ridge Rd
Elkhart IN 46516

Call Sign: WB9ARM
Nevin J Houston
1609 Evergreen Pl
Elkhart IN 46514

Call Sign: N9YVU
Scott M Hengert
55444 Falling Water Dr
Elkhart IN 46514

Call Sign: KB9JCN
Thomas L Spellins
1230 Fieldhouse Ave
Elkhart IN 46517

Call Sign: KC9IIF
Jess C Spry
28132 Fieldhouse Ave
Elkhart IN 465171066

Call Sign: KB9FK
Gregory K Mayes
23521 Florence St
Elkhart IN 46515

Call Sign: KI4UIG
Bill A Hardin
23454 Forest Ln
Elkhart IN 46516

Call Sign: KB9OYL
Martha J Wright
183 Foster Ave
Elkhart IN 46516

Call Sign: KB9VTW
Richard L Bowen
718 Fremont St
Elkhart IN 465162144

Call Sign: N9VTW
Richard L Bowen
718 Fremont St
Elkhart IN 465162144

Call Sign: KB9IAI
Benjamin D Chesser
1007 Fulton St
Elkhart IN 46514

Call Sign: KB9HKR
Robert L McClimon
1112 Fulton St
Elkhart IN 46514

Call Sign: KC9OHC
David L Nye
151 Gage Ave
Elkhart IN 46516

Call Sign: KB9GFM
Gregory P Williams
3200 Garden Blvd
Elkhart IN 46517

Call Sign: W9JWF
Dale W Bouwman
23005 Gardena Pl
Elkhart IN 46514

Call Sign: KA9VNS
Reuben E Zarria
23055 Gardena Pl
Elkhart IN 46514

Call Sign: W9GEK
Orbra W Bliss
59416 Garver Ave
Elkhart IN 46517

Call Sign: KC9OXR
Ryan S Cyrus
59821 Garver Ave
Elkhart IN 46517

Call Sign: KC9MIC
Rory W Kerwood
59828 Garver Ave
Elkhart IN 46517

Call Sign: KB9VPP
Robert W Peck
117 Graywood Ave
Elkhart IN 46516

Call Sign: KC9OXP
Michael W Rippey
2927 Green Tree
Elkhart IN 46514

Call Sign: W3DZN
Harold W Shira
1601 Greenbrier Dr
Elkhart IN 46514

Call Sign: N9EXO
Gerald D Glace
22841 Greenleaf Blvd
Elkhart IN 46514

Call Sign: WA9RNT
Herbert C Sommers
23530 Greenwood Blvd
Elkhart IN 465166137

Call Sign: N9VUH
Tracey M Stutzman
720 H Ln Apt 2C
Elkhart IN 46517

Call Sign: KA9GXY
Gary L Toland
26854 Hampton Woods
Dr
Elkhart IN 46514

Call Sign: N9MQJ
William A Hanscom
409 Harrison St
Elkhart IN 46516

Call Sign: KB9PFP
James F Zimmerman
57629 Hawthorne St
Elkhart IN 46517

Call Sign: KB9BTI
Bobby A Woolwine
1536 Holiday View Dr
Elkhart IN 46514

Call Sign: K9GIC
Cecil P Langdoc
201 Homan Ave
Elkhart IN 46516

Call Sign: N9FSL
Paul E Wilsey
159 Home Ave
Elkhart IN 46516

Call Sign: W9ZFA
Homer Houck Jr
54670 Homeland Rd

Elkhart IN 465144537

Call Sign: KB9MKF
Bradley S Saylor
58047 Homer Ave
Elkhart IN 46517

Call Sign: KB9BFM
Jerome J Larkin
155 Homewood Ave
Elkhart IN 46516

Call Sign: KB9WSX
Andrew J Newton
53801 Hyde Park Dr
Elkhart IN 46507

Call Sign: KA5IAE
Robert D Molen
53968 Ida Rd
Elkhart IN 46514

Call Sign: N9QIC
Alyssa M Schlosser
1913 Illinois Ave
Elkhart IN 46516

Call Sign: KA9CZO
Kenneth L Smith
23439 Ironwood Dr
Elkhart IN 46516

Call Sign: KB9PAJ
James P Soli
29940 Ivy Ln
Elkhart IN 46516

Call Sign: KB9PRU
David L Weaver
525 James St
Elkhart IN 46516

Call Sign: N9OJJ
Michael D Bennett
23140 Janiper Dr

Elkhart IN 46517   Elkhart IN 46517   Elkhart IN 46517

Call Sign: KF7VHF
Eric J Zehrung
1729 Johnson St
Elkhart IN 46514

Call Sign: K9CNZ
Pat A Taylor
28207 La Rue St
Elkhart IN 46516

Call Sign: KC9FZQ
Paul H Maurer
23337 Marydale Dr
Elkhart IN 46517

Call Sign: KA9PTV
Erik E Gravelle
600 K Ln 3D
Elkhart IN 46517

Call Sign: KB9OPR
Timothy B Brown
26231 Lakeview Dr
Elkhart IN 46514

Call Sign: KD8EB
David W Horst
2129 Mather
Elkhart IN 46517

Call Sign: KC9MQQ
Richard K Bowen
220 Kenwood Ave
Elkhart IN 46514

Call Sign: WB9OOJ
Raymond A Yoder
29559 Lehigh Dr
Elkhart IN 46514

Call Sign: N9ZMS
Kathleen Horst
2129 Mather Ave
Elkhart IN 46517

Call Sign: KC9MQM
Joshua M Stahl
54419 Kerryhaven Dr
Elkhart IN 46514

Call Sign: KC9BQG
Robert E Elliott
23536 Linden Dr
Elkhart IN 46516

Call Sign: KC9GMH
Adam M Wales
2201 Mather Ave
Elkhart IN 46517

Call Sign: WA5PSE
Michael D Hunton
53804 Kershner Ln
Elkhart IN 46514

Call Sign: KB1HXX
Peter W De Bonte
Links Dr
Elkhart IN 465145123

Call Sign: N9MAR
James W Cunningham
56769 Meadow Glen Dr
Elkhart IN 46516

Call Sign: K9QB
Michael D Hunton
53804 Kershner Ln
Elkhart IN 46514

Call Sign: KE9GM
Gregory E Stout
58232 Lowell St
Elkhart IN 46517

Call Sign: W9URX
James R Vaughn
328 Meisner Ave
Elkhart IN 46514

Call Sign: WA5PSE
Michael D Hunton
53804 Kershner Ln
Elkhart IN 46514

Call Sign: KB9UNU
Michael C Jones
1406 Magnolia Ave
Elkhart IN 46514

Call Sign: KC9RDP
James R Kaufman
24411 Merrimac Ln
Elkhart IN 46517

Call Sign: K9QXW
Jerry A Fivecoate
50781 Killian Ln
Elkhart IN 46514

Call Sign: K9RBJ
Paul W Richardson
1407 Maple Row
Elkhart IN 46514

Call Sign: KC9UAG
Nathan J Gingerich
59144 Merrimac Ln
Elkhart IN 46517

Call Sign: KB9GRO
Elizabeth L Thurston
23803 Kime Ave

Call Sign: KA9TAY
Harry R Strausborger
23369 Martin Ave

Call Sign: KC9IRP
Christine R Daly
23831 Mira Ct

Elkhart IN 46516

Call Sign: N9MHP
Michael A Daly
23831 Mira Ct
Elkhart IN 46516

Call Sign: AB9LU
Michael A Daly
23831 Mira Ct
Elkhart IN 46516

Call Sign: WD5BKM
Adam C Bull
2017 Morehouse Ave
Elkhart IN 46516

Call Sign: KC9FZS
Roger L Woods
58056 Morgan St
Elkhart IN 46517

Call Sign: KC9FZR
Samantha L Woods
58056 Morgan St
Elkhart IN 46517

Call Sign: KB9WSY
Joseph K Fuller
125 Myrtle St
Elkhart IN 46514

Call Sign: KB9QHX
Andrew M Massing
615 Myrtle St
Elkhart IN 46514

Call Sign: KB9MOG
James L Massing
615 Myrtle St
Elkhart IN 46514

Call Sign: KA9IBA
Chris G Arvanitis
1523 N Bay Dr

Elkhart IN 46514

Call Sign: KB8LHR
Jack W Kinney
1821 N Bay Dr
Elkhart IN 46514

Call Sign: WA9VID
David W Replogle
25310 N Shore Dr
Elkhart IN 46514

Call Sign: KB9QOJ
Joachim M Herzig
1923 N Striped Mapel Ln
Elkhart IN 46514

Call Sign: KB9TUK
Carl L Harrison
215 N Ward
Elkhart IN 46514

Call Sign: KC9CW
David A Miller
149 Nadel Ave
Elkhart IN 46516

Call Sign: KB9HGJ
Paul K Kelly
57279 Necedah Dr
Elkhart IN 46514

Call Sign: N9UUE
Debra J Byrket
2822 Oakland Ave
Elkhart IN 46517

Call Sign: N9YEW
Hollie C Byrket
2822 Oakland Ave
Elkhart IN 46517

Call Sign: N9UGT
Wayne K Jones
963 Oakland Estates Dr

Elkhart IN 46517

Call Sign: WN9EHN
Jon V Walker
54097 Old Mill Dr
Elkhart IN 46514

Call Sign: KA9ZFL
Matthew V Walker
54097 Old Mill Dr
Elkhart IN 46514

Call Sign: N9GUM
James D Chandler
56662 Old Orchard Ln
Elkhart IN 46516

Call Sign: AA9FH
Ronald A Curtis
2934 Old US 20 W
Elkhart IN 465141356

Call Sign: K9WU
Ronald A Curtis
2934 Old US 20 W
Elkhart IN 465141356

Call Sign: KB9ZUB
Robert J McDowell Jr
714 Osolo Rd
Elkhart IN 46514

Call Sign: WA2LPF
James E Gluckin
1506 Osolo Rd
Elkhart IN 46514

Call Sign: KB9QHV
Teresa L Manning
1901 Osolo Rd Lot 173
Elkhart IN 46514

Call Sign: KB9NTZ
Donna J Moore
1901 Osolo Rd Lot 50

Elkhart IN 46514   Elkhart IN 46517   Elkhart IN 465145316

Call Sign: N9GVC
Larry L Straw
56034 Outer Dr
Elkhart IN 46516

Call Sign: N9QJ
James I Carter
59060 Peppermint Dr
Elkhart IN 46517

Call Sign: KB8MAI
Andy S Benedict
58008 Riley St
Elkhart IN 46517

Call Sign: N9PEN
Harold I Miller
58573 Ox Bow Dr
Elkhart IN 46516

Call Sign: KC9BFR
Anthony J Peffley
59223 Peppermint Dr
Elkhart IN 46517

Call Sign: N9QYL
Andrew G Bogue
23527 River Manor Blvd
Elkhart IN 46516

Call Sign: W0WVV
Samuel H Rowley
60397 Pembrook Ln
Elkhart IN 46517

Call Sign: KA9HSU
Darlene M Wright
2401 Pleasant Plain
Elkhart IN 46517

Call Sign: KB6BRS
George P Kelsey
55925 River Shores Ln
Elkhart IN 46516

Call Sign: KB9HKF
James E Smith
57433 Penny Ln
Elkhart IN 46517

Call Sign: KA9HSV
Robert D Wright
2401 Pleasant Plain
Elkhart IN 46517

Call Sign: KB9HPG
Stephen M Jones
55791 Riverdale Dr
Elkhart IN 46514

Call Sign: WD9FUV
Edward M Hobson
2905 Peoria St
Elkhart IN 46517

Call Sign: KB9RQS
James A Null
57064 Porter Ave
Elkhart IN 46516

Call Sign: WB9VTZ
Thomas J Szerencse
23652 Riverlane Blvd
Elkhart IN 465166342

Call Sign: KB9AKO
James I Carter
59060 Peppermint Dr
Elkhart IN 46517

Call Sign: KB9OYK
Harry A Snyder
1221 Praire St
Elkhart IN 46516

Call Sign: KB9YCD
Charles R Wilson
103 Riverside Dr
Elkhart IN 46514

Call Sign: KC9NYH
James I Carter
59060 Peppermint Dr
Elkhart IN 46517

Call Sign: WB9SPT
Neil A Dodson
26242 Quail Ridge Dr
Elkhart IN 465146315

Call Sign: KC9LXR
William A Swartout
60191 Robinhood Ln
Elkhart IN 46517

Call Sign: N9QJ
James I Carter
59060 Peppermint Dr
Elkhart IN 46517

Call Sign: W9NU
Neil A Dodson
26242 Quail Ridge Dr
Elkhart IN 465146315

Call Sign: W9QXF
Arthur D Kiracofe
1229 Romain Ave
Elkhart IN 46514

Call Sign: KB9AKO
James I Carter
59060 Peppermint Dr

Call Sign: KB9TUM
John Merriman Jr
25080 Rex St

Call Sign: KB9PIJ
Dennis W Chamberlain
29616 Roscommon Dr

Elkhart IN 46514

Call Sign: N9PZN
Chris A Kratzer
26978 Roseland Rd
Elkhart IN 46514

Call Sign: KA1QNG
Jerry L Tucker
27846 Rosewood Dr
Elkhart IN 46517

Call Sign: N9KKO
Steven L Fath
1808 Roys Ave
Elkhart IN 46516

Call Sign: K9ME
Michael P Axman
2434 Roys Ave
Elkhart IN 465172042

Call Sign: KB9MYG
Billy W Moore Jr
417 S 5th St
Elkhart IN 46516

Call Sign: KB9ZSY
Adam M Kennedy
30513 S Elizabeth Dr
Elkhart IN 46516

Call Sign: W0FZY
Adam M Kennedy
30513 S Elizabeth Dr
Elkhart IN 46516

Call Sign: WB9PZL
John E Wilson
2230 S Main St
Elkhart IN 465172425

Call Sign: KC9LNN
Richard E Inglish
115 S Michigan St

Elkhart IN 46514

Call Sign: KC9LPW
Richard E Inglish
115 S Michigan St
Elkhart IN 46514

Call Sign: W7REI
Richard E Inglish
115 S Michigan St
Elkhart IN 46514

Call Sign: W9CSV
Melvin A Pieper
132 S Shore Dr
Elkhart IN 46516

Call Sign: KB8ILE
Nancy J Jesko
1853 S Striped Maple Ln
Elkhart IN 46514

Call Sign: WA9WTM
Neal F Thomas
54503 Saddle Brook
Crossing
Elkhart IN 465144667

Call Sign: WA3VLC
John W Parker
29523 Santa Cruz
Elkhart IN 46514

Call Sign: KB9TUJ
Robert D Thrapp
56620 Sapphire Blvd
Elkhart IN 46516

Call Sign: KE9YY
James E Glaum
28585 Schwalm Dr
Elkhart IN 46517

Call Sign: KB9BUH
Tammy L Glaum

28585 Schwalm Dr
Elkhart IN 46517

Call Sign: KA9MXY
Thomas W Butler
23027 Scottswood Ct
Elkhart IN 46514

Call Sign: N9JHQ
Roger D Myers
1901 Shaffer Ave
Elkhart IN 46517

Call Sign: N9LVK
Pamela E Pesola
55645 Sheridan Blvd
Elkhart IN 46514

Call Sign: N9GMS
Harold G Pesola
55645 Sheridan Blvd
Elkhart IN 465149364

Call Sign: KC9CUB
Robert J Roth
54235 Silver St
Elkhart IN 46514

Call Sign: W3SNV
George H Zensen Jr
59217 Spearmint Dr
Elkhart IN 465179411

Call Sign: KB9UEX
Paul F Corey
1535 Springbrook Dr
Elkhart IN 46514

Call Sign: K9MV
Paul F Corey
1535 Springbrook Dr
Elkhart IN 46514

Call Sign: KA9VTO
Thomas E Hively Sr

50678 SR 19 N
Elkhart IN 46514

Call Sign: N9NAD
Dale L Lechlitner
59039 SR 19 S
Elkhart IN 46517

Call Sign: KC9EXF
Timothy R Anderson
61531 SR 19
Elkhart IN 46517

Call Sign: KA9WLX
Patrisha A Hively
1704 St Charles Ave
Elkhart IN 46514

Call Sign: KB9LFB
Henry A Baskins
1719 St Charles Ave
Elkhart IN 46514

Call Sign: KB9ZXZ
Mary H Ollenburger
18 St Joesph Manor
Elkhart IN 46516

Call Sign: KC9SZJ
Larry R King Jr
315 State St
Elkhart IN 46514

Call Sign: N9PGE
James M Slater
2107 Stevens Ave
Elkhart IN 46517

Call Sign: WA8APA
Richard J Bolyard
666 Strong Ave
Elkhart IN 46514

Call Sign: W9VFI
Roy D Wiltrout

1119 Strong Ave
Elkhart IN 46514

Call Sign: KC9GQV
William F Genslinger
1153 Strong Ave
Elkhart IN 46514

Call Sign: W9JKX
Alexander C Berta
54636 Suburban Dr
Elkhart IN 46514

Call Sign: N9NNQ
Steven A Gattman
58377 Summer Chase Dr
Elkhart IN 46517

Call Sign: KA9SAZ
Kenneth A Holderman
23678 Sunnyside Ave
Elkhart IN 46516

Call Sign: WA9GMR
Curtis L Holmes
2 Surrey Ln
Elkhart IN 46514

Call Sign: KC9PJC
Hargis Wilson Jr
4 Surrey Ln
Elkhart IN 46514

Call Sign: N9WDE
Samuel A McGuire
60218 Surrey Ln
Elkhart IN 46517

Call Sign: KB9QGJ
Amy M Pauley
53520 Sweetspire Trl
Elkhart IN 46514

Call Sign: KB9DPZ
Louis A Antonelli

30431 Sycamore Ln
Elkhart IN 46514

Call Sign: WB9UJD
Robert F Fink
110 Sycamore St
Elkhart IN 46516

Call Sign: KA9PEE
Ronald A Heinrichs
2325 Sylvan Ln
Elkhart IN 46514

Call Sign: N9OIY
Kathleen Snyder
626 Thomas St
Elkhart IN 46516

Call Sign: WA9I
Edward L Snyder
626 Thomas St
Elkhart IN 465162108

Call Sign: KE9AV
Michael E Wolf
58989 Towne Rd
Elkhart IN 46517

Call Sign: KB9MOF
Joseph C Huffman Jr
53031 Tulain St
Elkhart IN 46514

Call Sign: K9FUP
Richard L Hurtle
23549 US 33 E
Elkhart IN 46517

Call Sign: KC9UMO
Steven D Crussemeyer
58189 Valleyview Dr
Elkhart IN 46517

Call Sign: N9XGE
Frank M Hoover

30035 Velma Ln
Elkhart IN 46514

Call Sign: K9PGR
Carlton M Osburn
906 Violet Rd
Elkhart IN 46514

Call Sign: KC9NAV
Charles R Reid Jr
600 W Beardsley Ave
Elkhart IN 46514

Call Sign: KA9TOD
David R Stalling
714 W Blaine Ave
Elkhart IN 46516

Call Sign: WB0OKJ
Stanley E Smith
401 W Hively
Elkhart IN 46517

Call Sign: KB9DNR
Carolyn E Smith
401 W Hively Ave
Elkhart IN 46517

Call Sign: KA5YXW
Evelyn M Smith
812 W Hively Ave
Elkhart IN 46517

Call Sign: K0EH
Maurice E Smith
812 W Hively Ave
Elkhart IN 46517

Call Sign: KB5HIT
Susan M Hanna
812 W Hively Ave
Elkhart IN 46517

Call Sign: W6TUA
Delbert G Stouder

1001 W Hively Ave
Rosewood Ter
Elkhart IN 46517

Call Sign: N0OGI
Andrew L Green
1610 W Indiana Ave
Elkhart IN 46516

Call Sign: N9UUF
James O Lowe
2301 W Lexington 107
1A
Elkhart IN 46516

Call Sign: KD6RAN
Tommy L Galloway
2301 W Lexington Apt
104 1B
Elkhart IN 46514

Call Sign: KF9GK
Paul D Axell
821 W Lusher Ave
Elkhart IN 46517

Call Sign: KB9OBI
Sam J Martin
28904 W Wynd
Elkhart IN 46516

Call Sign: KC9GSD
James D Pixey
508 West Blvd S
Elkhart IN 46514

Call Sign: K9HCT
Howard C Held
1130 Willowdale Ave
Elkhart IN 46514

Call Sign: N9HDP
George H Himebaugh Jr
1169 Willowdale Ave
Elkhart IN 46514

Call Sign: KC9OXQ
Shailyn M Owings
23889 Wilshire Blvd
Elkhart IN 46516

Call Sign: N9JGR
James E West
23701 Wilshire Blvd E
Elkhart IN 46516

Call Sign: N9GDE
Joseph D Carlson
51119 Winding Waters
Ln
Elkhart IN 46514

Call Sign: N9RSV
Jay D Ostrom
52425 Winding Waters
Ln S
Elkhart IN 46514

Call Sign: WB9VJD
Charles O Henderson
52106 Winding Waters S
Elkhart IN 46514

Call Sign: N9EY
Charles O Henderson
52106 Winding Waters S
Elkhart IN 46514

Call Sign: K9RKO
William S Van Patten Jr
127 Witmer Ave
Elkhart IN 46516

Call Sign: N9HPW
Eugene W Loy
30106 Wolf Ave
Elkhart IN 46516

Call Sign: KA9MIQ
Richard C Meyer

56561 Woodbine Ln
Elkhart IN 46516

Call Sign: KC9EDF
Daniel S Thomas
30042 Yellow Pine Ct
Elkhart IN 46514

Call Sign: N9HAS
James C Streitmatter
Elkhart IN 46515

Call Sign: N9ICS
Kenneth W Wagner Jr
Elkhart IN 46514

Call Sign: KB9NRH
Dale W Holden
Elkhart IN 46515

Call Sign: KC9IXU
Danny L Newcomer
Elkhart IN 465140723

Call Sign: KB9OCR
Christopher A Ferguson
Elkhart IN 465150562

Call Sign: KB9MIC
J Douglas Ferguson
Elkhart IN 465150562

Call Sign: W9LZX
Elkhart County Radio
Association
Elkhart IN 465152535

FCC Amateur Radio Licenses in Etna Green

Call Sign: N9GPB
Shawn M Rafferty
14019 Beech Rd
Etna Green IN 46524

Call Sign: KC9RRB
Keith A Claassen
226 E Pleasant St
Etna Green IN 46524

Call Sign: WB9ESE
Darwin Monesmith
5379 N SR 19
Etna Green IN 46524

Call Sign: KC9INF
Ross D Jacobs
9291 N SR 19
Etna Green IN 46524

Call Sign: KC9LVA
Jason T Kline
9321 N SR 19
Etna Green IN 46524

Call Sign: KC9QDK
Merril P Stouder
104 S Main St
Etna Green IN 46524

Call Sign: KC9TQW
Crista O Barker
8886 W CR 25 S
Etna Green IN 46524

Call Sign: N9GXO
Florence S Stauffer
Etna Green IN 46524

Call Sign: KC9ATI
Randy L Borkholder
Etna Green IN 46524

FCC Amateur Radio Licenses in Fairmount

Call Sign: N9JWG
Errol D Parsons
5740 E 1050 S
Fairmount IN 46928

Call Sign: KA9YID
James L Matney
2351 E 1100 S
Fairmount IN 46928

Call Sign: AA9RJ
Barry D Howard
605 E 975 S
Fairmount IN 46928

Call Sign: KB9ZYT
Gregory L Smith
523 E Jefferson St
Fairmount IN 46928

Call Sign: KB9UOV
Lawrence R Lamb
617 E Washington St
Fairmount IN 46928

Call Sign: KA9VFL
Vicki L Lamb
300 N Barclay 21
Fairmount IN 46928

Call Sign: N9FPC
Clyde D Lamb
300 N Barclay Lot 21
Fairmount IN 469281238

Call Sign: KA9ZJF
James T Nelson Jr
515 N Main St
Fairmount IN 46928

Call Sign: KB9UOT
Peggy S Barnes
102 N Wilson
Fairmount IN 46928

Call Sign: KF9RE
Michael P King
708 N Wilson St
Fairmount IN 46928

Call Sign: W9UCT
Forest C Kientz
9611 S 69 E
Fairmount IN 46928

Call Sign: WB9RMN
James A Sheedy
11580 S 700 W
Fairmount IN 46928

Call Sign: KA9DAN
Cassie Morgan
11371 S 800 W
Fairmount IN 46928

Call Sign: WD9HJM
James A Morgan
11371 S 800 W
Fairmount IN 46928

Call Sign: N9VUI
John R Strong
11800 S 932 E Wheeling
Pk
Fairmount IN 46928

Call Sign: WA9H
Rodney A De Shong
227 S Barclay St
Fairmount IN 46928

Call Sign: W9OCM
David G Mantor
203 S Buckeye St
Fairmount IN 46928

Call Sign: KB9GUZ
Charles A Hendricks
323 S Main
Fairmount IN 46928

Call Sign: KB9YPH
David E Cowart
10951 S SR 9

Fairmount IN 46928

Call Sign: WW9C
J Sam McGibbon
410 S Sycamore
Fairmount IN 46928

Call Sign: KB9ATF
Micah S McGibbon
410 S Sycamore St
Fairmount IN 46928

Call Sign: KA9JUB
Dennis D Clevenger
516 S Walnut
Fairmount IN 46928

Call Sign: KB9YLT
Dennis D Clevenger
516 S Walnut
Fairmount IN 46928

Call Sign: KA9VLD
Darlene S Clevenger
516 S Walnut St
Fairmount IN 46928

Call Sign: KB9LKB
Joni M Vermilion
11649 S Wheeling Pike
Fairmount IN 46928

Call Sign: N9PKK
Robert C Vermilion
11649 S Wheeling Pk
Fairmount IN 46928

Call Sign: KA9YIC
Mark R Matney
319 W 3rd St
Fairmount IN 46928

Call Sign: KF9RD
Thomas J King
220 W 4th St

Fairmount IN 46928

FCC Amateur Radio Licenses in Flora

Call Sign: KB9UZF
Steven B Walker
1150W
Flora IN 46929

Call Sign: KB9EOR
Curtis N Kell
Box 116A
Flora IN 46929

Call Sign: KC9QDN
Thomas J Schwartz
11939 CR 500 N
Flora IN 46929

Call Sign: KC9BPC
Thomas L Brower
108 Green Acres Dr
Flora IN 46929

Call Sign: K9NRA
Thomas L Brower
108 Green Acres Dr
Flora IN 46929

Call Sign: N9XYQ
Greg A Fridholm
3487 N 1150 W
Flora IN 469299514

Call Sign: KB9KLN
Carol L Rupp
707 S Center St
Flora IN 46929

Call Sign: K9EFY
Richard D Curts
903 South Dr
Flora IN 469291631

Call Sign: KC9DYK
Debra A Kelly
12169 W 350 N
Flora IN 46902

Call Sign: N9DEB
Debra A Kelly
12169 W 350 N
Flora IN 46929

Call Sign: KB9ZBF
Michael K Kelly
12169 W 350 N
Flora IN 46929

Call Sign: KC9LXD
Michael K Kelly Jr
12169 W 350 N
Flora IN 46929

**FCC Amateur Radio
Licenses in Fort Wayne**

Call Sign: W8JGC
Robert A Shaw
6950 46th Dr
Fort Wayne IN
468351502

Call Sign: KC9NDL
Ron G Marmelstein
Abbey Dr
Fort Wayne IN 46835

Call Sign: W9RGM
Ron G Marmelstein
Abbey Dr
Fort Wayne IN 46835

Call Sign: KA9IHA
John R Capin
Abbey Dr
Fort Wayne IN
468353112

Call Sign: KB9MGQ
Philip A Dery
2420 Abbey Dr 1
Fort Wayne IN
468353132

Call Sign: KB9JDT
Emery W McClendon II
2618 Abbey Dr Apt 5
Fort Wayne IN 46835

Call Sign: WD9IRX
Bret A Diehm
9811 Abbington Trl
Fort Wayne IN 46818

Call Sign: KB9MDR
William Shull
3115 Abbott
Fort Wayne IN 46806

Call Sign: KB9EVP
Paul V Murphy
3702 Abbott St
Fort Wayne IN 46806

Call Sign: KB9EVR
Sharon K Murphy
3702 Abbott St
Fort Wayne IN 46806

Call Sign: N9NNT
Douglas B Jones
4425 Aboite Lake Dr
Fort Wayne IN 46804

Call Sign: N9SCA
Susan R Jones
4425 Aboite Lake Dr
Fort Wayne IN 46804

Call Sign: N9OBL
Jonathan C Luckey
4438 Aboite Lake Dr
Fort Wayne IN 46804

Call Sign: W9OZ
Richard T Kidd
4413 Aboite Lk Dr
Fort Wayne IN 46804

Call Sign: KC9QHL
Michael S Lyons
9417 Acacia Psge
Fort Wayne IN 46835

Call Sign: WA9NCY
Allan C Thomas
6827 Adams Center Rd
Fort Wayne IN 46816

Call Sign: KC9RAC
Frederick R Fulkerson II
10210 Adobe Ct
Fort Wayne IN 46825

Call Sign: KC9RAJ
Paul A Stanton
1709 Alabama Ave
Fort Wayne IN 46805

Call Sign: N9VWY
William L Plant
4272 Albert Dr
Fort Wayne IN 46835

Call Sign: W9MIV
George A Schuller
7611 Allburn Rd
Fort Wayne IN 46825

Call Sign: N9RYE
Jay E Tipton
3010 Allegany Ave
Fort Wayne IN 46809

Call Sign: KB9QVG
David S Hippensteele
6011 Allendale Ct
Fort Wayne IN 46809

Call Sign: N8YUR
Randy E Dix
5806 Allendale Dr
Fort Wayne IN 46809

Call Sign: KB9ACW
Stephen M Garrett
6114 Almond Bluff Pass
Fort Wayne IN 46804

Call Sign: KB9EVX
Maria V Simo
609 Anderson Ave
Fort Wayne IN 46805

Call Sign: KA9THS
Kathy L Vardaman
6627 Angello Ct
Fort Wayne IN 46835

Call Sign: WB9UYT
Gary D Reece
5126 Ann Hackley Rd
Fort Wayne IN 46835

Call Sign: WB9KEP
Gerald L Schuster Sr
1605 Annette Ave
Fort Wayne IN 46805

Call Sign: KA9VAP
Victor A Bowers
7916 Anoka Dr
Fort Wayne IN 46809

Call Sign: W9DUY
Dennis L Free
604 Ansley Dr
Fort Wayne IN 46804

Call Sign: KE9ZE
Ronald L Barnhart
7239 Antebellum Dr
Fort Wayne IN 46815

Call Sign: AB9BR
Ronald L Barnhart
7239 Antebellum Dr
Fort Wayne IN 46815

Call Sign: AA9KN
Bienvenido C Peralta
7304 Antebellum Dr
Fort Wayne IN 46815

Call Sign: KB9HIO
Mary R Rose
4306 Anthony Wayne Dr
Fort Wayne IN 46806

Call Sign: WQ9H
Michael P Nomina
1307 Applewood
Fort Wayne IN 46825

Call Sign: KA9JTM
Howard P Fischer
835 Applewood Rd
Fort Wayne IN 46825

Call Sign: W9GHA
Robert J Bontempo Jr
914 Applewood Rd
Fort Wayne IN
468253704

Call Sign: WD9FAQ
J Allan Waters
1403 Apricot Ct
Fort Wayne IN
468253770

Call Sign: KB9IRG
Jon E Ashby
6022 Aragon Dr
Fort Wayne IN 46818

Call Sign: N9XPB
Robert L Hire

6217 Aragon Dr
Fort Wayne IN 46818

Call Sign: KB9VBV
Daniel B Baker
5907 Arbor Ave
Fort Wayne IN 46809

Call Sign: KB9VBK
Marygrace E Baker
5907 Arbor Ave
Fort Wayne IN 46809

Call Sign: KB9WWO
Susie K Baker
5907 Arbor Ave
Fort Wayne IN 46809

Call Sign: KB9TFC
Thomas C Baker
5907 Arbor Ave
Fort Wayne IN 46809

Call Sign: N9TB
Thomas C Baker
5907 Arbor Ave
Fort Wayne IN 46809

Call Sign: KA0PAU
Don R Trembly
10020 Arbor Trl
Fort Wayne IN 46804

Call Sign: KC9RDI
George M Visocky
667 Archer Ave
Fort Wayne IN 46808

Call Sign: WA9HPC
Ronald D Winn
2002 Ardis Dr
Fort Wayne IN
468191392

Call Sign: KA9SPP

Donna K Smith
12732 Auburn Rd
Fort Wayne IN 46845

Call Sign: K9VFE
Larry J Smith
12732 Auburn Rd
Fort Wayne IN 46845

Call Sign: W9LL
Larry J Smith
12732 Auburn Rd
Fort Wayne IN 46845

Call Sign: N9AQZ
Ronald D Hensley
2126 August Dr
Fort Wayne IN 46818

Call Sign: N3ZFQ
Gary L Miller Jr
831 Autumn Ridge Ln
Fort Wayne IN 46804

Call Sign: KC9KJH
Wayne L Ostman
7011 Avalon Dr
Fort Wayne IN 46819

Call Sign: N9SYE
David W Jones Sr
7515 Avalon Dr
Fort Wayne IN 46819

Call Sign: KB9JHB
Dorothy M Jones
7515 Avalon Dr
Fort Wayne IN 46819

Call Sign: KA9MIN
Martha L Fairbanks
1023 Aylesford Dr
Fort Wayne IN 46819

Call Sign: KA9PWO

William E Fairbanks III
1023 Aylesford Dr
Fort Wayne IN 46819

Call Sign: KA9PWR
William E Fairbanks Jr
1023 Aylesford Dr
Fort Wayne IN 46819

Call Sign: WD9FUY
David B Brineman
6440 Azalea Dr
Fort Wayne IN 46825

Call Sign: KA9FPZ
Oliver H Talbott
7115 Baer Rd
Fort Wayne IN 46809

Call Sign: KC9HQU
Christopher L Piano
10904 Baldham Pass
Fort Wayne IN 46845

Call Sign: KD9UF
Scott A Brune
9820 Banyan Ct
Fort Wayne IN 46835

Call Sign: KB9TEY
Jonathan A Wolter
9821 Banyan Ct
Fort Wayne IN
468359999

Call Sign: KC9OSA
Hugo A Ramos
223 Barouche Pl
Fort Wayne IN 46845

Call Sign: KC9SFE
Most Precious Blood
School
1529 Barthhold St
Fort Wayne IN 46845

Call Sign: KC9SUA
Most Precious Blood
School
1529 Barthold St
Fort Wayne IN 46808

Call Sign: K9MPB
Most Precious Blood
School
1529 Barthold St
Fort Wayne IN 46808

Call Sign: KC9NDH
Dennis W Spence
6530 Bayberry Dr
Fort Wayne IN 46825

Call Sign: KB9TUI
Gary L Gruesbeck
7312 Baylor Dr
Fort Wayne IN 46819

Call Sign: KB9YJI
Dionne A Pumphrey
1841 Bayview Dr
Fort Wayne IN 46815

Call Sign: AB9IZ
Philip J Hooper
2113 Bayview Dr
Fort Wayne IN 46815

Call Sign: KC9MNY
Terryn M Sears
8313 Beacon Ridge Pl
Fort Wayne IN 46835

Call Sign: KG7IO
William D Sears
8313 Beacon Ridge Pl
Fort Wayne IN
468354754

Call Sign: WD9DMC

Clark L Bradley
2210 Beacon St Apt 325
Fort Wayne IN 46805

Call Sign: KC9PUU
Melissa R Smith
8820 Beacon Woods Pl
Fort Wayne IN 46804

Call Sign: KC9LAF
Roger A Smith
8820 Beacon Woods Pl
Fort Wayne IN 46804

Call Sign: KC9CPG
Ryan M Smith
4101 Beaver Brook Dr
Fort Wayne IN 46815

Call Sign: KC9EJC
Robert W Tomsits
8133 Becketts Ridge Ln
Fort Wayne IN 46825

Call Sign: KC9QZX
Giselle R Bowser
1915 Beineke Rd
Fort Wayne IN 46808

Call Sign: KC9PUT
Mark A Bowser Sr
1915 Beineke Rd
Fort Wayne IN 46808

Call Sign: KE6SDK
Jack L Dooley Sr
2911 Belfast Dr
Fort Wayne IN
468053024

Call Sign: N9OOD
John B Webster
6726 Bellefield
Fort Wayne IN 46835

Call Sign: KB9DOX
Jessica M Voris
6335 Bellefield Dr
Fort Wayne IN 46835

Call Sign: KB9DOW
Nancy E Kelley
6335 Bellefield Dr
Fort Wayne IN 46835

Call Sign: KC9RAE
Carl D Lyvers
6430 Bellefield Dr
Fort Wayne IN
468353916

Call Sign: N9AVR
Walter E Wood
2096 Bellevue Dr
Fort Wayne IN 46825

Call Sign: KC9CGI
Ricky L Martin
2199 Bellevue Dr
Fort Wayne IN 46825

Call Sign: KC9NNP
Richard R Byers
3105 Bellshire Way
Fort Wayne IN 46815

Call Sign: W9RRB
Richard R Byers
3105 Bellshire Way
Fort Wayne IN 46815

Call Sign: K9VRP
David R Peterson
3130 Bellshire Way
Fort Wayne IN 46815

Call Sign: WA9TDH
Simpson United
Methodist Radio Club
9736 Berkshire Ln

Fort Wayne IN 46804

Call Sign: W9TDU
Charles M Cook
9736 Berkshire Ln
Fort Wayne IN
468044302

Call Sign: N9UKM
Teresa L Deventer
11418 Bethel Rd
Fort Wayne IN 46818

Call Sign: AB9JU
Thad S McCulloch
11232 Bittersweet Creek
Run
Fort Wayne IN
468143286

Call Sign: KA9LLH
Keith E Johnson
9405 Black Diamond Pl
Fort Wayne IN 46835

Call Sign: WA9YOF
Jack A Druckemiller
7210 Blackhawk Ln
Fort Wayne IN 46815

Call Sign: N0AWJ
Deborah A Snyder
5821 Blissfield Ct
Fort Wayne IN 46818

Call Sign: KD8BFS
Martin J Beem
7101 Blue Beech Dr
Fort Wayne IN 46815

Call Sign: N9MFX
David R Sanner
308 Blue Jacket Run
Fort Wayne IN 46825

Call Sign: N9MFN
John A Sanner
308 Blue Jacket Run
Fort Wayne IN 46825

Call Sign: W9FJT
Robert S Sievers
7021 Blue Mist Rd
Fort Wayne IN 46819

Call Sign: N9SBW
Michael R Sevcovic
9707 Blue Mound Dr
Fort Wayne IN 46804

Call Sign: KF9TE
Patricia G Bagby
3636 Bluegrass Ln
Fort Wayne IN 46815

Call Sign: KC9ORR
Ronald L Davis
1207 Bluff Pt Way
Fort Wayne IN 46845

Call Sign: KB9IGW
Pamela R Wolfe
5410 Bluffton Rd
Fort Wayne IN 46809

Call Sign: WB9TYJ
Donald P Sell
4528 Blum Dr
Fort Wayne IN 46835

Call Sign: WD9ECE
Kelly A Sell
4528 Blum Dr
Fort Wayne IN 46835

Call Sign: KB9MBP
Carol J Stedge
4784 Blum Dr
Fort Wayne IN 46835

Call Sign: KB9LOF
Clinton A Stedge
4784 Blum Dr
Fort Wayne IN 46835

Call Sign: KG9KS
James C Ransbottom
5220 Blum Dr
Fort Wayne IN 46835

Call Sign: KB9STY
David H Thompson
2703 Bolton Dr
Fort Wayne IN 46805

Call Sign: N9OBK
Lawrence L Kenner
3028 Bracebridge Pl
Fort Wayne IN 46815

Call Sign: KG4LPX
Sara M Glass
10132 Brandywine Dr
Fort Wayne IN 46825

Call Sign: W9WJR
William J Robertson
11408 Brantford Ct
Fort Wayne IN 46814

Call Sign: W8KHO
William J Robertson
11408 Brantford Ct
Fort Wayne IN
468047501

Call Sign: KH6GN
Charles F Raudonis
11420 Brantford Ct
Fort Wayne IN 46814

Call Sign: KA9WJG
Ronald L Hostetler
Bridgeway Cir
Fort Wayne IN 46816

Call Sign: N9SBD
David L Holland
8320 Bridgeway Dr Apt
1C
Fort Wayne IN 46816

Call Sign: WC0Y
Edward A Hall
11522 Brigadoon Ct
Fort Wayne IN 46814

Call Sign: KB9NQU
Patricia A Evans
5718 Brighton Dr
Fort Wayne IN 46825

Call Sign: KC9NDM
John W Little
2725 Brightwood Ct
Fort Wayne IN 46845

Call Sign: W5JWL
John W Little
2725 Brightwood Ct
Fort Wayne IN 46845

Call Sign: KA8QNI
Kent P Halloran
1706 Broken Oak Rd
Fort Wayne IN
468188800

Call Sign: WD8PGK
Kirk E Nygren
13707 Brook Hollow Ct
Fort Wayne IN 46804

Call Sign: N9ZNO
John G Cole
7806 Brookfield Dr
Fort Wayne IN 46835

Call Sign: WA0TVK
Steven C Hand

7831 Brookfield Dr
Fort Wayne IN 46835

Call Sign: KA9TPW
Annette M Yvinskas
2115 Brown St
Fort Wayne IN 46802

Call Sign: K3HZP
William E Rodgers
5727 Buckfield Ct
Fort Wayne IN 46804

Call Sign: K9BSQ
Donald E Schmutte
1408 Buckskin Dr
Fort Wayne IN 46804

Call Sign: K9EEJ
Mark J Kleppinger
5414 Buell Dr
Fort Wayne IN 46807

Call Sign: N9HYL
Kirk J Lyons
4318 Buesching Dr
Fort Wayne IN
468154812

Call Sign: KC9RQX
David J Miller
928 Burgess
Fort Wayne IN 46808

Call Sign: KB9VGU
John E Barchak
3630 Burrwood Ter
Fort Wayne IN 46815

Call Sign: W9PI
John E Barchak
3630 Burrwood Ter
Fort Wayne IN 46815

Call Sign: KC9UR

Robert E Billingsley
7724 Buttermore Ct
Fort Wayne IN 46804

Call Sign: N7BZB
Matthew J Beckstedt
11432 Cabriolet Run
Fort Wayne IN 46845

Call Sign: N8KKC
Frank J Silvagi
1832 Calais
Fort Wayne IN 46814

Call Sign: KB9MVP
Stephen J Slack
8129 Calera Dr
Fort Wayne IN 46818

Call Sign: KB9VML
Justin E Lange
2424 California Ave
Fort Wayne IN
468053512

Call Sign: KC9RAG
Bruce W Saylor
2612 Cambridge Blvd
Fort Wayne IN
468081954

Call Sign: N9RAG
Bruce W Saylor
2612 Cambridge Blvd
Fort Wayne IN
468081954

Call Sign: WA9FBK
Howard G Kennedy
505 Candlelite Ct
Fort Wayne IN
468073601

Call Sign: WA9EZP
Irene E Kennedy

505 Candlelite Ct
Fort Wayne IN
468073601

Call Sign: KB9YJJ
James L Angelo
744 Candlelite Ct
Fort Wayne IN 46807

Call Sign: KC9JMJ
Arthur W Kidd
9931 Canopy Ln
Fort Wayne IN 46835

Call Sign: WK9DD
Arthur W Kidd
9931 Canopy Ln
Fort Wayne IN 46835

Call Sign: N9NSP
Brad A Bohlender
3934 Captiva Dr
Fort Wayne IN 46815

Call Sign: KB9QI
Winston A Council
3638 Cardinal Ln
Fort Wayne IN 46815

Call Sign: KB9GY
James O Leimer
8020 Carnovan Dr
Fort Wayne IN 46835

Call Sign: KA9CZG
Nancy J Leimer
8020 Carnovan Dr
Fort Wayne IN 46835

Call Sign: WD9AJU
Timothy L Harding
8025 Carnovan Dr
Fort Wayne IN 46815

Call Sign: KB9FOH

John E Fletter
4218 Castell Dr
Fort Wayne IN 46835

Call Sign: KA9IOX
Donald H Ceckowski
12731 Cauthorn Ct
Fort Wayne IN
468452383

Call Sign: KB9GNY
Jennifer S Kaufeld
421 Cavalcade Ct
Fort Wayne IN 46845

Call Sign: KC9AIU
Tom L Rariden
3206 Cedar Run
Fort Wayne IN 46818

Call Sign: KC9JYL
Mark A Schroeder
613 Center St
Fort Wayne IN 46808

Call Sign: N9EVC
Dale W Anderson
6504 Centerton Dr
Fort Wayne IN 46815

Call Sign: KB9EWN
Joseph G Otero
4119 Central
Fort Wayne IN 46806

Call Sign: KB9RSY
Harold E Sinnes
3030 Central Dr
Fort Wayne IN 46806

Call Sign: KB9DPD
Andrew M Yoder
3809 Central Dr
Fort Wayne IN 46806

Call Sign: KA9PWP
Kathy S Waters
4107 Central Dr
Fort Wayne IN 46806

Call Sign: N9GSP
Rosamond L Polk Waters
4107 Central Dr
Fort Wayne IN 46806

Call Sign: N9NYM
Steven Bolin
4212 Central Dr
Fort Wayne IN 46806

Call Sign: KD9SX
David A Parnin
11734 Champagne Ct
Fort Wayne IN 46845

Call Sign: WD9FAH
Thomas C Wozniak
3614 Chancellor Dr
Fort Wayne IN 46815

Call Sign: WD9DYL
Robert J Reese
2727 Chandler Dr
Fort Wayne IN 46816

Call Sign: N9HXJ
Gaylord E Barnes
1516 Channel Ct
Fort Wayne IN 46825

Call Sign: N9RT
Gaylord E Barnes
1516 Channel Ct
Fort Wayne IN 46825

Call Sign: KB9WWN
Clay W Stahlka
1617 Channel Pl
Fort Wayne IN 46825

Call Sign: KC9SKE
Dan E Herrmann
8425 Chantclair Pl
Fort Wayne IN 46835

Call Sign: W9CB
Craig D Brown
1436 Chanterelle
Fort Wayne IN 46845

Call Sign: WB9FQM
Corwin E Ward
5422 Chantilly Dr
Fort Wayne IN 46815

Call Sign: KF9PQ
James W Napier
809 Charlotte Ave
Fort Wayne IN 46805

Call Sign: W9AZE
Robert R Berghoff
1622 Cherokee Rd
Fort Wayne IN 46808

Call Sign: WB9CUU
Donald M Armey
1922 Cherokee Rd
Fort Wayne IN 46808

Call Sign: KB9DSL
Kathleen W Herod
922 Cherry Blossom Ln
Fort Wayne IN 46825

Call Sign: KC0FNL
Kim I MacFeely
10433 Cherry Creek Rd
Fort Wayne IN
468188865

Call Sign: WD4KFW
Larry F Saum
10434 Cherry Creek Rd
Fort Wayne IN 46818

Call Sign: KC9AQB
Scott A Diehl
5912 Chesire Ct
Fort Wayne IN 46835

Call Sign: KA9UXG
Thomas N Towle
3511 Cheviot Dr 70
Fort Wayne IN 46816

Call Sign: KC9ORW
James J Holich
2606 Chichester Ln
Fort Wayne IN 46815

Call Sign: N9BZS
Ivan E Bosler
5709 Chilako Ct
Fort Wayne IN 46835

Call Sign: KA9FGC
Thomas E Bassett
1925 Chochtimar Trl
Fort Wayne IN 46808

Call Sign: W9AZC
Kenneth W Bradley
2104 Chochtimar Trl
Fort Wayne IN 46808

Call Sign: N8CFS
Joshua J Long
5123 Christian Ave
Fort Wayne IN 46835

Call Sign: KB9TBT
Kevin M Bryan
3320 Cilantro Cove
Fort Wayne IN 46818

Call Sign: KB9LYC
Joy A Reynolds
1134 Clara Ave
Fort Wayne IN 46805

Call Sign: KB5DFS
Frederick E Bailey
2421 Clara Ave
Fort Wayne IN 46805

Call Sign: KB9PQF
Nick D Heiny
16507 Claystone Ct
Fort Wayne IN
468072107

Call Sign: KD6ROA
Ronnie E Sarno
12926 Clydesdale Ct
Fort Wayne IN
468147490

Call Sign: KB9VLF
Marlise K Fletter
15530 Coldwater Rd
Fort Wayne IN 46845

Call Sign: W9VD
John D Fletter
15530 Coldwater Rd
Fort Wayne IN
468459706

Call Sign: N9AVT
Leonard P La Bundy
16006 Coldwater Rd
Fort Wayne IN 46845

Call Sign: KC9AZG
Richard L Chadwell
Coldwater Rd 101
Fort Wayne IN 46825

Call Sign: KV6AF
Alexandra D Fassett
Coldwater Rd 184
Fort Wayne IN 46825

Call Sign: N9WBE

Edward E Kimmel
1620 Colerick St
Fort Wayne IN 46806

Call Sign: KC9ZAM
Ben C Pinkowski
1749 Colony Dr
Fort Wayne IN 46825

Call Sign: K4RMU
James E Hinchee
1905 Colony Dr
Fort Wayne IN
468255009

Call Sign: KC9QZY
Clifford W Boyer
2015 Colony Dr
Fort Wayne IN 46825

Call Sign: K5EUY
Joseph P Randle
1417 Columbia Ave
Fort Wayne IN 46805

Call Sign: KJ9R
Joseph P Randle
1417 Columbia Ave
Fort Wayne IN 46805

Call Sign: KB9KKJ
Caleb J Cook
16610 Comer Rd
Fort Wayne IN 46819

Call Sign: WD9ACF
Leo R Trim
531 Constance
Fort Wayne IN 46805

Call Sign: KC9SJA
Northrop Grumman Fort
Wayne ARS
6112 Constitution Dr
Fort Wayne IN 46804

Call Sign: W9NGC
Northrop Grumman Fort
Wayne ARS
6112 Constitution Dr
Fort Wayne IN 46804

Call Sign: KC9UOQ
Jason R Eicholtz
6302 Constitution Dr
Fort Wayne IN 46804

Call Sign: KB9VMK
Jason S Lange
8730 Conway Ct
Fort Wayne IN
468252802

Call Sign: KB9YDZ
Joel P Lange
8730 Conway Ct
Fort Wayne IN
468252802

Call Sign: KB9ZHC
Mark P Lange
8730 Conway Ct
Fort Wayne IN
468252802

Call Sign: W9INA
Maynard J Mansfield
6412 Copper Creek Pl
Fort Wayne IN
468354733

Call Sign: WB5KRO
William A Arnold
6416 Copper Creek Pl
Fort Wayne IN 46835

Call Sign: N9NRQ
Steven L Smith
10314 Copper Tree Pl
Fort Wayne IN 46804

Call Sign: N9REA
Randy J Mays
3320 Copperhill Run
Fort Wayne IN 46804

Call Sign: N9PBQ
Angela M Jones
2316 Coral Bay Ct
Fort Wayne IN
468148942

Call Sign: N9NNR
David W Jones Jr
2316 Coral Bay Ct
Fort Wayne IN
468148942

Call Sign: N9ADM
Walter G Borland
11707 Coral Springs Dr
Fort Wayne IN 46845

Call Sign: WB9ZQW
Jearl W Nelson
12321 Corbin Rd
Fort Wayne IN 46845

Call Sign: WB9FZM
Keith E Hitchens
6221 Cordava Ct
Fort Wayne IN 46815

Call Sign: WB9VUN
Alan E Billings
2216 Cortland Ave
Fort Wayne IN 46808

Call Sign: W9GGA
Chad M Beach
2509.5 Cortland Ave
Fort Wayne IN 46808

Call Sign: KC9PRS
Frishly C Plaise

5612 Countess Dr
Fort Wayne IN 46815

Call Sign: KB9OT
Dimitrios Sgourakis
3414 Countrydale Dr
Fort Wayne IN 46815

Call Sign: KC9MOA
Thomas B Reinhart
9512 Courtyard Cove
Fort Wayne IN 46825

Call Sign: KB9SLW
Kyle S Smith
4107 Coventry Ln
Fort Wayne IN 46804

Call Sign: KA0AAW
Richard A Lammert
3 Coverdale Pl
Fort Wayne IN
468254928

Call Sign: WA9FCC
Ralph W Huhn
2512 Covington
Commons Dr
Fort Wayne IN
468047363

Call Sign: KC9ISY
Jon C Thomas
12709 Covington Maner
Farms Rd
Fort Wayne IN 46814

Call Sign: N9IGY
Kenneth G Simonsen
6506 Covington Rd A215
Fort Wayne IN 46804

Call Sign: N9XRG
Todd R Hargis
6510 Covington Rd E310

Fort Wayne IN 46804

Call Sign: KC9SXW
Michael A Shelby
4549 Craftsbury Cir
Fort Wayne IN 46818

Call Sign: AB9YA
Michael A Shelby
4549 Craftsbury Cir
Fort Wayne IN 46818

Call Sign: KC9SXV
Scott A Schilling
4676 Craftsbury Cir Apt
C
Fort Wayne IN 46818

Call Sign: KA9IOW
Larry D Branning
1826 Cramer Ave
Fort Wayne IN 46818

Call Sign: KC9DUH
Matthew S Ford
5220 Crandon Ln
Fort Wayne IN 46804

Call Sign: AB9UF
Matthew S Ford
5220 Crandon Ln
Fort Wayne IN 46804

Call Sign: KB9BNK
Jerald J Diehl
9609 Creek Bed Pl
Fort Wayne IN 46804

Call Sign: KC9KJG
Mark A Koeneman
2202 Crescent Ave
Fort Wayne IN
468054433

Call Sign: N9ZTD

Raymond J Resac
2415 Crescent Ave
Fort Wayne IN 46805

Call Sign: W0BBZ
Michael P Campbell
Crescent Cir
Fort Wayne IN 46825

Call Sign: KC9QZW
Kevin R Barwiler
5220 Cresthill Dr
Fort Wayne IN 46804

Call Sign: KC9MJU
Donald B Marshall II
5635 Cresthill Dr
Fort Wayne IN 46804

Call Sign: WE9N
George A Gust
909 Crestway Dr
Fort Wayne IN 46819

Call Sign: N9ZKY
Steve D Carter
1320 Curdes Ave
Fort Wayne IN 46805

Call Sign: W9FWI
Jack D Carter
2428 Curdes Ave
Fort Wayne IN 46805

Call Sign: KB9EM
John L De Turk
7706 Currie Hill Ct
Fort Wayne IN 46804

Call Sign: KC9BUT
Amos J Norman
5308 Curry Ford Ln
Fort Wayne IN 46804

Call Sign: KB9AJN

Amos J Norman
5308 Curry Ford Ln
Fort Wayne IN 46804

Call Sign: KB9RTA
Carl H Harz
2202 Dale Dr
Fort Wayne IN 46819

Call Sign: W9UJ
James K Boomer
4031 Dalewood Dr
Fort Wayne IN 46805

Call Sign: N9HDN
Dawn M Seelig
4715 Danbury
Fort Wayne IN 46835

Call Sign: N9EJA
John W Seelig
4715 Danbury
Fort Wayne IN 46835

Call Sign: N9GK
Victor L Keller
4011 Daner Dr
Fort Wayne IN 46815

Call Sign: KB9EBS
Richard A Stresser
4034 Daner Dr
Fort Wayne IN 46815

Call Sign: KV9B
Terry L Shoemaker
1728 Danny Dr
Fort Wayne IN 46808

Call Sign: KD9WH
James H Cosand
2606 Darlene Ct
Fort Wayne IN 46802

Call Sign: KB9LDU

Gregory J Carr
3924 Darwood Dr
Fort Wayne IN 46815

Call Sign: W9GT
Jack C Shutt
1820 Dawn Ave
Fort Wayne IN 46815

Call Sign: W9GGQ
Kenneth A Hanifan
1826 Dawn Ave
Fort Wayne IN 46815

Call Sign: KC9FMX
Terry J Bowman
1836 Dawn Ave
Fort Wayne IN 46815

Call Sign: K9FMX
Terry J Bowman
1836 Dawn Ave
Fort Wayne IN 46815

Call Sign: KC9ORP
Jerry M Bowers
608 Dayton Ave
Fort Wayne IN 46807

Call Sign: KC9ORQ
Mary P Bowers
608 Dayton Ave
Fort Wayne IN 46807

Call Sign: KB9NFY
Joan R Taylor
4540 De Rome Dr
Fort Wayne IN
468351536

Call Sign: W9EAB
John F Taylor
4540 De Rome Dr
Fort Wayne IN
468351536

Call Sign: N9XKO
Donald E Morris
7300 Decator Rd Apt 503
Fort Wayne IN
468163948

Call Sign: KC9GHY
Beth E Powell
2328 Deer Lodge Pl
Fort Wayne IN 46818

Call Sign: K9BEP
Beth E Powell
2328 Deer Lodge Pl
Fort Wayne IN 46818

Call Sign: N0APL
William R Powell
2328 Deer Lodge Pl
Fort Wayne IN 46818

Call Sign: W9WRP
William R Powell
2328 Deer Lodge Pl
Fort Wayne IN
468188890

Call Sign: WB9HTY
Joseph M Nicolosi
9417 Deer Trl
Fort Wayne IN 46804

Call Sign: WB9PXL
Edgar H Heller
2428 Deerwood Dr
Fort Wayne IN 46825

Call Sign: KC9NDF
William E Gerholt
1316 Delaware Ave
Fort Wayne IN 46805

Call Sign: K9ECE
Homer D Wibel

5115 Delaware Ave
Fort Wayne IN 46815

Call Sign: KB9IKK
Edwin H Martin
2025 Dellwood Dr
Fort Wayne IN 46803

Call Sign: WA9RJN
Stephen A Loeschner
2421 Dellwood Dr
Fort Wayne IN 46803

Call Sign: KB9UFX
James E Emmerson
3127 Delray Dr
Fort Wayne IN 46815

Call Sign: KC9BUS
Nancy A Emmerson
3127 Delray Dr
Fort Wayne IN 46815

Call Sign: N9FP
James E Emmerson
3127 Delray Dr
Fort Wayne IN 46815

Call Sign: W9OIF
Charles H Firks
4920 Desoto Dr
Fort Wayne IN 46815

Call Sign: KF9HB
Lee A Harris
2923 Devon Dr
Fort Wayne IN 46815

Call Sign: KB9BNH
Barbara W Mattoon
3719 Dewberry Dr
Fort Wayne IN 46815

Call Sign: WB9UBF
Gordon D Mattoon

3719 Dewberry Dr
Fort Wayne IN 46815

Call Sign: K9YXT
James E Cox
605 Dodane Rd
Fort Wayne IN 46819

Call Sign: WD9HIY
Kenneth S Buinowski
1217 Dodge Ave
Fort Wayne IN 46805

Call Sign: KA9QML
Tim A Holm
4634 Doenges Dr
Fort Wayne IN 46815

Call Sign: KA9FFZ
V Sue Holm
4634 Doenges Dr
Fort Wayne IN 46815

Call Sign: K9JDF
Bernard G Holm
4634 Doenges Dr
Fort Wayne IN
468154928

Call Sign: N9FNL
David M Erdman
12522 Donlee Ct
Fort Wayne IN 46845

Call Sign: KA9BXH
Jerald L Cox
13113 Drayton Pkwy
Fort Wayne IN
468459180

Call Sign: KB9WZF
Kyle P Shepherd
2004 Dublin Ct
Fort Wayne IN 46815

Call Sign: KC9RAK
David J Vachon
8932 Dune Creek Cove
Fort Wayne IN 46835

Call Sign: KC9BFU
Philip M Taylor
8718 Dunmore Ln
Fort Wayne IN 46804

Call Sign: KB9VGT
Alyn M Biddle
8809 Dunmore Ln
Fort Wayne IN 46804

Call Sign: KB9PFW
Edward A Fox
412 Dunnwood Dr Apt A
Fort Wayne IN 46805

Call Sign: KC9KOL
Ipfw ARC
2101 E Coliseum Blvd
Rm 221D
Fort Wayne IN
468051499

Call Sign: KM9DON
Ipfw ARC
2101 E Coliseum Blvd
Rm 221D
Fort Wayne IN
468051499

Call Sign: WA8NPF
Robert M O Dell
1618 E Cook Rd
Fort Wayne IN
468253765

Call Sign: K2OYG
Shirley A Sharan
1670 E Cook Rd
Fort Wayne IN 46825

Call Sign: KC9GTR
Frank J McNamara
205 E Cox Dr
Fort Wayne IN 46816

Call Sign: W9BRW
Robert F Rose
445 E Dupont Rd Apt 6
Fort Wayne IN 46825

Call Sign: KD6CUV
Ronald W Manuel
116 E Essex Ln
Fort Wayne IN 46825

Call Sign: K9CUV
Ronald W Manuel
116 E Essex Ln
Fort Wayne IN 46825

Call Sign: WA9OKV
William D Clark
905 E Fairfax Dr
Fort Wayne IN 46806

Call Sign: KC8IKJ
Benjamin J Hunsicker
4601 E Lafayette
Esplanade
Fort Wayne IN 46806

Call Sign: KA9DGB
Ivan E Garwood
3908 E Maple Grove
Fort Wayne IN 46806

Call Sign: KF9MW
Leander L Tarver
2505 E Paulding Rd
Fort Wayne IN 46816

Call Sign: K9QXC
Leonard O Goeglein
2534 E Saint Thomas Pt
Fort Wayne IN 46815

Call Sign: WB9JJN
John A Rinehart
4136 E State Blvd
Fort Wayne IN 46805

Call Sign: KC9QNE
Jeff H Lewis
6034 E State Blvd
Fort Wayne IN 46815

Call Sign: KC9BYE
Kekionga ARC
1600 E Washington Blvd
Fort Wayne IN 46803

Call Sign: KC9QDP
Jeffrey L Powell
1600 E Washington Blvd
Fort Wayne IN 46803

Call Sign: N9UWR
John A Martin
227 E Washington Blvd
Fort Wayne IN 46853

Call Sign: WA9ZLD
Gerald Marion
220 E Williams St
Fort Wayne IN
468033332

Call Sign: KB9JBR
Carole J Ster
6111 Eagle Creek Dr
Fort Wayne IN
468043213

Call Sign: W8ST
Robert D Ster
6111 Eagle Creek Dr
Fort Wayne IN
468143213

Call Sign: KC9NDG

Donna J Ster
6111 Eagle Creek Dr
Fort Wayne IN
468143213

Call Sign: W9DJS
Donna J Ster
6111 Eagle Creek Dr
Fort Wayne IN
468143213

Call Sign: KU8T
Thomas R Rupp
11710 Eagle Lake Ct
Fort Wayne IN 46814

Call Sign: KC9DRG
Fort Wayne Assembly
ARC
11710 Eagle Lake Ct
Fort Wayne IN 46814

Call Sign: N9SYF
Robert J Rose
3306 Eastbrook Dr
Fort Wayne IN 46805

Call Sign: W9HP
Joseph R Follrod Jr
2808 Easton Ridge Pl
Fort Wayne IN 46818

Call Sign: N9JFT
Wayne J Linkhart
319 Edgeknoll
Fort Wayne IN 46816

Call Sign: N9TMA
Keith L Spaulding
5206 Eicher Dr
Fort Wayne IN 46835

Call Sign: W9SLA
Richard J McNett
624 Elmer Ave

Fort Wayne IN 46808

Call Sign: K9DLZ
Thomas F Magdich
3520 Elmhurst Dr
Fort Wayne IN
468092016

Call Sign: K9GXF
John D Vandenberg
6811 Embers Ct
Fort Wayne IN 46815

Call Sign: KC9GU
Anthony J Colone Jr
7903 Emerald Canyon
Cove
Fort Wayne IN
468257402

Call Sign: N9CVF
Jeri S Colone
7903 Emerald Canyon
Cove
Fort Wayne IN
468257402

Call Sign: N9FZM
Andrew W O
Shaughnessy
3223 Emerald Lake Dr
Fort Wayne IN 46804

Call Sign: KC9INJ
Johnathan F Brouwer
431 Englewood Ct
Fort Wayne IN 46807

Call Sign: KC9RAI
Stephanie R
Schollenberger
209 Esmond St
Fort Wayne IN
468061092

Call Sign: W8IRE
Derek C Schollenberger
209 Esmond St
Fort Wayne IN
468061092

Call Sign: KB9TFB
Isaiah N Hathaway
5012 Ester Dr
Fort Wayne IN 46816

Call Sign: KB9MEA
Robert P Jones
7728 Evanwood Ct
Fort Wayne IN 46816

Call Sign: KA9QOM
Donald S Ladig
2720 Fairfield Ave
Fort Wayne IN 46807

Call Sign: KG9GW
Harold E McBride
5222 Fairfield Ave
Fort Wayne IN 46807

Call Sign: KB9EER
Judith M Mausser
1602 Fairhill Rd
Fort Wayne IN 46808

Call Sign: WA9LHP
Robert N Cobb Jr
2810 Fairoak Dr
Fort Wayne IN 46809

Call Sign: AD9R
Olen L Schibley
1312 Fairview
Fort Wayne IN 46803

Call Sign: KA9NLC
Meryl A Esslinger
12335 Falcatta Dr
Fort Wayne IN 46845

Call Sign: WA9FAC
Michael J Esslinger Sr
12335 Falcatta Dr
Fort Wayne IN 46845

Call Sign: KB7UDS
David F Stevenson
1119 Falcon Creek Pkwy
Fort Wayne IN
468459044

Call Sign: KR9V
Constantino Raptis
2013 Falconview Pl W
Fort Wayne IN 46818

Call Sign: WD9DGA
Kathy J Raptis
2013 Falconview Pl W
Fort Wayne IN 46818

Call Sign: N9HPY
Harold W Poulsen
8420 Fawncrest Pl
Fort Wayne IN 46835

Call Sign: AA9ZT
Michael M Imrick
6712 Felger Rd
Fort Wayne IN 46818

Call Sign: KA9QMK
Mary E Goller
1006 Ferguson Ave
Fort Wayne IN 46805

Call Sign: N9QME
Allen E Parks
3819 Finchley Ct
Fort Wayne IN 46815

Call Sign: KB9QIT
William T Turriff
3919 Finchley Ct

Fort Wayne IN 46815

Call Sign: KB8NH
James E Barnes
4022 Finchley Ct
Fort Wayne IN
468155351

Call Sign: KA9JAL
Adrianne L Hughes
910 Fiona Dr
Fort Wayne IN 46845

Call Sign: KC9HIY
Edward J Caylor III
14628 Firethorne Path
Fort Wayne IN 46814

Call Sign: N9PTQ
Ronald L Stabler
5016 Firwood Dr
Fort Wayne IN 46835

Call Sign: KB9WKG
Coleen K Christman
6005 Fitchburg Pl
Fort Wayne IN 46815

Call Sign: KC9ORX
Shawn E Mclain
1910 Flaugh Rd
Fort Wayne IN 46818

Call Sign: KD5VFK
Bruce W Freed Jr
1508 Flint Lock Ln
Fort Wayne IN 46845

Call Sign: W9CCF
Bruce W Freed Sr
1508 Flint Lock Ln
Fort Wayne IN 46845

Call Sign: KD5VBM
Martha L Freed

1508 Flint Lock Ln
Fort Wayne IN 46845

Call Sign: W9KTY
Martha L Freed
1508 Flint Lock Ln
Fort Wayne IN 46845

Call Sign: KC9PUY
Jessica L Thomas
1714 Flint Lock Ln
Fort Wayne IN 46845

Call Sign: KC9JMI
Thomas G Klapheke
2401 Florida Dr
Fort Wayne IN
468053539

Call Sign: K4CKQ
Thomas G Klapheke
2401 Florida Dr
Fort Wayne IN
468053539

Call Sign: N9MYI
David A Feustel
1123 Florida Dr Apt C12
Fort Wayne IN
468053558

Call Sign: N9NYL
Jeffrey D Pelz
8203 Flutter Rd
Fort Wayne IN 46835

Call Sign: KC9HJE
Dennis J Tippmann Jr
8930 Flutter Rd
Fort Wayne IN 46835

Call Sign: KC9LPQ
Bruce D Whitaker
1037 Forest Ave
Fort Wayne IN 46805

Call Sign: KC9Z
Kurt A Cripe
2232 Forest Park Blvd
Fort Wayne IN 46805

Call Sign: KP4US
Goshen Dx Assoc
2232 Forest Park Blvd
Fort Wayne IN 46805

Call Sign: N9GIW
Steven C Lewis
1631 Forest Valley Dr
Fort Wayne IN
468157801

Call Sign: KB9HJU
Darren R Herschberger
2205 Forest Valley Dr
Fort Wayne IN 46815

Call Sign: KB9RRS
Diane J Sparling
3833 Foresthill Ave
Fort Wayne IN 46805

Call Sign: K9DJS
Diane J Sparling
3833 Foresthill Ave
Fort Wayne IN 46805

Call Sign: KB9RPQ
Harold D Sparling
3833 Foresthill Ave
Fort Wayne IN
468051303

Call Sign: K9HDS
Harold D Sparling
3833 Foresthill Ave
Fort Wayne IN
468051303

Call Sign: WA9OHB

Richard M Charles
6816 Forestview Dr
Fort Wayne IN 46815

Call Sign: AA9DI
Christopher L Hambrock
8507 Forsythia Ct
Fort Wayne IN 46818

Call Sign: KA9QEA
James T Curtis Sr
2658 Fox Ave
Fort Wayne IN 46807

Call Sign: W9SAN
Steven A Nardin
7319 Fox Field Dr
Fort Wayne IN 46835

Call Sign: KB9ZOB
John E Nussbaum
5120 Fox Mill Run
Fort Wayne IN 46835

Call Sign: WA9BBN
Edward W Zobac
2211 Foxboro Dr
Fort Wayne IN 46818

Call Sign: KA9GKE
Rosalie K Zobac
2211 Foxboro Dr
Fort Wayne IN 46818

Call Sign: KC9QVT
Linda A Nardin
7319 Foxfield Dr
Fort Wayne IN 46835

Call Sign: W9LAN
Linda A Nardin
7319 Foxfield Dr
Fort Wayne IN 46835

Call Sign: W9TTL

Jason S Lange
8114 Franchesca Way
Fort Wayne IN
468253385

Call Sign: KA9RAU
James E Zehr
7202 Franke
Fort Wayne IN 46816

Call Sign: KB9DVO
Patricia A Zehr
7202 Franke Rd
Fort Wayne IN 46816

Call Sign: N9VCD
Stanley S Smith
1312 Franklin Ave
Fort Wayne IN 46808

Call Sign: KA9GBX
John A Webb
1525 Freehold Ln
Fort Wayne IN 46825

Call Sign: WB9QXF
Robert S Anderson
3716 Fritcha
Fort Wayne IN 46806

Call Sign: KB9DPG
Victor V Golaboff
4930 Galway Dr
Fort Wayne IN 46815

Call Sign: W9HMS
James Hatfield
5221 Gardenview Ave
Fort Wayne IN 46809

Call Sign: KC9HSJ
Gregory M Brown
1216 Garfield St
Fort Wayne IN 46805

Call Sign: KB9LOP
Jeffrey W Lindberg
7518 Gathings Dr
Fort Wayne IN 46816

Call Sign: KA9IRO
Rosanne Franke
5204 Gehring Ln
Fort Wayne IN 46818

Call Sign: W9TQA
Julian F Franke III
5204 Gehring Ln
Fort Wayne IN
468189775

Call Sign: KB9PQE
David A Witte
1841 Gillmore Dr
Fort Wayne IN 46818

Call Sign: KB9IHU
Terry O Miliczky
2126 Gillmore Dr
Fort Wayne IN 46818

Call Sign: K8ATY
Robert G Bailey
3523 Glenhurst
Fort Wayne IN 46805

Call Sign: KC8QHV
Susan F Crumrine
334 Glenmoor Dr
Fort Wayne IN 46804

Call Sign: WB9VOA
Herbert R Blombach
6040 Glenview Dr
Fort Wayne IN 46815

Call Sign: KD9ZU
Victor R Doughty
1310 Glenwood Ave
Fort Wayne IN 46805

Call Sign: N8BYI
Charles R Lewis
9229 Goldenrod Dr
Fort Wayne IN 46835

Call Sign: KC9EDZ
Sharon M Lewis
9229 Goldenrod Dr
Fort Wayne IN 46835

Call Sign: K9BLY
Joseph J Kaczmar
6537 Goodrich Rd
Fort Wayne IN 46804

Call Sign: KB9ZQG
Debra S Jenks
717 Goshen Ave
Fort Wayne IN 46808

Call Sign: KB9DEB
Debra S Jenks
717 Goshen Ave
Fort Wayne IN 46808

Call Sign: W9BGJ
Brian G Jenks
717 Goshen Ave
Fort Wayne IN 46808

Call Sign: KB9YWH
Don J Ingram
633 Goshen Ave 9
Fort Wayne IN 46808

Call Sign: KB9OXK
Jeremy Wells
5330 Goshen Rd
Fort Wayne IN 46818

Call Sign: KB9HQE
Gena F Duncan
10109 Goshen Rd
Fort Wayne IN 46818

Call Sign: KB9DET
John R Duncan
10109 Goshen Rd
Fort Wayne IN 46818

Call Sign: WA3ZKQ
Michael D Roe
5330 Goshen Rd Lot 136
Fort Wayne IN 46818

Call Sign: K9TP
Thomas O Piepenbrink
5330 Goshen Rd Lot 14
Fort Wayne IN 46818

Call Sign: WB9MRA
James D Bailey
5621 Graber Dr
Fort Wayne IN 46835

Call Sign: KA9BBC
Michael R Downs
11718 Grand River Dr
Fort Wayne IN 46845

Call Sign: KD9VN
John L Pfleiderer
11905 Grand River Dr
Fort Wayne IN 46845

Call Sign: N9NSR
Ted B Erick IV
511 Grapevine Ln
Fort Wayne IN 46825

Call Sign: W9KBV
William T Gibbons
535 Grapevine Ln
Fort Wayne IN 46825

Call Sign: KE9NY
Owen M Stiles
7925 Grayfield Ct
Fort Wayne IN 46825

Call Sign: KB9IBW
Emery W McClendon Sr
6116 Graymoor
Fort Wayne IN 46835

Call Sign: KC9HAJ
Amateur Radio Military
Appreciation Day
6116 Graymoor Ln
Fort Wayne IN 46835

Call Sign: KB9KCG
Richard S Galbreath
4615 Green Meadwos Dr
Fort Wayne IN 46825

Call Sign: K9YLR
William J Voors
4837 Greenfield Dr
Fort Wayne IN 46835

Call Sign: KC9SYP
Jon N Winther
10430 Greenoak Blvd
Fort Wayne IN 46514

Call Sign: KC9ML
Larrie A Gould
8320 Greenwich Ct
Fort Wayne IN 46835

Call Sign: W9NJR
Stanley M Robinson
8719 Greyhawk Dr
Fort Wayne IN 46835

Call Sign: W9SMR
Stanley M Robinson
8719 Greyhawk Dr
Fort Wayne IN 46835

Call Sign: KA3OPZ
Paul A Prestia
9507 Greyhawk Dr

Fort Wayne IN 46835

Call Sign: KB9UHF
Aaron D Prentice
6420 Hackberry Dr
Fort Wayne IN 46825

Call Sign: K9RKA
Billy A Trulock
4401 Haffner Dr
Fort Wayne IN 46835

Call Sign: KC9EPU
W9Bat Atv Club
4401 Haffner Dr
Fort Wayne IN 46835

Call Sign: W9BAT
W9Bat Atv Club
4401 Haffner Dr
Fort Wayne IN 46835

Call Sign: W9LMB
Robert J Beatty
205 Hamilton Forest
Cove
Fort Wayne IN 46814

Call Sign: KC9NDE
Ruth A Briggs
13311 Hammerhill Way
Fort Wayne IN 46845

Call Sign: N9UKE
Kristopher T Kruse
4822 Hanna St
Fort Wayne IN 46806

Call Sign: KB9KKG
Gene E Reed
12612 Hardisty Rd
Fort Wayne IN 46845

Call Sign: KC9NDI
Raymond L Parker Jr

3907 Hartzell Rd
Fort Wayne IN 46806

Call Sign: K9RLP
Raymond L Parker Jr
3907 Hartzell Rd
Fort Wayne IN 46806

Call Sign: KB9SLP
Rick P McCormick
3212 Harvster Ave
Fort Wayne IN 46803

Call Sign: WB9BCK
Gilbert A Walker
3705 Hastings Rd
Fort Wayne IN 46805

Call Sign: KC9APV
Roger A Treace Sr
2128 Hathaway Rd
Fort Wayne IN 46818

Call Sign: KC9NQX
Jeri D Elliott
2128 Hathaway Rd
Fort Wayne IN 46818

Call Sign: N9MPJ
John P Kaufeld
10409 Haverford Pl
Fort Wayne IN 46845

Call Sign: K9INK
John P Kaufeld
10409 Haverford Pl
Fort Wayne IN 46845

Call Sign: KA9CKN
David B Lupke
1407 Hawthorne Rd
Fort Wayne IN 46804

Call Sign: N9FNW
Lynn A Tuscan

7011 Hazelett Rd
Fort Wayne IN 46835

Call Sign: KA9GKH
Jerry K Davis
2212 Hazelwood Ave
Fort Wayne IN 46805

Call Sign: W9JSM
Robert J Bernhardt
2508 Hazelwood Ave
Fort Wayne IN 46805

Call Sign: WD9HFI
Mark P Heuer
6729 Hazlett Rd
Fort Wayne IN 46835

Call Sign: K9DPU
Mark P Heuer
6729 Hazlett Rd
Fort Wayne IN 46835

Call Sign: N9ZOD
Ted L Skeeters Sr
2228 Hearthstone Dr
Fort Wayne IN 46804

Call Sign: KB9DSO
Wendy H Furphy
6825 Heatherton Dr
Fort Wayne IN 46819

Call Sign: W9YRL
Paul M Burns
6908 Heatherton Dr
Fort Wayne IN 46819

Call Sign: N9SJV
Robert E Hilton
5809 Heatherview
Fort Wayne IN 46818

Call Sign: W9JJX
Allen C Moore

2817 Hedgerow Pass
Fort Wayne IN
468047849

Call Sign: AA9PX
Everett D Devine
4024 Hedwig Dr
Fort Wayne IN 46815

Call Sign: KC9AVW
Thomas G Palmer
5005 Hemlock Ln
Fort Wayne IN 46815

Call Sign: WA9ZVT
Steven R Holloway
7621 Hermitage Pl
Fort Wayne IN 46815

Call Sign: N9ZOF
James D Wilkins
7720 Hessen Cassel
Fort Wayne IN 46816

Call Sign: WA9KYX
Robert E Knapp
4125 Hiawatha Blvd
Fort Wayne IN
468091253

Call Sign: K9TZ
David A Beltz
7808 Hidden Hills Pl
Fort Wayne IN 46825

Call Sign: KC9BWH
Christopher B Bowser
9915 Hidden Meadows Pl
Fort Wayne IN 46825

Call Sign: AA9IT
Eric A Whitehill
6021 Highgate Pl
Fort Wayne IN 46815

Call Sign: KC9MOC
Karen A Karrer
6226 Highgate Pl
Fort Wayne IN 46815

Call Sign: K9KAK
Karen A Karrer
6226 Highgate Pl
Fort Wayne IN 46815

Call Sign: WB9PVK
Dennis C Keyfauver
4514 Hillegas Rd
Fort Wayne IN
468181916

Call Sign: KC9VAP
Matthew J Simerman
6727 Hiltonia Dr
Fort Wayne IN 46819

Call Sign: KF9TP
Mary C Bolin
1713 Hoagland Ave
Fort Wayne IN 46802

Call Sign: K9WJ
Willis G Bolin
1713 Hoagland Ave
Fort Wayne IN 46802

Call Sign: KC9PUX
Richard L Gilson
2928 Hoagland Ave
Fort Wayne IN 46807

Call Sign: KA9LTV
Victor Berko
4901 Hoagland Ave
Fort Wayne IN
468073226

Call Sign: KB9EOU
Jason A Wilson
1619 Hobson Rd

Fort Wayne IN 46805

Call Sign: WB9BEZ
John V Stiltner
2807 Hobson Rd
Fort Wayne IN
468052925

Call Sign: N9OJ
John V Stiltner
2807 Hobson Rd
Fort Wayne IN
468052925

Call Sign: N9ZNZ
Terence M Lee
2130 Hobson Rd Apt 107
Fort Wayne IN 46805

Call Sign: W9AJD
Eugene V Mount Sr
2930 Hoevelwood Dr
Fort Wayne IN 46806

Call Sign: N9XKV
Robert L Atkinson
6130 Holgate Dr
Fort Wayne IN
468161519

Call Sign: KB9NRL
Richard H Loney
6324 Holgate Dr
Fort Wayne IN
468161523

Call Sign: KE4GFU
Michael D Beadner
1115 Holly Ridge Run
Fort Wayne IN 46845

Call Sign: KC9ORN
Jennifer L Beadner
1115 Holly Ridge Run
Fort Wayne IN 46845

Call Sign: KC9CGM
Robert E Smith
4528 Holton Ave
Fort Wayne IN 46806

Call Sign: N9UNK
Gary L Cook
917 Home Ave
Fort Wayne IN 46707

Call Sign: KA9QNI
Marc T Jones
1351 Home Ave
Fort Wayne IN 46807

Call Sign: NJ0U
John P Carlson Jr
3832 Homestead Rd
Fort Wayne IN 46814

Call Sign: KA9SPO
Renata J Shore
5525 Hopkinton Dr
Fort Wayne IN 46804

Call Sign: KC9AUQ
Steven J Irving
2121 Huffman Blvd
Fort Wayne IN 46808

Call Sign: KA9SLN
Jeffrey S Badders
4308 Huntley Ct
Fort Wayne IN 46814

Call Sign: KC9EZP
Frederick A Gengnagel
4520 Hursh Rd
Fort Wayne IN 46845

Call Sign: N9GIS
Gary L Carpenter
4728 Hursh Rd

Fort Wayne IN
468459279

Call Sign: W9VHF
Arthur R King
5314 Hursh Rd
Fort Wayne IN 46845

Call Sign: KC9VAS
Dennis P Knepple
4017 Huth Dr
Fort Wayne IN 46804

Call Sign: KN9DPK
Dennis P Knepple
4017 Huth Dr
Fort Wayne IN 46804

Call Sign: KA9QDY
Yvonne G Constant
6112 Hystowe
Fort Wayne IN 46816

Call Sign: KA9PNM
William L Moore
4710 Illinois Rd
Fort Wayne IN 46804

Call Sign: K9JMT
Walter J Johnson
1119 Illsley Dr
Fort Wayne IN 46807

Call Sign: KC9OSB
Daniel P Rotondo
4120 Indiana Ave
Fort Wayne IN 46807

Call Sign: N9CMT
Thomas F Roffelsen
4811 Indiana Ave
Fort Wayne IN 46807

Call Sign: K9EEG
James J Nickels

7312 Inverness Commons
Fort Wayne IN 46804

Call Sign: KA0SSG
Steven P Phipps
2826 Inwood Dr
Fort Wayne IN 46815

Call Sign: WA9RDL
Laurel J Short
3219 Inwood Dr
Fort Wayne IN 46815

Call Sign: KB9JGG
Earl W Carpenter
2317 Inwood Ln
Fort Wayne IN 46815

Call Sign: KC9TPF
Kenneth A Helms
3627 Iowa Ct
Fort Wayne IN
468156611

Call Sign: W4UHF
Julie M Kaufman
2406 Island Club Dr Apt
B
Fort Wayne IN 46825

Call Sign: KC9IMW
Corey Wright
2418 Jacobs Creek Run
Fort Wayne IN 46825

Call Sign: N8VHO
David J Holdgreve
1816 Jessie Ave
Fort Wayne IN 46808

Call Sign: KC9VRN
Andrew J Danielson
6203 Justin Ct
Fort Wayne IN 46835

Call Sign: KC9IPR
Jonathan C Danielson
6203 Justin Ct
Fort Wayne IN 46835

Call Sign: W8ESE
Matthew M Palmer
7120 Kebir Ct
Fort Wayne IN 46815

Call Sign: W9HT
Joshua J Long
7212 Kebir Ct
Fort Wayne IN 46815

Call Sign: WB4CIU
Paul H Leiendecker
4420 Kekionga Dr
Fort Wayne IN 46809

Call Sign: KB9YTT
Garry W Pape
4515 Kenilworth St
Fort Wayne IN 46806

Call Sign: KB9NWX
David B Reed
922 Kensington
Fort Wayne IN 46805

Call Sign: KF4GGE
John R Long
1102 Kensington Blvd
Fort Wayne IN
468055316

Call Sign: WB9DIA
Gary F Kuntz
7226 Kensington Dr W
Fort Wayne IN 46818

Call Sign: N9IRX
Benjamin L Myers
7312 Kensington Dr W
Fort Wayne IN 46818

Call Sign: KA9CKK
Robert E Marshall
2109 Kentucky Ave
Fort Wayne IN 46805

Call Sign: KB9AYT
Jeffery L Freimuth Sr
2922 Kentucky Ave
Fort Wayne IN 46805

Call Sign: KC9JKA
John J Reitz
1401 Kenwood Ave
Fort Wayne IN
468052632

Call Sign: AB9RZ
John J Reitz
1401 Kenwood Ave
Fort Wayne IN
468052632

Call Sign: KE5NX
Donald G Corcoran
1626 Kenwood Ave
Fort Wayne IN 46805

Call Sign: KC9OWU
Stephen T Thompson
1704 Kenwood Ave
Fort Wayne IN 46805

Call Sign: KC9GVI
John D Nash III
2418 Kenwood Ave
Fort Wayne IN 46805

Call Sign: KB9VMN
Jerrod C Nash
2418 Kenwood Ave
Fort Wayne IN
468052756

Call Sign: N9KBV

Jerrod C Nash
2418 Kenwood Ave
Fort Wayne IN
468052756

Call Sign: WB9NEG
John D Nash Jr
2418 Kenwood Ave
Fort Wayne IN
468052756

Call Sign: KC9GVB
Jordan M Nash
2418 Kenwood Ave
Fort Wayne IN
468052756

Call Sign: N9FNK
William M Harrington
3326 Kenwood Ave
Fort Wayne IN 46805

Call Sign: KB9TEX
Andrew E Busch
7618 Kilbourn Dr
Fort Wayne IN 46809

Call Sign: WB9AA
Ronald E Busch
7618 Kilbourn Dr
Fort Wayne IN 46809

Call Sign: KA9JAY
Gene D Voelker
5511 Kimberley
Fort Wayne IN 46809

Call Sign: WB9HNW
Donald J Voelker
5511 Kimberley Rd
Fort Wayne IN 46809

Call Sign: KA9KUW
John Sutherland
5510 Kimberly Rd

Fort Wayne IN 46809

Call Sign: KC9HJO
Mark P Junk
601 Kimberton Dr
Fort Wayne IN 46816

Call Sign: KK9U
Mark P Junk
601 Kimberton Dr
Fort Wayne IN 46816

Call Sign: KE8OP
David A Murray
8624 Kings Mill Pl
Fort Wayne IN 46804

Call Sign: WB9VOG
Barbara L Smith
6721 Kingswood Blvd
Fort Wayne IN 46804

Call Sign: WB9UYU
Berdell O Smith
6721 Kingswood Blvd
Fort Wayne IN 46804

Call Sign: KI4YN
James H Baker
921 Kinnaird Ave
Fort Wayne IN
468071707

Call Sign: N9SYD
Veo F Boozel
715 Kinsmoor
Fort Wayne IN 46807

Call Sign: WD8APV
Eugene W Blazer
1722 Kinsmoor
Fort Wayne IN 46809

Call Sign: N8HGY
Ron A Blazer

1722 Kinsmoor
Fort Wayne IN 46809

Call Sign: WA9FCZ
Ralph W Huhn
823 Kinsmoor Ave
Fort Wayne IN 46807

Call Sign: N9QLX
Ernest Bacon
1301 Kitch
Fort Wayne IN 46803

Call Sign: N9VUN
Kyle R Lehman
6304 Kiwanis Dr
Fort Wayne IN 46835

Call Sign: KA9MIO
John G Homrig
2523 Knightsbridge Dr
Fort Wayne IN 46815

Call Sign: KB9ZQF
John K Earlywine
2806 Knightsbridge Pl
Fort Wayne IN 46815

Call Sign: AB9CX
John K Earlywine
2806 Knightsbridge Pl
Fort Wayne IN 46815

Call Sign: K1QB
John K Earlywine
2806 Knightsbridge Pl
Fort Wayne IN 46815

Call Sign: KA9KHP
Jeffrey A Eby
7416 Knightswood Dr
Fort Wayne IN 46819

Call Sign: N9ZNT
Robert M Graham

4224 Knoll Rd
Fort Wayne IN
468099721

Call Sign: KF9NN
Michael D Sunderman
3701 Knollcrest Rd
Fort Wayne IN 46835

Call Sign: N9RVM
Gerald L Roby
7306 Kristine Dr
Fort Wayne IN 46835

Call Sign: N9BMY
Robert S Farrer
7307 Kristine Dr
Fort Wayne IN 46835

Call Sign: KB9ZYY
John W Ray
2824 Kroemer Rd
Fort Wayne IN 46818

Call Sign: KB6SKW
Donna M Wescoatt
4230 Kroemer Rd
Fort Wayne IN 46818

Call Sign: KC9EEC
Brian R Thornhill
7306 Kumfer Ave
Fort Wayne IN 46809

Call Sign: KB9DPF
Dennis P Buesching
9031 La Bell Pl
Fort Wayne IN 46804

Call Sign: KB9SYF
Joshua P Buesching
9031 La Bell Pl
Fort Wayne IN 46804

Call Sign: KB9GVC

Kathy J Buesching
9031 La Bell Pl
Fort Wayne IN 46804

Call Sign: KB9SYG
Nathaniel J Buesching
9031 La Bell Pl
Fort Wayne IN 46804

Call Sign: KB9JVJ
Cliffton P Schenkel
2525 Ladue Cove
Fort Wayne IN 46804

Call Sign: W9VMG
George F Hatch
1022 Lake Ave
Fort Wayne IN 46805

Call Sign: AB9ND
Albert E Andreas Jr
1425 Lakeland Cove
Fort Wayne IN 46825

Call Sign: N9ISG
Tom A Jansen
1416 Lakewood Dr
Fort Wayne IN 46819

Call Sign: K9LSB
Jack D Forbing
1416 Lakewood Dr
Fort Wayne IN
468191330

Call Sign: N9PWM
Robert W Erb
13018 Lanark Pl
Fort Wayne IN 46814

Call Sign: KB9BNI
John B Rufner
5728 Lancashire Ct
Fort Wayne IN 46825

Call Sign: N9NO
Daniel P Roth
1714 Lancer Ln
Fort Wayne IN 46845

Call Sign: N9MR
Mark W Reese
6035 Landover Pl
Fort Wayne IN 46815

Call Sign: KB9NXY
Terry S Warner
6226 Landover Pl
Fort Wayne IN 46815

Call Sign: KC8BEX
Nathan J Yerian
5606 Larchwood Run
Fort Wayne IN 46825

Call Sign: KD9LQ
John C McLemore
1922 Lathrop
Fort Wayne IN
468081710

Call Sign: W9MYJ
Larrey A Wolever
6801 Laura Ln
Fort Wayne IN 46804

Call Sign: N9OOB
Brent A Krocker
5604 Le Steele Blvd
Fort Wayne IN 46818

Call Sign: KB9EWB
Jennifer L Krouse
3706 Leesburg Rd
Fort Wayne IN 46808

Call Sign: WB9DFI
Jacquelyn J Houck
12252 Leo Rd
Fort Wayne IN 46825

Call Sign: KA9JKJ
Samuel I Stephens
7411 Leswood Ct
Fort Wayne IN 46816

Call Sign: KB9YKV
Max G McCoy
6621 Liberty Dr
Fort Wayne IN 46819

Call Sign: KB8RTU
Norman R Hughes II
9612 Liberty Mills Rd
Fort Wayne IN 46804

Call Sign: KC9VDF
Scott A Wagner
13436 Liberty Mills Rd
Fort Wayne IN 46814

Call Sign: N9LFF
Perry G Ramsey
14617 Lightning Ridge
Run
Fort Wayne IN 46814

Call Sign: KC9SKJ
David E Clond
14628 Lightning Ridge
Run
Fort Wayne IN 46814

Call Sign: NT9F
Kelley Clond
14628 Lightning Ridge
Run
Fort Wayne IN 46814

Call Sign: KC9LPR
Douglas L Dilley
4025 Lillie St
Fort Wayne IN 46806

Call Sign: W9RJR

Larry G Hutchisson
1730 Lima Ln
Fort Wayne IN 46808

Call Sign: K9UOB
Paul L Girdner
7252 Linda Dr
Fort Wayne IN 46835

Call Sign: KC8ZH
David R Otto
11710 Linden Grove Dr
Fort Wayne IN 46845

Call Sign: KB9NRJ
Richard D Spenny
2214 Lindenwood
Fort Wayne IN 46808

Call Sign: KC9KN
Thomas F Cooney
5518 Lionel Dr
Fort Wayne IN 46815

Call Sign: N9VUP
James C Isaacs Jr
4214 Live Oak Blvd
Fort Wayne IN 46804

Call Sign: KC9UZF
James C Isaacs
4214 Live Oak Blvd
Fort Wayne IN 46804

Call Sign: K9YRS
Jack D Fisher
3625 Logan Ave
Fort Wayne IN 46803

Call Sign: KA9WFC
Michael J Fisher
3625 Logan Ave
Fort Wayne IN 46803

Call Sign: KB9SYH

Steven C Bryan
6011 Lois Ln
Fort Wayne IN 46804

Call Sign: K2KO
David A Maynard
10405 Lone Eagle Way
Fort Wayne IN
468451155

Call Sign: KB9TAF
Mark B Walker
5025 Lonesome Oak Trl
Fort Wayne IN
468459103

Call Sign: KA9VCL
Kyinkyin Lee
1737 Lough Nest
Fort Wayne IN 46804

Call Sign: KC9QGH
Zephyr Z Jaquish
1425 Louisdale Dr
Fort Wayne IN 46808

Call Sign: KC9LVH
Rigel Jaquish
1423 Louisedale Dr
Fort Wayne IN 46808

Call Sign: KD7ECM
Thomas E Jaquish
1423 Louisedale Dr
Fort Wayne IN 46808

Call Sign: KC9FZF
Tycho J Jaquish
1723 Louisedale Dr
Fort Wayne IN 46808

Call Sign: KB9FFA
Orvil E Schlatter
6114 Lower Huntington
Rd

Fort Wayne IN 46809

Call Sign: WA9RAD
James F McArdle
7331 Lower Huntington
Rd
Fort Wayne IN
468099762

Call Sign: KB9AYY
Glenn E Linsky
6732 Ludington
Fort Wayne IN 46816

Call Sign: N9ZOE
James A Strebig Jr
607 Lyell Ct
Fort Wayne IN 46825

Call Sign: N9LSA
Regis B Zachrel
5305 Lynhurst Dr
Fort Wayne IN 46835

Call Sign: KB9JRP
Eric L Johnston
1936 Lynn Av
Fort Wayne IN
468053661

Call Sign: KB9GAJ
John L Crawford
1907 Lynn Ave
Fort Wayne IN 46805

Call Sign: KB9VTJ
Daniel T Scheerer
2424 Lynn Ave
Fort Wayne IN
468053802

Call Sign: KA9ZQM
Carl C Flink
5022 Madiera Dr
Fort Wayne IN 46815

Call Sign: KC9OSD
Gordon J Smith
12112 Mallards Lake
Pkwy
Fort Wayne IN 46845

Call Sign: KB9LHV
William J Armstrong
4873 Mamie Dr
Fort Wayne IN 46835

Call Sign: W9LKH
David J Lindquist
6123 Manchester Dr
Fort Wayne IN 46835

Call Sign: WA9RRW
Stanley A Williams
9628 Manor Woods Rd
Fort Wayne IN 46804

Call Sign: W9CTK
Edwin S Beach
4519 Maple Ter Pkwy
Fort Wayne IN 46835

Call Sign: WB9NHC
Robert M Ostman
8235 Maple Valley Dr
Fort Wayne IN 48635

Call Sign: K9DMT
Richard E Roudebush
5436 Maplecrest Rd
Fort Wayne IN 46835

Call Sign: W9JOQ
Raymond J Yeranko
1717 Maplecrest Rd Apt
352
Fort Wayne IN 46815

Call Sign: WB9RKB
Stephen J Chobot

6505 Mapledowns Dr
Fort Wayne IN 46835

Call Sign: KC9HIU
Michael R Cumins
2019 Maples Rd
Fort Wayne IN 46816

Call Sign: W8HOM
James G Mast
4509 Maples Rd
Fort Wayne IN 46816

Call Sign: WB9UFS
Charles L Beardsley
9107 Maples Rd
Fort Wayne IN 46816

Call Sign: WA9PAB
Margaret L Palmer
1711 Maplewood Rd
Fort Wayne IN
468191636

Call Sign: KD9VV
Peter C Herman
3728 Marchfield Pl
Fort Wayne IN 46804

Call Sign: WB9FGI
Alan B Clemens
3435 Marias Dr
Fort Wayne IN 46815

Call Sign: WD9FAF
Frank S Hawk
1808 Marietta Dr
Fort Wayne IN 46804

Call Sign: KC9APT
Allan L Bowman
9117 Mariners Ridge Dr
Fort Wayne IN 46819

Call Sign: WA9FVY

Gene E Mann
10924 Marion Center Rd
Fort Wayne IN 46816

Call Sign: NQ9S
Joseph H Nolte
4319 Marquette Dr
Fort Wayne IN 46806

Call Sign: KC9VJF
Jonathan R Thomas
4521 Martin Creek Ct
Fort Wayne IN 46845

Call Sign: W9JRT
Jonathan R Thomas
4521 Martin Creek Ct
Fort Wayne IN 46845

Call Sign: N9MT
Martin R Thomas
4521 Martin Creek Ct
Fort Wayne IN 46845

Call Sign: KC9VAR
Michael M Thomas
4521 Martin Creek Ct
Fort Wayne IN 46845

Call Sign: W9MMT
Michael M Thomas
4521 Martin Creek Ct
Fort Wayne IN 46845

Call Sign: KB9PFX
Kristi D Rohrer
5608 Martys Hill Pl
Fort Wayne IN 46815

Call Sign: KB9ZQV
Memorial Park Middle
School ARC
2200 Maumee Ave
Fort Wayne IN 46803

Call Sign: W9LE
E Lewis Kester
5419 Maurane Dr
Fort Wayne IN 46804

Call Sign: KC4KK
Brian J Rehmer
3419 Maxim Dr
Fort Wayne IN 46815

Call Sign: N9UBC
Bradley L Pahmier
1238 Maxine Dr
Fort Wayne IN 46807

Call Sign: N9UOD
Mark E Miller
1242 Maxine Dr
Fort Wayne IN 46807

Call Sign: KC9JMK
Christopher R Barrell
3626 Mayapple Dr
Fort Wayne IN 46818

Call Sign: KB9VXT
Joshua T Robinson
4106 Mayberry St
Fort Wayne IN 46815

Call Sign: WA9LGX
Delbert V Ritter
9732 Maysville Rd
Fort Wayne IN 46805

Call Sign: WA9POL
Leila J Ritter
9732 Maysville Rd
Fort Wayne IN 46815

Call Sign: K9DMX
Roger P Ryan
6306 Maywood Cir
Fort Wayne IN 46819

Call Sign: KA9YYE
William H Eminger
6620 Maywood Cir
Fort Wayne IN 46819

Call Sign: KB9DOY
Jeremy T Lee
3603 McArthur Dr
Fort Wayne IN 46809

Call Sign: N9YHE
Carole L Harrigan
3333 McKinnie
Fort Wayne IN 46806

Call Sign: KB9HYD
William N Harrigan
3333 McKinnie
Fort Wayne IN 46806

Call Sign: N9ZNM
B John Bay
3524 Meda Pass
Fort Wayne IN 46809

Call Sign: KB9DOZ
Eric M Lawson
3524 Meda Pass
Fort Wayne IN 46809

Call Sign: N9MHB
Roger R Coon
3819 Meda Pass
Fort Wayne IN 46809

Call Sign: KV4EE
Craig L Hall
8731 Medicine Bow Run
Fort Wayne IN 46825

Call Sign: AF9M
Craig L Hall
8731 Medicine Bow Run
Fort Wayne IN 46825

Call Sign: KB9SLY
Robert J Fontaine III
8922 Merganser Ln
Fort Wayne IN 46818

Call Sign: W9RJF
Robert J Fontaine
8922 Merganser Ln
Fort Wayne IN 46818

Call Sign: KD7JNR
Michael W Barnes
4217 Meridith Dr
Fort Wayne IN 46815

Call Sign: KB9VFO
Everett D White
7226 Miahqueah Ct
Fort Wayne IN 46815

Call Sign: KB9RH
Joel M Tye
801 Mildred Ave
Fort Wayne IN
468082177

Call Sign: KB9TYU
Franke Park Radio Club
828 Mildred Ave
Fort Wayne IN 46808

Call Sign: KB9WHJ
Garald J Williams
2827 Miller Ridge Ct
Fort Wayne IN 46818

Call Sign: KA9LCF
Bradd J Davidson
10817 Millstone Dr
Fort Wayne IN 46818

Call Sign: KB9JCV
Kenneth C Campbell
11506 Millstone Dr
Fort Wayne IN 46818

Call Sign: WB9SSE
Albert G Burke III
11714 Millstone Dr
Fort Wayne IN 46818

Call Sign: WB9RUS
Carole L Burke
11714 Millstone Dr
Fort Wayne IN 46818

Call Sign: W9TE
Fort Wayne Radio Club
11714 Millstone Dr
Fort Wayne IN 46818

Call Sign: KC9TLT
Dennis E Spillers
5202 Millwright Pl
Fort Wayne IN 46835

Call Sign: N9FPT
Dennis E Spillers
5202 Millwright Pl
Fort Wayne IN 46835

Call Sign: KA9LVC
John T Swain
930 Milton St
Fort Wayne IN 46806

Call Sign: KB9PFY
Patrick J Murphy
6830 Mimosa
Fort Wayne IN 46825

Call Sign: KC9UOP
David W Shakley
2711 Misty Oaks Trl
Fort Wayne IN
468451968

Call Sign: N9FGP
David W Shakley
2711 Misty Oaks Trl

Fort Wayne IN
468451968

Call Sign: KB9TUF
Eric A Fetcho
1327 Misty River Dr
Fort Wayne IN 46808

Call Sign: KA9JTJ
Sandra M Williams
5110 Moeller Rd
Fort Wayne IN 46806

Call Sign: N9EPH
John E Wise
7227 Moeller Rd 57
Fort Wayne IN 46806

Call Sign: N9KFE
Joseph G Zeilbeck
6008 Moeller Rd 81
Fort Wayne IN 46806

Call Sign: KC9ORU
David A Hart
7515 Monaco Pl
Fort Wayne IN 46825

Call Sign: KA9HFC
Roger D Lowe
5516 Monarch Dr
Fort Wayne IN 46815

Call Sign: KB9DOQ
Gwen M Jordan
3512 Mono Gene Dr
Fort Wayne IN 46806

Call Sign: KB9DOR
Janice F Kumlien
3512 Mono Gene Dr
Fort Wayne IN 46806

Call Sign: KA9ASN
Lori J Shearer

3524 Montagne Dr
Fort Wayne IN 46816

Call Sign: KC9CGH
Christopher M Olry
3310 Montagne Dr
Fort Wayne IN 46816

Call Sign: KB9UTN
Junior E Wilcox
3402 Montana Dr
Fort Wayne IN
468156625

Call Sign: KC9UOO
Jeremy A Holmes
6624 Montecito Ct
Fort Wayne IN 46835

Call Sign: N0ASG
Donald M Shoop
6625 Montecito Ct
Fort Wayne IN 46835

Call Sign: N9AHS
Tony L Cayot
4119 Monument Dr
Fort Wayne IN 46815

Call Sign: KB9EWL
Brian P Marshall
10301 Moon Valley Dr
Fort Wayne IN 46825

Call Sign: KB9EWM
Christina L Marshall
10301 Moonvalley Dr
Fort Wayne IN 46825

Call Sign: N9XPL
Robert D Sluyter
7809 Morning Gate Ct
Fort Wayne IN 46804

Call Sign: N0AGC

Timothy L Sweeney
8003 Moss Grove Pl
Fort Wayne IN
468253551

Call Sign: KC9ACY
Joseph R Buchan
9120 Muldoon Rd
Fort Wayne IN 46819

Call Sign: KC9GQG
Richard E Malmstrom
5518 Myanna Ln
Fort Wayne IN 46835

Call Sign: KB9OZH
Wayne M Bergamino
2324 N Anthony Blvd
Fort Wayne IN 46805

Call Sign: WB9UYX
Joseph W O Keeffe
2711 N Anthony Blvd
Fort Wayne IN
468053664

Call Sign: KC9DPA
Dennis J Marshall
2725 N Anthony Blvd
Fort Wayne IN 46805

Call Sign: KC9ONM
Ivy Tech Northeast ARC
3800 N Anthony Blvd
Fort Wayne IN 46805

Call Sign: KU9I
Ivy Tech Northeast ARC
3800 N Anthony Blvd
Fort Wayne IN 46805

Call Sign: N8PCD
Frank L Bankson Jr
1002 N Anthony Blvd
Fort Wayne IN 46805

Call Sign: KB9HYE
Lynn R Shultz
5022 N Bend Dr
Fort Wayne IN 46804

Call Sign: KD9ZZ
James E Helm
616 N Camden Dr
Fort Wayne IN 46825

Call Sign: KB9EVY
Joseph A Scott Jr
2714 N Clinton St
Fort Wayne IN 46805

Call Sign: KF9ZE
Kendall G Sohaski
N Gate
Fort Wayne IN 46835

Call Sign: KA9UAY
Johnna S Temenoff
4415 N Wallen Rd
Fort Wayne IN 46818

Call Sign: KB9EVC
Margaret E Krawczewicz
2404 N Wells
Fort Wayne IN 46808

Call Sign: KB9CJB
James M Krawczewicz
2404 N Wells St
Fort Wayne IN 46808

Call Sign: KB9MIP
Lori E Miodus
5124 Nassau Dr
Fort Wayne IN 46815

Call Sign: KC9PUP
Linda A Deweese
7414 Nature Trl Dr
Fort Wayne IN 46835

Call Sign: KB9YES
Thomas Stachowiecz
7417 Nature Trl Dr
Fort Wayne IN 46835

Call Sign: N9KKG
Carole A Klaehn
9912 Neil Armstrong Ct
Fort Wayne IN 46804

Call Sign: KB9DOP
Richard J Klaehn
9912 Neil Armstrong Ct
Fort Wayne IN 46804

Call Sign: N9ANW
Alton N White
7258 Nelwood Dr
Fort Wayne IN 46835

Call Sign: KB9EVZ
Jodi M Leamon
1217 Nevada Ave
Fort Wayne IN 46805

Call Sign: KA8LCF
Jarett F Alwine
3405 New Haven Ave
Fort Wayne IN 46803

Call Sign: KB9OFC
Andrew M Schnelker
6611 Newburgh Pl
Fort Wayne IN 46835

Call Sign: K9FT
Michael A Schnelker
6611 Newburgh Pl
Fort Wayne IN 46835

Call Sign: KC9JM
Derek P De Mond
6626 Newburgh Pl

Fort Wayne IN
468351344

Call Sign: KA4BNY
James D Roberts
3810 Newport Ave 9
Fort Wayne IN 46805

Call Sign: W9KQU
George S Lewis
7112 Nighthawk Dr
Fort Wayne IN
468359395

Call Sign: WB8HQS
Donald A Gagnon
2805 Nordholme Ave
Fort Wayne IN 46805

Call Sign: KB9BNP
Mary R Gagnon
2805 Nordholme Ave
Fort Wayne IN 46805

Call Sign: KB9YLM
Evanita W Montalvo
111 Norfolk Ave
Fort Wayne IN 46805

Call Sign: N9LST
Glendon F Kierstead
1122 Normandale Dr
Fort Wayne IN 46808

Call Sign: KG9FM
Clark D Derbyshire
4107 North Dr
Fort Wayne IN 46815

Call Sign: KC9QHK
Cathleen L Huff
4329 North Dr
Fort Wayne IN 46815

Call Sign: NY6J

Robert I Helt
4329 North Dr
Fort Wayne IN 46815

Call Sign: N9PDT
Jack L Warfield
247 Northeast Dr
Fort Wayne IN 46825

Call Sign: N9OSL
Mitchell L Surface
4925 Northfield Dr
Fort Wayne IN 46804

Call Sign: N8SSK
Perry W Perisho
5040 Northfield Dr
Fort Wayne IN 46804

Call Sign: AB9YB
Joshua L Thorn
2701 Northgate Ave
Fort Wayne IN 46385

Call Sign: KB9AYS
Steven M Carbaugh
2822 Northgate Blvd Apt
1
Fort Wayne IN 46835

Call Sign: K9LCZ
Martin T Husar
2727 Northgate Blvd Apt
3
Fort Wayne IN
468352910

Call Sign: KB9OXN
James C Dee
2341 Northway Ave
Fort Wayne IN 46805

Call Sign: KB9IWM
Ronald R Dose
2517 Northway Ave

Fort Wayne IN 46805

Call Sign: N9LSS
James C Blee Jr
8687 Notestine Rd
Fort Wayne IN 46835

Call Sign: KB9BSA
John I Heath
8703 Notestine Rd
Fort Wayne IN 46835

Call Sign: K9EA
Daniel F Michnay
9406 Notestine Rd
Fort Wayne IN 46835

Call Sign: N9NSS
Tom R Hunkler
9720 Notestine Rd
Fort Wayne IN 46835

Call Sign: N9GFP
Ronnie M McChesney
10319 Nottawa Trl
Fort Wayne IN 46825

Call Sign: W9LHO
Donald R McKee
710 Nuttman Ave
Fort Wayne IN
468071844

Call Sign: KA9ZQL
Cynthia M Charbonneau
424 NW Passage Trl
Fort Wayne IN 46825

Call Sign: KA9WNE
Terrance W Charbonneau
424 NW Passage Trl
Fort Wayne IN 46825

Call Sign: AA9DZ
Gary W Brown

910 Oak Branch
Fort Wayne IN 46845

Call Sign: NI9N
Peter E Goodmann
5029 Oak Creek Ct
Fort Wayne IN 46835

Call Sign: KB9HLK
Eileen R Witte
6617 Oak Forest Trl
Fort Wayne IN 46835

Call Sign: KB9HLL
Erwin F Witte
6617 Oak Forest Trl
Fort Wayne IN 46835

Call Sign: W9KFU
F Lawrence Averbeck
7420 Oak Ln
Fort Wayne IN 46804

Call Sign: KA9GKD
Michael S Wakeland
3606 Oak Park Dr
Fort Wayne IN 46815

Call Sign: KC9SEZ
Robert P Curtis
10905 Oak Tree Rd
Fort Wayne IN 46845

Call Sign: N9PDX
Richard N Yergens
3723 Oakhurst Dr
Fort Wayne IN
468156238

Call Sign: KC9LUP
Adam M Advany
3808 Oakhurst Dr
Fort Wayne IN 46815

Call Sign: K7AMA

Adam M Advany
3808 Oakhurst Dr
Fort Wayne IN 46815

Call Sign: KA9MIA
Mohammed I Advany
3808 Oakhurst Dr
Fort Wayne IN 46815

Call Sign: KC9TIS
Charles W Summers II
4010 Oakleaf Dr
Fort Wayne IN 46815

Call Sign: KE4CYC
Philip J Hooper
5915 Oakmont Dr
Fort Wayne IN 46816

Call Sign: KC9HQI
Rebekah Hooper
5915 Oakmont Rd
Fort Wayne IN 46063

Call Sign: K9CRA
Earl E Hooper
5915 Oakmont Rd
Fort Wayne IN 46816

Call Sign: KB9YEA
David L Nold
1405 Old Lantern Trl
Fort Wayne IN 46845

Call Sign: KA9ZSK
Thomas E Kelble
5022 Old Maysville Rd
Fort Wayne IN 46815

Call Sign: WD9GKT
Janice K Hattendorf
4041 Old Mill Rd
Fort Wayne IN 46807

Call Sign: WA9CED

Don F Coombs
2944 Old Orchard Rd
Fort Wayne IN 46804

Call Sign: WB9TKJ
Livonia E Coombs
2944 Old Orchard Rd
Fort Wayne IN 46804

Call Sign: KC9BTJ
Lori A Seger
6904 Old Trl Rd
Fort Wayne IN 46809

Call Sign: N9ZFS
Michael G Collins
5014 Oliver St
Fort Wayne IN 46806

Call Sign: KB9LYD
Marvin F Porter
1632 Olladale Dr
Fort Wayne IN 46808

Call Sign: WJ0J
Jaiwant N Mulik
1619 Olladale Dr
Fort Wayne IN 46808

Call Sign: KB9LPG
Timothy P Rueger
12020 Orchard Pl
Fort Wayne IN 46845

Call Sign: KA9RWC
Mark A Murphy
12025 Orchard Pl
Fort Wayne IN 46845

Call Sign: KB9HLC
Brian M Dorsett
2933 Ormsby
Fort Wayne IN 46806

Call Sign: N9TMS

Jason L Dorsett
2933 Ormsby St
Fort Wayne IN 46806

Call Sign: N9TLZ
Johnnie L Dorsett
2933 Ormsby St
Fort Wayne IN 46806

Call Sign: KA9HPX
Marilynn M Ronk
2217 Otsego Dr
Fort Wayne IN 46825

Call Sign: KA9FQV
William E Ronk Jr
2217 Otsego Dr
Fort Wayne IN 46825

Call Sign: WA9TAL
Charles J Voors
2724 Otsego Dr
Fort Wayne IN 46825

Call Sign: KB9GYB
David A Gushwa
1430 Pacific Dr
Fort Wayne IN 46809

Call Sign: WB9VNK
Mark A Hart
7258 Pana Dr
Fort Wayne IN 46835

Call Sign: WB9NOO
Michael J Stein
1520 Park Ave
Fort Wayne IN 46807

Call Sign: N9NMW
Valerie L Stein
1520 Park Ave
Fort Wayne IN 46807

Call Sign: N9MKB

Clifford S Shreve II
3412 Parnell Ave
Fort Wayne IN 46805

Call Sign: WB8RNL
Tom M Wosniewski
3204 Pavilion Ct
Fort Wayne IN
468352033

Call Sign: KB9DOT
James I Machamer
6730 Pawawna Dr
Fort Wayne IN
468156342

Call Sign: KB9DOS
Kimberly K Machamer
6730 Pawawna Dr
Fort Wayne IN
468156342

Call Sign: N9CQC
Edward L Hobbs
717 Pellston Dr
Fort Wayne IN 46825

Call Sign: KA9NZQ
Nancy A Hobbs
717 Pellston Dr
Fort Wayne IN
468252277

Call Sign: KB9RLW
Kevin B Loughin
1406 Pemberton
Fort Wayne IN 46805

Call Sign: N9ZXG
Robert A Walchle
914 Pemberton Dr
Fort Wayne IN 46805

Call Sign: KB9DV
Carl W Vinyard

1709 Pemberton Dr
Fort Wayne IN
468055140

Call Sign: KC9OSC
Dianne M Rudig
362 Penn Ave
Fort Wayne IN 46805

Call Sign: KB9YWI
Wesley E Keisler
369 Penn Ave
Fort Wayne IN 46805

Call Sign: WB9WUY
Rose A Crist
8030 Pepperwood Ct
Fort Wayne IN 46818

Call Sign: K9CR
Clifford K Riley
311 Pequeen St
Fort Wayne IN 46804

Call Sign: WB2JFA
Christopher M Leyden
1318 Perry Lake Dr
Fort Wayne IN 46845

Call Sign: KA2EUK
Frederick L Strauss
13924 Piedmont Cove
Fort Wayne IN 46845

Call Sign: ND9F
Justin B Damerell
11116 Pine Orchard Cove
Fort Wayne IN
468451800

Call Sign: KA9SES
Bernard H Beckstedt
4705 Pinecrest Dr
Fort Wayne IN 46809

Call Sign: W9KHK
Theodore D Taylor
824 Pinehurst Dr
Fort Wayne IN 46815

Call Sign: W9TED
Theodore D Taylor
824 Pinehurst Dr
Fort Wayne IN 46815

Call Sign: K9LA
Roland C Luetzelschwab
1227 Pion Rd
Fort Wayne IN 46845

Call Sign: KB5EAM
Victoria A Luetzelschwab
1227 Pion Rd
Fort Wayne IN 46845

Call Sign: AE9YL
Victoria A Luetzelschwab
1227 Pion Rd
Fort Wayne IN 46845

Call Sign: KC9ACV
St Vincents School Radio
Club
1227 Pion Rd
Fort Wayne IN 46845

Call Sign: W9STV
St Vincents School Radio
Club
1227 Pion Rd
Fort Wayne IN 46845

Call Sign: KB9IKH
John E Cline
2811 Pittsburg St
Fort Wayne IN 46803

Call Sign: W9PWZ
Edward A Hildebrand
5202 Plaza Dr

Fort Wayne IN 46806

Call Sign: K9LSA
Paul C Fish
5205 Plaza Dr
Fort Wayne IN 46806

Call Sign: KA9LVB
John D Swain
5419 Plaza Dr
Fort Wayne IN
468063351

Call Sign: N9CYK
Ralph W Bracht
5515 Plaza Dr
Fort Wayne IN 46806

Call Sign: K3DCK
Dennis C Keyfauver
1932 Pleasant Ridge Dr
Fort Wayne IN
468199513

Call Sign: WA9LJD
Marvin R Gramling
3855 Plymouth Rd
Fort Wayne IN
468154619

Call Sign: N8WJR
Roy M Metzger Jr
3751 Plymouth Rd
Fort Wayne IN 46815

Call Sign: KC9LA
Charles A Hall
7433 Popp Rd
Fort Wayne IN
468459681

Call Sign: KD9DV
Clifford J Schmidt
5710 Port Royal

Fort Wayne IN
468158556

Call Sign: N9FGX
Katharine F Evans
5910 Port Royal
Fort Wayne IN 46815

Call Sign: KB9YKP
Douglas B Pritchett
3424 Portage Blvd
Fort Wayne IN 46802

Call Sign: KB9FVK
Lori A Auer
3535 Portage Blvd 2
Fort Wayne IN 46802

Call Sign: WA1ZRX
Christian R Caggiano
5130 Potomac Dr
Fort Wayne IN 46835

Call Sign: ND9T
Timothy R Kearney
12429 Preserve Blvd
Fort Wayne IN 46818

Call Sign: KC9SJB
Michael J Fiedeldey
2532 Princeton Ave
Fort Wayne IN 46808

Call Sign: N9ZKT
Dana L Cuney
2727 Princeton Ave
Fort Wayne IN 46808

Call Sign: KC9LYV
Mad Anthony Radio Club
1010 Production Rd Mail
Stop C2 5
Fort Wayne IN 46808

Call Sign: K9NCS

Mad Anthony Radio Club
1010 Production Rd Mail
Stop C2 5
Fort Wayne IN 46808

Call Sign: AB9JE
Joseph P Mcneely
6759 Pt Inverness Way
Fort Wayne IN 46804

Call Sign: NB9T
Joseph P Mcneely
6759 Pt Inverness Way
Fort Wayne IN 46804

Call Sign: KC9BQH
Saqib Jamil
2310 Pt W Dr Apt 3B
Fort Wayne IN 46808

Call Sign: N9SCF
Dennis P Carrier
1851 Purdue Dr
Fort Wayne IN 46808

Call Sign: N9BW
James R Weigand
8121 Purple Sage Cove
Fort Wayne IN 46804

Call Sign: KA9VPO
Jeanette M Weigand
8121 Purple Sage Cove
Fort Wayne IN 46804

Call Sign: KB5CTO
Theodore W Amadeus
664 Putnam St
Fort Wayne IN 46898

Call Sign: WD9AJS
Eddie Coble
809 Putnam St
Fort Wayne IN
468082336

Call Sign: WA9PIV
Lynn E Pequignot
7014 Raintree Rd
Fort Wayne IN 46825

Call Sign: WD9AMR
Edward L Williams
11133 Ransom Ct
Fort Wayne IN 46845

Call Sign: KC9RD
James E Jones
2013 Ransom Dr
Fort Wayne IN 46845

Call Sign: KB9PW
Larry D Coss
13235 Ravenswood Blvd
Fort Wayne IN 46845

Call Sign: KD9IY
Arthur A Brown
4919 Reckeweg Pl
Fort Wayne IN
468041786

Call Sign: KC9PUQ
Carol A Griffin
7933 Red Clover Ln
Fort Wayne IN 46815

Call Sign: KC9TQY
Ryan V Brammer
305 Red Eagle Pass
Fort Wayne IN 46845

Call Sign: WA9ALY
Homer A Evans
12529 Redding Dr
Fort Wayne IN 46804

Call Sign: KB9YAP
Juanita J Norem
12529 Redding Dr

Fort Wayne IN 46814

Call Sign: N9UBB
Marian E Girod
13305 Redding Dr
Fort Wayne IN 46814

Call Sign: N9RNV
Robert J Girod Sr
13305 Redding Dr
Fort Wayne IN 46814

Call Sign: K9CUZ
George P Geones
2614 Reed Rd
Fort Wayne IN
468156842

Call Sign: N9ZOZ
James B Montgomery Jr
4021 Reed Rd
Fort Wayne IN 46815

Call Sign: KC9RAM
Janice M Zavodny
4105 Reed Rd
Fort Wayne IN 46815

Call Sign: KC9RAN
Matthew S Zavodny
4105 Reed Rd
Fort Wayne IN 46815

Call Sign: AC9AT
Matthew S Zavodny
4105 Reed Rd
Fort Wayne IN 46815

Call Sign: AB9VD
Stephen A Zavodny
4105 Reed Rd
Fort Wayne IN
468154939

Call Sign: KB9ZHD

Paul O Porter
4270 Reed Rd
Fort Wayne IN
468154942

Call Sign: KB9DSK
Susie Y Tse
4959 Reed Rd
Fort Wayne IN 46835

Call Sign: W9MWS
Michael W Stover
5024 Reed Rd
Fort Wayne IN
468353552

Call Sign: N9QR
Michael W Stover
5024 Reed Rd
Fort Wayne IN
468353552

Call Sign: KC9VAT
Brandon L Stump
Reed Rd
Fort Wayne IN 46815

Call Sign: N9UIK
Ronald N Williams
1411 Reed Rd 4
Fort Wayne IN 46815

Call Sign: AB9PK
Charles W Berry
1727 Reed Rd Apt B
Fort Wayne IN 46815

Call Sign: KB9QAO
Thomas W Cartwright
4810 Reed St
Fort Wayne IN 46806

Call Sign: KB9MDW
Simon R Montalvo
5209 Reed St

Fort Wayne IN 46806

Call Sign: W4MOM
Kathryn M Kroemer
7408 Regina Dr
Fort Wayne IN 46815

Call Sign: KI4JMN
Michael K Kroemer
7408 Regina Dr
Fort Wayne IN 46815

Call Sign: WB9MDS
Jay M Farlow
3333 Regis Dr
Fort Wayne IN 46816

Call Sign: W9LW
Jay M Farlow
3333 Regis Dr
Fort Wayne IN 46816

Call Sign: N9XKU
Peggy A Farlow
3333 Regis Dr
Fort Wayne IN 46816

Call Sign: WB9NIE
Robert C Lipp
6433 Revere Pl
Fort Wayne IN 46815

Call Sign: WD9GFJ
Rose Marie Lipp
6433 Revere Pl
Fort Wayne IN 46815

Call Sign: KB9OZE
Joel E Esslinger
915 Rewill Dr
Fort Wayne IN 46804

Call Sign: KB9VXV
Kathleen Hartenstein
215 Rexford Dr

Fort Wayne IN 46816

Call Sign: WB9UDW
Robert J Hartenstein
215 Rexford Dr
Fort Wayne IN 46816

Call Sign: KA9SLX
Brian W Howard
3514 Reynolds St
Fort Wayne IN 46803

Call Sign: KB9SLV
William D West
10511 Richmond Dr
Fort Wayne IN
468451640

Call Sign: N9YBM
Wayne G Bartlett
4611 Ridgeland Dr
Fort Wayne IN 46804

Call Sign: W9HV
Walter Kowal
622 Ridgewood Dr
Fort Wayne IN 46805

Call Sign: KC9PVE
Brandon M Dills
832 Ridgewood Dr Apt 8
Fort Wayne IN 46805

Call Sign: KC9MRB
Robert V Erb
2624 River Cove Ln
Fort Wayne IN 46825

Call Sign: W9LE
Nelson E Preble
8304 River Oak Dr
Fort Wayne IN 46825

Call Sign: WA8VKS
William A Hossler

821 River Oak Run
Fort Wayne IN 46804

Call Sign: KC9UOZ
William A Hossler
821 River Oak Run
Fort Wayne IN 46804

Call Sign: WA8VKS
William A Hossler
821 River Oak Run
Fort Wayne IN 46804

Call Sign: WA9WTJ
Adolph J Wozniak
9936 River Rapids Run
Fort Wayne IN 46845

Call Sign: KB9EXZ
Holly H Weston
1840 River Run Trl
Fort Wayne IN 46825

Call Sign: N9LPV
Gavin J Roberts
5435 River Run Trl
Fort Wayne IN 46825

Call Sign: KB1IVA
Edward J Caylor III
5820 River Run Trl
Fort Wayne IN 46825

Call Sign: N8PHJ
Jerilyn J Rogers
River Run Trl
Fort Wayne IN 46825

Call Sign: KA9VNF
Thomas A Welch
River Run Trl
Fort Wayne IN 46825

Call Sign: N0USN
Shannon W Flinsbaugh

River Run Trl
Fort Wayne IN 46825

Call Sign: W9TLP
Tammy L Preble
8304 Riveroak Dr
Fort Wayne IN 46825

Call Sign: W9TP
Tammy L Preble
8304 Riveroak Dr
Fort Wayne IN 46825

Call Sign: N9WBO
Michael A Taylor
5105 Riviera Dr
Fort Wayne IN 46825

Call Sign: WA9RRY
Melvin D Whitesel
5120 Riviera Dr
Fort Wayne IN
468255704

Call Sign: KC9MOE
Matthew J Herald
5611 Roaring Fork Run
Fort Wayne IN 46825

Call Sign: KC9NRY
Midwest Geocachers
ARC
5611 Roaring Fork Run
Fort Wayne IN 46825

Call Sign: W9MWG
Midwest Geocachers
ARC
5611 Roaring Fork Run
Fort Wayne IN 46825

Call Sign: KC9LLC
David W Campbell
5620 Roaring Fork Run
Fort Wayne IN 46825

Call Sign: K9RYJ
David W Campbell
5620 Roaring Fork Run
Fort Wayne IN 46825

Call Sign: KC9ORS
Donald D Gregory
8208 Rockbrook Ct
Fort Wayne IN 46825

Call Sign: KB7JWE
Jed S Wilson
6609 Rockingham Dr
Fort Wayne IN 46835

Call Sign: N9AR
Harry C Harvey Jr
3021 Rockwood Dr
Fort Wayne IN 46815

Call Sign: WB9ZIY
Steven A Nardin
3030 Rockwood Dr
Fort Wayne IN 46815

Call Sign: KE9AG
Michael J Hughes
3123 Rockwood Dr
Fort Wayne IN 46815

Call Sign: NY9Y
Michael J Hughes
3123 Rockwood Dr
Fort Wayne IN 46815

Call Sign: N9FRS
Paul J Koehler
3323 Rockwood Dr
Fort Wayne IN 46815

Call Sign: KA9HIZ
Danny K Van Doorn
5922 Rolling Hills Dr
Fort Wayne IN 46804

Call Sign: KA9FQN
David L Van Doorn
5922 Rolling Hills Dr
Fort Wayne IN 46804

Call Sign: W9WEL
David L Van Doorn
5922 Rolling Hills Dr
Fort Wayne IN 46804

Call Sign: K1FJ
Frank J Jaworski
2911 Roscommon Dr
Fort Wayne IN 46805

Call Sign: KA9IFQ
Teresa L Jaworski
2911 Roscommon Dr
Fort Wayne IN 46805

Call Sign: KB9PNB
Carol J Shank
7533 Rose Ann Pkwy
Fort Wayne IN 46804

Call Sign: KB9PNA
Daniel E Shank
7533 Rose Ann Pkwy
Fort Wayne IN 46804

Call Sign: KB9POD
Philip M Shank
7533 Rose Ann Pkwy
Fort Wayne IN 46804

Call Sign: KB9OZP
Steven K Shannon
4618 Rose Hill Ln
Fort Wayne IN 46835

Call Sign: K9SKS
Steven K Shannon
4618 Rose Hill Ln
Fort Wayne IN 46835

Call Sign: KB9SCF
Gregory M Applegate
3307 Rosewood Dr
Fort Wayne IN
468046109

Call Sign: KB8MPL
Stephen M Harrigan
5416 Rothermere Dr
Fort Wayne IN 46835

Call Sign: N7KFT
James A Norton
5164 Rothman Rd
Fort Wayne IN
468351451

Call Sign: W9KFT
James A Norton
5164 Rothman Rd
Fort Wayne IN
468351451

Call Sign: KA9ULH
Lee C De La Barre
8617 Rothman Rd
Fort Wayne IN 46835

Call Sign: WD9FAR
Craig E Bienz
6021 Running Brook Ln
Fort Wayne IN 46835

Call Sign: N9QXO
Kenneth M Chlebik
1514 Runnion Ave
Fort Wayne IN 46808

Call Sign: N9QXP
Kevin W Chlebik
1514 Runnion Ave
Fort Wayne IN 46808

Call Sign: N9RVP

Roger A Lehman
2229 Rutgers Dr
Fort Wayne IN 46809

Call Sign: WA9RGB
Warren E Hoagland
4002 S Anthony Blvd
Fort Wayne IN
468061939

Call Sign: KF6CCN
Robert S Parisot
4619 S Anthony Blvd
Fort Wayne IN 46806

Call Sign: N9JZV
Herbert G Tipton
6701 S Anthony Blvd
Fort Wayne IN 46816

Call Sign: W9UC
Charles W Kronmiller
6723 S Anthony Blvd
Fort Wayne IN 46816

Call Sign: KB9HZB
David K West Jr
4417 S Calhoun St
Fort Wayne IN 46807

Call Sign: N9VHE
Gregory A Foote
315 S Cornell Cir
Fort Wayne IN 46807

Call Sign: KC9LAR
Zion Lutheran Academy
Radio Society
2313 S Hanna St
Fort Wayne IN 46803

Call Sign: W9TSF
Frank J Smith
4642 S Hanna St
Fort Wayne IN 46806

Call Sign: WB9DAH
Arthur W Sterling
4814 S Hanna St
Fort Wayne IN 46806

Call Sign: KA9QMI
Robert W Zollinger
6323 S Hanna St
Fort Wayne IN
468161138

Call Sign: KB9DRQ
Josh T Klugman
4112 S Harrison St
Fort Wayne IN 46807

Call Sign: KC9KTH
Steven B Dalton
4118 S Harrison St
Fort Wayne IN 46807

Call Sign: WA9JJX
Steven B Dalton
4118 S Harrison St
Fort Wayne IN 46807

Call Sign: KB9BRZ
Paul H Spear
6404 S Harrison St
Fort Wayne IN 46807

Call Sign: W9MGV
Eldon E Wood
4701 S Park Dr
Fort Wayne IN 46806

Call Sign: KB9GBF
Michael W Cassaday
4708 S Park Dr
Fort Wayne IN 46806

Call Sign: KB9IKJ
Nicholas M Cassaday
4708 S Park Dr

Fort Wayne IN 46806

Call Sign: WA9AJV
Robert E Johnson
7020 S River Rd
Fort Wayne IN 46803

Call Sign: KB9HQB
Christina R McCann
107 S Seminole Cir
Fort Wayne IN 46807

Call Sign: N9IBW
Andrew T Pettigrew
2607 S Wayne
Fort Wayne IN 46807

Call Sign: KC9HYX
Andrew T Pettigrew
2607 S Wayne
Fort Wayne IN 46807

Call Sign: N9VZJ
Scott A Price
5019 S Webster St
Fort Wayne IN 46807

Call Sign: W9KBW
Russell E Johnston
Saddleback Ct
Fort Wayne IN 46904

Call Sign: KB9BNX
F Ruth Priest
5415 Saint Joe Center Rd
Fort Wayne IN 46835

Call Sign: K9FNQ
Robert O Blessing
2209 Saint Joe Ctr Rd
Fort Wayne IN
468255099

Call Sign: KC9PAO
Forest D Musselman

10725 Saint Joe Rd
Fort Wayne IN 46835

Call Sign: N9ZNW
Donald E Harris
1705 Saint Louis Ave
Fort Wayne IN 46819

Call Sign: KC9GVA
Larry W Coffman
2891 Saint Louis Ave Apt
I
Fort Wayne IN 46809

Call Sign: WA9RQY
H Glenn Bogel
8427 Sakaden Pkwy
Fort Wayne IN 46825

Call Sign: KL0JW
J≈Rg Boggel-Trahe
8427 Sakaden Pkwy
Fort Wayne IN
468252932

Call Sign: KB9UHI
Kelvin M Duncan
5102 Salem Ln
Fort Wayne IN 46806

Call Sign: WB9WBM
Robert W Downing
7020 Salge Ct
Fort Wayne IN 46815

Call Sign: N9RYK
Richard G Fancher
5959 Salge Dr
Fort Wayne IN
468352451

Call Sign: KC9GAQ
Richard A Blair
6036 Salge Dr
Fort Wayne IN 46835

Call Sign: N9RVO
Robert F Berard
6431 Salge Dr
Fort Wayne IN 46835

Call Sign: KC9TRM
Jon R Preble
4933 Salt Trail Canyon
Pass
Fort Wayne IN 46808

Call Sign: K9TT
Don R Howe
10909 Sandpiper Cove
Fort Wayne IN 46845

Call Sign: WD9FAT
Douglas G R Knuth
5824 Sandra Lee
Fort Wayne IN
468191120

Call Sign: N5SRQ
Tommy L Lightfoot
4325 Sanford Ln
Fort Wayne IN 46816

Call Sign: WB9UZA
Victor L Guess
3311 Sanibel Dr
Fort Wayne IN 46815

Call Sign: N9XKQ
Mary L Huntley
8320 Santa Fe Trl
Fort Wayne IN 46815

Call Sign: N8RSP
Russell G Nicholson
6227 Sapphire Trl
Fort Wayne IN
468049203

Call Sign: N9NRP

Glen J Seward
9527 Saratoga Rd
Fort Wayne IN 46804

Call Sign: KB9VAQ
Richard C Andrew
2832 Sawgrass Trl
Fort Wayne IN 46808

Call Sign: N9HRA
Richard C Andrew
2832 Sawgrass Trl
Fort Wayne IN 46808

Call Sign: NK9B
Jason H Whiteaker
9528 Sea Pines Way
Fort Wayne IN 46819

Call Sign: KC9KLK
John J Sandor
1525 Seabrook Dr
Fort Wayne IN 46845

Call Sign: N9LPN
Scott M Boyd
6617 Sedgemore
Fort Wayne IN 46835

Call Sign: KA9JMR
Carole K Branning
3419 Senate Ave
Fort Wayne IN 46806

Call Sign: K9KB
Kenneth P Branning
3419 Senate Ave
Fort Wayne IN 46806

Call Sign: WB9YGD
Jerry J Hoffmann
5631 Senna Ct
Fort Wayne IN 46804

Call Sign: WD9GXR

Sandra K Hoffmann
5631 Senna Ct
Fort Wayne IN 46804

Call Sign: N9ANB
Charles H Whitaker Jr
3619 Shadow Creek Dr
Fort Wayne IN
468188992

Call Sign: KA9CLX
Charles H Whitaker Jr
3619 Shadow Creek Dr
Fort Wayne IN
468188992

Call Sign: AC9AG
Charles H Whitaker Jr
3619 Shadow Creek Dr
Fort Wayne IN
468188992

Call Sign: WB5NCB
William C Smith
6124 Shady Creek Ct
Fort Wayne IN 46814

Call Sign: WB9TWN
Herbert W Masenthin
2525 Shady Oak Dr
Fort Wayne IN
468065331

Call Sign: KA9JTE
Dick Stump
514 Shadyhurst Dr
Fort Wayne IN 46825

Call Sign: WB9FOC
Gerald E Prumm Jr
4024 Sheratan Dr
Fort Wayne IN 46808

Call Sign: N9FM
Robert L Waugh

2705 Sherborne Blvd
Fort Wayne IN
468053058

Call Sign: AA9SW
Sarah E Shurtz
1517 Sherman Blvd
Fort Wayne IN 46808

Call Sign: W9PRO
Harold E Norton Jr
1723 Sherman Blvd
Fort Wayne IN 46808

Call Sign: WD8ATQ
Robert G Hartung
2519 Sherman Blvd
Fort Wayne IN
468082005

Call Sign: KB9VTI
James R Brackeen
4222 Sherman Blvd
Fort Wayne IN 46808

Call Sign: KA9RVG
Ronald L Parker
8131 Silver Springs Run
Fort Wayne IN 46825

Call Sign: KA0DJW
Margaret M Bell
7003 Silverthorn Run
Fort Wayne IN 46835

Call Sign: KB9GVH
Roy T Holland
1117 Sinclair St
Fort Wayne IN 46808

Call Sign: KB9GYA
Ruth N Holland
1117 Sinclair St
Fort Wayne IN 46808

Call Sign: KA9ORK
Roy E Baker
1210 Sinclair St
Fort Wayne IN 46808

Call Sign: N9JFS
Kenneth E Saylor
1513 Sinclair St
Fort Wayne IN 46808

Call Sign: KC9HQH
Kristy L Anderson
1934 Sinclair St
Fort Wayne IN 46808

Call Sign: AB9PC
Kristy L Anderson
1934 Sinclair St
Fort Wayne IN 46808

Call Sign: KC9OAX
Nikolas A Moehring
2037 Sky Hawk Dr
Fort Wayne IN 46815

Call Sign: KB9WWM
James S Moehring
2037 Skyhawk Dr
Fort Wayne IN 46815

Call Sign: KB9YWG
Melodie J Moehring
2037 Skyhawk Dr
Fort Wayne IN 46815

Call Sign: WA9LHC
Richard G Sunderland
5808 Southbend Dr
Fort Wayne IN 46804

Call Sign: KC9EUT
Shane S Freeman
5921 Southcrest Rd
Fort Wayne IN 46816

Call Sign: KC9GAT
Rick L Cocklin
1103 Southerly Pt
Fort Wayne IN
468459756

Call Sign: KB9LSI
Richard L Bultemeyer
2719 Spring Creek Dr
Fort Wayne IN 46808

Call Sign: N9DSG
Carl Handshoe
1515 Spring Cress Rd
Fort Wayne IN 46814

Call Sign: WA9ROW
John C Louks
1618 Spring Cress Rd
Fort Wayne IN 46814

Call Sign: KA9CMC
Charles G Cary
10914 Spring Oak Rd
Fort Wayne IN 46845

Call Sign: WB9OCM
Martin L Didion
11011 Spring Oak Rd
Fort Wayne IN 46845

Call Sign: W9MLD
Martin L Didion
11011 Spring Oak Rd
Fort Wayne IN 46845

Call Sign: KA9YYF
Kurt S Frederick
1413 Spring St
Fort Wayne IN 46808

Call Sign: KA9UJF
Patrick D Faherty
1501 Spring St
Fort Wayne IN 46808

Call Sign: KA9YYG
Elise M Kriss
2701 Spring St
Fort Wayne IN 46808

Call Sign: N9KJA
Richard W Dugger
8929 Spring View Dr
Fort Wayne IN 46804

Call Sign: N9QYT
Ruth A Bassett
4012 Springwood Dr
Fort Wayne IN 46815

Call Sign: W9PEP
Roland A Mitchell
4115 Springwood Dr
Fort Wayne IN 46815

Call Sign: KB7DVK
Roy J Baker
1317.5 Spy Run Ave
Fort Wayne IN 46805

Call Sign: N8KR
Kenneth C Rogner
10032 St Clairs Retreat
Fort Wayne IN 46825

Call Sign: W9SQD
Charles H Marks
2209 St Joe Center Rd
Fort Wayne IN
468255099

Call Sign: KA9GME
Jackie D Smith
5415 St Joe Center Rd
Fort Wayne IN 46835

Call Sign: KC9IQJ
Michael R Ormiston

6142 St Joe Center Rd
141
Fort Wayne IN
468352505

Call Sign: W9MRO
Michael R Ormiston
6142 St Joe Center Rd
141
Fort Wayne IN
468352505

Call Sign: KC7EHE
Mark D Berke
5683 St Joseph Center Rd
Fort Wayne IN 46835

Call Sign: WA7NXI
Mark D Berke
5683 St Joseph Center Rd
Fort Wayne IN 46835

Call Sign: WD9DJU
Stephen M Engelman
3023 St Louis Ave
Fort Wayne IN
468092950

Call Sign: AA9NL
Ernest L Blazer
2100 St Marys Apt 111
Fort Wayne IN 46808

Call Sign: KD4DQM
Edith E Cummings
St Marys Ave
Fort Wayne IN 46808

Call Sign: W9SRG
Donald A Wolever
538 Stadium Dr
Fort Wayne IN 46805

Call Sign: N0EKN
Charles E Mantock Jr

9415 Stagecoach Dr
Fort Wayne IN 46804

Call Sign: KB9DQT
Richard H Sigmund
4407 Standish Dr
Fort Wayne IN 46806

Call Sign: KC9ACZ
Michael A Wasson
2701 Stanford Ave
Fort Wayne IN 46808

Call Sign: K9TCF
Timothy C Fox
4732 Stellhorn
Fort Wayne IN 46815

Call Sign: K9JMF
Jo Anne M Fox
4732 Stellhorn Rd
Fort Wayne IN 46815

Call Sign: KB9DKI
John W Ridgeway Sr
6710 Stellhorn Rd
Fort Wayne IN 46815

Call Sign: WB9CIJ
Roger D Miller
3217 Stepping Stone Ln
Fort Wayne IN
468352048

Call Sign: N9YNN
Christopher D Hartman
3820 Stone Creek Run
Fort Wayne IN 46804

Call Sign: KC9FLN
Brian S Kibiger
12536 Stoneboro Ct
Fort Wayne IN 46845

Call Sign: KC9GUX

James E Hinchee
5226 Stonehedge Blvd
Fort Wayne IN
468353004

Call Sign: K9GKC
Scott R Zehr
2227 Stonington Rd
Fort Wayne IN 46845

Call Sign: W9FNP
F Nelson Peters IV
9934 Stowaway Cove
Fort Wayne IN 46835

Call Sign: N9UAU
F Nelson Peters IV
9934 Stowaway Cove
Fort Wayne IN 46835

Call Sign: KB9JJI
Paul D Nash
4317 Strathdon Dr
Fort Wayne IN 46816

Call Sign: KB9BJA
Virginia A Miller
2805 Streamside Ct
Fort Wayne IN 46818

Call Sign: WB9NJY
Gary L Greer
2805 Streamside Ct
Fort Wayne IN
468189583

Call Sign: KA9VGI
Roxanna S Greer
2805 Streamside Ct
Fort Wayne IN
468189583

Call Sign: N9TJR
Ray L Drook
2912 Sugarmans Trl

Fort Wayne IN 46804

Call Sign: WD9CVI
John E Zumbaugh
10609 Summerhill Pl
Fort Wayne IN 46814

Call Sign: KC9GGV
Gary R Stebbins
8412 Summerset Pl
Fort Wayne IN
468256495

Call Sign: KB9OZI
Michael D Banks
3625 Summit View Pl
Fort Wayne IN 46808

Call Sign: WB9QAL
Arthur D Wortman
8923 Sunburst Ln
Fort Wayne IN
468043438

Call Sign: KB9NXZ
Curtis A Sople
6104 Sundance Dr
Fort Wayne IN 46825

Call Sign: KC9BUR
Kevin C Crews
6501 Sunland Dr
Fort Wayne IN 46815

Call Sign: W9LHM
Howard J Bradley
6825 Sunland Dr
Fort Wayne IN 46815

Call Sign: KB9LHT
Enrique R Sablan Jr
8221 Sunny Ln
Fort Wayne IN 46835

Call Sign: KB9LHU

Melindrina U Pablo
8221 Sunny Ln
Fort Wayne IN 46835

Call Sign: N9XKS
Brent S Hiatt
1925 Sunnymede Dr
Fort Wayne IN 46803

Call Sign: KB9STZ
Richard C Jentgen
8225 Surrey Ct
Fort Wayne IN 46815

Call Sign: N9PXG
R Scott Sides
4304 SW Anthony
Wayne Dr
Fort Wayne IN 46806

Call Sign: N9BNA
Richard K Erwin
4802 Tacoma Ave
Fort Wayne IN 46807

Call Sign: KB9KSM
John R Schutt
4940 Tacoma Ave
Fort Wayne IN
468073108

Call Sign: KB9OXL
Luke C Schutt
4940 Tacoma Ave
Fort Wayne IN
468073108

Call Sign: KB9JHS
Noel R Schutt
4940 Tacoma Ave
Fort Wayne IN
468073108

Call Sign: KB9OQO
Sharon M Schutt

4940 Tacoma Ave
Fort Wayne IN
468073108

Call Sign: KC9ENU
Ritchie Short
10334 Tairn Dr
Fort Wayne IN 46825

Call Sign: KA9FFX
Larry D Mallett
4308 Tamarack Dr
Fort Wayne IN 46835

Call Sign: KB9RDJ
James R Sulecki
13509 Tamiami Trl
Fort Wayne IN 46845

Call Sign: W9MZH
Eugene A Fisher
1815 Taylor St
Fort Wayne IN 46802

Call Sign: W9UKV
Maynard D Faith
1807 Tecumseh
Fort Wayne IN 46805

Call Sign: KB9NRK
Dwight A Troue
Tecumseh St
Fort Wayne IN 46805

Call Sign: N9VXM
Albert H Bennett
2615 Terrace Rd
Fort Wayne IN 46805

Call Sign: WD9ECN
Vilas E Deane
3326 Terry Ln
Fort Wayne IN 46835

Call Sign: WD9FAE

Robert C Harold
3330 Thames Dr
Fort Wayne IN 46815

Call Sign: N9FTF
Michael M Thomas
5710 The Prophets Pass
Fort Wayne IN 46845

Call Sign: N9WPA
David W Stark
10929 Thiele Rd
Fort Wayne IN 46819

Call Sign: N9CGH
John P Mitchell
5201 Thompson Rd
Fort Wayne IN 46816

Call Sign: KB9FZT
Andrew J Magner
5615 Thompson Rd
Fort Wayne IN 46816

Call Sign: KB9FZS
James A Magner
5615 Thompson Rd
Fort Wayne IN 46816

Call Sign: K8BNJ
Herbert L Heider
5925 Thoreau Ave
Fort Wayne IN 46815

Call Sign: K9AWA
Roland J Brown
5926 Thoreau Ave
Fort Wayne IN 46815

Call Sign: WB9ZHT
Dennis K Plank
4003 Thornbury Pl
Fort Wayne IN 46804

Call Sign: WB9MYQ

Gerald J Jacyno
1612 Thorny Meadow Ln
Fort Wayne IN 46825

Call Sign: N9KLR
Kenneth W Carmichael
7527 Thoroughbred Dr
Apt 2A
Fort Wayne IN 46804

Call Sign: W9LES
David W Ford
4009 Thorton Dr
Fort Wayne IN 46815

Call Sign: WB9QNE
William A Starn
3414 Three Oaks Dr
Fort Wayne IN 46809

Call Sign: KC9ORV
Wardell Hodges
716 Three River N
Fort Wayne IN 46802

Call Sign: KA9BMX
Daryl L Nicholson
7601 Thrush Ave
Fort Wayne IN 46816

Call Sign: KA9JDA
Craig A Sedery
7710 Thrush Ave
Fort Wayne IN 46816

Call Sign: WB9EAO
Joseph F Novosel
11623 Tillbury Cove
Fort Wayne IN 46845

Call Sign: AA9MD
David W Mauritzen
4918 Timberland Dr
Fort Wayne IN 46835

Call Sign: KB9NRA
James C Luttenbacher
7913 Tipperary Trl
Fort Wayne IN
468158148

Call Sign: K9JHE
Jerry A Young
5629 Tomahawk Trl
Fort Wayne IN 46804

Call Sign: N9JHS
William N Dansby
2826 Trentman Ave
Fort Wayne IN 46806

Call Sign: N9NRO
Carl E Rittenhouse
4661 Trier Rd
Fort Wayne IN 46815

Call Sign: KC9FAX
Richard E Buchanan
5340 Trier Rd
Fort Wayne IN
468155102

Call Sign: AA9FK
Jacob Derkach
4533 Trierwood Park Dr
Fort Wayne IN 46815

Call Sign: WD9HII
William C Hall
5027 Tristam Ct
Fort Wayne IN
468155060

Call Sign: K9SUX
James W Thomas
1820 Trotter Ct
Fort Wayne IN 46815

Call Sign: KC9PVF
Jonathan R Puckett

5133 Truemper Way Apt
8
Fort Wayne IN 46835

Call Sign: N9DGL
Bruce J Cadwell
1536 Tulip Tree Rd
Fort Wayne IN 46825

Call Sign: W9AY
Fredus N Peters III
5612 Tunbridge Crossing
Fort Wayne IN 46815

Call Sign: KC9RSD
Robert R Iden II
4837 Turbo Trl
Fort Wayne IN 46818

Call Sign: AE9Y
Donald G Guy
5318 Twilight Ln
Fort Wayne IN 46835

Call Sign: KC9OFR
Steven P Miller
5138 Tyrone Rd
Fort Wayne IN 46809

Call Sign: W9SPM
Steven P Miller
5138 Tyrone Rd
Fort Wayne IN 46809

Call Sign: N9WGE
Brian M Flinn
5968 Ullyot Dr
Fort Wayne IN 46804

Call Sign: KC9GAR
Allen J Householder
6519 Underwood Cove
Fort Wayne IN 46835

Call Sign: KR9U

James B Wolf
2415 Union Chapel Rd
Fort Wayne IN 46845

Call Sign: KB9HYF
Lisa G Wolf
2415 Union Chapel Rd
Fort Wayne IN 46845

Call Sign: W9PFO
Esther N Clifton
5621 Union Chapel Rd
Fort Wayne IN 46825

Call Sign: W9TC
Ted K Clifton
5621 Union Chapel Rd
Fort Wayne IN 46825

Call Sign: WB9YWC
James R Miller
12111 US 24th W
Fort Wayne IN 46814

Call Sign: KC9UXL
Steven D Blevins
10744 US 27 S Lot 216
Fort Wayne IN 46816

Call Sign: K9UV
Robert J Schram
10744 US 27S Lot199
Fort Wayne IN 46816

Call Sign: WB9ULN
Charles F Willer
5849 US 33 W
Fort Wayne IN 46818

Call Sign: KG9DX
Craig T Steadman
5001 US Hwy 30 W
Fort Wayne IN 46818

Call Sign: KC9GVC

Joseph A Rodecap
10206 Valley Hill Ln
Fort Wayne IN 46825

Call Sign: KA9TCT
Irving G Weigel
906 Valley O Pines Pkwy
Fort Wayne IN 46845

Call Sign: K9FW
Albert S Biddle
920 Vance Ave
Fort Wayne IN 46805

Call Sign: KB9AYR
Jeremy R Biddle
920 Vance Ave
Fort Wayne IN 46805

Call Sign: KA9CGX
Kay L Biddle
920 Vance Ave
Fort Wayne IN 46805

Call Sign: KE9YP
David G Sweigert
1522 Vance Ave
Fort Wayne IN 46805

Call Sign: N9LC
George H Sweigert
1522 Vance Ave
Fort Wayne IN 46805

Call Sign: K9ZNJ
Gerald Roemke
4107 Vance Ave
Fort Wayne IN 46815

Call Sign: KC9MNZ
Wallace T Smith
1606 Ventura Ln
Fort Wayne IN 46816

Call Sign: NA9C

Emmett J France
6603 Verandah Ln
Fort Wayne IN 46835

Call Sign: W9QOD
Eugene F Goshorn
7615 Verona Dr
Fort Wayne IN 46816

Call Sign: K9FZV
Frederick H Alberts
3406 Vesey Ave
Fort Wayne IN 46809

Call Sign: K9BLI
Robert H Marschand Jr
4204 Victoria Dr
Fort Wayne IN 46815

Call Sign: KC9KLE
Andrew M Alidai
8308 Victoria Woods Pl
Fort Wayne IN 46825

Call Sign: KC9UUG
Jahred S Gamez
607 Villa Park Ct
Fort Wayne IN 46808

Call Sign: WB8MWW
Larry L Carroll
830 Villa Park Ct
Fort Wayne IN 46808

Call Sign: N8ZWM
Christopher M Lewis
9028 Village Dr
Fort Wayne IN 46818

Call Sign: KC9KXK
Christopher M Lewis
9028 Village Dr
Fort Wayne IN 46818

Call Sign: K9TET

Christopher M Lewis
9028 Village Dr
Fort Wayne IN 46818

Call Sign: AB9SY
Christopher M Lewis
9028 Village Dr
Fort Wayne IN
468181069

Call Sign: KB9PSF
Christopher L Schubert
8817 Village Grove Dr
Fort Wayne IN 46804

Call Sign: K9IAK
Anthony H Berghoff
1609 W 3rd St
Fort Wayne IN 46808

Call Sign: KB9FEV
Andrew P Ambrose
1309 W 4th St
Fort Wayne IN 46808

Call Sign: N9SCE
Scott T Daniel
4737 W Arlington Park
Blvd
Fort Wayne IN 46835

Call Sign: K9EDI
Terry M Lentz
5212 W Arlington Park
Blvd
Fort Wayne IN 46835

Call Sign: W9FEZ
Mizpah Shrine Radio
Unit
407 W Berry St
Fort Wayne IN 46802

Call Sign: N9NAI
William A Meints

538 W Berry St Apt 704
Fort Wayne IN 46802

Call Sign: N9RJN
Harvey R Milligan
447 W Brackenridge St
Fort Wayne IN 46802

Call Sign: N9EDF
Maurice I Clinger
341 W Branning
Fort Wayne IN 46807

Call Sign: N9QJS
Daniel W Harrigan
412 W Branning
Fort Wayne IN 46807

Call Sign: KB9VNM
John C Patty
2922 W Coliseum Blvd
B3
Fort Wayne IN 46808

Call Sign: N9XXL
Jill A Henderson-
Coblentz
9625 W Cook Rd
Fort Wayne IN 46818

Call Sign: N9WOY
Robert L Coblentz
9625 W Cook Rd
Fort Wayne IN
468189452

Call Sign: KB9HKX
Dennis D Fett
2914 W County Line Rd
N
Fort Wayne IN 46818

Call Sign: N9UKF
Jeffrey L Patterson
416 W De Wald

Fort Wayne IN 46802

Call Sign: N9NRM
David W Oaks Sr
1522 W Dupont Rd
Fort Wayne IN
468251016

Call Sign: K9TZU
Kenneth P Hubler
145 W Essex Ln
Fort Wayne IN 46825

Call Sign: KD7USY
Alex N Hayward
489 W Essex Ln
Fort Wayne IN 46825

Call Sign: N9FDO
Duane L Yoder
606 W Fairfax Ave
Fort Wayne IN 46807

Call Sign: KA1YF
Arthur A Swanson
712 W Fairfax Ave
Fort Wayne IN 46807

Call Sign: KC9FAZ
Patricia A Moore
13120 W Hamilton Ln
Fort Wayne IN 46814

Call Sign: W9JJX
Patricia A Moore
13120 W Hamilton Ln
Fort Wayne IN 46814

Call Sign: KB9MEF
Beresford N Clarke
3723 W Hamilton Rd
Fort Wayne IN 46804

Call Sign: WB9BGR
Walter G Hackett

5208 W Hamilton Rd
Fort Wayne IN 46804

Call Sign: W9HF
Elvin L Miller
6409 W Hamilton Rd
Fort Wayne IN
468149771

Call Sign: N9CKG
William D Bathurst
401 W Lenox Ave
Fort Wayne IN 46807

Call Sign: KC9FBE
Brad L Hartz
1127 W Ludwig Rd
Fort Wayne IN 46825

Call Sign: KB9VXU
Carroll F Lockwood
1503 W Ludwig Rd
Fort Wayne IN 46825

Call Sign: KB9IHT
Donald E Madison
2416 W Ludwig Rd
Fort Wayne IN 46818

Call Sign: KB9TTY
Thomas E Presley
1631 W Main
Fort Wayne IN 46808

Call Sign: AA9FR
Owen J Hinkle Jr
120.5 W Oakdale Dr
Fort Wayne IN 46807

Call Sign: N9ZTG
Ronald L Sheets
1224 W Oakdale Dr
Fort Wayne IN
468071750

Call Sign: W9RLS
Ronald L Sheets
1224 W Oakdale Dr
Fort Wayne IN
468071750

Call Sign: N9RDZ
Claud C Sigman
815 W Packard Av
Fort Wayne IN 46807

Call Sign: WA9WTH
Lyle J Hamman
10820 W Rosewood Cir
Fort Wayne IN 46845

Call Sign: KC9EDJ
Joseph P Mcneely
330 W Rudisill Blvd
Fort Wayne IN 46807

Call Sign: N9ZNP
Richard E Douglas
603 W Rudisill Blvd
Fort Wayne IN 46807

Call Sign: KB9DPC
Ian M Slagle
125 W Sherwood Ter
Fort Wayne IN 46807

Call Sign: KB9DPE
Michael L Slagle
125 W Sherwood Ter
Fort Wayne IN 46807

Call Sign: KB9HYG
Deborah S White
657 W State Blvd
Fort Wayne IN 46808

Call Sign: KB9DDT
Serena L Smith
1418 W State Blvd
Fort Wayne IN 46808

Fort Wayne IN 46807

Call Sign: K9WUJ
George E Skordos
2517 W State Ct
Fort Wayne IN 46808

Call Sign: KB9YKU
Kenneth L Uhrick
742 W Superior St Apt B
Fort Wayne IN 46802

Call Sign: KC9ADN
Kent W Gildow
314 W Suttenfield St
Fort Wayne IN 46807

Call Sign: W9HT
Richard W Miller Jr
3924 W Taylor 67
Fort Wayne IN 46804

Call Sign: N9IWW
Kevin D Adam
1239 W Till Rd
Fort Wayne IN 46825

Call Sign: KC9JXP
Bobby R Wade
4810 W Till Rd
Fort Wayne IN 46818

Call Sign: AB9MR
Bobby R Wade
4810 W Till Rd
Fort Wayne IN 46818

Call Sign: AB9W
Bobby R Wade
4810 W Till Rd
Fort Wayne IN 46818

Call Sign: KC9JYK
Teresa G Wade
4810 W Till Rd
Fort Wayne IN 46818

Call Sign: K9TGW
Teresa G Wade
4810 W Till Rd
Fort Wayne IN 46818

Call Sign: N9VGP
Jeffrey L Stiltner
2111 W Wallen Rd
Fort Wayne IN 46818

Call Sign: KB9OS
Larry J Temenoff
4415 W Wallen Rd
Fort Wayne IN 46818

Call Sign: N9FWZ
Sandra S Temenoff
4415 W Wallen Rd
Fort Wayne IN 46818

Call Sign: N9QCK
John A Shelton
W Washington Center Rd
Fort Wayne IN 46818

Call Sign: KB9DSM
Kevin T Smith
2737 W Washington Cnt
Rd 279
Fort Wayne IN 46818

Call Sign: WA9ZPN
Terry L Crist
421 W Wildwood
Fort Wayne IN 46807

Call Sign: WA9TLC
Terry L Crist
421 W Wildwood
Fort Wayne IN 46807

Call Sign: KC9GLM
George V Williams Sr
1030 W Wildwood Ave

Call Sign: N9FGP
David W Shakley
10620 Wadsworth Ct
Fort Wayne IN 46845

Call Sign: W9EPD
James P Arnold
539 Wagner St
Fort Wayne IN
468054040

Call Sign: N9FNH
Robert L Brooks Jr
3124 Wakashan Pl
Fort Wayne IN 46815

Call Sign: WB9PUJ
Richard E Bokern
6409 Wakopa Ct
Fort Wayne IN 46815

Call Sign: AG9C
Robert D Morrison
6517 Wakopa Ct
Fort Wayne IN 46815

Call Sign: KC9IAV
Frank J Merritt
5703 Wald Rd
Fort Wayne IN 46818

Call Sign: KA9ZBA
Rebecca A Merritt
5703 Wald Rd
Fort Wayne IN 46818

Call Sign: KC9DPC
Lori J Wachtman
3418 Walden Run
Fort Wayne IN 46815

Call Sign: K9KUQ
Joseph H Vielkind

1441 Waldron Cir
Fort Wayne IN 46807

Call Sign: KB9IU
Max E Platt
5432 Wapiti Dr
Fort Wayne IN 46804

Call Sign: K9YXR
James A Chase
1311 Warren St
Fort Wayne IN
468032148

Call Sign: KB9ZQE
Charles W Humphries
1811 Watergrove Ct
Fort Wayne IN 46825

Call Sign: KB9TTW
Joel A Vilensky
8315 Waterswolde Ln
Fort Wayne IN 46825

Call Sign: K9WQI
Timothy N Thomson
3512 Waterton Cove
Fort Wayne IN 46804

Call Sign: KC9NNR
Ancil L Schilling
8608 Wave Cir Apt D
Fort Wayne IN 46825

Call Sign: KA9JSJ
John D Constant
4636 Wayne Trace
Fort Wayne IN 46806

Call Sign: W9CNU
Roy A Moore
5514 Wayne Trace
Fort Wayne IN
468062769

Call Sign: KA9FSG
Paul W Riley
8229 Wayne Trace
Fort Wayne IN
468162909

Call Sign: W9QWW
Phillip L Hyndman
2311 Wayside Dr
Fort Wayne IN 46818

Call Sign: KC9TGL
Albert Mcsweeney
12124 Wellingham Ct
Fort Wayne IN 46845

Call Sign: W9UFB
Francis E Madison
4131 Wenonah Ln
Fort Wayne IN
468091153

Call Sign: WD9ITN
Wardell Hodges
2827 Westbrook 402
Fort Wayne IN 46805

Call Sign: KB9WKH
Fergus E Moore
1117 Westerly Rd
Fort Wayne IN
468459334

Call Sign: K9GEN
Daniel G Mock
1204 Westerly Rd
Fort Wayne IN
468459755

Call Sign: KA9YYH
Phillip B Hudson Jr
6021 Westhampton Dr
Fort Wayne IN 46825

Call Sign: KD9FW

Neil H O Brien
8415 Westridge Rd
Fort Wayne IN 46825

Call Sign: KB9VTH
Mark D Ogden
8035 Wethersfield Cove
Fort Wayne IN 46835

Call Sign: K9DMA
Richard L Meyer
11527 Wexsford Dr
Fort Wayne IN 46804

Call Sign: KA9JCB
Rick I Brooks
7822 Weymouth Ct
Fort Wayne IN 46825

Call Sign: KA9JCQ
Sharon S Brooks
7822 Weymouth Ct
Fort Wayne IN 46825

Call Sign: KB9MJ
William D Livingston
7521 Wheelock Rd
Fort Wayne IN 46835

Call Sign: N9AVV
David M Disher
7628 Wheelock Rd
Fort Wayne IN 46835

Call Sign: KA9YYO
Susan S Billian
10022 White Cedar Rd
Fort Wayne IN
468045209

Call Sign: KA9ZAZ
Robert E Curts
7201 White Eagle Dr
Fort Wayne IN 46815

Call Sign: N9IWF
Mark L Vosmeier
2705 Whitegate Dr
Fort Wayne IN 46805

Call Sign: KB9IH
James D Boyer
3031 Wilderness Rd
Fort Wayne IN 46845

Call Sign: K9RFZ
Joseph D Lawrence
4624 Willard Dr
Fort Wayne IN 46815

Call Sign: KB9RFZ
Joseph D Lawrence
4624 Willard Dr
Fort Wayne IN 46815

Call Sign: N9ZKU
Janet M Maggart
1607 Willistead Pl
Fort Wayne IN 46845

Call Sign: N9BMX
Daniel L Farrer
11119 Willow Creek Dr
Fort Wayne IN 46845

Call Sign: KC9VCX
Rita L E Alvey
6107 Willow Green Dr
Fort Wayne IN 46818

Call Sign: N9ZNS
John B Gallagher
3106 Willow Oaks Dr
Fort Wayne IN 46809

Call Sign: KC8APZ
Thomas E Richards
5027 Willowbrook Dr
Fort Wayne IN 46835

Call Sign: WD9HSP
Ronald R Hall
5220 Willowwood Ct
Fort Wayne IN
468354355

Call Sign: N9XRF
Marilyn V Whitney
11012 Wilmington Ct
Fort Wayne IN 46814

Call Sign: KA9ZQN
James J Richardson
5214 Winchester Rd
Fort Wayne IN 46819

Call Sign: N9ADS
Howard R Pletcher
8704 Winchester Rd
Fort Wayne IN 46819

Call Sign: WB9YER
Allen County Amateur
Radio Emerg Club
8704 Winchester Rd
Fort Wayne IN 46819

Call Sign: WC9AAM
Allen County Amateur
Radio Emer Club
8704 Winchester Rd
Fort Wayne IN 46819

Call Sign: N9VHC
Patricia A Parisot
3709 Winding River Ct
Fort Wayne IN 46818

Call Sign: N9VGQ
Russell A Parisot
3709 Winding River Ct
Fort Wayne IN 46818

Call Sign: AA9UJ
Susan M Parisot

3709 Winding River Ct
Fort Wayne IN 46818

Call Sign: AA9QG
David M Snyder
4205 Winding Way Dr
Fort Wayne IN 46835

Call Sign: KB9KIO
Sarah K Snyder
4205 Winding Way Dr
Fort Wayne IN 46835

Call Sign: KB9RA
Lloyd D Hicks
2725 Windridge Ct
Fort Wayne IN
468451937

Call Sign: KZ9R
Thomas R Rush
10722 Windsor Woods
Blvd
Fort Wayne IN
468456127

Call Sign: N9XKT
Melissa R Fischer
906 Wingate Dr
Fort Wayne IN 46845

Call Sign: KC9ADB
Jeffrey W Lopshire
6325 Winnebago Ct
Fort Wayne IN 46815

Call Sign: K9KI
Raymond J Cronin
7225 Winnebago Dr
Fort Wayne IN 46815

Call Sign: WA8TGA
Ernest P Poole
1115 Winnsboro Pass
Fort Wayne IN 46835

Call Sign: KC9AYK
Donald V Rudy
7227 Wintergreen Dr
Fort Wayne IN 46814

Call Sign: KB9AYV
Benjamin L Grose
2507 Winters Rd
Fort Wayne IN 46809

Call Sign: N9FTK
Robert E Fiedler
5111 Wisteria Ln
Fort Wayne IN 46804

Call Sign: W9IOL
Clifford L Hardwick
7636 Wohama Dr
Fort Wayne IN 46819

Call Sign: KC9VAM
Michael L Boschet Jr
1029 Wolverton Dr
Fort Wayne IN 46825

Call Sign: AC9BE
Michael L Boschet Jr
1029 Wolverton Dr
Fort Wayne IN 46825

Call Sign: N1EET
Elizabeth E Toole
12213 Wood Glen Dr
Fort Wayne IN 46814

Call Sign: N1RU
James G Toole
12213 Wood Glen Dr
Fort Wayne IN 46814

Call Sign: KB9IRZ
Jon R Preble
5235 Wood Manor Run
Fort Wayne IN 46835

Call Sign: KB9HQF
Robert A Fiore
7224 Wood Meadows Ln
Fort Wayne IN 46835

Call Sign: KD6NT
Alan W Schmidt
2020 Wood Moor Dr
Fort Wayne IN 46804

Call Sign: KF6HIF
Jamie A Schnelker
7420 Woodbine
Fort Wayne IN 46825

Call Sign: KB9NVB
Lloyd C Patterson
15307 Woodcliffe Trl
Fort Wayne IN 46845

Call Sign: W9KPX
Robert E Snyder
7925 Woodcreek Ln
Fort Wayne IN
468158080

Call Sign: WB9EBX
Paul F Welty
4921 Woodford Dr
Fort Wayne IN
468351403

Call Sign: KE9PT
Joseph L Briggs
4946 Woodford Dr
Fort Wayne IN 46835

Call Sign: WB9RPW
Don T Bailey Jr
816 Woodland Crossing
Fort Wayne IN 46825

Call Sign: K9ODF
George L Johnson

1712 Woodland Lake
Pass
Fort Wayne IN
468257206

Call Sign: KB9UWA
Steven N Grimes
7101 Woodlyn Dr
Fort Wayne IN 46816

Call Sign: WB9ZMC
John R Seely
4602 Woodlynn Ct
Fort Wayne IN 46816

Call Sign: WA9RRZ
Lawrence D Pepple
5122 Woodmark Dr
Fort Wayne IN 46815

Call Sign: KA9YYD
Phillip S Bronicki
Woodshire Dr
Fort Wayne IN 46835

Call Sign: KC9PUR
Dennis J Redding
4622 Woodstock Dr
Fort Wayne IN 46815

Call Sign: KC9PUV
Thane L Ashcraft
4625 Woodstock Dr
Fort Wayne IN 46815

Call Sign: KC9PUW
Jennifer T Ashcraft
4625 Woodstock Dr
Fort Wayne IN 46815

Call Sign: N9LTM
Dorman K Walker
8732 Woodstream Dr
Fort Wayne IN 46804

Call Sign: AA9DU
Erik B Stirratt
8829 Woodstream Dr
Fort Wayne IN 46804

Call Sign: WB9HKO
Thomas M Schmidt
9909 Woodstream Dr
Fort Wayne IN
468047005

Call Sign: KB9DPB
Charles C Savage
2426 Woodward Ave
Fort Wayne IN 46805

Call Sign: KX9VHF
Blake A Prentice
2515 Woodward Ave
Fort Wayne IN 46305

Call Sign: KB9UHG
Blake A Prentice
2515 Woodward Ave
Fort Wayne IN 46805

Call Sign: KB9HII
Dolores C Kindred
4874 Woodway Dr
Fort Wayne IN 46835

Call Sign: WA9RAP
William E Kindred
4874 Woodway Dr
Fort Wayne IN
468353668

Call Sign: WD9DYM
Donald E Davison
7217 Wrangler Tr
Fort Wayne IN 46835

Call Sign: KD9DF
Perry K Falk
5202 Wyndemere Ct

Fort Wayne IN 46835

Call Sign: KB9VTG
Jack R Van Til
4634 Wyndemere Ln
Fort Wayne IN 46835

Call Sign: KB9HIP
Mohammed I Advany
Fort Wayne IN 46850

Call Sign: N9QYP
John A Whitney
Fort Wayne IN 46851

Call Sign: N9QYQ
Ronald J C Whitney
Fort Wayne IN 46851

Call Sign: N9VWX
Joel D Seiferman
Fort Wayne IN 46869

Call Sign: N9KST
Brock A Watters
Fort Wayne IN 46885

Call Sign: KB9HQA
Jedidiah R Watters
Fort Wayne IN 46885

Call Sign: KB9HPZ
Kevin N Watters
Fort Wayne IN 46885

Call Sign: W9INX
Allen Co Ama Rad
Technical Soc Inc
Fort Wayne IN 46806

Call Sign: KC9MOI
Larry G Casebere
Fort Wayne IN 46858

Call Sign: N9MEL

Steve M Haxby
Fort Wayne IN 46862

Call Sign: KB9OQN
David Thompson
Fort Wayne IN 46867

Call Sign: KC9MWS
Kevin M Mcconnell
Fort Wayne IN 46898

Call Sign: N9HZH
Ronald C Bishop
Fort Wayne IN
468561212

FCC Amateur Radio Licenses in Fowler

Call Sign: KB9PQC
Lisa M Stover
6927 E 100 N
Fowler IN 47944

Call Sign: KB9KLM
Mark R Stover
6927 E 100 N
Fowler IN 47944

Call Sign: KC9CDP
Ernest L Rappolt
106 E 2nd St
Fowler IN 47944

Call Sign: K9DUW
Garry A Guthridge
1037 E 400 S
Fowler IN 47944

Call Sign: KC9AFL
Elaine K Stone
1109 E 4th St
Fowler IN 47944

Call Sign: KB9FCG

David F Dorsey
203 E 5th St
Fowler IN 47944

Call Sign: KB9UPK
Jeffrey T Budreau
1576 N 200 W
Fowler IN 47944

Call Sign: KN9L
Robert T Datzman
1467 S 400 E
Fowler IN 47944

Call Sign: KB9VZE
Lon A Deno
3452 S Meridian
Fowler IN 47944

FCC Amateur Radio Licenses in Fowlerton

Call Sign: KC9HUN
Diane K Hill
219 E 2nd St Box 57
Fowlerton IN 46930

Call Sign: N9QJB
James E Thomason
201 W 2nd St
Fowlerton IN 46930

Call Sign: KS9E
Arnold E Click
Fowlerton IN 46930

FCC Amateur Radio Licenses in Fremont

Call Sign: N3YBE
Perry L Sidwell
700N
Fremont IN 46737

Call Sign: KC9QDO

Charles I Parsons
202 Charles Dr
Fremont IN 46737

Call Sign: WA9WBS
Warren J Hankes
6050 Coldwater St
Fremont IN 46737

Call Sign: KA9RVE
Barry L McDaniel
711 Cora Ln
Fremont IN 46737

Call Sign: KC9EPT
Joseph A Angel
705 E Spring St
Fremont IN 467370660

Call Sign: N9UTQ
William J Hooven
1125 Feathervalley Rd
Fremont IN 46737

Call Sign: KC8YEQ
Richard J Crist
801 Hope Dr
Fremont IN 46737

Call Sign: N9VGS
James A Bixler
578 Lake Dr Clear Lake
Fremont IN 467379559

Call Sign: W9MRE
Thomas F Wendt
891 Lake Dr Clear Lk
Fremont IN 46737

Call Sign: K9MNI
Ronald G Kane
649 Lake Dr Clearlake
Fremont IN 46737

Call Sign: KB9OR

Walter J David
575 Ln 101 Lk Pleasant
Fremont IN 46737

Call Sign: NL7GE
Lyle E Reiff II
680 Ln 301 Lake George
Rd
Fremont IN 46737

Call Sign: AA9AC
John R Boyd
15 Ln 340 B Jimmerson
Lk
Fremont IN 46737

Call Sign: KC9FWZ
Raymond J Schowe
860 Ln 340 Jimmerson
Lk
Fremont IN 46737

Call Sign: K9JKF
Nolan C Lowden
200 Ln 510D Lake James
Fremont IN 46737

Call Sign: KC9TGK
Michael D Smith
100 Ln 650A Snow Lake
Fremont IN 46737

Call Sign: KB9EZN
Paul D Motz
200 Ln 650Aa Snow
Lake
Fremont IN 46737

Call Sign: KC9LVN
Michael D Wyss
20 Ln 788 Snowlake
Fremont IN 46737

Call Sign: KB9WZ
Larry K Berndt

140 Ln 840 Snow Lake
Fremont IN 46737

Call Sign: KC9TXE
Robert B Rice Sr
4531 N 575 E
Fremont IN 46737

Call Sign: N9XPO
Dianne S Diehl
4705 N 725 E
Fremont IN 46737

Call Sign: N9LCF
Gene A Diehl
4705 N 725 E
Fremont IN 46737

Call Sign: N9CGE
Sandra J Smith
7120 N 925 E
Fremont IN 46737

Call Sign: KC9BXX
David D Diehl
301 S Reed Rd
Fremont IN 46737

Call Sign: KC9EDK
Barry A Wilcox
207 S Wayne St
Fremont IN 46737

Call Sign: KC9GDH
Melissa A Wilcox
207 S Wayne St
Fremont IN 46737

Call Sign: N9XPS
Lee B Jones
2840 W 600 N
Fremont IN 46737

Call Sign: KC9KNW
James A Swift

890 W 700 N
Fremont IN 46737

Call Sign: K9VPL
Marvin L Munger
3370 W Nevada Mills Rd
Fremont IN 46737

Call Sign: N8LUX
Paul J Limestahl
902 W Renee Dr
Fremont IN 46737

Call Sign: KB9NNR
Theresa J Limestahl
902 W Renee Dr
Fremont IN 46737

Call Sign: KC9SEN
Jimmy L James Jr
3980 W SR 120
Fremont IN 46737

Call Sign: KB9DMQ
William Bauhof
301 W Toledo St
Fremont IN 46737

Call Sign: KC9EDE
Russell L Amaden Jr
807 W Toledo St
Fremont IN 467370640

Call Sign: KB9QII
John J Holman
Fremont IN 46737

**FCC Amateur Radio
Licenses in Galveston**

Call Sign: K9HLG
Jan W Dibble
Box 162
Galveston IN 46932

Call Sign: KB9FTU
Bobbie G Foster
Box 172A
Galveston IN 46932

Call Sign: K9TF
Jan W Dibble
10690 E 1300 S
Galveston IN 46932

Call Sign: WA9TTB
Gladys N Sheetz
10891 E CR 1350 S
Galveston IN 46932

Call Sign: K9TQQ
Steven R Sheetz
10891 E CR 1350 S
Galveston IN 46932

Call Sign: W0PLA
Alvin W Wallace
11250 S 1000 E
Galveston IN 46932

Call Sign: W9IKX
Alvin W Wallace
11250 S 1000 E
Galveston IN 46932

Call Sign: AB9EA
Alvin W Wallace
11250 S 1000 E
Galveston IN 46932

Call Sign: W9IKX
Alvin W Wallace
11250 S 1000 E
Galveston IN 46932

Call Sign: N9ZMX
Julia M Haworth
13397 S 125 E
Galveston IN 46932

Call Sign: KX9F
Brian M Stavroff
9138 S 900 E
Galveston IN 46932

Call Sign: N9QPX
Christopher L Weaver
401 S California St
Galveston IN 46932

Call Sign: K9SXM
Roger L Weaver
502 S Maple St
Galveston IN 46932

Call Sign: WB9CZW
Donald L Turner
12657 S Pr 1040 E
Galveston IN 46932

Call Sign: KC9KRV
Marion L Shipley
4729 W 1300 S
Galveston IN 46932

Call Sign: N9XMD
Kim A Wallace
4587 W 1300 S
Galveston IN 46932

Call Sign: K9CFG
Ervin R Buehler
315 W Griffith St
Galveston IN 46932

Call Sign: N9LLZ
Stephen R Kitts
415 W Griffith St
Galveston IN 46932

Call Sign: WB9YVO
Jerry H Conwell
113 W Washington
Galveston IN 46932

Call Sign: KA9DLN
Brian S Sheetz
Galveston IN 46932

Call Sign: KC9ASY
James W Harris
Galveston IN 46932

Call Sign: N9WPR
Jane A Sheetz
Galveston IN 46932

Call Sign: N9RUX
Jeffrey A Packard
Galveston IN 46932

FCC Amateur Radio Licenses in Garrett

Call Sign: KC9NQS
Barbara J Harty
2048 CR 52
Garrett IN 46738

Call Sign: KC9NQT
Jeffrey R Harty
2048 CR 52
Garrett IN 46738

Call Sign: WB9UVI
Emory Heitz
1187 CR 60
Garrett IN 46738

Call Sign: N9HLH
Rae A Bean
4202 CR 7
Garrett IN 46738

Call Sign: KC9UGW
Brian J Smith
6692 CR 9A
Garrett IN 46738

Call Sign: KB9IKC

Gerald W Murphy
1301 E Quincy St
Garrett IN 46738

Call Sign: KB9IOR
Ryan J Murphy
1301 E Quincy St
Garrett IN 46738

Call Sign: K9PBR
Terry R Berkshire
309 Fairfax Ct
Garrett IN 46738

Call Sign: N9KSR
Karl W Luyben
811 Randolph St
Garrett IN 46738

Call Sign: KB9BRY
Steven M Sizelove
120 S 1st St
Garrett IN 46738

Call Sign: N9HCH
Randall K Hartman
1311 S Cowen St
Garrett IN 46738

Call Sign: KC9GVD
Joel A Rahrig
204 S Guilford St
Garrett IN 46738

Call Sign: WD9CJW
Steven E Davis Sr
415 S Guilford St
Garrett IN 46738

Call Sign: KC9VAN
Kevin E Wilkinson
808 S Ijams
Garrett IN 46738

Call Sign: W9LOW

John Freeze Jr
1311 S Lee St
Garrett IN 46738

Call Sign: KB9QG
Jeffrey K De Lucenay
919 S Peter St
Garrett IN 46738

Call Sign: KC9GEK
Terry R Berkshire
509 S Randolph St
Garrett IN 46738

Call Sign: KA9EEV
Bill Pelz
319 S Walsh
Garrett IN 46738

Call Sign: WD9IKW
William C Ort
71 Skyline Dr
Garrett IN 46738

Call Sign: WA9OTW
Henry A Greenfield
517 W Edgerton St
Garrett IN 46738

Call Sign: WB9RWE
David G Freeburn
318 W Keyser St
Garrett IN 46738

Call Sign: N9XYI
Ronald D Leland
914 W King St
Garrett IN 46738

Call Sign: KA9ZJO
Rick A Crunk
1200 W Quincy St
Garrett IN 46738

Call Sign: WG9K

John E Rostorfer
74 Westlake Dr
Garrett IN 46738

Call Sign: KB8LGW
Carolanne Davis
Garrett IN 46738

Call Sign: KA9KOH
Jack E McHenry Sr
Garrett IN 46738

FCC Amateur Radio Licenses in Gary

Call Sign: N9JRV
David C Chary
6409 Ash Ave
Gary IN 46403

Call Sign: AA9XS
David C Chary
6409 Ash Ave
Gary IN 464031912

Call Sign: KB9LZM
Thomas J Summers
350 Buchanan St
Gary IN 46402

Call Sign: KA9ISG
William G Walters
4155 Buchanan St
Gary IN 464082535

Call Sign: KC9NTD
Steve P Barath
243 Calhoun St
Gary IN 46406

Call Sign: N9BZM
Bill E Raymond
4020 Calhoun St
Gary IN 464081707

Call Sign: W9NYW
Thomas Shields
1808 Central Dr
Gary IN 46407

Call Sign: N9OIQ
Ronald E Lane Sr
337 Chase St
Gary IN 46404

Call Sign: WD9HYQ
William M Prince
5100 Chase St
Gary IN 46408

Call Sign: K9OES
Frank Editz
334 Cleveland St
Gary IN 46404

Call Sign: N9OHI
George M Modrak
4784 Cleveland St
Gary IN 46408

Call Sign: N9HFO
Charles G Pickett
4207 Colfax
Gary IN 46408

Call Sign: KC9BDI
Carlton M Biro
3828 Colonial Dr
Gary IN 46408

Call Sign: W9JSY
Quintette E McDuffie
2452 Conn St
Gary IN 46407

Call Sign: WB9TYZ
Alexander Mitic
4013 Connecticut St
Gary IN 46409

Call Sign: W9JEX
Andrew J Pruvenok
614 Durbin St
Gary IN 46406

Call Sign: WD9JJJ
James E Alexander
839 E 14th Ave
Gary IN 46407

Call Sign: KB9T
Opal L Courtney
1008 E 35th Ct
Gary IN 46409

Call Sign: K9VDO
James Bottando
4200 E 6th Pl
Gary IN 464032779

Call Sign: KB9APT
Diane E Weems
4620 E 7th Ave
Gary IN 46403

Call Sign: KA9RBO
Mark J Stern
7535 E Harold Ave
Gary IN 46403

Call Sign: KA9BCB
Patricia A Riley
2529 E Oakwood Dr
Gary IN 46406

Call Sign: KA9GKT
Henry O Sheets Jr
4220 Georgia St
Gary IN 46409

Call Sign: KC9KSW
Henry O Sheets Sr
Memorial ARC
4220 Georgia St
Gary IN 46409

Call Sign: WA9SPR
Henry O Sheets Sr
Memorial ARC
4220 Georgia St
Gary IN 46409

Call Sign: KB9OZW
Jonathan S Fisher
3009 Gerry St
Gary IN 464063356

Call Sign: KC9BXB
Ronald S Hogg
751 Grant St
Gary IN 46404

Call Sign: N9IBT
James C Treat
3004 Hanley St
Gary IN 46406

Call Sign: WD9FDD
Charlotte J Runyon
4620 Harrison
Gary IN 46408

Call Sign: WD9CTS
Gerald E Runyon
4620 Harrison
Gary IN 46408

Call Sign: N9YRU
Samuel T Woods
7117 Hemlock Ave
Gary IN 46403

Call Sign: KB9VFI
Tim J Boyle
8239 Indian Boundry
Gary IN 46403

Call Sign: WA9WNA
Reverend R McCraney
558 Jefferson Ave

Gary IN 46402

Call Sign: WB9WZN
William P Braswell
3648 Madison St
Gary IN 46408

Call Sign: W9QB
William P Braswell
3648 Madison St
Gary IN 46408

Call Sign: W9IYB
Leon Crass
3831 Marshall Pl
Gary IN 46408

Call Sign: KB9NWM
Ronald J Bruno
408 Marshall St
Gary IN 46404

Call Sign: KB9QZK
Judith Bruno
408 Marshall St
Gary IN 464041058

Call Sign: KB9RRK
Ladonna H Lewis
410 Marshall St
Gary IN 46404

Call Sign: KB9RRG
Daryl A Lewis
410 Marshall St
Gary IN 464041058

Call Sign: KB9REP
Gabriel J Lewis
410 Marshall St
Gary IN 464041058

Call Sign: KB9RRF
John A Lewis
410 Marshall St

Gary IN 464041058

Gary IN 464041058

Gary IN 46408

Call Sign: KB9RYP
Samuel D Lewis
410 Marshall St
Gary IN 464041058

Call Sign: KG9LY
Ronald J Bruno Jr
456 Marshall St
Gary IN 464041058

Call Sign: N9OWJ
Norman W Walton
3700 Roosevelt St
Gary IN 46408

Call Sign: KB9REQ
Dontae J Dennis
433 Marshall St
Gary IN 464041035

Call Sign: KG9MH
Ronald J Bruno III
456 Marshall St
Gary IN 464041058

Call Sign: KB9PQX
Cary W Hmurovic
3940 Ross Rd
Gary IN 46408

Call Sign: KB9RRH
Jeremy M Slatton
435 Marshall St
Gary IN 46404

Call Sign: KB9SEG
Sarah L Bruno
456 Marshall St
Gary IN 464041058

Call Sign: KB9QCZ
Kimberly I Hmurovic
3940 Ross Rd
Gary IN 46408

Call Sign: KB9RVV
Shawn T Doston
435 Marshall St
Gary IN 464041057

Call Sign: N9EWC
George W Stowell
4863 Maryland Pl
Gary IN 46409

Call Sign: KC9JQN
Roy E Gillis
435 Rutledge St
Gary IN 46404

Call Sign: KC9BSI
Judah T Bruno
456 Marshall St
Gary IN 46404

Call Sign: KC9HMZ
Mark A Balog
264 N Lake St
Gary IN 464031963

Call Sign: N9WEN
Karen J Basham
3600 Tompkins Ct
Gary IN 46408

Call Sign: KB9RHO
Jeffrey S Bruno
456 Marshall St
Gary IN 464041058

Call Sign: KB9CTC
Dorothy G Harvey
1066 N Vermillion St
Gary IN 46403

Call Sign: W9TY
William E De Geer
3601 Tyler St
Gary IN 46408

Call Sign: KB9RER
Joshua D Bruno
456 Marshall St
Gary IN 464041058

Call Sign: W9RQG
Victor H Voss
4112 Oak Ln
Gary IN 46408

Call Sign: N9ZDG
Robert M Olszanski
1001 Vanderburg
Gary IN 46403

Call Sign: KB9RVX
Pamela S Bruno
456 Marshall St
Gary IN 464041058

Call Sign: KC9HVF
Benjamin H Davis
360 Roosevelt St
Gary IN 46404

Call Sign: K9KIQ
John A Banks
4011 Vermont
Gary IN 46409

Call Sign: KB9SEF
Pauline H Dennis
456 Marshall St

Call Sign: KB9HPF
Norman W Walton
3700 Roosevelt St

Call Sign: KA5MRI
Joe W McCarty
7237 W 21st Ave

Gary IN 46406

Call Sign: N9DJB
Lionel Spears
4052 W 22 Ave
Gary IN 46404

Call Sign: W9LIO
Lionel Spears
4052 W 22 Ave
Gary IN 46404

Call Sign: KA9SQJ
David H Price
5820 W 25th Ave
Gary IN 46406

Call Sign: KA9SVV
David J Valentine
1634 W 39th Ct
Gary IN 46408

Call Sign: KA9VMP
Robin D Atchley
4025 W 41st Ave
Gary IN 46408

Call Sign: KD9X
Richard L Brown
234 W 46 Ave
Gary IN 46408

Call Sign: KA9CTT
Edward A Rice
2813 W 47th Ave
Gary IN 464084109

Call Sign: KC9USJ
Chris W Cowley
4315 W 47th Ave
Gary IN 46408

Call Sign: KB9FHN
Benjamin H Davis
2306 W 5th Ave

Gary IN 46404

Call Sign: KB9MCD
Drake L Cheatham
5724 W 6th Ave
Gary IN 46406

Call Sign: KB9DJW
Sarah B Wingfield
5732 W 7th Ave
Gary IN 46406

Call Sign: KB9JAK
Clarence J Wolfe
4520 W Ridge Rd Lot
201
Gary IN 46408

Call Sign: KC9HJS
Maurice C Stanley
2319 Wabash Ave
Gary IN 46404

Call Sign: KB9TEQ
Eddie V Harvey
1148 Waite St
Gary IN 46404

Call Sign: KC9SIZ
Christopher G De Bie
3961 Wallace Pkwy
Gary IN 46408

Call Sign: KA9USR
Vernard L Green Sr
1328 Whitcomb
Gary IN 46404

Call Sign: KB9CCT
Richard S Grey II
2021 Williams St
Gary IN 46404

Call Sign: KB9QBN
Latanza R Kemp

1736 Wilson St
Gary IN 46404

Call Sign: N9TGK
Lawrence Hutton
Gary IN 46401

Call Sign: N9MLL
Michael J Comsa
Gary IN 46403

FCC Amateur Radio Licenses in Gas City

Call Sign: K9LDV
Merle W Schmidt
500 Ash Ln
Gas City IN 469331520

Call Sign: KA9VEW
Angie K Walters
617 Beach Dr
Gas City IN 46933

Call Sign: WD9IHJ
Albert E Eckstein
504 Chestnut Dr
Gas City IN 46933

Call Sign: KB9CRA
Kevin M McNeely
716 Chestnut Dr
Gas City IN 469331249

Call Sign: N9LPO
Margaret A Mcneely
716 Chestnut Dr
Gas City IN 469331249

Call Sign: W9EBN
Grant County ARC
716 Chestnut Dr
Gas City IN 469331249

Call Sign: W9POX

William A Koontz
334 E Main St
Gas City IN 46933

Call Sign: WD9FVM
Phil M Adrianson
601 E N A St
Gas City IN 46933

Call Sign: W9PMA
Phil M Adrianson
601 E N A St
Gas City IN 46933

Call Sign: KF9PK
Gilbert C Topliff
608 E N A St
Gas City IN 46933

Call Sign: KA9FAF
Diane C Topliff
608 E N A St
Gas City IN 46933

Call Sign: KB9OMB
Robert G McHarry
121 E N B St
Gas City IN 46933

Call Sign: KC9RIT
Shad A Barkdull
214 E N B St
Gas City IN 46933

Call Sign: WA9SHG
Robert E Hutcheson
603 E N B St
Gas City IN 46933

Call Sign: KB4KUZ
Fred E Reitz
218 E N H St
Gas City IN 46933

Call Sign: KC9DOF

Charles W Ellis
724 E N H St
Gas City IN 46933

Call Sign: KB9YEN
Bryan M Mcwhirt
725 E S D St
Gas City IN 46933

Call Sign: KB9UOU
Richard L Francis
105 Locust Dr
Gas City IN 469331134

Call Sign: W9UOU
Richard L Francis
105 Locust Dr
Gas City IN 469331134

Call Sign: K9PQM
John L Keeling
958 N 10th
Gas City IN 46933

Call Sign: WD8CVT
Wallace T Greene
972 N 10th St
Gas City IN 46933

Call Sign: KA9TBM
Jerry L Everhart
724 N Grant St
Gas City IN 46933

Call Sign: KA9YFS
Sheryl A Everhart
724 N Grant St
Gas City IN 46933

Call Sign: WB9WIU
Larry W Bryant
813 Rockshire Ct
Gas City IN 46933

Call Sign: N9OCE

Terry D Davis
5155 S 700 E
Gas City IN 46933

Call Sign: KB9YKT
Craig L Couch
965 Virgil Dr
Gas City IN 46933

Call Sign: KC9EQW
Frank L Butterworth III
Gas City IN 46933

Call Sign: KB9MCV
Jerry L Horner
Gas City IN 46933

Call Sign: N9SCV
Robert E Antrim Jr
Gas City IN 46933

Call Sign: KC9GHD
Suzan H Butterworth
Gas City IN 46989

FCC Amateur Radio Licenses in Geneva

Call Sign: N9LSU
Nolan E Liechty
Box 40L
Geneva IN 46740

Call Sign: KA9YFE
Scott D Steenburg
Box 6B
Geneva IN 46740

Call Sign: KC5TLM
Carla D Steury
3496 E 900 S
Geneva IN 46740

Call Sign: WA9ABI
Raymond K Milligan

205 E Pyle St
Geneva IN 467400083

Call Sign: KB9MVK
John M Butcher
11020 S 150 E
Geneva IN 467409289

Call Sign: KB9SCA
Jerry W Armstrong
11505 S 150E
Geneva IN 46740

Call Sign: KB9SBZ
Nancy Armstrong
11505 S 150E
Geneva IN 46740

Call Sign: AA9KI
Harold E Nelson
10961 S 300 W
Geneva IN 46740

Call Sign: KA9YFD
Paul D Steenburg
9454 S US Hwy 27
Geneva IN 46740

Call Sign: KC9QGR
Kevin D Nussbaum
944 W 950 S
Geneva IN 46740

Call Sign: AB9KN
Kevin D Nussbaum
944 W 950 S
Geneva IN 46740

Call Sign: KB9UYI
Ruth Miller
310 Washington St
Geneva IN 46740

Call Sign: KB9ZHE
Donald F Snow

570 Winchester Rd
Geneva IN 46740

FCC Amateur Radio Licenses in Glen Park

Call Sign: N9TDJ
Alphonso P Shaw
3730 Johnson St
Glen Park IN 46408

FCC Amateur Radio Licenses in Goodland

Call Sign: K9RUD
Robert G Smith
318 N Benton St
Goodland IN 47948

Call Sign: N9MQL
Louis R Sainte
Goodland IN 47948

FCC Amateur Radio Licenses in Goshen

Call Sign: AG4YI
Edward E Slater
621 Amberwood Dr
Goshen IN 46526

Call Sign: AI9J
Edward E Slater
621 Amberwood Dr
Goshen IN 465265529

Call Sign: KC8ICY
Walter G Ryder
20713 Antler Ct
Goshen IN 46528

Call Sign: N9MFV
Karen A Stutzman
57334 Arabian Dr
Goshen IN 46526

Call Sign: WD9GXY
James I Stembel
57343 Arabian Dr
Goshen IN 46526

Call Sign: KC9RDO
Stan Kolesnitchenko
57425 Arabian Dr
Goshen IN 46528

Call Sign: KB9GFG
William K Warner
2405 Berkey Ave
Goshen IN 46526

Call Sign: N5LMN
Kristie J Scott
17698 Bramblewood
Goshen IN 46526

Call Sign: WA9FTP
Donald D Rhude
2113 Cambridge Dr
Goshen IN 46526

Call Sign: KC9CUC
Donald L Stringfellow
1237 Camden Ct
Goshen IN 465266453

Call Sign: K9DLS
Donald L Stringfellow
1237 Camden Ct
Goshen IN 465266453

Call Sign: KC9UMS
William C Stucky
208 Carter Rd
Goshen IN 46526

Call Sign: KC9QPB
Andrew S Ahlersmeyer
1320 Cedar Brook Ct Apt
G

Goshen IN 46526

Call Sign: N3UZS
Timothy D Wagner
1325 Cedarbrook Ct Apt D
Goshen IN 46526

Call Sign: N9IWB
Duff Middleton
66192 Chamfers Ln
Goshen IN 46526

Call Sign: W6MQE
Esther L Huhta
22750 Chestnut Ln
Goshen IN 46528

Call Sign: W8GXB
L Wayne Huhta
22750 Chestnut Ln
Goshen IN 46528

Call Sign: N9PZO
Thomas D Holtzinger
1002 College Ave
Goshen IN 46526

Call Sign: N9NDX
Richard J Putz
2400 College Ave
Goshen IN 46526

Call Sign: WA9AQZ
Orton S Kauffman
2605 College Ave
Goshen IN 465285013

Call Sign: N9IOV
Donna J White
2400 College Ave
Carriage Manor Rm 224
Goshen IN 46528

Call Sign: KC9MQP

Dohn Cunningham
405 Colorado Dr
Goshen IN 46526

Call Sign: KC9DOC
Mark D Pettifor
62270 Country Rd 11
Goshen IN 46526

Call Sign: KB9ORC
Donald A Pettifor
62458 CR 11
Goshen IN 46526

Call Sign: KC9DOD
David W Pittifer
62458 CR 11
Goshen IN 46562

Call Sign: WB9QLA
Richard L Putz
57305 CR 117
Goshen IN 46526

Call Sign: KA9RIY
Douglas A Moore
22512 CR 118
Goshen IN 46526

Call Sign: KA9RIZ
Edwin C Moore
22512 CR 118
Goshen IN 46526

Call Sign: KA8MMX
David E Geiman
61528 CR 13
Goshen IN 46526

Call Sign: N9LZC
Amos D Yontz
16087 CR 138 R 4
Goshen IN 46526

Call Sign: KC9SIG

Matthew S Lievore
17821 CR 14
Goshen IN 46528

Call Sign: WD9HIU
Clair S Hoover
61323 CR 15
Goshen IN 46526

Call Sign: K9DHC
Arthur R Tait
57207 CR 17
Goshen IN 46528

Call Sign: KA9PPL
John R Vrydaghs
20659 CR 18
Goshen IN 46526

Call Sign: KC9NYI
James L Leichty
57869 CR 18
Goshen IN 46528

Call Sign: KB9RVY
Danny D Hanna
20456 CR 19
Goshen IN 46528

Call Sign: KF9IC
Taras Sawchuk
60050 CR 19
Goshen IN 46528

Call Sign: KB9KGB
Dale E Moore
60730 CR 19
Goshen IN 46528

Call Sign: KC9GSE
Brad J Hooley
15700 CR 20
Goshen IN 46528

Call Sign: N9XYU

Maxwell S Dehaven
18135 CR 20
Goshen IN 46526

Call Sign: WB9TEN
David T Menges
18890 CR 20
Goshen IN 46528

Call Sign: KC9ONC
Jaime R Yoder
59100 CR 21
Goshen IN 46528

Call Sign: KD4JTB
Philip W Miller
60182 CR 21
Goshen IN 46528

Call Sign: N9SBB
Franklin K Oyer
64409 CR 21
Goshen IN 46526

Call Sign: WA9WOO
John E Harris
21335 CR 26
Goshen IN 465289098

Call Sign: KB9KGC
Darrell E Moore
57765 CR 27
Goshen IN 46528

Call Sign: N9HZ
Robert B Zook
23772 CR 30
Goshen IN 46527

Call Sign: KB9OKJ
Burton L Showalter
66761 CR 31
Goshen IN 46526

Call Sign: KB9AVS

Stephen O Arnold
68059 CR 31
Goshen IN 46526

Call Sign: KC9UMP
Jenson J Long
63726 CR 33
Goshen IN 46528

Call Sign: KB9OPS
Charlotte R Long
63726 CR 33
Goshen IN 46528

Call Sign: KB9MLE
David H Long
63726 CR 33
Goshen IN 46528

Call Sign: KA9ERQ
Richard L Dubbs
22659 CR 36
Goshen IN 46526

Call Sign: W9XD
Dennis A Drudge
27901 CR 36
Goshen IN 46526

Call Sign: KC9PNN
Timothy S Yoder
62815 CR 37
Goshen IN 46528

Call Sign: KA9VVP
Brian E Maust
12743 CR 38
Goshen IN 46526

Call Sign: W9DOT
Brent A Graybill
22381 CR 38
Goshen IN 46526

Call Sign: KB9QOT

Terry L Ernsberger
15655 CR 40
Goshen IN 46526

Call Sign: W9JOE
Sanford C
Swartzendruber
16722 CR 40
Goshen IN 46526

Call Sign: KA9SRZ
Philip C Swartzendruber
16722 CR 40
Goshen IN 46526

Call Sign: K9WJU
Goshen ARC
16722 CR 40
Goshen IN 46526

Call Sign: N9YOD
John V Baer
17063 CR 40
Goshen IN 46526

Call Sign: WB9LUJ
Kenneth C Ames
18009 CR 40
Goshen IN 46526

Call Sign: KA9RTH
Gary L Kaufman
21150 CR 40
Goshen IN 46526

Call Sign: KC9BQD
Steven G Eddy
64542 CR 43
Goshen IN 46528

Call Sign: KC5BFK
Jerry D Hapner
15461 CR 44
Goshen IN 465289323

Call Sign: KC5ZAY
Sofia C Hapner
15461 CR 44
Goshen IN 465289323

Call Sign: KC9FZV
Earl Hapner
15491 CR 44
Goshen IN 46528

Call Sign: N9GNU
Rita C Plough
21993 CR 45
Goshen IN 46526

Call Sign: KB9QOS
Richard C Hurlbert
61108 CR Lot 114
Goshen IN 46526

Call Sign: KB9USX
Melvin E Troyer
122.5 Crescent St
Goshen IN 46528

Call Sign: KB9OYN
Russell E Byerly
17565 Cross Rd
Goshen IN 46526

Call Sign: KC9LXP
Beth A Housour
58399 Debra Dr
Goshen IN 46528

Call Sign: W9BAD
Beth A Housour
58399 Debra Dr
Goshen IN 46528

Call Sign: KC9FZT
Rod A Housour
58399 Debra Dr
Goshen IN 46528

Call Sign: W9RAM
Rod A Housour
58399 Debra Dr
Goshen IN 46528

Call Sign: KB9GKT
Clark E Schweitzer
1513 Dogwood Ct
Goshen IN 46526

Call Sign: KC9TCI
Doug Pettifor
18091 Dundee Ct
Goshen IN 46528

Call Sign: K9YEO
Herman J Hartzler
1318 E Douglas St
Goshen IN 46528

Call Sign: KE9OJ
Elmer J Bowers
309 E Kercher Rd
Goshen IN 465265319

Call Sign: KB9WHK
Larry C Koskie
410 E Plymouth Ave
Goshen IN 46526

Call Sign: KC9FZU
Carl Thompson
716 E Reynolds St
Goshen IN 46526

Call Sign: K9IAP
Gene F Haberstich
907 E Reynolds St
Goshen IN 46526

Call Sign: KC9IHP
Daniel R Wakefield
1213 E Reynolds St
Goshen IN 46528

Call Sign: KD7MSN
Kimber Beachy
520 E Washington St
Goshen IN 46528

Call Sign: KC9TQ
John A Sawatsky
19691 Edgewaters Dr
Goshen IN 46526

Call Sign: KA9LWT
Albert J Meyer
708 Emerson St
Goshen IN 465263904

Call Sign: KA9LWU
Mary E Meyer
708 Emerson St
Goshen IN 465263904

Call Sign: KC9BQB
Vladimir Stefanov
66035 Evergreen Dr
Goshen IN 46526

Call Sign: KB9LMG
Gerald L Reeder
2713 Evergreen Ln
Goshen IN 46526

Call Sign: N9DUZ
James M Kehr
18 Fairfield Park
Goshen IN 46526

Call Sign: KC9CDS
Roger W Mertz
328 Fairview Dr
Goshen IN 46528

Call Sign: WB7OTR
Steven R Holmgren
915 Galen Ct
Goshen IN 46526

Call Sign: N9RED
Caroll S Stottlemyer
1511 Garland Dr
Goshen IN 46526

Call Sign: W9ENG
Richard L Putz
19523 Gentle Stream Cir
Goshen IN 465286281

Call Sign: KB9PUB
Daniel J Slabach Jr
918 Georgia
Goshen IN 46526

Call Sign: KC9BQC
Kevin R Mohney
224 Gorham Rd
Goshen IN 46528

Call Sign: N9RIB
Suzanne M Huffman
417 Gra Roy Dr
Goshen IN 46526

Call Sign: KB9ECI
Thane A Huffman
417 Gra Roy Dr
Goshen IN 46526

Call Sign: KB9NRF
Esther L Kawira
611 Gra Roy Dr
Goshen IN 46526

Call Sign: KC9NYG
John Morehouse
1801 Greencroft Blvd
Goshen IN 46526

Call Sign: W0NCQ
Jacob M Buzzard
1801 Greencroft Blvd
228
Goshen IN 46526

Call Sign: N8DLY
Garfield H Thompson
1801 Greencroft Blvd
411
Goshen IN 46526

Call Sign: N9KKR
Howard W Trumbull
1801 Greencroft Blvd
Apt 142
Goshen IN 46526

Call Sign: N9FJZ
Benjamin F Byler
1422 Greencroft Dr
Goshen IN 46526

Call Sign: WA9LJI
Dorothy I Pruitt
1425 Greencroft Dr 212
Goshen IN 46526

Call Sign: KB9KFX
Kent L Hartman
1413 Harvest Dr
Goshen IN 46526

Call Sign: KB9VPM
Frederick W Scribner Jr
1523 Harvest Dr
Goshen IN 46526

Call Sign: KC9MIB
David A Zollinger
201 Hawthorne Dr
Goshen IN 46526

Call Sign: W9DAZ
David A Zollinger
201 Hawthorne Dr
Goshen IN 46526

Call Sign: KB9VPO
Leo J Akins

1205 Hickory St
Goshen IN 46526

Call Sign: N9OTH
Graham S Pearson
57405 Horseshoe Ct
Goshen IN 46528

Call Sign: N9SIY
Nathan A Cripe
57265 Horseshoe Ct
Goshen IN 46528

Call Sign: KB9OZ
Gary T Fields
57009 Hummingbird Ct
Goshen IN 46526

Call Sign: N9HSO
James M Crabille
1922 Lynwood Dr
Goshen IN 465261134

Call Sign: WA9LBC
Floyd L Rheinheimer
109 Mallard Ln
Goshen IN 46526

Call Sign: K9UHI
G Weldon Troyer
3201 Mallard Ln
Goshen IN 465266196

Call Sign: KA9SYE
John H Allyn
3209 Mallard Ln
Goshen IN 46526

Call Sign: KC9TPI
Goshen ARC
3209 Mallard Ln
Goshen IN 46526

Call Sign: KF9BU
Philip W Miller

401 Marilyn Ave
Goshen IN 46526

Call Sign: N7GVD
George C Vasbinder
2607 Martin Manor Dr
Goshen IN 46526

Call Sign: N9KLX
Darrell W Burch
22198 Mohawk Dr
Goshen IN 46526

Call Sign: KC9ADA
Darrell W Burch
22198 Mohawk Dr
Goshen IN 46526

Call Sign: K9YRB
Clifford H Sharp
22927 Mulberry Ct
Goshen IN 46528

Call Sign: N9KJS
David L Willig
526 N 6th St
Goshen IN 46528

Call Sign: N9TRF
Terry J Haney
917 N 6th St
Goshen IN 46526

Call Sign: KC9STF
Gary W Condict
101 N 8th St
Goshen IN 46526

Call Sign: N9QEY
David W Phebus
503 N Chicago Ave Apt
A
Goshen IN 465282315

Call Sign: KC9OE

Young E Snodgrass
919 N Green Rd
Goshen IN 465261122

Call Sign: W9YWF
Norman J Harner
706 N Greene Rd
Goshen IN 46526

Call Sign: KA9NNZ
Marion Yoder
105 N Wheatland Dr
Goshen IN 465261622

Call Sign: KD6YEV
Gregory G Van Fossen
59342 Old CR 17
Goshen IN 46528

Call Sign: KB9USZ
Karilyn J Kilmer
20033 Opal Ct
Goshen IN 46528

Call Sign: N0PHI
Kevin J Kilmer
20033 Opal Ct
Goshen IN 46528

Call Sign: KB9SDU
Ronald J Burton
64925 Orchard Dr
Goshen IN 465269117

Call Sign: KA9SRY
Calvin F Swartzendruber
415 Park Ct
Goshen IN 465288843

Call Sign: KC9IRO
Randall S Perry
1925 Park W Dr
Goshen IN 46526

Call Sign: W9BHX

Henry D Weaver Jr
1332 Pebble Ct
Goshen IN 46528

Call Sign: KC9MIE
Frasney A Dumka
66148 Prairie View Dr
Goshen IN 46526

Call Sign: K9VTN
Paul E Beck
625 Pringle Dr
Goshen IN 465261348

Call Sign: KB9UXC
Brian Messier
606 Revere Dr Apt B
Goshen IN 46526

Call Sign: N9LZB
Donald L Metzler
59638 Ridgewood
Goshen IN 46526

Call Sign: KC9HAH
Stuart J Meade
312 River Vista Dr
Goshen IN 46526

Call Sign: KC9PW
Richard D Rose
19937 Rosetta Dr
Goshen IN 46526

Call Sign: N2UDV
Alan J Shea
141 Roxbury Park
Goshen IN 46526

Call Sign: KB9BIF
Charlie M Short
1609 S 10th St
Goshen IN 46526

Call Sign: KC9BPL

Maple City Amateur
Repeater Society
1609 S 10th St
Goshen IN 46526

Call Sign: KC9DUP
Josh M Hunton
1120 S 11th St
Goshen IN 46526

Call Sign: AB9A
Ralph O Yoder
815 S 12th St
Goshen IN 465264459

Call Sign: WB9THE
A Raymond Mann
915 S 12th St
Goshen IN 46526

Call Sign: KB9NTY
Cheryl L Cripe
916 S 15th St
Goshen IN 46526

Call Sign: N9SPI
Tim E Cripe
916 S 15th St
Goshen IN 46526

Call Sign: KD9TF
Richard A Stern
1108 S 16th St
Goshen IN 46526

Call Sign: KB9WHI
Kenneth E Horst
1303 S 16th St
Goshen IN 46526

Call Sign: N9WKU
Kevin S Miller
1015 S 16th St Apt B
Goshen IN 46526

Call Sign: KB9RUB
William D Lower
215 S 27th St
Goshen IN 46528

Call Sign: NV7R
Robert J Ryan
620 S 3rd St
Goshen IN 46526

Call Sign: KC9JSH
John M Looney
806 S 3rd St
Goshen IN 46526

Call Sign: KB9CWV
Joel N Hathaway
410 S 6th St
Goshen IN 46526

Call Sign: KB9CWW
Max W Hathaway
410 S 6th St
Goshen IN 46526

Call Sign: W9CG
Ronald D Yoder
513 S 6th St
Goshen IN 46526

Call Sign: K9WPV
Larry R Yoder
805 S 7th St
Goshen IN 465264016

Call Sign: N9RAJ
Darin R Batten
323 S 8th St Apt 1
Goshen IN 465283428

Call Sign: N9VUO
Aaron L Kreider
1700 S Main St
Goshen IN 46526

Call Sign: WA9NJU
Goshen College ARC
1700 S Main St
Goshen IN 46526

Call Sign: N9VML
Steven D Jarvis
1703 S Main St
Goshen IN 46526

Call Sign: AA9DG
David W Evans
2308 S Main St
Goshen IN 46526

Call Sign: KC9MAG
Ivan J Conrad
307 S Riverside Blvd
Goshen IN 46526

Call Sign: N9ZZX
Donald R Stevens
57047 Sequoia Dr
Goshen IN 46526

Call Sign: KC9LLZ
Allan C Currier
22331 SR 119
Goshen IN 46526

Call Sign: KB9MOH
Kellie A Edwards Smith
58143 Steiner Dr
Goshen IN 46528

Call Sign: KB9WHL
Cynthia L Charles
58550 Sun Bow Dr
Goshen IN 46528

Call Sign: KB9BBI
Edward B Charles
58550 Sun Bow Dr
Goshen IN 465287754

Call Sign: WB2L
Robert C Moore
1908 Sweetbriar Dr
Goshen IN 46526

Call Sign: KC9STE
William L Bainter Jr
1522 Sycamore Ct
Goshen IN 46526

Call Sign: KC5BAV
Daniel L Wiley
207 Tanglewood Dr Apt
A
Goshen IN 465261715

Call Sign: N9UDH
David J Whitehead
1123 Tramore Cir
Goshen IN 46526

Call Sign: N9XVF
Kimberly A Whitehead
1123 Tramore Cir
Goshen IN 46526

Call Sign: KB9ASF
Thurl D Stiver
67939 US 33
Goshen IN 46526

Call Sign: KC9NYC
Jeannie A Pennington
1910 W Clinton St
Goshen IN 46526

Call Sign: KC9NYD
Michael N Pennington
1910 W Clinton St
Goshen IN 46526

Call Sign: N9XVD
Francis J Coyne
607 W Kplymouth Ave
Goshen IN 46526

Call Sign: KD9UQ
George C Trenshaw
1407 W Lincoln Ave
Goshen IN 46526

Call Sign: K9TSM
Goshen ARC
1407 W Lincoln Ave
Goshen IN 46526

Call Sign: WD9AKG
Myron D Yoder
601.5 W Pike St
Goshen IN 465262334

Call Sign: N9KFQ
Paul H Buller
410 Waneta Dr
Goshen IN 46526

Call Sign: N9LZA
Darl K Stump
1401 West Ave
Goshen IN 46526

Call Sign: K9PYF
Dean F Brubaker
1504 West Ave
Goshen IN 46526

Call Sign: N9IUS
Steven J Yoder
15 Winchester Trl
Goshen IN 46526

Call Sign: KB9MKD
Paul F Koepke
1319 Winsted Dr
Goshen IN 46526

Call Sign: N9VKQ
Arden K Ball
1802 Woodgate Dr
Goshen IN 465266455

Call Sign: KC9CZD
Mark A Kurtz
105 Woodlawn Dr
Goshen IN 465265435

Call Sign: K9MAK
Mark A Kurtz
105 Woodlawn Dr
Goshen IN 465265435

Call Sign: W9BIF
Maple City Amateur
Repeater Society
Goshen IN 46527

Call Sign: W5DHM
David H Martin
Goshen IN 465270278

Call Sign: K9HYU
Jonathan H Hoke
Goshen IN 465270534

Call Sign: K9BIF
Charlie M Short
Goshen IN 465270554

**FCC Amateur Radio
Licenses in Grabill**

Call Sign: KB9KKI
Edward L De Bolt
15824 Bayview Blvd
Grabill IN 46741

Call Sign: WA1URA
Frank N Moore
16025 Bayview Blvd
Grabill IN 46741

Call Sign: KB9JUP
Ted J Wells
12824 Country Shoal Ln
Grabill IN 46741

Call Sign: N9BNB
Barry J Coe
12827 Country Shoal Ln
Grabill IN 46741

Call Sign: W9CLZ
David Bertsch
11520 Grabill Rd
Grabill IN 46741

Call Sign: KD8PF
Paul L Bailey
12430 Grabill Rd
Grabill IN 46741

Call Sign: WD9HFN
Mark A Downing
14701 Hurshtown Rd
Grabill IN 467419617

Call Sign: WD9EWS
Ronald D Cleven
12305 Schwartz Rd
Grabill IN 46741

Call Sign: WB9YFL
Jim Schweickart
13319 Schwartz Rd
Grabill IN 46741

Call Sign: K9LI
Donald L Glick
9503 Sienna Springs Dr
Grabill IN 46741

Call Sign: KA9ZQO
Eric J Savio
13913 Surrey Trace
Grabill IN 46741

FCC Amateur Radio Licenses in Granger

Call Sign: KB9KLL

James E Haugh
11845 Adams Rd
Granger IN 46530

Call Sign: KB9KGA
Michael J Haugh
11845 Adams Rd
Granger IN 46530

Call Sign: KI9C
Paul J Leeser
51262 Amesburry Way
Granger IN 46530

Call Sign: N9ZVG
Joshua L Wiggins
10122 Anderson Rd
Granger IN 46530

Call Sign: KB9ZOA
Eric W Grashorn
51205 Ashley Dr
Granger IN 46530

Call Sign: KC9RPP
Joseph H Bishop
53593 Ashwood Dr
Granger IN 46530

Call Sign: KC9ERP
Daniel J Sams
52140 Barrington Pl
Granger IN 46530

Call Sign: KB9MSY
Charles L Konopinski
17244 Barryknoll Way
Granger IN 46530

Call Sign: KC9PJX
Michael J Anglin
52058 Bellflower Ln
Granger IN 46530

Call Sign: KF9PY

Dennis P Berg
16100 Branchwood Ln
Granger IN 46530

Call Sign: KA9LXN
Ronald W Logsdon
13619 Brick Rd
Granger IN 46530

Call Sign: N9LWC
James R Fowler
50766 Buckboard Tr
Granger IN 46530

Call Sign: KC9CLO
Jonathan C Dosmann
50607 Cherry Rd
Granger IN 46530

Call Sign: KC9PKB
Jacob R Dylewski
50627 Cherry Rd
Granger IN 46530

Call Sign: KB8CIE
Richard E Whiteman
51611 Cherry Rd
Granger IN 465308632

Call Sign: KC9PF
Frank A Maples
51988 Cheryl Dr
Granger IN 46530

Call Sign: N9DCJ
Joseph L Torzewski
51625 Chestnut Rd
Granger IN 46530

Call Sign: KC9PJY
Eugene A Dylewski
51945 Chestnut Rd
Granger IN 46530

Call Sign: KC9PKY

Tom E Kelsey
13988 Cleveland Rd
Granger IN 46530

Call Sign: N9SPQ
Betty A Gray
15431 Cleveland Rd
Granger IN 46530

Call Sign: ND2U
Michael J Chapple
15651 Cold Spring Ct
Granger IN 46530

Call Sign: WM9A
Ronald L Flick
51950 Copperfield Ct
Granger IN 46530

Call Sign: N9IBA
Vickie L Flick
51950 Coppperfield Ct
Granger IN 46530

Call Sign: KC9LXQ
Taylor A Frend
10039 Donald Ln
Granger IN 46530

Call Sign: N9PSW
Marilyn A Gray
15401 E Cleveland Rd
Granger IN 46530

Call Sign: N9MRZ
Robert B Gray
15401 E Cleveland Rd
Granger IN 46530

Call Sign: KB9QOH
David A Harsanyi
52122 Farmington Sq Dr
Granger IN 46530

Call Sign: AB9X

Steven N Ginn
50770 Fawn Dale Ct
Granger IN 46530

Call Sign: KC9OYP
Catherine J Brown
12460 Frontier Ct
Granger IN 465308970

Call Sign: KC9PJS
Brian C Kempa
51930 Gentian Ln
Granger IN 46530

Call Sign: N9ZSY
Jason A Ciastko
16650 Gerald St
Granger IN 46530

Call Sign: N9IIA
John R Hriczo
50655 Glen Meadow Ln
Granger IN 46530

Call Sign: N9HN
Thomas M Overman
13919 Hearthside Dr
Granger IN 465304960

Call Sign: KD9IJ
Louis B Macakanja
51906 Hedge Ln
Granger IN 46530

Call Sign: N9FIK
Michael R Rosenberg
52020 Iron Forge Ln
Granger IN 465306414

Call Sign: N9YB
Michael R Rosenberg
52020 Iron Forge Ln
Granger IN 465306414

Call Sign: KC9NAJ

Nicholas J Laneman
51585 James Lawrence
Pkwy
Granger IN 46530

Call Sign: N9WPI
Stephen L Eslinger
12281 Lariat Ln
Granger IN 46530

Call Sign: KB9NWV
Michael T Heider
52391 Liberty Mills Ct
Granger IN 46530

Call Sign: KC8MGQ
Matthew S Wolf
30880 Lincoln Dr
Granger IN 46530

Call Sign: W9RXU
Melvyn A Silver
50778 Lincroft Ln
Granger IN 46530

Call Sign: WQ8A
James E Wilson
50601 Little John Ln
Granger IN 46530

Call Sign: KC9IXW
Ryan M Toth
50610 Little John Ln
Granger IN 46530

Call Sign: KB9NII
Scott B Watson
52117 Mallard Pt Dr
Granger IN 46530

Call Sign: AA9ZC
Scott B Watson
52117 Mallard Pt Dr
Granger IN 46530

Call Sign: N9TJG
Richard D Nimtz Jr
15285 Monterosa Dr
Granger IN 46530

Call Sign: N9YHI
Mary A Nimtz
15285 Monterosa Dr
Granger IN 46530

Call Sign: KC9SBW
Sally P Norton
10628 N Pheasant Cove
Granger IN 46530

Call Sign: KB8IR
Randall L Shaull
10928 Nottinghamshire
Dr
Granger IN 46530

Call Sign: KG9QF
Randall L Shaull
10928 Nottinghamshire
Dr
Granger IN 46530

Call Sign: W8NBP
Randall L Shaull
10928 Nottinghamshire
Dr
Granger IN 46530

Call Sign: KF4ZHL
Kenneth M Froehlke
51138 Old Cottage Dr
Granger IN 46530

Call Sign: WA9YUL
Roderick C Abbott Jr
12310 Painted Ridge Trl
Granger IN 46530

Call Sign: KB9ZRW
Anne L Lanvin

50900 Park Ln
Granger IN 46530

Call Sign: KB9ZVI
Ivan P Lebrun
50900 Park Ln
Granger IN 46530

Call Sign: KC9DZL
Thomas A Closurdo Jr
14296 Park Ridge Dr
Granger IN 46530

Call Sign: KC9QYE
Robert W Collins
10492 Patricia Church Dr
Granger IN 46530

Call Sign: N9AFO
Patrick B Campbell
51114 Pheasant Run Dr
Granger IN 46530

Call Sign: KC9SIH
Alexander P Norton
10628 Phesant Cove
Granger IN 46530

Call Sign: N9KXR
John A Verduin
10801 Pine Cone Ct
Granger IN 46530

Call Sign: KC9AUP
John P Schroeder Jr
50500 Prestonwood Ct
Granger IN 465304963

Call Sign: KB9YGO
Michael R Hardy
50785 Prtrdige Woods Dr
Granger IN 46530

Call Sign: KC9MTK
Paul S Morse

12222 Saddle Horn Ct
Granger IN 46530

Call Sign: KC9CLP
Drew G Olson
10255 Shadow Wood Ct
Granger IN 46530

Call Sign: KB9STV
Keith M Gligorich
10111 Shadow Wood Dr
Granger IN 46530

Call Sign: KB9STU
Martin W Tschida
15480 Siena Ct
Granger IN 46530

Call Sign: W9NXH
Myrtle T Jamieson
13838 SR 23
Granger IN 46530

Call Sign: KB9MVN
Douglas R Pettifor
50721 SR 23
Granger IN 46530

Call Sign: KC9GTL
Aaron A Koszyk
51555 Steeple Chase Ct
Granger IN 46530

Call Sign: WB9YPJ
Stephen A Koszyk
51555 Steeple Chase Ct
Granger IN 46530

Call Sign: KA9BJT
Jeffrey W Miller
14709 Stonington Ct
Granger IN 46530

Call Sign: KB9RVZ
Michael W Lueneburg

15151 Stransbury Ct
Granger IN 46530

Call Sign: WD9FJP
Timothy W Bath
10155 Terri Brook Cir
Granger IN 46530

Call Sign: N9OIZ
James R Snyder
52811 Timberland Dr
Granger IN 46530

Call Sign: WD9GYJ
Payton T Garnand
52811 Timberland Dr
Granger IN 46530

Call Sign: WB9HRU
David M Brown
52897 Timberland Dr
Granger IN 46530

Call Sign: N9QWL
Shane L Borders
51520 Timberline Trace
W
Granger IN 46530

Call Sign: KC9FIO
Matthew T Wolff
5525 Town Center Dr 5
Granger IN 46530

Call Sign: KD0LND
Matthew D Bell
5630 Town Center Dr
Apt 5
Granger IN 46530

Call Sign: KC9GTP
Brenda J Trumble
16745 Trenton Ct
Granger IN 46530

Call Sign: KC9MHW
Dean L Strycker
51758 Wexford Dr
Granger IN 46530

Call Sign: WA9OYL
H David Collins
16361 Wild Cherry Dr
Granger IN 465308544

Call Sign: KC9SDS
Thomas M Williams
15609 Windfield Ln
Granger IN 46530

Call Sign: KC9MTM
John D St Pierre
51100 Woodcliff Ct
Granger IN 46530

Call Sign: KC9MTO
Andrew M St Pierre
51100 Woodcliff Ct
Granger IN 46530

Call Sign: KC9MTN
Daniel A St Pierre
51100 Woodcliff Ct
Granger IN 46530

Call Sign: N9ONB
Brian E Heimbaugh
13694 Woods Trl
Granger IN 46530

Call Sign: N8EYO
Joyce L Alpiner
16690 Yorktown Rd
Granger IN 46530

Call Sign: N9IZZ
Gary L Reese
Granger IN 46530

FCC Amateur Radio Licenses in Greentown

Call Sign: KB9IQI
Dustin G Karns
50S
Greentown IN 46936

Call Sign: N9AQY
William T Kerby
Box 150
Greentown IN 46936

Call Sign: KC9UIX
Michael A Gillogly
6912 Cassell Dr
Greentown IN 46936

Call Sign: KB9MDZ
Mark A Kady
11961 E 100 S
Greentown IN 46936

Call Sign: KB9QXN
Robert A Maines
8585 E 180 S
Greentown IN 46936

Call Sign: N9DGJ
Erskine H Carter Jr
9116 E 200 S
Greentown IN 46936

Call Sign: W9ENE
Omer R Brown
11653 E 300 S
Greentown IN 46936

Call Sign: W9GWU
Anthony M Marsh
12313 E 300 S
Greentown IN 469369761

Call Sign: N9JXX
Kevin J Hawes

6766 E 50 N
Greentown IN 46936

Call Sign: WD9CQV
Daryll G Heath
950 E 52 S
Greentown IN 46936

Call Sign: N9TQY
Barry T Childs
850 E 647 S
Greentown IN 46936

Call Sign: KA9KXN
Michael A Giles
505 E Hall St
Greentown IN 46936

Call Sign: KC9MY
Robert A Giles
505 E Hall St
Greentown IN 46936

Call Sign: KB9IQE
Sheila R Estes
627 E Hall St
Greentown IN 46936

Call Sign: KC9GHE
Jeffrey C Bennett
624 E Main
Greentown IN 46936

Call Sign: N9BHT
Jack D Alexander
9983 E Oon S
Greentown IN 46936

Call Sign: KB9SEA
Garry N Hill
1021 Eastcrest Dr
Greentown IN 469361612

Call Sign: KC9CTY
James L Silver

135 Holiday Dr
Greentown IN 46936

Call Sign: N9RPH
Thomas R Silver
313 Holiday Dr
Greentown IN 46936

Call Sign: KB9RYN
Michael T Silver
313 Holiday Dr
Greentown IN 469361632

Call Sign: K9AYD
Russell W Pogue
603 Knoll Wood Ln
Greentown IN 469369617

Call Sign: N9EVD
Mark A Pollard
321 Meadows Dr
Greentown IN 46936

Call Sign: N9LRO
Ronald L Julius
607 Meadows Dr
Greentown IN 46936

Call Sign: KC9DHJ
John R Mullett
3353 N 1000 E
Greentown IN 46936

Call Sign: KB9REW
Gregory S Peterson Sr
1783 N 1100 E
Greentown IN 46936

Call Sign: AB9I
Gregory S Peterson Sr
1783 N 1100 E
Greentown IN 46936

Call Sign: KB9SAE
Mary L Peterson

1783 N 1100 E
Greentown IN 46936

Call Sign: KB9SAF
Gregory S Peterson Jr
1783 N 1100 E
Greentown IN 469369606

Call Sign: N9JOG
Sharon A Eikenberry
1487 N 1250 E
Greentown IN 46936

Call Sign: KB9IQD
Philip W Bogue
2789 N 850 E
Greentown IN 46936

Call Sign: W9IJ
Thomas V Cornell
3631 N 900 E
Greentown IN 469368837

Call Sign: K9LHB
Kevin T Cornell
3631 N 900 E Rd
Greentown IN 46936

Call Sign: N9ZEZ
Jordan J Buckley
824 N 950 E
Greentown IN 46936

Call Sign: KA9VRJ
Sam K Coate
228 N Carter St
Greentown IN 469361009

Call Sign: N9QGM
Bonnie S Coate
228 N Carter St
Greentown IN 469361009

Call Sign: N9JOV
Roger L Kring

1487 N CR 1250 E
Greentown IN 46936

Call Sign: KG4IEQ
Justin R Johnson
318 N Green St
Greentown IN 469361125

Call Sign: ND9A
Michael K Leazenby
612 N Meridian St
Greentown IN 46936

Call Sign: KC9QPN
Robert J Timme
2143 S 1000 E
Greentown IN 46936

Call Sign: W9TNY
Robert J Timme
2143 S 1000 E
Greentown IN 46936

Call Sign: KA9CPU
Sherry L Van Matre
1572 S 1038E
Greentown IN 46936

Call Sign: W9XX
Gordon P Howlett
2448 S 1050 E
Greentown IN 46936

Call Sign: KC9IXY
Wayne A Sozansky
2161 S 1250 E
Greentown IN 46936

Call Sign: N9HYK
Jerry P Loomis
53 S 700 E
Greentown IN 46936

Call Sign: N9NKV
Charles E Childs

647 S 850 E
Greentown IN 46936

Call Sign: KB9SEB
Shawna I Werst
4705 S 900 E
Greentown IN 46936

Call Sign: N9YJT
Tommy C Werst
4705 S 900 E
Greentown IN 46936

Call Sign: WA9FKA
Larry E Foust
28 S 950 E
Greentown IN 46936

Call Sign: N9SCX
Aaron M Barnard
603 S Harvey Dr
Greentown IN 46936

Call Sign: N9ZFA
Stephen L Combs
630 S Maple Ave
Greentown IN 46936

Call Sign: KB9IIM
Michael D Elftman
6743 Stone Ct
Greentown IN 46936

Call Sign: KB9SBN
Brent A Tobin
647 Stone Dr
Greentown IN 46936

Call Sign: KD9EN
George M Gaskill
580 Villa Manor Ct
Greentown IN 46936

Call Sign: KB9PKA
Audrey L Pawlak

8406 Villa Manor Dr
Greentown IN 46936

Call Sign: N9ZUY
Steve J Pawlak
8406 Villa Manor Dr
Greentown IN 46936

Call Sign: KC9HWD
Michael R Baker
403 W Grant St
Greentown IN 46936

Call Sign: KB9OX
Wayne A Powell
212 W Main St
Greentown IN 46936

Call Sign: N9UKQ
Dawn M Shupperd
128 W Main St
Greentown IN 46936

Call Sign: N9UKN
Eric S Shupperd
128 W Main St
Greentown IN 46936

Call Sign: KB9UWD
Joel Matthews
208 W Walnut St
Greentown IN 46936

Call Sign: KC9HFY
Samuel N Roberts
Greentown IN 46936

**FCC Amateur Radio
Licenses in Griffith**

Call Sign: KA9WDF
Henry B Schendera
812 E 40th Pl
Griffith IN 46319

Call Sign: N9DTG
Lucille M Schendera
812 E 40th Pl
Griffith IN 463191745

Call Sign: WA9VWN
Richard A Lovin
617 E Ash St
Griffith IN 46319

Call Sign: KA9MXG
Kimberly M Griffin
2016 E Elm St
Griffith IN 46319

Call Sign: WZ9E
Mary S Luetschwager
1624 E Main
Griffith IN 46319

Call Sign: N9CXR
Venessa M Wagner
1549 E Main St
Griffith IN 46319

Call Sign: N9HGM
Charles D Aldrin
829 E Woodside Dr
Griffith IN 463192007

Call Sign: N9TXM
Joshua J Hines
1549 Main St
Griffith IN 46319

Call Sign: KE9FZ
Joseph T Butcher
429 Manchester Ct
Griffith IN 46319

Call Sign: KA9EWZ
Bonnie R Olar
818 N Arbogast Ave
Griffith IN 46319

Call Sign: KA9EWY
Louis G Olar
818 N Arbogast Ave
Griffith IN 46319

Call Sign: WA9CZU
Walter S Woods
2017 N Arbogast Ave
Griffith IN 46319

Call Sign: KA9WPB
Harry Hanson Sr
207 N Arbogast St
Griffith IN 46319

Call Sign: KC9AYZ
Eugene A Metcalf
756 N Arbogast St
Griffith IN 46319

Call Sign: N9DLI
Michael J Chiaro
814 N Broad
Griffith IN 46319

Call Sign: KB9GIK
Craig R Burgans
339 N Dwiggins
Griffith IN 46319

Call Sign: KC9QOG
Marc A Bonomini
730 N Elmer St
Griffith IN 46319

Call Sign: WA9CXQ
Harold W Clark
825 N Glenwood St Apt
2L
Griffith IN 46319

Call Sign: W9BOR
Harold W Clark
825 N Glenwood St Apt
2L

Griffith IN 46319

Call Sign: N9JXS
Brian E Malik
1213 N Indiana Apt 3A
Griffith IN 46319

Call Sign: KB9UOZ
Michael D Schutter
815 N Indiana St
Griffith IN 46319

Call Sign: WA9JLN
Robert G Lamprecht
1325 N Indiana St
Griffith IN 46319

Call Sign: W9UM
Nicholas G Cominos
402 N Indiana St
Griffith IN 46319

Call Sign: KC9MQG
Darrell Gottschammer
825 N Lafayette
Griffith IN 46319

Call Sign: WD9FOS
Frederick J Loomis Sr
1931 N Lafayette
Griffith IN 46319

Call Sign: KC9GYG
Gary R Clark
546 N Lillian St
Griffith IN 46319

Call Sign: N9EZE
Joseph A Lubrant
1020 N Oakwood
Griffith IN 46319

Call Sign: KC9HCO
David D Kepple
717 N Raymond Ave

Griffith IN 46319

Call Sign: KA9FDC
Walter S Kozol
624 N Rensselaer St
Griffith IN 46319

Call Sign: WA9WCH
Jon O Grasch
806 N Wheeler
Griffith IN 46319

Call Sign: KC9VJV
Ahui G Herrera
735 N Wiggs Ave
Griffith IN 46319

Call Sign: K9TAW
Ahui G Herrera
735 N Wiggs Ave
Griffith IN 46319

Call Sign: WA9UZR
James M Hennes
517 Oxford Cir
Griffith IN 46319

Call Sign: WA9GXZ
Warren G Shulz
847 S Indiana Ave
Griffith IN 46319

Call Sign: KB9WIN
Eugene P Keown
111 W Glenpark Ave
Griffith IN 46319

Call Sign: KC9WH
Robert L Wyatt Jr
319 W Main St
Griffith IN 46319

Call Sign: KC9OMG
Paul D Valentas
1047 Wheeler Ave

Griffith IN 46319

Call Sign: N9NES
Joann F Boulles
706 Wren Ct
Griffith IN 46319

Call Sign: W9GAB
George A Boulles
706 Wren Ct
Griffith IN 463193753

Call Sign: N9GX
George A Boulles
706 Wren Ct
Griffith IN 463193753

Call Sign: WN9SA
George A Boulles
706 Wren Ct
Griffith IN 463193753

FCC Amateur Radio Licenses in Grovertown

Call Sign: KB9YMK
Bob J Grimble
1025E
Grovertown IN 46531

Call Sign: N9VXO
Dwayne L Brashere
950E
Grovertown IN 46531

Call Sign: KB9GRR
Stuart H Short Jr
Box 198
Grovertown IN 46531

Call Sign: KC9UKX
Daniel D Craft
11302 E 150 N
Grovertown IN 46531

Call Sign: W9LEW
Lewis W Tuttle
3315 N 1100 E
Grovertown IN 46531

Call Sign: KA9WLM
Norman L Brashere
3275 N 950 E
Grovertown IN 46531

Call Sign: KC9PLZ
Sharon K Genis
Grovertown IN 46531

FCC Amateur Radio Licenses in Hamilton

Call Sign: N9XPP
Stacy W Hagerty
4265 Bellefontaine Rd
Hamilton IN 467429635

Call Sign: N9XPQ
Kelly J Hagerty
103 Center Ct
Hamilton IN 467420084

Call Sign: KB9MYV
Ronald A Greenfield
892 CR 53
Hamilton IN 46742

Call Sign: KC9RHZ
Jimmy Eric F James
1002 CR 61
Hamilton IN 46742

Call Sign: WB9ENB
William N Peckhart
5415 E 700 S
Hamilton IN 46742

Call Sign: KC8UBC
William J Cance
5455 E 775 S

Hamilton IN 46742

Call Sign: KB9TXL
Lucy L La Hurreau
3885 E Beecher St
Hamilton IN 46742

Call Sign: KB9SYM
Howard A Lahurreau
3885 E Beecher St
Hamilton IN 467420337

Call Sign: KC9TUQ
Frederick C Walker
5290 S 300 E
Hamilton IN 46742

Call Sign: KA9OJB
Robert C Parker
2030 S 475 E
Hamilton IN 46742

Call Sign: KA9RNY
Sandra K Parker
2030 S 475 E
Hamilton IN 46742

Call Sign: KC9EED
Daniel L Mcmillan
7340 S 575 E
Hamilton IN 46742

Call Sign: KB7QHU
Raymond J Jones
3135 S 800 E
Hamilton IN 46742

Call Sign: KC9MOB
Raymond J Jones
3135 S 800 E
Hamilton IN 46742

Call Sign: N9VXR
Henry R Lewis Jr
3135 S 800 E

Hamilton IN 46742

Call Sign: K9FZG
Thomas A Laffey
3215 S CR 800 E
Hamilton IN 467429215

Call Sign: N9XPR
Wayne E Hagerty
Hamilton IN 46742

FCC Amateur Radio Licenses in Hamlet

Call Sign: KB9INO
Larry D Fritz
5335 E 500 N
Hamlet IN 46532

Call Sign: KC9JRX
David L Fretz
607 E Oak St
Hamlet IN 46532

Call Sign: KC9GEU
Steven M Poloncak
501 N Maple St
Hamlet IN 46532

Call Sign: N0DXP
Robb K French
9053 S 125 E
Hamlet IN 465329640

Call Sign: KC9IOP
Hugh M Vales
8384 S 300 E
Hamlet IN 46532

Call Sign: WO0P
Hugh M Vales
8384 S 300 E
Hamlet IN 46532

Call Sign: KC9KNB

Steven W Hause
10635 S US Hwy 35
Hamlet IN 46532

Call Sign: N9HXV
John B Genis
Hamlet IN 46532

Call Sign: KA5MLZ
Kenneth S Folse
Hamlet IN 465320072

FCC Amateur Radio Licenses in Hammond

Call Sign: W9VIZ
John A Delegan
1131 167th St
Hammond IN 463241605

Call Sign: WB9HVU
John E Gutknecht
736 169th St
Hammond IN 46324

Call Sign: W9PUC
Purdue Calumet ARS
2200 169th St
Hammond IN 46323

Call Sign: KC9JHS
Adrienne Gadling
3544 170 Pl
Hammond IN 46324

Call Sign: N9IKQ
Joseph T Dancho
842 170th St
Hammond IN 46324

Call Sign: WB9ZFK
Howard V Marion
2645 170th St
Hammond IN 463232105

Call Sign: N9ZJM
Robert L Massey
1517 174 St
Hammond IN 46324

Call Sign: KB9PHE
Joseph J Sinde
830 175 St
Hammond IN 46324

Call Sign: KB9ZB
Walter M Sackett
175th
Hammond IN 46324

Call Sign: KB9ESK
Jeff T Polczynski
1669 175th St
Hammond IN 46324

Call Sign: K9GYM
Louis J Novak
426 176th Ct
Hammond IN 46324

Call Sign: W9RXB
John Kicho
3316 176th Pl
Hammond IN 46323

Call Sign: KB9NSB
Thomas J Sexton
3834 176th Pl
Hammond IN 463233004

Call Sign: KF9BT
Joseph G Phares
823 176th St
Hammond IN 46324

Call Sign: KA9YKV
Larry W White
1560 177th St
Hammond IN 46324

Call Sign: KB9AMS
Robert A Clark
3505 43rd St
Hammond IN 463223134

Call Sign: N9ZDO
Robert A Hill
3727 43rd St
Hammond IN 46322

Call Sign: WD9HYE
Arnold C Nemcek
7345 Alabama Ave
Hammond IN 46323

Call Sign: N9XUH
Carl N Larkin
6120 Alexander
Hammond IN 46323

Call Sign: KC9GMO
Sean M Cantrell
6924 Alexander
Hammond IN 46326

Call Sign: N9RIZ
Michael D Hendricks
6123 Alexander Ave
Hammond IN 46323

Call Sign: KB9LEP
Shawn W McDaniel
6132 Alexander Ave
Hammond IN 46323

Call Sign: W9HPD
Shawn W McDaniel
6132 Alexander Ave
Hammond IN 46323

Call Sign: K9EEN
Anthony J Sahulcik Sr
6918 Alexander Ave
Hammond IN 46323

Call Sign: WB9WFT
Robert T Miller
7346 Alexander Ave
Hammond IN 46323

Call Sign: KC9PLX
Grasiela Reyna
6940 Arizona Ave
Hammond IN 46323

Call Sign: N4NKK
James Brill
4844 Ash Ave
Hammond IN 46327

Call Sign: N9DLR
Frank N Kotlarz
4417 Baltimore Ave
Hammond IN 46327

Call Sign: KA9PPW
Frank N Kotlarz Jr
4417 Baltimore St
Hammond IN 46327

Call Sign: N9EHS
Judy Kotlarz
4417 Baltimore St
Hammond IN 46327

Call Sign: K9GSV
Charles J Hanusin
7020 Baring Ave
Hammond IN 463242204

Call Sign: KB9DVJ
Samuel Jackson
908 Bauer St
Hammond IN 46320

Call Sign: KB9FAU
Betty J Harris
916 Becker St
Hammond IN 46320

Call Sign: KB9FAT
Leroy F Harris
916 Becker St
Hammond IN 46320

Call Sign: N9JFQ
Paul W Szymkowski
7948 Belmont
Hammond IN 46324

Call Sign: WD9FMS
Gregory L Zonca
7617 Bertram
Hammond IN 46324

Call Sign: K9NKP
William D De Long
7606 Bertram Ave
Hammond IN 463243136

Call Sign: W9ZWY
Theodore J Mysliwiec
7030 Birch Ave
Hammond IN 46324

Call Sign: KA9QJG
Donald L Crozier Sr
7824 Birch Dr
Hammond IN 46324

Call Sign: KC9ATX
David A Terpstra
6238 California Ave
Hammond IN 463231125

Call Sign: W9BUM
Francis E Buxton
6248 California Ave
Hammond IN 46323

Call Sign: KB9ALM
Joy E Thierer
7211 Calumet Ave 222
Hammond IN 46324

Call Sign: WD9HZA
Reuben W Schluntz Jr
7701 Catalpa Ave
Hammond IN 46324

Call Sign: KB9IDH
David P Nowaczyk
4904 Cedar Ave
Hammond IN 46327

Call Sign: KC9BXC
Erik D Hill
4846 Chestnut
Hammond IN 463271709

Call Sign: N9EDH
Erik D Hill
4846 Chestnut
Hammond IN 463271709

Call Sign: KB9JSR
Jamie O Oller
7605 Chestnut Ave
Hammond IN 46324

Call Sign: N9ZUM
Adel A Haddad
725 Chicago Ave 100
Hammond IN 46327

Call Sign: KB9GSY
Ayman J Azar
4421 Clark Ave
Hammond IN 46327

Call Sign: KC9CAR
Frank J Gil
7426 Cline Ave
Hammond IN 46323

Call Sign: N9UFG
Barbara J Loeffler
3123 Crane Pl
Hammond IN 46323

Call Sign: N9NAE
Donald R Loeffler
3123 Crane Pl
Hammond IN 46323

Call Sign: KC9ICM
Miguel Morales
908 E Wilcox St
Hammond IN 46320

Call Sign: KB9HQZ
John Contreras
4831 Elm Ave
Hammond IN 46327

Call Sign: KA9VRN
James C McCarty
3223 Farmer Dr
Hammond IN 46322

Call Sign: KA9DGX
Michael A Warot
532 Florence St
Hammond IN 46324

Call Sign: W9TQT
Corliss A Beck
6340 Forest Ave
Hammond IN 46324

Call Sign: W9BUN
Thomas L Rutherford
6721 Forestdale Ave
Hammond IN 46323

Call Sign: WD9HYG
Harold M Boswinkle
2949 Franklin
Hammond IN 46322

Call Sign: KB9KXL
Peter R Wayne
6234 Garfield Ave
Hammond IN 46324

Call Sign: KB9ESL
Justin F Morey
6316 Garfield Ave
Hammond IN 46324

Call Sign: N9ZNX
Maury J Kleinman
7545 Golfway
Hammond IN 463243144

Call Sign: KB9HEK
April M Ybarra
550 Gostlin St
Hammond IN 46327

Call Sign: N9ZDH
Roque Ybarra III
550 Gostlin St
Hammond IN 46327

Call Sign: W9UVR
George R Hanson
4032 Henry Ave
Hammond IN 46327

Call Sign: KC9IP
Kenneth R Hines Jr
4322 Hickory Ave
Hammond IN 46327

Call Sign: WA9PZY
Joseph S Bolsega
4822 Hickory Ave
Hammond IN 46327

Call Sign: W9KH
Kenneth R Hines
4322 Hickory St
Hammond IN 46327

Call Sign: N9CSO
Mary L Hines
4322 Hickory St
Hammond IN 46327

Call Sign: W9PDN
Peter D Novak Sr
3738 Higgins Park S St
Hammond IN 46323

Call Sign: N9MJW
Carl D Cluck Sr
505 Highland St
Hammond IN 46320

Call Sign: N4GIX
William L Leaming
511 Hoffman St
Hammond IN 46327

Call Sign: N9PCW
Trinidad Hernandez
1150 Hoffman St
Hammond IN 46327

Call Sign: N9HZJ
Eugenia R Callais
5946 Hohman 314
Hammond IN 46320

Call Sign: KB9DVH
David E Ellis
5946 Hohman Ave
Hammond IN 46320

Call Sign: N9ZUL
Rodney A Clark
6805 Huron St
Hammond IN 46323

Call Sign: KC9DHE
Paul W Lane
7050 Idaho Ave
Hammond IN 46323

Call Sign: KE9ZI
Herbert E Greene
6743 Idaho St
Hammond IN 46323

Call Sign: N9GEM
Arthur L Jones
7141 Jefferson Ave
Hammond IN 46324

Call Sign: KC9MTW
Robert W Brooks Jr
7519 Jefferson Ave
Hammond IN 46324

Call Sign: N9KBP
Nate R Mahns
4234 Johnson Ave
Hammond IN 46327

Call Sign: KA9VRP
David Cudzilo
6705 Kentucky Ave
Hammond IN 46323

Call Sign: KB9WIO
Phillip S Merritt
2707 Kenwood St
Hammond IN 46323

Call Sign: KB9DHC
Steve E Vockell
6927 Knickerbocker
Hammond IN 46323

Call Sign: KB9GDJ
John R Evak
6711 Leland Ave
Hammond IN 46323

Call Sign: AB9EL
John R Evak
6711 Leland Ave
Hammond IN 46323

Call Sign: KB9DGF
Keith J Pieniazek
506 Locust
Hammond IN 46324

Call Sign: KB9NYX
Joseph A Svoboda Jr
634 Locust St
Hammond IN 46324

Call Sign: KC9MQI
Steven P Szczepanski
535 Logan Dr Apt 205
Hammond IN 46320

Call Sign: KB9DVE
Frederick F Heth
965 Logan St
Hammond IN 46320

Call Sign: N9ZUN
Jeffrey A Gladish
7611 Madison Ave
Hammond IN 46324

Call Sign: KC9CMS
Michael E Clark
6731 Magoun Ave
Hammond IN 46324

Call Sign: W9DDK
Michael E Clark
6731 Magoun Ave
Hammond IN 46324

Call Sign: KB9HEH
Shay P O Hearn
7123 Maplewood
Hammond IN 46324

Call Sign: KA9PCE
Harry F Larimer Sr
7537 Maplewood Ave
Hammond IN 46324

Call Sign: KB9DVG
Thaddeus H Janowski Jr
7125 Marshall Ave
Hammond IN 46323

Call Sign: KC9BDK
Charles T Lewis
7539 Marshall Ave
Hammond IN 46323

Call Sign: N9RII
Thomas L Rutherford
6519 McCook
Hammond IN 46323

Call Sign: KB9HYR
John W Sheridan
7218 McCook
Hammond IN 46323

Call Sign: KA9YEI
Melissa A Wozniak
7226 McLaughlin Ave
Hammond IN 46324

Call Sign: N9MWI
Yvonne M Bockel
6525 Monroe Ave
Hammond IN 46324

Call Sign: KA9DUG
Albert A Res
7617 Monroe St
Hammond IN 46324

Call Sign: KB9DGW
Kellie A Myers
6230 Moraine Ave
Hammond IN 46324

Call Sign: KC9CHR
Eric J Foust
6403 Nebraska Ave
Hammond IN 46323

Call Sign: KC9CHS
Mark R Foust
6403 Nebraska Ave
Hammond IN 46323

Call Sign: KA9IGW
Larry D Patterson
6419 Nebraska Ave
Hammond IN 46323

Call Sign: KB9MUZ
Donald E Harney
6327 Nevada Ave
Hammond IN 46323

Call Sign: W9PVQ
John A Theodore
6843 New Jersey
Hammond IN 46323

Call Sign: KB9PWS
Michael A Frangello
4839 Oak Ave
Hammond IN 46327

Call Sign: KB9MCA
Timothy J Reidelbach
234 Oakwood
Hammond IN 46324

Call Sign: KT9OC
Garrett E Moseley
7044 Olcott Ave
Hammond IN 463232040

Call Sign: WG9M
Garrett E Moseley
7044 Olcott Ave
Hammond IN 463232040

Call Sign: KC9HCN
Steven E Alexander
6732 Osborn Ave
Hammond IN 463231403

Call Sign: W9SEA
Steven E Alexander
6732 Osborne Ave
Hammond IN 463231403

Call Sign: KB9LHN
Alex B Gayer
7345 Parrish Ave
Hammond IN 46323

Call Sign: KB9KND
Guy L Gayer
7345 Parrish Ave
Hammond IN 463232305

Call Sign: KA9YSQ
Stuart M Sinisi
8729 Parrish Ave
Hammond IN 46322

Call Sign: KC9QYD
Milton J Skorupa
6941 Rhode Island
Hammond IN 46323

Call Sign: KB9FAP
Jerome Oberc
6423 Rhode Island Ave
Hammond IN 46323

Call Sign: KB9HEP
Angie M Farris
6817 Ridgeland Ave
Hammond IN 46324

Call Sign: WB9ENZ
Richard D Linsenmann
6904 Ridgeland Ave
Hammond IN 46324

Call Sign: WB9WWD
Larry C Moss
1001 River Dr
Hammond IN 46324

Call Sign: N9KFS
Terrance K Mehler
1113 Roosevelt St
Hammond IN 463201341

Call Sign: N9DRD
Stephen Buvala
5946 S Hohman Ave 103
Hammond IN 463202563

Call Sign: W9ZRO
Bryan C Majoch
4044 S Wabash Ave
Hammond IN 46327

Call Sign: KB9DGG
Joseph M Flores
6738 Schneider
Hammond IN 46323

Call Sign: KA9CFG
Bill F Sheahan
7015 Schneider
Hammond IN 46323

Call Sign: NV9C
Mary H Sheahan
7015 Schneider
Hammond IN 46323

Call Sign: KA9BKL
William F Sheahan
7015 Schneider
Hammond IN 46323

Call Sign: KA9LKI
Lowell L Crom
7133 Schneider Ave
Hammond IN 46323

Call Sign: KB9DGH
Eric M Osborne
719 Sibley St
Hammond IN 46320

Call Sign: KB9PQ
Robert McCarty
7605 Southeastern
Hammond IN 46324

Call Sign: KB9YUN
Julie Evak
7242 Southeastern Ave
Hammond IN 46324

Call Sign: KC9LUG
Wade S Downing
1112 State St
Hammond IN 46320

Call Sign: KC9IIJ
Kevin D Hamming
7203 Tilly Dr
Hammond IN 46324

Call Sign: K9HYW
Frank J Sowa
3946 Torrence Ave
Hammond IN 46327

Call Sign: KB9DHB
Brian J Long
4135 Torrence Ave
Hammond IN 46327

Call Sign: KB9PEQ
Noelia Ramirez
4630 Torrence Ave
Hammond IN 46327

Call Sign: KB9PER
Noel Ramirez
4630 Torrence Ave
Hammond IN 46327

Call Sign: KA9QDQ
Virginia L Eagle
6634 Van Buren
Hammond IN 46324

Call Sign: KB9HIF
Acy W Wartsbaugh II
6434 Van Buren Ave
Hammond IN 46324

Call Sign: KB9ESM
Greg J Williams
7124 Van Buren Ave
Hammond IN 46324

Call Sign: KB9JKS
Chris W Gootee
7532 Van Buren Ave
Hammond IN 46324

Call Sign: KB9EEZ
Rachel A La Velle
3618 Vine St Apt 1D
Hammond IN 46323

Call Sign: WB9KYJ
Walter C Youngs
3922 Wabash Ave
Hammond IN 463271103

Call Sign: KB9IOB
David W Templeton
7626 Walnut Ave
Hammond IN 46324

Call Sign: KB9IDG
Amanda Wolfe
4 Warren St
Hammond IN 46320

Call Sign: KB9DHG
Darin Rosellini
7950 White Oak Ln
Hammond IN 46324

Call Sign: KB9YHK
John M Hawthorne
901 Wilcox
Hammond IN 46320

Call Sign: KB9FIA
Heather E Hanning
50 Wildwood Rd
Hammond IN 46324

Call Sign: KB9ONR
Ryan G Reeder
50 Williams St
Hammond IN 46320

Call Sign: KC9SQC
Delores M Vitullo
718 Willow Ct
Hammond IN 46320

Call Sign: N9KLE
Shawn S Fleming
7023 Woodlawn
Hammond IN 46324

Call Sign: KD9VH
Sherrell D Poole
7450 Woodmar Ave
Hammond IN 46323

Call Sign: AA9XN
Sherrell D Poole
7450 Woodmar Ave
Hammond IN 46323

Call Sign: WP4FYB
Pedro Ortiz
Hammond IN 46223

Call Sign: K9DBX
Edward Barus
Hammond IN 46325

Call Sign: KC9CMR
Paula A Stone
Hammond IN 46323

Call Sign: N9IVL
David A Klingensmith
Hammond IN 46324

Call Sign: N9GSR
Michael A Thierer
Hammond IN 46324

Call Sign: K9DL
James R Hohenberger
Hammond IN 463250952

FCC Amateur Radio Licenses in Hanna

Call Sign: AE9T
Charles J Galbreath
1200S
Hanna IN 46340

Call Sign: KC9JMY
Zacc E Sweet
12998 S 450 W
Hanna IN 46340

Call Sign: N9YMK
Deanna L Vandiver
14588 S 550 W
Hanna IN 46340

Call Sign: W4DLV
Deanna L Vandiver
14588 S 550 W
Hanna IN 46340

Call Sign: W4SV
Stanley L Vandiver
14588 S 550 W
Hanna IN 46340

Call Sign: KC9PNQ
Qcwa Chapter 36
14588 S 550 W
Hanna IN 46340

Call Sign: KC9PTV
Qcwa Chapter 36
14588 S 550 W
Hanna IN 46340

Call Sign: W9EGQ
Qcwa Chapter 36
14588 S 550 W

Hanna IN 46340

Call Sign: K9QCW
Qcwa Chapter 36
14588 S 550 W
Hanna IN 46340

Call Sign: N9AWA
Thaddeus W Gorski
12345 SR 39
Hanna IN 46340

FCC Amateur Radio Licenses in Harlan

Call Sign: KI4MGE
Charles W Lane
26326.5 N County Line
Rd E
Harlan IN 46743

Call Sign: KI4MGF
Terri Jo Lane
26326.5 N County Line
Rd E
Harlan IN 46743

Call Sign: W9BUZ
Lawrence D Eager
16211 Scipio Rd
Harlan IN 46743

Call Sign: KB9NRB
Ray W Bender
Harlan IN 46743

FCC Amateur Radio Licenses in Hartford City

Call Sign: KB9KFH
Darryl P Hannon
3141 E 200 S
Hartford City IN 47348

Call Sign: KC9DOB
Michael L Sparger
404 E Conger St
Hartford City IN 47348

Call Sign: K9MOU
John K McVicker
414 E Elm St
Hartford City IN 47348

Call Sign: KE5DVQ
John E Esslinger
802 E Elm St
Hartford City IN 47348

Call Sign: KC9DNK
William R Bolling
111 E Hickory Grove Rd
Hartford City IN 47348

Call Sign: KC9OYW
Chadney J Sullivan
984 E Old SR 22
Hartford City IN 47348

Call Sign: KB9NZQ
Michael L Glass
222 E Patterson St
Hartford City IN 47348

Call Sign: W9NPA
Walter R Ring Sr
201 Greenwood Dr
Hartford City IN 47348

Call Sign: N9XQW
Janet M Wallace
1312 Harrison Dr
Hartford City IN
473482348

Call Sign: N9ONX
Walter M Wallace Sr
1312 Harrison St

Hartford City IN
473482348

Call Sign: KC9GQD
Rob E Moery
300 Hillside Dr
Hartford City IN 47348

Call Sign: KB9WWA
William R Bosworth
415 N Cherry St
Hartford City IN 47348

Call Sign: KC9CTT
Aaron M Henderson
1519 N High St
Hartford City IN 47348

Call Sign: KC9AKW
Matthew E Trice
423 N Jefferson St
Hartford City IN 47348

Call Sign: K9LQT
Marion A Slater
421 S 200 W
Hartford City IN 47348

Call Sign: KC9RNO
Jeffrey D Kieffer
147 S 300 E
Hartford City IN 47348

Call Sign: KC9RNP
Levi J Kieffer
147 S 300 E
Hartford City IN 47348

Call Sign: AA9Z
Tracy N Michael
1326 S 600 E
Hartford City IN 47348

Call Sign: KB9UQQ
Zachary G Michael

1326 S 600 E
Hartford City IN 47348

Call Sign: WD9ADM
Kay F Wolfe
310 S High St
Hartford City IN 47348

Call Sign: KC9DOH
Clifford L Bell
1212 S Jefferson St
Hartford City IN 47348

Call Sign: KB9ZRZ
David J Lyding
1617 S Poplar St
Hartford City IN 47348

Call Sign: KC9HEN
Robert W Medows
30 S Shamrock
Hartford City IN 47348

Call Sign: WD9BHT
Robert W Medows
30 S Shamrock
Hartford City IN 47348

Call Sign: K9VND
James R Hasty
3041 S SR 3
Hartford City IN 47348

Call Sign: KC9JQZ
Michael D Esslinger
1710 S Walnut Lot 86
Hartford City IN 47348

Call Sign: KA9VEX
Darlene K Clark
2424 W 500 N
Hartford City IN 47348

Call Sign: KC9DJY
Jewel A Binegar

542 W Commercial
Hartford City IN 47348

Call Sign: KC9DCR
Lennie L Binegar
542 W Commercial
Hartford City IN 47348

Call Sign: KC9CGY
Kenneth R Curtis
536 W Commercial St
Hartford City IN 47348

Call Sign: WB9HLA
Oral E Henderson Jr
622 W Elm
Hartford City IN 47348

Call Sign: N9GEU
Alan G Pugh
101 W Hickory Grove Rd
Hartford City IN 47348

Call Sign: KC9DQJ
Barbara L Walker
110 W Main St Apt B
Hartford City IN 47348

Call Sign: KC9AZN
Robert R Dodds Jr
514 W McDonald St
Hartford City IN
473481327

Call Sign: KC9JOP
Caleb Franks
2667 W Mohee Rd
Hartford City IN 47348

Call Sign: KC9JSG
John-Paul W Franks
2667 W Mohee Rd
Hartford City IN 47348

Call Sign: KA9VIS

Gregory E Bantz Sr
511 W Ohio Ave
Hartford City IN 47348

Call Sign: KA9UMY
Harold Dill
210 W Park Ave
Hartford City IN 47348

Call Sign: N9GMD
Billie R Uncapher
1747 W SR 18
Hartford City IN
473489225

Call Sign: W9JJU
Richard L Creamer
2330 W SR 18
Hartford City IN 47348

Call Sign: N9XWE
Toby J Sills
2476 W SR 26
Hartford City IN
473489532

Call Sign: WD9HJK
Donald E Carmichael
Hartford City IN 47348

Call Sign: KC9NHR
Blackford ARC
Hartford City IN 47348

Call Sign: K9VND
Blackford ARC
Hartford City IN 47348

FCC Amateur Radio Licenses in Hebron

Call Sign: KB9KDW
Crystal A Martin
16155 Colorado St
Hebron IN 46341

Call Sign: WB9SLT
James H Koepke
16887 Colorado St
Hebron IN 46341

Call Sign: N9JBR
Mary A Hernandez
285 Fieldstone Dr
Hebron IN 46341

Call Sign: W9BLK
Brandie L Krajacic
648 S 300 W
Hebron IN 46341

Call Sign: WB9SCS
Lyndon B Jacobs
7125 E 157th
Hebron IN 46341

Call Sign: KC9LMA
Rob D Hagle
15526 Hancock St
Hebron IN 46341

Call Sign: N9TAX
Joseph F Krajacic Jr
648 S 300 W
Hebron IN 46341

Call Sign: KB9ODX
Eric S Grant
3315 E 157th Ave
Hebron IN 463419007

Call Sign: KC9DJL
Patrick J Zurawik
24 Marvin Gardens
Hebron IN 46341

Call Sign: K9WHK
Donald W Buchanan
648 S 400 W
Hebron IN 46341

Call Sign: N9DWY
Henry W Theile
6808 E 173rd Ave
Hebron IN 46341

Call Sign: KB9UOY
Timothy M Kirby
506 N Main St
Hebron IN 46341

Call Sign: N9ZVX
George Bazil
77 S 600 W
Hebron IN 46341

Call Sign: N9YRQ
Antoni A Tokarz
4804 E 181st Ave
Hebron IN 46341

Call Sign: KC9DJM
Paul E Patterson
25 Park Pl
Hebron IN 46341

Call Sign: KA9FOI
Frank E Santaquilani
223 S 725 W
Hebron IN 46341

Call Sign: KC9FPW
Dawn M Erdelles
608 E Bates St
Hebron IN 46341

Call Sign: W9PEP
Paul E Patterson
25 Park Pl
Hebron IN 46341

Call Sign: NU9G
Juan Gutierrez
320 S 725 W
Hebron IN 46341

Call Sign: KA9LQA
Neil E Simpson
212 E Sigler St
Hebron IN 46341

Call Sign: AE9P
Paul E Patterson
25 Park Pl
Hebron IN 46341

Call Sign: KC9UFG
Michael A Steffel
811 S 800 W
Hebron IN 46341

Call Sign: KC9DHD
Dwight L Brown
106 Falawater Dr Lot 135
Hebron IN 463419366

Call Sign: W9DEI
Dwayne Dobson
190 Park Pl
Hebron IN 463419125

Call Sign: KC9MHY
Theodore A Fitzgerald
9 S Beulah Vista
Hebron IN 46341

Call Sign: N9IXJ
Manuel P Hernandez
285 Fieldstone Dr
Hebron IN 46341

Call Sign: KC9PCJ
Brandie L Krajacic
648 S 300 W
Hebron IN 46341

Call Sign: KC9VEE
Christian M Burns
208 S Madison St
Hebron IN 46341

Call Sign: KC9EQF
Thomas G Fry
681 S SR 2
Hebron IN 46341

Call Sign: WD9FNA
Joseph P Balczo
871 S SR 2
Hebron IN 46341

Call Sign: KA9DKW
Ernest E Hero
1089 S SR 231
Hebron IN 46341

Call Sign: KB9OCF
Pete Theodoratos
614 W 100 S
Hebron IN 463419731

Call Sign: AB9BC
Pete Theodoratos
614 W 100 S
Hebron IN 463419731

Call Sign: KB9WPR
Jason A Clement
656 W 250 S
Hebron IN 46341

Call Sign: KB9WSG
Heather R Burton
660 W 250 S
Hebron IN 46341

Call Sign: N9CVV
Kenneth G Burton
660 W 250 S
Hebron IN 46341

Call Sign: N9CV
Kenneth G Burton
660 W 250 S
Hebron IN 46341

Call Sign: N9KB
Kenneth G Burton
660 W 250 S
Hebron IN 46341

Call Sign: KD9EU
Laurie M Burton
660 W 250 S
Hebron IN 46341

Call Sign: KJ9V
Laurie M Burton
660 W 250 S
Hebron IN 46341

Call Sign: N9HRB
Heather R Burton
660 W 250 S
Hebron IN 46341

Call Sign: KC9HW
Daniel B R Ziegler
583 W 350 S
Hebron IN 46341

Call Sign: N9EZB
Andrew D Blough
617 W 50 S
Hebron IN 46341

Call Sign: KB9FHZ
Frances R Mitch
668 W 725 S
Hebron IN 46341

Call Sign: N9JTR
William G Mitch
668 W 725 S
Hebron IN 46341

Call Sign: KB9QXC
James L Gorby
423 W 900 S
Hebron IN 46341

Call Sign: K9KLR
Nick G Lash
458 W 900 S
Hebron IN 46341

Call Sign: KC8NTA
Gerald E Hunt
200 W McAlpin
Hebron IN 46341

Call Sign: KB9FEW
Donald E Largent Jr
604 W Sigler St
Hebron IN 46341

Call Sign: KA9MMY
Tobi J Fisher
315 W SR 8
Hebron IN 46341

Call Sign: KA9SQK
David W Howenstine
757 Walter Dr
Hebron IN 46341

**FCC Amateur Radio
Licenses in Hemlock**

Call Sign: W9YUW
Clyde H Abbott
4571 E 410 S
Hemlock IN 46937

**FCC Amateur Radio
Licenses in Highland**

Call Sign: AA9FC
Thomas G Gountanis
3024 100 Pl
Highland IN 46322

Call Sign: KC9GQZ
Robert E Gomez
2908 38th St

Highland IN 46322   Highland IN 46322   Highland IN 46322

Call Sign: K9WRH
Frederick J Zimmerman
3648 41st Ln
Highland IN 46322

Call Sign: W9FXT
Andrew Finick Jr
3006 98th St
Highland IN 46322

Call Sign: N9TEW
Robert A Bieker
9528 Farmer Dr
Highland IN 46322

Call Sign: KB9HHT
Charles P Progar
2716 41st St
Highland IN 46322

Call Sign: N9OID
Patricia A Finick
3006 98th St
Highland IN 46322

Call Sign: WD9FOU
George Wolotka
9443 Forrest Dr
Highland IN 46322

Call Sign: WA9OTL
Jack S Watts
3332 41st St
Highland IN 46322

Call Sign: N9FXT
Patricia A Finick
3006 98th St
Highland IN 46322

Call Sign: KC9SZF
Chris A Tucker
3329 Franklin St
Highland IN 46322

Call Sign: N9QXC
Marc S Johnson
3433 42nd Pl
Highland IN 46322

Call Sign: WD9O
Juan A Contreras
9034 Cline Ave
Highland IN 463222204

Call Sign: N9CZH
Fred J Salmon
3224 Garfield Ave
Highland IN 463221750

Call Sign: WB9YPD
Nicholas P Karin
3523 42nd St
Highland IN 46322

Call Sign: WB9VJL
Alexander Opach
2845 Condit St
Highland IN 46322

Call Sign: KC9RLG
Thomas A Black
3515 Garfield Ave
Highland IN 46322

Call Sign: KA9EOB
Earle G Gummerson
8116 4th Pl W
Highland IN 46322

Call Sign: KB9PYK
James S Dal Santo
8939 Cottage Grove Ave
Highland IN 46322

Call Sign: K9ASE
Thomas A Black
3515 Garfield Ave
Highland IN 46322

Call Sign: WB9FQS
Larry A Brechner
2736 81st St
Highland IN 46322

Call Sign: WA9HXF
Saad Spott
9228 Cottage Grove Ave
Highland IN 46322

Call Sign: KB9URY
Keith M Tokoly
3520 Garfield St
Highland IN 46322

Call Sign: N9FXT
Andrew Finick Jr
3006 98th St
Highland IN 46322

Call Sign: KC9BDJ
Steven M Schroers
9741 Delaware Pl Apt 5
Highland IN 46322

Call Sign: KF9OV
Gregory S Miller
3127 Glenwood St
Highland IN 46322

Call Sign: AA9YJ
Andrew Finick Jr
3006 98th St

Call Sign: N9PBG
Henry J Boone
3129 Duluth

Call Sign: KA9ARB
Harry Ranney
9232 Grace St

Highland IN 46322

Highland IN 463222648

Highland IN 46322

Call Sign: WU9D
Michael L Rohwedder
3305 Grand Blvd
Highland IN 46322

Call Sign: W9TAW
Alexander Jackson
2606 Jewett St
Highland IN 46322

Call Sign: WA9VKA
Edward Payo
2923 Lincoln St
Highland IN 46322

Call Sign: WY9R
Meyer Evanson
2329 Hart Rd
Highland IN 46322

Call Sign: KA9MDB
Christopher W Tussey
9316 Kennedy
Highland IN 46322

Call Sign: KC9UXH
Jeffrey Bogusz
3704 Manor Dr
Highland IN 46322

Call Sign: KB9OUB
Robert C Daily
9203 Highland Pl
Highland IN 46322

Call Sign: WD9ADZ
John C Van Willigan
8830 Kennedy Av
Highland IN 46322

Call Sign: KC9QYH
Brian Hoogeveen
3238 North Dr
Highland IN 46322

Call Sign: N9VBF
Donald J Bunting
8838 Highland St
Highland IN 46322

Call Sign: N9HEM
Laveta L Wolotka
10016 Kennedy Ave
Highland IN 46322

Call Sign: KD8FWU
Paul M Casault
8042 North Dr
Highland IN 46322

Call Sign: KB9MCJ
Ronald M Smolen
2645 Hwy Ave
Highland IN 46322

Call Sign: KB9OOB
Pamela G Wimberly
3424 La Verne Dr
Highland IN 463222167

Call Sign: WA9DJY
Victor I Lypka
9201 Oday Dr
Highland IN 46322

Call Sign: KC9NWR
Matthew B Landry
8811 Idlewild Ave
Highland IN 46322

Call Sign: W9TWU
John W Horvath
3019 Lakeside Dr
Highland IN 46322

Call Sign: KC9UVT
Paul W Sanusky
9002 Ohio Pl
Highland IN 46322

Call Sign: W9IA
David R Wojcinski
9005 Idlewild Dr
Highland IN 46322

Call Sign: KB9OOA
Thomas C Wimberly
3424 Laverne Dr
Highland IN 46322

Call Sign: KB9PXU
Lloyd D Thomas
8540 Orchard Dr
Highland IN 46322

Call Sign: K9EO
Eugene J Orzechowicz
9210 Idlewild Dr
Highland IN 46322

Call Sign: KC9GSC
Michael C Pepelea
3541 Lincoln Pl
Highland IN 46322

Call Sign: N9HHY
Susan Sinisi
8729 Parrish Ave
Highland IN 46322

Call Sign: WA9HHJ
Thomas O Newberry
9445 Indianapolis Blvd

Call Sign: WA9EXA
James G Austgen
2449 Lincoln St

Call Sign: W9WTW
Kenneth E Brechner
2908 Pkwy Dr

Highland IN 46322

Call Sign: KA9OOB
Kenneth R Williams
8830 Pkwy Dr
Highland IN 46312

Call Sign: W9OCH
Ralph E Skoog
9336 Pkwy Dr
Highland IN 46322

Call Sign: KF9CQ
Richard E Van Strien
9148 Southmoor Ave
Highland IN 46322

Call Sign: N9SSX
John D McGehee
8008 Spruce St
Highland IN 46322

Call Sign: N9RWP
Robert W Pasternak
8818 St James Pl
Highland IN 46322

Call Sign: W9CTO
James W Millsap
3535 Wicker Ave
Highland IN 46322

Call Sign: KC9CBB
Ronald Grochowski
3535 Wicker Ave
Highland IN 46322

Call Sign: W9RGX
Ronald Grochowski
3535 Wicker Ave
Highland IN 46322

Call Sign: N9JHK
Michael R Markus
3842 Wicker Ave

Highland IN 46322

Call Sign: N9CWG
Gary L Cooper
8206 Wicker Park Dr
Highland IN 46322

Call Sign: KA9EMU
Frank R Michalak
9400 Wildwood
Highland IN 46322

Call Sign: N9HQY
Daniel E Arnold
3702 Wirth Rd
Highland IN 46322

Call Sign: KC9SNN
Heidi S Harshman
Highland IN 46322

Call Sign: KB9TUC
Mark W Harshman
Highland IN 46322

**FCC Amateur Radio
Licenses in Hoagland**

Call Sign: KF9YP
Larry J Eckerley
13811 Emanuel Rd
Hoagland IN 467459736

Call Sign: WB9PDW
Robert E Theurer
12408 Flatrock Rd
Hoagland IN 467459548

Call Sign: KC9TAI
Nathan A Buuck
8728 Hoagland Rd
Hoagland IN 46745

Call Sign: KB9TBU
Michael E Mourey

10601 Hoagland Rd
Hoagland IN 467459701

Call Sign: KC9LOH
Eric E Kiess
11003 Hoagland Rd
Hoagland IN 46745

Call Sign: KC9LPP
Scott A Shepherd
12135 Hoagland Rd
Hoagland IN 46745

Call Sign: WD9ACE
Jerry L Miller
8626 Monroeville Rd
Hoagland IN 46745

Call Sign: WD9EUI
Albert R Oberneder Jr
15136 Witte Rd
Hoagland IN 46745

**FCC Amateur Radio
Licenses in Hobart**

Call Sign: KC9TMO
Michael D Mccombs
4526 16th St
Hobart IN 46342

Call Sign: K9UIF
Walter R Cummings
9162 Ainsworth Rd
Hobart IN 46342

Call Sign: W9MN
Claude E Gormley
4134 Alabama St
Hobart IN 46342

Call Sign: KC9KRX
Bradley J Curtis
3773 Barnes St
Hobart IN 46342

Call Sign: N9OLH
John R Burk Sr
1648 Brookview Ct
Hobart IN 46342

Call Sign: N9CLX
Michael L Roberts
928 Capitol Dr
Hobart IN 46342

Call Sign: N9ULA
Donald P Trail
400 Center St
Hobart IN 46342

Call Sign: N9XGH
Kenneth Zajac
3813 Colbourne
Hobart IN 46342

Call Sign: KB9KXM
Marcella A Zajac
3813 Colbourne St
Hobart IN 46342

Call Sign: WE9C
Gene D Kemp
2648 Coral Dr
Hobart IN 46342

Call Sign: KA9RBP
Richard C Packham
207 Court St
Hobart IN 46342

Call Sign: KF9YH
Robert A Scott
2919 Drexel Dr
Hobart IN 46342

Call Sign: KF9WW
Michael A Frank
1221 E 10th St
Hobart IN 46342

Call Sign: WB9KBV
Everett C Pence
435 E 11th St
Hobart IN 46342

Call Sign: N9XGB
Frank A Settles
23650 E 32nd Ct
Hobart IN 46342

Call Sign: KA9JCM
Gene D Kemp
3690 E 33rd Ln
Hobart IN 46342

Call Sign: W9GDK
Gene D Kemp
3690 E 33rd Ln
Hobart IN 46342

Call Sign: KA9DBW
Jack H Johnson
1319 E 34th Ave
Hobart IN 46342

Call Sign: KC7FQZ
Cassandra A Morrill
1730 E 34th Ave
Hobart IN 46342

Call Sign: N9UYS
Robert A Craigin
3604 E 34th Ln
Hobart IN 46342

Call Sign: K9ULU
Edward J Martin
3990 E 34th Ln
Hobart IN 46342

Call Sign: N9IPS
Michael Modrak
22 E 36th Pl
Hobart IN 46342

Call Sign: KB9UUO
Jeffrey W Depper
534 E 37th Ave Lot 447
Hobart IN 46342

Call Sign: N9VGL
Gerald G Price
1101 E 5th St
Hobart IN 46342

Call Sign: N9JLZ
Brian J Depper
2875 E 62nd Pl
Hobart IN 46342

Call Sign: K9UIF
Mark W Cummings Jr
6509 E 62nd Pl
Hobart IN 46342

Call Sign: KC9IHM
James R Martin
1408 E 6th St
Hobart IN 46342

Call Sign: N9HQV
Bernard J Tucker
2122 E Cleveland Ave
Hobart IN 46342

Call Sign: WA9PQM
Milo M Roscoe
1411 E High St
Hobart IN 463423313

Call Sign: WB9MDL
Michael C Fields
1001 E Home Ave
Hobart IN 46342

Call Sign: KB9KXQ
James A Rodgers
1040 E Rand St
Hobart IN 46342

Call Sign: KB9NLB
Kevin M Trinosky
937 Garfield St
Hobart IN 46342

Call Sign: KC9JAN
Terry B Adams
1229 Garfield St
Hobart IN 463426033

Call Sign: N9DCR
Marvin R Bernard
6430 Grand Blvd
Hobart IN 46342

Call Sign: WA9PBD
Norman J Pera
1005 Lake George Dr
Hobart IN 46342

Call Sign: KC9LQR
William H Kistler
7462 Lincoln Mill Rd
Hobart IN 46342

Call Sign: N9GGA
Margaret D Veiner
851 Lincoln St
Hobart IN 46342

Call Sign: W9CCH
Christopher C Hedges
11602 Maryland St
Hobart IN 46307

Call Sign: KB9SRH
Robert D Hayes
3001 McAfee Dr
Hobart IN 46342

Call Sign: KA9ALE
Terry L Shaw
652 N 700 W
Hobart IN 46342

Call Sign: WB9RQQ
Michael J Fenchak
325 N 725 W
Hobart IN 46342

Call Sign: KC9BCM
Mark W Cummings
554 N Guyer St
Hobart IN 46342

Call Sign: WV9O
Marvin M Boetcher
225 N Indiana St
Hobart IN 463423225

Call Sign: KB9RRI
John E Rhynearson
444 N Indiana St
Hobart IN 46342

Call Sign: KB9WXS
Joe Griffith
400 N Lake Park Ave Apt
K12 S
Hobart IN 46342

Call Sign: KA9FAX
Anthony J Kostelnik
21 N Linda St
Hobart IN 46342

Call Sign: KC9FWU
Robert J Allen
555 N Union St
Hobart IN 46342

Call Sign: W9FDM
Robert J Allen
555 N Union St
Hobart IN 46342

Call Sign: KB9IKD
Donald W Duncan
55 N Washington St

Hobart IN 46342

Call Sign: W9MEM
Marlin E Mosher
258 N Washington St
Hobart IN 46342

Call Sign: KB9PIZ
William R Kriess
8901 Park Valley Ct
Hobart IN 46342

Call Sign: N9XJP
George Sladic
3402 Randolph Pl
Hobart IN 463421415

Call Sign: W9AYH
Hamline W Robinson
230 S Ash
Hobart IN 46342

Call Sign: KA9HKB
Donald K Denbow
129 S California St
Hobart IN 46342

Call Sign: N9OHJ
Michael H Schuffert
1300 S Delaware St
Hobart IN 46342

Call Sign: N9HPT
Thomas A Rees
1333 S Hobart Rd
Hobart IN 46342

Call Sign: N9HSB
Clifford R Belz
112 S Indiana St
Hobart IN 46342

Call Sign: KC9BCQ
Nancy C Belz
112 S Indiana St

Hobart IN 46342

Call Sign: KA9FCP
Eugene L Shirey
838 S Linda St
Hobart IN 463425270

Call Sign: W9SC
Philip M Buzolitz
971 S Linda St
Hobart IN 46342

Call Sign: N8NAH
Michael R Kraynik III
521 S Wabash Pl
Hobart IN 46342

Call Sign: KC9HV
Charles W Eichelberger
1224 W 37th Pl
Hobart IN 46342

Call Sign: KA9WWL
Michelle A Eichelberger
1224 W 37th Pl
Hobart IN 463422017

Call Sign: KC9MIL
Walter E Wojciechowski
2925 W 38th Ave
Hobart IN 46342

Call Sign: KB9WIQ
David A Timmer
910 W 3rd Pl
Hobart IN 46342

Call Sign: WD9HYK
Ralph Gonzales
1611 W 4th St
Hobart IN 46342

Call Sign: KC9OKQ
John A Tonello
780 W 600 N

Hobart IN 46342

Call Sign: AA9SO
Robert Pisarski
1401 W Cleveland
Hobart IN 46342

Call Sign: AB9SU
Robert Pisarski
1401 W Cleveland
Hobart IN 46342

Call Sign: KA9IVA
Robert S Yetsko
800 W Joliet Rd
Hobart IN 463427067

Call Sign: KC9EYE
Paul W Lane
4002 Willow St
Hobart IN 46342

FCC Amateur Radio Licenses in Howe

Call Sign: KB9AHV
Patricia J Chapman
602 6th St
Howe IN 46746

Call Sign: KC9KXW
James V Mcfall
4285 N SR Lot 52
Howe IN 46746

Call Sign: KC9KXX
Diana L Mcfall
4285 N SR9 Lot 52
Howe IN 46746

Call Sign: KA9NNG
Sherrel M Elliott
Howe IN 46746

FCC Amateur Radio Licenses in Hudson

Call Sign: KA9YFJ
Wayne L Keen
Box 60
Hudson IN 46747

Call Sign: KC9EDD
Holly M Stewart
120 Collins St
Hudson IN 467470053

Call Sign: KB9TXN
Judy C Young
580 Ln 201 McClish
Lake
Hudson IN 467479245

Call Sign: N9RYD
William E Young
580 Ln 201 McClish
Lake
Hudson IN 467479245

Call Sign: KA9KHF
Michael E Lucas
295 Ln 201 Turkey Lake
Hudson IN 46747

Call Sign: KC9GUY
Mark E Tritch
4340 S 1000 W
Hudson IN 46747

Call Sign: KA9RVF
Bruce D McDaniel
3970 S 800 W
Hudson IN 46747

Call Sign: N9QYR
Zara D Claudy
5380 S 850 W
Hudson IN 46747

Call Sign: KC9FLO
Eugene L Kennedy
604 Smathers St
Hudson IN 467470193

Call Sign: N9YCD
Harold L Wickizer
610 Smathers St
Hudson IN 467470054

Call Sign: KA9WUA
Fred J Fender
8555 W 400 S
Hudson IN 46747

Call Sign: W9SKQ
Wilho R Roy
10785 W 650 S
Hudson IN 46747

FCC Amateur Radio Licenses in Huntertown

Call Sign: KB9AZH
Deborah K Greer
1423 Ashville Dr
Huntertown IN
467489316

Call Sign: WD9EQF
Gene J Garrett
Box 70
Huntertown IN 46748

Call Sign: KA9CZE
Lillian G Garrett
Box 70
Huntertown IN 46748

Call Sign: W6JXZ
John J De Muth
15719 Chilkat Trl
Huntertown IN 46748

Call Sign: KC9GZ

Alan J Dunn
16317 Coldwater Rd
Huntertown IN 46748

Call Sign: KA9ULN
Vincent S Cook
18742 Coldwater Rd
Huntertown IN 46748

Call Sign: KB9NGM
Daniel L Soper
18436 Doug Dr
Huntertown IN 46748

Call Sign: WB9TPW
Nelson E Preble
1309 Duesenberg Dr
Huntertown IN 46748

Call Sign: KA9JEG
Tammy L Preble
1309 Duesenberg Dr
Huntertown IN 46748

Call Sign: AF9Y
Michael W Cook
501 E Cedar Canyon Rd
Huntertown IN 46748

Call Sign: N9MTC
David D Atkison
2112 Edgerton
Huntertown IN 46748

Call Sign: N5GEJ
Marcus J Wagner
15127 Hedgebrook Dr
Huntertown IN 46748

Call Sign: KB9MW
Marcus J Wagner
15127 Hedgebrook Dr
Huntertown IN 46748

Call Sign: KB9IFW

Michael F Fisher
1819 Hunter St
Huntertown IN 46748

Call Sign: KA9ZTB
Jacob W Burke
18605 Lima Rd
Huntertown IN 46748

Call Sign: N9VKR
Jeannette L Burke
18605 Lima Rd
Huntertown IN 46748

Call Sign: N9HVP
Larry S Burke
18605 Lima Rd
Huntertown IN
467489785

Call Sign: WB3GSU
Benjamin B Johnson
4431 McComb Rd
Huntertown IN 46748

Call Sign: KA8VJU
Ronald C Reece
1809 Mill Wheel Dr
Huntertown IN 46748

Call Sign: KC9UXN
Adam C Thomas
324 Osprey Pass
Huntertown IN 46748

Call Sign: KB9ZGC
Nicholas C Voorhees
1215 Simon Rd
Huntertown IN 46748

Call Sign: KB9OZF
Adam M Esslinger
1113 Thornwillow Ct
Huntertown IN 46748

Call Sign: N9JJX
Susan K Demerly
16210 Thrundebird Rd
Huntertown IN 46748

Call Sign: K9JUI
William A Demerly Jr
16210 Thunderbird Rd
Huntertown IN 46748

Call Sign: KB9MDT
John L Schaefer
16211 Thunderbird Rd
Huntertown IN 46748

Call Sign: WZ8Y
Robert A Kaminski
16230 Thunderbird Rd
Huntertown IN 46748

Call Sign: KT8O
Eric J Shook
15501 Walnut St
Huntertown IN 46748

Call Sign: KB9WNY
James M Reid
Huntertown IN 46748

**FCC Amateur Radio
Licenses in Huntington**

Call Sign: KA9VGQ
Wanda L Case
1000N
Huntington IN 46750

Call Sign: N9DPY
Carl E Hoag
100S
Huntington IN 46750

Call Sign: KB9KIJ
Richard W Huffman
100W

Huntington IN 46750

Call Sign: K9GYS
Don P Jones
734 1st St
Huntington IN 46750

Call Sign: WD9HRX
Jerry L Platt
1034 1st St
Huntington IN 46750

Call Sign: W9IGV
L D Williams
200W
Huntington IN 46750

Call Sign: N9IEW
Reo W Parrett
400W
Huntington IN 46750

Call Sign: N9GZD
Dennis R Miller
494N
Huntington IN 46750

Call Sign: KA9WIN
Harold E Reeves
700W
Huntington IN 46750

Call Sign: KC9HOX
Melvyn L Scott
1370 Ash
Huntington IN 46750

Call Sign: KB9OGG
Michael D Thomas
1725 Aspen Ave
Huntington IN 46750

Call Sign: KB9GBM
Thomas E Wilson Jr
1905 Aspen Ct

Huntington IN 46750

Call Sign: KB9MBQ
James D Greenwell
641 Byron St
Huntington IN 46750

Call Sign: KB9NYA
Brenda E Lewis
1138 Byron St
Huntington IN 46750

Call Sign: KA9WIR
Ward R Lewis
1138 Byron St
Huntington IN 46750

Call Sign: KB9KIH
Christopher A Meyer
955 Cherry St
Huntington IN 46750

Call Sign: N9NNW
Michael R Nei
1428 Cherry St
Huntington IN 46750

Call Sign: KB9DEU
Heribert O Kruse
1232 College Ave
Huntington IN 46750

Call Sign: KB9DQW
Jason L McConnell
1709 College Ave
Huntington IN 46750

Call Sign: KB9DQX
Linda C McConnell
1709 College Ave
Huntington IN 46750

Call Sign: WA9OPG
K F Triggs ARC
1709 College Ave

Huntington IN 46750

Huntington IN 46750

Huntington IN 46750

Call Sign: KB9GAR
Edward J High
1641 Condit St Lot 116
Huntington IN 46750

Call Sign: KC9GYO
Ray E Rittenhouse
2218 E 600 N
Huntington IN 46750

Call Sign: KG9EX
James T Wittke
568 E Lamont Rd
Huntington IN 46750

Call Sign: WB9EBI
Lea E Allman
210 Cottonwood
Huntington IN 46750

Call Sign: K9SH
Steven L Hart
2955 E 630 N
Huntington IN 46750

Call Sign: W9NNH
Quentin O Corkhill
1355 E Market St
Huntington IN 46750

Call Sign: N9JQX
Ronald K Martin
604 Court St
Huntington IN 46750

Call Sign: KC9HRZ
Brian J Baird
304 E 700 N
Huntington IN 46750

Call Sign: N9MHD
Dale E Banker Jr
641 E Market St Apt C
Huntington IN 46750

Call Sign: KC9AYU
Angela M Hunter
704 Court St
Huntington IN 46750

Call Sign: KC9MWR
Amanda L Minton
516 E Franklin St
Huntington IN 46750

Call Sign: N9QVJ
David L Melching
1095 E Markle Rd
Huntington IN 46750

Call Sign: KB9FJS
David M Swain
416 Crescent Ave
Huntington IN 46750

Call Sign: KA9MZD
John S Beeching
516 E Franklin St
Huntington IN 46750

Call Sign: N9GEJ
Ronald E Canvin
289 E Markle Rd
Huntington IN 46750

Call Sign: WA9VEF
Robert A Koehlinger
3107 Cumberland Way
Huntington IN 46750

Call Sign: WD8PIF
Donald L Dinius
540 E High St
Huntington IN 46750

Call Sign: KB9RGJ
Miriam A Shull
2245 E SR 114 92
Huntington IN 46750

Call Sign: N9IOD
Linda P Wyatt
695 Dimond St
Huntington IN 46750

Call Sign: KB9DON
Kent A Dinius
540 E High St
Huntington IN 46750

Call Sign: KA9BLY
Earl F Dinius
519 E State St
Huntington IN 46750

Call Sign: N9NRL
John P Moran Jr
720 Dimond St
Huntington IN 46750

Call Sign: KA9PDV
Mark A Dinius
540 E High St
Huntington IN 46750

Call Sign: KA9ZHA
Benjamen D Schmidt
760 E Taylor St
Huntington IN 46750

Call Sign: KA9IDZ
James L Kline
1247 E 300 N

Call Sign: KB9DOO
Shirley J Dinius
540 E High St

Call Sign: K9DKB
Carl T Clipp
426 E Tipton St

Huntington IN 46750

Call Sign: KB8QES
Aida A Shoemaker
715 E Tipton St
Huntington IN 46750

Call Sign: KA9NIW
Fred E Bolinger Jr
624 Etna Ave
Huntington IN 46750

Call Sign: WA9DKQ
Sylvia N McHenry
813 Evergreen Rd
Huntington IN 46750

Call Sign: WA9DKP
Verl R McHenry
813 Evergreen Rd
Huntington IN 46750

Call Sign: W9AJS
Donald A Bennett
1215 Evergreen Rd
Huntington IN 46750

Call Sign: KC8MOC
Charles D Haynes
1215 Evergreen Rd Lot
12
Huntington IN 46750

Call Sign: WF9F
William R Shaneyfelt
1585 Flaxmill Rd
Huntington IN
467508954

Call Sign: W2FHS
Richard W Mcconnell
4005 Flint Ridge Ct
Huntington IN 46750

Call Sign: KC9QGE

Daniel L Zimmerman
1540 Freedom St
Huntington IN 46750

Call Sign: WA9BZZ
Charles E Reith
1405 Garfeild Apt 15
Huntington IN 46750

Call Sign: KA9YIF
Monte C Sieberns
511 Garfield St
Huntington IN 46750

Call Sign: N9MTE
John T McIntosh
845 Gragg St
Huntington IN 46750

Call Sign: KC9AIV
Matthew R Taylor
1255 Grayston Ave
Huntington IN 46750

Call Sign: KB9QVH
Westley A Dirr
1243 Green St
Huntington IN 46750

Call Sign: KC9GUO
Daniel W Wintrode
637 Guilford St
Huntington IN 46750

Call Sign: W9NCI
Tony P Ehler
908 Guilford St
Huntington IN 46750

Call Sign: AA9TE
Tony P Ehler
908 Guilford St
Huntington IN 46750

Call Sign: KA9VEC

E Joseph Homier Jr
1335 Guilford St
Huntington IN 46750

Call Sign: WB0PHP
Earl A Coolman
3009 Hawk Spring Hill
Huntington IN
467507836

Call Sign: KE9WI
David S Kendall
401 Himes St
Huntington IN 46750

Call Sign: N9NOA
Joan L Kendall
401 Himes St
Huntington IN 46750

Call Sign: N9JJW
Robert J Foster
1950 Indiana St
Huntington IN 46750

Call Sign: N9NNS
Sandy B Foster
1950 Indiana St
Huntington IN 46750

Call Sign: KC9GX
Burl D Covey
1752 Kocher St
Huntington IN 46750

Call Sign: N9ONC
Anna M Doerscher
716 Leopold
Huntington IN 46750

Call Sign: K9RIT
Stephen J Doerscher
716 Leopold St
Huntington IN 46750

Call Sign: KC9PNO
Michael C Rankin
935 Leopold St
Huntington IN 46750

Call Sign: N9NNX
Richard D Ziegler
633 Mayne
Huntington IN 46750

Call Sign: K9NIC
Charles N Stanley
1250 Memorial Ln
Huntington IN 46750

Call Sign: KB9JDN
Larry L Richey
Memorial Ln
Huntington IN 46750

Call Sign: N9ONE
Gary J Gill
1247 Mishler Rd
Huntington IN 46750

Call Sign: W9NJD
Doyle V Strandlund
2849 N 035 W
Huntington IN
467504012

Call Sign: KA9ZQH
Paul E J Coy
7801 N 100 W
Huntington IN 46750

Call Sign: AB9IB
Jeffrey G Geese
10330 N 100 W
Huntington IN 46750

Call Sign: KC9RMP
Dennis D Watkins
10699 N 200 W
Huntington IN 46750

Call Sign: W9YFS
Willard J Harman
8880 N 300W
Huntington IN 46750

Call Sign: N9IEX
Jana C Parrett
9821 N 400 W
Huntington IN 46750

Call Sign: KB9SWZ
Matt A Brown
2705 N 500 E
Huntington IN
467509520

Call Sign: KC9PXC
Patricia R Tullis
624 N 500 W
Huntington IN 46750

Call Sign: WA9QGL
Samuel N Tullis Sr
624 N 500 W
Huntington IN 46750

Call Sign: W9BFL
Allan A Nostwick
4625 N 615 W
Huntington IN 46750

Call Sign: N9REC
Stephen R Herman
4321 N 635 W
Huntington IN 46750

Call Sign: KC5FUF
Kevin R Le Cavalier
4306 N 641 W
Huntington IN 46750

Call Sign: KB9EHX
Cameron Douglas
9280 N 700 W

Huntington IN 46750

Call Sign: KC9JVM
Charles N Stanley
7287 N Clear Creek Rd
Huntington IN 46750

Call Sign: KA9VTB
Jack W Oberholtzer
8385 N Clear Creek Rd
Huntington IN 46750

Call Sign: KC9HOV
Jon R Knecht
8454 N Clear Creek Rd
Huntington IN 46750

Call Sign: KC9TFR
Huntington County
Emergency
Communications Club
6830 N Goshen Rd
Huntington IN 46750

Call Sign: KC9TIV
Huntington County
Emergency
Communications Club
6830 N Goshen Rd
Huntington IN 46750

Call Sign: WX9EC
Huntington County
Emergency
Communications Club
6830 N Goshen Rd
Huntington IN 46750

Call Sign: W9ECC
Huntington County
Emergency
Communications Club
6830 N Goshen Rd
Huntington IN 46750

Call Sign: W6DSP
David S Pratt
6830 N Goshen Rd
Huntington IN
467507726

Call Sign: WB9LWA
John T Sees
1110 N Jefferson St
Huntington IN 46750

Call Sign: W9LWA
John T Sees
1110 N Jefferson St
Huntington IN 46750

Call Sign: WA9DRI
Bernard J Miller
225 N La Fontaine St
Huntington IN 46750

Call Sign: KA9LDI
Edward E Campbell Jr
1333 N La Fontaine St
Huntington IN 46750

Call Sign: N9VAN
Thomas H Rupert
224 N Lafontaine
Huntington IN 46750

Call Sign: K9WHA
Ralph M Reed
5340 N Mishler Rd
Huntington IN 46750

Call Sign: KB9JDH
David L Lloyd
6618 N Old Ft Wayne Rd
Huntington IN 46750

Call Sign: K9ROZ
John W Miller
3892 N Rangeline Rd
Huntington IN 46750

Call Sign: KA9IJC
George M Amick
1630 N Shutt Hill Rd
Huntington IN 46750

Call Sign: N9ZOC
Steven D Morris
5812 N US 24 E
Huntington IN 46750

Call Sign: WD9JFM
Warren F Myers
260 Northcrest
Huntington IN 46750

Call Sign: N9NNY
John W Hohe
1585 Oak St
Huntington IN 46750

Call Sign: N9BHA
Dennis L Conner
125 Orchard Ln
Huntington IN 46750

Call Sign: N9FYO
Linda J Conner
125 Orchard Ln
Huntington IN 46750

Call Sign: WA9HKA
Keith E James
1044 Poplar St
Huntington IN 46750

Call Sign: KA9LDM
Orvin A Koher
1545 Poplar St
Huntington IN
467501331

Call Sign: KB9OYZ
Kent D Hathaway
427 Riverside Dr

Huntington IN 46750

Call Sign: K9RRN
Edward M Raynes Jr
200 Riverside Dr Apt 5
Huntington IN 46750

Call Sign: KD9SQ
Robert J Anderson
216 Roche St
Huntington IN 46750

Call Sign: KA9NCB
Frank L Pyle Sr
711 Rocky Run
Huntington IN
467501332

Call Sign: WB9GEQ
Joseph Y Shaw
929 S 200 E
Huntington IN 46750

Call Sign: K9AS
Robert L Worsham
929 S 200 E
Huntington IN 46750

Call Sign: K9HC
Huntington County ARS
929 S 200 E
Huntington IN 46750

Call Sign: KA9WIO
James R Radtke Sr
712 S Briant St
Huntington IN 46750

Call Sign: KC9ABK
Walter V McCann
1010 S Jefferson St
Huntington IN
467503707

Call Sign: KC8DTP

Sally J Evans
1086 S Warren Rd
Huntington IN 46750

Call Sign: KB9JDK
Candy L Richardson
2104 Sabine St
Huntington IN 46750

Call Sign: KB9JDL
Emil E Richardson
2104 Sabine St
Huntington IN 46750

Call Sign: KC9BKN
Jerry L Waters
2134 Sabine St
Huntington IN 46750

Call Sign: KB9JEL
Richard P Miller
170 Studebaker Dr
Huntington IN 46750

Call Sign: AB9OK
Richard P Miller
170 Studebaker Dr
Huntington IN 46750

Call Sign: KA9ZPU
Jeffrey G Geese
1225 Superior St
Huntington IN 46750

Call Sign: KB9VUM
Judy K Zumbrun
4222 W 100 S
Huntington IN 46750

Call Sign: NQ9O
Ronald E Pressler
2750 W 200 S
Huntington IN 46750

Call Sign: WV9Y

Sonya L Ciriilo
8141 W 250 S
Huntington IN 46750

Call Sign: WB8FKT
Jay B Ballard
6139 W 465 N
Huntington IN 46750

Call Sign: W9NZX
Dwight V Ericsson
4963 W 539 N
Huntington IN 46750

Call Sign: KB9RSX
Allen A Thorn
2857 W 550 S
Huntington IN 46750

Call Sign: KA9ZRT
Harold C Riggle
4553 W 600 N
Huntington IN 46750

Call Sign: WB9FVZ
Leroy R Rinehart
4615 W 600 N
Huntington IN 46750

Call Sign: KC9BHK
William A Davis Sr
5810 W 600 S
Huntington IN 46750

Call Sign: KC9AZQ
William A Davis
5813 W 600 S
Huntington IN
467509158

Call Sign: N9YVQ
Titus A Lloyd
4484 W 700 N
Huntington IN 46750

Call Sign: KB9YLO
Robert S Linker
5008 W 800 N
Huntington IN 46750

Call Sign: N9VOD
Jeffrey E Miller
8845 W 800 N
Huntington IN 46750

Call Sign: AB7CC
Michael C Warner
3152 W 800 N
Huntington IN 46750

Call Sign: WB9YZL
Gary L Oliver
2848 W 853N
Huntington IN
467509709

Call Sign: N9QVR
Matt L Bridge
3664 W Division Rd
Huntington IN 46750

Call Sign: KB9OFF
Lincoln G Cocklin
5350 W Division Rd
Huntington IN 46750

Call Sign: KB9NSP
David V English
6861 W Maplegrove Rd
Huntington IN 46750

Call Sign: KC9NQV
Steve M Butts
148 W McCrum St
Huntington IN 46750

Call Sign: WU9Z
Jack A Smith
4714 W River Rd
Huntington IN 46750

Call Sign: KC9APZ
William R Scheer
201 W State St Apt A
Huntington IN 46750

Call Sign: WB9VOB
Larry W Smith
404 W Tipton
Huntington IN 46750

Call Sign: KC9AZR
Sheila A Hibler
502 Wabash Cir
Huntington IN
467508413

Call Sign: KB9KII
Daniel N Kelly
5035 Wabash Rd
Huntington IN 46750

Call Sign: KB9GBN
William R Whitesell
1428 Walnut St
Huntington IN 46750

Call Sign: KB5WLD
Carol E Price
1200 Walnut St
Huntington IN 46750

Call Sign: WB9GCH
Larry F Price
1200 Walnut St
Huntington IN 46750

Call Sign: KB9VBQ
Barbara J Roberts
11 Water St
Huntington IN 46750

Call Sign: KB9VBP
Darin S Redding
11 Water St

Huntington IN 46750

Call Sign: K9MKK
Ray A Clark
1120 Waterworks Rd
Huntington IN 46750

Call Sign: N9SOU
Cheryl L Belville
538 Wilkerson St
Huntington IN 46750

Call Sign: KC9AYV
Thomas E Beeching
1259 William St
Huntington IN 46750

Call Sign: KB9UMI
Mark C Cassatt
521 William St Apt 202
Huntington IN 46750

Call Sign: N9NNV
James C Kneller
441 Zahn St
Huntington IN 46750

Call Sign: KC9HYW
Betty J Hopson
Huntington IN 46750

Call Sign: KA9DTZ
Gregory H Watson
Huntington IN 46750

Call Sign: KB9OUN
Mark T Carnes
Huntington IN 46750

FCC Amateur Radio Licenses in Idaville

Call Sign: KC9UBP
Rob B Craig
10471 E US Hwy 24

Idaville IN 47950

FCC Amateur Radio Licenses in Jonesboro

Call Sign: KB9YXY
George M Perry
4129 E 900 S
Jonesboro IN 46938

Call Sign: KB9VUL
Jacquelynn M Perry
4129 E 900 S
Jonesboro IN 46938

Call Sign: W9MGA
Jacquelynn M Perry
4129 E 900 S
Jonesboro IN 469389750

Call Sign: KB9UOW
Rod L Perry
4129 E 900 S
Jonesboro IN 469389750

Call Sign: W9ROD
Rod L Perry
4129 E 900 S
Jonesboro IN 469389750

Call Sign: KC9SSY
Timothy J Catanese
5415 E 975 S
Jonesboro IN 46938

Call Sign: WA9ZEX
Kenneth E Ellis
1110 River Ave
Jonesboro IN 46938

Call Sign: KB9ISU
David M Payne
202 S 4th Ave
Jonesboro IN 46938

Call Sign: KB9YLP
Stephen J Robinson
415 S 4th Ave
Jonesboro IN 46938

Call Sign: WA9ZIS
John D Wade
504 S Main
Jonesboro IN 469381117

Call Sign: N9PKL
James H Hahn
207 S Main St
Jonesboro IN 46938

Call Sign: N9SMD
Annette L Hahn
207 S Main St
Jonesboro IN 46938

Call Sign: N9DDM
Gary L Wade
500 S Main St
Jonesboro IN 469381117

Call Sign: KC9RIY
James L Windle Jr
904 S Water St
Jonesboro IN 46938

Call Sign: WQ9K
John W Wilhelm
8037 S Wheeling Pike
Jonesboro IN 46938

Call Sign: KB9YXX
Linda S Mark
704 W 12th St
Jonesboro IN 46938

Call Sign: KB9YXW
Brendi D Mark
704 W 12th St
Jonesboro IN 46938

Call Sign: KB9OZT
Scott W Morris
376 W 650 S
Jonesboro IN 46938

Call Sign: KB9NZR
Tobey W Morris
376 W 650 S
Jonesboro IN 46938

Call Sign: KH6EKY
Edward J Joy
618 W 9th St
Jonesboro IN 46938

Call Sign: K9SUB
Edward J Joy
618 W 9th St
Jonesboro IN 46938

**FCC Amateur Radio
Licenses in Kendallville**

Call Sign: N9RYO
Kenneth L Bodenhafer
828 Allen Chapel Rd
Kendallville IN 46755

Call Sign: WB9NFD
Richard A Gard Sr
240 Angling Rd Apt 214
Kendallville IN 46755

Call Sign: KC9GYX
David J Rhea
108 Crescent Ave
Kendallville IN 46755

Call Sign: N7ZKQ
Larry W Leonhardt
11413 E 850 N
Kendallville IN 46755

Call Sign: KB9ZDI
Timothy S Murray

1567 E Appleman Rd
Kendallville IN 46755

Call Sign: KB9VTK
David W Spence
8548 E Circle Dr
Kendallville IN 46755

Call Sign: KC9DSB
Kendallville Contesters
Club Ars
7817 E Cree Lake S
Kendallville IN 46755

Call Sign: KC9RAH
Carrie A Schlichtenmyer
1486 E Kammerer Rd
Kendallville IN 46755

Call Sign: KB9PT
David L Fulk
3270 E Mapes Rd
Kendallville IN 46755

Call Sign: N9XPU
Roy S Williams
2756 E North St
Kendallville IN 46755

Call Sign: WA9BVW
James F Holbrook
2010 E Wallace Rd
Kendallville IN 46755

Call Sign: KC9UHU
Robert E Dean Jr
440 Freeman St
Kendallville IN 46755

Call Sign: W9JWS
James W Stout
2002 Jonathan St
Kendallville IN 46755

Call Sign: KC9MTA

Donald G Buckler
1346 Knoll Crest Dr
Kendallville IN 46755

Call Sign: WA9GCA
George E Workman
454 Lake St
Kendallville IN 46755

Call Sign: KC9KNV
Kevin D Martin
426 Lewis St
Kendallville IN 46755

Call Sign: KA9HQC
Gregory R Johnson
403 McIntosh Ave
Kendallville IN 46755

Call Sign: N9XPT
Paul E Williams
9838 N 1100 E
Kendallville IN 46755

Call Sign: KC9UXM
Hobart M Poyser
11076 N 1100 E
Kendallville IN 46755

Call Sign: N9EXM
Hobart M Poyser
11076 N 1100 E
Kendallville IN 46755

Call Sign: KC9GYV
Joe W Travis
970 N Allen Chapel Rd
Kendallville IN 46755

Call Sign: W9BXV
Kenneth G Harp
722 N Main St
Kendallville IN 46755

Call Sign: N9RBS

Maurice L Marouart
950 N McKinley Ln
Kendallville IN 46755

Call Sign: KC9VEI
Kaleb B Thacker
11748 N SR 3
Kendallville IN 46755

Call Sign: N9MQB
Shelby Miller
301 N Wood St
Kendallville IN 46755

Call Sign: WA9WFS
Adam A Kacprowicz
2114 Pueblo Dr
Kendallville IN 46755

Call Sign: W9AAK
Adam A Kacprowicz
2114 Pueblo Dr
Kendallville IN 46755

Call Sign: KB9PQH
Kemper S Powell
314 Red Oak Dr
Kendallville IN 46755

Call Sign: N9JGE
Matthew A Fulk
Rr 5
Kendallville IN 46755

Call Sign: KC9IPL
Roger I Correa
1452 S Allen Chapel
Kendallville IN 46755

Call Sign: KD6UAN
Randall S Bishop
719 S Main St
Kendallville IN 46755

Call Sign: KC9MOF

Randall S Bishop
719 S Main St
Kendallville IN 46755

Call Sign: KB9PQG
Samuel W Woods
1403 S Main St
Kendallville IN 46755

Call Sign: N9RYP
Hugh T Mullen
121 S Morton
Kendallville IN
467550163

Call Sign: W9BTZ
John C Marty
213 S Oak St
Kendallville IN 46755

Call Sign: KC9NYE
Don Hoover
902 S State St
Kendallville IN 46755

Call Sign: KC9LUT
Eric J Keck
1220 S State St
Kendallville IN 46755

Call Sign: KB9BTJ
Ronald J Miller
1612 W Rimmel Rd
Kendallville IN 46755

Call Sign: AB4CN
William M Grossman
2011 W Rimmel Rd
Kendallville IN
487552527

Call Sign: KC9OWD
Matthew I Coplin
125 W Rush St
Kendallville IN 46755

Call Sign: KC9OWE
Justin M Coplin
125 W Russ St
Kendallville IN 46755

Call Sign: WA9HUP
John M Green
117 W Shalley Dr
Kendallville IN 46755

Call Sign: WB9IHR
Thomas E Trowbridge Sr
601 Wedgewood Pl
Kendallville IN 46755

Call Sign: K9RGY
C Gene Browand
313 Wood St
Kendallville IN 46755

Call Sign: WD9EMJ
Ollie D Hamdin
Kendallville IN 46755

FCC Amateur Radio Licenses in Kentland

Call Sign: KA9UGN
Gregory A Sumner
304 E Maple St
Kentland IN 47951

Call Sign: WA9GUH
Charles R Rheude
302 E Maple St
Kentland IN 47951

Call Sign: KC5LFJ
James E Large
704 N 1st St
Kentland IN 47951

Call Sign: N9KCH
David S Dennis

Kentland IN 47951

FCC Amateur Radio Licenses in Kewanna

Call Sign: N9PCP
Jeffrey J Hoffman
Box 35
Kewanna IN 46939

Call Sign: N9TJQ
N Starr Hoffman
Box 35
Kewanna IN 46939

Call Sign: KB9RHH
5 Star Repeater Club
420 S 1175 W
Kewanna IN 46939

Call Sign: KB9MWN
Michael A Beckley
9870 S 475 W
Kewanna IN 46939

Call Sign: KB9BIM
Francis G Hudkins
9268 W 100 N
Kewanna IN 46939

FCC Amateur Radio Licenses in Keystone

Call Sign: WA9WUA
Andrew F Stiltner
6924 E 900 S
Keystone IN 46759

Call Sign: K9DAW
Don A Wallace
10197 S 100 E
Keystone IN 46759

Call Sign: KB9QEV
David M Carpenter

9950 S 200 W
Keystone IN 46759

FCC Amateur Radio Licenses in Kimmell

Call Sign: WC9T
Laron P Beyer
2067 N US 33
Kimmell IN 467609634

Call Sign: KB9DDU
Marla M Beyer
2067 N US 33
Kimmell IN 467609634

Call Sign: N9MTF
Bradley K Peterson
2237 S 700 W
Kimmell IN 46760

Call Sign: N9NRN
Kendra M Peterson
2237 S 700 W
Kimmell IN 46760

Call Sign: N9YWA
Patricia A Luckey
5038 W 1005
Kimmell IN 46760

Call Sign: KC9VCY
Cameron J Meyers
Kimmell IN 46760

Call Sign: KC9HUR
James K Snyder
Kimmell IN 46760

Call Sign: KC9RRH
Nolen J Meyers
Kimmell IN 46760

Call Sign: KC9RRN
Stan L Meyers

Kimmell IN 46760

**FCC Amateur Radio
Licenses in Knox**

Call Sign: N9QYK
Paul C Lisowski
100N
Knox IN 46534

Call Sign: KC9JBB
Gregory T Hostetler
201 Allen Dr
Knox IN 465341620

Call Sign: N9OVO
Philip L Singleton
Box 122
Knox IN 46534

Call Sign: KA9VRM
Tom E Singleton
Box 128
Knox IN 46534

Call Sign: K9POT
John A Simkus
Box 320
Knox IN 46534

Call Sign: N9UVU
Eric D Scherf
Box 362
Knox IN 46534

Call Sign: KA4UKS
Max F Wolff
Box 627
Knox IN 46534

Call Sign: N9USE
Nancy J Wilson
Box 717
Knox IN 46534

Call Sign: KB9QMQ
Willard N Case
Box 98
Knox IN 46534

Call Sign: KC9ACJ
Robert D Fosnough
3604 CR 210 S
Knox IN 46534

Call Sign: NR5F
Robert D Fosnough
3604 CR 210 S
Knox IN 46534

Call Sign: KA9VFO
James H Byrd
2555 E 100 S
Knox IN 46534

Call Sign: KA9WGJ
Robert W Byrd
2555 E 100 S
Knox IN 46534

Call Sign: KC9LUR
Patrick L Mccarty Jr
4620 E 150 N
Knox IN 46534

Call Sign: KC9MQD
Kenneth R Norberg
535 E 150 S
Knox IN 46534

Call Sign: KF9IG
Sherman C Combs
2320 E 200 S
Knox IN 46534

Call Sign: KC9ISH
Randall S Brown
4060 E 200 S
Knox IN 46534

Call Sign: N9CPX
Randall S Brown
4060 E 200 S
Knox IN 46534

Call Sign: KC9GLB
Jack R Hudgens
6525 E 200 S
Knox IN 46534

Call Sign: KC9HUC
Raymond N Flory
7695 E 25 N
Knox IN 46534

Call Sign: KC9LHO
William C Husk
8160 E 25 N
Knox IN 46534

Call Sign: WC2O
William C Husk
8160 E 25 N
Knox IN 46534

Call Sign: KC9HUF
Jack R Hudgens
1875 E 250 S
Knox IN 46534

Call Sign: KB9MSX
Christopher S Simoni
3380 E 400 N
Knox IN 46534

Call Sign: KC9HUB
Roy D Bradley
1520 E 400 S
Knox IN 46534

Call Sign: N9ZUO
David E White
8075 E 50 S
Knox IN 46534

Call Sign: K9JGY
Gerald J Haney
4867 E 850 S
Knox IN 46534

Call Sign: KD9U
David J Oliver
6840 E Oakwood Ave
Knox IN 46534

Call Sign: N9DAF
Melody S Day
1915 N 300 E
Knox IN 46534

Call Sign: KC9SWR
Richard L Dennis Jr
1203 E Culver Rd
Knox IN 46534

Call Sign: KB9SCE
Daniel R Case
760 E SR 10
Knox IN 46534

Call Sign: KC9ND
Patrick H Day
1915 N 300 E
Knox IN 46534

Call Sign: KC9MAJ
Charles E Fugate
405 E Danker St
Knox IN 46534

Call Sign: KA9MBC
Daniel F Kawka
1311 E Washington
Knox IN 465341330

Call Sign: N9TJU
Mike A Wilson
15.5 N Main St
Knox IN 46534

Call Sign: KC9JQP
Michael D Martin
11968 E Division Rd
Knox IN 46534

Call Sign: N9VJS
Kathi L Browne
302 E Washington St
Knox IN 46534

Call Sign: K9CIV
Richard A Lochner
1635 N US 35
Knox IN 46534

Call Sign: WB9L
Michael D Martin
11968 E Division Rd
Knox IN 46534

Call Sign: N9VJT
Timothy E Browne
302 E Washington St
Knox IN 46534

Call Sign: KC9GKZ
Garland Collins
5920 S 100 E
Knox IN 46534

Call Sign: N9BGK
Elmer R Fritz
6855 E Hickory Dr
Knox IN 46534

Call Sign: KC9LHM
David A Regalado
5540 Edgewood Way
Knox IN 46534

Call Sign: KA9WMW
Michael A Vician
3382 S 300 E
Knox IN 46534

Call Sign: KB9OGZ
David W Tompkins
8900 E Long Ln
Knox IN 46534

Call Sign: N9QFE
Joseph J Lisowski
1360 N 1025 E
Knox IN 46534

Call Sign: KB9WXE
Joe V Thompson
2428 S 450 E
Knox IN 46534

Call Sign: KC9NFD
Joseph D Oliver
6840 E Oakwood Ave
Knox IN 46534

Call Sign: KB9VBJ
Gayla B Day
1915 N 300 E
Knox IN 46534

Call Sign: KB9WIM
James J Johnson II
8 S Cleveland St
Knox IN 46534

Call Sign: KC9MRS
David J Oliver
6840 E Oakwood Ave
Knox IN 46534

Call Sign: KB9JMO
Kenneth W Day
1915 N 300 E
Knox IN 46534

Call Sign: KC9JQO
Nancy C Fosnough
3604 S CR 210
Knox IN 46534

Call Sign: KC9OIM
Herbert L Ross Jr
406 S East St
Knox IN 46534

Call Sign: N9LU
Melissa D Moore
708 S East St
Knox IN 46534

Call Sign: N9JU
Russell J Moore
708 S East St
Knox IN 46534

Call Sign: W9QBF
Hibbert C Eckroad Sr
6729 S Lombardy
Knox IN 46534

Call Sign: KC9LCY
David E King
406 S Main
Knox IN 46534

Call Sign: KA4HWX
John M Poindexter
204 S Main St
Knox IN 46534

Call Sign: W3ML
John M Poindexter
204 S Main St
Knox IN 46534

Call Sign: KC9PTU
Kn9Ox Repeater
Association
204 S Main St
Knox IN 46534

Call Sign: KN9OX
Kn9Ox Repeater
Association
204 S Main St

Knox IN 46534

Call Sign: KC9OUN
Logan G Owens
205 S Main St
Knox IN 46534

Call Sign: KC9LHN
Gina R King
406 S Main St
Knox IN 46534

Call Sign: W9MTE
Kenneth W Whiles
408 S Pearl
Knox IN 46534

Call Sign: KD9T
Eugene W Cook
108 S Pearl St
Knox IN 46534

Call Sign: KC9IBM
Ethan P Price
303 S Shield St
Knox IN 46534

Call Sign: KC9KBI
Mark A Lovins
509 S Shield St
Knox IN 46534

Call Sign: KC9ISI
Robert E Tingley
601 S Williams St
Knox IN 46534

Call Sign: KA9ZGM
Donald J Carli
1013 Virginia Ln
Knox IN 46534

Call Sign: N9CQD
Robert A Brown
502 W Delaware St

Knox IN 46534

Call Sign: W9QN
Thomas L Troike
405 W Jackson St
Knox IN 46534

Call Sign: KC9KPE
Melissa D Moore
328 W Spruce Dr
Knox IN 46534

Call Sign: KC9KPF
Russell J Moore
328 W Spruce Dr
Knox IN 46534

Call Sign: N9HSV
Jesse D Day
Knox IN 46534

FCC Amateur Radio Licenses in Kokomo

Call Sign: WD9FKG
Kenneth A Young
200E
Kokomo IN 469024128

Call Sign: N9SDV
James R Buchanan
344E
Kokomo IN 46902

Call Sign: KD7XG
John A Lind
3803 Albright Rd
Kokomo IN 469024456

Call Sign: ND9B
Robert J Donahue
5301 Algonquin Trl
Kokomo IN 46902

Call Sign: N9NKM

Genevieve E Selley
5323 Algonquin Trl
Kokomo IN 46902

Call Sign: K9MXG
Frederick A Selley
5323 Algonquin Trl
Kokomo IN 46902

Call Sign: N9KGC
Craig A Wilson
2713 Alto Rd
Kokomo IN 46902

Call Sign: W9MJM
W James West
915 Alto Rd E
Kokomo IN 46902

Call Sign: N9MG
Michael W Gardner
4519 Anna Ln
Kokomo IN 46902

Call Sign: KB7ORP
Donald E Kesler
5409 Arrowhead Blvd
Kokomo IN 46902

Call Sign: W9OOK
James T Gotshall
3314 Artisan Dr
Kokomo IN 469028115

Call Sign: KA9ZZS
Mark E Schneider
1308 Arundel Dr
Kokomo IN 46901

Call Sign: KC9EPL
Barten E Gilbert
1317 Avalon Ct
Kokomo IN 469023103

Call Sign: WA9SCX

Charles M Cord
2217 Avalon Ct
Kokomo IN 46902

Call Sign: NM8G
Wayne A Madsen
2915 Bagley Dr
Kokomo IN 46902

Call Sign: KA9QEK
Doreen M Kiehl
2938 Bagley Dr
Kokomo IN 46902

Call Sign: WB9RUF
Alan R Anderson
2715 Bagley Dr W
Kokomo IN 469023228

Call Sign: N9LLO
Christopher S Nicholson
2513 Balmoral Blvd
Kokomo IN 46902

Call Sign: KA8DOS
James E Beckwith
2207 Baton Rouge Dr
Kokomo IN 46902

Call Sign: N9SCZ
Cathy S Weaver
909 Bellevue Pl
Kokomo IN 46901

Call Sign: W9GY
Jeffrey M Stricker
1305 Belvedere Dr
Kokomo IN 469025605

Call Sign: N9KQL
Max T Shadley
1529 Belvedere Dr
Kokomo IN 46902

Call Sign: N9SBR

Dawn R Wysong
1100 Birchwood Dr
Kokomo IN 46901

Call Sign: N9RUY
Howard M Wysong Jr
1100 Birchwood Dr
Kokomo IN 46901

Call Sign: KB9MSE
David P Goodridge
11912 Birdie Ct
Kokomo IN 469019717

Call Sign: N9LRD
Kim E Goodridge
11912 Birdie Ct
Kokomo IN 469019717

Call Sign: WB8ROE
Kim J Kochersperger
807 Boston Dr
Kokomo IN 46902

Call Sign: KG9EP
Robert D Lukes
1715 Bramoor
Kokomo IN 46902

Call Sign: KB9WRK
Brian J Denta
1521 Bramoor Dr
Kokomo IN 46902

Call Sign: N9VZU
Jan A Summers
300 Branded Blvd
Kokomo IN 46901

Call Sign: N9NKQ
Richard L Himelick
2785 Bridgestone Cir
Kokomo IN 469027009

Call Sign: KC9IPK

Brent D Gilles
1002 Brookhaven Ct
Kokomo IN 46901

Call Sign: WB9TRO
Gregory W Latus
2611 Brookshire Dr
Kokomo IN 46902

Call Sign: W8IX
Larry R Ditmer
4200 Brookside Dr
Kokomo IN 46902

Call Sign: KG9NK
Ricky A Duncan
5402 Buckskin Dr
Kokomo IN 46902

Call Sign: KC4HUF
Donald E McCoy
5509 Buckskin Dr
Kokomo IN 46902

Call Sign: KB8LS
Hilton A Turner Jr
1513 Buick Ln
Kokomo IN 469022523

Call Sign: N9VZV
Randy E Conaway
2402 Burgundy Dr
Kokomo IN 46902

Call Sign: WA9SCY
Leslie B Claxton
2408 Burningtree Ln
Kokomo IN 469021365

Call Sign: W9RZX
Maurice E Rogers
1716 Cadillac Dr W
Kokomo IN 46902

Call Sign: WB2JKY

Jimmy R Schroeder
2157 Cameron Dr
Kokomo IN 46902

Call Sign: KB9LYZ
Sarah E Wills
1609 Candy Ct N
Kokomo IN 46902

Call Sign: KC9DCT
Dale L Hawkins
3115 Carter St S
Kokomo IN 46901

Call Sign: K9HG
Dale L Hawkins
3115 Carter St S
Kokomo IN 46901

Call Sign: KC9FMV
Nancy A Hawkins
3115 Carter St S
Kokomo IN 46901

Call Sign: K9NAN
Nancy A Hawkins
3115 Carter St S
Kokomo IN 46901

Call Sign: N9HYT
Brian D Coate
513 Cassville Rd
Kokomo IN 46901

Call Sign: KB9EOS
Dale J Kumke
3500 Cedar Ct
Kokomo IN 46902

Call Sign: W9LOF
Wayne E Agnew
1012 Columbus Blvd
Kokomo IN 46901

Call Sign: N9UJB

Leslie C Renn
1712 Columbus Blvd
Kokomo IN 46901

Call Sign: W9DO
Roland F Frye
1810 Columbus Blvd
Kokomo IN 46901

Call Sign: KC0ENA
Robert M Edmond
1105 Columbus Blvd
Kokomo IN 46901

Call Sign: N9JAV
Jeffrey S Coote
2105 Corvette Dr
Kokomo IN 46902

Call Sign: KA4YGK
Richard E Glover Sr
4907 Council Ring Blvd
Kokomo IN 469025324

Call Sign: KC9PIW
Donald G Prunty
5911 Council Ring Blvd
Kokomo IN 46902

Call Sign: KC9RF
Russell H Perry
CR 400 S
Kokomo IN 46902

Call Sign: N9SCY
Thomas A Tygart
CR 650 W
Kokomo IN 46901

Call Sign: KB9JPJ
Richard Z Badders
1517 Cranbrook Dr
Kokomo IN 46902

Call Sign: KA5NGI

Richard C Walton
900 Crescent Dr
Kokomo IN 46901

Call Sign: WB9VJR
Scott W Brown
3028 Crooked Stick Dr
Kokomo IN 46902

Call Sign: N9SCB
Laura B Garman
5812 Dartmouth Ct
Kokomo IN 46902

Call Sign: K8ASX
Gerd Klingler
5909 Dartmouth Dr
Kokomo IN 46902

Call Sign: KC9UQZ
Todd M Brandenburg
1900 Dee Ann Dr
Kokomo IN 46902

Call Sign: WJ9D
Todd M Brandenburg
1900 Dee Ann Dr
Kokomo IN 46902

Call Sign: KA9QIQ
Bruce A Daulton
493 Delray St
Kokomo IN 46901

Call Sign: W9QIQ
Bruce A Daulton
493 Delray St
Kokomo IN 46901

Call Sign: N8PQX
Eugenio J De Leon
230 Devonshire Dr
Kokomo IN 46901

Call Sign: N8BRB

James H Schuelke
2002 Diplomat Ln
Kokomo IN 46902

Call Sign: W9QHC
Harold E Dague
2811 Doral Park Ct
Kokomo IN 46901

Call Sign: KA9CWB
Ralph J Baxter
2674 E 00 N S
Kokomo IN 46901

Call Sign: KB9MGJ
Craig P Millard
4113 E 00 N S
Kokomo IN 469016620

Call Sign: N9ZZD
Roger D Mitchell
4113 E 00 N S
Kokomo IN 469026620

Call Sign: KB9AVB
Michael A Thomas
1643 E 100 N
Kokomo IN 46901

Call Sign: N8JCA
Edwin J Lossing
1716 E 100 N
Kokomo IN 46901

Call Sign: KC9JSX
Kevin M Cooney
2132 E 100 N
Kokomo IN 469013455

Call Sign: N9YTA
Roger D Sand
4260 E 100 N
Kokomo IN 46901

Call Sign: N9JMX

Robert J Atkins
4356 E 100 S
Kokomo IN 46902

Call Sign: KB9QNY
Mary C Hayes
4356 E 100 S
Kokomo IN 469029335

Call Sign: WB9GXA
William I Orttel
1203 E 1350 S
Kokomo IN 46901

Call Sign: N9QGG
William H Barnard
2115 E 200 S
Kokomo IN 46902

Call Sign: KB9JBJ
Merrell L Campbell
700 E 2662 S
Kokomo IN 46902

Call Sign: N9SDP
Darlton L Bontrager
3586 E 300 N
Kokomo IN 46901

Call Sign: KC9CSM
Darlton L Bontrager
3586 E 300 N
Kokomo IN 46901

Call Sign: KF9XD
Glen T Bontrager
3586 E 300 N
Kokomo IN 46901

Call Sign: WA9LXK
Herman G Locke
3174 E 300 S
Kokomo IN 469029252

Call Sign: KC9ULG

Robert J Clark
3354 E 300 S
Kokomo IN 46902

Call Sign: KB9RGF
Charlie W McClish
3613 E 300 S
Kokomo IN 46902

Call Sign: KC9KAA
Jo D Mcclish
3613 E 300 S
Kokomo IN 46902

Call Sign: N9WPU
Debra A McKee
265 E 400 S
Kokomo IN 46902

Call Sign: KA9WCM
Dennis L Cook
4149 E 400 S
Kokomo IN 46904

Call Sign: N9YFQ
Dustin E McKee
265 E 400 S
Kokomo IN 46902

Call Sign: N9XLU
Gerald E McKee
265 E 400 S
Kokomo IN 46902

Call Sign: N9LRJ
Jan M Loisch
3878 E 50 N
Kokomo IN 46901

Call Sign: KK9I
Robert L Taylor
4609 E 50 N
Kokomo IN 46901

Call Sign: KB9MSD

Noah J Herschberger
4823 E 600 N
Kokomo IN 46901

Call Sign: N9UKO
Carole B Brantley
1901 E Alto Rd
Kokomo IN 46902

Call Sign: KD3EF
Richard D Brantley
1901 E Alto Rd
Kokomo IN 46902

Call Sign: KB9KRX
Thomas E Inderhees
2432 E Baxter Rd
Kokomo IN 46902

Call Sign: WB9YZK
Jerry L Rosselot
2117 E Carter
Kokomo IN 46901

Call Sign: KC9CBA
Duane K Kelly
1013 E Cornell Rd
Kokomo IN 46901

Call Sign: N9AWR
Larry L Amthauer
4758 E CR 00Ns
Kokomo IN 46901

Call Sign: KD9BT
Norman L Gingerich
2408 E CR 1400 S
Kokomo IN 469017588

Call Sign: KB9PXV
Brian M West
1200 E Firmin St
Kokomo IN 46902

Call Sign: KB9RLN

Gerald B West
1200 E Firmin St
Kokomo IN 46902

Call Sign: KB9SOA
Danny R McCain
1817 E Firmin St
Kokomo IN 46902

Call Sign: KB9VIE
Robert R Rosenbaum II
717 E Fischer St
Kokomo IN 46901

Call Sign: KC9ELH
Terry L Brown
1113 E Fischer St
Kokomo IN 46901

Call Sign: N9SAO
Raymond G Gresley
1108 E Gerhart
Kokomo IN 46901

Call Sign: AA9GV
Jason R Seabolt
918 E Harrison St
Kokomo IN 46901

Call Sign: N9RLP
John A Seabolt
918 E Harrison St
Kokomo IN 46901

Call Sign: N9PWJ
Thomas C Lossing
1223 E Laguna
Kokomo IN 46902

Call Sign: KB9SWV
Robert A McGimpsey
505 E Lordeman St
Kokomo IN 469012311

Call Sign: KB9MNZ

Bobby Riley
1400 E Monroe
Kokomo IN 46901

Call Sign: W9KMY
Joseph M McClain
700 E North St
Kokomo IN 46901

Call Sign: WA9QWM
Oliver Cobb
1051 E North St
Kokomo IN 46901

Call Sign: WA9WBD
Hobert E Dodd
4073 E Oo N S
Kokomo IN 46902

Call Sign: KA9OZA
William E Daugherty
308 E Taylor
Kokomo IN 46901

Call Sign: KB9TRR
John T Watkins
1312 E Taylor
Kokomo IN 46901

Call Sign: WB9HEW
Ted A Weber
301 Edgewater Ln
Kokomo IN 46902

Call Sign: N9NKO
Werner Zackschewski
2235 Edward Dr
Kokomo IN 46902

Call Sign: WD9HQD
Richard J Sanders
1955 Elizabeth Ln
Kokomo IN 46902

Call Sign: K9RJS

Richard J Sanders
1955 Elizabeth Ln
Kokomo IN 46902

Call Sign: KA9SDR
Stephen E Ewbank
1806 Elva Dr
Kokomo IN 46902

Call Sign: KB9AUZ
Jeffrey L Kingery
1810 Elva Dr
Kokomo IN 46902

Call Sign: KB9RQ
Jerry A Johnson
3106 Elva Dr
Kokomo IN 46902

Call Sign: WD9HZQ
Steven M Fisher
1628 Executive Dr
Kokomo IN 46902

Call Sign: WN9O
Kevin E McClure
1610 Fairway Dr
Kokomo IN 46901

Call Sign: W9NCC
J Dane Ridenour
2501 Friendship Blvd Apt
118
Kokomo IN 46901

Call Sign: K9PHL
Jeffrey L Ellison
3455 Ginger Ct
Kokomo IN 46901

Call Sign: KB9TEZ
Thomas E Sanders
1624 Gleneagles Dr
Kokomo IN 469023171

Call Sign: W9ITT
Herman W Gross
1705 Gordon Dr
Kokomo IN 46902

Call Sign: W9IU
Don A Coulter
1600 Green Acres Dr
Kokomo IN 46901

Call Sign: KC9IZ
James D Henson Jr
304 Greenbriar
Kokomo IN 46901

Call Sign: KB9IWI
Ronnie L Nearon
239 Greenbriar St
Kokomo IN 46901

Call Sign: K9EYV
Bill H Phipps
2208 Grey Twig Dr
Kokomo IN 46901

Call Sign: W9BFF
Jerry M Mason
2306 Grey Twig Dr
Kokomo IN 46902

Call Sign: KA9RCN
Linda D Grady
6001 Harvard Dr
Kokomo IN 46902

Call Sign: K9OPO
Roger A Grady
6001 Harvard Dr
Kokomo IN 46902

Call Sign: KC9BNR
Charles N Elwood
2227 Hazelnut Ln
Kokomo IN 46902

Call Sign: KC9SDU
Frank D Momot
2555 Hazelnut Ln
Kokomo IN 46902

Call Sign: KC9SWX
Dennis W Hesselman
2833 Heritage Dr
Kokomo IN 46901

Call Sign: KB9AUY
Daniel E Beaver
516 Hillcrest Dr
Kokomo IN 46901

Call Sign: KC9AOA
Casey Heaton
608 Holly Ln
Kokomo IN 46902

Call Sign: N9LRC
Merril T Glentzer
1401 Honey Ln
Kokomo IN 469023921

Call Sign: WA9YVS
Perry E Grieb
1405 Honey Ln
Kokomo IN 46902

Call Sign: KD9LP
Leslie V Cattin
913 James Dr
Kokomo IN 46902

Call Sign: KB9VAP
Jeffrey H Burns
3210 Janice Dr
Kokomo IN 46902

Call Sign: AB9AO
Jeffrey H Burns
3210 Janice Dr
Kokomo IN 46902

Call Sign: KC9AEF
Lynne M Burns
3210 Janice Dr
Kokomo IN 469023922

Call Sign: K9CTH
William H Hubbard
909 Jeff Dr
Kokomo IN 469016707

Call Sign: WB9ZGW
William B Morgan III
4207 Kelly Ct
Kokomo IN 46902

Call Sign: KB9IG
Richard J Rush
2114 Kerri Lynn Ln
Kokomo IN 46902

Call Sign: KB9YIL
Tony E Forsythe
1611 Kingston Rd
Kokomo IN 46901

Call Sign: WB9VEI
Mickey D Arvin
6001 Kiowa
Kokomo IN 46902

Call Sign: N4BKA
Jon P Kelley
4160 Lake Windemere
Ln
Kokomo IN 46902

Call Sign: KA9JXP
Robert D Newburn
983 Lakeside Ct
Kokomo IN 46901

Call Sign: KU9D
Michael J Young
3109 Lamplighter Ln
Kokomo IN 46902

Call Sign: K9MIT
Charles C McCoy
4206 Lance Ct
Kokomo IN 469024109

Call Sign: N9HOO
David J Gatchell
213 Laramie Ln
Kokomo IN 46901

Call Sign: KA9OVB
Homer S Ericson
124 Leafy Ln
Kokomo IN 46902

Call Sign: W9CRC
Russell B Rennaker Sr
1011 Linda Dr
Kokomo IN 46902

Call Sign: KC9DHG
Owen L Lowe
5514 Long Bow Dr
Kokomo IN 46902

Call Sign: KC9NNH
John M Mansur
2112 Lynn Dr
Kokomo IN 46902

Call Sign: K9HIA
William C Thornton
2236 Lynn Dr
Kokomo IN 46902

Call Sign: N9PWI
Mark A Koors
3607 Lyons Dr
Kokomo IN 46902

Call Sign: WA9GKT
Russell C Allen
532 Magnolia Dr
Kokomo IN 46901

Call Sign: K9MJZ
Kent H Blacklidge
814 Maplewood Dr
Kokomo IN 46902

Call Sign: WB9UGI
Robert E Moredock
1000 Maplewood Dr
Kokomo IN 46902

Call Sign: KA9NPF
Alice M Reecer
406 Marilyn Ct
Kokomo IN 46902

Call Sign: N9AEI
Willard M Puranen
717 Marsha Dr
Kokomo IN 469024339

Call Sign: W9GO
Kokomo ARC
717 Marsha Dr
Kokomo IN 469024339

Call Sign: W9ASC
Philip P Porter
720 Marsha Dr
Kokomo IN 46902

Call Sign: W9JU
Robert J Ropes
3009 Mayfair Dr
Kokomo IN 46902

Call Sign: N9XSB
Philip R Stavroff
3033 Mayfair Dr
Kokomo IN 46902

Call Sign: WB9RDN
Robert Stavroff
3033 Mayfair Dr
Kokomo IN 469023932

Call Sign: KC9AKU
Christopher K Smith
2921 Mayor Dr
Kokomo IN 46902

Call Sign: KA9KXP
Harold W Harrington
1524 Meadowbrook Dr
Kokomo IN 46902

Call Sign: N9EKN
Stephen L Inman
3404 Melody Ln E
Kokomo IN 46902

Call Sign: N9XYS
Jon R Padfield
3408 Melody Ln E
Kokomo IN 46902

Call Sign: N9DBU
Larry C Durbin
3412 Melody Ln E
Kokomo IN 46902

Call Sign: KC9CCI
Debra A Kelly
805 Miami Blvd
Kokomo IN 46902

Call Sign: K9GEP
Kenneth M Hunt
Mill St
Kokomo IN 46902

Call Sign: KA9YOE
Jerry L Logan
1907 Mohr Dr
Kokomo IN 46902

Call Sign: N9ZNE
Robert N Logan
1907 Mohr Dr
Kokomo IN 46902

Call Sign: W9CUO
Lester J Maibaum
2302 Mohr Dr
Kokomo IN 46901

Call Sign: KB9MBW
Ricky A Dempsey
5900 Monona Dr
Kokomo IN 46902

Call Sign: N9KYB
Steven M Jones
1703 N 1050 W
Kokomo IN 46901

Call Sign: KC9BRU
Julie A Miller
5194 N 300 W
Kokomo IN 46901

Call Sign: KC9NND
Shayne A Riley
2708 N 500 W
Kokomo IN 46901

Call Sign: KC9GJP
Micah J Fivecoate
210 N 600 W
Kokomo IN 46901

Call Sign: AB9JG
Ian C Offer
852 N 600 W
Kokomo IN 46901

Call Sign: N9XG
Ian C Offer
852 N 600 W
Kokomo IN 46901

Call Sign: KC9UMI
Douglas C Martin
3497 N 650 W
Kokomo IN 46901

Call Sign: KC9JSW
David S Maxey
1668 N 700 E
Kokomo IN 46901

Call Sign: WD9GWU
Roger L Willits
2260 N 700 E
Kokomo IN 46401

Call Sign: KB9MDP
Brenda K Willits
2260 N 700 E
Kokomo IN 46901

Call Sign: KB9RZF
Jeffrey J Marrah
235 N 820 W
Kokomo IN 46901

Call Sign: WB9FLK
Lawrence D Huffer Sr
2900 N Appersonway Lot
357
Kokomo IN 46901

Call Sign: W9FLK
Lawrence D Huffer Sr
2900 N Appersonway Lot
357
Kokomo IN 46901

Call Sign: KB9UTK
Molly M Foland
1408 N Bell
Kokomo IN 46901

Call Sign: N9XYT
Brent A Snow
2316 N Bell
Kokomo IN 46901

Call Sign: KB9ZGD
Brian J Mula

601 N Berkley Rd
Kokomo IN 46901

Call Sign: KB9ZRU
Brian J Mula
601 N Berkley Rd
Kokomo IN 46901

Call Sign: WB9WIG
Patricia A Mula
601 N Berkley Rd
Kokomo IN 46901

Call Sign: WB9WJN
Roddy Mula
601 N Berkley Rd
Kokomo IN 46901

Call Sign: N9NKN
Mary L Corey
1021 N Berkley Rd
Kokomo IN 46901

Call Sign: N9ZEY
David B Bricknell
2010 N Buckeye
Kokomo IN 46901

Call Sign: KB9WRG
Eric P Muffley
2323 N Buckeye St
Kokomo IN 46901

Call Sign: N9LRI
Byron N Rhodes
1134 N Burk
Kokomo IN 46901

Call Sign: KA9OWN
Richard L Mitchell
2184 N CR 300 W
Kokomo IN 469019104

Call Sign: KJ9G
Richard L Mitchell

2184 N CR 300 W
Kokomo IN 469019104

Call Sign: KB9AVA
Espie P Mitchell
2184 N CR 300 W
Kokomo IN 469019104

Call Sign: KC9UBQ
Grephen Latif
3267 N Davis Rd
Kokomo IN 46901

Call Sign: N9AA
Scott A Manthe
914 N Forest Dr
Kokomo IN 46901

Call Sign: KA9NCX
Dale E Lewis
919 N Forest Dr
Kokomo IN 46901

Call Sign: W9MJN
Fred B Kearney
235 N Hickory Ln
Kokomo IN 469013826

Call Sign: N9HZU
Timothy D Martin
805 N Hickory Ln
Kokomo IN 46901

Call Sign: KC9VAO
Larry J Sparks
1401 N Hickory Ln
Kokomo IN 46901

Call Sign: N9NKW
Randy L Dempsey
1605 N Jay St
Kokomo IN 469012443

Call Sign: KG9AP
Fred A Murphy

1902 N Jay St
Kokomo IN 46901

2152 N Market St
Kokomo IN 46901

113 N Rd 820 W
Kokomo IN 46901

Call Sign: KB9QNZ
Robert E Chalmers
2419 N Jay St
Kokomo IN 46901

Call Sign: N9UVT
Jeffery L Miller
2152 N Market St
Kokomo IN 46901

Call Sign: KB9BCA
Sandra J Luckey
2405 N Union St
Kokomo IN 46901

Call Sign: N9OHO
Gene R Tippy
2312 N La Fountain
Kokomo IN 46901

Call Sign: N9UNI
Terry L Miller
2152 N Market St
Kokomo IN 46901

Call Sign: N9UES
Julie A Parks
1134 N Wabash
Kokomo IN 46901

Call Sign: KA9FAA
John O Lee II
1413 N Leeds
Kokomo IN 46901

Call Sign: N9JSN
Joanne L Kelly
4814 N Pkwy
Kokomo IN 46901

Call Sign: K9VIF
Meredith R Kingery
1112 N Wabash Ave
Kokomo IN 469012606

Call Sign: N9NKT
Chris W Fidler
1516 N Lindsay St
Kokomo IN 46901

Call Sign: KE9WT
Phillip W Kelly
4814 N Pkwy
Kokomo IN 46901

Call Sign: W9QUI
Raymond L Snyder
1216 N Wabash Ave
Kokomo IN 469015005

Call Sign: N9XSD
Douglas A Gelzleichter
2136 N Locke St
Kokomo IN 46901

Call Sign: KA9KHD
Bryan C Byers
4832 N Pkwy
Kokomo IN 46901

Call Sign: KA9ZXF
Linda L Sams
2310 N Waugh
Kokomo IN 46901

Call Sign: KF4ODE
Keith S Smitt
606 N Market St
Kokomo IN 46901

Call Sign: KB9BOS
Samuel J Humphries Sr
807 N Purdum
Kokomo IN 46901

Call Sign: N9YAX
Jerry R Rust
400 N Western Ave
Kokomo IN 46901

Call Sign: KC9PQU
Charles R Sanders
1408 N Market St
Kokomo IN 46901

Call Sign: W9WWJ
Wesley W Jeffries
1519 N Purdum St
Kokomo IN 46901

Call Sign: KA9OMP
John A Lundmark
4705 North Pkwy
Kokomo IN 46901

Call Sign: K9MOS
Charles R Sanders
1408 N Market St
Kokomo IN 46901

Call Sign: N9NKS
William R Ballenger
4567 N Rd 150 W
Kokomo IN 46901

Call Sign: W9PUK
Ross G Jordan Jr
4811 North Pkwy
Kokomo IN 46901

Call Sign: N9ZZC
Elaine Miller

Call Sign: WA9OPV
Robert L Harding

Call Sign: KC9TA
Jimmy E Bass

2009 Northview
Kokomo IN 46901

2320 Pinehurst Ln
Kokomo IN 46902

4702 Pumpkin Leaf Dr
Kokomo IN 46902

Call Sign: KA9ZDZ
Rhonda G Watson
1633 Oakhill Rd
Kokomo IN 46902

Call Sign: K9MXE
Frederick W Selley
1726 Pinetree Ln
Kokomo IN 46902

Call Sign: KB9ZYU
Sarah B Mock
4805 Pumpkin Leaf Dr
Kokomo IN 46902

Call Sign: W9KRC
Kokomo Repeater Club
3604 Oakhurst Dr
Kokomo IN 46902

Call Sign: KC9DHH
Benjamin L Moses
1965 Player Pl
Kokomo IN 46902

Call Sign: WD9IHF
Charlotte R Alley
512 Rainbow Dr E
Kokomo IN 46902

Call Sign: KB9RYO
Robert D Obenchain
3604 Oakhurst Dr
Kokomo IN 469023613

Call Sign: WA9SCZ
Steve A Golding
1611 Pontiac Dr
Kokomo IN 46902

Call Sign: WD9HUA
James F Alley
512 Rainbow Dr E
Kokomo IN 46902

Call Sign: W9NWN
Robert D Obenchain
3604 Oakhurst Dr
Kokomo IN 469023613

Call Sign: N9QGH
Edward J Hyland
5704 Princeton
Kokomo IN 46902

Call Sign: K9VIB
Joseph V Randall
1305 Red Bird Ct
Kokomo IN 46902

Call Sign: KC9TLE
John W Danley
4601 Orleans Dr
Kokomo IN 46902

Call Sign: N9PWH
Sue A Hyland
5704 Princeton Ct
Kokomo IN 46902

Call Sign: N9HZV
Donald K Goodin
3820 Red Bud Ln
Kokomo IN 469024381

Call Sign: KC9FGW
James E Irwin
3200 Oxford St
Kokomo IN 469021500

Call Sign: KB9VMM
Craig A Lechlitner
4607 Pumpkin Leaf Dr
Kokomo IN 46902

Call Sign: W9AIR
Michael D Ringeisen
1309 Redbird Ct
Kokomo IN 46901

Call Sign: W9LU
Gordon L Smith
4504 Parkwood Dr
Kokomo IN 46901

Call Sign: N9KDP
Larry D Lechlitner
4607 Pumpkin Leaf Dr
Kokomo IN 46902

Call Sign: KB9UBA
James D Wheeler
200 Redwood Dr
Kokomo IN 469023625

Call Sign: KC9QVE
Anthony O Ridlen
432 Pillars Pl Apt 8
Kokomo IN 46902

Call Sign: N9KDQ
Marguerite A Lechlitner
4607 Pumpkin Leaf Dr
Kokomo IN 46902

Call Sign: KB9BCB
Bradley B Jones
800 Ridge Ave
Kokomo IN 46901

Call Sign: KG9FE
William W Parks

Call Sign: N9ZZB
Benjamin E McNally

Call Sign: KB9WPP
Michael W Blazier

1317 Roberts Dr
Kokomo IN 46902

13097 S 300E
Kokomo IN 46901

3468 S 400 W
Kokomo IN 46902

Call Sign: K5PSI
Michael W Blazier
1317 Roberts Dr
Kokomo IN 46902

Call Sign: KA9TAE
Gregory L Richardson
2861 S 350 E
Kokomo IN 46902

Call Sign: KB9NSU
Michaele K Aldridge
3468 S 400 W
Kokomo IN 46902

Call Sign: N9CYN
Christopher W Jones
4502 Rolland Dr
Kokomo IN 46902

Call Sign: K9TAE
Gregory L Richardson
2861 S 350 E
Kokomo IN 46902

Call Sign: KB9FM
James R Wright
3312 S 400 W Airport Rd
Kokomo IN 46902

Call Sign: KA9MRR
Kenneth E Nelson
Rr 3
Kokomo IN 46901

Call Sign: KA9GFS
David A Cregar
3420 S 350 W
Kokomo IN 46902

Call Sign: N9SJL
Robert E Gust
4536 S 450 E
Kokomo IN 46902

Call Sign: N4PCV
Daniel R Payne
1400 Ruhl Garden Ct
Kokomo IN 469029702

Call Sign: KA9YRY
Tonna K Cregar
3420 S 350W
Kokomo IN 46902

Call Sign: W9CE
William G Rickey
3461 S 600 E
Kokomo IN 46902

Call Sign: N9DRP
Daniel R Payne
1400 Ruhl Garden Ct
Kokomo IN 469029702

Call Sign: KC9DHF
Jerry L Price
759 S 400 E
Kokomo IN 46902

Call Sign: WA9UJY
Richard A Kennedy
606 S 750 W
Kokomo IN 46901

Call Sign: KA9OYM
Mark A Elkins
4108 S 00 Ew
Kokomo IN 46902

Call Sign: KB9WE
Robert H Obremski
3321 S 400 E Rd
Kokomo IN 469029358

Call Sign: K9FTQ
Owen Wright
3204 S Albright Rd
Kokomo IN 46901

Call Sign: N9ZFD
John A Shrock
11971 S 100 W
Kokomo IN 46901

Call Sign: KY9F
Robert H Obremski
3321 S 400 E Rd
Kokomo IN 469029358

Call Sign: N9YFT
Charles L Dusenberry
3611 S Albright Rd
Kokomo IN 46902

Call Sign: KA9ERD
Rebecca A Ulerick
12670 S 200 W
Kokomo IN 46901

Call Sign: KC9TJM
Bob Japundza
3384 S 400 W
Kokomo IN 46902

Call Sign: KC9OEW
Rex A Cook
904 S Bell St
Kokomo IN 46901

Call Sign: WD9JKR
George M Gaskill Jr

Call Sign: KB9MDB
Gregory E Aldridge

Call Sign: W9REX
Rex A Cook

904 S Bell St
Kokomo IN 46901

Call Sign: KB9KCE
Lizbeth C Welch
409 S Brooks St
Kokomo IN 46901

Call Sign: KC9NNG
Daniel F Doyle
1115 S Buckeye
Kokomo IN 46901

Call Sign: N5NBU
Donald A Lane
1603 S Courtland
Kokomo IN 469022055

Call Sign: KC9AOB
Mary Jo Russell
2305 S Courtland Ave
Kokomo IN 46902

Call Sign: WD9HUC
Robert B Longshore
4463 S CR 0 E W Box 92
Kokomo IN 46902

Call Sign: KB9SIS
Raymond L Silver
2669 S CR 400 E
Kokomo IN 46902

Call Sign: W9WPH
Arthur L Anderson
4329 S CR 50 E
Kokomo IN 46902

Call Sign: KA9AFU
William I Summers
4587 S CR 50 E
Kokomo IN 46902

Call Sign: KA9SDN
Bernadine A Hulka

4678 S CR 500 E
Kokomo IN 46902

Call Sign: WB9FND
Robert S Hulka
4678 S CR 500 E
Kokomo IN 46902

Call Sign: N9SGQ
Robert L Moloch
4422 S CR 600 E
Kokomo IN 46902

Call Sign: WB9TXV
Vernon R Fowler
3287 S CR 800E
Kokomo IN 46902

Call Sign: KB9EFX
Gary K Mitchell
3324 S Dixon Apt 227
Kokomo IN 46902

Call Sign: KE9HA
Lori A Kis
3304 S Dixon Ln Apt 145
Kokomo IN 46902

Call Sign: K9MWC
Frances L Fulwider
1929 S Dixon Rd
Kokomo IN 46902

Call Sign: KB9WRL
Jerome A Schneider
2709 S Dixon Rd
Kokomo IN 46902

Call Sign: N0JM
Jerry Malone
900 S Elizabeth
Kokomo IN 469015674

Call Sign: KC9GDR
William D Bird

1214 S Elizabeth
Kokomo IN 46902

Call Sign: N9ZYW
David E Hoy
116 S Forest Dr
Kokomo IN 46901

Call Sign: N9VZT
Ivan E Rohrer
137 S Forest Dr
Kokomo IN 46901

Call Sign: KA9IAM
Leo G Whitney
1830 S Goyer Rd
Kokomo IN 46902

Call Sign: KJ9Y
M Ellen Whitney
1830 S Goyer Rd
Kokomo IN 46902

Call Sign: KC9KGQ
James R Hunt
901 S Hickory Ln
Kokomo IN 46901

Call Sign: K9GTJ
James R Hunt
901 S Hickory Ln
Kokomo IN 46901

Call Sign: KC9LIM
Jeri A Hunt
901 S Hickory Ln
Kokomo IN 46901

Call Sign: W9CLD
Cliff L Duke
1515 S Home Ave
Kokomo IN 46902

Call Sign: KB9TBF
Leota I Duke

1515 S Home Ave
Kokomo IN 46902

5011 S Park Rd
Kokomo IN 46902

3503 S Webster
Kokomo IN 46902

Call Sign: N9IPA
Francis R Elliott Jr
1745 S Indiana
Kokomo IN 46902

Call Sign: KG9T
Martin S Young
1413 S Styer Ave
Kokomo IN 46902

Call Sign: N9NKU
Leslie W Shelley
616 S Webster Apt 1
Kokomo IN 46901

Call Sign: W9FPJ
Francis R Elliott Jr
1745 S Indiana
Kokomo IN 46902

Call Sign: W9MQS
Vincent C Guerin
1811 S Union
Kokomo IN 46901

Call Sign: KB9GKW
Philip M Brown
522 S Webster St
Kokomo IN 46901

Call Sign: KB9PJO
Jeremiah D White
719 S Leeds
Kokomo IN 46901

Call Sign: KB9MNY
Jon A Scheetz
1058 S Union St
Kokomo IN 46902

Call Sign: WC9ABQ
Howard Cty Emerg
Mngmnt Agency
3600 S Webster St
Kokomo IN 46502

Call Sign: KC9PLV
James E Mcguire Jr
1245 S Locke St
Kokomo IN 46902

Call Sign: KB9THN
Wesley W Jeffries
1818 S Wabash Ave
Kokomo IN 46902

Call Sign: KA9YYU
William S Aburn
3600 S Webster St
Kokomo IN 46902

Call Sign: KB9QYU
John V La Free
1319 S Main St
Kokomo IN 46902

Call Sign: KB9WTE
Gregory R Mccoy
2501 S Wabash Ave
Kokomo IN 469023313

Call Sign: KB9PVQ
Pac ARC
140 S Western Ave
Kokomo IN 46901

Call Sign: WB9JOI
Jimmie J Gibson
2922 S Park Rd
Kokomo IN 46901

Call Sign: KA9BWP
John W Kennedy
1431 S Washington St
Kokomo IN 46901

Call Sign: WD9HWO
Sharon S Kelly
403 Sagebrush Dr
Kokomo IN 469017014

Call Sign: N9EBZ
Evelyn W Fewell
3406 S Park Rd
Kokomo IN 46902

Call Sign: KC9DOI
Bruce C Moss
1435 S Washington St
Kokomo IN 46902

Call Sign: KC9RZF
Jerry N Titus Jr
1812 Saint Charles Ct
Kokomo IN 46902

Call Sign: N9DZY
Waldo F Fewell
3406 S Park Rd
Kokomo IN 46902

Call Sign: N9PWG
Steven P Ballenger
1200 S Waugh
Kokomo IN 46902

Call Sign: N9VZS
Gordon D Williams
800 Salem Dr
Kokomo IN 46902

Call Sign: KB9GKG
Kenneth E Gaines

Call Sign: KE4YPO
John L Amos

Call Sign: KD9YF

Oliver F Justice
5810 Seneca Trl
Kokomo IN 46902

Call Sign: N9VOB
John D Fulton
2000 Sibley Dr
Kokomo IN 46902

Call Sign: N9DGR
Donald E Vandercook
26 Southdowns Dr
Kokomo IN 46902

Call Sign: N9DGC
Teresa L Vandercook
26 Southdowns Dr
Kokomo IN 46902

Call Sign: W9DJJ
Howard F Johnson
33 Southdowns Dr
Kokomo IN 46902

Call Sign: K9FB
John N Reigler
1108 Southway Blvd E
Kokomo IN 46902

Call Sign: WD9JLP
Teresa M Reigler
1108 Southway Blvd E
Kokomo IN 46902

Call Sign: K9JDU
Tom V Pfaffenbach
2005 Southway Blvd E
Kokomo IN 46902

Call Sign: N9MBJ
Steven J Engelder
2501 Spring Grove Dr
Kokomo IN 46902

Call Sign: KB9OYB

George W Grills
3303 Springdale Dr
Kokomo IN 46902

Call Sign: N9RRM
Shawn R Zackschewski
4037 Springmill Dr
Kokomo IN 46902

Call Sign: WH6CDU
Lloyd M Deem II
737 Springwater Rd
Kokomo IN 46902

Call Sign: NI9J
Larry D Ousley
2706 St Dennis Ct
Kokomo IN 46902

Call Sign: NW8O
James K Harrison
1314 Styer Ave
Kokomo IN 46902

Call Sign: KC9SFM
Martin M Pendergast
3705 Sugar Ln
Kokomo IN 46902

Call Sign: KB9PXX
Aaron S Morehead
2812 Sundown Dr
Kokomo IN 46901

Call Sign: N9NKL
Burtron D Schertz
3205 Susan Ct
Kokomo IN 46902

Call Sign: KA9GJC
Philip A Inman
1505 Tally Ho Ct
Kokomo IN 46902

Call Sign: N9FGH

James M Caddell
3120 Tally Ho Dr
Kokomo IN 46902

Call Sign: N9UKS
John D Lawler
3313 Tally Ho Dr
Kokomo IN 46902

Call Sign: N9XMC
Sean D Lawler
3313 Tally Ho Dr
Kokomo IN 46902

Call Sign: N9JHJ
Monte M Sanders
3709 Tallyho Dr
Kokomo IN 46902

Call Sign: W9HTA
John E Ross
2428 Tam O Shanter Rd
Kokomo IN 46902

Call Sign: KB9EYW
Ian T Bowen
1008 Tee Pee Dr
Kokomo IN 46902

Call Sign: WB9EPF
James W Arnett
1006 Tepee Dr
Kokomo IN 46901

Call Sign: K9PEF
Laverne F Stewart
3101 Terrace Dr
Kokomo IN 469023730

Call Sign: KC9AZU
Vic P Thacker
3005 Timber Valley Dr
Kokomo IN 469025064

Call Sign: WD9HLA

David A Pogue
3901 Tulip Ln
Kokomo IN 46901

Call Sign: KB9UFZ
Kenneth S Uhle
1918 Verasailles Dr
Kokomo IN 46902

Call Sign: KB9QNV
Marshall L Wisehart
2207 Versailles Dr
Kokomo IN 46902

Call Sign: KC9IWQ
Joshua P Beckner
3077 Vinton Cir
Kokomo IN 46902

Call Sign: WD8DXA
Kevin T Hankins
7594 W 00 Ns
Kokomo IN 46901

Call Sign: KC9CHE
Gregory M Winn
4208 W 100 N
Kokomo IN 46901

Call Sign: K9QAU
Glenn E Wilson
5281 W 100 N
Kokomo IN 46901

Call Sign: WA9ESN
Rosemary Wilson
5281 W 100 N
Kokomo IN 46901

Call Sign: KC9IYD
Neil E Winn
4208 W 100N
Kokomo IN 46901

Call Sign: KB9CUS

Andrew N Crum
12888 W 200 N
Kokomo IN 46901

Call Sign: N9NKR
Ray T Vandergriff
3621 W 250 S
Kokomo IN 46902

Call Sign: KA9ERC
Thomas G Bowen
9506 W 300 N
Kokomo IN 46901

Call Sign: W9YIE
Arthur M Wood
581 W 300 S
Kokomo IN 46902

Call Sign: KC9CUU
John M Konold
1079 W 300 S
Kokomo IN 46902

Call Sign: KC9NNB
John M Engelhardt
4293 W 350 N
Kokomo IN 46901

Call Sign: W9LJH
Larry J Hawks
2647 W 400 S
Kokomo IN 46902

Call Sign: KC9KAM
Adam S Hartman
10463 W 500 N
Kokomo IN 46901

Call Sign: W9GIB
Howard N Louden
2138 W Carter St
Kokomo IN 46901

Call Sign: K9ROE

Glenn E Hobbs
2911 W Carter St
Kokomo IN 46901

Call Sign: KC9TWT
Roger L Murphy
10313 W CR 00 Ns
Kokomo IN 46901

Call Sign: K9VEZ
James I Moyer
3019 W CR 300 S
Kokomo IN 46902

Call Sign: KA9BSJ
Wilbur G Eikenberry
450 W CR 400 S
Kokomo IN 46902

Call Sign: WD9GKK
Ronald E Hite
269 W CR 600 N
Kokomo IN 46901

Call Sign: N9KJM
William A Peacock
711 W Foster
Kokomo IN 46902

Call Sign: AA9YX
William A Peacock
711 W Foster
Kokomo IN 46902

Call Sign: KG9QL
William A Peacock
711 W Foster St
Kokomo IN 469026269

Call Sign: W9YPR
Donald E Tomaszewski
1904 W Havens Dr
Kokomo IN 46901

Call Sign: KC9LNS

Laura M Taylor
1928 W Havens St
Kokomo IN 46901

Mary K Lamb
26 W Lake Dr
Kokomo IN 46901

Terry L McCray
3260 W SR 18
Kokomo IN 46901

Call Sign: WA9BPO
Laura M Taylor
1928 W Havens St
Kokomo IN 46901

Call Sign: N9XLT
David A Wallace
419 W Lincoln Rd P 4
Kokomo IN 46902

Call Sign: WM9D
Michael L Pelgen
840 W State St
Kokomo IN 46902

Call Sign: KC9IQK
Cliff A Rikard
1328 W Jefferson St
Kokomo IN 46901

Call Sign: N9BTX
Patrick F Collins
1611 W Madison
Kokomo IN 46901

Call Sign: KA9MTQ
Michael D Collins
2603 W Sycamore
Kokomo IN 46901

Call Sign: N9BWO
William L Coy
1404 W Jefferson St
Kokomo IN 46901

Call Sign: KB9NIK
David L Moon
1911 W Madison
Kokomo IN 469011827

Call Sign: KC9NNC
Virgil W Weitzel
1512 W Tate St
Kokomo IN 46901

Call Sign: N9ZFC
John F Keller
1722 W Jefferson St
Kokomo IN 46901

Call Sign: WA9QWA
Noel M Goddard
1304 W Madison St
Kokomo IN 469013217

Call Sign: KA9OVD
Allen E McKinney
1023 W Taylor
Kokomo IN 46901

Call Sign: WB9HVG
Shirley W Young
1904 W Jefferson St
Kokomo IN 46901

Call Sign: W9BYN
John F De Long
903 W Maplewood Dr
Kokomo IN 469023358

Call Sign: KA9ZXE
Daniel R Gaskill
1215 W Taylor St
Kokomo IN 46901

Call Sign: KA9WZA
William P Anderson
3315 W Jefferson St
Kokomo IN 46901

Call Sign: KC9ACN
Werner J Hingst
1710 W Mulberry
Kokomo IN 469014268

Call Sign: KB9MYP
Steven L Robertson
2021 W Vaile Ave
Kokomo IN 469015088

Call Sign: KE4ZEZ
Jerry L Gatlin
608 W Jefferson St
Kokomo IN 46904

Call Sign: W9CNE
Robert M Graham Sr
1908 W Murden St
Kokomo IN 46901

Call Sign: W9SO
Dan R Lawson
802 W Virginia Aave
Kokomo IN 46902

Call Sign: WB9HKJ
Robert L Moss
2714 W Judson Rd
Kokomo IN 46901

Call Sign: N9MBW
Brian E Wilson
1623 W North St
Kokomo IN 46901

Call Sign: KB9CSJ
Thomas R Downs
1424 W Walnut St
Kokomo IN 46901

Call Sign: N4AMC

Call Sign: N8SPV

Call Sign: N9XMF

Jon-Eric Eliker
1531 W Walnut St
Kokomo IN 46901

Call Sign: KB9JTR
Erin M Eliker
1531 W Walnut St
Kokomo IN 469014213

Call Sign: WB9DWP
Jerral A Long
3608 Walton Way
Kokomo IN 469024181

Call Sign: W9LAL
Edward L Lopke
1583 Waterview Way
Kokomo IN 46902

Call Sign: N9QLR
Douglas W Zackschewski
2008 Wellesley Ln
Kokomo IN 46902

Call Sign: N9UTM
Douglas E Eglen
4656 Wexmoor Dr
Kokomo IN 46902

Call Sign: W0WIE
Douglas E Eglen
4656 Wexmoor Dr
Kokomo IN 46902

Call Sign: W9DEE
Douglas E Eglen
4656 Wexmoor Dr
Kokomo IN 46902

Call Sign: AE9DE
Douglas E Eglen
4656 Wexmoor Dr
Kokomo IN 46902

Call Sign: W9KWG

Richard S Stroud
4707 Wexmoor Dr
Kokomo IN 469029596

Call Sign: KA9DXO
Michael A Ward
3002 Williams Ct
Kokomo IN 46902

Call Sign: KC8GRP
Jeffrey R Lipchik
3503 Williams Dr
Kokomo IN 469027505

Call Sign: KE9UZ
Douglas D Herbert
802 Williamsburg Dr
Kokomo IN 46902

Call Sign: W9KQD
Donald J Gross
780 Willow Ridge Dr
Kokomo IN 46901

Call Sign: W9DKR
William J Smiley
906 Witherspoon Dr
Kokomo IN 46901

Call Sign: KC9HOD
Ryan G Hensler
921 Wynterbrooke Dr
Kokomo IN 46901

Call Sign: K9MET
Ryan G Hensler
921 Wynterbrooke Dr
Kokomo IN 46901

Call Sign: KB9ZTH
Scott W Bridge
2657 Wynterpointe Ct
Kokomo IN 46901

Call Sign: WD9FNR

Cheryl A Genovese
1316 Zartman Rd
Kokomo IN 46902

Call Sign: WD9BEW
Clarence R Lane
Kokomo IN 46901

Call Sign: KC9ELF
Jeffery A Collins
Kokomo IN 46903

Call Sign: WB6PYN
Joel M Werbelow
Kokomo IN 46904

Call Sign: KC9USW
Justin M Crowell
Kokomo IN 46904

Call Sign: W9GAV
Robert E Hillis
Kokomo IN 46904

Call Sign: KC9NNF
William D Mezick
Kokomo IN 46904

FCC Amateur Radio Licenses in Kouts

Call Sign: N9VDH
Patricia A Yuraitis
308 Daumer Rd
Kouts IN 46347

Call Sign: KC9VJS
Shannon J Combs
1010 Diana Dr
Kouts IN 46347

Call Sign: KA9FGP
Robert E Hott
482 E SR 8
Kouts IN 46347

Call Sign: WA9LZP
George R Barbee
501 Jefferson Ave
Kouts IN 46347

Call Sign: WA9SCT
Joseph D Lincoln Sr
900 Strong St
Kouts IN 46347

Call Sign: W9JKZ
Harold Kazen
410 Woodland Ave
Kouts IN 46347

Call Sign: N9VDI
Louis M Yuraitis
Kouts IN 46347

FCC Amateur Radio Licenses in La Fontaine

Call Sign: KA9IUU
Richard L Wolfgang
106 Armstrong St
La Fontaine IN 46940

Call Sign: AB8BJ
Michael J Timmerman
3291 E 1050 S 6
La Fontaine IN 46940

Call Sign: N9BNC
Joan E Manning
5199 E SR 218
La Fontaine IN 46940

Call Sign: N9AFI
Larry D Manning
5199 E SR 218
La Fontaine IN 46940

Call Sign: KB9LDZ
Wabash County ARC Inc

5199 E SR 218
La Fontaine IN
469409232

Call Sign: WB9JNS
Henry C McAlister
9325 S 900 W 35
La Fontaine IN 46940

Call Sign: KA9IYA
Donald E Garwood
10689 S Marion Rd
La Fontaine IN 46940

Call Sign: KA9GQK
Rebecca K Larsh
201 W Grant St
La Fontaine IN 46940

Call Sign: KC9RNR
Sarah J Andrews
214 W Kendall St
La Fontaine IN 46940

Call Sign: KA9EBV
Janice L Zellers
La Fontaine IN 46940

Call Sign: KA9EYC
Larry J Zellers
La Fontaine IN 46940

FCC Amateur Radio Licenses in La Porte

Call Sign: KA9ZUM
Thomas D Lewis Jr
250E
La Porte IN 46350

Call Sign: W9FZQ
Altus N Salzwedel
810 2nd St
La Porte IN 46350

Call Sign: WA9NGO
Thomas M Travis
500S
La Porte IN 463506675

Call Sign: W9BBC
Archie R McBrayer
50W
La Porte IN 46350

Call Sign: KB9EGX
Paul F Killian
1501 A St
La Porte IN 46350

Call Sign: KA9FAW
Chester E Konopacki
1505 Andrew Ave
La Porte IN 46350

Call Sign: KB9NWL
Randall S Slease
2400 Andrew Ave 418
La Porte IN 46350

Call Sign: N0BIL
William W Brewer
2400 Andrew Ave Apt 724
La Porte IN 46350

Call Sign: KB9HUG
Donald J Pelz
323 Bordeaux Dr
La Porte IN 46350

Call Sign: KB9ESQ
Michael J Pelz
323 Bordeaux Dr
La Porte IN 46350

Call Sign: KB9PUY
Roberta J Marrapode
605 C St
La Porte IN 46350

Call Sign: KB9ZDC
Kenneth R Lunce Jr
702 C St
La Porte IN 463505510

Call Sign: KC9TDH
Kevin T Gould
5 Clark Dr
La Porte IN 46350

Call Sign: N6SYJ
Rev Dr John E Lemley
503 Clay
La Porte IN 46350

Call Sign: WA9OKQ
Donna R Newton
142 Country Club Dr
La Porte IN 463501961

Call Sign: WA9NUU
Melvin G Newton
142 Country Club Dr
La Porte IN 463501961

Call Sign: WA9OCQ
Earl R Yoder
193 Country Club Dr
La Porte IN 46350

Call Sign: N9QZP
Richard A Lute
516 D St
La Porte IN 46350

Call Sign: WA9AZR
George L Morley
712 E 18th St
La Porte IN 46350

Call Sign: KB9KMC
Michael K Sanders
891 E 300 N
La Porte IN 46350

Call Sign: KB9VKX
Robin M Sanders
891 E 300 N
La Porte IN 46350

Call Sign: KB9GSJ
Kathleen A Dudley
3577 E 300 S
La Porte IN 46350

Call Sign: WD9ENA
Wayne W Dudley
3577 E 300 S
La Porte IN 46350

Call Sign: WA9YNE
Wayne W Dudley
3577 E 300 S
La Porte IN 46350

Call Sign: K9TMK
Timothy E Krueger
1911 E 300 S Apt 2
La Porte IN 46350

Call Sign: KA6OJX
Barbara J Cave
834 E 400 S
La Porte IN 46350

Call Sign: WA6UOO
Gary N Cave
834 E 400 S
La Porte IN 46350

Call Sign: WB9VUX
Troy M Harrison
1102 E 700 N
La Porte IN 46350

Call Sign: NE9E
Bruce A McCoy
203 E 9th St
La Porte IN 46350

Call Sign: KB9VET
William P Desmond
1503 E Lincoln Way 12
La Porte IN 46350

Call Sign: KG9QE
William P Desmond
1503 E Lincoln Way 12
La Porte IN 46350

Call Sign: AA9XL
William P Desmond
1503 E Lincolnway Lot
12
La Porte IN 46350

Call Sign: W9EMS
Billie J Fonte
911 E Sportsman Ln
La Porte IN 46350

Call Sign: K9FI
James M Fonte
911 E Sportsman Ln
La Porte IN 46350

Call Sign: KB9HIN
Shaunna M Fonte
911 E Sportsman Ln
La Porte IN 46350

Call Sign: KC9GFN
David B Henry
3672 E SR 4
La Porte IN 46350

Call Sign: N9EVZ
Allen A Schoof Jr
2313 Elm Dr
La Porte IN 46350

Call Sign: KB9ZAU
Katherine M Rozinski
811 F St

La Porte IN 46350

Call Sign: K9JUE
James R Peterson
102 Farrand Ave
La Porte IN 46350

Call Sign: K9KSS
Christina M Fields
1609 Farrand Ave
La Porte IN 46350

Call Sign: KB9GSG
Kathryn A Warner
116 Fox St
La Porte IN 46350

Call Sign: WB9TSC
Lynn L Warner
116 Fox St
La Porte IN 46350

Call Sign: N9QZQ
Suzanna E Warner
116 Fox St
La Porte IN 46350

Call Sign: N9SWV
Timothy J Warner
116 Fox St
La Porte IN 46350

Call Sign: KB9ZDF
Christina M Fields
120 Franklin Ct
La Porte IN 46350

Call Sign: K9KAN
Alex J Kostelnik
120 Franklin Ct
La Porte IN 463505129

Call Sign: N9TPD
Pat A Heuer
216 G St

La Porte IN 46350

Call Sign: WB9YGF
Frank H Zahrt
136 Garden St
La Porte IN 46350

Call Sign: KB9MAR
Carrie A Salzer
424 Glenwood St
La Porte IN 46350

Call Sign: KA9WNQ
David E Reberg
154 Grand Ave
La Porte IN 463505350

Call Sign: WA9HIA
Craig E Scott
350 Grayson Rd
La Porte IN 463502249

Call Sign: KC9NWI
Mark R Rumbaugh
294 Grayson Rd
La Porte IN 46350

Call Sign: N9XGG
Gaelen P Lehker
416 Green Leaf S7
La Porte IN 463503012

Call Sign: KC9ONH
George M Gibbons
1004 H St
La Porte IN 46350

Call Sign: K9RIF
David S Riffel Jr
364 Hawthorne St
La Porte IN 46350

Call Sign: KC9LCW
Roger W Rosenbaum
1407 I St

La Porte IN 46350

Call Sign: N9VVG
Terry A Glancy
2105 I St
La Porte IN 46350

Call Sign: N9UNC
Daniel P Cubel
1013.5 Indiana Ave
La Porte IN 46350

Call Sign: KA9PGE
Jason A De Vaux
1305 Indiana Ave
La Porte IN 46350

Call Sign: KB9UKZ
David G Potter
1210 Indiana Ave 4
La Porte IN 46350

Call Sign: KE9HM
Bruce A McCoy
312 J St
La Porte IN 46350

Call Sign: AA9XQ
Bruce A McCoy
312 J St
La Porte IN 46350

Call Sign: KB9BLF
Ben F Lemley
283 Johnson Rd
La Porte IN 46350

Call Sign: KB9BLN
Jane F Lemley
283 Johnson Rd
La Porte IN 46350

Call Sign: KA9LSS
Mark A Nelson
110.5 Kingsbury Ave

La Porte IN 46350

La Porte IN 46350

La Porte IN 46350

Call Sign: K9TZS
Robert W Wiles
1206 L St
La Porte IN 46350

Call Sign: N9RVR
Robert J Swanson III
1524 Monroe St
La Porte IN 46350

Call Sign: N9TPB
Robert J Swanson
4266 N 525 W
La Porte IN 46360

Call Sign: W1LES
Robert W Wiles
1206 L St
La Porte IN 46350

Call Sign: W9ID
Lester J Chadwick
2427 Monroe St
La Porte IN 46350

Call Sign: KA9ZUL
William C Crowl
2944 N Fail Rd
La Porte IN 46350

Call Sign: KA9MFO
Marton J Danitschek
1301 Lincolnway
La Porte IN 46350

Call Sign: KA6QMW
Brian G Cave
2104 Mustang Dr
La Porte IN 46350

Call Sign: KB9MAS
James J Jesko
3907 N Fail Rd
La Porte IN 46350

Call Sign: KA9JYO
Carlos E Santini
3773 Malaga Dr E
La Porte IN 46350

Call Sign: N9JTY
Harold D Hutchinson
6116 N 125 W
La Porte IN 46350

Call Sign: N9WZR
Georgette M Behenna
4754 N Fail Rd
La Porte IN 46350

Call Sign: KC9FPA
Michael J Broviak
313 Miller St
La Porte IN 46350

Call Sign: KC9LYI
George M Hayes
2346 N 150 E
La Porte IN 46350

Call Sign: W9WQA
Thomas F Marrapode
7667 N Fail Rd
La Porte IN 46350

Call Sign: N9MIK
Michael J Broviak
313 Miller St
La Porte IN 46350

Call Sign: N9RCN
James W Pickhardt
5636 N 300 E
La Porte IN 46350

Call Sign: KB9BVK
Dennis J Behenna
4754 N Fail Rd
La Porte IN 46350

Call Sign: KA9BIL
Ronald J Broviak
313 Miller St
La Porte IN 46350

Call Sign: N9MDM
Florian M Predd
152 N 400 W
La Porte IN 46350

Call Sign: N9XGF
James D Vaughn
424 N Forrester Rd
La Porte IN 46350

Call Sign: WA9RON
Ronald J Broviak
313 Miller St
La Porte IN 46350

Call Sign: KA9MJH
Ronald W Lewis
4148 N 400 W
La Porte IN 46350

Call Sign: KA9VSM
James F Vaughn
424 N Forrester Rd
La Porte IN 46350

Call Sign: N9TPA
Robert J Swanson Jr
1524 Monroe Ave

Call Sign: N9VVI
Christopher P Tanger
6293 N 50 W

Call Sign: KC9VJT
John A Fry
2796 N Goldring Rd

La Porte IN 46350

La Porte IN 46350

La Porte IN 46350

Call Sign: N9WZU
Patricia A Nunes
5224 N Pawnee Trl
La Porte IN 46350

Call Sign: KC9KNZ
Timothy E Krueger
8152 N Wilhelm Rd
La Porte IN 46350

Call Sign: KB9LRA
Lester F Gillespie
208 Pine Lake Ave 341
La Porte IN 46350

Call Sign: N9MDO
Lindybergh Nunes Jr
5224 N Pawnee Trl
La Porte IN 46350

Call Sign: KC9CAV
Lynnette M James
404 Niesen St
La Porte IN 46350

Call Sign: KB9LWT
Martha A Taylor
208 Pine Lake Ave 341
La Porte IN 46350

Call Sign: KB9VSL
Kevin Palmer
3592 N Promanade Cir
La Porte IN 46350

Call Sign: KB9DEA
Jason M Ott
404 Niles St
La Porte IN 46350

Call Sign: KO9K
Robert W Kepler
100 Regency Pkwy
La Porte IN 46350

Call Sign: N9AS
Arthur L Simpson
5757 N Range Rd
La Porte IN 463508696

Call Sign: WD9BDO
David A Rykhus
609 Niles St
La Porte IN 46350

Call Sign: W9ISM
George E Forrest
1614 Richards St
La Porte IN 46350

Call Sign: N9OJX
Annette M Clark
4967 N Remington Sq
La Porte IN 46350

Call Sign: KB9ECF
Charles E Krcilek
214 Norton Apt B
La Porte IN 46350

Call Sign: N9NKK
Scott T Tharp
503 Rockwood St
La Porte IN 46350

Call Sign: N9OJY
Eric L Clark
4967 N Remington Sq
La Porte IN 46350

Call Sign: KC9TWX
Travis R Taylor
2913 Oakdale Ave
La Porte IN 46350

Call Sign: KC9ACR
Stacy J Tharp
503 Rockwood St
La Porte IN 46350

Call Sign: N9LAS
Mark L Clark
4967 N Remington Sq
La Porte IN 46350

Call Sign: KC9FPB
Murry J Winslett
304 Ohio St
La Porte IN 46350

Call Sign: KC9MXA
Adam S Tharp
503 Rockwood St
La Porte IN 46350

Call Sign: KA3ECT
Kathryn Dumbauld
8757 N SR 39
La Porte IN 46350

Call Sign: N9GCP
James D Walker
407 Park St
La Porte IN 46350

Call Sign: KC9HLE
Jeffrey Jesko
104 Roosevelt St
La Porte IN 46350

Call Sign: N9TPE
Todd W Henry
6969 N SR39

Call Sign: N9PYK
Mylan L Hill
1227 Pennsylvania Ave

Call Sign: N9XID
Phillip C Rozinski
104 Rose St

La Porte IN 463505528

Call Sign: N9ZNJ
Curtiss R Yeater
4925 S 200 E
La Porte IN 46350

Call Sign: KB9CAU
Stephen M Kelly
1222 S 300 E
La Porte IN 46350

Call Sign: KC9CQV
John J Wren
4367 S 300 E
La Porte IN 46350

Call Sign: KC9BJB
Jason M Ott
2382 S 350 E
La Porte IN 46350

Call Sign: KC9JYW
Ronald D Brenneman
2901 S 350 E
La Porte IN 46350

Call Sign: WA9ZDN
Steven W Osborn
2995 S 75 W
La Porte IN 46350

Call Sign: WA9ZMZ
Thomas E Ault
3553 S 75 W
La Porte IN 463509311

Call Sign: KC9HCS
Donna S Gillespie
2634 S Collins Dr
La Porte IN 46350

Call Sign: N9SFR
Gail M Frieden
531 S Holmesville Rd

La Porte IN 46350

Call Sign: N9YHJ
John R Jones
2692 S Nowak Ave
La Porte IN 46350

Call Sign: KA9LST
Terry R Nelson
2787 S Nowak Dr
La Porte IN 46350

Call Sign: N9IFU
Kelly R Nelson
2787 S Nowak Dr
La Porte IN 46350

Call Sign: N9SWW
Callie M Straub
566 S Wozniak Rd
La Porte IN 46350

Call Sign: N9QZN
Danielle K Straub
566 S Wozniak Rd
La Porte IN 46350

Call Sign: WZ9N
Neil D Straub
566 S Wozniak Rd
La Porte IN 46350

Call Sign: KA9UKW
Paul R Janisch
134 Sagamore Pkwy
La Porte IN 46350

Call Sign: KA9THY
Katherine M Rozinski
307 Scott St
La Porte IN 46350

Call Sign: K9JSI
La Porte ARC
307 Scott St

La Porte IN 46350

Call Sign: N9ROH
Clarence J Rozinski
307 Scott St
La Porte IN 46350

Call Sign: KB9DNY
Jeffrey L Daily
1822 Springville Rd Lot
18
La Porte IN 46350

Call Sign: N9VCZ
James E Weiss
403.5 State St
La Porte IN 46350

Call Sign: KB9TKQ
Jason R Kish
1409.5 State St
La Porte IN 46350

Call Sign: KE7LHX
Alex A Jakubin
3384 Tracy Allyn Dr
La Porte IN 463507781

Call Sign: KI9E
James A Jakubin
3384 Tracy Allyn Dr
La Porte IN 46350

Call Sign: AA9HP
Carl D Galloway Jr
618 Vine St
La Porte IN 46350

Call Sign: N9OZW
Patrick L Malott Sr
1515 W 1000 N
La Porte IN 46350

Call Sign: KC9KC
Lee T Whetzell

1203 W 10th St
La Porte IN 46350

9274 W 200 S
La Porte IN 46350

6534 W 450 N
La Porte IN 46350

Call Sign: N9LYN
Lynnette M James
1105 W 10th St 10
La Porte IN 46350

Call Sign: W9ZDV
Ronald B Stelter
1000 W 24th St
La Porte IN 46350

Call Sign: WA9GKA
Alan K Rutz
7102 W 500 S
La Porte IN 46350

Call Sign: N9TOZ
Brian J Broviak
705 W 11th
La Porte IN 46350

Call Sign: WB9PQE
Larry D Welsh
9132 W 250 S
La Porte IN 46350

Call Sign: WB9LSC
Fred S Hirt
255 W 625 N
La Porte IN 46350

Call Sign: KC9HTW
Robert L Ofcky Jr
7255 W 125 N
La Porte IN 46350

Call Sign: NU9H
David B Daley
6954 W 275 N
La Porte IN 46350

Call Sign: N9ITB
Jack L Albert
4126 W Andrea Dr
La Porte IN 46350

Call Sign: KE9PU
Albert E Kolvek Jr
8872 W 125 S
La Porte IN 46350

Call Sign: KC9EUG
Joseph A Bayne
5566 W 300 N
La Porte IN 46350

Call Sign: N9ROM
Robert E Smith
4144 W Andrea Dr
La Porte IN 46350

Call Sign: N9OKB
Lewis J Kyes Jr
803 W 12th St
La Porte IN 46350

Call Sign: AB9SK
Joseph A Bayne
5566 W 300 N
La Porte IN 46350

Call Sign: N9WUU
Michael J Adams
2461 W Butternut Dr
La Porte IN 46350

Call Sign: AA9UP
Ronald G Kinsey
708 W 13th St
La Porte IN 46350

Call Sign: N9APO
Harry J Brasel
8118 W 350 S
La Porte IN 46350

Call Sign: N9XSN
Kirk L Burnett
6766 W Cross Trl
La Porte IN 46350

Call Sign: WA9TOI
Virginia M Yoder
111 W 14th St
La Porte IN 46350

Call Sign: N9ZCG
Donna K Halley
6183 W 400 N
La Porte IN 46350

Call Sign: K9IRK
Kirk L Burnett
6766 W Cross Trl
La Porte IN 46350

Call Sign: WB9PJH
Jerry L Way
311 W 14th St
La Porte IN 46350

Call Sign: WD9EPP
Joseph F Reese
151 W 450 N
La Porte IN 46350

Call Sign: KC9FPC
Brian L Salzer
2284 W Elm
La Porte IN 46350

Call Sign: KC9EJK
Dale A Wienhoft

Call Sign: KA9WZI
Ronald J Kerwin

Call Sign: KB9HMR
Brian L Salzer

2284 W Elm
La Porte IN 46350

Call Sign: N9KEH
James D Forrest
6455 W Forrester
La Porte IN 46350

Call Sign: N9VVH
Douglas S Heller
337 W Johnson Rd
La Porte IN 46350

Call Sign: KC9HCR
Robert E Gaekle
654 W Maple Ln
La Porte IN 46350

Call Sign: WD9EIV
David S Luther
2222 W Oak St
La Porte IN 46350

Call Sign: K9DSL
David S Luther
2222 W Oak St
La Porte IN 46350

Call Sign: KB9MFK
Waldo E Baker
2302 W Oak St
La Porte IN 46350

Call Sign: N9WZQ
Brian D Perla
5404 W Schultz Rd
La Porte IN 46350

Call Sign: K9EGY
Paul G Kuhlen
3422 W Small Ct
La Porte IN 46350

Call Sign: KC9RTE
Timothy R Sandy

1532 W Springville Rd
La Porte IN 46350

Call Sign: KC9BTN
Paul V Brenda
5065 W Tokay Dr
La Porte IN 46350

Call Sign: WD9FFR
John A Baumer
3336 W Waverly Rd
La Porte IN 46350

Call Sign: N9OPO
Robert W Weber Sr
3621 W Windsor Hills
La Porte IN 46350

Call Sign: WB9OMF
Robert W Weber Jr
3621 W Windsor Hills
La Porte IN 46350

Call Sign: N9WZW
Ernest W Gregory
1307 Walton Ave
La Porte IN 46350

Call Sign: N9MDN
Joel B Predd
703 Waverly Rd
La Porte IN 46350

Call Sign: N9OOJ
Martin F Predd
703 Waverly Rd
La Porte IN 46350

Call Sign: N9OKA
Michael W Curley
202 Worden St
La Porte IN 46350

Call Sign: KC9HXH
Jacob Brown

1109 Wright Ave
La Porte IN 46350

Call Sign: KA9TEH
Donald G Whitmore
La Porte IN 46352

Call Sign: KF9YZ
John B Gens
La Porte IN 46352

Call Sign: WB9BSL
David L Kliss
La Porte IN 463520391

FCC Amateur Radio Licenses in La Crosse

Call Sign: KB9TGS
Paul J Adams
3 N Monroe St
LaCrosse IN 46348

Call Sign: KC9KYB
Robert C Rosenbaum
11152 W 1800 S
LaCrosse IN 46348

FCC Amateur Radio Licenses in LaGrange

Call Sign: KA9FOU
Leslie D Wagner
050N
LaGrange IN 467619419

Call Sign: KB9BLS
Norman D Beverly
200E
LaGrange IN 46761

Call Sign: KB9FQK
Craig E Treesh
Box 83
LaGrange IN 46761

Call Sign: KC9GYW
James W Stout
1445 E 75 N
LaGrange IN 46761

Call Sign: N9YTG
Delmar G Abel
302 E Central
LaGrange IN 46761

Call Sign: WS9S
Michael E Cole
870 N 00Ew
LaGrange IN 46761

Call Sign: N9XPM
Debra C Cole
870 N 00Ew
LaGrange IN 46761

Call Sign: KA9ERV
William C Parham
210 N 010 W
LaGrange IN 46761

Call Sign: KC9CTS
Tammi R Murray
775 N 150 E
LaGrange IN 46761

Call Sign: W9THD
Timothy S Murray
775 N 150 E
LaGrange IN 46761

Call Sign: WB9DNT
Wayne J Walter
4570 S 050 W
LaGrange IN 46761

Call Sign: KF9SC
Hershel J Mullins
3845 S 1175 E
LaGrange IN 46761

Call Sign: KB9MEC
Kim B Hummel
301 S Detroit St
LaGrange IN 46761

Call Sign: N9PXO
James H Pocklington Jr
2205 S SR 9
LaGrange IN 46761

Call Sign: N9MAH
Mc Kinley Woodworth Jr
345 W Central Ave
LaGrange IN 46761

Call Sign: W9LTR
Calvin J Evans
327 W Spring St
LaGrange IN 46761

Call Sign: KC9IPQ
Kim B Hummel
LaGrange IN 46761

Call Sign: KC9IQL
Kim B Hummel
LaGrange IN 46761

FCC Amateur Radio Licenses in Lagro

Call Sign: N9HTX
Jeffrey S Van Ness
1568 N 750 E
Lagro IN 46941

Call Sign: N9DVQ
Patricia A Van Ness
1568 N 750 E
Lagro IN 46941

Call Sign: N9CUB
Wayne L Van Ness
1568 N 750 E

Lagro IN 46941

Call Sign: WB9SHY
Steven R Wilson
875 S 650 E
Lagro IN 46941

FCC Amateur Radio Licenses in Lake Station

Call Sign: WA9YOZ
Anthony E Bodo
4623 E 25th Ave
Lake Station IN 46405

Call Sign: W9FVE
Edwin L Dahlstrom
2888 Elkhart St
Lake Station IN 46405

Call Sign: KB9SEE
Darrell Goldsmith
3448 Iowa St
Lake Station IN 46405

Call Sign: W9PLW
Le Roy W Hulvey
2615 Montgomery St
Lake Station IN 46405

Call Sign: KB9RVI
Christopher E Curdes
2242 Newton St
Lake Station IN
464051170

Call Sign: KB9WXI
Pamela A Curdes
2242 Newton St
Lake Station IN
464051170

Call Sign: W9ANJ
John A Shudick Jr
2200 Putnam St

Lake Station IN 46405

Call Sign: KB9MIA
Timothy L Marsee
3540 Revere Ct
Lake Station IN 46405

Call Sign: KB9OGX
Sarah J Watts
2324 Spencer
Lake Station IN 46405

Call Sign: KA9WVH
Roger K Watts
2324 Spencer St
Lake Station IN 46405

Call Sign: WA9DHH
John P Saul
2825 Utah St
Lake Station IN 46405

Call Sign: NC9A
Woodrow W Warren
2851 Vermillion
Lake Station IN 46405

Call Sign: WB9IZL
Fred L Newman
2262 Vigo St
Lake Station IN 46405

Call Sign: KB9YGD
Norman P Triantafilos
2634 Warren St
Lake Station IN 46405

Call Sign: KC9AXT
Thomas W Malinoff
2581 Wells St
Lake Station IN 46405

Call Sign: KB9RZL
Keith L Curtis
3398 Wisconsin St

Lake Station IN 46405

Call Sign: AB9CM
Djurica Maletin
Lake Station IN
464050132

FCC Amateur Radio Licenses in Lake Village

Call Sign: AC4TK
Coburn G Faucher
950N
Lake Village IN 46349

Call Sign: WN9HWV
James W Howe
Box 217
Lake Village IN 46349

Call Sign: KC9ILM
John A Hardin Sr
7793 N 100 E
Lake Village IN 46349

Call Sign: N9QFT
Paul W Faucher
8739 N 400 W
Lake Village IN 46349

Call Sign: KC9QIS
Derek W Yakimow
8855 N 471 W
Lake Village IN 46349

Call Sign: NY9X
John D Wertman Jr
6525 N 700 W Rd
Lake Village IN 46349

FCC Amateur Radio Licenses in Laketon

Call Sign: KB9JCX
Jeffery R Cook

40 S Main St
Laketon IN 46943

FCC Amateur Radio Licenses in Lakeville

Call Sign: WC9X
Roger K Kiefer
68099 Kenilworth Rd
Lakeville IN 46536

Call Sign: KC9HLF
Stephen P Thomas
67855 Linden Rd
Lakeville IN 46536

Call Sign: N9YYG
Robert A Krizmanich
64901 Maple Rd
Lakeville IN 46536

Call Sign: KC9R
Frederick M Whitlock
66400 Oak Rd
Lakeville IN 46536

Call Sign: KB9AVG
Donald L Fries
66711 Oak Rd
Lakeville IN 46536

Call Sign: N9LZO
Larry L Burnside
21962 Osborne Rd
Lakeville IN 46536

Call Sign: KA9MAU
Louis R Stroup
20538 Pierce Rd
Lakeville IN 46536

Call Sign: KA9IVQ
Randy S Murowski
22454 Riley Rd
Lakeville IN 46536

Call Sign: KC9KYA
William T Thompson
21640 SR 4
Lakeville IN 46536

Call Sign: N9ZUP
David L Adams
67875 US 31 S
Lakeville IN 46536

Call Sign: N9MKC
David A Deventer
1075E
LaOtto IN 46763

Call Sign: KC9AM
Diane L Sizelove
11445 E 200 S
LaOtto IN 467639748

Call Sign: N9CCT
Paul T Sizelove
11445 E 200 S
LaOtto IN 467639748

Call Sign: KC9OWG
Craig L Hunnicutt
11167 E 550 S
LaOtto IN 46763

Call Sign: N9LOV
David L Evans
5685 S 800 E
La Otto IN 46763

Call Sign: N9TMB
Chad J Harpel
4170 S School St
La Otto IN 46763

Call Sign: KB9YTU
Michael E Harris
3095 S 950 E
LaOtto IN 46763

Call Sign: KB9KUM
Kevin R Norton
223 W 1st Rd
LaPaz IN 46536

Call Sign: N9IME
David L Keefer
Box 16
Larwill IN 46764

Call Sign: N9WNJ
Rodney L Shull
5575 W 100 S
Larwill IN 46764

Call Sign: WB9JKN
Gary P Schuster
7251 W Lincolnway
Larwill IN 46764

Call Sign: N9PSO
Ramona L Bennett
5308 E 450 N
Leesburg IN 46538

Call Sign: K9HOO
Robert L Friddle
34 Ems B4 Oai Ln
Leesburg IN 46538

Call Sign: KC9SQN

Robert L Prado
209 Ems B40A Ln
Leesburg IN 46538

Call Sign: KA9POF
Robert L Prado
209 Ems B40A Ln
Leesburg IN 46538

Call Sign: KC9TRL
James D Patterson
139 Ems B7 Ln
Leesburg IN 46538

Call Sign: N9XCT
Charles F Adams
52 Ems T29 Ln
Leesburg IN 46538

Call Sign: KE9GC
Patrick R Morgan
31 Ems T30 B Ln
Leesburg IN 46538

Call Sign: N9NRW
Robert J Herendeen
123 Ems T31 Ln
Leesburg IN 46538

Call Sign: KC9PFQ
Keith T Obenchain
56 Ems T34 D2 Ln
Leesburg IN 46538

Call Sign: N8QKJ
Lonnie W Fisher
4 Ems T34 Ln
Leesburg IN 46538

Call Sign: KB9RLJ
Eric W Gunderson
17 Emst 7B Ln
Leesburg IN 46538

Call Sign: AA9JV

Jerry S Godshalk
6403 N 400 W
Leesburg IN 46538

Call Sign: N9ZBV
Janet H Chiddister
5817 N 450 E
Leesburg IN 46538

Call Sign: W2GO
Albert H Jones
274 N Bell Rohr Dr Rt 2
Leesburg IN 46538

Call Sign: KB0VEX
Todd E Holsten
5182 N Sawgrass Ln
Leesburg IN 46538

Call Sign: WX9TOD
Todd E Holsten
5182 N Sawgrass Ln
Leesburg IN 46538

Call Sign: N9FMJ
Richard L Robinson
207 W Plum St
Leesburg IN 465380272

Call Sign: N9REE
Justin R Hartman
Leesburg IN 46538

FCC Amateur Radio Licenses in Leo

Call Sign: WB9YBI
Carl W Thomas
11205 Alta Vista Dr
Leo IN 46765

Call Sign: KC9KTG
Renee K Thomas
11205 Alta Vista Dr
Leo IN 46765

Call Sign: N9GST
Marilyn M Thomas
11205 Alta Vista Dr
Leo IN 46765

Call Sign: N9IJB
Gary L Sturm
15231 Amstutz Rd
Leo IN 467650010

Call Sign: KB9VXS
Terry L Williams
13005 Cherry St
Leo IN 46765

Call Sign: N9YNM
Eric S Fuller
10021 Donald Ave
Leo IN 46765

Call Sign: N9FGO
Lani K Sell
10013 Garman Rd
Leo IN 46765

Call Sign: NO9H
Noel L Sell
10013 Garman Rd
Leo IN 46765

Call Sign: KC9VLW
Philip J Johnson
7116 Hosler Rd
Leo IN 46765

Call Sign: KB9JNU
William L Cook
17307 Hull Rd
Leo IN 46765

Call Sign: KF9UG
Michael D Day
17313 Juniper Ln
Leo IN 46765

Call Sign: KB9FPR
James J Julius
9702 Lakeshore Dr
Leo IN 46765

Call Sign: K8BU
Gary R Straub
14301 Leo Rd
Leo IN 46765

Call Sign: WD9GBU
George L Bachinsky Jr
14826 Marsha Ave
Leo IN 46765

Call Sign: KA9AVJ
Mark E Steffen
5708 N Shore Dr
Leo IN 46765

Call Sign: AJ8A
Walter Gage
16601 Painter Rd
Leo IN 46765

Call Sign: K1EBZ
Joseph A Artioli
16725 Pine Ridge Pass
Leo IN 467659210

Call Sign: N9PXF
Jean M Goller
4836 Ranch Rd
Leo IN 46765

Call Sign: K9UWA
John C Goller
4836 Ranch Rd
Leo IN 46765

Call Sign: W9NVU
Melvin R Lee
6611 Schlatter Rd
Leo IN 46765

Call Sign: WB9PXT
Joseph F Knight Sr
9227 Schlatter Rd
Leo IN 46765

Call Sign: N9YNP
Allen M Schwartz
11305 Shoreline Dr
Leo IN 46765

Call Sign: KC9MRZ
Aaron E Nedd
14811 SR 1
Leo IN 46765

Call Sign: WN9FMU
Aaron E Nedd
14811 SR 1
Leo IN 46765

Call Sign: W9LSU
Richard R Sterling
16817 Tonkel Rd
Leo IN 46765

Call Sign: KB9NPC
Dan Leeper
10514 Walnut St
Leo IN 46765

Call Sign: KA9FEX
Raymond F Ulrich
Leo IN 46765

Call Sign: WB9ZGY
Steven E Ervin
Leo IN 467650158

FCC Amateur Radio Licenses in Liberty Center

Call Sign: N9KKW
Barry E Clark

300S
Liberty Center IN 46766

Call Sign: K9EKI
Barry E Clark
300S
Liberty Center IN 46766

Call Sign: N9KKX
Nancy C Clark
300S
Liberty Center IN 46766

Call Sign: W9BRN
Ruth E Stroud
3139 S Main
Liberty Center IN 46766

Call Sign: W9SR
Richard W Stroud
Liberty Center IN 46766

FCC Amateur Radio Licenses in Ligonier

Call Sign: N9HUP
David P Houser
Box 79H
Ligonier IN 46767

Call Sign: KH2AH
Michael W Snavely
11034 CR 50
Ligonier IN 46767

Call Sign: KC9MGM
Phillip M Mossburg
209 E Northwood St
Ligonier IN 46767

Call Sign: KC9BKL
Billy J Moore Jr
982 North St
Ligonier IN 46767

Call Sign: KC9UEJ
John V Lutton
1000 North St
Ligonier IN 46767

Call Sign: N9DBQ
E Virginia Moore
1200 S Martin St
Ligonier IN 46767

Call Sign: W9WM
William S Moore
1200 S Martin St
Ligonier IN 46767

Call Sign: K9DWJ
Fred M Schultz
1107 W 2nd St
Ligonier IN 46767

Call Sign: KA9ALZ
Cinda L Kelly
506 W 3rd St
Ligonier IN 46767

Call Sign: K9OOP
Lanny D Kelly
506 W 3rd St
Ligonier IN 46767

Call Sign: KC9RAF
Eric W Moser
6114 W Albion Rd
Ligonier IN 46767

Call Sign: K9EMO
Eric W Moser
6114 W Albion Rd
Ligonier IN 46767

Call Sign: KC9PJO
Adam R Rohrer
7769 W Circle Dr S
Ligonier IN 46767

Call Sign: KC9GUW
Kenneth R Shaw
415 W Lawn Dr
Ligonier IN 46767

Call Sign: WD9DDZ
John V Lutton
100 W Miller St
Ligonier IN 46767

Call Sign: N9DHU
Stanley J Le Mieux
607 W Union St
Ligonier IN 467672504

Call Sign: N0DUL
David C Alspach
702 Westfield Dr
Ligonier IN 46767

FCC Amateur Radio Licenses in Logansport

Call Sign: WA8HSU
William C Wells
1012 19th St
Logansport IN
469474504

Call Sign: N9ZMY
Terry D Groninger Jr
830 20th St
Logansport IN 46947

Call Sign: N9YHK
Lillian Roberts
1003 21 St
Logansport IN 46947

Call Sign: N9PCO
Brian S Roberts
1003 21st St
Logansport IN 46947

Call Sign: AA9JU

Aja D Hollon
926 22nd St
Logansport IN 46947

Call Sign: N9OYK
Scott C Farnham
975 E
Logansport IN 46947

Call Sign: KB9ZAT
Veronica J Lear
312 Barrow St
Logansport IN 46947

Call Sign: N9RNR
William A Harrison
512 Bartlett St
Logansport IN 46947

Call Sign: KB9NEA
Rex R Robison
113 Beal St
Logansport IN 46947

Call Sign: KC9PG
Arnold O Foust
Box 238D
Logansport IN 46947

Call Sign: KA9BYO
Walter T Rehm
Box 69
Logansport IN 46947

Call Sign: WB6UCO
Robert T Buck
321 Burlington Ave
Logansport IN
469474834

Call Sign: KC9SWW
Aaron W Benner
629 Burlington Ave
Logansport IN 46947

Call Sign: N9QFH
Allen L Minter
2330 Capitol St
Logansport IN 46947

Call Sign: N9QJT
Debra S Minter
2330 Capitol St
Logansport IN 46947

Call Sign: KB9BDG
Virginia L Bell
CR 300E
Logansport IN 46947

Call Sign: W9ALT
Walter L Downham
CR 325S
Logansport IN 46947

Call Sign: K9AYF
William D Morrow
CR 350N
Logansport IN
469479217

Call Sign: K9GMH
Ronald K Blume
1206 Cummings
Logansport IN 46947

Call Sign: N9YFW
Robert A Ervin
530 Day St
Logansport IN 46947

Call Sign: KC9NTE
Aaron K Boughton
6037 E 925 N
Logansport IN 46947

Call Sign: KC0TAM
Ian M Boughton
6037 E 925 N
Logansport IN 46947

Call Sign: KB9SIR
John W Boughton
6037 E 925 N
Logansport IN 46947

Call Sign: KF9WP
Duane C Watts
1414 E Broadway
Logansport IN 46947

Call Sign: N9ZMU
Joe D Watts
1431 E Broadway
Logansport IN 46947

Call Sign: WA9KTZ
Jerry A Anderson
2610 E Broadway
Logansport IN 46947

Call Sign: WB9OKR
George L Voltz
3117 E Broadway
Logansport IN 46947

Call Sign: N9THJ
Ronald L Harrell
1218 E Broadway Apt 4
Logansport IN 46947

Call Sign: N9LMC
Michael E Laird
122 E Colfax St
Logansport IN 46947

Call Sign: N9WYT
Delia H Hartoin
5538 E CR 150 N
Logansport IN 46947

Call Sign: AA9IR
Thomas W Hartoin
5538 E CR 150 N
Logansport IN 46947

Call Sign: KC9FFU
Shayne A Leffert
5571 E CR 150 N
Logansport IN 46947

Call Sign: N9ZMV
Marjorie A Morrow
1565 E CR 350 N
Logansport IN 46947

Call Sign: N9SBU
Bernhard G Ulfers
3734 E CR 500 S
Logansport IN 46947

Call Sign: K9DVL
David R Rothermel
3680 E CR 75 N
Logansport IN 46947

Call Sign: KA9ZAH
Edwin C Moss
3830 E CR 75N
Logansport IN 46947

Call Sign: AA9FM
Gregory C Bell
5983 E Division Rd
Logansport IN 46947

Call Sign: KC9LNO
Buddy R McLay
10 E Linden Ave
Logansport IN 46947

Call Sign: N9OYI
Douglas M Swank Jr
1822 E Market
Logansport IN 46947

Call Sign: KB9LUR
Ward V Nickell Jr
812 E Market St
Logansport IN 46947

Call Sign: WA9OWH
Bailey Frye
117 E Roselawn
Logansport IN 46947

Call Sign: KB9NDI
Brian C Jarrett
2706 Emmet Dr
Logansport IN 46947

Call Sign: K9AWH
Robert D Minnick
2715 Emmet Dr
Logansport IN
469473805

Call Sign: KC9SWV
Morgen F Benner
1524 George St
Logansport IN 46947

Call Sign: N9WCQ
David L Wandrei
2403 George St
Logansport IN
469473738

Call Sign: N9MBX
John R Hopper
4412 Grandview Dr
Logansport IN 46947

Call Sign: KC9SCQ
Travis M Grandstaff
1544 Grant St
Logansport IN 46947

Call Sign: N9VXL
Janet S Flinn
429 Grove St
Logansport IN 46947

Call Sign: WZ9Z
Michael N Flinn

429 Grove St
Logansport IN 46947

Call Sign: N9TTU
Joanna F Haworth
420 Helm St
Logansport IN 46947

Call Sign: N9VFT
Robert J Pilles
832 Helm St
Logansport IN 46947

Call Sign: KC9AWR
Wilson S Fickle
530 Henry St
Logansport IN 46947

Call Sign: KC9AWS
Robert S Fickle
530 Henry St
Logansport IN
469471920

Call Sign: KN9M
Everett L Partridge
2600 High SR
Logansport IN 46947

Call Sign: W9CFI
Randolph G Lanning
3939 High SR Apt 119
Logansport IN 46947

Call Sign: WB9GOY
Carl D Cain
1913 High St
Logansport IN 46947

Call Sign: WB9SZH
Robert W Brown
4504 High St
Logansport IN 46947

Call Sign: N9ONK

Ned L Gochenour
4401 Jamestown Dr
Logansport IN 46947

Call Sign: N9YCO
Lisa J Ervin
2101 Jefferson Ave
Logansport IN 46947

Call Sign: N9PVQ
Todd A Ervin
2101 Jefferson St
Logansport IN 46947

Call Sign: N9OJA
Lloyd B Perry
4424 Kensington Dr
Logansport IN 46947

Call Sign: W9ZYR
Robert C Gharis
1116 Kiesling Rd
Logansport IN 46947

Call Sign: KB9JPV
Michael E Kutzner
511 King St
Logansport IN 46947

Call Sign: K9PSR
William E Norris
103 Lakenheath Way
Logansport IN 46947

Call Sign: N9ZBU
Sue E Norris
103 Lakenheath Way
Logansport IN
469472415

Call Sign: WD9FXD
Carl J Elpers Sr
203 Minor St
Logansport IN 46947

Call Sign: KA9UCN
Joseph F Yard
2118 Murdock St
Logansport IN 46947

Call Sign: N9VHF
Christine Farnham
1711 N 975 E
Logansport IN 46947

Call Sign: KC9LCA
John R Acuff
3284 N CR 275 E
Logansport IN 46947

Call Sign: KA9BYN
Marion E Bell Jr
2383 N CR 300 E
Logansport IN
469476759

Call Sign: WA9DTT
Woodrow S Tarver
2710 N CR 450 E
Logansport IN 46947

Call Sign: K9EQT
Donald E Hyman
2818 N Indian Creek Rd
Logansport IN 46947

Call Sign: WA9VZD
Scott W Schafer
1378 N SR 25
Logansport IN
469478030

Call Sign: W9LVY
Philip M Snider
1915 North St
Logansport IN 46947

Call Sign: W9VMW
Cass County ARC
1915 North St

Logansport IN 46947

Call Sign: N9NLI
William A Corn
2122 North St
Logansport IN 46947

Call Sign: KB9MIO
Larry W McCarter
3916 Parkmont Dr
Logansport IN 46947

Call Sign: KA9PAL
Donald E Albert
2725 Perrysburg Rd
Logansport IN
469471338

Call Sign: N9LMB
Michael A Marchal
4005 Pottawatomic Rd
Logansport IN 46947

Call Sign: N9RAA
Michael J Marchal
4005 Pottawatomie Rd
Logansport IN 46947

Call Sign: K9HFC
Harry E Burkhart Jr
6567 S CR 50 E
Logansport IN 46947

Call Sign: KB9ZGK
Scott D Grenert
1731 Smead St
Logansport IN 46947

Call Sign: KC9IDO
Anna L Hendrickson
1916 Smead St
Logansport IN 46947

Call Sign: KC9JFU
Marisa N Hendrickson

1916 Smead St
Logansport IN 46947

Call Sign: N9UNH
Gerald J Giecko
1814 Spear St
Logansport IN 46947

Call Sign: KB9YIN
Martin L Maxwell
2214 Spear St
Logansport IN 46947

Call Sign: N9ZMZ
William P Dexter
2600 Usher St
Logansport IN 46947

Call Sign: KB9VMW
Thomas R Denton
1309 Van Tower Dr
Logansport IN
469473380

Call Sign: KC9GCL
Jeffrey A Krysevig
5750 W 400 S
Logansport IN 46947

Call Sign: WB9RAE
Harold G Watson
25 W Columbia St
Logansport IN 46947

Call Sign: WA9AYT
Steven C Cress
4447 W CR 300 N
Logansport IN
469478500

Call Sign: WB9GHL
William T Barrett
722 W Linden
Logansport IN 46947

Call Sign: KB9SDY
Lonnie V Hall
1801 W Market St Lot 34
Logansport IN 46947

Call Sign: WB9TUR
Clarence H Easley
1001 W Melbourne Ave
Logansport IN 46947

Call Sign: KU9F
Woodrow L Hammon
615 W Miami Ave
Logansport IN 46947

Call Sign: N9ZBT
Roy J Abrams
17 W Mimia Ave
Logansport IN 46947

Call Sign: N9OJC
John E Timmons
1112 W Wabash Ave
Logansport IN 46947

Call Sign: W9YIU
Edward E Bosh
917 Wheatland
Logansport IN 46947

Call Sign: KB9JPW
Darrell E Edwards
514 Wheatland Ave
Logansport IN 46947

FCC Amateur Radio Licenses in Long Beach

Call Sign: W0FBV
Frank B Vardeman
1613 Indianapolis Ave
Long Beach IN 46360

Call Sign: W4VRI
Frank B Vardeman

1613 Indianapolis Ave
Long Beach IN 46360

Call Sign: KA9GVD
Alice S Garba
2002 Somerset Rd
Long Beach IN 46360

**FCC Amateur Radio
Licenses in Lowell**

Call Sign: KC9KFI
Nicola Ambrosini
5711 154th Ct
Lowell IN 46356

Call Sign: KB9CKB
Daniel R Balla
5778 177th
Lowell IN 46356

Call Sign: W9JEC
Robert H Gill
312 Amber Ln
Lowell IN 46356

Call Sign: KC9KGD
Mark D James
3553 Belshaw Rd
Lowell IN 46356

Call Sign: K9LBI
Donald W Ford
134 Burnham St
Lowell IN 46356

Call Sign: N9WGU
Martin N Semrau
17604 Camelot Dr
Lowell IN 46356

Call Sign: AI5H
Mark L Carbone
206 Cherokee Dr
Lowell IN 46356

Call Sign: K5IA
Mark L Carbone
206 Cherokee Dr
Lowell IN 46356

Call Sign: N9TEZ
Cornelis E Van Wijk
457 Cheyenne Dr
Lowell IN 46356

Call Sign: KB9JCP
Dennis J Fleener
22512 Colfax
Lowell IN 46356

Call Sign: KC9BOJ
Kathleen M Ryan
588 Driftwood Ct
Lowell IN 46356

Call Sign: N9JKJ
Jimmie D Baker
1101 E Commercial Ave
Lowell IN 46356

Call Sign: KC9EXH
Kristopher O'Connell
16348 Fulton St
Lowell IN 46356

Call Sign: KB9BFY
Brian T Terpstra
645 Gatewood Dr
Lowell IN 46356

Call Sign: WN9Z
Richard L Terpstra
645 Gatewood Dr
Lowell IN 46356

Call Sign: KB9VBB
Lake County Emergency
Mgmt Commun
645 Gatewood Dr

Lowell IN 46356

Call Sign: WE9M
Lake County Emergency
Mgmt Commun
645 Gatewood Dr
Lowell IN 46356

Call Sign: W9BO
Robert C Ores
16479 Grant
Lowell IN 463569506

Call Sign: N9FOD
Dennie L House
1242 Harrison St
Lowell IN 46356

Call Sign: KA9WLN
James A Baker
1226 Harrison St Apt B
Lowell IN 463561936

Call Sign: KA9JXF
Richard J Berzinski
18915 Idaho Ct
Lowell IN 46356

Call Sign: KA9JXE
Richard M Berzinski
18915 Idaho Ct
Lowell IN 46356

Call Sign: WB9QIB
Walter Swanson
502 Joe Martin Rd
Lowell IN 46356

Call Sign: KB9ZXI
Edward M Yura
687 Joe Martin Rd
Lowell IN 46356

Call Sign: WA9USW
William R McKinney

5403 Main St
Lowell IN 46356

Call Sign: KB9ZDA
Herchell G Northcutt
143 Oak
Lowell IN 46356

Call Sign: K9HGN
Herchell G Northcutt
143 Oak St
Lowell IN 46356

Call Sign: AA9XE
Daniel Blaschke
733 S Lakeview Dr
Lowell IN 46356

Call Sign: AA9EI
Timothy M Layer Sr
733 S Lakeview Dr
Lowell IN 46356

Call Sign: KB9QV
John C Masepohl
323 Spruce Ct
Lowell IN 463561768

Call Sign: KC9VPN
Dustin M Schmidt
328 Sweet Briar Ct
Lowell IN 46356

Call Sign: KC9LXN
Craig G Flanders
9441 W 157th Pl
Lowell IN 46356

Call Sign: KC9HNZ
Mark E Vendl
9189 W 158th Ct
Lowell IN 46356

Call Sign: N9ZOG
Henry K Holevinsky

7425 W 159th Ave
Lowell IN 46356

Call Sign: WB9DPN
Richard A Burdan
5313 W 171st Ave
Lowell IN 46356

Call Sign: NW6D
Donald A Defrance
7774 W 174th Ave
Lowell IN 46356

Call Sign: N9MEK
August L Blissmer
9610 W 189 Pl
Lowell IN 46356

Call Sign: KA9VLJ
Rudolph W Jakubin
5910 W 249th Ave
Lowell IN 46356

Call Sign: KB9MZA
Mark E Pflughoeft
621 W Commercial Ave
Lowell IN 46356

Call Sign: KC9VPO
Ryan Boldin
210 W Lakeview Dr
Lowell IN 46356

Call Sign: N9OHK
Mark C Zelesky
18266 White Oak
Lowell IN 46356

Call Sign: KA9OOI
Mark J Zelesky
18266 White Oak
Lowell IN 463569356

Call Sign: KC9HLW
Matthew J Coppens

17607 White Oak Ave
Lowell IN 46356

Call Sign: N9IRS
Joseph A Krupa
16218 Wicker Ave
Lowell IN 46356

Call Sign: KB9PIY
Dawn M Baggech
320 Woodland
Lowell IN 46356

Call Sign: KB9NBL
James P Baggech
320 Woodland Ct
Lowell IN 46356

Call Sign: KB9NHZ
Michael F Pawlak
206 Woodland Dr
Lowell IN 46356

Call Sign: WF5P
Mikeal R Hughes
211 Woodland Dr
Lowell IN 46356

FCC Amateur Radio Licenses in Lucerne

Call Sign: KC9MVQ
John W Flint
9216 N 100 E
Lucerne IN 46950

FCC Amateur Radio Licenses in Macy

Call Sign: N9HWT
Deborah A Hammond
Box 228
Macy IN 46951

Call Sign: WC5W

Dwight Hammond
2975 E Jefferson St
Macy IN 46951

Call Sign: N3VYS
Wes Bowen
4469 E SR 16
Macy IN 46951

Call Sign: KC9JOQ
Steven J Samsel
3147 Main St
Macy IN 46951

Call Sign: KC9QZF
Daniel J Fox
11324 N 100 W
Macy IN 46951

Call Sign: KC9NQY
Anthony R Waggoner
4420 W 1050 N
Macy IN 46951

Call Sign: KA9PYZ
Charles E Hall
4210 W CR 1150 N
Macy IN 46951

Call Sign: KC9BVJ
Linda R Scrivner
Macy IN 46951

Call Sign: KC9CCY
Mandy J Scrivner
Macy IN 46951

**FCC Amateur Radio
Licenses in Marion**

Call Sign: KC9MPT
Trevis L Bright
738 600 E
Marion IN 46953

Call Sign: N9ONF
Dannie L Case
71 Bobby Ave
Marion IN 46953

Call Sign: N9GRE
Stephen T Barley
1612 Broadview Dr
Marion IN 469521318

Call Sign: KB9KTQ
Shirley A Dillman
405 Campbell Ave
Marion IN 46952

Call Sign: KO9F
Verlis L Dillman
405 Campbell Ave
Marion IN 46952

Call Sign: KC9TIJ
George Cooper
7 Colonial Park Dr
Marion IN 46953

Call Sign: N9JMU
Jerry L Rowe
4420 E 100 N
Marion IN 46952

Call Sign: K9LIR
John U Robinson
3996 E 100 S
Marion IN 46952

Call Sign: KB9YXZ
Stephen P Swan
5360 E 100 S
Marion IN 46953

Call Sign: N9PWK
John W Jones
3131 E 200 N
Marion IN 46952

Call Sign: WD9EZA
Floyd A Johnson
3179 E 200 N
Marion IN 46952

Call Sign: N9SMC
Janet C Johnson
3179 E 200 N
Marion IN 46952

Call Sign: KA9EBU
Delbert A Frazier
3225 E 200 N
Marion IN 46952

Call Sign: KC9PWI
Douglas M Poore
8416 E 200 S
Marion IN 46953

Call Sign: N9IBI
Orlin T Planck
1022 E 29th St
Marion IN 46953

Call Sign: N9FHJ
David L Fox
1201 E 29th St
Marion IN 46953

Call Sign: KB4MDR
Michael D Robinette
917.5 E 30th St
Marion IN 46953

Call Sign: WA9LFA
Conrad C Shields
1078 E 38th St
Marion IN 46953

Call Sign: KA9NZG
Jessamine L Shields
1078 E 38th St
Marion IN 469534459

Call Sign: W9MXV
Sheldon A Whitcomb
1323 E 38th St
Marion IN 46953

Call Sign: N9HQU
Marvin A Calvert
1000 E 39th St
Marion IN 46953

Call Sign: KC9GZN
Mindy R Ballinger
7453 E 400 S
Marion IN 46953

Call Sign: KA9DAM
Barbara E Morgan
1620 E 450 N
Marion IN 46952

Call Sign: KB9EHC
Benjamin J Watkins
104 E 45th St
Marion IN 46953

Call Sign: N9VFZ
James D Downing
215 E 46th
Marion IN 46953

Call Sign: WB8ETJ
Philip D Moorhead
715 E 48th St
Marion IN 46953

Call Sign: KB9TTZ
Dennis G McHarry
718 E 500 S
Marion IN 46953

Call Sign: K9IX
Calumet Amateur Radio
Enthusiasts
2340 E Bocock Rd
Marion IN 46952

Call Sign: AJ9C
Michael A Kasrich
2340 E Bocock Rd
Marion IN 46952

Call Sign: KA9CVI
Rollie E Clouse
605 E Bond Ave
Marion IN 46952

Call Sign: KB9UBF
Walter E Whitlock Jr
1006 E Bradford
Marion IN 46952

Call Sign: N9SYL
Scott A Roll
1772 E Charles Rd
Marion IN 46952

Call Sign: N9NGO
Harold E Kellogg
1415 E Daisy St
Marion IN 46953

Call Sign: KB9FKZ
Amanda J Brooksher
1010 E Grant St
Marion IN 46952

Call Sign: KC9EGW
Richard A Deshong
640 E Grant St
Marion IN 46952

Call Sign: KB9ZBI
Amanda J Rudicel
203 E Highland Ave
Marion IN 46952

Call Sign: W9JOY
Amanda J Rudicel
203 E Highland Ave
Marion IN 46952

Call Sign: KB9OMC
Charles D Rudicel
203 E Highland Ave
Marion IN 46952

Call Sign: KB9OME
Vicki A Rudicel
203 E Highland Ave
Marion IN 46952

Call Sign: KB9PMA
Faron R Freeman
5612 E Lakewood Ct
Marion IN 46953

Call Sign: KB9CQZ
Jeffery G Banter
1111 E Marshall
Marion IN 46952

Call Sign: KB9VEH
Raymond L Abston
5498 E Montpelier Pike
Marion IN 46953

Call Sign: N9LLI
Kennith R Baldridge
4356 E Montpilier Pk
Marion IN 46953

Call Sign: K9CVH
David W Dodge
132 E N Deerwood Ct
Marion IN 46953

Call Sign: KB9AQN
Carl A Brookshire
4386 E Noos
Marion IN 46953

Call Sign: KA9VIT
Ray D Elzey II
4770 E Noos
Marion IN 46953

Call Sign: KC9RNN
Gary D Thorne
337 E Sherman St
Marion IN 46952

Call Sign: KC9GKC
Ronald D Dakin
613 E Swayzee St
Marion IN 46952

Call Sign: KB9OMD
Larry E Rudicel
411 E Wiley St
Marion IN 46952

Call Sign: KE4FY
Gregory F Broyles
1402 Eagle Ln
Marion IN 46952

Call Sign: K1NT
Benjamin C Hofmann
3265 Frances Slocum Trl
Marion IN 46952

Call Sign: K2ARI
Karen A Hofmann
3265 Frances Slocum Trl
Marion IN 46952

Call Sign: KB9GWR
James A Gray
2318 Home Ave
Marion IN 46953

Call Sign: KA9YJQ
Philip M Benbow
708 Ivanhoe Dr
Marion IN 46952

Call Sign: N9UTE
Floyd R McNeely
505 Keal Ave
Marion IN 46952

Call Sign: N9EVV
Robert L Hoke
1624 Mason Blvd
Marion IN 46953

Call Sign: KB9YPI
Jerry W Bennett
4412 Minto Dr
Marion IN 46952

Call Sign: KC9FCP
James C Davis
3834 N 100 E
Marion IN 46952

Call Sign: W9JCD
James C Davis
3834 N 100 E
Marion IN 46952

Call Sign: N9RPB
Claude A Rust
1058 N 400 E
Marion IN 469528736

Call Sign: KA9RUZ
Val G McIntire
4987 N 500 E
Marion IN 46952

Call Sign: KB9VCJ
Floyd S Marshall
3271 N 600 E
Marion IN 46952

Call Sign: N7HAN
Claude J Lemert
458 N Adams St
Marion IN 46952

Call Sign: N9LPB
Kevin S Nordstrom
302 N Boots St
Marion IN 46952

Call Sign: W9RWM
Richard W Masters
505 N Bradner Ave
Marion IN 46952

Call Sign: N9WE
Daniel J Edwards
3259 N Charles Rd
Marion IN 46952

Call Sign: KC9RAX
Scott Shepler
101 N D St
Marion IN 46952

Call Sign: KB9YLQ
Larry L Simons
1806 N Dumont Dr
Marion IN 46952

Call Sign: WA9SPT
Charles W Bartholomew
Sr
6981 N E00W
Marion IN 46952

Call Sign: KB9ISY
Christian W
Bartholomew
6981 N Eoow
Marion IN 46952

Call Sign: KA9DLJ
Jerry W Richards
808 N Fenton Rd
Marion IN 46952

Call Sign: N9TSD
Rodney R McClain
6089 N Francis Slocum
Tr
Marion IN 46952

Call Sign: K9NQW

Lynn B Nickerson
517 N Hendricks Ave
Marion IN 46952

Call Sign: KA6NQW
Lynn B Nickerson
517 N Hendricks Ave
Marion IN 469522319

Call Sign: N9ZNL
Warren E Arnett
723 N Horton St
Marion IN 469522228

Call Sign: KC9OTD
Richard E Martin
4329 N Huntington Rd
Marion IN 46952

Call Sign: KC9OTB
Tanner L Martin
4329 N Huntington Rd
Marion IN 46952

Call Sign: KB9YHS
Marissa M Castillo
5060 N Huntington Rd
Marion IN 46952

Call Sign: N9LRY
Peter M Castillo
5060 N Huntington Rd
Marion IN 46952

Call Sign: WD9HLU
William C McCarty
619 N Ivanhoe Dr
Marion IN 46952

Call Sign: KC9AZP
Eric D Creech
973 N King Rd
Marion IN 469528653

Call Sign: WD9EOI

James F Allman Jr
612 N Lenfesty
Marion IN 46952

Call Sign: WB9TOX
Kenneth E Hoke
611 N Lenfesty Ave
Marion IN 46952

Call Sign: N9UJP
Gary A Clendenin
1309 N Manor Dr
Marion IN 46952

Call Sign: KA9BFK
Robert E Swarts
1408 N Marlin Dr
Marion IN 46952

Call Sign: N9DGD
Alberta R Metz
2311 N Meridian St
Marion IN 46953

Call Sign: KC9EPB
Jerry R Jones
1836 N Michael Dr
Marion IN 46952

Call Sign: W9JED
Jerry R Jones
1836 N Michael Dr
Marion IN 46952

Call Sign: KA9YNO
Emil R Trautvetter
1880 N Michael Dr
Marion IN 46952

Call Sign: KB9IZP
Robert D Holley
4410 N Minto Dr
Marion IN 46952

Call Sign: KA7NME

Chris H Brevick
205 N Nebraska St
Marion IN 46952

Call Sign: KD7GQZ
Stephen M Mitchell
3825 N Penbrook Dr
Marion IN 46952

Call Sign: KD7FKD
William E Mitchell
3825 N Penbrook Dr
Marion IN 46952

Call Sign: KD7NEF
Darlene Mitchell
3825 N Penbrook Dr
Marion IN 46952

Call Sign: KC9MWQ
Kevin D Hicks
1215 N Quarry Rd
Marion IN 46952

Call Sign: W6UT
Randall P Wagaman III
1411 N Richard Rd
Marion IN 46952

Call Sign: N9AX
Randall P Wagaman III
1411 N Richard Rd
Marion IN 46952

Call Sign: KB9PNJ
Matthew D Hon
4489 N Wabash Rd
Marion IN 46952

Call Sign: KB9VEG
Laura L Zumbrun
853 N Washington
Marion IN 46952

Call Sign: KB9GTS

Douglas S Zumbrun
853 N Washington St
Marion IN 46952

Call Sign: KB9YLR
Cissy J Zumbrun
853 N Washington St
Marion IN 46952

Call Sign: N9KIH
Robert L Rust
121 N Washington St Apt
115
Marion IN 46952

Call Sign: KA9YJR
Candy S Elzey
N00S
Marion IN 46953

Call Sign: W9RWC
Richard W Cloud
1 Prairie Ct
Marion IN 46953

Call Sign: KB5YOD
Richard L Clymer
1909 S 400 E
Marion IN 46953

Call Sign: KA9YTX
Phillip L Ruley
6420 S 500 E
Marion IN 46953

Call Sign: KC9LAN
Richie E Hendey
1454 S 525 E
Marion IN 46953

Call Sign: KC9PWH
Adam L Hendey
1492 S 600 E
Marion IN 46953

Call Sign: KB9OQF
Mark E Banter
1782 S 900 E
Marion IN 46953

Call Sign: KB9CNV
Allan R Humbert
5514 S Adams
Marion IN 46953

Call Sign: KB9VUO
Eddie D Dennis
5101 S Adams 21
Marion IN 46953

Call Sign: N8DKT
George R Spencer
4405 S Adams St
Marion IN 46953

Call Sign: KC9SPX
Grant County Races
401 S Adams St Ste 601
Marion IN 46953

Call Sign: WB9HQA
Gary G Galbraith
3703 S Blair
Marion IN 46952

Call Sign: WD9HLY
Merrilee K Galbraith
3703 S Blair
Marion IN 46953

Call Sign: WB9EAP
William B Clark
2202 S Boots St
Marion IN 46953

Call Sign: K9CHV
Vernon C Wood
3611 S Boots St
Marion IN 46952

Call Sign: KC9FMW
Michael J Aldrich
3717 S Boots St
Marion IN 46953

Call Sign: KB9NTE
Martin M Ferguson
3011 S Branson
Marion IN 46953

Call Sign: N9LLG
Joseph A Major
1521 S Branson St
Marion IN 46953

Call Sign: N9GTL
Paul E Brown Jr
211 S D St
Marion IN 46952

Call Sign: N9HUJ
Terry L Dull
423 S Gallatin St
Marion IN 46953

Call Sign: N9ETM
Purdle H Briscoe
1702 S Gallatin St
Marion IN 46953

Call Sign: WA9HBF
Warren E Turner
2719 S Gallatin St
Marion IN 46952

Call Sign: KB9WJO
Glen E Hollinger
3706 S Gallatin St
Marion IN 46953

Call Sign: N9HQS
Frank T Sinclair
4705 S Harmon St
Marion IN 46953

Call Sign: WB9KMA
Thomas L Shane
1324 S Michigan Ave
Marion IN 46953

Call Sign: WD9EOH
Lewis A Inskeep
1612 S Washington
Marion IN 46953

Call Sign: AB9FW
Don R Lahr
3758 Shadeland Ct
Marion IN 46952

Call Sign: KB9ZRS
Michael L Miller
106.5 S Nebraska St
Marion IN 469523816

Call Sign: W9GZE
Stephen E Johnson
4501 S Washington
Marion IN 46952

Call Sign: N9ITV
Donald L Moon
3783 SR E
Marion IN 469520948

Call Sign: KT9Z
Dennis G McHarry
5597 S Nebraska St
Marion IN 46953

Call Sign: W9OGH
Donald N Dille
2302 S Washington St
Marion IN 46953

Call Sign: KA9QCS
Richard W Moore
3783 SR 18E
Marion IN 46952

Call Sign: KB9YLN
Jerry C Brown Sr
2218 S Race St
Marion IN 46953

Call Sign: W9FDC
Clyde L Brookshire
3323 S Washington St
Marion IN 46953

Call Sign: KB9JRM
Ray L Parker
910 Vinson Dr Apt C
Marion IN 46952

Call Sign: KB9RPT
Ralph O Craig
4624 S Selby St
Marion IN 46953

Call Sign: N9GVG
Evelyn J Brookshire
3323 S Washington St
Marion IN 46953

Call Sign: KA9QCL
Jess W Roll Jr
1009 W 10th St
Marion IN 46953

Call Sign: AB9AB
Ralph O Craig
4624 S Selby St
Marion IN 46953

Call Sign: WS9C
Jon R Nordstrom
5522 Scott Rd
Marion IN 46953

Call Sign: KC9QZE
Chris L Paul
1427 W 10th St
Marion IN 46953

Call Sign: KB9ISX
Samuel L Hornbuckle
2801 S Stone Rd 21
Marion IN 469534708

Call Sign: K9YN
Jon R Nordstrom
5522 Scott Rd
Marion IN 46953

Call Sign: WB9GFS
Richard E Sprong
2435 W 12th St
Marion IN 46953

Call Sign: N9HTU
Lydia J Hines
2801 S Stone Rd Lot 149
Marion IN 46953

Call Sign: N9LPP
Pamelia A Nordstrom
5522 Scott Rd
Marion IN 46953

Call Sign: KC9LNR
Michael P Raver
2743 W 17th L59
Marion IN 46953

Call Sign: WD9EOE
Thomas J Hines
2801 S Stone Rd Lot 149
Marion IN 46953

Call Sign: N9FBB
Don R Lahr
3758 Shadeland Ct
Marion IN 46952

Call Sign: KB9EJ
Ervin W Bartz
516 W 1st
Marion IN 46952

Call Sign: N9LKE
Paul D Hughes Jr
310 W 20th St
Marion IN 46953

Call Sign: N9AUV
David F Hulley
915 W 26th St
Marion IN 46953

Call Sign: KB9FLL
Nereece H Baird
921 W 26th St
Marion IN 46953

Call Sign: N9EXA
Richard W Masters
729 W 35th St
Marion IN 46953

Call Sign: WB9YCV
Phyllis S Knost
1529 W 38th St
Marion IN 46953

Call Sign: WA9ULM
Richard N Knost
1529 W 38th St
Marion IN 46953

Call Sign: KA9EDD
Paul A Leaming
1621 W 38th St
Marion IN 46952

Call Sign: AG9I
Donald D Hoke
619 W 3rd St Apt210
Marion IN 46952

Call Sign: K9OHA
Shelby J Whitcomb Gretz
2198 W 50th St
Marion IN 469539369

Call Sign: N8LPA
Amy A Rayment
1020 W 5th St
Marion IN 46953

Call Sign: KC9TCD
Richard M Graff
1430 W 5th St
Marion IN 46953

Call Sign: KC9OTE
Gary W Hurt
1601 W 5th St
Marion IN 46953

Call Sign: KB9TLR
Jason R Stepp
557 W 600 N
Marion IN 469529736

Call Sign: KC9JRA
Philip A Keifer
211 W 6th St
Marion IN 46953

Call Sign: KC9RNQ
Jon Altman
2347 W 8th
Marion IN 46952

Call Sign: W9CUC
Robert M Manor
923 W Chapel Pike
Marion IN 469521846

Call Sign: KC9UNY
Jedidiah Harvey
3598 W Delphi Pike
Marion IN 46952

Call Sign: KB9UZE
Daniel E Durkes
1420 W Forest Ln
Marion IN 46952

Call Sign: KB9ZNU
Andrew E White
803 W Nelson
Marion IN 46952

Call Sign: W9AEW
Andrew E White
803 W Nelson
Marion IN 46952

Call Sign: KC9GQB
Michael D Robinette
1412 W North Dr
Marion IN 46952

Call Sign: KB9JZ
Arlen G Schmidt
1421 W North Dr
Marion IN 46952

Call Sign: W4WIZ
James W Purvis
1516 W Spencer Ave
Marion IN 46952

Call Sign: N9GRD
Elizabeth A O'Donell
2025 W Westholme Dr
Marion IN 469529333

Call Sign: KC9OTC
Brian K Shrader
2003 W Wilno Dr
Marion IN 46952

Call Sign: KA9YTH
Brian R Goff
1814 Wenlock Dr
Marion IN 46952

Call Sign: W9NTB
Carl G Butsch
210 Wharton Dr
Marion IN 46952

Call Sign: KA9IYJ
Daniel S Cornett
3819 Wildwood Dr
Marion IN 46952

Call Sign: KA9IYI
Russell S Cornett
3819 Wildwood Dr
Marion IN 46952

Call Sign: W7DIZ
George M Kilmer
4265 Wilshire Dr
Marion IN 46952

Call Sign: KC9KML
Stephen Shepler
Marion IN 46952

Call Sign: WA9RVM
Stephen Shepler
Marion IN 46952

Call Sign: KC9NQW
Floyd E Broegman
Marion IN 46953

Call Sign: K9DRA
Floyd E Broegman
Marion IN 46953

FCC Amateur Radio Licenses in Markle

Call Sign: N9VUK
Joshua D Morris
335 Clay St
Markle IN 46770

Call Sign: K9WDP
John W Stockman
4761 E 500 S
Markle IN 46770

Call Sign: WD9IOV

Robert D Jackson
180 E Hall St
Markle IN 46770

Call Sign: KC9EJB
Nolan J Hartzler
9617 N 300 W 90
Markle IN 46770

Call Sign: KC9ELG
Scott E Moser
365 N Clark St
Markle IN 46770

Call Sign: K9MRI
Joseph L Stroud
3124 W 900 N
Markle IN 46770

Call Sign: N9RYI
Brian G Jenks
317 W Hoover Ln
Markle IN 46770

Call Sign: KB9YOX
Adam J Rodenbeck
Markle IN 46770

FCC Amateur Radio Licenses in Matthews

Call Sign: KG9O
Kenneth J Narducci
507 Cumberland Ln
Matthews IN 46957

Call Sign: N9RHZ
Michael D Horton
303 E 11th St Apt 1
Matthews IN 46957

Call Sign: KB9OQR
Gary J Skinner Jr
121 E 7th St
Matthews IN 46957

Call Sign: W9CSY
Charles L Newlin
Matthews IN 46957

Call Sign: W2ORG
Merritt F Malvern
Matthews IN 469570095

Call Sign: KA9FDN
Harold A Biggs
Matthews IN 469570186

FCC Amateur Radio Licenses in Medaryville

Call Sign: KE9I
Gerard Jendraszkiewicz
1600W
Medaryville IN 47957

Call Sign: KB9NSC
Nancy A Jendraszkiewicz
1600W
Medaryville IN 47957

Call Sign: KA9SKF
Kenneth R Williams
Box 308
Medaryville IN 47957

Call Sign: N9XIA
Michael G Gentry
3676 N 1000 W
Medaryville IN 47957

Call Sign: KC9HMV
Flying Iguana Contest
Group
2505 N 1600 W
Medaryville IN 47957

Call Sign: N9QX
Flying Iguana Contest
Group

2505 N 1600 W
Medaryville IN 47957

Call Sign: KB9TMC
Tri County ARC
2505 N 1600 W
Medaryville IN 47957

Call Sign: K9IZ
Tri County ARC
2505 N 1600 W
Medaryville IN 47957

Call Sign: K9KFT
Wayne D Mayhew Jr
2073 N 1650 W
Medaryville IN 47957

Call Sign: WD9DKW
Max L White
Medaryville IN 47957

Call Sign: KA9BZM
William E Shortz
Medaryville IN 47957

Call Sign: K9BZM
William E Shortz
Medaryville IN 47957

FCC Amateur Radio Licenses in Mentone

Call Sign: KC9RRV
Troy A Craig
20755 Birch Rd
Mentone IN 46539

Call Sign: N9ISW
Paul A Vandermark
Box 106
Mentone IN 46539

Call Sign: KC9RRG
Edward A Rock

514 E Jackson St
Mentone IN 46539

Call Sign: W9CDW
Dale J Wallace
102 Millers Dr Lot 13
Mentone IN 465390085

Call Sign: KA9DKP
Dennis K Baker
7834 N 900 E
Mentone IN 46539

Call Sign: KB9RHG
Wayne K Baker
1426 SR 25
Mentone IN 46539

Call Sign: KB9SBJ
John E Hart
202 W Maple St
Mentone IN 46539

Call Sign: N5MRD
Harriet A Guillaume
5769 W Martin Dr
Mentone IN 465399311

Call Sign: KC9NWK
Gary R McDaniel
6734 W SR 25
Mentone IN 46539

Call Sign: K9ISD
Joseph C Good
112 Yale St
Mentone IN 46539

Call Sign: KC9FJZ
Kevin G Hileman
Mentone IN 46539

Call Sign: KC9RQP
Terry L Reed
Mentone IN 46539

FCC Amateur Radio Licenses in Merrillville

Call Sign: W9KLI
George W Mattox
7250 Arthur Dr
Merrillville IN 46410

Call Sign: K9WWT
George D Kelly
5900 Arthur St
Merrillville IN
464102343

Call Sign: WD9ETJ
Nancy A Kelly
5900 Arthur St
Merrillville IN
464102343

Call Sign: W2SMO
Clarence L Huginnie
5555 Broadway
Merrillville IN 46410

Call Sign: KA9RBN
David A Staniszewski
7439 Chase St
Merrillville IN 46410

Call Sign: N9QLS
William R Young
7830 Chase St
Merrillville IN 46410

Call Sign: N9YUB
Robert E Petit Jr
5659 Connecticut
Merrillville IN 46410

Call Sign: KC9HCY
Ken J Vitullo
6680 Connecticut
Merrillville IN 46410

Call Sign: KA9EHU
Roger L Heiser
2 Deerpath Rd
Merrillville IN 46410

Call Sign: KB9NYV
John A Kadelak
130 E 52nd Ave
Merrillville IN 46410

Call Sign: N9SCH
Phillip E Bradshaw
193 E 53rd Ave
Merrillville IN 46410

Call Sign: N9TER
Alan L Neff
230 E 59th Ave 6C
Merrillville IN 46410

Call Sign: KB9RVW
James E Wirick
735 E 61 Ave
Merrillville IN 46410

Call Sign: N9SYU
Nathan N Schrock
1000 E 61st Pl
Merrillville IN 46410

Call Sign: KA9JWX
Paul L Webster
29 E 67th Ave
Merrillville IN
464103503

Call Sign: KB9VSH
Bryon S Mesarch
201 E 68th Pl
Merrillville IN
464103509

Call Sign: K7SVO
Bryon S Mesarch

201 E 68th Pl
Merrillville IN
464103509

Call Sign: KC9MLN
Douglas Anoman
3440 E 69th Ave
Merrillville IN 46410

Call Sign: WA9RMT
Philip W Zobel
2304 E 73rd Ave
Merrillville IN 46410

Call Sign: WA9JNO
Earl T Gumm
2502 E 73rd Ave
Merrillville IN 46410

Call Sign: N9IJJ
Harry J Duggan
3603 E 73rd Ave
Merrillville IN 46410

Call Sign: KC9HST
John Wood School Ham
Radio Club
6100 E 73rd St
Merrillville IN 46410

Call Sign: WB9WLB
Gary L Martin
7155 E 86 Ct
Merrillville IN 46410

Call Sign: N9YBL
Dustin B Stevenson
6873 Fillmore Dr
Merrillville IN 46410

Call Sign: N9QVF
George A Snure
7820 Hanley St
Merrillville IN 46410

Call Sign: N9MXP
Matthew A Sigstad
7820 Hanley St
Merrillville IN 46410

Call Sign: W9MAL
Malcolm A Lunsford
6721 Harrison Ct
Merrillville IN 46410

Call Sign: K9SAL
Shirley A Lunsford
6721 Harrison Ct
Merrillville IN 46410

Call Sign: K9OVC
Charles B Runions
5920 Hayes Pl
Merrillville IN 46410

Call Sign: KB9ENH
Greg J Runions
5920 Hayes Pl
Merrillville IN 46410

Call Sign: KC9TKM
Daniel J Olinger
5319 Jennings Pl
Merrillville IN 46410

Call Sign: K9SGA
Daniel J Olinger
5319 Jennings Pl
Merrillville IN 46410

Call Sign: WD9GQO
Lee A Raue
6401 Kentucky Pl
Merrillville IN 46410

Call Sign: KB9CYR
Joseph D Moke
5469 Madison Ave
Merrillville IN 46410

Call Sign: WF9U
William S Jachim
7470 Madison St
Merrillville IN 46410

Call Sign: WD9EZB
Robert W Wiberg Jr
7513 Marshall Pl
Merrillville IN 46410

Call Sign: KB9CYG
Larry D Johnson
6973 Pierce Dr
Merrillville IN 46410

Call Sign: K9OSB
James L Campbell
7214 Roosevelt Cir
Merrillville IN 46410

Call Sign: N9ELH
Eugene P Smith
8330 Taft St
Merrillville IN 46410

Call Sign: K9DNR
Richard J Tlapa
6350 Taft St Sr 55
Merrillville IN 46410

Call Sign: KB9TNQ
Lloyd B Fravel Jr
7608 Taney Pl
Merrillville IN
464104431

Call Sign: N9TUH
Herman C Neuliep
6823 Tyler
Merrillville IN 46410

Call Sign: W9TJH
Boris N Nastoff
320 W 56th Pl
Merrillville IN 46410

Call Sign: KB9CXR
William R Miller
2701 W 57 Ave
Merrillville IN
464101127

Call Sign: KB9HNY
Frank Ardizzone
2230 W 57th Ave
Merrillville IN 46410

Call Sign: W9JEA
James E Ausenbaugh
2709 W 57th Pl
Merrillville IN 46410

Call Sign: KC9CAZ
Terry D Shotliff
1855 W 58th Ave
Merrillville IN
464102305

Call Sign: K9TDS
Terry D Shotliff
1855 W 58th Ave
Merrillville IN
464102305

Call Sign: K9TZT
Edward T Perosky
2736 W 60th Dr
Merrillville IN 46410

Call Sign: KF9EX
James W Harney Sr
2600 W 61 Pl
Merrillville IN 46410

Call Sign: W9BYA
Michael R Kollar
2397 W 61st Pl
Merrillville IN 46410

Call Sign: KA9WWW

Winton H Hansen
813 W 65th Ln
Merrillville IN 46410

Call Sign: K9JCU
Theodore A Editz
973 W 67th Pl
Merrillville IN 46410

Call Sign: WB9BRP
Ted F Hathaway
201 W 68th Pl
Merrillville IN 46410

Call Sign: KA9YPL
Debra J Wojtyska
764 W 70th Pl
Merrillville IN 46410

Call Sign: KB9ERY
Lawrence W Brunansky
24 W 71st Pl
Merrillville IN 46410

Call Sign: WB9VQO
Donald T Artka
2938 W 74th Ave
Merrillville IN 46410

Call Sign: K9DLJ
George W Kepshire
3268 W 75th Ln
Merrillville IN 46410

Call Sign: KA9AQZ
Robert A Toby
2957 W 76 Ln
Merrillville IN 46410

Call Sign: WD9EOO
Larry A Thomas
2920 W 76th Ave
Merrillville IN 46410

Call Sign: KB9CNC

Judith A Hill
2958 W 76th Ln
Merrillville IN 46410

Call Sign: KB9CND
Timothy P Hill Sr
2958 W 76th Ln
Merrillville IN 46410

Call Sign: KC9DJN
Steven A Condos
3233 W 76th Ln
Merrillville IN
464104413

Call Sign: WD9DYQ
Fredrick C Miller
3203 W 76th Pl
Merrillville IN 46410

Call Sign: KB9NCJ
Russell E Lash
440 W 84th Dr
Merrillville IN 46410

Call Sign: K9PIA
Cheryl L Johnson
1256 W 84th Ln
Merrillville IN 46410

Call Sign: NA9U
John M Nason
2641 W 85th Ave
Merrillville IN 46410

Call Sign: N9WXW
Rafael Cruz Jr
1130 W 85th Ave
Merrillville IN 46410

Call Sign: WA8FIB
Harold T Ruggles
3819 W 90th Ct
Merrillville IN
464106838

Call Sign: W8FIB
Harold T Ruggles
3819 W 90th Ct
Merrillville IN
464106838

Call Sign: WB9SRR
James Kelly
7323 Whitcomb St
Merrillville IN 46410

Call Sign: KC9UNS
Benjamin A Straw
5344 Wilson St
Merrillville IN 46410

Call Sign: K9SAC
Steven A Condos
Merrillville IN 46411

Call Sign: KF4FPW
Theresa P Johnson
Merrillville IN
464111791

FCC Amateur Radio Licenses in Mexico

Call Sign: KB9YQP
Donald C Greer
51 N Fillmore St
Mexico IN 46958

Call Sign: K9LVV
Blaine J Keyes
Mexico IN 46958

Call Sign: KB9ZAQ
Debra K Hull
Mexico IN 46958

Call Sign: KB9RUZ
Patrick R Townsend
Mexico IN 46958

Call Sign: KB9EOD
Michael H Rendel
Mexico IN 46970

Call Sign: KC9GWC
John M Stoeckert
Mexico IN 469580315

FCC Amateur Radio Licenses in Michigan City

Call Sign: W9DZ
Allen E Jones
100N
Michigan City IN
463609451

Call Sign: KB9BYY
Thomas M Carr
950W
Michigan City IN 46360

Call Sign: WB9YZC
James A Maguire
201 Avalon Ct
Michigan City IN
463606203

Call Sign: WB9RXS
William L Stoakes
316 Barker Rd
Michigan City IN 46360

Call Sign: KB9HGE
Todd M Martinson
421 Black Oak Dr
Michigan City IN 46360

Call Sign: KB9IEI
Peter A Pizarek
316 Bolka Ave
Michigan City IN 46360

Call Sign: KC9HTY
Scott A Foster
309 Chestnut St
Michigan City IN 46360

Call Sign: KC9UUO
Barbara S Murray
336 Chestnut St
Michigan City IN 46360

Call Sign: KC9UUN
Dave L Pfeiffer
336 Chestnut St
Michigan City IN 46360

Call Sign: AJ9T
Charles F Zeese
508 Cleveland Ave
Michigan City IN 46360

Call Sign: KA9PGA
Dorothy I Lyles
4300 Cleveland Ave Villa
13
Michigan City IN 46360

Call Sign: KC9RCY
Alvious E Pack
336 Cloud St
Michigan City IN 46360

Call Sign: KB9YGF
Alan F Pitts
1614 Colorado Ave
Michigan City IN
463608416

Call Sign: W1PIT
Alan F Pitts
1614 Colorado Ave
Michigan City IN
463608416

Call Sign: KB9FET
Scott P Neitzel

105 Concord Dr
Michigan City IN 46360

Call Sign: N9BBJ
Edwin C Linsemeyer
203 Congress St
Michigan City IN 46360

Call Sign: KC9CP
Charles Ware Jr
165 Crestwood Dr
Michigan City IN 46360

Call Sign: KB9EUZ
Kara L Kienitz
113 Decatur St
Michigan City IN 46360

Call Sign: KB9KOJ
Daniel R Kelly
401 Derby
Michigan City IN 46360

Call Sign: KC9NWJ
Russell M Rumbaugh
3233 Dody Ave Apt 2
Michigan City IN 46360

Call Sign: KB9NDE
Marvin Eugene Scott
1604 E 8th St
Michigan City IN 46360

Call Sign: N9SJR
Roland H Sherwood
413 E 9th St
Michigan City IN 46360

Call Sign: WO9ODY
Roland H Sherwood
413 E 9th St
Michigan City IN 46360

Call Sign: N9SJS
Elbert M Ladd

1816 E Coolspring Ave
Michigan City IN
463606404

Call Sign: N9HMQ
Jeffrey E Sax
506 E Eckman St
Michigan City IN 46614

Call Sign: KA9LOW
Mark A Fisher
2902 E Michigan Blv
Michigan City IN 46350

Call Sign: KC5SSL
Barbara J Fisher
2902 E Michigan Blvd
Michigan City IN 46360

Call Sign: KC9DKX
Richard B Krentz
9801 E US 12 Lot 75
Michigan City IN 46360

Call Sign: K9IDE
William R Crawford
1115 Earl Rd
Michigan City IN 46360

Call Sign: KE4JQS
Richard E Hooper
3116 Edgebrook Dr
Michigan City IN 46360

Call Sign: N9PTA
Michael A Kmak Jr
715 Faulknor St
Michigan City IN 46360

Call Sign: K9GLK
Warren G Sherwood
711 Gardena St
Michigan City IN 46360

Call Sign: KC9KUV

Charles B Blair
105 Garrettson Ave
Michigan City IN 46360

Call Sign: K9CBB
Charles B Blair
105 Garrettson Ave
Michigan City IN 46360

Call Sign: N9MSE
Christopher A Oberg
601 Greentree
Michigan City IN 46360

Call Sign: W9HW
William E Voltz
1312 Greenwood Ave
Michigan City IN 46360

Call Sign: WD9BDW
Phillibert D Geoffrion
2014 Greenwood Ave
Michigan City IN 46360

Call Sign: KB9ORJ
Timothy P Volckmann
147 Hendricks St
Michigan City IN 46360

Call Sign: KC9OB
David D Kowalski
909 Henry St
Michigan City IN 46360

Call Sign: K9ET
Robert A Lyles
507 Hobart St
Michigan City IN
463610168

Call Sign: KA9PGB
Wilbert E Green
2944 Hollywood Ave
Michigan City IN 46360

Call Sign: WB9SUL
Jack L Siddall
1110 Hoyt St
Michigan City IN 46360

Call Sign: KA9PIM
Clarence W Rollason Jr
1555 Illinois Ave
Michigan City IN 46360

Call Sign: KC9LUQ
Leonard L Dineen
3011 Jackson St
Michigan City IN 46360

Call Sign: W9EDU
Kenneth P Humbert
500 Johnson Rd
Michigan City IN
463606513

Call Sign: KC9RPI
Stephen E Whitehead
1012 Lake Shore Dr
Michigan City IN 46360

Call Sign: N9QKW
John P Locke
3519 Lake Shore Dr
Michigan City IN 46360

Call Sign: KB9UIO
Richard A Doperalski
119 Lakehills Rd
Michigan City IN 46360

Call Sign: N9HPB
Joseph S Gembala
501 Laurel Dr T C
Michigan City IN 46360

Call Sign: KC9VDZ
Larry J Fleck
1727 Liberty Ave
Michigan City IN 46360

Call Sign: KC9ITE
Jeremy J Denton
201 Long Beach Ln
Michigan City IN 46360

Call Sign: K9HTJ
Jeremy J Denton
201 Long Beach Ln
Michigan City IN 46360

Call Sign: W9VBJ
Roger C Holloway
417 Madison St
Michigan City IN 46360

Call Sign: WB9WRG
Paul L Fane Jr
2808 Maple St
Michigan City IN 46360

Call Sign: WD9EOU
Michael O Silverthorne
40 Marine Dr 7
Michigan City IN 46360

Call Sign: WD9FGZ
Steven F Peterka
215 Meadowlark Dr
Michigan City IN
463605747

Call Sign: NT9T
Ronald J La Mothe
1917 Monrovia Dr
Michigan City IN
463601417

Call Sign: N9TPC
Ronald J Stahoviak
5802 N 400 W
Michigan City IN
463609721

Call Sign: N9UCN

Rowena F Stahoviak
5802 N 400 W
Michigan City IN
463609721

Call Sign: WE9H
Stanley M Kmak
1451 N 425 E
Michigan City IN 46360

Call Sign: W9TAD
Carl G Konefsky
1392 N 600 E
Michigan City IN 46360

Call Sign: KC9HCP
Jon Jesko
3237 N 950 W
Michigan City IN 46360

Call Sign: K9MZW
James E Moore
1965 N Country Ln
Michigan City IN 46360

Call Sign: KA9UPJ
Chad W Dyer
6981 N E Suburban Dr
Michigan City IN 46360

Call Sign: KA9UOJ
Billy J Dyer
6981 N E Suburban Dr
Michigan City IN 46360

Call Sign: KA9LTU
Allan L Wozniak
2399 N Orchard Dr
Michigan City IN 46360

Call Sign: KB9MCG
William A Newton
218 N Porter St
Michigan City IN 46360

Call Sign: N9LUM
Dale L Warren
1037 N Roeske Ave
Michigan City IN 46360

Call Sign: WB9SAF
Richard G Morman
9801 N US 12E Lot B
Michigan City IN 46360

Call Sign: KC9TWW
Billy J Halfacre
3434 N Wozniak Rd
Michigan City IN 46360

Call Sign: AG9S
James R Sjoberg Jr
4333 N Wozniak Rd
Michigan City IN 46360

Call Sign: N9CTQ
Ronald E Long
2322 Normandy Dt Apt
2A
Michigan City IN 46360

Call Sign: W9AAY
Howard L Smith
3016 Northmoor Trl
Michigan City IN 46360

Call Sign: K9FTO
George J Van Gieson
1504 Oak St
Michigan City IN 46360

Call Sign: N9WQA
Mark G Marz
321 Oakland Ave
Michigan City IN 46360

Call Sign: N9XLS
Anil Verma
430 Ogden Ave
Michigan City IN 46360

Call Sign: N9KOD
Joseph I Diab
1210 Ohio St
Michigan City IN 46360

Call Sign: KC9HL
Dean D Willson
217 Overhill Trl
Michigan City IN 46360

Call Sign: KB9EUN
Jessica L Ammerman
2109 Pear St
Michigan City IN 46360

Call Sign: KA9IXZ
Claudette H Harrison
1207 Pine St
Michigan City IN 46360

Call Sign: KC9E
Troy M Harrison
1207 Pine St
Michigan City IN 46360

Call Sign: N9HEK
Lane Wilhelm
205 Roberta Ave
Michigan City IN 46360

Call Sign: N9DSN
George J Kassal
2921 Roslyn Trl
Michigan City IN 46360

Call Sign: KB9DPQ
Paul G Kassal
2921 Roslyn Trl
Michigan City IN 46360

Call Sign: N9ZMJ
Seth A Lakin
505 S Ashland Ave
Michigan City IN 46360

Call Sign: KC9IUX
Chris E Parks
529 S Carroll Ave
Michigan City IN 46360

Call Sign: KC9KZS
Eugenia A Schwanke
721 S Dickson St
Michigan City IN 46360

Call Sign: N9ZIP
Kenneth R Osborne
721 S Dickson St
Michigan City IN 46360

Call Sign: KB9WFP
Kenneth L Smith
2324 S Ohio St
Michigan City IN 46360

Call Sign: N9ZDK
James R Wallace Jr
223 S Porter St
Michigan City IN 46360

Call Sign: N9WZS
Brian E Melson
3305 Salem Ct
Michigan City IN 46360

Call Sign: KC9HLR
Carl R Howard
1017 Salem St
Michigan City IN 46360

Call Sign: N9QKX
R David Oberle Sr
109 Sherman Ave
Michigan City IN 46360

Call Sign: N9WGS
William D Ortiz
111 South Ct
Michigan City IN 46360

Call Sign: K9FVS
Wallace E Reuer
215 South St
Michigan City IN 46360

Call Sign: KA9WHP
Donald A Zukaus
425 Springland
Michigan City IN 46360

Call Sign: WH6BHH
Richard F Gillon
405 Spruce Dr
Michigan City IN 46360

Call Sign: KB9FMR
Shane W Russell
405 Swasick Ave
Michigan City IN 46360

Call Sign: WD9EIX
Robert H Harris
206 Thurman Ave
Michigan City IN 46360

Call Sign: WD9BDR
Stanley D Freed
125 Tilden Ave
Michigan City IN
463605510

Call Sign: K9TEK
Stanley D Freed
125 Tilden Ave
Michigan City IN
463605510

Call Sign: NC9Q
Robert C Snyder
202 Tomahawk Dr
Michigan City IN 46360

Call Sign: KC9QAL
Matthew A Waters

108 Trunk Ct
Michigan City IN 46360

Call Sign: KA9PGF
George R Armbrust
2030 Tryon Rd
Michigan City IN 46360

Call Sign: KC9KZX
David H Spencer
123 Vail St
Michigan City IN 46360

Call Sign: W3RHJ
David H Spencer
123 Vail St
Michigan City IN 46360

Call Sign: KD8YB
Robert W Cooley
10055 W 100 N
Michigan City IN 46360

Call Sign: KC9LCX
Matthew Bilderback
1427 W 10th St
Michigan City IN 46360

Call Sign: K9URA
William E Jones
11765 W 125 N
Michigan City IN
463609456

Call Sign: N9HVI
Michael A Kmak Sr
8273 W 200 N
Michigan City IN 46360

Call Sign: WA9FPU
Allen R Short
7521 W 275 N
Michigan City IN 46360

Call Sign: KC9AHO

Mary Ann Short
7521 W 275 N
Michigan City IN 46360

Call Sign: KC9MDS
William H Newcomb
2744 W 675 N
Michigan City IN 46360

Call Sign: W9BFZ
Adam Q Ramey Jr
5556 W 800 N
Michigan City IN 46360

Call Sign: KA7PHF
Curtis E Johnston
5655 W 800 N
Michigan City IN 46360

Call Sign: KC9GFO
Danny L Foster
1214 W Coolspring Ave
Michigan City IN 46360

Call Sign: WA9HTA
Charles Struyf
2704 W Dunes Hwy
Michigan City IN 46360

Call Sign: N9EVI
Roy E Ramsey
7134 W Lynnwood Dr
Michigan City IN 46360

Call Sign: KC9NP
Robert E East
7057 W Red Apple Dr
Michigan City IN 46360

Call Sign: KC9HJI
David P Haas
228 Walnut St
Michigan City IN 46360

Call Sign: KB9NGL

Charles R Stone
731 Warnke Rd
Michigan City IN 46360

Call Sign: WB9JPA
John L Bayler
2012 Welnetz Rd
Michigan City IN 46360

Call Sign: WB9JGQ
Jerome D Piotrowski
111 Willow Ct
Michigan City IN 46360

Call Sign: WB9JEF
Metto D Hernandez
903 Willow Springs Dr
Michigan City IN 46360

Call Sign: KC9JHR
Erin M Phillips
3522 Windsor Rd
Michigan City IN 46360

Call Sign: KA9PGC
John H Phillips
3522 Windsor Rd
Michigan City IN 46360

Call Sign: W9GJX
John F Baird
3651 Windsor Rd
Michigan City IN 46360

Call Sign: W9LY
Michigan City ARC
Michigan City IN 46361

Call Sign: N6QYA
Michael D Maxfield
Michigan City IN
463619477

**FCC Amateur Radio
Licenses in Middlebury**

Call Sign: KB9NRG
Thomas L Del Vecchio
10267 Cottage Grove Dr
Middlebury IN 46540

Call Sign: KC9GSB
Paul J Cohen
54376 Country Rd 8
Middlebury IN
465409515

Call Sign: KA9IBL
James E Rhodes
14113 CR 12
Middlebury IN 46540

Call Sign: KB9QOY
Joseph A Riegsecker
55605 CR 33
Middlebury IN 46540

Call Sign: WW3L
Edward E Trayford Jr
59645 CR 35
Middlebury IN 46540

Call Sign: W8IIS
Lawrence W Benjamin
13689 CR 8
Middlebury IN 46540

Call Sign: N9WNF
Kraig A Kaminsky
14770 CR 8
Middlebury IN 46540

Call Sign: WA9YPI
Ben R Cohen
54376 CR 8
Middlebury IN 46540

Call Sign: KA9PPH
Jill E Cohen
54376 CR 8

Middlebury IN 46540

Call Sign: WA9YKR
Joel N Cohen
54376 CR 8
Middlebury IN 46540

Call Sign: K9ZBM
James S Sellers
54676 CR 8
Middlebury IN
465408710

Call Sign: KA9ZEE
Louise Sellers
54676 CR 8
Middlebury IN
465408710

Call Sign: KB9USY
David E Otto
51331 E Co Line
Middlebury IN 46540

Call Sign: KB9QOV
Randy H Smith
306 Eastern Star Dr
Middlebury IN 46540

Call Sign: KF9XT
Eric G Landaw
100 Greenfield Dr
Middlebury IN 46540

Call Sign: N9TRG
Danny R Smith
119 N Brown
Middlebury IN 46540

Call Sign: N7CCL
Charles C Hostetler III
508 Redbud Ln
Middlebury IN 46540

Call Sign: WD9HHS

John H Christner
523 S Main St
Middlebury IN 46540

Call Sign: K9SRI
Theodore M Smith
SR 13
Middlebury IN 46540

Call Sign: KB9UJT
Stanton J Hoover
517 Sunset Ln
Middlebury IN
465409585

Call Sign: KA9AAN
Rosalie A White
315 Twin Oaks Dr
Middlebury IN 46540

Call Sign: KC9KO
Wallace B White
315 Twin Oaks Dr
Middlebury IN 46540

Call Sign: WD9EPY
Jerry W Kindy
57154 Westlake Dr
Middlebury IN 46540

FCC Amateur Radio Licenses in Milford

Call Sign: KB9OZD
Armand J Fight Jr
203 E Forth
Milford IN 46542

Call Sign: WR9J
Michael A Gumz
251 E Nelson Dr
Milford IN 46542

Call Sign: WA9ZQV
Patrick E Neibert

909 E Shady Banks Ln
Waubee Lake
Milford IN 46542

Call Sign: KC9ATH
William L Weaver
11904 N 175 E
Milford IN 46542

Call Sign: K9DGA
Richard A Brunjes
12697 N 60 W
Milford IN 46542

Call Sign: WD9AUO
Michael A West
10554 N Grove Rd
Milford IN 46542

Call Sign: KB9ZCF
Jason L Mullett
20303 US 6
Milford IN 46542

Call Sign: KB9ZJS
Barbara A Mullett
20303 US 6
Milford IN 46542

Call Sign: KB9WQA
Freeman E Mullett
20303 US 6
Milford IN 46542

Call Sign: N9SKG
Anna M Reese
511 W 1st St
Milford IN 46542

Call Sign: KC9EQG
Jason A Mcdowell
506 W Emeline St
Milford IN 46542

Call Sign: KC9RQT

Jacob W Bowerman
Milford IN 46542

Call Sign: KB9QGI
Paul D Strycker
Milford IN 46542

Call Sign: KA9YFI
Allen A Frailey
Milford IN 465420706

FCC Amateur Radio Licenses in Mill Creek

Call Sign: N9RVS
Joseph D Nixon
600E
Mill Creek IN 46365

Call Sign: N9OKC
Larry D Nixon
100 N 600 E
Mill Creek IN 46365

Call Sign: N9OOI
Mary M Nixon
100 N 600 E
Mill Creek IN 46365

Call Sign: KC9PHC
William F Barr III
656 N 875 E
Mill Creek IN 46365

Call Sign: WR9L
Lance N Corley
Mill Creek IN 46365

FCC Amateur Radio Licenses in Millersburg

Call Sign: N9SIW
Barton L Black
11638 CR 42
Millersburg IN 46543

Call Sign: KB9CWX
Clifford A Green
67329 CR 43
Millersburg IN 46543

Call Sign: KB9CWY
David C Green
67329 CR 43
Millersburg IN 46543

Call Sign: KB9NRI
Mark A Beachy
3560 S 1000 W
Millersburg IN 46543

Call Sign: KC9GOR
Ricky J Kline
110 W Washington St
Millersburg IN 46543

FCC Amateur Radio Licenses in Mishawaka

Call Sign: KF4TAD
Gregory E High
4120 Anchor Dr
Mishawaka IN
465449142

Call Sign: KC9DMG
Larry A Rodino
11047 Archer Ave
Mishawaka IN 46544

Call Sign: NY9S
Larry A Rodino
11047 Archer Ave
Mishawaka IN 46544

Call Sign: KC9CTU
Robert A Hummer
214 Bain Ave
Mishawaka IN 46544

Call Sign: N9FXW
William D Hummer
214 Bain Ave
Mishawaka IN 46544

Call Sign: KR9BH
William D Hummer
214 Bain Ave
Mishawaka IN 46544

Call Sign: KO9R
William D Hummer
214 Bain Ave
Mishawaka IN 46544

Call Sign: N9VR
William D Hummer
214 Bain Ave
Mishawaka IN 46544

Call Sign: KC9JFG
Brian P Dunn
15633 Baintree Way
Mishawaka IN 46545

Call Sign: KE8AC
Cordell G Loken
322 Ballard Ave
Mishawaka IN
465443814

Call Sign: WB9WJK
David C Olson
1002 Barrington Pl
Mishawaka IN 46545

Call Sign: W9BRM
Willis K Shirk Jr
117 Bastogne Ave
Mishawaka IN 46545

Call Sign: KB3BUU
Joshua A Ickes
105 Bercado Pl Unit 3
Mishawaka IN 46544

Call Sign: N9GMG
Lois J Liebert
1504 Berkley Cir
Mishawaka IN 46544

Call Sign: K9CMJ
Vernon M Daly Jr
54661 Bethany Dr
Mishawaka IN
465452218

Call Sign: KB9KUK
Edward M Sheriff
2913 Birchwood Dr
Mishawaka IN 46545

Call Sign: N9WAJ
Larry J Carpenter
54525 Bittersweet Rd
Mishawaka IN 46545

Call Sign: KB9MJM
Louis G Motz
60535 Breman Hwy
Mishawaka IN 46544

Call Sign: KC9HGE
William F Breining
1208 Brookrun Rd Apt
2A
Mishawaka IN 46544

Call Sign: WA9DGI
Gerald D Hogue
56333 Buckeye Rd
Mishawaka IN 46545

Call Sign: KC9NAH
Lori A Gresso
3316 Cambridge Ct
Mishawaka IN 46545

Call Sign: KC9VN
Louis W Horvath

55965 Candace Ln
Mishawaka IN 46545

Call Sign: KB9NQV
Brian H Garrett
12366 Carleton Dr
Mishawaka IN 46545

Call Sign: N9WPB
Richard J Miller
15344 Carriage Ln
Mishawaka IN 46545

Call Sign: AB9DV
Richard J Miller
15344 Carriage Ln
Mishawaka IN 46545

Call Sign: KY9M
Richard J Miller
15344 Carriage Ln
Mishawaka IN
465451531

Call Sign: KC9NAQ
John W Kowalski III
426 Cedar Crest Ln
Mishawaka IN 46545

Call Sign: N9LBD
Larry M Mollis
16128 Chandler Blvd
Mishawaka IN
465446465

Call Sign: WA9OKC
Roger M Tinti
59925 Clover Rd
Mishawaka IN 46544

Call Sign: KB9ZJA
Stephen M Patterson
1602 Cobblestone Cir N
Mishawaka IN 46544

Call Sign: N9ZZW
Louis J Sharp Jr
1630 Cobblestone Cir N
Mishawaka IN 46544

Call Sign: KB9QYD
Sally J Sharp
1630 Cobblestone Cir N
Mishawaka IN 46544

Call Sign: WA9GND
Roy E Gulbranson
3306 Colony Ct
Mishawaka IN
465453158

Call Sign: N9VPN
Jeffrey A Coppes
13905 Creston St
Mishawaka IN 46544

Call Sign: KC9GUE
Pamela A Kronewitter
1322 Darien Ct
Mishawaka IN 46544

Call Sign: N9KWI
Elmer C Whitteberry
1322 Darien Ct
Mishawaka IN 46544

Call Sign: N9TOX
Mica W Wilson
514 Dittman
Mishawaka IN 46544

Call Sign: KC9LYH
Robert F Cook
712 Division St
Mishawaka IN 46545

Call Sign: KA9DVL
Ritchie L Williams
57550 Dogwood Rd
Mishawaka IN 46544

Call Sign: N9VGK
Keren J Williams
57550 Dogwood Rd
Mishawaka IN
465446336

Call Sign: KC9MAI
Timothy M Bognar
57600 Dogwood Rd
Mishawaka IN
465446329

Call Sign: KB9TBD
David C Douberteen
59301 Downey Rd
Mishawaka IN 46544

Call Sign: KB9PND
Thomas W Wood
1312 E 11th St
Mishawaka IN 46544

Call Sign: N9EIS
Donald R Hudson
416 E 13th St
Mishawaka IN 46544

Call Sign: KB9MLD
Mark E Trowbridge
1217 E 3rd St
Mishawaka IN 46544

Call Sign: KE9FE
Fred J Boehnlein
733 E 4th St
Mishawaka IN
465442228

Call Sign: N9OVK
James W Hurst
942 E 4th St
Mishawaka IN 46544

Call Sign: N9KUE

Joseph W Moysin
113 E 6th St
Mishawaka IN 46544

Call Sign: K9UTZ
Dale E Kindley
227 E 6th St
Mishawaka IN 46544

Call Sign: K9UTY
Marilyn R Kindley
227 E 6th St
Mishawaka IN 46544

Call Sign: KB9ITN
Peter V Chabot
13367 E 7th St
Mishawaka IN 46544

Call Sign: N9QMD
David G Thompson
13513 E 7th St
Mishawaka IN 46544

Call Sign: KB9LKM
Robert W Arnold
201 E 8th St
Mishawaka IN 46544

Call Sign: KB9JWK
Kevin A Schultz
804 E 8th St
Mishawaka IN 46544

Call Sign: KC9MID
Chris L Vanlue
13382 E 8th St
Mishawaka IN 46544

Call Sign: K9ADW
Dennis L Miller
822 E 9th
Mishawaka IN 46544

Call Sign: N9RHP

Warren K Brown
210 E Broadway St
Mishawaka IN 46545

Call Sign: N9XYV
Blaine D Plencner
416 E Broadway St
Mishawaka IN 46545

Call Sign: KF9VT
Timothy J Kobb
310 E Colfax Ave
Mishawaka IN 46544

Call Sign: KB9BDU
Tim J Kobb Jr
310 E Colfax Ave
Mishawaka IN 46545

Call Sign: KA9KLR
Joseph A Furore
1940 E Jefferson
Mishawaka IN 46545

Call Sign: W8MCG
Walter D Cornell
1959 E Jefferson Blvd
Mishawaka IN 46545

Call Sign: KC9OGZ
Robert P Anderson
12591 E Jefferson Blvd
Mishawaka IN 46545

Call Sign: KC9RPL
Diego A Delgado
415 E Lasalle Ave
Mishawaka IN 46545

Call Sign: KC9RPO
Diego N Delgado
415 E Lasalle Ave
Mishawaka IN 46545

Call Sign: KB9OIO

Kent C Johnson
223 E Lawrence Ave
Mishawaka IN 46545

Call Sign: KF9MA
Wayne J Drescher
724 E Lawrence St Apt 5
Mishawaka IN 46545

Call Sign: WA9EWL
Dominic A Perri
409 E Lowell Ave
Mishawaka IN 46545

Call Sign: KB9OSQ
Zack E Teeter
607 E Lowell Ave
Mishawaka IN 46545

Call Sign: KG5SS
Randy R Lehr
702 E Lowell Ave
Mishawaka IN 46545

Call Sign: KB9SRL
John M Keb
1219 E Mishawaka Ave
Mishawaka IN 46545

Call Sign: N0AFC
Ernest E Bird
56465 East Ave
Mishawaka IN 46545

Call Sign: K9AWT
David E Hinshaw
3006 Easton Ct Apt B
Mishawaka IN 46545

Call Sign: NJ9S
Bruno Trimboli
2116 Eastwood Cir
Mishawaka IN 46545

Call Sign: KB9SOG

Brian J Simpson
55501 Elder Rd
Mishawaka IN 46545

Call Sign: N9XAU
Bruce E Friedline
2739 Eller Ln Apt D
Mishawaka IN
465443625

Call Sign: KC9INC
Sarah A Friedline
2739 Eller Ln Apt D
Mishawaka IN
465443625

Call Sign: WA9SWZ
Edward J Jacobs
710 Elm Rd
Mishawaka IN 46545

Call Sign: KA9JBG
Maynard A Williams
58159 Elm Rd
Mishawaka IN 46544

Call Sign: KA9PHF
Roberta M Williams
58159 Elm Rd
Mishawaka IN 46544

Call Sign: W9AQA
Albert L Courtney
16150 Elmwood St
Mishawaka IN 46544

Call Sign: W9AQB
Norma J Courtney
16150 Elmwood St
Mishawaka IN
465446550

Call Sign: KT5H
Michael P Strong
55970 Erhart Dr

Mishawaka IN 46545

Call Sign: N9ID
Michael P Strong
55970 Erhart Dr
Mishawaka IN 46545

Call Sign: KA9SKH
Charles D Tuesburg
1643 Fallcreek Dr
Mishawaka IN
465445845

Call Sign: NI9Y
Dan G Caesar
55966 Fir Rd
Mishawaka IN 46545

Call Sign: N9NXV
Jerry A Kretchmer
55993 Fir Rd
Mishawaka IN 46545

Call Sign: WB9CKV
Wayne A Clark
1309 Forest Ave
Mishawaka IN
465455801

Call Sign: K9CDT
James O Coursey Jr
14397 Fox Trl Ct
Mishawaka IN 46545

Call Sign: WB9VTY
Thomas J Fields
56225 Frances Ave
Mishawaka IN 46545

Call Sign: KB9AND
Jerry L Niswonger
513 Geyer St
Mishawaka IN
465441552

Call Sign: N9WHZ
Norman G Shearer
1021 Geyer St
Mishawaka IN 46544

Call Sign: KC9GJK
Joseph R Nania
928 Handlebar Rd
Mishawaka IN 46544

Call Sign: W9JRN
Joseph R Nania
928 Handlebar Rd
Mishawaka IN 46544

Call Sign: N9RSW
Ronald C Post
801 Hendricks
Mishawaka IN 46544

Call Sign: WA9DTW
Garifeld L Walker
55430 Hickory Rd
Mishawaka IN 46545

Call Sign: N9ZMR
James A Taylor
4234 Hickory Rd 3D
Mishawaka IN 46545

Call Sign: K9UHY
Robert F Bonamarte Jr
1803 Homewood Ave
Mishawaka IN 46544

Call Sign: KA9ZLZ
Robert M Gonzales
414 Honey Cycle Rd Apt
6
Mishawaka IN 46514

Call Sign: N8VWN
Karen S Hewitt
56040 Hoosier Ave
Mishawaka IN 46545

Call Sign: N9UFC
George T Moser
2602 Huntington Pl
Mishawaka IN 46544

Call Sign: N8HYD
Michael J Breza
2704 Huntington Pl
Mishawaka IN 46544

Call Sign: N9MMQ
Andrew A Cannoot
640 Indiana Ave
Mishawaka IN 46544

Call Sign: W9WDV
Herman L Hums
58709 Ireland Trl
Mishawaka IN 46544

Call Sign: KC9GTS
Edward F Hums
58847 Ireland Trl
Mishawaka IN 46544

Call Sign: W9TIL
Dale G Miller
15130 Jackson Rd
Mishawaka IN 46544

Call Sign: KB9QOM
Doris J Miller
15130 Jackson Rd
Mishawaka IN 46544

Call Sign: KD9PA
Paul D Young
11851 Jefferson Blvd
Mishawaka IN 46545

Call Sign: N9LAU
John C Bunch
14800 Kelly Rd
Mishawaka IN 46544

Call Sign: W9NNC
Donald G Misch
15600 Kern Rd
Mishawaka IN 46544

Call Sign: N9UNJ
Royce J Reeder
14380 Kitch Rd
Mishawaka IN 46544

Call Sign: WA9CBN
Glen V Revell
1908 Liberty Dr
Mishawaka IN 46545

Call Sign: N9QNQ
Jason L Hanson
124.5 Lincoln Way E
Mishawaka IN 46656

Call Sign: KB9UZC
John M Konrath
1442 Lincoln Way E
Mishawaka IN 46544

Call Sign: KA9YDL
Erika K Humphrey
2029 Lincoln Way W Apt
C
Mishawaka IN 46544

Call Sign: KA3QIC
Cathy Heiner
3320 Lincolnway E
Mishawaka IN 46544

Call Sign: KA3OXM
George M Heiner Jr
3320 Lincolnway E
Mishawaka IN 46544

Call Sign: KB9CCS
Jeffrey W Hums
3634 Lindahl Dr

Mishawaka IN 46544

Call Sign: W9NAR
Raymond J Ramsey
1621 Linden Ave
Mishawaka IN 46544

Call Sign: WB0ICI
David R Wyatt
1910 Linden Ave
Mishawaka IN 46544

Call Sign: KC9NAF
James L Mester
11870 Loughlin Dr
Mishawaka IN 46545

Call Sign: KB9RDT
Raymond L Goddard
1727 Lowell Wood W
Mishawaka IN 46545

Call Sign: KA9ZLK
Carol J Laidig
14450 Madison Rd
Mishawaka IN 46544

Call Sign: KJ4DQ
Wyn D Laidig
14450 Madison Rd
Mishawaka IN 46544

Call Sign: N9GXM
Tommy J Atwood
1504 Marblehead
Mishawaka IN 46544

Call Sign: N9IDA
Samuel P Beavo
1520 Marblehead
Mishawaka IN 46544

Call Sign: KB9SDT
Timothy L Putman
2419 Marshall Dr

Mishawaka IN 46544

Call Sign: KC9TEL
William E Ziegler
11920 McKinley Hwy
Mishawaka IN 46545

Call Sign: N9EER
Ray O Townsend
14433 Meadows Ct
Mishawaka IN
465451868

Call Sign: N9VXW
Michael L Wolfe
819 Meridian St
Mishawaka IN 46544

Call Sign: W9KDW
George R Green
54720 Merrifield Dr
Mishawaka IN 46545

Call Sign: NR9F
Allen G Viduka Sr
541750 Merrifield Rd
Mishawaka IN 46545

Call Sign: N9CZB
Beverly J Weiss
120 Miami Club Dr
Mishawaka IN 46544

Call Sign: N9CXT
Leonard E Weiss
120 Miami Club Dr
Mishawaka IN 46544

Call Sign: KC9DAS
Kimberly K Hengert
204 Miami Club Dr
Mishawaka IN 46544

Call Sign: KB9TFH
Joe P Humberger

1710 Milburn Blvd
Mishawaka IN 46544

Call Sign: KB9TOY
David P Humberger
1710 Milburn Blvd
Mishawaka IN 46544

Call Sign: N9BDD
Osborne J Taman
452 N Ballard Ave
Mishawaka IN 46544

Call Sign: KA9IIU
Marjorie J Goebel
100 N Center St Apt 304
Mishawaka IN 46544

Call Sign: WG9E
Richard C Griffin
100 N Center St Apt 412
Mishawaka IN 46544

Call Sign: KA9ZNE
Gary C Ehresman
100 N Center St Apt 611
Mishawaka IN 46544

Call Sign: KC9GPQ
Macon S Hanback Jr
612 N Chestnut St
Mishawaka IN 46545

Call Sign: N9MMR
Christian A Lattimer
618 N Indiana Ave
Mishawaka IN 46544

Call Sign: N9NDW
Daniel A Lattimer
618 N Indiana Ave
Mishawaka IN 46544

Call Sign: N9UYD
Benjamin K Smith

3600 N Main St Apt 2
Mishawaka IN 46545

Call Sign: KC9IIE
Alan G Schrader
215 N Oakland Ave
Mishawaka IN 46544

Call Sign: KB9ZYZ
Ronald W Armstrong
436 N Oakland Ave
Mishawaka IN 46544

Call Sign: N9KIX
Dennis P Laffin
507 N Oakland Ave
Mishawaka IN 46544

Call Sign: KB9GWS
Steven L Ward
13409 New Rd
Mishawaka IN 46544

Call Sign: KC9AYP
Michael L Cocanower
13691 Nora Ln
Mishawaka IN 46544

Call Sign: N9OVL
Gregory A Swan
716 Oak St
Mishawaka IN 46545

Call Sign: W9OCK
Howard E King
57839 Oakside Ave
Mishawaka IN
465446309

Call Sign: KB9NWW
Raymond A Henry
57564 Oakside St
Mishawaka IN 46544

Call Sign: N9RKN

Scott D Meyer
54450 Old Bedford Tr
Mishawaka IN 46545

Call Sign: N9YDE
John H Vandenbosch Jr
5733 Ottawa Ct Apt 2B
Mishawaka IN 46545

Call Sign: N9GSQ
Robert A Nash
2021 Panama St
Mishawaka IN 46544

Call Sign: W8MGL
George W Simpson Sr
4105 Parkwood Cir 1C
Mishawaka IN 46545

Call Sign: KB9UNT
Erik S Oberlin
4005 Parkwood Cir 3B
Mishawaka IN 46545

Call Sign: KC9RJX
Harvey A Gluck
3428 Portsmouth Ct Apt
B
Mishawaka IN 46545

Call Sign: KB9PDE
Charles F Norton
2983 Princeton Dr
Mishawaka IN 46544

Call Sign: N4NFM
William W Wenger
1008 Prospect Dr
Mishawaka IN 46544

Call Sign: N9TRD
Thomas E Pawlak
816 Reddick St
Mishawaka IN 46544

Call Sign: K9SUH
Kenneth P Reising
2530 Riviera Dr
Mishawaka IN 46544

Call Sign: W9NAS
Daniel J Sabade
210 Roseland Ave
Mishawaka IN 46544

Call Sign: KC9NIU
Andy J Anderson
814 S Main St
Mishawaka IN 46544

Call Sign: KA9DVA
June Waterman
1311 S Main St
Mishawaka IN 46544

Call Sign: WA9NJM
Emil T De Boe
611 S Russell Ave
Mishawaka IN 46544

Call Sign: W8LAL
Thomas W Weber
325 S West St
Mishawaka IN 46544

Call Sign: W9XJ
Joseph J Fujawa
1416 S West St
Mishawaka IN 46544

Call Sign: KC9NAL
Kimnerly J Loughlin
208 Saint Lo Ave
Mishawaka IN 46545

Call Sign: N9JPO
Howard E Slayton
2604 Schumacher Dr
Mishawaka IN 46545

Call Sign: N9HWQ
Norris J Ward
2811 Schumacher Dr
Mishawaka IN 46545

Call Sign: KC9PJV
Tyler L Loughridge
1618 Shelton Dr
Mishawaka IN 46544

Call Sign: N9KUF
Bruce W Moysin
1528 Southwood Dr
Mishawaka IN 46544

Call Sign: N9JOT
Adolph P Van Haver
1605 Southwood Dr
Mishawaka IN 46544

Call Sign: W9SIQ
William A Davidson
701 Steeplechase Dr
Mishawaka IN 46544

Call Sign: N9BVI
Samuel D Richards
530 Tanglewood Ln Apt
215
Mishawaka IN
465452653

Call Sign: KC9MQS
Don D Sorrell
1903 Tea Rose Ln
Mishawaka IN 46544

Call Sign: N9GID
Joseph M Mergen
2030 Trailridge N
Mishawaka IN 46544

Call Sign: KE9MU
Margaret M Mergen
2030 Trailridge N

Mishawaka IN
465446622

Call Sign: KD6BMI
David S Younger
5608 Trippel Dr
Mishawaka IN 46545

Call Sign: W4UIV
George D Bible
5620 Trippel Dr
Mishawaka IN 46545

Call Sign: N9TZN
Albert A Spagnola Jr
16400 Valley Trl
Mishawaka IN 46544

Call Sign: KB9TEP
Deborah K Spagnola
16400 Valley Trl
Mishawaka IN 46544

Call Sign: WB9VUA
Robert L Sproston
113 W 12th St
Mishawaka IN 46544

Call Sign: KC9DZJ
Scott A Wasulko
502 W 12th St
Mishawaka IN 46544

Call Sign: KB9ZP
Robert E Bowen
830 W 13th
Mishawaka IN 46544

Call Sign: KA9SOA
George Caesar
522 W 15th St
Mishawaka IN 46544

Call Sign: KA9NEC
David E Caesar

522 W 15th St
Mishawaka IN
465445007

Call Sign: WB9JWZ
Wallace J Kronewitter
2719 W 6th St
Mishawaka IN 46544

Call Sign: KB9MOP
Zachery W Wolfinger
612 W 9th St
Mishawaka IN 46544

Call Sign: KC9PJW
Betsy J Fox
434 W Battell
Mishawaka IN 46545

Call Sign: KC9PJU
Phillip F Fox
434 W Battell
Mishawaka IN 46545

Call Sign: KK9G
Daniel L Dews Sr
529 W Broadway
Mishawaka IN 46545

Call Sign: WD9HNA
Peter D McQueen
325 W Broadway St
Mishawaka IN 46545

Call Sign: K9PDM
Peter D McQueen
325 W Broadway St
Mishawaka IN 46545

Call Sign: N9RXR
Walter D James
423 W Broadway St
Mishawaka IN 46544

Call Sign: KG9QT

Mark D Smith
529 W Broadway St
Mishawaka IN 46545

Call Sign: KA9OVN
Mark D Smith
529 W Broadway St
Mishawaka IN 46545

Call Sign: N9WNE
Ronald R Songer
521 W Catalpa
Mishawaka IN 46545

Call Sign: N9ROQ
Gregory A Snider
319 W Grove St
Mishawaka IN 46545

Call Sign: N9QIL
Kenneth R Wezeman
602 W Grove St
Mishawaka IN 46545

Call Sign: W9MLM
Michael L Morrison
214 W La Salle Ave
Mishawaka IN 46546

Call Sign: N9GXX
Wayne A Chodzinski Sr
806 W Lawrence
Mishawaka IN 46545

Call Sign: N9GVU
David E Fox
111 W Marion St
Mishawaka IN
465456117

Call Sign: KB9WW
Floyd J Kuzan
55475 Weber Dr
Mishawaka IN 46544

Call Sign: KE6WFT
Kermit R Eby Jr
1027 Wheatstone Dr
Mishawaka IN 46544

Call Sign: KB9LZK
Brian D Rodgers
11907 Willard Dr
Mishawaka IN 46545

Call Sign: KC9RPQ
James E Huston
1127 Willow Bridge Ln
Mishawaka IN 46545

Call Sign: KC9JHO
Roberta L Holtzinger
2628 Woodwinds Ct
Mishawaka IN 46544

Call Sign: KB9PRV
Ronald E Mize
3306 York St
Mishawaka IN 46544

Call Sign: N9WIG
De Wayne W Moss
5615 Zappia Dr
Mishawaka IN 46545

Call Sign: KA9WIL
Cheryl L Dazey
Mishawaka IN 46544

Call Sign: KB7OJJ
Paul B Kellner
Mishawaka IN 46546

Call Sign: N9OCB
Robert D Henning
Mishawaka IN 46546

FCC Amateur Radio Licenses in Monon

Call Sign: KC9DKC
Paul D Hurd
502 N Arch St
Monon IN 47959

Call Sign: KB9BDA
John D Dyrek III
10505 N Meridian Rd
Monon IN 47959

Call Sign: W9EHU
John D Dyrek Jr
10707 N Meridian Rd
Monon IN 47959

Call Sign: KA9NHN
Lois C Dyrek
10707 N Meridian Rd
Monon IN 47959

Call Sign: W9CSJ
Paul R Irons
Monon IN 479590476

FCC Amateur Radio Licenses in Monroe

Call Sign: KC9OWV
Kent D Whitacre
2182 S Salem Rd
Monroe IN 46772

Call Sign: W9ZK
Kent D Whitacre
2182 S Salem Rd
Monroe IN 46772

FCC Amateur Radio Licenses in Monroeville

Call Sign: KA9LHE
Michael L Coomer Sr
12335 Aljean Dr
Monroeville IN 46774

Call Sign: KC9IAU
Robert D Bleeke
20828 Alliger Rd Lot 2
Monroeville IN 46773

Call Sign: KC9GLK
Ryan D Bleeke
20828 Alliger St Lot 43
Monroeville IN 46773

Call Sign: KC9GLL
Raymond A Higgins
204 Elm St
Monroeville IN 46773

Call Sign: KC9ORY
Edward R Mitchell
401 Elm St
Monroeville IN 46773

Call Sign: KA9NSF
Robert C Hart
23222 Hoagland Rd
Monroeville IN 46773

Call Sign: KA9NSE
Robert J Hartman
22821 Hoffman Rd
Monroeville IN 46773

Call Sign: WB9VCI
Paul E Taylor
23112 Lincoln Hwy E
Monroeville IN 46773

Call Sign: KC9HJF
Dale R Hood
402 Monroe St
Monroeville IN 46773

Call Sign: KC9RAL
Joseph A Voirol
9321 Morgan Rd
Monroeville IN 46773

Call Sign: WA9GFR
Lynn A Gerig
Morgan Rd
Monroeville IN 46773

Call Sign: KA9SJB
Michael J Johnson
5707 Roy Ln
Monroeville IN 46773

FCC Amateur Radio Licenses in Monterey

Call Sign: KC9CTV
Ursula J Carey
250E
Monterey IN 46960

Call Sign: W9OLD
Martin O Piepenburg
500N
Monterey IN 46960

Call Sign: N9HXT
Chris E Whiting
9180 E 850 S
Monterey IN 469609323

FCC Amateur Radio Licenses in Monticello

Call Sign: KA9NYR
Richard C Cochran
1200W
Monticello IN 47960

Call Sign: KA9ZPT
Curtis L Weida
716 Bluewater Dr
Monticello IN 47960

Call Sign: N9MOI
William E Funcheon Jr
Box 419F
Monticello IN 47960

Call Sign: N9TIU
Randall J Miller
Box 719
Monticello IN 47960

Call Sign: WB9SOJ
Marilyn A Wilson
901 Calley Dr
Monticello IN 47960

Call Sign: N9MOU
Ivan R Aldrich Jr
5270 E Bay Front Ct
Monticello IN 479607343

Call Sign: AA9ST
Jimmy D Looney
5571 E Grande Vista Ct
Monticello IN 47960

Call Sign: KA9DRS
Jack R Ames
207 E Marion St
Monticello IN 47960

Call Sign: KA0HDB
David C Mote
1207 E Ohio St
Monticello IN 47960

Call Sign: KF9NX
Joe A Bougher
5147 E Oriole Dr
Monticello IN 47960

Call Sign: KB9FII
Richard A Marshall Jr
7002 E Red Maple Ave
Monticello IN 47960

Call Sign: KC9CLK
Guy C Poore
5976 E Redwood Ct
Monticello IN 43960

Call Sign: KC9CLT
Janet M Poore
5976 E Redwood Ct
Monticello IN 47960

Call Sign: KG9BU
Eugene C Simon
704 E Terrace Bay Ct
Monticello IN 47960

Call Sign: N9MUZ
Margaret A Christensen
7106 Lakewood Dr Lot
102F
Monticello IN 47960

Call Sign: K9JZI
Wesley L Christensen Sr
7106 Lakewood Dr Lot
102F
Monticello IN 47960

Call Sign: KC9CSB
Ken E Wolfe
945 Lee Ave
Monticello IN 47960

Call Sign: KD9TY
Ken E Wolfe
945 Lee Ave
Monticello IN 47960

Call Sign: WB9SVA
W R Jones
11741 N 950 W
Monticello IN 47960

Call Sign: KB9YUG
David A Naville
8402 N Claverts Dr
Monticello IN 47960

Call Sign: KC9BWB
Michael D Lewis

1904 N Francis St Main
House
Monticello IN 47950

Call Sign: KC9TAF
Thomas D Taylor
7724 N Hambridge Dr
Monticello IN 47960

Call Sign: KC9TDT
Tom D Taylor
7724 N Hambridge Dr
Monticello IN 47960

Call Sign: KB9CCU
Eric N Ward
322 N Illinois St
Monticello IN 47960

Call Sign: N9UMB
Andrew J Roeske
3951 N Lake Rd 26 E
Monticello IN 47960

Call Sign: WA9ZEW
Frank J Loughery
3422 N Shore Acres Ct
Monticello IN 47960

Call Sign: W9BSV
Donald G Davis
8789 N US 421
Monticello IN 47960

Call Sign: K9ZQJ
Jack A Ward
203 Oak Dr
Monticello IN 479602546

Call Sign: KA9ZZZ
Robert L Warner
1775 Royal Oaks Dr N
Monticello IN 479602486

Call Sign: N9GBM

Gary D Stein
300 S 650 E
Monticello IN 47960

Call Sign: WD9EXI
Byron C Robbins
571 S Bluff
Monticello IN 47960

Call Sign: KB9LKC
David D Went
4473 S Freeman Rd
Monticello IN 47960

Call Sign: KC9SIN
David A Trueb
3783 S Jamaica Ct
Monticello IN 47960

Call Sign: AC9AU
David A Trueb
3783 S Jamaica Ct
Monticello IN 47960

Call Sign: WB9SUQ
Leroy R Mason
562 S Maple St
Monticello IN 47960

Call Sign: N9BEE
Charles C Harvey
4367 S Miami Trl
Monticello IN 47960

Call Sign: KC9PQA
White County ARS
4455 S Nicole Dr
Monticello IN 47960

Call Sign: N9RLA
Robert L Aldrich
4455 S Nicole Dr
Monticello IN 47960

Call Sign: KC9ZB

Sandra M Foley
307 S Park Dr
Monticello IN 47960

Call Sign: W9JFF
Robert F Ellsworth
508 Twin Lakes Ave
Monticello IN 47960

Call Sign: N9XNJ
Cecil L Shinneman
11768 US Hwy 421 N
Monticello IN 47960

Call Sign: WB9UJJ
Adrienne J Adams
406 W Marion St
Monticello IN 47960

Call Sign: KB9FIK
Wesley A Molencupp
Monticello IN 47960

FCC Amateur Radio Licenses in Montpelier

Call Sign: KB9NNB
Chris A Snyder
153 E Chesnut St
Montpelier IN 47359

Call Sign: KF9JB
Robert D White Sr
301 S Washington St
Montpelier IN 47359

Call Sign: WB9GAT
Howard W Pence
524 S Washington St
Montpelier IN 473591443

Call Sign: WM9E
Richard L Slentz
435 W High St
Montpelier IN 47359

Call Sign: KC9CHB
Dennis M Atkinson
448 W Plate Glass St
Montpelier IN 47359

Call Sign: KC9CHA
Marty L Atkinson
448 W Plate Glass St
Montpelier IN 47359

Call Sign: KC9GFC
Donovan T Stone
Montpelier IN 47359

Call Sign: KC9GFB
Kathryn S Stone
Montpelier IN 47359

FCC Amateur Radio Licenses in Morocco

Call Sign: KB9LAT
Willie E Alexander
100N
Morocco IN 47963

Call Sign: N9WJH
Thomas P Szewczyk
507 S Clay St
Morocco IN 47963

Call Sign: N4ODG
Dennis B McDonald
42 W Beaver
Morocco IN 47963

Call Sign: KB9QLK
June M Rushmore
520 W Sunshine Dr
Morocco IN 47963

FCC Amateur Radio Licenses in Mount Ayr

Call Sign: KB9RLK
Betty J Pritchard
Mount Ayr IN 47964

FCC Amateur Radio Licenses in Munster

Call Sign: W9WJU
Joel R Miner
500 45th Ave
Munster IN 46321

Call Sign: AJ9N
Charles R Sufana
1137 Azalea Dr
Munster IN 46321

Call Sign: WB9ZDH
Philip C Wagner
319 Belmont Pl
Munster IN 46321

Call Sign: KA9JLJ
James J Della Rocco III
1110 Bluebird
Munster IN 46321

Call Sign: K9UDG
James P Della Rocco
1110 Bluebird
Munster IN 46321

Call Sign: KC9DVA
Robert P Della Rocco
1110 Bluebird Dr
Munster IN 46321

Call Sign: N9BCF
Arden D Harmon
9051 Bunker Hill
Munster IN 46321

Call Sign: KF9WN
Kenneth E Prasco

7935 Calumet Ave Rm
324
Munster IN 46321

Call Sign: KF9GW
John L Gianotti
1513 Camellia Dr
Munster IN 46321

Call Sign: W9WY
John L Gianotti
1513 Camellia Dr
Munster IN 46321

Call Sign: WA9MIF
Foster H Johnson
1708 Camellia Dr C1
Munster IN 46321

Call Sign: N9RX
David G Clark
1521 Cardinal Ct
Munster IN 46321

Call Sign: KI4HP
Stephen G Mican
1627 Cardinal Dr
Munster IN 46321

Call Sign: K9YWO
Dennis E Senchak
537 Cedar Ct
Munster IN 46321

Call Sign: N9NAW
Robert J Markovich
9500 Chestnut Ln
Munster IN 46321

Call Sign: KB9PR
Harold D Harris
8034 Columbia Ave
Munster IN 46321

Call Sign: N9ZDU

Nick G Papageorge
8203 Columbia Ave
Munster IN 46321

Call Sign: K9UEE
David Kaymark
8100 Euclid Ave
Munster IN 463211706

Call Sign: KB9TSC
David A Jones
549 Evergreen Ln
Munster IN 46321

Call Sign: KB9NCI
Timothy H Brown
532 Fisher Pl
Munster IN 46321

Call Sign: KA1ONT
Marsha E Johnstone
543 Fisher Pl
Munster IN 46321

Call Sign: KB9NSM
Joseph P Sopata
7823 Forest Ave
Munster IN 46321

Call Sign: W9BHJ
Irwin L Greenspon
8215 Forest Ave
Munster IN 46321

Call Sign: KB9HOZ
John A Lindeman
8120 Greenwood Ave
Munster IN 46321

Call Sign: KB9MCF
Kenneth E Beard
8645 Greenwood Ave
Munster IN 46321

Call Sign: KB9NNO

Cecil D Medlin
8330 Harrison
Munster IN 46321

Call Sign: WF9FCC
Cecil D Medlin
8330 Harrison
Munster IN 46321

Call Sign: KB9ALG
Jerry M Janco
8750 Harrison
Munster IN 463212335

Call Sign: KB9IAY
George B Smundin
8020 Harrison Ave
Munster IN 46321

Call Sign: KC9BAO
James T MacDonald
8400 Hawthorne Dr
Munster IN 46321

Call Sign: W9MAQ
James T MacDonald
8400 Hawthorne Dr
Munster IN 46321

Call Sign: KA9VRO
Frederic W Martin
508 Hickory Ln
Munster IN 46321

Call Sign: N9TDQ
Michael L Sassone
8205 Highland Pl
Munster IN 46321

Call Sign: K9DIR
Aurelia D Senchak
8605 Hohman Ave
Munster IN 46321

Call Sign: N9LIW

David W Talabay
9123 Holly
Munster IN 46321

Call Sign: N9SON
Scott R Holly
7918 Jackson Ave
Munster IN 46321

Call Sign: N9ULE
Mary Jo Holly
7918 Jackson Ave
Munster IN 46321

Call Sign: W9WFI
Stephen Branyik
8246 Jackson Ave
Munster IN 46321

Call Sign: KC9OVR
Miles W Hastings
8730 Jefferson Ave
Munster IN 46321

Call Sign: NM9G
Stanley J Mucha Jr
9519 Lilac Ln
Munster IN 46321

Call Sign: W9QPR
Leonard Kraus
8039 Linden Ave
Munster IN 46321

Call Sign: KC9VEG
Robert J Groszewski III
8719 Linden Ave
Munster IN 46321

Call Sign: KF9RL
Gregory G Zivich
1512 MacArthur Blvd
Munster IN 46321

Call Sign: K9GZ

Gregory G Zivich
1512 MacArthur Blvd
Munster IN 46321

Call Sign: N9ZXT
Karen Zivich
1512 MacArthur Blvd
Munster IN 463213127

Call Sign: WA9ZIU
James P Landowski
8767 Madison Ave
Munster IN 46321

Call Sign: KB9WIL
Cory C Glasen
1914 Magnolia Ln
Munster IN 46321

Call Sign: KC9NTJ
Kurt M Popovich
1934 Magnolia Ln
Munster IN 46321

Call Sign: KA9RBS
Edward H Travis Jr
8659 Manor Ave Apt C
Munster IN 46321

Call Sign: WB9YRT
Daniel M Shudick Jr
1908 Martha St
Munster IN 46321

Call Sign: KB9CDQ
Bobby L Hutsenpiller
8618 Monroe Ave
Munster IN 46321

Call Sign: KB9SLO
John W Sikora
8747 N Cote Ave
Munster IN 463212726

Call Sign: WB9IWN

John W Sikora
8747 N Cote Ave
Munster IN 463212726

Call Sign: K9KJ
Thomas A Johnson Jr
10156 New Devon
Munster IN 46321

Call Sign: KA9YHC
Mark Banaszak
8835 Oakwood Ave
Munster IN 46321

Call Sign: W9BEE
Larry L Emsweller
1839 Oriole Dr
Munster IN 46321

Call Sign: NS9D
John S Palenik
9900 Redbud Rd
Munster IN 463214214

Call Sign: KA9DBV
Irene M Fuss
8934 Revere Ct
Munster IN 46321

Call Sign: KB9KXJ
Matthew J Majszak
911 Ridgeway
Munster IN 46321

Call Sign: WB9PVQ
Bill M Cummings
919 River Dr
Munster IN 46321

Call Sign: KB9OJ
Gerald J Markovich
1200 River Dr
Munster IN 46321

Call Sign: WA9WWH

Robert A Bukvich
8821 Schreiber Dr
Munster IN 46321

Call Sign: WB9KAM
James A Florek
1608 Sea Breeze Ct
Munster IN 463215105

Call Sign: KA9KBM
James S Smith
1920 Somerset Dr
Munster IN 46321

Call Sign: WD9GLR
Robert F Frankowiak
9531 Southwood Dr
Munster IN 46321

Call Sign: WA9MIZ
Edward J Schwoegler
7533 State Line Ave
Munster IN 46321

Call Sign: W9ZHW
William L Erickson Sr
232 Terrace Dr
Munster IN 46321

Call Sign: KC9JSK
Christopher G Markovich
9017 University Dr
Munster IN 46321

Call Sign: K9OHM
Christopher G Markovich
9017 University Dr
Munster IN 46321

Call Sign: KC9UQB
Darlene M Markovich
9017 University Dr
Munster IN 46321

Call Sign: KC9ODF

Holly M Markovich
9017 University Dr
Munster IN 46321

Call Sign: KC9UQA
Michael J Markovich
9017 University Dr
Munster IN 46321

Call Sign: KB9OI
Joseph G Markovich
9017 University Dr
Munster IN 46321

Call Sign: N9ING
Michael B Lumbrazo
9457 Walnut Dr
Munster IN 46321

Call Sign: N9HAH
Christopher R Harrison
Sr
2140 Washington Cir
Munster IN 46321

Call Sign: N9TWF
Gene A Borgo
8652 White Oak Ave
Munster IN 46321

Call Sign: KB9YHL
Brent A Torrenga
9833 Wildwood Cir Apt
20
Munster IN 46321

Call Sign: KA9EGB
Eugene J Barlog
1818 Wren Dr
Munster IN 463213424

Call Sign: KB9DGX
Omar A Porras
1819 Wren Dr
Munster IN 46321

Call Sign: W9HEI
Maurice A Kraay
Munster IN 46321

FCC Amateur Radio Licenses in Nappanee

Call Sign: N9KKN
Henri L Richards Jr
1299 Beech Rd
Nappanee IN 46550

Call Sign: WW9M
Henri L Richards Jr
1299 Beech Rd
Nappanee IN 46550

Call Sign: KA9UPN
Ralph D Anderson
1513 Brooks Dr
Nappanee IN 46550

Call Sign: KC9IXS
Roger A Zeglin
501 Buffalo Ct
Nappanee IN 46550

Call Sign: WB9FUT
Stephen D Price
70776 CR 7 Rr 4
Nappanee IN 46550

Call Sign: KA9RTA
Dana L Hollar
502 E Van Buren St
Nappanee IN 465501454

Call Sign: KB9ZJQ
Conrad J Hershberger
1044 Franklin St
Nappanee IN 46550

Call Sign: N9HHO
Lauretha M Schmucker

104 Hartman Knoll Ct
Nappanee IN 465501322

Call Sign: WD9ATU
Tod R Schmucker
104 Hartman Knoll Ct
Nappanee IN 465501322

Call Sign: N9FVQ
David H Stalnaker
425 Hickory Ln
Nappanee IN 465501113

Call Sign: KB9GRV
Paula L Housour
Meadow
Nappanee IN 46550

Call Sign: W9MSF
Lester R Mast
12925 N 850 W
Nappanee IN 46550

Call Sign: KC9KPG
Michael J Slattery
1200 N Main St Apt 508
Nappanee IN 46550

Call Sign: N9JPQ
Donald R Freed
151 N Summit
Nappanee IN 46550

Call Sign: N9EZQ
James E Shawgo
452 N Williams St
Nappanee IN 46550

Call Sign: N9EZN
Henri L Richards Sr
605 Northwood Cir
Nappanee IN 46550

Call Sign: KA9UOD
James E Shawgo II

256 Park Dr
Nappanee IN 46550

Call Sign: NN9X
Alexander H Orn
1354 Pickwick Ct
Nappanee IN 46550

Call Sign: KB9KUS
Alric P Bolt
327 Pinecroft
Nappanee IN 46550

Call Sign: KC9HXS
Dennis W Henry
451 S Main St
Nappanee IN 465502529

Call Sign: N9DWH
Dennis W Henry
451 S Main St
Nappanee IN 465502529

Call Sign: KB9ATP
Arlene M Currier
451 S Nappanee St
Nappanee IN 46550

Call Sign: N9JDL
Larry A Housour
253 S Summit
Nappanee IN 46550

Call Sign: KC9CUA
Seth R Jacobs
657 W Centennial St
Nappanee IN 465501501

Call Sign: KC9RAD
Maxwell S Heckathorn
152 W High St
Nappanee IN 46550

Call Sign: N9QEW
Dawn L Heckathorn

152 W High St
Nappanee IN 465502566

Call Sign: N9QEX
Steven D Heckathorn
152 W High St
Nappanee IN 465502566

Call Sign: KB9EFR
Henry L Oge
152 W Randolph
Nappanee IN 46550

Call Sign: KB9EFQ
James R L Oge
152 W Randolph
Nappanee IN 46550

Call Sign: KB9ATS
Steven M Smith
356 W Randolph St
Nappanee IN 46550

Call Sign: KB5VNV
J Lee Hochstetler
1752 Waterfall Dr
Nappanee IN 465508954

FCC Amateur Radio Licenses in New Carlisle

Call Sign: AA9IN
Donald R Bryant
900E
New Carlisle IN 46552

Call Sign: W9EY
Jerome Tannenbaum
31891 Chicago Trl Apt 52
New Carlisle IN 46552

Call Sign: KC9GTV
Suzie S Burkhart
7048 Cottage Grove

New Carlisle IN 46552

Call Sign: KC9GTX
Donovan R Burkhart
7048 Cottage Grove Ave
New Carlisle IN 46552

Call Sign: K9GXD
Donald E Schrader
213 Dunn Rd
New Carlisle IN 46552

Call Sign: KB9FEX
Dale K Kovas
7722 E 1000 N
New Carlisle IN 46552

Call Sign: N9HXU
Richard A Lewis
8473 E Avalon Dr
New Carlisle IN 46552

Call Sign: WB9RYB
Charles E Miller
7166 E Chicago Rd
New Carlisle IN 46552

Call Sign: N9ODI
David M Washburn
7670 E Chicago Trl
New Carlisle IN 46552

Call Sign: N9OZJ
Thomas W Washburn
7670 E Chicago Trl
New Carlisle IN 46552

Call Sign: W9DW
David W Washburn
7670 E Chicago Trl
New Carlisle IN 46552

Call Sign: KA9UUE
Beverly R Schrader
213 E Dunn

New Carlisle IN
465520711

Call Sign: KA9BEV
Beverly R Schrader
213 E Dunn
New Carlisle IN
465520711

Call Sign: WD9EOW
John A Schroeder
7303 E Hwy 20
New Carlisle IN 46552

Call Sign: KB9YKQ
Todd M Demeyer
8395 E Lakeshore Dr
New Carlisle IN 46552

Call Sign: KA9OXN
Richard L Lewis
494 E Michigan St Lot 29
New Carlisle IN 46552

Call Sign: N9COP
Robert A Neitzel
494 E Michigan St Lot 3
New Carlisle IN 46552

Call Sign: N9ODH
Brian J Borders
8354 E Tulip Ln
New Carlisle IN 46552

Call Sign: W9RJM
Robert J Mattasits
7355 E US Hwy 20
New Carlisle IN 46552

Call Sign: KB9FWM
Curtis A Gill
33837 Early Rd
New Carlisle IN 46552

Call Sign: KB9JOL

Brian A Thompson
29445 Edison Rd
New Carlisle IN 46552

Call Sign: KC9OTG
Michael R Ondrovich
33800 Ferncrest Ct
New Carlisle IN 46552

Call Sign: KC9KYG
Scott E Vanlue
30341 Fillmore Rd
New Carlisle IN 46552

Call Sign: K9KS
Kenneth H Sytsma
Grapevine Ln
New Carlisle IN 46552

Call Sign: KA9MRN
Daniel E Cherrone
330 Marvel Ln
New Carlisle IN 46552

Call Sign: KC9GEV
The Nerdherd
4488 N 900 E
New Carlisle IN 46552

Call Sign: NC9IN
The Nerdherd
4488 N 900 E
New Carlisle IN 46552

Call Sign: KA9CKZ
Glen P Kenfield
7639 N Cedar Ln
New Carlisle IN 46552

Call Sign: N9ROE
Kelli D Derkach
7238 N Chicago Rd
New Carlisle IN 46552

Call Sign: N9OJW

Patrick G Heminger
7865 N Grapevine Ln
New Carlisle IN 46552

Call Sign: K9TMD
Todd M Demeyer
7593 N Vaughn Blvd
New Carlisle IN 46552

Call Sign: N9YKR
Susan E Barrett
7760 N Walker Rd
New Carlisle IN 46552

Call Sign: N9FMC
J Edmond Higgins
107 S Cherry St
New Carlisle IN 46552

Call Sign: WR9K
Gerald R Wallis II
56276 Sage Rd
New Carlisle IN 46552

Call Sign: KC9ISB
Brian L Gray
30675 SR 2
New Carlisle IN 46552

Call Sign: KC9TJB
Kenneth X Cecil
33906 Sumerset Ln
New Carlisle IN 46552

Call Sign: KF9EB
Jim A Buszkiewicz
715 Thunderbird Dr
New Carlisle IN 46552

Call Sign: KC9MQR
Michael K Jacobs
56555 Tulip Rd
New Carlisle IN 46552

Call Sign: KB9JAC

Michael K Jacobs
56555 Tulip Rd
New Carlisle IN 46552

Call Sign: N9XRI
Timothy M Vanslager
29417 US 20
New Carlisle IN 46552

Call Sign: K9TMV
Timothy M Vanslager
29417 US 20
New Carlisle IN 46552

Call Sign: KB9PJA
N9Xri-N9Nry Repeater
Group
29417 US 20
New Carlisle IN 46552

Call Sign: N9LUB
Robert G Houk
102 W Ben St Box 486
New Carlisle IN 46552

Call Sign: KB9ZPH
James N Clark
306 W Elm St
New Carlisle IN 46552

Call Sign: WD9AOZ
Robert J Mattasits
221 W Michigan St
New Carlisle IN
465520987

Call Sign: WD9EJR
Earl C Schimmel
709 Willow Ln
New Carlisle IN 46552

Call Sign: KB9OVB
John R Higgins
129 Ziglor St
New Carlisle IN 46552

Call Sign: AB9OZ
John R Higgins
129 Ziglor St
New Carlisle IN 46552

Call Sign: N9DX
John R Higgins
129 Ziglor St
New Carlisle IN 46552

Call Sign: N9UOC
Douglas S Lambert
New Carlisle IN 46552

Call Sign: N9MXK
Jamie R Borders
New Carlisle IN 46552

Call Sign: KG9DL
James A Buszkiewicz Jr
New Carlisle IN 46552

Call Sign: KB9KVQ
Jessica A Buszkiewicz
New Carlisle IN 46552

Call Sign: KB9MDO
Sylvia A Buszkiewicz
New Carlisle IN 46552

**FCC Amateur Radio
Licenses in New Haven**

Call Sign: W9BYR
Edward L Braidwood
1305 Aberdeen Ln
New Haven IN 46774

Call Sign: N9VDE
Sarah A Digangi
1321 Aberdeen Ln
New Haven IN 46774

Call Sign: WD9BKT

Richard B Slayton Sr
532 Adams St
New Haven IN 46774

Call Sign: K9RBS
Richard B Slayton Sr
532 Adams St
New Haven IN 46774

Call Sign: KF6FNS
Carolina B Rutz
1825 Berwick Ln
New Haven IN
467742019

Call Sign: KC9BKK
Laura A Marschand
586 Brandford Ct
New Haven IN 46774

Call Sign: KA9SPQ
Paul D Payne
618 Brandford Ct
New Haven IN
467742619

Call Sign: KA9MZQ
Jerry W Womack
4324 Bruick Rd
New Haven IN 46774

Call Sign: N9JFN
Daniel B Harper
1144 Canal St
New Haven IN 46774

Call Sign: KB9HQD
Denise L Schuckel
1337 Canal St
New Haven IN 46774

Call Sign: KB9HQC
Raymond D Schuckel
1337 Canal St
New Haven IN 46774

Call Sign: KC9HEP
Michael K Reynolds
4532 Castlerock Dr
New Haven IN 46774

Call Sign: WB9QEZ
Michael E Claymiller
887 Chamberlin Ct
New Haven IN
467742123

Call Sign: K9UNN
Dominic V Christofaro
2725 Cherokee Run
New Haven IN 46774

Call Sign: N9BGZ
John M Bissontz
1574 Dundee Dr
New Haven IN 46774

Call Sign: KC9MUT
Charles R Ward
533 Eben St
New Haven IN 46774

Call Sign: KC9JML
David A Benner
8519 Edgerose Dr
New Haven IN 46774

Call Sign: WD9AVW
John P Morton
8526 Edgerose Dr
New Haven IN 46774

Call Sign: KB9SLX
Constance L Morton
8526 Edgerose Dr
New Haven IN
467741007

Call Sign: KC9MOG
Timothy K Benson

4429 Fenwick Dr
New Haven IN 46774

Call Sign: KD9VQ
William T Needham
8915 Forest Dale Dr
New Haven IN 46774

Call Sign: W8IXN
David M Kunkel
3136 Golden Years
Homestead Dr
New Haven IN
467743012

Call Sign: K9WEZ
Roy F Rath
3724 Green Rd
New Haven IN 46774

Call Sign: N9SJU
Alvin B Berry
1659 Hartzell Rd Apt 1C
New Haven IN 46774

Call Sign: N9AIV
Joseph D Police
9549 Iroquois Trace
New Haven IN 46774

Call Sign: KF9DT
Timothy K Harrison
10960 Isabelle Dr Apt 13
New Haven IN 46774

Call Sign: KC9JOM
Neill P Germann
9155 Lake Shore Ct
New Haven IN 46774

Call Sign: KC9TJ
Robert P Easterday
1720 Lincoln Hwy E
New Haven IN
467741741

Call Sign: KB9IQW
Wilbur N Ort
15925 Lincoln Hwy E
New Haven IN 46774

Call Sign: K9LLZ
Jack K Riner
16005 Lincoln Hwy E
New Haven IN 46774

Call Sign: KA9IPA
Dennis D Fry
234 Lincoln Hwy Lot 15
New Haven IN 46774

Call Sign: KB9MEE
Jon J Dreyer
1345 Melbourne Dr
New Haven IN 46774

Call Sign: KA9ZNN
Henry A Goulet
1351 Melbourne Dr
New Haven IN 46774

Call Sign: W6AZO
Conrad O Lunde
1404 Melbourne Dr
New Haven IN 46774

Call Sign: KA9HWM
Harold A Yoder
1407 Melbourne Dr
New Haven IN 46774

Call Sign: N9SKK
Carl W Berry
1605 Melbourne Dr
New Haven IN 46774

Call Sign: KC9TSC
Larry R Pensinger
9017 N River Rd
New Haven IN 46774

Call Sign: W9LRP
Larry R Pensinger
9017 N River Rd
New Haven IN 46774

Call Sign: NC9D
Clyde R Treadway
1709 N Tyland
New Haven IN 46774

Call Sign: KF9TH
Don W Easterday
9311 Parent Rd
New Haven IN 46774

Call Sign: W9JBC
James B Coleman
1135 Powers St
New Haven IN 46774

Call Sign: WA9SNV
Mark A Ellsworth
1710 Richfield Dr
New Haven IN 46774

Call Sign: WD9HIF
Stephen M Kirby
1745 Richfield Dr
New Haven IN 46774

Call Sign: KA9FFT
David A Smith
586 Royalton Dr
New Haven IN 46774

Call Sign: KC9DGH
North East Indiana Dx
Association
9924 S Country Knoll
New Haven IN 46774

Call Sign: N9KNJ
Ronald L Kaufman
9924 S Country Knoll

New Haven IN
467741992

Call Sign: WB9RKZ
Roderick Vandermotten
305 Sara Dr
New Haven IN 46774

Call Sign: KC9ABJ
Steven C Marlowe
441 Sara Dr
New Haven IN
467142314

Call Sign: KC9NDJ
Neil T Meyer
8708 Seiler Rd
New Haven IN 46774

Call Sign: WB9SEF
Jerry W Stephens
3061 Shawnee Trl
New Haven IN 46774

Call Sign: W8SGX
Vance E Sheets
8812 Shordon Rd
New Haven IN
467741040

Call Sign: NA9H
David P Lonis
4037 Shoreline Blvd
New Haven IN 46774

Call Sign: KC9PEI
Marc E Siegel
2917 Sioux Pt
New Haven IN 46774

Call Sign: KC9YVT
Marc E Siegel
2917 Sioux Pt
New Haven IN 46774

Call Sign: KA9YYK
Janice L Schrenk
18431 Slusher Rd
New Haven IN 46774

Call Sign: KA9YYL
Richard D Schrenk
18431 Slusher Rd
New Haven IN 46774

Call Sign: KA9YYM
Steven Schrenk
18431 Slusher Rd
New Haven IN 46774

Call Sign: NR9H
Robert E Peck
342 SR 930 E
New Haven IN
467741381

Call Sign: WD9BHU
Roy D Hosfield
1108 Straford Rd
New Haven IN 46774

Call Sign: KC9EZQ
Michael R Brenton
205 Sturm St
New Haven IN
467741142

Call Sign: N8SGF
John K Schaefer
1215 Summit St
New Haven IN 46774

Call Sign: W9BHR
Kekionga ARC
14539 US Hwy 24 E
New Haven IN 46774

Call Sign: W9BHR
Kekionga ARC
14539 US Hwy 24 E

New Haven IN
467749546

Call Sign: WB9RMA
Edward J Paragi
14539 US Hwy 24 E
New Haven IN
467749546

Call Sign: K9AXM
Wayne A Doenges
932 W Circle Dr
New Haven IN 46774

Call Sign: KB9GAE
Joseph L Morris
9414 Waterside Ct
New Haven IN 46774

Call Sign: WB9FDH
Robert L Wroblewski Sr
140 West St
New Haven IN 46774

Call Sign: KB9YUK
Dennis J Nichter
1706 Woodmere
New Haven IN
467742351

Call Sign: KB9RQN
John S Grantham
New Haven IN 46774

**FCC Amateur Radio
Licenses in New Paris**

Call Sign: KC9QHV
Byrel R Mitchell
69420 CR 27
New Paris IN 46553

Call Sign: KA9AAT
Alvin W Cripe
31024 CR 46 Rt 1

New Paris IN 46553

Call Sign: KB9WMY
John Dick
18561 CR 48
New Paris IN 46526

Call Sign: KD9SK
Ronald A Juday
18765 E 4th St Box 461
New Paris IN 46553

Call Sign: KB5CHV
Gregory L Campbell
69131 Marietta Dr
New Paris IN 46553

Call Sign: KB9RUA
Kevin D Pressler
19077 Oak St
New Paris IN 46553

Call Sign: KB9OYM
George E Kalich Jr
19107 Oak St
New Paris IN 46553

Call Sign: KB9VDZ
Judy E Kalich
19107 Oak St
New Paris IN 46553

Call Sign: N9GNV
Roger E Kaufman
22333 US 6
New Paris IN 46553

Call Sign: KC9CMV
Edward P Ponzetti
18993 Wild Rose Rd
New Paris IN 46553

Call Sign: WA9MZW
David D Fox
New Paris IN 46553

Call Sign: N9WOX
Thomas F Cartmel
New Paris IN 46553

Call Sign: KF9WG
Thomas N Van
Diepenbos
New Paris IN 46553

FCC Amateur Radio Licenses in North Judson

Call Sign: KA9VOI
Mathew W Quaife
900S
North Judson IN 46366

Call Sign: N9TJP
Jeffery T Dixon
Box 374
North Judson IN 46366

Call Sign: KB9GQS
Joe J Vanek Jr
Box 388
North Judson IN 46366

Call Sign: N9QKC
Floyd C Rowe Sr
Box 77
North Judson IN 46366

Call Sign: KC9ISJ
Randall D Stafford
615 Cherry St
North Judson IN 46366

Call Sign: KA9ZVS
Colleen M Alva
304 High St
North Judson IN 46366

Call Sign: KC9QFS

Donald E Martin
304 Jones St
North Judson IN 46366

Call Sign: KC9UYZ
Wesley E Klinkhammer
513 Laurel St
North Judson IN 46366

Call Sign: KB9LRK
Richard C Cinert
703 Laurel St
North Judson IN 46366

Call Sign: N9JXP
Ned B Hillers
6800 S 100 E
North Judson IN 46366

Call Sign: W9AL
Anthony J Langer
8530 S 100 E
North Judson IN 46366

Call Sign: KC9RXO
Starke County Ares
Races Group
8530 S 100 E
North Judson IN 46366

Call Sign: K9ARG
Starke County Ares
Races Group
8530 S 100 E
North Judson IN 46366

Call Sign: KC9HUG
Janet M Langer
8530 S 100 E
North Judson IN 46366

Call Sign: KB9TBO
Anthony J Langer
8560 S 100 E
North Judson IN 46366

Call Sign: KC9OVG
Keith J Gum
1560 S 150 W
North Judson IN 46366

Call Sign: KB9JMP
Joseph L Klecka
7495 S 500 W
North Judson IN 46366

Call Sign: AA9YQ
Joseph L Klecka
7495 S 500 W
North Judson IN 46366

Call Sign: W9JOZ
Starke County ARC
7495 S 500 W
North Judson IN 46366

Call Sign: K9PFQ
Gerald J Razus
4500 S 600 W
North Judson IN
463668894

Call Sign: KB9PVM
Margaret A Razus
4500 S 600 W
North Judson IN
463668894

Call Sign: WB9CAO
Levi B Mayes
4650 S 650 W
North Judson IN
463668739

Call Sign: N9EOX
Seirra S Mayes
4650 S 650 W
North Judson IN
463668739

Call Sign: KB9GPW
Stephen E Scamerhorn Jr
8360 S 700 W
North Judson IN 46366

Call Sign: KC9TWV
Robert D Short Sr
3143 S Angela Dr
North Judson IN 46366

Call Sign: KC9UGS
Helen M Short
3143 S Angela Dr
North Judson IN 46366

Call Sign: WA9KRT
Donald N Smith
3157 S Angela Dr
North Judson IN 46366

Call Sign: KE9ML
Bryan W Ness
509 S Garfield
North Judson IN
463661345

Call Sign: W9ME
Morris E Teague
4180 S Range Rd
North Judson IN 46366

Call Sign: KC9QAP
Pamela L Andress
6500 S SR 39
North Judson IN 46366

Call Sign: KC9MFC
Joseph J Vanek Jr
7135 S SR 39
North Judson IN 46366

Call Sign: KB9GQS
Joseph J Vanek Jr
7135 S SR 39
North Judson IN 46366

Call Sign: KC9QAR
Kerry L Madsen Sr
7420 S SR 39
North Judson IN 46366

Call Sign: KB9OLZ
Gary E Kletz Sr
6455 S Walnut St
North Judson IN 46366

Call Sign: KC9MQC
Scott D Helmcke
2683 W 1st Ave
North Judson IN
463668366

Call Sign: KC9HGF
Roger A Fort Sr
1520 W 450 S
North Judson IN 46366

Call Sign: KC9FQA
Leonard S Bartkowiak
1255 W 450S
North Judson IN 46366

Call Sign: KA9RLA
Kevin C Zee
7175 W 850 S
North Judson IN 46366

Call Sign: WA9AVE
Kevin C Zee
7175 W 850 S
North Judson IN 46366

Call Sign: KC9GLA
Robert K Eberhardt
7175 W 850 S
North Judson IN 46366

Call Sign: KB9OEL
Bobbi K Zee
7175 W 850 S

North Judson IN
463668867

Call Sign: KC9HUD
Dawn M Manns
3180 W 900 S
North Judson IN 46366

Call Sign: W9MWQ
Mathew W Quaife
3180 W 900 S
North Judson IN 46366

Call Sign: N9LV
Mathew W Quaife
3180 W 900 S
North Judson IN 46366

Call Sign: KC9BJA
Michael E King
604 W Vine St
North Judson IN 46366

FCC Amateur Radio Licenses in North Liberty

Call Sign: KC9AKE
Robert D Wise
59130 Crumstown Hwy
North Liberty IN 46554

Call Sign: N9MBQ
Tracey T Herzeg
61725 Crumstown Trl
North Liberty IN
465549615

Call Sign: KD9MC
Denis M Richardson
27907 Holler
North Liberty IN 46554

Call Sign: KA9DUZ
Richard M Ramsbey

25703 Layton Rd
North Liberty IN 46554

Call Sign: KC9IUW
Anthony R Rubio
28800 Madison Rd
North Liberty IN 46554

Call Sign: KB9STX
Dale R Kulwickz
212 N Lafayette
North Liberty IN 46554

Call Sign: AA5XX
Stephen A Wojcik
305 N Main St
North Liberty IN 46554

Call Sign: N9VGC
Aloysius T Nowicki
63400 Pine Rd
North Liberty IN 46554

Call Sign: K9TXF
Ronald J Yoder
68909 Pine Rd
North Liberty IN 46554

Call Sign: KC9LFF
Karen E Taylor
67820 Primrose Rd
North Liberty IN 46554

Call Sign: KC9DMF
Shad P Taylor
67820 Primrose Rd
North Liberty IN 46554

Call Sign: WA6NFZ
Gene L Schrader
66230 Redwood Rd
North Liberty IN 46554

Call Sign: KC9OND
Larry B Bunch

203 S Jefferson St
North Liberty IN 46554

Call Sign: KA9OVQ
Roger A Lawson
65401 SR 23
North Liberty IN 46554

Call Sign: WB9TXQ
A Jerry Kendall
27589 SR 23
North Liberty IN 46554

Call Sign: N9NVK
James A Rutkowski
64691 SR 23
North Liberty IN
465549307

Call Sign: KC9NAP
Jeffrey E Lewis
66990 Tamarack Rd
North Liberty IN 46554

Call Sign: KA9CVQ
Charles L Ross
103 W Mill St
North Liberty IN 46554

Call Sign: KB9GLU
Corey A Ross
103 W Mill St
North Liberty IN 46554

Call Sign: KB9CUV
Nancy C Dowlut
North Liberty IN 46554

Call Sign: KB9HGV
Scott C Rimbaugh II
North Liberty IN 46554

Call Sign: KC9HCM
Audrey M Wood
North Liberty IN 46554

Call Sign: KB9MJK
Gary C Peterson
North Liberty IN 46554

Call Sign: KC9ACX
John E Ramsey
North Liberty IN 46554

Call Sign: KB9MQA
Keith Price Jr
North Liberty IN 46554

Call Sign: KG9FW
Keith A Price
North Liberty IN 46554

Call Sign: KC9HCL
Kenneth E Drapinski
North Liberty IN 46554

Call Sign: KB9LOY
Nicholas C Peterson
North Liberty IN 46554

Call Sign: KC9AHS
David S Riffel Jr
North Liberty IN 46654

**FCC Amateur Radio
Licenses in North
Manchester**

Call Sign: N7ZOQ
Bradan D Pyrah
705 Bond
North Manchester IN
46962

Call Sign: N9SKH
Karin M Drawert
609.5 College Ave
North Manchester IN
46962

Call Sign: KC9TRF
Matthew R Enyeart
3188 E 1300 S
North Manchester IN
46962

Call Sign: KC9TGU
Stanley E Kurtz
4898 E 1400 N
North Manchester IN
46962

Call Sign: KF9LS
L Dwight Farringer
1407 E Orchard Dr
North Manchester IN
46962

Call Sign: WA9DRQ
R Lowell Yohe
2201 East St
North Manchester IN
46962

Call Sign: N9NMX
Randall E Cook
407 Groff St
North Manchester IN
46962

Call Sign: W9BOL
Howard N Uhrig
306 Hickory Ln
North Manchester IN
469629606

Call Sign: K9ORX
Floyd E Fisher
312 Hickory Ln
North Manchester IN
469629606

Call Sign: KC9TRO
Stephen R Rockwell
703 Meadowdale Dr

North Manchester IN
46962

Call Sign: KC9GIS
Bradan D Pyrah
11568 N 500 E
North Manchester IN
46962

Call Sign: K9BP
Bradan D Pyrah
11568 N 500 E
North Manchester IN
46962

Call Sign: KC9GKN
Bryce B Pyrah
11568 N 500 E
North Manchester IN
46962

Call Sign: KC9VAW
Gabriel E Fetters
12504 N 500 E
North Manchester IN
46962

Call Sign: KB7PKY
Barbara A Pyrah
11568 N 500 E
North Manchester IN
46962

Call Sign: KC9OKN
Clint A Wilson
9529 N 600 E
North Manchester IN
46962

Call Sign: W9OSU
Clint A Wilson
9529 N 600 E
North Manchester IN
46962

Call Sign: KB9AYW
Glenn A Hawkins
106 N Front St
North Manchester IN
46962

Call Sign: KC9HSK
Robin Brubaker
10764 N Ogden Rd
North Manchester IN
46962

Call Sign: K9RUE
Littleton L Lefforge
408 N Sycamore St
North Manchester IN
46962

Call Sign: KB6GJF
Max F Purdy
3315 N Wabash Ave
North Manchester IN
469628281

Call Sign: KA9PTT
Robert C Orn
715 N Wayne St
North Manchester IN
46962

Call Sign: W9ETT
Francis H Barr
21 Oak Dr
North Manchester IN
46962

Call Sign: KB9OZG
Charles V Craig
717 Ruse St
North Manchester IN
46962

Call Sign: KE9RO
David L Coburn
1505 Villa Ct

North Manchester IN
46962

Call Sign: KB9OUM
Nelson P Drudge
5760 W 1400 N
North Manchester IN
46962

Call Sign: KB9ORV
Duncan N Swan
306 W 2nd St
North Manchester IN
46962

Call Sign: KB9VBE
Ladona J Webb
405 W 6th St
North Manchester IN
46962

Call Sign: K9GPQ
Thomas H Kane
400 W 7th
North Manchester IN
46962

Call Sign: KB9WLN
Joel M Benz
2297 W 900 N
North Manchester IN
46962

Call Sign: KC9NKT
Tina M Evans
165 Woodring
North Manchester IN
46962

Call Sign: N9VSG
David A Clark
North Manchester IN
46962

Call Sign: KB9UB

J F Trick Sr
North Manchester IN
46962

Call Sign: N9VDF
Troy N Schuler
North Manchester IN
46962

Call Sign: NM9K
Maurice E Kessler
North Manchester IN
46962

**FCC Amateur Radio
Licenses in North
Webster**

Call Sign: KB9GVP
Gary L Gerber
705 Asbury
North Webster IN 46555

Call Sign: KC9HWL
Danny L Warrick
8788 E 500 N
North Webster IN 46555

Call Sign: KB9VMJ
Anthony A Ryl Kuchar
9407 E Backwater Rd
North Webster IN 46555

Call Sign: KC9KRI
Nathaniel I Enyeart
301 E George St
North Webster IN 46555

Call Sign: KC9HUQ
Gregory A Smith
28 Ems W15 Ln
North Webster IN 46555

Call Sign: KB9OIZ
Joseph James

362 Ems W17 Ln
North Webster IN
465559509

Call Sign: W3JUB
Joseph James
362 Ems W17 Ln
North Webster IN
465559509

Call Sign: KC9DSE
James S Hill
6 Ems W21 Ln
North Webster IN
465559535

Call Sign: KB4PVF
Patricia R Dean
10 Ems W28 Ln
North Webster IN 46555

Call Sign: KB4QOP
Robert C Dean
10 Ems W28 Ln
North Webster IN 46555

Call Sign: KB9EXM
Donald E Gerber Jr
6605 N 2nd Trl
North Webster IN 46555

Call Sign: KC9RRX
Cristine D Guy
6665 N 2nd Trl
North Webster IN 46555

Call Sign: KC9NWM
Kenneth B Ledgerwood
5284 N 850 E
North Webster IN 46555

Call Sign: N9VKS
Joshua R Church
5063 N 900 E
North Webster IN 46555

Call Sign: N9AN
Galen L Haney
7533 N Syr Web Rd
North Webster IN 46555

Call Sign: W9DLF
Daryl L Woodward
North Webster IN 46555

Call Sign: W9VPK
Donald M Pemberton
North Webster IN 46555

Call Sign: KB9DJB
John K Rayburn
North Webster IN 46555

Call Sign: N9FLR
Mindy N Twombly
North Webster IN 46555

Call Sign: N9OBM
Richard A Stoddard
North Webster IN 46555

Call Sign: N9NRU
Sabrina S Stoddard
North Webster IN 46555

FCC Amateur Radio Licenses in Notre Dame

Call Sign: KA9NLO
Richard W Fessenden
Andre Pl Apt 315
Notre Dame IN
465560303

Call Sign: ND1U
Notre Dame ARC
226 Coba College Of Bus
U ND
Notre Dame IN 46556

Call Sign: KC9OOJ
Daniel E Guerrero
231 Dillon Hall
Notre Dame IN 46556

Call Sign: KC9IXT
William A Bezouska
289 Dillon Hall
Notre Dame IN 46556

Call Sign: KC9THI
Ian Duncan
327 Duncan Hall
Notre Dame IN 46556

Call Sign: KC5GQD
Aaron A Prager
Fischer Grad Res
Notre Dame IN 46556

Call Sign: N1EWO
Yaakov Sloman
257 Fitzpatrick Hall Of
Engineering
Notre Dame IN 46556

Call Sign: KB9SRK
Robert M Zwaska
152 Zham Hall
Notre Dame IN 46556

Call Sign: KC9GUK
James H O'Donnell
Notre Dame IN 46556

Call Sign: KC9TSM
Thomas J Mylod
Notre Dame IN
465560303

FCC Amateur Radio Licenses in Oakford

Call Sign: KB9OYD
Jason L Millard

Oakford IN 46965

FCC Amateur Radio Licenses in Ogden Dunes

Call Sign: KC9GUA
Jeffrey R Shapiro
40 Shore Dr
Ogden Dunes IN 46368

Call Sign: NX9X
Ernest E Larson
12 Sunset Trl
Ogden Dunes IN
463688718

Call Sign: W9GSN
Melvin L Griem
44 Sunset Trl
Ogden Dunes IN
463688718

FCC Amateur Radio Licenses in Onward

Call Sign: W9HST
Charles R Mays
Onward IN 46967

FCC Amateur Radio Licenses in Orland

Call Sign: N8ZFG
Wayne L Davis
11110 E 750 N
Orland IN 467769500

Call Sign: KG9HZ
Max E Warner Jr
7885 N 650 W
Orland IN 467769722

Call Sign: W9ROA
Roger L Railsback

7025 N 850 W
Orland IN 467769736

Call Sign: KC9TUG
Jerry A Bystry
8645 W SR 120
Orland IN 46776

Call Sign: K8QQI
Donald J Baad
Orland IN 46776

Call Sign: KC9QCE
Michael L Garrison Jr
Orland IN 46776

Call Sign: KB9LHP
Calvin T Oliver
Orland IN 46776

Call Sign: KC9QCF
Charles E Smith
Orland IN 46776

Call Sign: KC9BEX
Ian T Smith
Orland IN 467760196

FCC Amateur Radio Licenses in Osceola

Call Sign: N9YHH
Donald C Holst
11845 3rd St
Osceola IN 46561

Call Sign: KA9TZZ
Mark A Bailey
55078 Andrew Ln
Osceola IN 46561

Call Sign: N9SDR
Terence L Bird
662 Apple Rd
Osceola IN 46561

Call Sign: KB9RUC
Linda J Ostapchuk
59425 Apple Rd
Osceola IN 46561

Call Sign: N9SFX
Peter L Ostapchuk
59425 Apple Rd
Osceola IN 46561

Call Sign: KC9KFY
Richard Perzyna
59425 Apple Rd
Osceola IN 465619393

Call Sign: AB9SL
Richard Perzyna
59425 Apple Rd
Osceola IN 465619393

Call Sign: WB9TYB
Ronald E Lusk
41 Arlington Dr
Osceola IN 46561

Call Sign: KC9VRV
Douglas J Southworth
54514 Ash Rd
Osceola IN 46561

Call Sign: KA9ZLY
Amy L Gonzales
56801 Ash Rd
Osceola IN 46561

Call Sign: NI9A
Lowell M Friesner
56801 Ash Rd
Osceola IN 46561

Call Sign: KB9REC
Ralph T Bennett
54152 Ash Rd 243
Osceola IN 46561

Call Sign: KC9GTW
James L Carter
54152 Ash Rd 265
Osceola IN 465619006

Call Sign: KB9FYD
Curtis D Heitzman
54152 Ash Rd Lot 137
Osceola IN 46561

Call Sign: KC9MQO
Melonie S Clark
55175 Barksdale St
Osceola IN 46561

Call Sign: N9ASP
Paul E Overhulser
81 Beverly Ln
Osceola IN 46561

Call Sign: KA9DVF
Ruth A Overhulser
81 Beverly Ln
Osceola IN 46561

Call Sign: NV9L
David W Blystone
56231 Birch Rd
Osceola IN 46561

Call Sign: KA9TOC
Jeffery D Wynegar
11385 Birchway Dr
Osceola IN 46561

Call Sign: N9ZMQ
Eugene I Keranen
10342 Charles
Osceola IN 46561

Call Sign: N8ITM
Anne Marie Hideg
54710 Dawn Dr
Osceola IN 465619352

Call Sign: N8HSC
Istvan G Hideg
54710 Dawn Dr
Osceola IN 465619352

Call Sign: KA9SUF
Eldon H Haden
10399 Douglas
Osceola IN 46561

Call Sign: KB9DTJ
Christine M Haden
10399 Douglas Rd
Osceola IN 46561

Call Sign: KA9SUG
Patricia A Haden
10399 Douglas Rd
Osceola IN 465619436

Call Sign: KB9GTG
Raymond L Balogh Jr
10165 Dunn Rd
Osceola IN 46561

Call Sign: AA9VM
Geron Reynolds
10168 Edison Rd
Osceola IN 46561

Call Sign: KB9OLV
William P Asherman
10982 Edison Rd
Osceola IN 46561

Call Sign: KC9NAS
Roderick A Powell
11650 Edison Rd
Osceola IN 46561

Call Sign: KC9LYK
Paul F Hyde
10994 Fairview Ave
Osceola IN 46561

Call Sign: KC9OHA
Jean Marie Thompson
10350 Inwood Rd
Osceola IN 46561

Call Sign: WB9NJU
Lawrence K Reising
10860 Ireland Rd
Osceola IN 46561

Call Sign: N9OBX
John A Somheil
55936 Jefferson Knolls
Osceola IN 46561

Call Sign: W9GQQ
William J Jamieson Sr
10334 Jefferson Rd
Osceola IN 46561

Call Sign: KB9IVA
Robert W Reiman
30711 Kevin Ct
Osceola IN 46561

Call Sign: K9UPS
Robert R Henry
502 Lamport St
Osceola IN 46561

Call Sign: KA9MQK
David M Lindenlaub
54155 Landes Dr
Osceola IN 465619018

Call Sign: N9ZIW
Kimothy S Moser
10310 Lindwood Ct
Osceola IN 46561

Call Sign: K9BZS
Frederic K Baldauf
322 N Beech Rd
Osceola IN 46561

Call Sign: WB9WOV
Albert R Ludwig
325 N Grand Ave
Osceola IN 46561

Call Sign: KB9NRE
Eugene K Cocanower
116 N Olive
Osceola IN 46561

Call Sign: WB9MUD
Robert L Kollar Jr
10295 Neely St
Osceola IN 46561

Call Sign: K9JCA
James O Butler
55962 Oakview Ln
Osceola IN 46561

Call Sign: N9SQC
Robert J Pate
11810 Owens Dr
Osceola IN 46561

Call Sign: KC9GTZ
Robert F Helbing
10925 Pewamo Dr
Osceola IN 46561

Call Sign: KC9RFH
Robert F Helbing
10925 Pewamo Dr
Osceola IN 46561

Call Sign: N9OC
Harold C Arnold
11815 Price St
Osceola IN 46561

Call Sign: KB9RYE
Bi County Radio
Amateurs
11815 Price St

Osceola IN 465611833

Call Sign: WO9A
Theodore L Schafer
55654 Springdale Ct
Osceola IN 46561

Call Sign: KC9KYH
Ellen M Rathburn
10327 Sunview Dr
Osceola IN 46561

Call Sign: KC9MIA
Joseph A Sipocz
10327 Sunview Dr
Osceola IN 46561

Call Sign: KC9KYE
Vincent J Sipocz
10327 Sunview Dr
Osceola IN 46561

Call Sign: N9ROP
Jovan Skocajic
10224 Vistula Rd
Osceola IN 46561

Call Sign: K9FII
Richard L Mecklenburg
11905 Vistula Rd
Osceola IN 46561

Call Sign: N9MAX
David A McGinnis
11269 Wildwood Dr
Osceola IN 46561

Call Sign: KA9TSD
Paul S Geer
11050 Wildwood Dr
Osceola IN 46561

Call Sign: KB9HUZ
James R Massey Jr
Osceola IN 46561

Call Sign: W9QQT
Rolland D Jackson
Osceola IN 46561

Call Sign: W9SJ
Samuel J Jamieson Sr
Osceola IN 46561

Call Sign: W1HJA
Myron D Shoaf
Osceola IN 465610192

Call Sign: KE4RIT
Richard S Zimmerman
Osceola IN 465610373

Call Sign: KB9TYZ
Saint Joseph County
ARC
Osceola IN 465610512

**FCC Amateur Radio
Licenses in Ossian**

Call Sign: K9WQU
David F Houser
Box 135
Ossian IN 46777

Call Sign: WD9SPB
Stephen P Butler
1819 Brook Ct
Ossian IN 46777

Call Sign: KB9YEB
Thomas C Robison
703 Country Dr
Ossian IN 46777

Call Sign: KB9BNJ
Scott A Diehl
302 Countryside Dr
Ossian IN 46777

Call Sign: KC9VRR
Neil T Ainslie
5126 E 1000 N
Ossian IN 46777

Call Sign: KC9VRQ
Russell T Ainslie
5126 E 1000 N
Ossian IN 46777

Call Sign: WB9HNL
John K Melching
5872 E 1000 N
Ossian IN 46777

Call Sign: N9VAJ
Jonathan J Mitchell
1388 E 900 N
Ossian IN 46777

Call Sign: WA9TMU
Douglas B Nyffeler
1650 E 950 N
Ossian IN 46777

Call Sign: N0SQG
Stephen P Butler
120 E Lafever St
Ossian IN 46777

Call Sign: KC9CGO
Nancy J Vysniauskas
2030 E US 224
Ossian IN 46777

Call Sign: KC9MOM
Nancy J Vysniauskas
2030 E US 224
Ossian IN 46777

Call Sign: W8BYA
Gedas C Vysniauskas
2030 E US 224
Ossian IN 46777

Call Sign: WB9CHI
Ronald E Yoss
2451 E Water St
Ossian IN 46777

Call Sign: KC9GCM
Robert C Smith
321 Eagle Ct
Ossian IN 46777

Call Sign: KC9GCP
Robert J Smith
321 Eagle Ct
Ossian IN 46777

Call Sign: KB9PDW
Richard A Mink
513 Greenwood Trl
Ossian IN 46777

Call Sign: K9ZE
Ron A Hensel
8792 N 500 E
Ossian IN 46777

Call Sign: AA9MO
Susan I Hensel
8792 N 500 E
Ossian IN 46777

Call Sign: W9KNP
David J Pyard
8657 N Diane Dr
Ossian IN 46777

Call Sign: KC9DFQ
Lukus S Hurt
206 N Jefferson St
Ossian IN 46777

Call Sign: N9RJA
Thomas C Nahrwold
210 N Maxine Dr
Ossian IN 46777

Call Sign: KB9EWA
Benjamin L Carr
11080 N SR 1 Lot 90
Ossian IN 46777

Call Sign: KB9MHS
Michael D Hippensteele
918 S Countyline
Ossian IN 46777

Call Sign: AB9QA
Michael D Hippensteele
918 S Countyline
Ossian IN 46777

Call Sign: N9NST
Kenneth W Kaletta
125 W Craig St
Ossian IN 46777

Call Sign: KC9APO
Ron E Kunze
813 W Mill St
Ossian IN 46777

Call Sign: KD9GJ
Lloyd E Dawson
Ossian IN 46777

FCC Amateur Radio Licenses in Oxford

Call Sign: KA9DNY
Linden L Fell
201 E Enota
Oxford IN 47971

Call Sign: WB9WHT
Jayne A Hale
Oxford IN 47971

Call Sign: WB9WHU
Raymond L Hale
Oxford IN 47971

Call Sign: K8DER
Donald E Robinson
Oxford IN 479710371

FCC Amateur Radio Licenses in Pennville

Call Sign: KB9STJ
Randall L Morgan
650W
Pennville IN 47369

Call Sign: WA9HFF
James I Wheeler
225 Broadway Box 294
Pennville IN 47369

Call Sign: KB9SZU
Patricia S Morgan
3365 N 650 W
Pennville IN 47369

Call Sign: KC9APX
April R Coleman
5789 W 300 N
Pennville IN 47369

Call Sign: KC9APW
Eric E Coleman
5789 W 300 N
Pennville IN 47369

Call Sign: KB9UMJ
Laura L Coleman
5789 W 300 N
Pennville IN 47369

Call Sign: KB9YMS
Perry R Coleman
5789 W 300 N
Pennville IN 47369

Call Sign: N9WQU
Jerry L Welch
10811 W 450 N

Pennville IN 47369

Call Sign: KB9MVJ
Mildred J Duke
6815 W 500 N
Pennville IN 47369

Call Sign: KB9KFG
Hershel T Duke
Pennville IN 47369

Call Sign: KB9JSP
Janet L Downing
Pennville IN 47369

Call Sign: KB9KFF
Keith R Farmer
Pennville IN 47369

Call Sign: KC9GRW
Ralph Frazee
Pennville IN 47369

Call Sign: WA9BFF
Joseph E Downing
Pennville IN 473690186

FCC Amateur Radio Licenses in Pershing

Call Sign: N9WHF
Susan K Fisher
302 E Main St
Pershing IN 47370

Call Sign: K9DLF
Donald L Fisher
302 Main St
Pershing IN 47370

FCC Amateur Radio Licenses in Peru

Call Sign: KB9WQW
Bonnie J Mathis

300N
Peru IN 46970

Call Sign: N9JIP
James A Childs
10 Airport Rd
Peru IN 46970

Call Sign: KA9NYY
Norman R Leasor
112 Arnold Ave
Peru IN 46970

Call Sign: WB9FNR
Paul G Hoffarth
22 Barkley Ave
Peru IN 46970

Call Sign: W9QXL
Harold E Rendel
Box 158
Peru IN 46970

Call Sign: N9MOT
Phyllis A Gable
Box 182A
Peru IN 46970

Call Sign: N9XSA
Jeffrey S Stinson
Box 23A
Peru IN 46970

Call Sign: N9LBL
John W Shank
Box 244A
Peru IN 46970

Call Sign: N9XFU
Christopher L Newport
Box 269D
Peru IN 46970

Call Sign: K9SBW
Byron B Wilson

Box 337
Peru IN 46970

Call Sign: KB9EFV
Joseph N Catanzaro
Box 50
Peru IN 46970

Call Sign: KB9QYT
Teri A Vermilion
Box 59
Peru IN 46970

Call Sign: N9RGQ
Aaron T Dunkle
2670 Capehart Ave
Peru IN 46970

Call Sign: N6JYF
Thomas R Appleton
8 Delores Ave
Peru IN 46970

Call Sign: W9LCS
Donald W Murphy
23 Delores Ave
Peru IN 46970

Call Sign: K9LVK
Guy R Mathis
5576 E 300 N
Peru IN 46970

Call Sign: KB9IXC
Leo R Irving
276 E 3rd
Peru IN 46970

Call Sign: KC9RJE
Jeremiah B Gilbert
582 E 3rd St
Peru IN 46970

Call Sign: N9MTG
Matthew T Gruel

67 E 5th St
Peru IN 46970

Call Sign: N9VXS
Ronald R Morris
527 E 5th St Apt 2
Peru IN 46970

Call Sign: N9IMA
Wayne E Guillaume
165 E 6th St
Peru IN 46970

Call Sign: KK5JI
John R Bowman
281 E 9th St
Peru IN 46970

Call Sign: W9EJC
Carl L Redmon
260 E Canal St
Peru IN 46970

Call Sign: N9MFP
Kenneth E Marks
276 E Canal St
Peru IN 46970

Call Sign: WQ9J
James R Bradley
3986 E Daniels Rd
Peru IN 46970

Call Sign: KC9KHU
Layne R Bradley
278 E Elm Wood
Peru IN 46970

Call Sign: KB9VAW
Teresa G Butzin
497 E Main St Apt 3
Peru IN 46970

Call Sign: KA9BAL
James E Cassel

701 E Main St Apt 326
Peru IN 46970

Call Sign: N9LBK
Blaine J O Neil
2496 E Paw Paw Pike
Peru IN 46970

Call Sign: KB9DTN
Iris J Lewis
2025 E Rachel Ln
Peru IN 46970

Call Sign: KB9DVM
Stephen E Lewis
2025 E Rachel Ln
Peru IN 46970

Call Sign: KC9AZS
Leon L Pearson II
65 E Riverside Dr
Peru IN 46970

Call Sign: K9LZC
William E Goodwin
4946 E SR 124
Peru IN 46970

Call Sign: N9XLX
Terry W Vermilion
3775 E SR 218
Peru IN 46970

Call Sign: W9SFZ
Don C Murphy
1567 E Victory School
Rd
Peru IN 46970

Call Sign: N9LAO
James R Pogue
126 Ewing St
Peru IN 46970

Call Sign: KC9GVE

James M Baldwin
469 Jackson Ave
Peru IN 46970

Call Sign: KF9GD
Richard E Galbreath
16 Lakeview Dr
Peru IN 46970

Call Sign: WD9EBS
Frederick J Gutohrel
115 Logan St
Peru IN 46970

Call Sign: KC9RQU
Terry L Harris
403 Madison Ave
Peru IN 469701246

Call Sign: N9PCQ
Alma J Jackson
23 McKinstry Ave
Peru IN 46970

Call Sign: KB9YQQ
Aaron C Greer
4611 N 190 W
Peru IN 46970

Call Sign: KB9MSC
Christopher D Rife
631 N 670 E
Peru IN 46970

Call Sign: N9TIV
Anita L Rife
743 N 670 E
Peru IN 46970

Call Sign: WA9RRL
Claude D Rife
743 N 670 E
Peru IN 46970

Call Sign: KA9UUB

Joseph A Sutton Sr
15 N Benton St
Peru IN 469700444

Robert W Smalley II
28 Rose Dr<
Peru IN 46970

Frederick W Weil
1840 S Donald Pl
Peru IN 46970

Call Sign: KC9KLL
Frederick W Schumacher
85 N CR 400 W
Peru IN 46970

Call Sign: WA8PNZ
Richard R Wolf
946 Rosewood Dr
Peru IN 46970

Call Sign: N9KNM
Larry A Rand
5105 US 31 S
Peru IN 46970

Call Sign: KC9TSD
Danny R Hughart Jr
112 N Fremont St
Peru IN 46970

Call Sign: WD9GIU
William E McAlpin
1118 Rosewood Dr
Peru IN 46970

Call Sign: K9CWG
Leland Booher
5238 US 31 S
Peru IN 46970

Call Sign: KK9DAN
Danny R Hughart Jr
112 N Fremont St
Peru IN 46970

Call Sign: KB9PKC
Alan D Adkins
6243 S 160 W
Peru IN 46976

Call Sign: KC9RRT
Stanley M Higgins III
714 Van Buren Ave
Peru IN 46970

Call Sign: KB9RKB
Laura M Hileman
4769 N Paw Paw Pike
Peru IN 46970

Call Sign: KB9PQB
Belerma Adkins
6243 S 160 W
Peru IN 469707771

Call Sign: N9MOS
Danny A Webb
636 W 11th St
Peru IN 46970

Call Sign: N9WHX
Laura M Hileman
4769 N Paw Paw Pike
Peru IN 46970

Call Sign: N9XMA
Julie A Hamman
2911 S 50 W
Peru IN 46970

Call Sign: N9XRY
Charles D Freeman
1011 W 250 S
Peru IN 46970

Call Sign: WD9FPL
Shirley A Kerns
979 Orchid Pl
Peru IN 46970

Call Sign: N9SCK
Francis C Venters
723 S Broadway
Peru IN 46970

Call Sign: KC9CCX
Joshua D Hyrman
71 W 2nd St
Peru IN 469702158

Call Sign: KB9IWK
John C Lewis
1345 Rachel Ln
Peru IN 46970

Call Sign: KB9IFU
Frank C Venters
723 S Broadway
Peru IN 46970

Call Sign: KB8WVA
Sharon A Hartman Ms
462 W 2nd St
Peru IN 46970

Call Sign: N9YXG
Stephen E Lewis II
2025 Rachel Ln
Peru IN 46970

Call Sign: WB9YXR
Inez I Hiner
6510 S CR 125W
Peru IN 46970

Call Sign: N9LRF
Jack M Gable
39 W 500 S
Peru IN 46970

Call Sign: N9YOF

Call Sign: W8FOF

Call Sign: W9RAT

Michael S Ratican
851 W 500 S
Peru IN 46970

Call Sign: KC9JFW
April M Confer
87 W 570 S
Peru IN 46970

Call Sign: KC9JFV
Bradley S Fisher
87 W 570 S
Peru IN 46970

Call Sign: KC9JSV
Vernon V Keller
2111 W 600 S
Peru IN 46970

Call Sign: KC9GWB
Kenneth E Rhoads Jr
204 W 6th
Peru IN 46970

Call Sign: N9LRQ
Donald L West
359 W Blvd
Peru IN 46970

Call Sign: KC9HIR
Gregory A Fisher
87 W CR 570 S
Peru IN 46970

Call Sign: KC9HIS
Jennifer A Fisher
87 W CR 570 S
Peru IN 46970

Call Sign: KC9ROE
Colin A Sherrill
1785 W Farview Dr
Peru IN 46970

Call Sign: KG4BQH

Ray A Hostetler
1888 W Farview Dr
Peru IN 46970

Call Sign: KG4CAS
Kristie L Hostetler
1888 W Farview Dr
Peru IN 46970

Call Sign: KC9GLN
Justin N Zook
2202 W Leffel Ln
Peru IN 46970

Call Sign: KC9BLB
Linda K Robinson
2202 W Leffel Ln
Peru IN 46970

Call Sign: WB9VCL
Robert S Robinson Jr
2202 W Leffel Ln
Peru IN 46970

Call Sign: W9RSR
Robert S Robinson Jr
2202 W Leffel Ln
Peru IN 46970

Call Sign: KC9HTJ
Tyler M Fromm
474 W Main St
Peru IN 46970

Call Sign: KB9VAU
John D Moon
570 W Main St
Peru IN 46970

Call Sign: KC9INB
Aaron J Wakal
1002.5 W Main St
Peru IN 46970

Call Sign: KC9ULC

Robert M Peconga
2460 W Pebble Dr
Peru IN 46970

Call Sign: KB9ZAR
David L Thorpe
165 W Riverside Dr
Peru IN 46970

Call Sign: KF9QW
Angela K Flory
2205 W Willow Ln
Peru IN 46970

Call Sign: KF9NU
Eric R Flory
2205 W Willow Ln
Peru IN 46970

Call Sign: KC9FAW
Mark A Brown
3400 Westover St
Peru IN 46970

Call Sign: N9QEV
Robert L Allison
Peru IN 46970

Call Sign: K9ZEV
Miami County ARC
Peru IN 46970

**FCC Amateur Radio
Licenses in Pierceton**

Call Sign: N9HJZ
Kevin L Myers
Box 328
Pierceton IN 46562

Call Sign: KC9THA
Torre S Owens
8285 E 250 S
Pierceton IN 46562

Call Sign: KB9VRH
Thomas E Church
5627 E 350 S
Pierceton IN 46562

Call Sign: KV9P
Charles D Reinhart
6278 E 350 S
Pierceton IN 46562

Call Sign: N8LAM
Diana K Reinhart
6278 E 350 S
Pierceton IN 46562

Call Sign: KB9QQO
Brandon A Pletcher
5919 E Van Ness Rd
Pierceton IN 46562

Call Sign: KC9ZE
Tom L Pletcher
5919 E Van Ness Rd
Pierceton IN 46562

Call Sign: N9FKN
Vicki L Pletcher
5919 E Van Ness Rd
Pierceton IN 46562

Call Sign: KD6OTT
Emma L Long
5069 E Wooster Rd
Pierceton IN 46562

Call Sign: N1LL
Lyle L Long
5069 E Wooster Rd
Pierceton IN 46562

Call Sign: WB7EED
Healthcare America
Radio Club
5069 E Wooster Rd
Pierceton IN 46562

Call Sign: KB9OZO
Lisa R Stoddard
301 Ems R4 Ln
Pierceton IN 46562

Call Sign: KB9MYW
Mark A Stoddard
301 Ems R4 Ln
Pierceton IN 46562

Call Sign: KB9UKL
Julia S Harrison
465 Ems R4 Ln
Pierceton IN 465629019

Call Sign: NR9M
David T Schaefer
70 Ems R4C Ln
Pierceton IN 46562

Call Sign: N9VPA
James A Stoddard
41 Ems R4I Ln
Pierceton IN 46562

Call Sign: KA9UOH
Sandra F Schaefer
70 Ems Ruc Ln
Pierceton IN 46562

Call Sign: KA9YAN
Jason W Burnworth
508 N 1st St
Pierceton IN 46562

Call Sign: N9FIT
Bill D Burnworth
508 N 1st St
Pierceton IN 46562

Call Sign: KF9AY
Deljon R Fisher
207 N 4th St
Pierceton IN 46562

Call Sign: KB9TUE
Jesse D Fisher
207 N 4th St
Pierceton IN 46562

Call Sign: KC9RRD
Andrew L Emerick Sr
1179 N 850 E
Pierceton IN 46562

Call Sign: W9NUZ
Theodore J Lenox
302 N Indiana St
Pierceton IN 46562

Call Sign: KA9ESM
Jonathan M Townsend
4886 S 750 E
Pierceton IN 46562

Call Sign: N9IPU
Whitney J Townsend
4886 S 750E
Pierceton IN 46562

Call Sign: KB9JBV
John M Arter
383 S 900 W
Pierceton IN 46562

Call Sign: KA9STX
John A Arter
383 S 900 W 92
Pierceton IN 46562

Call Sign: KB9CZX
Jason P Carpenter
Pierceton IN 46562

Call Sign: KB9CSI
Jerry N Hartman
Pierceton IN 46562

Call Sign: KC9RQS

Chad L Pletcher
Pierceton IN 46562

Call Sign: KB9MOS
Chris W Dean
Pierceton IN 46562

FCC Amateur Radio Licenses in Pleasant Lake

Call Sign: K8BPD
Brad A Mcconn
560 E Bellefontaine Rd
Pleasant Lake IN 46779

Call Sign: KC9LVQ
William L Perry
4905 S 150 W
Pleasant Lake IN 46779

Call Sign: KC9LVR
Kathy L Moor
4905 S 150 W
Pleasant Lake IN
467799528

Call Sign: WW6Q
Roy S Jolly
3205 S 325 W
Pleasant Lake IN 46779

Call Sign: N9QPA
Paul D McDaniel
4325 S 500 W
Pleasant Lake IN 46779

Call Sign: KC9GDD
Anna S Keller
3525 S 600 W
Pleasant Lake IN 46779

Call Sign: KC9EDB
David L Keller
3525 S 600 W

Pleasant Lake IN
467799771

Call Sign: KC9EDA
Norene K Keller
3525 S 600 W
Pleasant Lake IN
467799771

Call Sign: N9ZKZ
Neal A Puff
5945 S 725 W
Pleasant Lake IN 46779

Call Sign: KA9IYK
Clarence A Seitz
5395 S 800 W
Pleasant Lake IN 46779

Call Sign: KB9ICD
Mary Jo Seitz
5395 S 800 W
Pleasant Lake IN 46779

Call Sign: KC9GGE
Lewis G Erwin Jr
6517 S Meridian Rd
Pleasant Lake IN 46779

Call Sign: KX9V
Lewis G Erwin
6575 S Meridian Rd
Pleasant Lake IN 46779

Call Sign: KC9LVP
Greta K Ross-Hill
1980 W 500 S
Pleasant Lake IN 46779

Call Sign: KC9GDC
Stephen A Hill
1980 W 500 S
Pleasant Lake IN 46779

Call Sign: K9GDC

Stephen A Hill
1980 W 500 S
Pleasant Lake IN 46779

Call Sign: KC9CXZ
Lori A Henderson
5845 W Lake Valley Rd
Pleasant Lake IN 46779

Call Sign: KC9BES
Roy L Henderson
5845 W Lake Valley Rd
Pleasant Lake IN 46779

Call Sign: KC9BEZ
Virginia L Stroh
1605 W Long Lake Rd
Pleasant Lake IN 46779

Call Sign: KB9TXK
Tracy L Stroh
1605 W Long Lk Rd
Pleasant Lake IN 46779

Call Sign: WD9DSP
Sharon L Brown
905 W Pkwy Dr
Pleasant Lake IN 46779

Call Sign: WD9DSN
William N Brown
905 W Pkwy Dr
Pleasant Lake IN
467799503

Call Sign: KC9BEY
Jeri L Treesh
1235 W South Dr
Pleasant Lake IN 46779

Call Sign: KC9BFA
Tyler J Treesh
1235 W South Dr
Pleasant Lake IN 46779

Call Sign: KA9ZCB
Robert W Green
Pleasant Lake IN 46779

Call Sign: KC9VEJ
Charles W Moore
Pleasant Lake IN 46779

Call Sign: WA9KKC
Richard L McMillen
2060 N US 33
Pleasant Mills IN 46780

**FCC Amateur Radio
Licenses in Plymouth**

Call Sign: KB9JMR
Wayne L Hollenbaugh
17684 10B Rd
Plymouth IN 46563

Call Sign: KB9KZC
Elouise M Hollenbaugh
17684 10B Rd
Plymouth IN 46563

Call Sign: KC9NFC
Dan D Cummins
19515 10B Rd
Plymouth IN 46563

Call Sign: KB9MDI
Dexter E Funk
8865 11th Rd
Plymouth IN 46563

Call Sign: KA9T
Larry M Gibson
12287 11th Rd
Plymouth IN 46563

Call Sign: N9DCV
Linda J Gibson
12287 11th Rd
Plymouth IN 46563

Call Sign: WA9BGW
Richard L Craft
18800 12th Rd
Plymouth IN 46563

Call Sign: N9INJ
Jeffrey D Zechiel
12839 2C Rd
Plymouth IN 46563

Call Sign: WA9CFK
Ronald G Prusinski
13559 3rd Rd
Plymouth IN 46563

Call Sign: K9OSZ
Richard E Ward
11060 4A Rd
Plymouth IN 46563

Call Sign: WB9MAF
Melvin R Mahler
13402 4B Rd
Plymouth IN 46563

Call Sign: N9CLI
Adam A Morie
18752 6th B Rd
Plymouth IN 46563

Call Sign: W9IZJ
Kenneth E Kunze
805 Baker Lot 38
Plymouth IN 46563

Call Sign: W1OJB
Carlton W McAvey
700 Berkley Sq Lot 318
Plymouth IN 465631863

Call Sign: KB9GRD
William F Genslinger Sr
Box 70
Plymouth IN 46563

Call Sign: KC9BDP
John A Sellers
10201 Carriage Dr
Plymouth IN 46563

Call Sign: K9JAS
John A Sellers
10201 Carriage Dr
Plymouth IN 46563

Call Sign: KC9HSR
Andrew J Tomasik
11418 Castle Dr
Plymouth IN 46563

Call Sign: KC9BOI
Steven L Towne
325 Conger St
Plymouth IN 46563

Call Sign: N9FCM
Deborah A Morgan
338 Conger St
Plymouth IN 46563

Call Sign: N9RDH
Sean W Franklin
12363 Coral Ct
Plymouth IN 46563

Call Sign: KG9MB
Yaqoob A Rana
11461 Crocus Ct
Plymouth IN 46563

Call Sign: KA9JOZ
Tunis C Ross Jr
1010 Ferndale
Plymouth IN 46563

Call Sign: KF9JW
Thomas A Nowicki
1120 Ferndale St
Plymouth IN 46563

Call Sign: NG9O
Thomas A Nowicki
1120 Ferndale St
Plymouth IN 46563

Call Sign: NF9I
James E Easterday
11855 Lawndale Ave
Plymouth IN 46563

Call Sign: AB9AU
Donel D Hathaway
16770 Mill Pond Trl
Plymouth IN 46563

Call Sign: N9RT
Thomas A Nowicki
1120 Ferndale St
Plymouth IN 46563

Call Sign: WA9VRK
Clarence E Shaffer
128 Lemler Ln
Plymouth IN 46563

Call Sign: KB9AGB
David D Babcock
10557 Muckshaw Rd
Plymouth IN 465638558

Call Sign: KB9BST
B Clark Phillips
325 Franklin
Plymouth IN 46563

Call Sign: KA9KUN
Kathryn E Rowe
15557 Lincoln Hwy W
Plymouth IN 46563

Call Sign: WB9CEQ
Richard T Cushman
614 N Michigan St
Plymouth IN 46563

Call Sign: KB9VJF
Roger W Risner
329 Franklin Ave
Plymouth IN 46563

Call Sign: N9ABN
Mario J Meribela
3922 Maple Rd
Plymouth IN 46563

Call Sign: KC9HGG
Randall A Neirynck Sr
3840 N Nutmeg Rd
Plymouth IN 46563

Call Sign: KC9RYQ
Amy S Hostetler
217 Gideon St
Plymouth IN 46563

Call Sign: N9WPE
Marvin Balogh
3863 Michigan Rd
Plymouth IN 46563

Call Sign: N9JEU
Tommy L Conrad
3327 Nutmeg Rd
Plymouth IN 46563

Call Sign: WA9INM
Wayne D Zehner Jr
6386 Hwy 17
Plymouth IN 465639464

Call Sign: WB5KVE
Gene R Siddall
5625 Michigan Rd
Plymouth IN 46563

Call Sign: WB9MLG
Rosemary Listenberger
10451 Nutmeg Rd
Plymouth IN 46563

Call Sign: K9WZ
Wayne D Zehner Jr
11317 Iris Ct
Plymouth IN 465637667

Call Sign: N9AYW
Frank J Barracca
2403 Michigan Rd Lot 82
Plymouth IN 46563

Call Sign: WB0SIT
Gerald R McCoid
10938 Nutmeg Rd
Plymouth IN 465637502

Call Sign: WB9YDC
Lois J Zehner
11317 Iris Ct
Plymouth IN 465637667

Call Sign: KB9SCI
Donel D Hathaway
16770 Mill Pond Trl
Plymouth IN 46563

Call Sign: N9ZLR
Mike C Layman
704 Oak Hill Ave
Plymouth IN 46563

Call Sign: KB9LRJ
Rex A Sullivan
10516 King Rd
Plymouth IN 46563

Call Sign: KB9WJK
Donel D Hathaway
16770 Mill Pond Trl
Plymouth IN 46563

Call Sign: KC9GDB
Dwayne A Golden
12398 Olive Tr
Plymouth IN 46563

Call Sign: N9EMA
Melvin R Snyder
829 Pearl
Plymouth IN 46563

Call Sign: KC9DOJ
Christopher A Carpenter
9676 Sunnyside
Plymouth IN 46563

Call Sign: WB9YID
Larry D Norman
14840 W 14B Rd
Plymouth IN 46563

Call Sign: KF9TW
Edward A Friberg
231 Pennsylvania Ave
Plymouth IN 46563

Call Sign: KB9BLT
Sue A Kostreba
17224 Tomahawk Trl
Plymouth IN 46563

Call Sign: N9MJV
Mike McFarland
16081 W 14th Rd
Plymouth IN 465639331

Call Sign: KB9WQX
James J Muday
9881 Pine Rd
Plymouth IN 46563

Call Sign: KC9RPT
Timothy J Pletcher
7791 Tulip Rd
Plymouth IN 46563

Call Sign: KB9LWR
Rebecca S Hartman
14789 W 16th Rd
Plymouth IN 46563

Call Sign: K9JHU
James J Muday
9881 Pine Rd
Plymouth IN 46563

Call Sign: WB9WJL
Donald P Abbott
12041 US 6
Plymouth IN 46563

Call Sign: KB9KGI
Francis T Kennedy
9076 W County Line Rd
Plymouth IN 46563

Call Sign: N9KQU
Janice Badell
10337 Quince Rd
Plymouth IN 46563

Call Sign: KB9WTZ
Bruce A Stutsman
13409 US 6
Plymouth IN 46563

Call Sign: KB9PZI
Sonia A Rana
1216 W Jefferson St
Plymouth IN 46563

Call Sign: K9KRT
Dale L Schrom
913 S Pearl St
Plymouth IN 46563

Call Sign: KB9JHZ
Roger L Wheatbrook
12269 W 11th Rd
Plymouth IN 46563

Call Sign: K9GYR
J Douglas Badell
120 W Washington St
Plymouth IN 46563

Call Sign: KB9MJL
Samia L Schrom
913 S Pearl St
Plymouth IN 46563

Call Sign: KA9BCS
Violet J Gilbert
13567 W 12th Rd
Plymouth IN 46563

Call Sign: KC9PKH
Chuck G Rowe
609 W Washington St
Plymouth IN 46563

Call Sign: KB9JMQ
Darrin K Lyon
9557 SR 17
Plymouth IN 46563

Call Sign: N9GUT
Jon E Harrington
11385 W 13th Rd
Plymouth IN 46563

Call Sign: KC9PRJ
Charles A Turner
17900 Walnut St
Plymouth IN 46563

Call Sign: KB9KRV
Jana L Lyon
9557 SR 17
Plymouth IN 46563

Call Sign: KB9PLW
Sarah A Norman
14840 W 14 B Rd
Plymouth IN 46563

Call Sign: KC9LTO
Ann M Stoub
1907 Westgate Ave
Plymouth IN 46563

Call Sign: K9ZLQ
Marshall County ARC
Plymouth IN 46563

FCC Amateur Radio Licenses in Poneto

Call Sign: KC9CGZ
Rick A Velasquez
9770 S 200 W
Poneto IN 46781

Call Sign: AB9HP
Rick A Velasquez
9770 S 200 W
Poneto IN 46781

Call Sign: W9AYW
Wells County ARC
9770 S 200 W
Poneto IN 46781

Call Sign: N9CBC
Thomas E Wade
5010 S 400 W
Poneto IN 46781

FCC Amateur Radio Licenses in Portage

Call Sign: KC9ANX
Drennen J Gaffney
6802 Ava Ave
Portage IN 46368

Call Sign: AF9U
Drennen J Gaffney
6802 Ava Ave
Portage IN 46368

Call Sign: KC9ABM
Scott B Reel
45 Bass Dr
Portage IN 46368

Call Sign: KA9YSW
David E Foster
2925 Blake Rd
Portage IN 463682776

Call Sign: KC9MXC
Philip G Martin
3951 Bluebell St
Portage IN 46368

Call Sign: KC9PHE
Margaret A Schick
6148 Brie Ave
Portage IN 46368

Call Sign: W8MSN
Margaret A Schick
6148 Brie Ave
Portage IN 46368

Call Sign: KB9OYU
John J Schick Sr
6148 Brie Ave
Portage IN 463683654

Call Sign: W8OCG
John J Schick Sr
6148 Brie Ave
Portage IN 463683660

Call Sign: KC9KGB
Norman L Haskell
5471 Bruce Ave
Portage IN 46368

Call Sign: K9CAW
Norman L Haskell
5471 Bruce Ave
Portage IN 46368

Call Sign: KC9JHP
Joshua A Lloyd
5779 Bruce Ave
Portage IN 46368

Call Sign: KC9HWN
Kurtis M Lloyd
5779 Bruce Ave
Portage IN 46368

Call Sign: KC9HWO
Teresa L Lloyd
5779 Bruce Ave
Portage IN 46368

Call Sign: KC9KQC
Northern Indiana ARC
5779 Bruce Ave
Portage IN 46368

Call Sign: N9TUE
Earl D Williams
1448 Burns Dr
Portage IN 46368

Call Sign: KA9DLM
Elbert Fife Jr
512 Camelot Manor
Portage IN 46368

Call Sign: W9TUE
Robert W McKay Sr
1161 Camelot Manor
Portage IN 46368

Call Sign: KC9OYC
Richard A Eason
1302 Camelot Manor
Portage IN 46368

Call Sign: N9PR
Richard J Podolak
5717 Chapman Ave
Portage IN 46368

Call Sign: KC9JMZ
Dwayne Dobson
2918 Christy St
Portage IN 46368

Call Sign: WJ9Q
Peter L Lombardo
2943 Christy St
Portage IN 46368

Call Sign: WO9H
Don Frye
5076 Concord Ave
Portage IN 46368

Call Sign: WA9UPD
George S Romich
3040 Cooley St
Portage IN 46368

Call Sign: N9DLF
Thomas W Parent
126 Coral
Portage IN 46368

Call Sign: WD9GDC
James L Leighty
2716 Costello Dr
Portage IN 46368

Call Sign: ND9Y
Glenn E Yerby
2025 Crisman Rd
Portage IN 46368

Call Sign: N9YAC
Cruz Rosales
5096 Danube Ave
Portage IN 46368

Call Sign: N9RRG
Donald B Valenti
3042 Debra St
Portage IN 46368

Call Sign: K9RRG
Donald B Valenti
3042 Debra St
Portage IN 46368

Call Sign: KC9JHK
Eugene L Barksdale
2341 Dombey Rd
Portage IN 463681444

Call Sign: KC9JHM
Sarah A Manuel-
Barksdale
2341 Dombey Rd
Portage IN 463681444

Call Sign: KB9SFR
Mario Vasquez
2885 Edgewood St
Portage IN 46368

Call Sign: KB9OGV
John J Matta Jr
2746 Engle St
Portage IN 46368

Call Sign: KA9YBR
Kenneth D Dossett
5724 Evergreen Ave
Portage IN 46368

Call Sign: KC9IRQ
Lewis A Miko Jr
2504 Fern St
Portage IN 46368

Call Sign: AA9DC
Henry J Hansen Jr
2680 Hickory St
Portage IN 46368

Call Sign: W9HXO
August L Flassig Jr
75 Hill Crest Od 210
Portage IN 46368

Call Sign: KA9HNE
William F Kayes

87 Hillcrest Rd Ogden
Dunes
Portage IN 46368

Call Sign: KB4ZBX
Donald G Hoover
5099 Honeysuckle Ave
Portage IN 46368

Call Sign: N9TFR
Dennis R Gregory
173 Honeysuckle Trl
Portage IN 463684606

Call Sign: W9DRG
Dennis R Gregory
173 Honeysuckle Trl
Portage IN 463684606

Call Sign: KA4ACX
Harold W Shaw
516 Indigo Ave
Portage IN 46368

Call Sign: N9HRX
Catherine M Dranchak
2131 Jackson St
Portage IN 46368

Call Sign: NT9V
Edward Dranchak
2131 Jackson St
Portage IN 463682311

Call Sign: KJ9ED
Portage ARC
2131 Jackson St
Portage IN 463682311

Call Sign: WB9SER
George A Stewart
6319 Lake Wood Ave
Portage IN 46368

Call Sign: W9JZA

Gilbert G Galambus
3175 Lancer
Portage IN 463684496

Call Sign: N4YHC
David C Clark
2154 Landmark St
Portage IN 46368

Call Sign: KA9HWK
Keith J Heitmann
2128 Lapine
Portage IN 463681420

Call Sign: KB9EGD
Dave W Lasayko
6178 Lute Rd
Portage IN 46368

Call Sign: KC9KUD
Matthew D Lasayko
6178 Lute Rd
Portage IN 46368

Call Sign: KA9YAS
James M Smith
6218 Lute Rd
Portage IN 46368

Call Sign: NS9A
Jamie B Veiner
6218 Lute Rd
Portage IN 46368

Call Sign: N9JJH
Joseph R Drasich
3166 May
Portage IN 46368

Call Sign: KA9MNC
Lynne R Mahoney
5665 McCasland
Portage IN 46368

Call Sign: N9RJI

Scott S Gerrie
5520 Melton Rd 41
Portage IN 46368

Call Sign: KB9OCE
Michael A Truax
2784 Monnier Rd
Portage IN 463683425

Call Sign: KF9UB
Paul E Sosa
2739 Monnier St
Portage IN 46368

Call Sign: W9KOE
Richard P Zajac
6581 Monument Ave
Portage IN 46368

Call Sign: W9VQP
Robert F Sass
Ogden Dunes
Portage IN 46368

Call Sign: N9SZT
Deborah R Peterson
6070 Old Porter Rd
Portage IN 46368

Call Sign: N9SLQ
Deborah R Peterson
6070 Old Porter Rd
Portage IN 46368

Call Sign: N9SZS
Elisabeth G Peterson
6070 Old Porter Rd
Portage IN 46368

Call Sign: N9LL
William L Peterson
6070 Old Porter Rd
Portage IN 46368

Call Sign: N9IN

Portage ARC
6070 Old Porter Rd
Portage IN 46368

Call Sign: N9UNB
Ruby B Peterson
6070 Old Porter Rd
Portage IN 463681616

Call Sign: KC9TMS
Clarence A Miller Jr
6702 Old Porter Rd
Portage IN 46368

Call Sign: KC9HXG
Robert E Berquist III
2165 Pennsylvania St
Portage IN 46368

Call Sign: N9BTU
Edward W Liedtke Jr
2128 Pico Ct
Portage IN 46368

Call Sign: KA9SJX
Michael J Boller
129 Piney Bend
Portage IN 463684612

Call Sign: KB9EU
James K Prevo
Plaza Dr
Portage IN 46368

Call Sign: KC9BVG
Jerome S Ruschak Sr
2209 Poinsettia St
Portage IN 46368

Call Sign: N9ROC
Clifton R Leggett
6552 Portage Ave
Portage IN 46368

Call Sign: WB9UUP

Paul O Bell
6654 Portage Ave
Portage IN 46368

Call Sign: KB9QEA
Alex M Mulvihill
6922 Prairie Run Ave
Portage IN 46368

Call Sign: N9WEI
Bryan K Mulvihill
6922 Prairie Run Ave
Portage IN 46368

Call Sign: N9AEF
William R Davis
2561 Pryor St
Portage IN 46368

Call Sign: KY9Z
Kevin W Damerell
6826 Rio Grande Ave
Portage IN 46368

Call Sign: KC9QAM
Melvin J Riffett
6127 Robbins Rd
Portage IN 46368

Call Sign: KA9QAV
Robert J Szczudlo Sr
6473 Robbins Rd
Portage IN 463684575

Call Sign: WD9FYX
Darren A Duvall
2846 Russell
Portage IN 46368

Call Sign: N9TPF
Donald E Farris
2886 Russell St
Portage IN 46368

Call Sign: KA9REP

Virgil M Wozniak
2281 Sandwood St
Portage IN 46368

Call Sign: KR4CM
Thomas J Hollifield
5171 Sherwin Ave
Portage IN 46368

Call Sign: N9FKD
Ronald M Cutler
7006 Sherwood Ave
Portage IN 46368

Call Sign: N9WTR
John A Blumer
519 Sienna Ave
Portage IN 46368

Call Sign: KA9KIA
Marie R Baer
626 Sienna Ct
Portage IN 46368

Call Sign: KA9EFD
Allan E Lloyd
628 Sienna Ct
Portage IN 46368

Call Sign: K9SNQ
Northern Indiana ARC
628 Sienna Ct
Portage IN 46368

Call Sign: W9ZQE
Thomas W Tittle
60 Stagecoach Rd
Portage IN 46368

Call Sign: KC9DAX
Vernon H Podgorski
5747 Stone Ave
Portage IN 46368

Call Sign: KA9HJZ

Anthony F Altese
6355 Valley View
Portage IN 46368

Call Sign: N9QVH
John F Altese
6355 Valleyview Ave
Portage IN 46368

Call Sign: N9GAD
Alvin R De Lisle
6286 Victory Ave
Portage IN 46368

Call Sign: KF9CC
Robert J Boyle
2855 Vivian St
Portage IN 46368

Call Sign: KB8BUN
Charles T Moyar
3277 W Bend Dr Apt 105
Portage IN 46368

Call Sign: KA9OTI
Harold D Hilty
5180 Westchester Ave
Portage IN 46368

Call Sign: KA9FDV
Alan D Johnson
5230 Westchester Ave
Portage IN 46368

Call Sign: KB9WIP
Michael J Smith
2088 Whippoorwill St
Portage IN 46368

Call Sign: KB9DVD
John J Netherton
5944 Whispering Pl Apt 1
Portage IN 46368

Call Sign: N9ZZM

David A Trail
2019 Willow Creek
Portage IN 46368

Call Sign: W9JGH
Michael R Burdett
5675 Willowdale Ln 208
Portage IN 46368

Call Sign: KB9QWV
Ernest E Wilson
2145 Woodlawn St
Portage IN 46368

Call Sign: N9JAC
Jason A Clement
6292 Wyandot Ave
Portage IN 46368

Call Sign: KF4BWT
Aaron A Johnson
Portage IN 46368

FCC Amateur Radio Licenses in Porter

Call Sign: N9JDJ
John W Lane
216 Arrowhead Trl
Porter IN 46304

Call Sign: KB9NCE
Pamela S Tharp
1001 Babcock Rd
Porter IN 46304

Call Sign: KB9PFK
Aaron J Mullet
30 Burrwell Dr
Porter IN 46304

Call Sign: K9UHF
Edwin G Weimer
1020 Cardinal Ct
Porter IN 46304

Call Sign: N9ROK
Timothy W Savage
1160 Cardinal Ct
Porter IN 46304

Call Sign: KC9OYB
Samuel R Stemler
730 E Oak Hill Rd
Porter IN 46304

Call Sign: KC8DHP
Matthew D Walker
963 Eugene St
Porter IN 46304

Call Sign: KB9PFJ
Jacob B Donley
320 Indiana St
Porter IN 463041728

Call Sign: KB9TAS
Charles E Lawson
1330 Lawson Ln
Porter IN 46304

Call Sign: K9HKY
Charles E Lawson
1330 Lawson Ln
Porter IN 46304

Call Sign: W9LOZ
Jack Shepard
207 Michigami Trl
Porter IN 46304

Call Sign: KC9MCU
Donald H Puent III
218 Michigan St
Porter IN 46304

Call Sign: KB9KWO
Robert E Fulton Jr
221 Monroe St
Porter IN 46304

Call Sign: KA9WPH
Patrick J Abretske
1394 N Cloverleaf Rd
Porter IN 46304

Call Sign: N9WLS
John A Kugler
845 Pearson Rd
Porter IN 46304

Call Sign: KB9RWV
William A Dawson
1417 Port Cove Dr
Porter IN 46304

Call Sign: KB9ONS
Beth M Harris
809 Portage Ave
Porter IN 46304

Call Sign: KB7RTP
Barbara J Liles
333 Porter Ave
Porter IN 46304

Call Sign: N7ZFK
Samuel P Liles
333 Porter Ave
Porter IN 46304

Call Sign: KB7ZTY
Samuel P Liles III
333 Porter Ave
Porter IN 46304

Call Sign: KB9WAG
Todd M Waugh
500 Pottowatamie Trl
Porter IN 463041838

Call Sign: W9MED
Christopher E Curdes
262 Springwood Ct
Porter IN 46304

Call Sign: KC9ICN
Tristan J Deford
262 Springwood Ct
Porter IN 46304

Call Sign: K1EMT
Pamela A Curdes
262 Springwood Ct
Porter IN 463048826

Call Sign: KC9QPE
Benjamin M Fair
904 W Oak Hill Rd
Porter IN 46304

Call Sign: KA9DFH
Dolores A Slater
506 Wagner Rd
Porter IN 46304

Call Sign: W9KES
Kenneth E Slater
506 Wagner Rd
Porter IN 46304

Call Sign: KC9AWO
Brian D Erxleben
606 Wagner Rd
Porter IN 46304

Call Sign: KC9BJL
Nathan D Erxleben
606 Wagner Rd
Porter IN 46304

Call Sign: KB9FZP
Charles V Jones
1000 Waverly Rd
Porter IN 46304

Call Sign: KA9NFJ
Donald C Bender
390 Wood Lawn Ave
Porter IN 46304

FCC Amateur Radio Licenses in Portland

Call Sign: KC9LQY
Lester J Landers
4380 W 350 S
Portland IN 47371

Call Sign: WE9T
Lavon D Rds Jr
1105 Boundry Pike
Portland IN 473719190

Call Sign: N9UIS
Julie A Roll
Box 306
Portland IN 47371

Call Sign: N9QAY
Liza H Poole
Box 333A
Portland IN 47371

Call Sign: N9PXT
Timothy A Poole
Box 333A
Portland IN 47371

Call Sign: WB9RTO
Gerald E Jellison
Box 96
Portland IN 47371

Call Sign: KC9GRI
Aaron J Daniels
869 E 200 S
Portland IN 47371

Call Sign: N9AJD
Aaron J Daniels
869 E 200 S
Portland IN 47371

Call Sign: N9EVJ

Darrel J Bisel
596 E 300 S
Portland IN 47371

Call Sign: W9SNQ
Darrel J Bisel
596 E 300 S
Portland IN 47371

Call Sign: N9ERK
Randal D Dunmoyer
215 E 3rd St
Portland IN 473712505

Call Sign: KB9UMO
Todd S Miller
1763 E 400 N
Portland IN 47371

Call Sign: KB9MVI
Betty M Woolslager
709 E Arch St
Portland IN 473711615

Call Sign: N9EDJ
John J Woolslager
709 E Arch St
Portland IN 473711615

Call Sign: AA9OM
Darrell L Borders
869 E CR 200S
Portland IN 473719408

Call Sign: WA9BDS
James D Jacobs
1520 E Division Rd
Portland IN 47371

Call Sign: K9HAY
Marion C Bubp
816 E North
Portland IN 47371

Call Sign: AA9NT

Robert A Clamme
1423 E SR 26
Portland IN 47371

Call Sign: W9GKF
David L Peters
3585 E SR 26
Portland IN 47371

Call Sign: KC9GJS
Wabash River Repeater
Association
5126 E SR 26
Portland IN 47371

Call Sign: WA9JAY
Wabash River Repeater
Association
5126 E SR 26
Portland IN 47371

Call Sign: WB9QQB
Adrian K Daniels
5126 E SR 26
Portland IN 47371

Call Sign: WA9DAN
Adrian K Daniels
5126 E SR 26
Portland IN 47371

Call Sign: WB9VGA
Judith A Daniels
5126 E SR 26
Portland IN 47371

Call Sign: KD8BCB
David L Sparks
5929 E SR 26
Portland IN 47371

Call Sign: KG9GY
James E Chapman
3582 E Treaty Line Rd
Portland IN 47371

Call Sign: WD9CNA
Harold D Milthaler
421 E Water St
Portland IN 47371

Call Sign: N9VAL
Jerry W Wheeler
320 Elder St
Portland IN 47371

Call Sign: W9OAC
John B Warner
420 N Charles St
Portland IN 47371

Call Sign: KB9MVM
Jason R Woolslager
1112 N Franklin St
Portland IN 473711015

Call Sign: KC9GRJ
Donald D Green
614 N Harrison
Portland IN 47371

Call Sign: KC9GRL
Caleb D Rouch
532 N Western Ave
Portland IN 47371

Call Sign: N9HQF
David L Poole
209 Oak St
Portland IN 47371

Call Sign: KB9CFR
Keith A Green
213 Pittsburg Ave
Portland IN 47371

Call Sign: KB9UMH
John F Brigham
114 Rayburn Dr
Portland IN 47371

Call Sign: N9PTJ
Randall L Roll
4154 S 200 W
Portland IN 47371

Call Sign: AA9OM
Darrell L Borders
3168 S Boundary Pike
Portland IN 47371

Call Sign: W9PSS
Darrell L Borders
3168 S Boundary Pike
Portland IN 473718108

Call Sign: W9STG
Kenneth R Smith
3461 S Boundary Pike
Portland IN 473718109

Call Sign: N9WQV
Jeffry L Harker
447 S Meridian St
Portland IN 47371

Call Sign: K9UO
Robert E Sours
2949 S US 27
Portland IN 47371

Call Sign: KB9ATH
Marvin C Teel
5731 S US 27
Portland IN 473718959

Call Sign: N9EAM
Gary W Kelly
912 S Vine St
Portland IN 47371

Call Sign: KB9MVL
Michael J Woolslager
685 S Western Ave
Portland IN 47371

Call Sign: KB9KQB
Larry W Brown
210 W 100 N
Portland IN 47371

Call Sign: KB9OFG
Philip S Gross
5181 W 200 N
Portland IN 47371

Call Sign: KB9QVN
George A McGinnis
2327 W 300 N
Portland IN 47371

Call Sign: KA9AQL
Robert V Avey
2371 W 300 N
Portland IN 47371

Call Sign: KC9LYQ
Barbara A Landers
4380 W 350 S
Portland IN 47371

Call Sign: KC9CJK
Donald H Minch
2825 W 400 N
Portland IN 47371

Call Sign: KC9EVA
Susan K Minch
2825 W 400 N
Portland IN 47371

Call Sign: KB9KQC
Joyce A Landers
711 W 7th
Portland IN 47371

Call Sign: N9YXU
Jeff K Landers
711 W 7th St
Portland IN 47371

Call Sign: W9JKL
Jeff K Landers
711 W 7th St
Portland IN 47371

Call Sign: KC9IYQ
Jay County ARC
711 W 7th St
Portland IN 47371

Call Sign: W9JCA
Jay County ARC
711 W 7th St
Portland IN 47371

Call Sign: N9YBN
Priscilla J McFarland
721 W Arch St
Portland IN 47371

Call Sign: K9YXS
James A Cox
903 W Arch St
Portland IN 47371

Call Sign: K9ZHV
Charles D Turner
931 W High St
Portland IN 47371

Call Sign: K9VXH
Homer Evans Jr
440 W Race St
Portland IN 47371

Call Sign: KB9QVO
Francis G Betts
3351 W SR 26
Portland IN 47371

Call Sign: KB9UMK
Jack H Cullen
6317 W SR 26
Portland IN 47371

Call Sign: N9XQZ
Edwin J Friend
Portland IN 47371

FCC Amateur Radio Licenses in Redkey

Call Sign: KB9PPK
Byron A Daugherty
246 E Bell Ave
Redkey IN 47373

Call Sign: KC9NHV
John D Nixon
7045 S 1150 W
Redkey IN 47373

Call Sign: W9JDN
John D Nixon
7045 S 1150 W
Redkey IN 47373

Call Sign: WD9DCN
Richard L Henry
6767 W 500 S
Redkey IN 47373

Call Sign: KA9ENY
Virginia S Henry
6767 W 500 S
Redkey IN 47373

Call Sign: KB9UMM
Darrel P Kaufman
627 W Main St
Redkey IN 47373

Call Sign: KB9ZZG
James E Alberson
10642 W SR 28
Redkey IN 47375

Call Sign: KB9RPZ
Gary W Gillespie

11213 W SR 28
Redkey IN 47373

Call Sign: KB9FXH
Terry L Moore
8704 W SR 67
Redkey IN 47373

FCC Amateur Radio Licenses in Remington

Call Sign: N9FRU
Donald R Atkinson
Box 43
Remington IN 47977

Call Sign: KC9SCM
Daniel J Marin
524 N Iowa St
Remington IN 47977

Call Sign: KB9VFH
Amy L Black
13248 S 280 W
Remington IN 47977

FCC Amateur Radio Licenses in Rensselaer

Call Sign: WA9MSF
Homer V Taulbee Sr
Box 136
Rensselaer IN 47978

Call Sign: KC9ENG
Richard E Allison
603 E Angelica St
Rensselaer IN 47978

Call Sign: KC9HVT
Jasper County Amateur
Radio Group
603 E Angelica St
Rensselaer IN 47978

Call Sign: KC9GHO
Craig M Smart
1030 E Eger Rd
Rensselaer IN 47978

Call Sign: W9KDT
Paul R Goldsberry
414 E Maple
Rensselaer IN 47978

Call Sign: N9DAL
Thomas F Grzesik
5942 Fairway Dr
Rensselaer IN 47978

Call Sign: N9BVL
Larry A Clark
901 Kannal Apt 18
Rensselaer IN 47978

Call Sign: KC9KTV
James B Beckner Sr
3961 N 250 E
Rensselaer IN 47978

Call Sign: KC9NEB
Nancy S Beckner
3961 N 250 E
Rensselaer IN 47978

Call Sign: KB9THP
James K McEwen Jr
4401 N 250 E
Rensselaer IN 47978

Call Sign: AC7EX
Daniel J Blankenship
10858 N Fairway Dr
Rensselaer IN 47978

Call Sign: KB9ZHO
Austin W Ruuska
1113 S 850 W
Rensselaer IN 47978

Call Sign: KB9ZHN
Eric A Ruuska
1113 S 850 W
Rensselaer IN 47978

Call Sign: KC9JYY
Bradley W Mushett
5744 S 850W
Rensselaer IN 47978

Call Sign: KC9PHD
Will D Orchard
5267 S Airport Rd
Rensselaer IN 47978

Call Sign: KC9IBW
Robert L Peck
312 S McKinley Ave
Rensselaer IN 47978

Call Sign: KC9HJK
John C Baggerly
320 S McKinley Ave
Rensselaer IN 47978

Call Sign: KB9KNN
Brad L Wood
318 S Melville St
Rensselaer IN 47978

Call Sign: KC9RKM
Robert J Byrd
439 S Romaine St
Rensselaer IN 47978

Call Sign: KB9OGU
Harold W Williams
328 S Van Rensselaer St
Rensselaer IN 47978

Call Sign: AC9BG
David D Chesak
420 S Weston St
Rensselaer IN 47978

Call Sign: KC9JYX
Jerry D Flanigan
9467 W 100S
Rensselaer IN 47978

Call Sign: AB9VV
John C Shepherd
5452 W 300 N
Rensselaer IN 47978

Call Sign: WA1PLY
Robert R Murfitt
11358 W Bunkum Rd
Rensselaer IN 47978

Call Sign: KB9OQB
Rick L Flynn
216 W Clark St
Rensselaer IN 47978

Call Sign: N9BLK
Kenneth C Murray
640 W Fleming Blvd
Rensselaer IN 479783080

Call Sign: KB9KNO
David W Harsha
825 W Kannal Ct Apt 5
Rensselaer IN 47978

Call Sign: KB9RLL
Cindy A Pritchard
825 W Kannal Ct Apt 5
Rensselaer IN 479782786

Call Sign: KA9EWF
Marvin E Nesius
2225 W McCoysburg Rd
Rensselaer IN 47978

Call Sign: K9MEN
Marvin E Nesius
2225 W McCoysburg Rd
Rensselaer IN 479787297

Call Sign: KF9H
Edward R Cercone
424 W Vine St
Rensselaer IN 47979

Call Sign: KC9URV
Kumar
Kadimisettysatyasesh
891 Winding Rd
Rensselaer IN 47978

FCC Amateur Radio Licenses in Reynolds

Call Sign: KA9FGI
Geoffrey J Furrer
2358 W 50 N
Reynolds IN 47980

Call Sign: KA9DRR
Alvin J Furrer
2381 W 50 N
Reynolds IN 47980

FCC Amateur Radio Licenses in Roachdale

Call Sign: KB9YWB
Ivan T Deaton
9023 N CR 400 W
Roachdale IN 46172

Call Sign: KB9BQG
Lisa M Dews
9198 N CR 825E
Roachdale IN 46172

Call Sign: KJ4IRH
Matthew R Rose
4667 W CR 1000 N
Roachdale IN 46172

FCC Amateur Radio Licenses in Roann

Call Sign: KA9OVF
Andrew J Pfaffenbach
13504 N 700 E
Roann IN 46974

Call Sign: WD9EMM
Karel S Long
420 W Adams St
Roann IN 46974

Call Sign: W9JOO
Terry A Long
420 W Adams St
Roann IN 46974

Call Sign: KC9MZI
Daniel J Yocum
Roann IN 46974

FCC Amateur Radio Licenses in Roanoke

Call Sign: WA9CQU
Vernon V Allmandinger
1100N
Roanoke IN 46783

Call Sign: KB9OGF
Daniel A Hall
1200N
Roanoke IN 46783

Call Sign: KF9BK
Thomas E Shepherd
600W 90
Roanoke IN 467839001

Call Sign: N9ICI
Steve L Easterday
376 Aaron Corner
Roanoke IN 46783

Call Sign: N9AKF
Bart D Antonides
1140 Allen St

Roanoke IN 46783

Roanoke IN 46783

Roanoke IN 46783

Call Sign: WB9RAB
Raymond E Morris
3065 E 1000 S 92
Roanoke IN 467839222

Call Sign: WD9JFC
Michael C Brooker
16836 Feighner Rd
Roanoke IN 46783

Call Sign: KC9PAP
Owen F Wade
8556 N Mayne Rd
Roanoke IN 46783

Call Sign: WA9LXO
Thomas J Brewer
1921 E 1100 N
Roanoke IN 46783

Call Sign: KB9EUL
Matthew L Pinkerton
13135 Hamilton Rd
Roanoke IN 46783

Call Sign: K9YBU
James A Hartley
9745 S 500 E 92
Roanoke IN 46783

Call Sign: WA9LXP
Thomas J Brewer Jr
1921 E 1100 N
Roanoke IN 46783

Call Sign: KB9CJC
Ted L Pinkerton
13135 Hamilton Rd
Roanoke IN 46783

Call Sign: WB9IBE
Lee J Harvey
9109 S 600 E 92
Roanoke IN 46783

Call Sign: WB9YBZ
James H Emley
5900 E 1100 N
Roanoke IN 46783

Call Sign: KC9HOY
Lesley M Scholl Md
14727 Hamilton Rd
Roanoke IN 46783

Call Sign: KB9LYE
Deana G Harvey
9109 S 600E 92
Roanoke IN 46783

Call Sign: WB9YBY
Carl J Emley
5990 E 1100 N
Roanoke IN 46783

Call Sign: K1KLR
Lesley M Scholl Md
14727 Hamilton Rd
Roanoke IN 46783

Call Sign: N9GCS
Bill G Rogers
547 S Main St
Roanoke IN 46783

Call Sign: KB9BGW
Steven G Berrier
2081 E 1200 N
Roanoke IN 46783

Call Sign: W9FFT
James E Cox
11233 Kress Rd
Roanoke IN 46783

Call Sign: N9REM
George E Bowlin
10215 Snowy Owl Ln
Roanoke IN 46783

Call Sign: WB9VLE
Randy J Fisher
5105 E 1200 N
Roanoke IN 46783

Call Sign: N9XFC
Jeffrey S Moore
10476 N 400 E
Roanoke IN 467839441

Call Sign: N9UKH
Eric T Marshall
14330 Zubrick Rd
Roanoke IN 46783

Call Sign: KB9PCF
Robin M Berrier
2081 E 1200 N
Roanoke IN 46783

Call Sign: N9QZO
Alethea J Gilpin
6263 N 440 E
Roanoke IN 46783

**FCC Amateur Radio
Licenses in Rochester**

Call Sign: K9SSH
Max R Waggoner
100N
Rochester IN 46975

Call Sign: KA9PLU
Tim E Zehr
15015 Feighner Rd

Call Sign: KB9ORI
Todd A Gilpin
6263 N 440 E

Call Sign: KC8LCO
Bruce W Hess
100W
Rochester IN 46975

Call Sign: K9ZLM
Robert D Newcomb
1312 Bancroft Ave
Rochester IN 46975

Call Sign: KA9DEM
Gregory R Agnew
2129 Blvd St
Rochester IN 46975

Call Sign: KA9CNU
Marjorie A Tobey
Box 163
Rochester IN 46975

Call Sign: KA9CDL
Marjorie A Carrico
Box 362
Rochester IN 46975

Call Sign: KB9DRB
Emily M Erp
Box 423
Rochester IN 46975

Call Sign: KB9DRC
Linda L Erp
Box 423
Rochester IN 46975

Call Sign: KE4NDB
John J Pontius
905 Cherry Tree Ln
Rochester IN 46975

Call Sign: K9TRK
John J Pontius
905 Cherry Tree Ln
Rochester IN 46975

Call Sign: KC9BGK
Larry G Murray
500 Clay St
Rochester IN 46975

Call Sign: N9MTH
Sherry L Roberts
903 Clover St
Rochester IN 46975

Call Sign: N9GCG
Philip D Roberts
903 Clover St
Rochester IN 46975

Call Sign: KB9VWR
Charles F Greer
5467 E 650 N
Rochester IN 46975

Call Sign: KA9YQM
Rolland D Calvert
5655 E Race St Talma
Rochester IN 46975

Call Sign: WD9GYW
Dennis G Morin
5060 E SR 14
Rochester IN 46975

Call Sign: N9LOU
Brett A Shaske
1718 Gregory Farm
Village
Rochester IN 46975

Call Sign: KC9DKD
Robin M Dusley
916 Jefferson Ave
Rochester IN 46975

Call Sign: KA9RQC
Francis D Hughes
3180 Kent Dr
Rochester IN 46975

Call Sign: K9RQC
Francis D Hughes
3180 Kent Dr
Rochester IN 46975

Call Sign: KC9JFD
Cody M Cox
530 Lakeview Dr
Rochester IN 46975

Call Sign: KB9MEB
Nancy A Jackson
1708 Monroe St
Rochester IN 46975

Call Sign: KA9HYH
Gerald W Beattie Jr
3310 Monticello Rd
Rochester IN 46975

Call Sign: KC9JMH
Steven E Reese
1784 N 500 E
Rochester IN 46975

Call Sign: KB9ZHA
Ron E Bruner
3548 N 600 E
Rochester IN 46975

Call Sign: KC9OCI
James L Kerr
4676 N 600 W
Rochester IN 46975

Call Sign: KC9HUA
Terry L Porter
6940 N 600 W
Rochester IN 46975

Call Sign: N9ZNU
Benjamin L Greenwood
6147 N Elm Ln
Rochester IN 46975

Call Sign: N9ZNV
Sharon L Greenwood
6147 N Elm Ln
Rochester IN 46975

Call Sign: N9ZLS
Dean A Shinneman
6147 N Elm Ln
Rochester IN 46975

Call Sign: KB9QYS
Gary J Wyatt
5863 N Old US 31
Rochester IN 46975

Call Sign: N9JGV
James P Erp
6623 N SR 25
Rochester IN 46975

Call Sign: KA9RTD
Larry W Fisher
6586 N SR 2S
Rochester IN 46975

Call Sign: KC9BJY
Richard R Kowal
788 N Sweet Gum Rd
Rochester IN 46975

Call Sign: KC9JOR
Richard S O'Dell
104 Owl Dr
Rochester IN 46975

Call Sign: W9KLC
Raymond J Kerr
212 Pontaic St
Rochester IN 46975

Call Sign: N9CKD
Clifton J Wilkins
180 Pontiac St
Rochester IN 46975

Call Sign: KC9IXX
Roger M Olinger
212 Pontiac St
Rochester IN 46975

Call Sign: NN9R
Harold R Masterson
2199 S 500 E
Rochester IN 469757738

Call Sign: KC9CFG
Birch F Long
3385 S 75 W
Rochester IN 46975

Call Sign: N8HSN
Gerald R Jones
1271 S Appletree Ln
Rochester IN 469758175

Call Sign: KB9YQH
Russ Allen
6139 S Burch Ln
Rochester IN 46975

Call Sign: N9KQG
Gary C Donaldson
1074 S Hawthorne Ln
Rochester IN 46975

Call Sign: KF9KR
Charles G Azbell
591 S School View Dr
Rochester IN 46975

Call Sign: KC5UKZ
Donald W Meyer
1987 S Southway 31
Rochester IN 469758196

Call Sign: KC9TDZ
Larry E Sayger
4425 SR 25 N
Rochester IN 46975

Call Sign: KC9LAG
Carolyn S Waggoner
6264 W 100 N
Rochester IN 46975

Call Sign: W9NKC
Louis Van Doren
2939 W 500 N
Rochester IN 46975

Call Sign: N9DYN
James N Tobey
516 W 5th St
Rochester IN 46975

Call Sign: KC9HYV
William J Stokes
1165 W 9th St
Rochester IN 46975

Call Sign: K9ZHX
William J Stokes
1165 W 9th St
Rochester IN 46975

Call Sign: WG9D
Rickey E Layman
4556 W McCarty Ln
Rochester IN 46975

Call Sign: N8VZM
William A Bryant
4556 W McCarty Ln
Rochester IN 46975

Call Sign: KB9WSL
Ralph T Murray
1010 W Monticello
Rochester IN 46975

Call Sign: KA9HOL
James I Mathias
1084 W Monticello Rd
Rochester IN 46975

Call Sign: N9ZLT
Tami B Weeden
8100 W Olson Rd
Rochester IN 46975

Call Sign: KB9CAZ
Thomas J Long
4576 W SR 14
Rochester IN 46975

Call Sign: N9PVP
Lyman E Jones
1205 Wabash Ave
Rochester IN 46975

Call Sign: KG9KV
Larry E Himes Jr
1523 Wallace Ave
Rochester IN 469752313

Call Sign: W9ZLN
Phillip S Grau
1406 Washington St
Rochester IN 46975

Call Sign: WB9RLE
Myron E Alderfer
2321 Water View Dr
Rochester IN 46975

Call Sign: W9EOW
Charles R Green
2306 Wolf Pt Dr
Rochester IN 46975

FCC Amateur Radio Licenses in Rockfield

Call Sign: WD9GHZ
Norman C Been
Rockfield IN 46977

Call Sign: KB9JPX
Guy A Baker

Rockfield IN 46977

FCC Amateur Radio Licenses in Rolling Prairie

Call Sign: N9ZGW
Loren N Vermilyer
8088 E 200 N
Rolling Prairie IN 46371

Call Sign: KB9SIN
Carol A Vermilyer
8088 E 200 N
Rolling Prairie IN 46371

Call Sign: KB9LHG
Andrew W Crowl
8062 E 350 N
Rolling Prairie IN 46371

Call Sign: N9YSV
Timothy N Pilarski
6583 E Bootjack Rd
Rolling Prairie IN
463719581

Call Sign: N9RHR
Wendell R Magley
606 E Michigan
Rolling Prairie IN 46371

Call Sign: KA9IXD
Kenneth B Freeman
4976 E Robin Ct
Rolling Prairie IN 46371

Call Sign: N9ROG
Dennis P Wozniak
4475 N 350 E
Rolling Prairie IN 46371

Call Sign: N9YKS
Linda J Baginski
9425 N 600 E

Rolling Prairie IN 46371

Call Sign: KF9XS
Stanley E Baginski
9425 N 600 E
Rolling Prairie IN 46371

Call Sign: W9ESU
Robert C Eddy
2982 N 800 E
Rolling Prairie IN
463719425

Call Sign: N6ACP
William D Bradford
7642 N Emery Rd
Rolling Prairie IN 46371

Call Sign: N9LWD
Dennis E Houk
108 W Mechanic St
Rolling Prairie IN 46371

Call Sign: N9SWX
Penny S Houk
108 W Mechanic St
Rolling Prairie IN 46371

Call Sign: N9UOB
Tiffany J Houk
Rolling Prairie IN 46371

Call Sign: N9WZT
Larry A Cummings
Rolling Prairie IN 46371

Call Sign: KB9OIN
John P Loughnane
Rolling Prairie IN
463710188

FCC Amateur Radio Licenses in Rome City

Call Sign: N9QVS

Eugene K Knight
9869 N Eagle Island Rd
Rome City IN 46784

Call Sign: N9RVN
Paul C Philips
1030 W Pleasant Pt
Rome City IN 46784

FCC Amateur Radio Licenses in Roselawn

Call Sign: K9RNC
Benny E Devitt
Roselawn IN 46372

Call Sign: KC9QBL
Mark D Stanek
Roselawn IN 46372

FCC Amateur Radio Licenses in Royal Center

Call Sign: N9ONJ
Glenn D Gaddis III
CR 250N
Royal Center IN 46978

Call Sign: K9FOC
Philip L McDonald
7177 N 350 W
Royal Center IN 46978

Call Sign: N4YFD
Daniel M McDonald
7551 N CR 350W
Royal Center IN 46978

Call Sign: KV9N
Daniel M McDonald
7551 N CR 350W
Royal Center IN 46978

Call Sign: N9DZT

Wayne O Leach
4665 W CR 400 N
Royal Center IN 46978

Call Sign: KF9AB
Norman C Felker
Royal Center IN 46978

FCC Amateur Radio Licenses in Russiaville

Call Sign: N9JLJ
Daniel F Porter
100S
Russiaville IN 46979

Call Sign: K9FHQ
Donald K Lybrook
Box 26R
Russiaville IN 469799803

Call Sign: KA9GIO
Gary M McQuilling
4112 Honey Creek Blvd
Russiaville IN 46979

Call Sign: WA9DPO
Mary Jane Lybrook
380 Kinsey Apt 17
Russiaville IN 46979

Call Sign: KB9UUZ
Thomas A Grobengieser
950 Meadow Run Ct
Russiaville IN 46979

Call Sign: K9CK
Corwin L Kelly
430 N West St
Russiaville IN 46979

Call Sign: KC9IXZ
Wade J Pekarske
2849 S 500 W
Russiaville IN 46979

Call Sign: WX9LEE
Leon L Pearson II
3771 S 500 W
Russiaville IN 46979

Call Sign: KB9WRH
Susan E Muffley
4444 S 500 W
Russiaville IN 46979

Call Sign: KB9QOA
Fred A Aldridge
4314 S 580 W
Russiaville IN 46979

Call Sign: KB9SUR
Towana K Aldridge
4314 S 580 W
Russiaville IN 46979

Call Sign: KC9AEE
Max L Young
2642 S 700 W
Russiaville IN 46979

Call Sign: KB9RZE
Jay B Miller
3092 S 700 W
Russiaville IN 46979

Call Sign: KB9UFY
Curtis L Parker
1872 S 870 W
Russiaville IN 46979

Call Sign: N9YOZ
Anthony D Weber
2299 S CR 870 W
Russiaville IN 469799729

Call Sign: KB9BBZ
L Stephen Sciortino
4447 W 100 S
Russiaville IN 46979

Call Sign: N9SXZ
Roger Davis
9063 W 150 S
Russiaville IN 46979

Call Sign: W9JBS
Russell E Kelly
6019 W 160 S
Russiaville IN 46979

Call Sign: N9QGL
Chester A Moore
4167 W 180 S
Russiaville IN 46979

Call Sign: WB9ZDE
Arthur K Boe
3131 W 200 S
Russiaville IN 46979

Call Sign: KA9AKJ
Robert S Hulka Jr
8615 W 200 S
Russiaville IN 46979

Call Sign: KA7YMI
Patricia R Bryant
7545 W 233 S
Russiaville IN 46979

Call Sign: KB9WTD
Michael L Perry
9866 W 250 S
Russiaville IN 46979

Call Sign: KB9WRJ
Dahl M Perry
9866 W 2505
Russiaville IN 46979

Call Sign: K9JRE
William E Davis
5179 W 300 S
Russiaville IN 46979

Call Sign: KA9RCO
Teresa D Brewer
5719 W 400 S
Russiaville IN 46979

Call Sign: KB9ONG
Douglas E Aldridge
7962 W 460 S
Russiaville IN 46979

Call Sign: KB9ONH
Edie A Aldridge
7962 W 460 S
Russiaville IN 469799118

Call Sign: KC9NAM
Chris Cady
9146 W 500 S
Russiaville IN 46979

Call Sign: KC9NAC
Nancy Hopper-Cady
9146 W 500 S
Russiaville IN 46979

Call Sign: N9UKP
Ronnie N Arnett
11672 W 600 N
Russiaville IN 46979

Call Sign: KB9JTP
Jerry L Scott Jr
11385 W 600 N
Russiaville IN 46979

Call Sign: KB9JTQ
Vanessa V Scott
11385 W 600 N
Russiaville IN 46979

Call Sign: KG0GE
Michael B Shockney
380 W Chandler Lot 5
Russiaville IN 46979

Call Sign: KB9UBE
Shari L Shockney
380 W Chandler Lot 5
Russiaville IN 46979

Call Sign: KC9NNE
John W Sherman
380 W Chandler Lot 7
Russiaville IN 46979

Call Sign: KA9NPH
Joan Kelly
6019 W CR 160 S
Russiaville IN 46979

Call Sign: N9BFF
Gerald W Martin
8886 W CR 250S Rr 1
Russiaville IN 46979

Call Sign: N9EYH
Paul V Newport
6985 W CR 400 S R1
Russiaville IN 46979

Call Sign: KB9QNW
Charles A Rider
150 W Marshall
Russiaville IN 46979

Call Sign: WD9FZF
James R Sipes
Russiaville IN 46979

FCC Amateur Radio Licenses in Saint Joe

Call Sign: KB9GWK
Kathryn J Hoversland
6303 CR 51
Saint Joe IN 46785

Call Sign: N9MKA
Roger C Hoversland

6303 CR 51
Saint Joe IN 46785

Call Sign: N9LSV
Virgil H Stomberg
7832 CR 56
Saint Joe IN 46785

Call Sign: KA9QWE
Greg E Carnes
7380 CR 60
Saint Joe IN 46785

Call Sign: KA9ZJL
Wayne A McKean
6925 CR 62
Saint Joe IN 46785

Call Sign: N9NRS
Dirk Van Der Duim
6192 CR 64
Saint Joe IN 46785

Call Sign: KC9GUZ
Eric A Zerkle
307 Spencer St
Saint Joe IN 46785

Call Sign: KC9GRX
Katherine E Zerkle
307 Spencer St
Saint Joe IN 46785

Call Sign: KB9TXM
Sharilyn D Greenfield
5131 SR 101
Saint Joe IN 46785

FCC Amateur Radio Licenses in Saint John

Call Sign: KB9NIA
Janet E Pawlak
11835 105th St
Saint John IN 46373

Call Sign: WA8ZAZ
Cliff M Burns
9660 Acorn Dr
Saint John IN 46373

Call Sign: KA9CBH
Clarence P O Connor
9992 Belmont Ct
Saint John IN 46373

Call Sign: WB9WVD
Frank L Nagy
8509 Christopher Dr
Saint John IN 46373

Call Sign: KA9BCE
Paul D Ingram
8960 Columbia Ave
Saint John IN 46373

Call Sign: N9QVG
Lon S Baczkowski
8625 Fairway Dr
Saint John IN 46373

Call Sign: WD9HMT
Joseph L Payonk
9212 Kardel Dr
Saint John IN 46373

Call Sign: KB9YOY
Michael D Bond
10550 Knickerbocker Ct
Saint John IN 46373

Call Sign: KA9CMN
Norman S Warns Jr
8238 Knickerbocker Pl
Saint John IN 46373

Call Sign: W8GFG
Ralph D Kelley
9010 Marquette St
Saint John IN 46373

Call Sign: N9XWZ
John M Gervais
9260 Marquette St
Saint John IN 46373

Call Sign: KB9TXS
Gordon W Molenaar
8301 Meadow Ln
Saint John IN 46373

Call Sign: AD9U
John A Beatrice
9853 Northcote Ave
Saint John IN 46373

Call Sign: WD9EVN
Pam M Beatrice
9853 Northcote Ave
Saint John IN 46373

Call Sign: KA9GMB
Sandy A Ores
10157 Northcote Ave
Saint John IN 46373

Call Sign: KA9BOM
Kenneth L Ores
10157 Northcote Ct
Saint John IN 463739500

Call Sign: K9KO
Kenneth L Ores
10157 Northcote Ct
Saint John IN 463739500

Call Sign: KA9OWW
Arvin B Levin
10198 Olcott Ave
Saint John IN 46373

Call Sign: WB9NUG
Robert E Popiela
9040 Schafer Dr
Saint John IN 46373

Call Sign: N9UTT
Daniel L Offerman
12930 Snowberry Ln
Saint John IN 46373

Call Sign: WB9WHV
Carl G Miller
11303 Valley Dr
Saint John IN 46373

Call Sign: KA9CBJ
Walter J Kline
11338 Valley Dr
Saint John IN 46373

Call Sign: N9QKB
Robert F Lukes
11429 Valley Dr
Saint John IN 46373

Call Sign: KC9RTB
Robert J Rimkus
11931 W 103rd Ct
Saint John IN 46373

Call Sign: K9CRS
Robert J Rimkus
11931 W 103rd Ct
Saint John IN 46373

Call Sign: N9CR
Clayton E Ruth
8540 W 105th Ave
Saint John IN 463738615

Call Sign: KA9YNB
Wayne J Van Gilder
8580 W 105th Ave
Saint John IN 46373

Call Sign: W9QEF
John D Takish
10916 W 82nd Ct
Saint John IN 46373

Call Sign: KB9WZW
Timothy B Campbell
12325 W 85th Ave
Saint John IN 46373

Call Sign: KB9IPT
Louis E Gasper
12507 W 87th Ave
Saint John IN 46373

Call Sign: KB9WTO
Karen C Erwin
13724 W 90th Ave
Saint John IN 46373

Call Sign: KA9YLV
Chad L McClellan
13724 W 90th Ave
Saint John IN 463739305

Call Sign: K9MQ
Mark A Skowronski
8640 W 92nd Ln
Saint John IN 46373

Call Sign: KC9UAC
W9Aub / W9Puc Alumni
Group
8640 W 92nd Ln
Saint John IN 463739073

Call Sign: W9AUB
W9Aub / W9Puc Alumni
Group
8640 W 92nd Ln
Saint John IN 463739073

Call Sign: WD9GXN
Charles W Smith
9211 W Spring Hill
Saint John IN 46373

Call Sign: N9KCP
Michael A Smith

12051 Wildwood Dr
Saint John IN 46373

Call Sign: W9MAS
Michael A Smith
12051 Wildwood Dr
Saint John IN 46373

FCC Amateur Radio Licenses in San Pierre

Call Sign: KA9VRD
Daniel L Germann Jr
Box 23
San Pierre IN 46374

Call Sign: W9BHK
Richard W Bratton
12 S Webster St
San Pierre IN 46374

Call Sign: WY9J
Albert A Cox
355 Sandy Knob Dr
San Pierre IN 46374

Call Sign: WB9DPH
Raymond G Ledvina
10840 W SR 10
San Pierre IN 46374

FCC Amateur Radio Licenses in Schererville

Call Sign: W8UKW
David L Shanks
6817 73rd Ct
Schererville IN 46375

Call Sign: N9JWO
William J Fayta
1105 Auburn Meadow Ln
Schererville IN
463751381

Call Sign: KB9THY
Kevin N Krikau
201 Barbara Jean Dr
Schererville IN 46375

Call Sign: K9OTR
Martin J Dzik
412 Gregory St
Schererville IN 46375

Call Sign: AB9OH
Victor Vasilenko
54 Heather Ct
Schererville IN 46375

Call Sign: KC9EKX
Mark T Ernst
1031 Brooke Ln
Schererville IN 46375

Call Sign: WJ9Q
Martin J Dzik
412 Gregory St
Schererville IN 46375

Call Sign: KC9LKO
Aleksey Romanov
54 Heather Ct
Schererville IN 46375

Call Sign: N9CKR
Ilus C Wood Jr
127 E Elizabeth Dr
Schererville IN 46375

Call Sign: N0AQG
Harold G Snure
7820 Hanley St
Schererville IN 46375

Call Sign: WX0X
Zoran B Mladenovic
54 Heather Ct
Schererville IN 46375

Call Sign: KB9UOX
Mark E Butler
961 E Joliet St Apt 16
Schererville IN 46375

Call Sign: WD9JBB
Rebecca E Bailey
6927 Hawk Dr
Schererville IN 46375

Call Sign: AB9OD
Evangelos Gkekas
54 Heather Ct
Schererville IN 46375

Call Sign: KC9UZB
David J Pickard
940 Evergreen Ln
Schererville IN 46375

Call Sign: AB9OG
Evgeny Kuleshov
54 Heather Ct
Schererville IN 46375

Call Sign: W3FN
Evangelos Gkekas
54 Heather Ct
Schererville IN 46375

Call Sign: KB9CMG
Gregory N Markey
52 Gleneagles Dr
Schererville IN 46375

Call Sign: KB9WRP
Hranislav M Milosevic
54 Heather Ct
Schererville IN 46375

Call Sign: KB9EOW
Francine B Ryann
845 High Ridge Dr
Schererville IN 46375

Call Sign: KC9EOJ
Susan L Cramer
312 Golfview Dr
Schererville IN 46375

Call Sign: N9YU
Hranislav M Milosevic
54 Heather Ct
Schererville IN 46375

Call Sign: K9OXE
Albert C Stahnke
512 Iroquois Rd
Schererville IN 46375

Call Sign: KA4ZUI
Leslie M Crouch
7431 Greenfield St
Schererville IN 46375

Call Sign: AB9OE
Mladen Bogdanov
54 Heather Ct
Schererville IN 46375

Call Sign: N9OWW
Kimberly D Kozak
681 James Wittchen Dr
Schererville IN 46375

Call Sign: N9NEQ
Martin J Dzik
412 Gregory St
Schererville IN 46375

Call Sign: AB9OF
Roman Tkachenko
54 Heather Ct
Schererville IN 46375

Call Sign: WB9IRX
Gerald A Kozak
681 James Wittehen Dr
Schererville IN 46375

Call Sign: KC9CGR
Jesse D Browning
1424 Kennedy Ave
Schererville IN 46375

Call Sign: KB9QZD
George F Blush Jr
1839 Kennedy Ave
Schererville IN 46375

Call Sign: KC9JBK
David A Peterson
2243 Lori Ln
Schererville IN 46375

Call Sign: KB9DIR
Roy K Harrison
304 Maid Marion Dr S
Schererville IN 46375

Call Sign: W9KKL
Robert E Pearson
304 Maid Marion S
Schererville IN 46375

Call Sign: KB9HMR
Clyde Crutchfield
2231 Meadow Ln
Schererville IN 46375

Call Sign: WA9EMU
Joseph J Payer
1641 Michael Dr
Schererville IN 46375

Call Sign: W9ABN
Edward S Moskalick
5320 Mount Dr
Schererville IN
463753374

Call Sign: W8AG
Catalpa ARS
5426 Mount Dr
Schererville IN 46375

Call Sign: N8COQ
Kenneth R Barnes
5426 Mount Dr
Schererville IN
463753376

Call Sign: KC9HUL
Rick L Ward
7819 Mount St
Schererville IN 46375

Call Sign: WD9HXX
Timothy M Maksymczak
121 Mulerry Ln
Schererville IN
463751113

Call Sign: K9MNQ
Mark A Skowronski
2627 Naples Dr
Schererville IN 46375

Call Sign: N9AYZ
Richard F Devine
Newcastle Dr
Schererville IN 46375

Call Sign: WA9AKM
Paul W Muller
108 North Rd
Schererville IN 46375

Call Sign: KC9OKP
Kenneth A Barlo
4916 Oriole Ave
Schererville IN 46375

Call Sign: KB9YYA
Mark E Fullgraf
2216 Rde River Dr
Schererville IN 46375

Call Sign: N9SUB
Robert A Deakin

2323 Robinhood Blvd
Schererville IN 46375

Call Sign: KA9GLZ
Sam R Winer
301 Saint Andrews Dr
Schererville IN 46375

Call Sign: N9VMI
David R Olivencia
2011 Scherwood Lakes
Dr
Schererville IN 46375

Call Sign: KB9TXR
Mark E Hardig
1112 Schilling
Schererville IN 46375

Call Sign: N9GFU
James A Nemeth
1139 Schilling Dr
Schererville IN 46375

Call Sign: K9BH
Ira J Roberts
1148 Schilling Dr
Schererville IN 46375

Call Sign: KB9LHK
Courtney L Godsoe
652 Seberger Rd
Schererville IN 46375

Call Sign: N9ZDP
Stephen J Semeth Jr
1667 Selo Dr
Schererville IN 46375

Call Sign: N9ZDN
Michael A Mis
1907 Sherman St
Schererville IN 46375

Call Sign: KC9KEN

Michael A Huppert
920 Sherwood Lake Dr
Schererville IN 46375

Call Sign: N9FBA
Stephen J Arent
2120 Sherwood Lake Dr
11
Schererville IN 46375

Call Sign: WB9VRT
Bernard Baltrushaitis
436 Siebert Dr
Schererville IN 46375

Call Sign: W9NYO
Alfred E Seymour Sr
6948 Swan Ln
Schererville IN 46375

Call Sign: KC9DBT
Charles T St Clair
1925 Terri Ln
Schererville IN 46375

Call Sign: W9MRS
John M Hollis
4830 W 73rd Ave
Schererville IN 46375

Call Sign: KB9SIM
Robert L Hall
8803 W 85th Ave
Schererville IN 46375

Call Sign: N9MRQ
Edward A Bohney
12 W Joliet
Schererville IN 46375

Call Sign: KB9KXR
Henry J Blake
331 Whitewood Dr
Schererville IN 46375

Call Sign: KB9QHZ
John J Kocoj
1342 Willow Ct
Schererville IN 46375

Call Sign: KB9CBY
Benford R Frye
915 Woodhollow Dr
Schererville IN 46375

Call Sign: KD4CXG
Douglas D Kiser
Schererville IN 46375

FCC Amateur Radio Licenses in Shipshewana

Call Sign: W9EFA
Robert E Dillon
1470 N 500 W
Shipshewana IN 46565

Call Sign: WA9DRA
Harold J Knowles Jr
2120 N 675 W
Shipshewana IN 46565

Call Sign: KC9ENT
Devon J Lengaches
3325 N 675 W
Shipshewana IN 46565

Call Sign: N9YVT
Matthew A Yordy
935 N 740 W
Shipshewana IN 46565

Call Sign: K9EJZ
Robert E Pruitt
3585 N 900 W
Shipshewana IN 46565

Call Sign: WU9Y
Devon L Hochstetler

7245 W 200 N
Shipshewana IN 46565

Call Sign: N9EQL
Eli M Mast
7400 W 650 N
Shipshewana IN 46565

Call Sign: KB9FMZ
Andy R Keil
10935 W 805 N
Shipshewana IN
465659576

Call Sign: WA6HTU
Carroll W Brown
9780 W SR 120
Shipshewana IN 46565

FCC Amateur Radio Licenses in Silver Lake

Call Sign: KA9FDP
Robert L Moery Jr
Box 260B
Silver Lake IN 46982

Call Sign: N9MZY
Joseph B Slone
Box 95 SR 15
Silver Lake IN 46982

Call Sign: KC9EIM
David D Tofson
15887 E 375 S
Silver Lake IN 46982

Call Sign: N9TSB
Diane L Keel
208 N High St
Silver Lake IN 46982

Call Sign: KB9DQV
Medard H Murfin
202 N Jefferson St

Silver Lake IN 46982

Call Sign: K9BTV
Harold E Sensibaugh
Rr 2
Silver Lake IN 46982

Call Sign: KC9IXV
Daniel J Compagnari Jr
10256 S Edgewater Dr
Silver Lake IN 46982

Call Sign: W9ERP
Floyd R Rittenhouse
8929 S Hill Dr
Silver Lake IN 46982

Call Sign: KB9DQM
Jason A Schaefer Sr
5440 W High St
Silver Lake IN 46982

Call Sign: KB9DQL
Nancy A Schaefer
5440 W High St
Silver Lake IN 46982

Call Sign: N9IXI
Wesley L Schaefer
5440 W High St
Silver Lake IN 46982

Call Sign: KE6BIQ
Katherine A Kieper
3280 W Hilltop Ln
Silver Lake IN 46982

FCC Amateur Radio Licenses in Simms

Call Sign: KC9GKD
Richard W Cloud
203 W Howard St
Sims IN 46986

Call Sign: KC9VHT
Franklin C Dooley
108 W Taylor St
Sims IN 46986

Call Sign: WD9GRX
Franklin C Dooley
108 W Taylor St
Sims IN 46986

FCC Amateur Radio Licenses in Somerset

Call Sign: KB9JSO
Ruth E Lord
11 Maple St
Somerset IN 469840224

Call Sign: KB9JSM
Kenton M Lord
11 Maple St
Somerset IN 469840224

FCC Amateur Radio Licenses in South Bend

Call Sign: KF9BS
Thomas J Berger
54678 28th St
South Bend IN 46635

Call Sign: KB9BZL
Allen G Viduka Jr
518 30th St
South Bend IN 46615

Call Sign: W9MYI
George Allinger
710 31st St
South Bend IN 46615

Call Sign: WD9AQF
Richard L Mead
53196 34th St
South Bend IN 46635

Call Sign: W9AQF
Richard L Mead
53196 34th St
South Bend IN 46635

Call Sign: WD9AQF
Richard L Mead
53196 34th St
South Bend IN 46635

Call Sign: KC9MCH
Robert C Irish
18371 Abbot Ct
South Bend IN 46637

Call Sign: W9RCI
Robert C Irish
18371 Abbot Ct
South Bend IN 46637

Call Sign: W9PDF
Kenneth C Kuespert
5910 Aberdeen Dr
South Bend IN
466146382

Call Sign: KD7RLZ
Mark Little
22658 Adams Rd
South Bend IN 46628

Call Sign: KA9TOQ
Oscar L Fielder
1213 Alpine Dr
South Bend IN 46614

Call Sign: KB8LTV
Ernest Tetirick
711 Altgeld St
South Bend IN 46614

Call Sign: K9MZA
Allan S Varner
1312 Apple Ridge Ct

South Bend IN 46614

Call Sign: KA9MXX
Constance J Butler
2813 Appletree Ln
South Bend IN 46615

Call Sign: K9BQN
William N Butler
2813 Appletree Ln
South Bend IN 46615

Call Sign: KA9MXW
Harold E Brueseke
52741 Arbor Dr
South Bend IN
466351205

Call Sign: KA9YDI
Dan P Sumption
22676 Arbor Pt Dr
South Bend IN 46628

Call Sign: KC9GUG
Jeanne M Mahoney
22780 Arbor Pt Dr
South Bend IN 46628

Call Sign: KB3RTI
Georgia A Warrix
23001 Arbor Pt Dr
South Bend IN 46628

Call Sign: K9CJW
Candice J Warnke
23299 Arbor Pt Dr
South Bend IN 46628

Call Sign: N9UPW
Derek S Warnke
23299 Arbor Pt Dr
South Bend IN 46628

Call Sign: N9IOW
Thomas F Gustafson

1633 Arcadia Ave
South Bend IN 46635

Call Sign: KB9QOX
Ronald L Johnson
1434 Argyle Dr
South Bend IN
466143459

Call Sign: KB8OJH
Ethan L Blanton
19039 Auten Rd
South Bend IN 46637

Call Sign: NN9Q
Andre J Desrosiers
53051 Ba J Er Ln
South Bend IN 46635

Call Sign: KB9CXB
Carol A Saunders
1125 Belmont Ave
South Bend IN 46615

Call Sign: N9LHM
Brian L Hoover
1714 Belmont Dr
South Bend IN 46615

Call Sign: WD9FSK
James R Crawford
1238 Berkshire Dr
South Bend IN 46614

Call Sign: WB9MCU
Kingsley J Becker
1306 Berkshire Dr
South Bend IN 46614

Call Sign: K9KJB
Kingsley J Becker
1306 Berkshire Dr
South Bend IN 46614

Call Sign: KB9QYB

Robert E Wrzesien
748 Birchwood
South Bend IN 46619

Call Sign: N9ZNK
Duane L Boen
506 Blaine Ave
South Bend IN 46616

Call Sign: KC9GTO
Clarence M Blakley
537 Blaine Ave
South Bend IN
466161025

Call Sign: KA9EXC
Richard C Farkas
3216 Boynton Ave
South Bend IN
466153822

Call Sign: N9YIM
Andrew J Marshall
3126 Boynton Ave
South Bend IN
466153820

Call Sign: KB1AGA
William W Allen
52633 Brandel Dr
South Bend IN 46635

Call Sign: N9NPU
Robert O MacWilliams
20365 Brick Rd
South Bend IN 46637

Call Sign: KB9GFN
Joseph W Springstead Jr
23683 Brick Rd
South Bend IN 46628

Call Sign: KC9NWN
Douglas J Hazel
25641 Brick Rd

South Bend IN 46628

Call Sign: KA9DVC
John R P Northage Sr
26027 Brush Trl
South Bend IN 46628

Call Sign: WB9JXH
Robert W Pasternak Sr
2704 Buckskin Ln 34
South Bend IN 46628

Call Sign: K9VNV
Elden E Reinhold
141 Burbank Ave
South Bend IN 46619

Call Sign: K9RYJ
Clyde E Perkins Sr
18894 Burke St
South Bend IN 46637

Call Sign: KC9TLR
Brandon R Ludwig
1149 Byron Dr
South Bend IN 46614

Call Sign: KA9ZFJ
David R Bennett
1255 Byron Dr
South Bend IN 46614

Call Sign: N9WFZ
James L Yeager
1311 California Ave
South Bend IN 46628

Call Sign: K9GZR
Jack A Mathews
1446 Cambridge Dr
South Bend IN 46614

Call Sign: N9MML
Robert S Binder
1477 Cambridge Dr

South Bend IN 46614

Call Sign: WD4MSM
Barry P Keating
1839 Campeau St
South Bend IN 46617

Call Sign: KD9QF
Frank G Koloszar Jr
1329 Canterbury Dr
South Bend IN 46628

Call Sign: KC9GBE
Bruce Wukovits
5209 Canton St
South Bend IN 46614

Call Sign: KA9VKL
Cynthia S Antonelli
26310 Carol Lou Dr
South Bend IN
466199528

Call Sign: WB9QML
Nicholas L Antonelli
26310 Carol Lou Dr
South Bend IN
466199528

Call Sign: KC9PGP
Randy A Custard
1611 Caroline St
South Bend IN 46613

Call Sign: N9SLG
James M Snow
53344 Catalina Ct
South Bend IN 46635

Call Sign: N9VTE
Eric L Smith
1917 Catalpa St
South Bend IN 46613

Call Sign: W9FS

Jerry W Daugherty
1921 Catalpa St
South Bend IN 46613

Call Sign: K9IBW
William B Haselton
1238 Catherwood Dr
South Bend IN 46614

Call Sign: KC9UAD
Surasak Mainoi
1920 Charles St
South Bend IN 46637

Call Sign: N9UZN
Bradley J Ball
18343 Chaucer Ln
South Bend IN 46637

Call Sign: KC9NAW
William H Nash
1316 Chester St
South Bend IN 46615

Call Sign: K9FXV
Walter A Jaqua
1218 Chimes Blvd
South Bend IN 46615

Call Sign: N9VGJ
Brian M Burns
1226 Chimes Blvd
South Bend IN 46615

Call Sign: N9YSU
Jerry F Ryan
1845 Churchill Dr
South Bend IN 46617

Call Sign: KC9SMA
Christopher A Harman
17663 Cleveland Rd
South Bend IN 46635

Call Sign: W9EKK

George N Spillman
19053 Cleveland Rd
South Bend IN 46637

Call Sign: KB9YRY
Renee A Putman
3828 Clydesdale Dr 3B
South Bend IN 46628

Call Sign: KB9ILI
Robert M Vernon
1033 Colfax St
South Bend IN 46616

Call Sign: KE6BPC
Timothy J McGrath
1309 College St
South Bend IN 46628

Call Sign: KC9IHZ
Raymond W W Dalgliesh
4310 Coral Dr
South Bend IN 46614

Call Sign: KA9ZRW
Herschel L Hickman
624 Cottage Grove Ave
South Bend IN 46616

Call Sign: K9YCA
James A Sumption
55057 Country Club Rd
South Bend IN
466285603

Call Sign: WA9ND
Peter M Metcalf
18170 Courtland Dr
South Bend IN
466376014

Call Sign: N9LYS
James D Madsen
1825 Cross Creek Dr
South Bend IN 46628

Call Sign: KC9GJL
John W MacDonald
4340 Cross Creek Dr
South Bend IN 46628

Call Sign: KC9HXI
Thomas R Cook
60422 Crown Ridge Dr
South Bend IN 46614

Call Sign: W9LLQ
William E Ulbricht
18221 Crownhill Dr
South Bend IN 46637

Call Sign: NE9I
E Elliott Hood
5627 Danbury Dr
South Bend IN
466146023

Call Sign: KC9GVK
James E Doyle
17310 Darden Rd
South Bend IN 46635

Call Sign: KB9MFL
Gary E Wright
19499 Darden Rd
South Bend IN 46637

Call Sign: KC9PJT
Phil Nowak
19439 Detroit Ave
South Bend IN 46614

Call Sign: KC9MEC
Gene D Kaiser
913 Diamond Ave
South Bend IN 46628

Call Sign: KC9MQL
Rebecca M Kaiser
913 Diamond Ave

South Bend IN 46628

Call Sign: KC9EGC
Brendan E Krueger
1611 Dorwood Dr
South Bend IN 46617

Call Sign: KC9NAU
Jim W Connelly
1808 Dorwood Dr
South Bend IN 46617

Call Sign: KA9RGS
Frances Ganser
18532 Douglas Rd
South Bend IN 46637

Call Sign: K9IFX
William J Ganser
18532 Douglas Rd
South Bend IN 46637

Call Sign: WS9O
Walter E Beatty
19069 Dresden Dr
South Bend IN 46637

Call Sign: W9MCJ
Arthur G Bauernfeind
19600 Dubois Ave
South Bend IN 46637

Call Sign: KB9TGK
Harold D Sparling
1516 Dunbarton Ct
South Bend IN 46614

Call Sign: KB9ERP
Donald L Neely
20945 Dunwoody Ct
South Bend IN 46614

Call Sign: KB9KBX
James T Hurdt
901 E Altgeld

South Bend IN 46614

South Bend IN 46613

South Bend IN 46613

Call Sign: W9OEZ
John F Magerkurth
1728 E Altgeld
South Bend IN 46614

Call Sign: KB9ZVJ
Stephen G Huston
1717 E Calvert St
South Bend IN 46613

Call Sign: KC9IXN
Dean V Engle
34 E Dubail St
South Bend IN 46613

Call Sign: KC8HHC
Brett A Blankenship
1167 E Bowman
South Bend IN 46613

Call Sign: N9KAP
Nellie O Yoder
303 E Chippewa
South Bend IN 46614

Call Sign: KC9IXM
Sandra L Engle
634 E Dubail St
South Bend IN 46613

Call Sign: WH6ARF
James K Ahia III
1207 E Bowman St
South Bend IN 46613

Call Sign: KC9NAR
Alexander M Liby
2019 E Colfax Ave
South Bend IN 46617

Call Sign: KA9EXD
Mary P Koontz
713 E Dubail St
South Bend IN 46613

Call Sign: KA9EWP
Delcia M De Groff
1910 E Bowman St
South Bend IN 46613

Call Sign: KB9YMX
Micheal W Gillam Jr
231 E David St
South Bend IN 46637

Call Sign: N9YOU
Brian D Jennings
633 E Fairview Ave
South Bend IN 46614

Call Sign: KB9NWT
Bruce A Hunter
1930 E Bowman St
South Bend IN 46613

Call Sign: KA9REI
Paul R Clark
404 E Dean St
South Bend IN 46614

Call Sign: KB9ORX
Larry D Jennings
633 E Fairview Ave
South Bend IN 46614

Call Sign: WB9VRP
James E Miller
1631 E Byron Dr
South Bend IN 46614

Call Sign: N9NIW
Michael G Bird
1207 E Donald St
South Bend IN 46613

Call Sign: KC9NAD
Michael W Mccray Sr
637 E Fairview Ave
South Bend IN 46614

Call Sign: N9NSU
Patrick A Meeks
1145 E Calvert
South Bend IN 46613

Call Sign: KA9VIW
Matthew D Hunckler
1829 E Donald St
South Bend IN 46613

Call Sign: N9VCK
David L Batz
1156 E Fox St
South Bend IN 46613

Call Sign: K9HQO
Joseph E Bell
1125 E Calvert St
South Bend IN 46613

Call Sign: KB9STW
Nicholas R Orisich
1830 E Donald St
South Bend IN 46613

Call Sign: KC9PJZ
Konrad Badillo
1902 E Fox St
South Bend IN 46613

Call Sign: N9PGT
Marvin D Humerickhouse
1348 E Calvert St

Call Sign: WA9NJM
Nicholas R Orisich
1830 E Donald St

Call Sign: K9FLX
Konrad Badillo
1902 E Fox St

South Bend IN 46613

Call Sign: KC9PKC
Marcey L Badillo
1902 E Fox St
South Bend IN 46613

Call Sign: KC9PNM
Teodolfo S Badillo
1902 E Fox St
South Bend IN 46613

Call Sign: K9EUJ
Walter E Parker
2926 E Hastings St
South Bend IN 46615

Call Sign: N9GHJ
Ralph R Greer
529 E Ind
South Bend IN 46613

Call Sign: KC9UWI
Severt G Natvig
1216 E Jackson Rd
South Bend IN
466145919

Call Sign: N9HLA
John C Hooley
1826 E Jackson Rd
South Bend IN 46614

Call Sign: W9AB
Michiana ARC Inc
3220 E Jefferson Blvd
South Bend IN 46615

Call Sign: KC9GTY
John M Ross
801 E Johnson Rd
South Bend IN 46614

Call Sign: KB9ICR
Millard H Hill Jr

1015 E Madison St
South Bend IN 46617

Call Sign: W9CWE
John J Pine
209 E Marion
South Bend IN 46601

Call Sign: KC9FJF
Rachel M Timm
1709 E McKinley
South Bend IN 46617

Call Sign: KB9RNH
Greg E Cheak
801 E Oakside St
South Bend IN 46614

Call Sign: WB2QWR
George E Molnar Jr
217 E Pokagon St
South Bend IN 46617

Call Sign: KC9RPS
John M Lackman
1348 E South St
South Bend IN 46615

Call Sign: KA9IYR
Howard W Snyder
601 E Tasher
South Bend IN 46614

Call Sign: KB9BLD
Anthony D Young
1006 E Victoria St
South Bend IN 46614

Call Sign: KC9GPV
Edward N Russell
1211 E Victoria St
South Bend IN 46614

Call Sign: KA9VGV
Douglas F Mead

1238 E Victoria St
South Bend IN 46614

Call Sign: K9SMI
Douglas F Mead
1238 E Victoria St
South Bend IN 46614

Call Sign: KB9FZL
Paul V Bolger
1003 E Washington
South Bend IN 46617

Call Sign: KB9SY
Robert J Wolosin
1322 E Wayne St
South Bend IN 46615

Call Sign: KB9FBN
Nancy W Saunders
1507 E Wayne St
South Bend IN
466151331

Call Sign: KB9DLH
Richard G Saunders
1507 E Wayne St
South Bend IN
466151331

Call Sign: W9UKD
Lew W Ehresman
807 E Woodside Dr
South Bend IN 46614

Call Sign: KD7PVC
Steven J Kaniewski
1303 Edgewood Dr
South Bend IN 46616

Call Sign: W9YXX
Robert R Lee
19410 Edinburgh Dr
South Bend IN 46614

Call Sign: N9NDY
Jeffrey A Wallis
2726 Edison Rd
South Bend IN 46615

Call Sign: KB9QCE
Larry D Martin
26632 Edison Rd
South Bend IN 46628

Call Sign: WB9DFR
Thomas N Birdsell
17565 Eldorado Ln
South Bend IN
466351359

Call Sign: KB9MPZ
Robert A Kossakowski
17157 Ethel Ave
South Bend IN 46635

Call Sign: KC9IOX
William J Horvath
18245 Eugene St
So Bend IN 46635

Call Sign: N9FAS
John D Kubsch Jr
18290 Eugene St
South Bend IN 46637

Call Sign: KA9ZBQ
Linda S Moreno
932 Evergreen Ave
South Bend IN 46619

Call Sign: KB9QON
Deborah S Bickel
53901 Fairview Dr
South Bend IN 46628

Call Sign: N9KQD
Fred A Bickel
53901 Fairview Dr
South Bend IN 46628

Call Sign: W9EQJ
Darwin Mormon
18374 Farm Ln
South Bend IN
466374382

Call Sign: KC9DSC
Patrick G Gordon
61530 Fellows St
South Bend IN 46614

Call Sign: KC9RKL
Glenn G Brown Jr
625 Fellows St Apt 2
South Bend IN 46601

Call Sign: KC9GUF
John D Shaw
17304 Fergus Dr
South Bend IN 46635

Call Sign: KB9ZRV
Peter F Shaw
17304 Fergus Dr
South Bend IN 46635

Call Sign: WA9BJM
Carl D Tuveson Jr
928 Finch Dr
South Bend IN 46614

Call Sign: W9SBT
Carl D Tuveson Jr
928 Finch Dr
South Bend IN 46614

Call Sign: WA9PYH
James E Kocsis
53180 Flicker Ln
South Bend IN 46637

Call Sign: N9SNH
Ernest I Wroblewski
2531 Flint Ct 7

South Bend IN 46628

Call Sign: KA8JUN
Matthew J Honkanen
2218 Foxfire Dr
South Bend IN 46628

Call Sign: N1NHU
Frank E Lawrence
1606 Fremont St
South Bend IN 46628

Call Sign: KA9UZZ
Rick W Rish
55192 Glenn Rd
South Bend IN 46628

Call Sign: KC9IOW
John S Ames
55582 Grandview Ave
So Bend IN 46628

Call Sign: KC9KYC
Jeffrey M Nicholas
26237 Grant Rd
South Bend IN 46619

Call Sign: KB9TVH
Barry A Toth
60166 Grass Rd
South Bend IN 46614

Call Sign: K9FIJ
Allie A Jojo Jr
51405 Green Hill Dr
South Bend IN 46628

Call Sign: N9QEO
Millard H Hill Sr
62230 Greenbrier Crt
South Bend IN 46614

Call Sign: KC9IIC
June M Hill
62230 Greenbrier Ct

South Bend IN 46614

Call Sign: W9KFH
Donald W Yates Sr
61465 Greentree Dr
South Bend IN 46614

Call Sign: KC9LMC
Dean A Woodcox
22776 Grove St
South Bend IN 46628

Call Sign: KC9FOJ
Jeffrey G Breining
53230 Haddington Dr
South Bend IN 46635

Call Sign: W9OGZ
Robert G Kasa
27290 Harrison Rd
South Bend IN 46619

Call Sign: KB9SWQ
Bradley J May
27390 Harrison Rd
South Bend IN 46619

Call Sign: WD9ACP
James F Tisdale
1927 Hartman Dr
South Bend IN 46617

Call Sign: N9RXP
H Stephen Nye
3420 Hays Ct
South Bend IN
466142334

Call Sign: N9TJE
Kirk A McIntyre
19090 Helen Ave
South Bend IN 46637

Call Sign: KM9CQ
Kirk A McIntyre

19090 Helen Ave
South Bend IN 46637

Call Sign: N9UUD
Terry M Sholty
19090 Helen Ave
South Bend IN 46637

Call Sign: WA9BIG
Roy J Meilner
1316 Helmen Dr
South Bend IN 46615

Call Sign: KC9MQN
Roland A Antonelli Sr
727 Hickory Rd
South Bend IN 46615

Call Sign: WA9SIQ
Michael L Kauffman
52995 Highlands Dr
South Bend IN 46635

Call Sign: K9SIQ
Michael L Kauffman
52995 Highlands Dr
South Bend IN 46635

Call Sign: KC9LKE
Ted S Niespodziany
50988 Hollyhock Rd
South Bend IN 46637

Call Sign: KC9MHZ
Bruce A Hummel
51327 Hollyhock Rd
South Bend IN 46637

Call Sign: N9YYH
Craig B Francis
51724 Hollyhock Rd
South Bend IN 46637

Call Sign: KC9IRY
James G Shelley

52794 Hollyhock Rd
South Bend IN 46637

Call Sign: KC9NAT
Edward L Carrico
59341 Hollywood Blvd
South Bend IN 46614

Call Sign: N9FDR
Terri R Reynolds
2320 Hollywood Pl
South Bend IN 46616

Call Sign: KC9TCB
Edward J Bonczynski Jr
55193 Holmes Rd
South Bend IN 46628

Call Sign: N9YYF
Michael R Shaw
55310 Holmes St
South Bend IN 46628

Call Sign: KC9FGM
Cheryl A Schaeper
52855 Hound Trl
South Bend IN 46628

Call Sign: N9VDG
Mike P Wheeler
719 Howard St
South Bend IN 46617

Call Sign: AE6RV
Robert W Stewart
2115 Inglewood Pl
South Bend IN 46616

Call Sign: KB9IGL
Virgil G Jewell
17607 Ireland Rd
South Bend IN 46614

Call Sign: KB9KXV
Victor M Brulez

4010 Irish Hills Dr 2C
South Bend IN 46614

Call Sign: N9OFX
Jim I Hurst
4423 Irish Hills Dr 3C
South Bend IN 46614

Call Sign: KC9NAN
Kenneth J Andrysiak
4225 Irish Hills Dr Apt
1C
South Bend IN 46614

Call Sign: N9OJZ
Patrick H Predd
4244 Irish Hills Dr Apt
2C
South Bend IN 46614

Call Sign: KB9RSW
Paul I Watkins
Irish Hills Dr Apt 3D
South Bend IN 46614

Call Sign: N9DLP
Michael A Ciesiolka
20105 Jane St
South Bend IN 46637

Call Sign: N9IHV
Allan E Sikes
20336 Johnson Rd
South Bend IN
466145116

Call Sign: N9TJF
Mara L Lula
56771 Joseph Ln
South Bend IN 46619

Call Sign: WB9WXO
Ronald L Lula
56771 Joseph Ln
South Bend IN 46619

Call Sign: KC9TSJ
Stefan M Lula
56772 Joseph Ln
South Bend IN 46619

Call Sign: KC9GTM
Ivan D Snow
52621 Juniper Rd
South Bend IN 46637

Call Sign: WA9DTV
Ivan D Snow
52621 Juniper Rd
South Bend IN 46637

Call Sign: KC9HCQ
Robert A Streebel
19966 Kelly St
South Bend IN 46637

Call Sign: KB9WHM
Isaac P Howard
2126 Kendall St
South Bend IN 46613

Call Sign: W9HQ
Richard A Davis
52666 Kenilworth Rd
South Bend IN 46637

Call Sign: KC9MHV
Jennifer E Tobey
19181 Kern Rd
South Bend IN 46614

Call Sign: W9YME
Kenneth A Tyson
19329 Kern Rd
South Bend IN 46614

Call Sign: KA9WNR
Robert L Denniston
21970 Kern Rd

South Bend IN
466149295

Call Sign: KC9IXQ
Eric M Mammolenti
22155 Kern Rd
South Bend IN 46614

Call Sign: KB9MT
Douglas L Neumann
22175 Kern Rd
South Bend IN
466149244

Call Sign: KB9HAV
Joan Z Madsen
1301 Kessler Pl
South Bend IN 46616

Call Sign: N9AIU
Robert S De Buysser
2713 Kettering Dr
South Bend IN 46635

Call Sign: KC9TSK
Benjamin J Monges
63833 Kingsway Ct
South Bend IN 46614

Call Sign: KC9TSL
Charlene V Monges
63833 Kingsway Ct
South Bend IN 46614

Call Sign: KC9ETP
John R Marshall
3836 Langley
South Bend IN 46614

Call Sign: KC9UTD
Lloyd R Matthews Jr
3544 Langley Dr
South Bend IN 46614

Call Sign: WB9AGX

Saint Joseph County Ema
4714 Lathrop St
South Bend IN 46628

Call Sign: KA9OUX
Charles R McGinnis Jr
59701 Lee Rd
South Bend IN 46614

Call Sign: N9NRZ
Andrew Chmielowiec
51115 Lilac Rd
South Bend IN 46628

Call Sign: AA9WQ
Larry L Yaw
52535 Lilac Rd
South Bend IN 46628

Call Sign: W9AMR
Larry L Yaw
52535 Lilac Rd
South Bend IN 46628

Call Sign: N9DX
Lawrence J Higgins
52757 Lilac Rd
South Bend IN 46628

Call Sign: N9VRZ
Dean R De Vries
51138 Lily Rd
South Bend IN 46637

Call Sign: KC9IOV
Michael W Kopec
1819 Lincoln Way W
South Bend IN 46628

Call Sign: KA9TWK
Wayne M Kopec
1819 Lincoln Way W
South Bend IN 46628

Call Sign: KB9HGF

Jason R Lula
25853 Little Fox Trl
South Bend IN 46628

Call Sign: N9KYL
Norma K Miller
61734 Locust Rd
South Bend IN 46614

Call Sign: N9TUD
Lloyd R Matthews Jr
62430 Locust Rd Lot 74
South Bend IN
466149795

Call Sign: KC9MIF
Mike J Padberg
21200 London Plane Ct
South Bend IN 46614

Call Sign: KB9DTL
Brian K Le Baron
301 Luelde St
South Bend IN 46614

Call Sign: W9ART
Arthur D Visser
306 Luelde St
South Bend IN 46614

Call Sign: W9WWW
Arthur D Visser
306 Luelde St
South Bend IN 46614

Call Sign: W9ART
Arthur D Visser
306 Luelde St
South Bend IN 46614

Call Sign: N9RIE
Lucinda L Visser
306 Luelde St
South Bend IN 46614

Call Sign: KB9SFW
Michael D Warren
311 Luelde St
South Bend IN 46614

Call Sign: KC9IIB
Andrew P Byers
2526 MacArthur Blvd
South Bend IN 46615

Call Sign: W7KUM
Arthur A Ullery
16901 Madison Rd
South Bend IN 46614

Call Sign: N9EJQ
Robert G Yates
22285 Madison Rd
South Bend IN 46614

Call Sign: KO9H
Eugene L Runyan
1525 Madora St
South Bend IN 46628

Call Sign: N9GCX
Mary L Runyan
1525 Madora St
South Bend IN 46628

Call Sign: KA9EKA
Junior E Bradshaw
4135 Manor Dr
South Bend IN 46614

Call Sign: WD9FSW
Lillian M Bradshaw
4135 Manor Dr
South Bend IN 46614

Call Sign: KC9QYG
Rocky L Baisden
3029 Maple Hilll Ct
South Bend IN 46628

Call Sign: WB9WSJ
Roland L Seguin
5024 May Fair Pl
South Bend IN 46619

Call Sign: KC9IXR
Carol J Rowland
1001 Mayflower Rd
South Bend IN 46619

Call Sign: WA9WQG
Earl D Smith
2705 Miami
South Bend IN 46614

Call Sign: AA9AM
Eugene M Myers Jr
6450 Miami Cir
South Bend IN 46614

Call Sign: N1OUL
Raymond G Rushing
61527 Miami Meadows
Ct
South Bend IN 46614

Call Sign: KB9FWN
David R Anderson Sr
5914 Miami Rd
South Bend IN 46614

Call Sign: W9RKE
Norman B Melick
63951 Miami Rd
South Bend IN 46614

Call Sign: N9OBZ
Philip R Melick
63951 Miami Rd
South Bend IN 46614

Call Sign: KC9JFF
Jonathan Sloman
2405 Miami St
South Bend IN 46614

Call Sign: KC9JFK
Renee R Sloman
2405 Miami St
South Bend IN 46614

Call Sign: N9WAH
Timothy M Cherrone
3929 Miami St
South Bend IN 46614

Call Sign: N9HGZ
Ron R Campbell
3010 Mishawaka Ave
South Bend IN
466152348

Call Sign: KC9UMD
Adam C Warner
3843 Morgan St Apt 3 A
South Bend IN 46628

Call Sign: KJ9J
Newton F Straup
55194 Moss Rd
South Bend IN
466285203

Call Sign: KC9NAO
Mike W Lewis
55298 Moss Rd
So Bend IN 46628

Call Sign: WA9KGR
Edward D Borowski
52196 Myrtle Ave
South Bend IN 46637

Call Sign: KA9SCP
Randall K Spicher
61801 Myrtle Ave
South Bend IN 46614

Call Sign: N9TRE
Alfred L Lemmon II

2021 N Brookfield
South Bend IN 46628

Call Sign: N9UZK
Therese A Sarah
2021 N Brookfield St
South Bend IN 46601

Call Sign: KA9TWI
Richard L Mcclure
217 N Burbank
South Bend IN 46619

Call Sign: W9KWC
William J Stogdill
520 N Coquillard
South Bend IN 46617

Call Sign: N9LHN
Martyn J Ballestero
1415 N Elmer St
South Bend IN 46628

Call Sign: KC9AGS
Kirkland B Stewart Jr
1757 N Fremont St
South Bend IN
466283102

Call Sign: WB9SSJ
Allen J Wujcik
1623 N Illinois St
South Bend IN 46628

Call Sign: W9BJ
Burton Jaffe
1105 N Ironwood Dr
South Bend IN 46615

Call Sign: KC9CAU
Christopher M Smith
1318 N Meade St
South Bend IN 46628

Call Sign: KC9GUB

Terry L Smith
300 N Michigan St
South Bend IN 46601

Call Sign: N9MAL
Kevin P Six
2124 N Olive St
South Bend IN 46628

Call Sign: KC2KFK
Wayne C Smith
420 N Walnut St
South Bend IN 46628

Call Sign: KC9GUI
Mark A Hockaday
53222 Nadine St
South Bend IN 46637

Call Sign: K9CLM
Kathryn Colten
3910 Nall Ct
South Bend IN 46614

Call Sign: W9CZI
Jerrold L Colten
3910 Nall Ct
South Bend IN
466142313

Call Sign: N9WKT
Daniel P Armstrong
1534 Nash St
South Bend IN 46613

Call Sign: KC9NAI
David A Hamilton
3524 Northside Blvd
South Bend IN 46615

Call Sign: N9YJQ
Danny W Duke
3018 Norway Maple Ct
South Bend IN 46628

Call Sign: KB9ZRY
Ronald A Delaere
1735 Oak Park Dr
South Bend IN 46617

Call Sign: N9CWI
Philip D Halasz
62154 Oak Rd
South Bend IN 46614

Call Sign: KC9RPN
Dale W West Jr
62323 Oak Rd
South Bend IN 46614

Call Sign: KC9FGL
Sarah A Clauser
63934 Oak Rd
South Bend IN 46614

Call Sign: N9DKT
Gertrude R Kerger
53190 Oakmont Central
Dr
South Bend IN
466373515

Call Sign: KB9CY
Robert E Kerger
53190 Oakmont Central
Dr
South Bend IN
466373515

Call Sign: WB9KDW
Richard A Wachs
1221 Oakridge Dr
South Bend IN 46617

Call Sign: KC9UWG
Nathan J Ladwig
53080 Oakton Dr
South Bend IN 46635

Call Sign: KB9KFY

Nicholas J Carlo
63006 Orange Rd
South Bend IN 46614

Call Sign: WA9GOP
Melvin H Dzialak
63280 Orange Rd
South Bend IN 46614

Call Sign: KA9DIG
Charles J Vance
19387 Orchard
South Bend IN 46637

Call Sign: W9NRV
John W Hanson
19459 Orchard St
South Bend IN 46637

Call Sign: KB9BIT
Thomas M Laskowski
3420 Oxford Ln
South Bend IN
466153737

Call Sign: KB9IYR
Anthony G Van
Himbergen
25683 Pack Trl
South Bend IN 46628

Call Sign: AB9NJ
Anthony G
Vanhimbergen
25683 Pack Trl
South Bend IN 46628

Call Sign: KB8YHP
William R Read Jr
3804 Palomino Cir Apt
3A
South Bend IN 46628

Call Sign: N9VFO
Russell L Duckwall

58491 Pam Dr
South Bend IN 46619

Call Sign: AA9RD
Russell L Duckwall
58491 Pam Dr
South Bend IN 46619

Call Sign: KC9GTN
Edward P Benchik
626 Park Ave
South Bend IN 46616

Call Sign: KB9QOW
Andy T Evans
527 Parry St
South Bend IN 46617

Call Sign: KA9RIT
Marcus E Bartz
2109 Peachtree Ln
South Bend IN 46617

Call Sign: KC9ADR
Troy E Dewey
58045 Pear Rd
South Bend IN 46619

Call Sign: KC9TSI
Michael P Downs
57302 Peggy Dr
South Bend IN 46619

Call Sign: KC9ZRT
Michael P Downs
57302 Peggy Dr
South Bend IN 46619

Call Sign: KC9RPK
Zuolei Liao
19303 Pendle Rd
South Bend IN 46637

Call Sign: W9WCE
John G Kuespert

56262 Peppermint Rd
South Bend IN 46619

Call Sign: N9PFX
Charles G Koczan III
25013 Pin Oak Dr
South Bend IN 46614

Call Sign: KC9AEY
Robert L Wood
56281 Pine Rd
South Bend IN 46619

Call Sign: KC9KYN
Theodore G Johnson
57360 Pine Rd
South Bend IN 46619

Call Sign: KI4JHA
Ward L Kremer
57262 Poppy Rd
South Bend IN
466199775

Call Sign: KB9BFI
Geoffrey C Nieboer
1943 Portage Ave
South Bend IN 46616

Call Sign: K9KCN
Kourtney C Nieboer
1943 Portage Ave
South Bend IN 46616

Call Sign: KB9NND
Thomas L Hadrick
2608 Powder Horn
South Bend IN 46628

Call Sign: W9SMW
Paul P Stockinger
3114 Prairie Ave
South Bend IN 46614

Call Sign: KB9QCD

Ronald A Wood Sr
51226 Prescott Av
South Bend IN 46637

Call Sign: KB1LVX
Zachariah Silver
422 Preston Dr
South Bend IN
466153326

Call Sign: W9DGP
Edwin Gonter Jr
534 Preston Dr
South Bend IN
466153328

Call Sign: W8KKJ
Vernon M Daly Sr
4310 Queens Row Apt A
South Bend IN 46637

Call Sign: KB9MHZ
Charles R Wigent
54657 Quince Rd
South Bend IN 46628

Call Sign: KB9YGA
Joseph R Wojtasik
54678 Quince Rd
South Bend IN 46628

Call Sign: N9UUI
Robert P Wojtasik
54678 Quince Rd
South Bend IN
466284524

Call Sign: WA1NXL
Allen R Gale
3116 Red Maple Ct
South Bend IN
466283708

Call Sign: WA9S
Charles K Wishmeier

1834 Ribourde Dr
South Bend IN 46628

Call Sign: KB9KUJ
Paul A Klockow
51310 Righter Ln
South Bend IN
466289679

Call Sign: KB9KRW
Roland A Klockow
51310 Righter Ln
South Bend IN
466289679

Call Sign: N5JYU
Tony J Lala
524 River Ave
South Bend IN 46601

Call Sign: N9JCZ
Joseph J Taschetta
1029 Riverside Dr
South Bend IN
466161402

Call Sign: K9KBR
Joseph J Taschetta
1029 Riverside Dr
South Bend IN
466161402

Call Sign: K9IXT
Betty J Werts
1889 Riverside Dr
South Bend IN 46616

Call Sign: N9ZZR
James R Lupa
2029 Riverside Dr
South Bend IN 46616

Call Sign: N9LJI
Robert E Brown
3821 Riverside Dr

South Bend IN 46628

Call Sign: W1EEP
Hiroshi C Bowman
1667 Riverside Dr Apt C
South Bend IN
466161636

Call Sign: AB9UI
Hiroshi C Bowman
1667 Riverside Dr Apt C
South Bend IN
466161636

Call Sign: KC9DZH
James J Bettcher
1624 Rockne Dr
South Bend IN 46617

Call Sign: KC9LKD
Larry Marosz
1355 Roelke Dr
South Bend IN 46614

Call Sign: KB9GP
Stephen Elek Jr
20087 Roosevelt Rd
South Bend IN
466145026

Call Sign: ND9O
Stephen Elek Jr
20087 Roosevelt Rd
South Bend IN
466145026

Call Sign: NY9G
Milford G Billhimer
21400 Roosevelt Rd
South Bend IN
466144828

Call Sign: KC9QZZ
Mark F Chabot
23564 Roosevelt Rd

South Bend IN 46614

Call Sign: WB0ZPQ
Doyle A Bush
25020 Roosevelt Rd
South Bend IN 46614

Call Sign: WB0ZRA
Doyle E Bush
25020 Roosevelt Rd
South Bend IN 46614

Call Sign: AB9UL
Benson R Mitchell
1430 Rosemary Ln Apt B
South Bend IN 46637

Call Sign: KC9MHX
Yan He
1440 Rosemary Ln Apt E
South Bend IN 46637

Call Sign: N9CHV
George E Hollis
3914 Roxbury Plz
South Bend IN 46628

Call Sign: KC9GTU
Stellus R Pereira
3026 Rue Montesquieu
Apt 2204
South Bend IN 46615

Call Sign: N9SAA
Munesh G Makhija
3120 Rue Renoir Apt 208
South Bend IN 46615

Call Sign: N9WXD
Troy E Leiter
941 S 23rd St
South Bend IN 46615

Call Sign: N9VPB
Dennis D Freeman

524 S 25th St
South Bend IN 46615

Call Sign: KC9MCG
Michael L Morrison
602 S 25th St
South Bend IN 46615

Call Sign: NY9A
Alan B Seifert
705 S 25th St
South Bend IN 46615

Call Sign: KB9INT
Reda J Seifert
705 S 25th St
South Bend IN 46615

Call Sign: KC9KEA
Tony J Lala
919 S 25th St
South Bend IN 46615

Call Sign: KA9GDX
Richard L Spicer
1009 S 26th St
South Bend IN
466151717

Call Sign: KA9IYU
Stephen H Rippey
609 S 27th St
South Bend IN 46615

Call Sign: N9NYH
Jerry D Boyer Sr
810 S 27th St
South Bend IN 46615

Call Sign: K9EMS
Jamie R Borders
717 S 28th St
South Bend IN 46615

Call Sign: KI4YXL

Jason M Bray
1114 S 28th St
South Bend IN 46615

Call Sign: KC9CYI
James J Scott
837 S 29th St
South Bend IN 46615

Call Sign: KC9DZI
Graham D Troyer
842 S 29th St
South Bend IN 46615

Call Sign: KB9BBK
Randy W Viduka
518 S 30th St
South Bend IN 46615

Call Sign: KB9LTS
Dennis R Whittaker
1012 S 30th St
South Bend IN 46615

Call Sign: K6TEX
James D Dees
1233 S 31st St
South Bend IN 46615

Call Sign: KC9LYG
Richard H Allriedge
1302 S 32nd St
South Bend IN 46615

Call Sign: KC9IXP
Keith A Barker
713 S 33rd St
South Bend IN 46615

Call Sign: KB9OIP
Lisa L Ciastko
806 S 33rd St
South Bend IN
466152323

Call Sign: WB9OYL
Dennis A Niemier
813 S 33rd St
South Bend IN 46615

Call Sign: K9AIM
Edward H Richmond
829 S 33rd St
South Bend IN 46615

Call Sign: N9NRY
Timothy L Fye
942 S 34th St
South Bend IN 46615

Call Sign: N9OVI
Charles R Babbitt
1014 S 34th St
South Bend IN 46617

Call Sign: KC9NIV
Dawn M Kemble
606 S 36 St
South Bend IN 46615

Call Sign: KE9BR
Ricky A Hollar
1338 S Bend Ave
South Bend IN 46617

Call Sign: WA9UIM
John M Rosenbaum
2043 S Bend Ave Box
193
South Bend IN
466375642

Call Sign: K9ATR
Milton E Gibson
5707 S Bridgeton Ln
South Bend IN 46614

Call Sign: K9MNF
Frederick A Jones
2218 S Catalpa Ave

South Bend IN 46613

Call Sign: N9JMH
Jeff A Mais
2211 S Chapin
South Bend IN 46613

Call Sign: KC9PRI
Kurt R Sells
18622 S Cypress Cir
South Bend IN 46637

Call Sign: N9ZSX
Richard L Motz
1810 S Douglas
South Bend IN 46613

Call Sign: N9ZSU
Trell M Schlundt
1717 S Douglas St
South Bend IN 46613

Call Sign: W9LPD
Frank J Giszewski
2211 S Douglas St
South Bend IN 46613

Call Sign: N9FMH
Nona S Binder
738 S Dundee St
South Bend IN 46619

Call Sign: N8FQC
Douglas C Hall
127 S Ellsworth Pl
South Bend IN 46617

Call Sign: KB9GBD
Tony J Kuzmits
3728 S Fellows St
South Bend IN 46614

Call Sign: W9MWY
Virgil E Dunkin
4131 S Fellows St

South Bend IN 46614

Call Sign: N9JDB
Michael J Detlef
114 S Holiday Dr
South Bend IN 46615

Call Sign: N9EWL
Stephen Pajor
3602 S Ironwood Dr Apt
172E
South Bend IN 46614

Call Sign: KB9WQB
Bradford A Haimbaugh
718 S Lake St
South Bend IN 46619

Call Sign: KC9NZ
Jefferson T Rans
837 S Logan St
South Bend IN 46615

Call Sign: N9WAK
Jerry A Sherwood
902 S Lombardy Dr
South Bend IN
466194133

Call Sign: KC9KYJ
Michael P Morris
3885 S Main St
South Bend IN 46614

Call Sign: KB9RQT
Raymond D Miller
1001 S Mayflower 389
South Bend IN 46619

Call Sign: KC9RPJ
Robert G Ross
1001 S Mayflower Rd
Lot 267
South Bend IN 46619

Call Sign: W9RGR
Robert G Ross
1001 S Mayflower Rd
Lot 267
South Bend IN 46619

Call Sign: KB9DBZ
John T Hartman
2810 S Michigan St
South Bend IN 46614

Call Sign: KB9TVI
Mark D Straup
2822 S Michigan St
South Bend IN 46614

Call Sign: N9TAG
Jack R Styles Jr
211 S Michigan St Apt
608
South Bend IN 46601

Call Sign: WA9GOH
Charles A Hemenway
1830 S Pulaski St
South Bend IN 46613

Call Sign: N9ICP
Jeffrey W Waters
829 S Sheridan St
South Bend IN 46619

Call Sign: WD9GBN
Joseph P Illes
56869 S Sundown
South Bend IN 46619

Call Sign: WB9TPY
Randal L Rockwell
1006 S Twyckenham
South Bend IN 46615

Call Sign: KD9FO
Dale T Stuart
1814 S Twyckenham

South Bend IN 46613

Call Sign: N9FAX
David W Martin Sr
2715 S Twyckenham Dr
South Bend IN
466141441

Call Sign: N9KMD
Eric E Rector
3510 S Wise Cir
South Bend IN
466141930

Call Sign: N9ZNI
Tomar R Thomas
237 Sadie St
South Bend IN 46628

Call Sign: N9IQF
Ronald C Mathia
20830 Segway Ct
South Bend IN 46614

Call Sign: WB9LOK
Donald L Rice
4822 Selkirk Dr
South Bend IN 46614

Call Sign: KB9MVO
Justin R Heim
52579 Shellbark Ave
South Bend IN 46628

Call Sign: WA9RFY
David H Kepple
22034 Silver Spring Dr
South Bend IN 46628

Call Sign: WA9JVU
Thomas L De Von
22021 Silverspring Dr
South Bend IN 46628

Call Sign: KC9GUC

Lynne M Palmer
4519 Silvery Ln
South Bend IN 46619

Call Sign: KA9YVT
Brian S Morehouse
4829 Skye Ct
South Bend IN 46614

Call Sign: N9DD
Thomas E Frisz
4148 Spring Hill Ct
South Bend IN 46628

Call Sign: N9OCD
Maryo Pasarel
3522 Springbrook Dr
South Bend IN 46614

Call Sign: N9YRM
Neil E Beckwith
1361 Squire Dr Apt F
South Bend IN
466374045

Call Sign: NE2B
Neil E Beckwith
1361 Squire Dr Apt F
South Bend IN
466374045

Call Sign: K9BXD
Allen W Bickel
25609 SR 2
South Bend IN 46619

Call Sign: N9IQP
Elizabeth M Bickel
25609 SR 2
South Bend IN 46619

Call Sign: N9MDX
Richard C Bakos
25833 SR 2

South Bend IN
466174736

Call Sign: KA9TOB
William Klute
17763 SR 23
South Bend IN 46660

Call Sign: KB9TML
Patricia L Mead
20072 State Line Rd
South Bend IN 46637

Call Sign: N9LFJ
Clarence R Wisner
18188 Stoneridge St Unit
E
South Bend IN 46637

Call Sign: N9CMC
Marion P Williams
18188 Stoneridge Unit E
South Bend IN 46637

Call Sign: KC9SUY
Michael T Tinny
1516 Strathmore Ct
South Bend IN 46614

Call Sign: KC9DZK
Ryan P Bartkus
3610 Sullivan Ct
South Bend IN 46614

Call Sign: WB9SCC
George A Scheuer
1726 Sunnymede Ave
South Bend IN
466151330

Call Sign: KC9IIG
Russel L Mehler
3117 Sunnymede Ave
South Bend IN 46615

Call Sign: KQ9Q
Jeffrey W Oursler
19642 Sunset Ln
South Bend IN 46637

Call Sign: KB9NIL
Joel M Wallis
923 Sussex Dr
South Bend IN 46628

Call Sign: KC9NQE
Michiana Amateur
Repeater Association
1001 Sussex Dr
South Bend IN 46628

Call Sign: W9LVS
Michiana Amateur
Repeater Association
1001 Sussex Dr
South Bend IN 46628

Call Sign: K9FIV
Donald A Lightner
1001 Sussex Dr
South Bend IN
466281232

Call Sign: W9EZS
Radio Teleprinters Soc
Of Northern Ind
1001 Sussex Dr
South Bend IN
466281232

Call Sign: N9KBV
Gerald R Wallis
1122 Sussex Dr
South Bend IN 46628

Call Sign: KA9HZE
Michael P Young
203 Swanson Cir NW
South Bend IN 46615

Call Sign: KB9ACX
Thomas E White
226 Sylvan Glen Dr
South Bend IN 46615

Call Sign: W9TEW
Thomas E White
226 Sylvan Glen Dr
South Bend IN 46615

Call Sign: KB9BDW
Carl O Zahart
2646 Tamarac Pl
South Bend IN 46615

Call Sign: WA9YWE
Thomas M Mayse
2732 The Royal
Huntsman Ct
South Bend IN 46637

Call Sign: KC9EOT
Harry E Robinson
1912 Trentway
South Bend IN 46614

Call Sign: KC9KYI
Barry A Greene
26408 US 20 W
South Bend IN 46628

Call Sign: N8VKC
Jamie G Dennis
6414 US 31 S
South Bend IN 46614

Call Sign: KC9NIR
Heather M Stansbury
61430 US 31 S
South Bend IN 46614

Call Sign: KC9NIS
Jeremy M Stansbury
61430 US 31 S
South Bend IN 46614

Call Sign: KG9PW
Brian S Olmstead
27695 US Hwy 20
South Bend IN 46628

Call Sign: AA9YI
Brian S Olmstead
27695 US Hwy 20
South Bend IN 46628

Call Sign: W9BY
Brian S Olmstead
27695 US Hwy 20
South Bend IN 46628

Call Sign: KB9IGK
Shirley D Lowe
23730 Vine St
South Bend IN 46614

Call Sign: N8XQR
Jerry M Buckhanan
607 W Calvert St
South Bend IN 46613

Call Sign: N9SQE
Charles R Hohenstein
624 W Colfax Ave Apt E
South Bend IN 46601

Call Sign: KB9MLF
Steven E Baker
120 W Cripe St
South Bend IN 46637

Call Sign: WB9YPA
Michael P Sienicki
751 W Ewing
South Bend IN 46613

Call Sign: W9ZBK
Benjamin M Krusniak
1229 W Ford St
South Bend IN 46619

Call Sign: K9WFF
Alfred Koczan
20301 W Jewel Ave
South Bend IN 46614

Call Sign: KC9HCX
Larry C Clough Sr
19923 W Oakdale Ave
South Bend IN
466371754

Call Sign: KB9DSR
Dennis S Wesolowski
1037 W Thomas St
South Bend IN 46625

Call Sign: KC2KOA
Jarett T Deangelis
508 W Washington St
South Bend IN 46601

Call Sign: N9SNG
Paula L Spart
5024 W Western Ave
South Bend IN 46619

Call Sign: KB9GQG
Timothy W Kinney
1401 Wall St
South Bend IN 46615

Call Sign: N9XKW
David L Russell
20189 Weller Ave
South Bend IN 46614

Call Sign: N9XTB
Jonathan D Russell
20189 Weller Ave
South Bend IN 46614

Call Sign: KA4SDR
Herbert J Stevens III
20806 Wellesley Ct

South Bend IN
466371369

Call Sign: KC9TSH
Mathew A Chrystal Jr
52156 Wembley Dr
South Bend IN 46637

Call Sign: KC9LBW
Richard J Fox
3714 Whitcomb St
South Bend IN 46614

Call Sign: KC9KYF
Georgia L Hinds
1022 Whitehall Dr
South Bend IN 46615

Call Sign: W9PRA
Michael P Hinds
1022 Whitehall Dr
South Bend IN 46615

Call Sign: ND9X
Michael P Hinds
1022 Whitehall Dr
South Bend IN 46615

Call Sign: KD7TM
Michael P Hinds
1022 Whitehall Dr
South Bend IN 46615

Call Sign: KC9JHQ
Jeffrey A Eskildsen
53770 Whitesell Dr
South Bend IN 46628

Call Sign: N9FLB
Charles A Lightner
20660 Windrush Ct
South Bend IN 46614

Call Sign: KB9PNE
George M Wlochowski

58080 Windsor Rd
South Bend IN 46619

Call Sign: N9SKI
Robert F Litzkow Jr
3032 Woodmont Dr
South Bend IN 46614

Call Sign: KA9TPG
John J Wieczorek
17710 Woodridge Dr
South Bend IN 46635

Call Sign: W1GSM
John J Mitchell
17720 Woodthrush Ln
South Bend IN 46635

Call Sign: KC9GPR
Joseph G O'Rourke
1063 Woodward Ave
South Bend IN 46616

Call Sign: N9JIC
Ralph M Applegate
4432 York Rd
South Bend IN 46614

Call Sign: N9VXU
Bryan T Newport
6021 York Rd
South Bend IN 46614

Call Sign: W9VVJ
Richard C Ferguson
South Bend IN 46624

Call Sign: KA9OYJ
Evelyn J Feder
South Bend IN 46637

Call Sign: KC9VEA
Dawn M Phelps
South Bend IN 46624

Call Sign: N9OCA
M Myer Blatt
South Bend IN 46624

Call Sign: N9VXK
Bentley B Phelps Sr
South Bend IN 46634

Call Sign: N9KIL
Lisa A Haimbaugh
South Bend IN 46634

Call Sign: KB9VDH
Benjamin L Kanoff
South Bend IN 46660

Call Sign: WD8ARZ
William F Stamps Jr
South Bend IN 46660

FCC Amateur Radio Licenses in South Whitley

Call Sign: N9ONY
Eugene L Vogely
350W
South Whitley IN 46787

Call Sign: N9ICA
Howard E Harnish
505 E Front St
South Whitley IN 46787

Call Sign: KF9VZ
James N Nagano
110 N Jefferson St
South Whitley IN 46787

Call Sign: N9FSC
Gale R Brown
203 N State St
South Whitley IN 46787

Call Sign: N9YGY

Estel W Easterday Jr
706 N State St
South Whitley IN
467871127

Call Sign: KC9GZC
Homer R Crowder
202 S Line St
South Whitley IN 46787

Call Sign: N9HRC
Homer R Crowder
202 S Line St
South Whitley IN 46787

Call Sign: KC9MJT
Melanie M Dahms
303 S Main St
South Whitley IN 46787

Call Sign: WB9DNE
Charles S Bollinger
602 S State St
South Whitley IN 46787

Call Sign: WD9DBM
Nancy N Bollinger
602 S State St
South Whitley IN 46787

Call Sign: N9MHC
Carl E Keuneke
2749 W 1000 S
South Whitley IN 46787

Call Sign: KC9CTZ
Dennis A Basinger
5585 W 1000 S
South Whitley IN 46787

Call Sign: KD1DW
Robert J Fontaine
2399 W 900 S
South Whitley IN 46787

Call Sign: N5TMP
Dawn M Fontaine
2399 W 900 S
South Whitley IN
467879715

Call Sign: WF9Q
Fred J Fisher
405 W Buffalo
South Whitley IN 46787

Call Sign: W6RDJ
John B Harmon
405 W Buffalo St
South Whitley IN 46787

Call Sign: K6EXV
Lucille M Harmon
405 W Buffalo St
South Whitley IN 46787

Call Sign: N9OSM
Dorothy G Hollingsworth
6866 W River Rd
South Whitley IN 46787

Call Sign: N9MTD
Roger A Hubble
8515 W S R 14
South Whitley IN 46787

Call Sign: KB9DOH
Paul W Woods
South Whitley IN 46787

FCC Amateur Radio Licenses in Spencerville

Call Sign: WB9SLQ
Robert G Metcalf
18113 Beechwood Ln
Spencerville IN 46788

Call Sign: WR9V
Robert G Metcalf

18113 Beechwood Ln
Spencerville IN 46788

Call Sign: N8ODI
Sharon V Metcalf
18113 Beechwood Ln
Spencerville IN 46788

Call Sign: KC9TLS
Robert A Murbach
17631 Breezewood Dr
Spencerville IN 46788

Call Sign: KC9ORO
Carl O Bodinka
7250 CR 39
Spencerville IN 46788

Call Sign: W9QR
Larry W Wheeler
5904 CR 64
Spencerville IN 46788

Call Sign: KA9USA
Tri State 440 Club
5904 CR 64
Spencerville IN
467889715

Call Sign: W9ISE
Indiana Special Events
Radio Association
5904 CR 64
Spencerville IN
467889715

Call Sign: KC9MOH
Barbara J Richards
17510 Devall Rd
Spencerville IN 46788

Call Sign: AB9OJ
Thomas E Richards
17510 Devall Rd
Spencerville IN 46788

Call Sign: KY9I
Thomas E Richards
17510 Devall Rd
Spencerville IN 46788

Call Sign: N9XKP
Edward A La Rocque III
18801 Lochner Rd
Spencerville IN 46788

Call Sign: KC9OH
George F Deebel
15128 N County Line Rd
Spencerville IN 46788

Call Sign: KA9UJE
Mark E Deebel
15128 N County Line Rd
Spencerville IN 46788

Call Sign: K9TVZ
Howard V Eicher
24414 N County Line Rd
Spencerville IN 46788

Call Sign: KA9CZF
Dennis W King
17103 N SR 1
Spencerville IN 46788

Call Sign: KC9QCD
Jeffrey F Dailey
17206 N SR 1
Spencerville IN 46788

Call Sign: KA9VIH
Bradley K Compton
7091 SR 1
Spencerville IN 46788

Call Sign: WA9RJF
John D Carpenter
17436 SR 1 Rfd 1
Spencerville IN 46788

FCC Amateur Radio Licenses in Star City

Call Sign: KA9KZF
Robert M Thomas
8971 S 200 W
Star City IN 46985

Call Sign: KB9ZKF
Frank T Allen
7805 S SR 119
Star City IN 46985

Call Sign: KD7NUW
Robert L Galbreath
861 W 600 S
Star City IN 46985

Call Sign: W9RLG
Robert L Galbreath
861 W 600 S
Star City IN 46985

Call Sign: K9OPK
John Binkley
626 W 750 S
Star City IN 469858873

Call Sign: N9LUE
Scott L Moss
Star City IN 46985

Call Sign: K9OXT
Raymond E Penn
Star City IN 46985

FCC Amateur Radio Licenses in Stroh

Call Sign: KB9NNU
Harry W Williams
425 S 11665 E
Stroh IN 46789

Call Sign: KB9SFP
Gary P Kocher
Stroh IN 467890296

FCC Amateur Radio Licenses in Swayzee

Call Sign: N9ONW
Richard K Smith
204 E Grant St
Swayzee IN 46986

Call Sign: WB9AQA
James L Shroyer Jr
6793 W 300 S
Swayzee IN 46986

Call Sign: KB9BAK
Rebecca A Shroyer
6793 W 300 S
Swayzee IN 46986

Call Sign: KB9FJB
Robert M Shroyer
6793 W 300 S
Swayzee IN 46986

Call Sign: KC9VOT
Joshua A Rennaker
7262 W 700 S
Swayzee IN 46986

Call Sign: W9CVO
Earl O Simon
Swayzee IN 46986

Call Sign: WD9IZA
Jay M Beall Jr
Swayzee IN 46986

FCC Amateur Radio Licenses in Sweetser

Call Sign: KB9ZNT
Ned A Yauger

619 Allen Dr
Sweetser IN 46987

Call Sign: W9NAY
Ned A Yauger
619 Allen Dr
Sweetser IN 46987

Call Sign: N9NDR
Richard E Treber Jr
110 S Greenberry St
Sweetser IN 46987

Call Sign: KB9YPR
Troy L Freeman
Sweetser IN 46987

FCC Amateur Radio Licenses in Thayer

Call Sign: KB9VVV
Robert L Robbins
Thayer IN 46381

Call Sign: WA9ORS
John E Alexander
Thayer IN 46381

Call Sign: KC9CKD
Larry N Stevens
Thayer IN 46381

FCC Amateur Radio Licenses in Tippecanoe

Call Sign: KC9RRM
Evan J Rock
3295 E 18 B Rd
Tippecanoe IN 46570

Call Sign: KA9CDN
Michael W Baker
7569 N SR 25
Tippecanoe IN 46570

Call Sign: KB9MDQ
Michael D Stephan
16998 SR 331
Tippecanoe IN 46570

Call Sign: KC9RRL
Wyatt M Stephan
16998 SR 331
Tippecanoe IN 46570

FCC Amateur Radio Licenses in Topeka

Call Sign: N9LAI
Judith I Ress
214 Morrow St Apt 503
Topeka IN 46571

Call Sign: N9APH
Daniel L Pruitt
Topeka IN 46571

FCC Amateur Radio Licenses in Trail Creek

Call Sign: KA9ZGR
Kenneth T Johnston
308 Black Oak Dr
Trail Creek IN 46360

Call Sign: KB9TLW
Donald B Westphal
439 Johnson Rd
Trail Creek IN
463606510

Call Sign: KC9IRR
Bill C Carter
1927 Welnetz Rd
Trail Creek IN 46360

Call Sign: AB9QU
Bill C Carter
1927 Welnetz Rd
Trail Creek IN 46360

FCC Amateur Radio Licenses in Twelve Mile

Call Sign: W9HQV
Daniel L Elkins
7580 E CR 600 N
Twelve Mile IN 46988

Call Sign: KC9EQB
Gerald W Mathis
8499 E SR 16
Twelve Mile IN 46988

Call Sign: K9ACX
Bonnie J Mathis
8499 SR 16 E
Twelve Mile IN 46988

Call Sign: AC9X
Guy R Mathis
8499 SR 16 E
Twelve Mile IN 46988

Call Sign: KC9ESB
Lois R Mathis
8499 SR 16 E
Twelve Mile IN 46988

Call Sign: KC9GOW
Eugene F Williams
Twelve Mile IN 46988

Call Sign: W9MCI
Eugene F Williams
Twelve Mile IN 46988

Call Sign: KC9SDT
Fonda J Williams
Twelve Mile IN 46988

Call Sign: K9MCI
Fonda J Williams
Twelve Mile IN 46988

FCC Amateur Radio Licenses in Union Mills

Call Sign: KB9RNX
Charles A Neill
1100S
Union Mills IN 46382

Call Sign: KC9IBN
David P Jones
1212 E 2nd St
Union Mills IN 46382

Call Sign: K9DPJ
David P Jones
1212 E 2nd St
Union Mills IN 46382

Call Sign: KD4MSH
Charles C Hildreth
9828 S 100 W
Union Mills IN 46382

Call Sign: K9FIM
Marvin G Freeman
5764 W 800 S
Union Mills IN 46382

Call Sign: KB9TKP
Dale V Hewitt
1168 W 850 S
Union Mills IN 46382

Call Sign: AB9AS
Dale V Hewitt
1168 W 850 S
Union Mills IN 46382

Call Sign: KC9HXE
Dennis C Davis
2283 W 950 S
Union Mills IN 46382

FCC Amateur Radio Licenses in Uniondale

Call Sign: KA9DMO
Timothy D Garwood
6152 N 200 W
Uniondale IN 46791

Call Sign: KC9VDE
Katherine I Triplett
5916 N Miller St
Uniondale IN 46791

Call Sign: WB9FTW
Richard L Triplett
5916 N Miller St
Uniondale IN 46791

Call Sign: KB9VNL
Alan M Lance
1189 W 600 N
Uniondale IN 46791

Call Sign: N9VDW
Timmy J Griner
164 W 800 N
Uniondale IN 46791

Call Sign: W9HRC
Ronald L Dvorak
2223 W US 224
Uniondale IN 46791

FCC Amateur Radio Licenses in Upland

Call Sign: KB9EZI
Evelyn M Harriman
124 Bragg Ave E
Upland IN 46989

Call Sign: KB9RUM
Joan C Hobbs
Catalina Dr
Upland IN 46989

Call Sign: KB9NVN

Patrick D Coyle
10635 E 1100 S
Upland IN 46989

Call Sign: N9RLO
John R Hill
10820 E 500 S
Upland IN 46989

Call Sign: N9MNW
Gregg A Ballinger
8015 E 500 S Box 237
Upland IN 46989

Call Sign: KA9QZB
Jonette S Gilley
10908 E 600 S
Upland IN 469899773

Call Sign: KB9ZNY
David L Voss
8651 E 700 S
Upland IN 46989

Call Sign: KB9ZNZ
Henry D Voss
8651 E 700 S
Upland IN 46989

Call Sign: KB9ZNW
Jonathan C Voss
8651 E 700 S
Upland IN 46989

Call Sign: W7YIG
James H Kleist
11600 E 700 S
Upland IN 46989

Call Sign: WB9BAT
Leon W Amstutz
714 Harsax D Fcc
Upland IN 46989

Call Sign: KA9ISH

Malcolm R Holland
217 Lake St
Upland IN 469890426

Call Sign: KB9TTX
Larry J Shipley
434 N Half St
Upland IN 46989

Call Sign: KC9QCJ
Harrold W Williamson
7217 S 1150 E
Upland IN 46989

Call Sign: KB9ZNV
Brent E Gerig
1016 S 1st St
Upland IN 46989

Call Sign: KA9DKQ
Leonard D Scheidt
304 S 5th St Box 214
Upland IN 46989

Call Sign: KB9IJN
Eric C Himelick
5275 S 800 E
Upland IN 46989

Call Sign: WA7ZPZ
Robert D Hodge
1305 S 8th St
Upland IN 46989

Call Sign: WA9YJB
McCulloch Middle
School ARC
4371 S 900 E
Upland IN 46953

Call Sign: KC9RGN
Elizabeth G Goldsmith
236 W Reade Ave
Upland IN 46989

Call Sign: KB9ZNX
Scott W Wohlfarth
236 W Reade Ave
Upland IN 46989

Call Sign: KC9OUK
Thomas D Nicol
236 W Reade Ave
Upland IN 46989

Call Sign: N9EWH
Carl R Daudt
540 Warkentin Ct
Upland IN 46989

Call Sign: N9INA
Jon D Vandegriff
232 Wengatz Hall Taylor
University
Upland IN 46989

Call Sign: KC9IFK
Douglas S Zumbrun
Upland IN 46989

Call Sign: KB9GTS
Douglas S Zumbrun
Upland IN 46989

Call Sign: KB9PRN
Stephen A Olsen
Upland IN 469890615

**FCC Amateur Radio
Licenses in Urbana**

Call Sign: AA9SH
Alan F Wojtkowiak
370 E Mill St
Urbana IN 46990

Call Sign: N9TIH
David A Peden Jr
250 S Washington St
Urbana IN 46990

Call Sign: WB9NEU
Joseph D Gifford
Urbana IN 46990

Call Sign: N9PZI
Eric L Cohee
Urbana IN 469900149

**FCC Amateur Radio
Licenses in Valparaiso**

Call Sign: K9EFX
John R Harbeck
300N
Valparaiso IN 463839549

Call Sign: W9HHO
George W Kalas
600N
Valparaiso IN 46383

Call Sign: N9QKI
Charles J Myers
830N
Valparaiso IN 46383

Call Sign: K9KO
Don Fredrick
405 Andover Dr
Valparaiso IN 46383

Call Sign: KC9KRW
Brian S Rosendaul
1313 Aspen Dr
Valparaiso IN 46385

Call Sign: KC9GUD
Dawn L Hamel
744 Baltimore Rd
Valparaiso IN 46385

Call Sign: N9OUB
William J Watts Sr
766 Baltimore Rd

Valparaiso IN 46383

Call Sign: N9OUC
William J Watts Jr
766 Baltimore Rd
Valparaiso IN 46383

Call Sign: N9WYU
Darrin C Young
1703 Bartz Rd
Valparaiso IN 46383

Call Sign: N9WXY
Riley A Lemay
2601 Bartz Rd
Valparaiso IN 46383

Call Sign: K9MJS
Michael J Smith
178 Bayberry Ct
Valparaiso IN 46383

Call Sign: N9IVQ
Jay W Shoup
1002 Beech St
Valparaiso IN 46383

Call Sign: KB9IRL
Ryan M Watson
1909 Beech St 107
Valparaiso IN 46383

Call Sign: KC9LQP
David R Massner
1911 Beech St Apt 301
Valparaiso IN 46383

Call Sign: KB9WSF
Melvin R Hansen
2901 Black Partridge Ln
Valparaiso IN 46383

Call Sign: W9OTN
Bruce H Balsley
195 Blackthorn Dr

Valparaiso IN 46383

Call Sign: N9HDF
Eric A Dennin
3504 Bloomingdale Ave
Valparaiso IN 46383

Call Sign: KB9QE
Ross J Mack
1305 Boca Lago Dr
Valparaiso IN 46383

Call Sign: NY9K
Daniel D Bowker
2608 Boca Raton Dr
Valparaiso IN 46383

Call Sign: N9DNU
Judith A Steimel
1401 Boca Teeka Dr E
Valparaiso IN 46383

Call Sign: KU9U
Lynn P Steimel
1401 Boca Teeka Dr E
Valparaiso IN 46383

Call Sign: KB9ZDL
Christopher A Cole
306 Brown St
Valparaiso IN 46383

Call Sign: KB9FUM
Michael G Wilder
202 Bullseye Lake Rd
Valparaiso IN 463831863

Call Sign: KC9OYE
Charles E Hill
254 Butternut Ln
Valparaiso IN 46383

Call Sign: W9GPP
Richard D Evans
2503 Camilla Dr

Valparaiso IN 46383

Valparaiso IN 46385

Valparaiso IN 46385

Call Sign: KJ4EYX
Gene P Moore Jr
757 Capitol Rd
Valparaiso IN 46385

Call Sign: N9CRK
William S Davis
3907 Colonial Dr
Valparaiso IN 46383

Call Sign: KC9RTD
Tyler G Wahl
1772 Danvers Pkwy
Valparaiso IN 46385

Call Sign: KC9NKV
Connor A Ritzi
45 Castleton Rd
Valparaiso IN 46385

Call Sign: KC9UGR
Larry Whitlow
2904 Columbine Cir
Valparaiso IN 46383

Call Sign: N9EGB
Roger J Kneeland
632 Deer Meadow Tr
Valparaiso IN 46383

Call Sign: KB9VMB
Brian P Sexton
706 Center St
Valparaiso IN 46385

Call Sign: KC9VEF
Jordan A Chadwick
3002 Comeford Rd
Valparaiso IN 46383

Call Sign: KC9IIM
Kevin S Ribordy
382 Deer Ridge Rd
Valparaiso IN 46385

Call Sign: N4XPM
Don R Peltonen
432 Chadwick Cir
Valparaiso IN 46385

Call Sign: KC9KOB
Sotirios Bakas
1107 Cortland Dr
Valparaiso IN 46383

Call Sign: KC9IIK
Kyle D Ribordy
382 Deer Ridge Rd
Valparaiso IN 46385

Call Sign: KB9YST
Tabitha G Luecker
2302 Chandana Trl
Valparaiso IN 46383

Call Sign: KO9B
Sotirios Bakas
1107 Cortland Dr
Valparaiso IN 46383

Call Sign: KB9WTQ
John A Miller
1504 Del Vista Dr
Valparaiso IN 46385

Call Sign: W9ORW
Robert A Pence
256 Chestnut St
Valparaiso IN 46383

Call Sign: N9EZH
Charles F Schmetzer
704 Coventry Ln
Valparaiso IN 46383

Call Sign: KB9HFR
William M Williams
794 Devonshire
Valparaiso IN 46383

Call Sign: KC9DTY
Thomas J Deskouich
452 Chestnut St
Valparaiso IN 46385

Call Sign: N9TRH
Gail A Rebus
23 Covington Dr
Valparaiso IN 46383

Call Sign: WB9FOR
Samuel H Reisinger Jr
785 Devonshire Rd
Valparaiso IN 46383

Call Sign: KB9BSH
Ronald F Haberkamp Sr
373 Clear Creek
Valparaiso IN 46383

Call Sign: N8HBG
George J Rebus
23 Covington Dr
Valparaiso IN 46383

Call Sign: WD9HYZ
Timothy E Anderson
2604 Dorset Dr
Valparaiso IN 46383

Call Sign: KC9UZA
Jason M Jones
1902 Clover Ln

Call Sign: KC9RTC
Frank W Cunningham
1772 Danvers Pkwy

Call Sign: AA9QC
David S Watkins
2106 Dunwoddy Dr

Valparaiso IN 46383

Valparaiso IN 46383

Valparaiso IN 46383

Call Sign: KB9KJD
Daniel B Riley
459 E 200 N
Valparaiso IN 46383

Call Sign: N9ZVZ
James R Staub
1402 E Evans Ave
Valparaiso IN 46383

Call Sign: KB9OZU
Nicole R Miller
304 Fair St
Valparaiso IN 46383

Call Sign: K9RVW
James E Wirick
392 E 300 S
Valparaiso IN 46383

Call Sign: N9MRR
Brent M Barber
1102 E Glendale Blvd
Valparaiso IN 46383

Call Sign: KB9QJX
Casey L Schuetz
404 Fordwick
Valparaiso IN 46383

Call Sign: K9YH
Robert A Scott
403 E 300 S
Valparaiso IN 46383

Call Sign: KA9QIN
Thomas C Vrydaghs
76 E US 6 Lot 227
Valparaiso IN 46383

Call Sign: KC9KKG
Ilija K Labovic
435 Forest Wood Dr
Valparaiso IN 46385

Call Sign: KB9TDV
Peter J Weber
121 E 700 N
Valparaiso IN 46383

Call Sign: KB9YGG
John Romeo
76 E US Hwy 6 Lot 34
Valparaiso IN 46383

Call Sign: KC9KKH
Jelisaveta B Labovic
435 Forest Wood Dr
Valparaiso IN 46385

Call Sign: KD9BO
Steven E Weber
121 E 700 N
Valparaiso IN 46383

Call Sign: KB9NLA
John W Sinclair
725 Eagle Cr Rd
Valparaiso IN 46383

Call Sign: KA9TWH
Mark O Williams
Fox River Rd
Valparaiso IN 46383

Call Sign: KB9WOI
Jordan M Gray
121 E 700 N
Valparaiso IN 46383

Call Sign: WB9AJG
Charles D Marrs
827 Elm St
Valparaiso IN 46383

Call Sign: KA9OSU
Mary L Reid
712 Fremont
Valparaiso IN 46383

Call Sign: WB9JOV
John W Ruppert
420 E 900 N
Valparaiso IN 46383

Call Sign: WB9AJH
Sandra L Marrs
827 Elm St
Valparaiso IN 46383

Call Sign: KA9UNT
Tiffanie L Reid
712 Fremont
Valparaiso IN 46383

Call Sign: KC5BRI
Crisley R Handly
436 E 900 N
Valparaiso IN 46383

Call Sign: N9DWK
Dennis P Landry
300 Evans
Valparaiso IN 46383

Call Sign: KB9UYG
Peter T Weiss
559 Gene Ln
Valparaiso IN 46385

Call Sign: N9SLH
Irene D Candiano
503 E Chicago

Call Sign: KB9JKF
Jay L Williams Jr
301 Fair St

Call Sign: N9DQD
Erik I Gustafson
1802 Georgia St

Valparaiso IN 46383

Call Sign: N9AVD
Gustav I Gustafson
1802 Georgia St
Valparaiso IN 46383

Call Sign: N6NNZ
Margaret A Johnson
89 Gingerwood Ct
Valparaiso IN 46383

Call Sign: KB9JMT
Sarah E Black
610 Glade Pl
Valparaiso IN 46383

Call Sign: K3USV
Alan D Strauss
217 Golden Eagle Dr
Valparaiso IN 463859073

Call Sign: KC9QYF
Michael A Gavaller
4905 Goodrich Rd
Valparaiso IN 46385

Call Sign: AB9VP
Michael A Gavaller
4905 Goodrich Rd
Valparaiso IN 46385

Call Sign: KC9MII
Joseph Parrett
766 Governor Rd
Valparaiso IN 46385

Call Sign: NS8M
Orfeo Di Biase
254 Green Acres Dr
Valparaiso IN 46383

Call Sign: N8ZAX
Mary Di Biase
254 Green Acres Dr

Valparaiso IN 46383

Call Sign: KC9FRO
Dennis P Pflughaupt
476 Grove Ave
Valparaiso IN 46385

Call Sign: N9DPP
Dennis P Pflughaupt
476 Grove Ave
Valparaiso IN 46385

Call Sign: KA9HKA
Paul G Domazet
83 Hawick Dr
Valparaiso IN 46383

Call Sign: WD9GCY
Richard A Miko
708 Heritage Rd
Valparaiso IN 46383

Call Sign: W9KTP
Jerome E Hess
484 High Meadow Cir
Valparaiso IN 46383

Call Sign: KF9QM
Thomas E Calloway
2959 Hundred Rd
Valparaiso IN 46383

Call Sign: KC9ADP
Steve D Cavinder
1005 Illinois St
Valparaiso IN 46383

Call Sign: K9JSG
Ronald J Draus
Joliet Rd
Valparaiso IN 46383

Call Sign: KC9UH
Phillip G Springer
758 Juniper Rd

Valparaiso IN 463858400

Call Sign: N9WAG
Dennis E Powell
380 Keystone Dr
Valparaiso IN 46385

Call Sign: N9ODW
Steve P Tylisz
203 Kimrich Cir
Valparaiso IN 46385

Call Sign: KK9F
Albert L Reichle
4405 Kingsdale Dr
Valparaiso IN 46383

Call Sign: KA9FAT
Lynn E Reichle
4405 Kingsdale Dr
Valparaiso IN 46383

Call Sign: N9ZRJ
Jeffrey D Kwok
1804 Lafayette St
Valparaiso IN 46383

Call Sign: KB9LHO
Paul D Leyden
332 Lahonda Dr
Valparaiso IN 46385

Call Sign: N9USQ
Terry A Powell Jr
372 Lahonda Dr
Valparaiso IN 46385

Call Sign: KC9ECR
Brad W Cicenas
3605 Lake Meadow Dr
Valparaiso IN 46385

Call Sign: KC9DJO
Richard A Cicenas
3605 Lake Meadow Dr

Valparaiso IN 46385   Valparaiso IN 46385   Valparaiso IN 463835081

Call Sign: W9LVW   Call Sign: KB9TYS   Call Sign: KC9FWW
Michael O Smith   Kimberly A Crotty   Wayne L Stowers
2101 Lakeview Rd   530 Lismore Ln   339 Midway Dr
Valparaiso IN 46383   Valparaiso IN 46385   Valparaiso IN 46385

Call Sign: K9DQJ   Call Sign: W9QBS   Call Sign: KC8YIP
Earl C Pace   Maurice H Martin   Michael J Mulder
502 Lancaster Dr   Long Lake Rd   1408 Monticello Park Dr
Valparaiso IN 46384   Valparaiso IN 46383   Valparaiso IN 46383

Call Sign: KG9OD   Call Sign: KA9JWT   Call Sign: N9YZO
Raymond E Anderson   Collyn B Summers   Michael S Graves
570 Lantern Walk   1601 Loveland Ct   1105 Monticello Pk Dr
Valparaiso IN 46385   Valparaiso IN 463858546   Valparaiso IN 46383

Call Sign: KC9VJW   Call Sign: WA9FLV   Call Sign: WA9ECW
Kevin A Bottorff   James L Van Wienen   Richard A Halstead
380 Larimar Tr   313 Madison St   302 Morgan Blvd
Valparaiso IN 46385   Valparaiso IN 46383   Valparaiso IN 46383

Call Sign: KB9UQO   Call Sign: KA9OFF   Call Sign: WX9X
Adam J Stepanek   Gregory S Walls   Richard A Halstead
2159 Lennox Ln   1054 Marion St   302 Morgan Blvd
Valparaiso IN 463857110   Valparaiso IN 46383   Valparaiso IN 46383

Call Sign: KC0FSS   Call Sign: KU9W   Call Sign: KB9UCJ
Jill A Stepanek   Carroll L Walls   Qsl Printers ARC
2159 Lennox Ln   1054 Marion St   302 Morgan Blvd
Valparaiso IN 463857110   Valparaiso IN 46385   Valparaiso IN 46383

Call Sign: KB9KWN   Call Sign: KC9HLQ   Call Sign: WV9R
Earl C Uban   Ronald R Goble   Raymond D Morehouse
235 Lincoln Hills Dr   1100 McCord Rd   731 N 200 E
Valparaiso IN 46383   Valparaiso IN 46383   Valparaiso IN 46383

Call Sign: N9PYE   Call Sign: N9PON   Call Sign: N9NIZ
Arnold E Felten   Walter L Dunivan   Margaret L Cushman
807 Linwood Ave   2607 McCord Rd   944 N 200 W
Valparaiso IN 46383   Valparaiso IN 46383   Valparaiso IN 46383

Call Sign: KB9TLL   Call Sign: K9ZTX   Call Sign: WB9AOU
Brien P Crotty   Bruce Shinabarger   Diane M Belcher
530 Lismore Ln   404 Michigan Av Apt 1   956 N 200 W

Valparaiso IN 46383

Valparaiso IN 46383

Valparaiso IN 46383

Call Sign: N9QLQ
Richard D Ard
1001 N 200 W
Valparaiso IN 46383

Call Sign: KB9QDY
Susan E Wigent
895 N 500 E
Valparaiso IN 46383

Call Sign: KB9WFQ
Phillip A Simcich
502 N College Ave
Valparaiso IN 46383

Call Sign: KC9QPR
Jeffrey C Langan
494 N 250 W
Valparaiso IN 46385

Call Sign: KC9TMN
Bernardus T Maas
184 N 500 W
Valparaiso IN 46385

Call Sign: KB9BBF
Charles A Morse
450 N SR 149
Valparaiso IN 46385

Call Sign: KA9PLR
Margaret E Mollman
682 N 300 E
Valparaiso IN 46383

Call Sign: KB9YEC
Caleb P Lachmann
35 N 575 E
Valparaiso IN 46383

Call Sign: N9JAH
Dianna D Cutler
680 N SR 149
Valparaiso IN 46385

Call Sign: N9IMK
Dennis R Cannon Sr
523 N 325 W
Valparaiso IN 46383

Call Sign: KB9SID
Joshua J Lachmann
35 N 575 E
Valparaiso IN 46383

Call Sign: K9GC
Gregory C Ganz
132 N Timber Pt Ct
Valparaiso IN 463859312

Call Sign: KD9HI
Donald J Sims
188 N 350 W
Valparaiso IN 46385

Call Sign: KC9OHJ
Edward A Hansen
160 N 600 W
Valparaiso IN 46385

Call Sign: KB9KXK
Frederick G Stavitzke
355 Nathan Ter
Valparaiso IN 46383

Call Sign: K0EEN
Dennis D Vadies
863 N 350E
Valparaiso IN 46383

Call Sign: KC9MTR
Zachary P Ziollcowski
95 N 656 W
Valparaiso IN 46385

Call Sign: WB9PEK
Vernon D Hislope
369 Nathan Ter
Valparaiso IN 46383

Call Sign: WB9FWQ
William F Bear
416 N 475 W
Valparaiso IN 463859238

Call Sign: KC9FWV
John J Demchak
140 N 750 W
Valparaiso IN 46385

Call Sign: KC9KOA
Thomas M Bingham
425 Norfolk St
Valparaiso IN 46385

Call Sign: W9DN
David J Nicolaus
709 N 50 W
Valparaiso IN 46385

Call Sign: AB9JB
John J Demchak
140 N 750 W
Valparaiso IN 46385

Call Sign: KA9CRF
Don F Driver
161 Northview Dr
Valparaiso IN 46383

Call Sign: N9GRJ
Lawrence R Wigent
895 N 500 E

Call Sign: W9GVI
Phillip A Simcich
502 N College Ave

Call Sign: WC9ABM
Porter County Civil
Defense

161 Northview Dr
Valparaiso IN 46383

Call Sign: N9IAA
Kevin J Babich
2600 Nottingham
Valparaiso IN 46383

Call Sign: KB9ONV
Michael E Brown
189 NW Hills
Valparaiso IN 46383

Call Sign: KA9YLZ
Michelle A Hoover
635 Osage Rd
Valparaiso IN 46385

Call Sign: N9FDF
Toby Hoover
635 Osage Rd
Valparaiso IN 46385

Call Sign: KB9JVW
Brad A La Coss
645 Oxbow Ct
Valparaiso IN 46385

Call Sign: KB9OLY
Walter F Benson Jr
2206 Penwick Dr
Valparaiso IN 46383

Call Sign: WD9IEF
Dale M Howell
Piedmont Rd
Valparaiso IN 46383

Call Sign: N9FPU
Wanda J Horak
1310 Pkwy Ave
Valparaiso IN 46383

Call Sign: KC9EKY
Steven J Pazanin

922 Plantation Rd
Valparaiso IN 46385

Call Sign: WD9HYM
Garry A Kotvasz
2109 Powderly Rd
Valparaiso IN 46383

Call Sign: KC9QAJ
Charles W Castle Jr
2209 Powderly Rd
Valparaiso IN 46383

Call Sign: KB9UWG
Gregory G Adair
2103 Powderly Rd
Valparaiso IN 46383

Call Sign: KB9AXL
Jennifer L Wall
543 Raven Rd
Valparaiso IN 46383

Call Sign: KB9MCC
Patrick J Harwood
356 Rickenbacker Ct
Valparaiso IN 46383

Call Sign: W9PQQ
Samuel G Saar
954 Ridgeland Ave
Valparaiso IN 46383

Call Sign: N9VSN
Paul P Werner
528 Robyn Rd
Valparaiso IN 46383

Call Sign: KB9SPR
Lyle C Werner
528 Robyn Rd
Valparaiso IN 46385

Call Sign: N9GCY
Dawn M Kujawski

542 Robyn Rd
Valparaiso IN 46383

Call Sign: NF9G
Kathlyn L Kujawski
542 Robyn Rd
Valparaiso IN 46383

Call Sign: NN9J
Steve T Kujawski
542 Robyn Rd
Valparaiso IN 46383

Call Sign: W9ZG
John M Miller
63 Rosewood Ln
Valparaiso IN 46383

Call Sign: KB9NLD
Brian J Iske
1284 Rowley St
Valparaiso IN 46385

Call Sign: N9UIQ
Leslie C Iske
1284 Rowley St
Valparaiso IN 46385

Call Sign: KC9IU
Larry R Sargent
409 S 150 E
Valparaiso IN 46383

Call Sign: AB9WJ
Loren P Clay
124 S 450 W
Valparaiso IN 46385

Call Sign: KC9JUH
Robert W Witters
456 S Morgan
Valparaiso IN 46383

Call Sign: KD9PAN
Robert W Witters

456 S Morgan
Valparaiso IN 46383

Call Sign: KC9ASP
David K Gaddis
356 S Morgan Blvd
Valparaiso IN 46383

Call Sign: N9WTS
Craig A Ingram
4 S Quinn St
Valparaiso IN 46385

Call Sign: N9GBT
Steven J Genovese
116 S Sager Rd
Valparaiso IN 46383

Call Sign: W9UJE
Larry A Hall
93 S Smoke Rd
Valparaiso IN 46383

Call Sign: KC9KOH
Porter County Emergency
Mgmt
1995 S SR 2
Valparaiso IN 46385

Call Sign: KI9EMA
Porter County Emergency
Mgmt
1995 S SR 2
Valparaiso IN 46385

Call Sign: KC9OKO
Anthony B Capriglione
416 Sable Dr
Valparaiso IN 46385

Call Sign: KB9E
Ronald P Emerson
418 Sable Dr
Valparaiso IN 46385

Call Sign: KC9OPF
Emily Qualkinbush
Sable Dr
Valparaiso IN 46385

Call Sign: KC9NZL
Scott C Mueller
34 Sager Rd
Valparaiso IN 46383

Call Sign: W9HQX
Arthur E Olsen Jr
1955 Sager Rd 56
Valparaiso IN 46383

Call Sign: KA9YHZ
Ross J Himes
386 Salt Creek Pkwy
Valparaiso IN 46383

Call Sign: KB9WEL
Steven H Nosek
390 Salt Creek Pkwy
Valparaiso IN 463858126

Call Sign: KB9IRX
Garry S Martin
397 Sassafras Dr
Valparaiso IN 46383

Call Sign: KB9MZJ
Bart J Wolf
417 Shadeland Dr
Valparaiso IN 463837905

Call Sign: W4EZT
David Whiteley Jr
505 Shamrock Ln
Valparaiso IN 46385

Call Sign: W9CWG
Donald E Wiggins
951 Sheffield Dr
Valparaiso IN 463852851

Call Sign: KA9JNH
John E Vittoe
103 Shorewood Dr
Valparaiso IN 463858067

Call Sign: KF8EY
Robert A Ingram
653 Slalom Ln
Valparaiso IN 46383

Call Sign: N9XIC
Daniel P Mehlman
676 Slalom Ln
Valparaiso IN 46383

Call Sign: N9WEH
Linda R Mehlman
676 Slalom Ln
Valparaiso IN 46383

Call Sign: W9PM
Phillip Mehlman
676 Slalom Ln
Valparaiso IN 46383

Call Sign: N9YQD
Nancy E Halstead
676 Slalom Ln
Valparaiso IN 46383

Call Sign: KB9KRI
Duneland Amateur
Repeater Group
676 Slalom Ln
Valparaiso IN 46383

Call Sign: AA9FI
John M Dziedziejko
265 Springhill Dr
Valparaiso IN 46383

Call Sign: K9JMD
John M Dziedziejko
265 Springhill Dr
Valparaiso IN 46385

Call Sign: KC9ILL
Joseph E Wisniewski
530 SR 149
Valparaiso IN 46385

Call Sign: KA9FAV
Russell D Ingram
12 Stoner Dr
Valparaiso IN 46385

Call Sign: KB9FIC
Matthew D Mitch
19 Stoner Dr
Valparaiso IN 46385

Call Sign: KC9MTQ
Aaron D Lovall
408 Sturgeon Dr
Valparaiso IN 46385

Call Sign: KC9BZO
Julie A Tuesburg
1011 Sun Valley Dr
Valparaiso IN 46385

Call Sign: N9GFV
Gerald W Cook Jr
52 Tanglewood Trl
Valparaiso IN 46385

Call Sign: W9THB
Thomas H Booth
4504 Thornbury Dr W
Valparaiso IN 46383

Call Sign: WA9CUW
Andrew S Fortunak
383 Tremont Ct
Valparaiso IN 46385

Call Sign: WR9U
Bryant S Mitol
508 Valparaiso St
Valparaiso IN 46383

Call Sign: KC9MCS
William R Johnson
4008 Victoria Dr
Valparaiso IN 46383

Call Sign: KA9YSG
Gregory S Gora
200 Virginia Ct
Valparaiso IN 46383

Call Sign: N9PYC
Greg A Hamilton
646 W 100 N
Valparaiso IN 46383

Call Sign: KC9ILK
Brad Hines
788 W 100 N
Valparaiso IN 463859220

Call Sign: KC9IJT
Wheeler Hs Engineering
Radio Club
587 W 300 N
Valparaiso IN 46385

Call Sign: K9EJF
Joseph D Shudick
727 W 50 N
Valparaiso IN 46383

Call Sign: K9TDM
Ida E Shudick
727 W 50 N
Valparaiso IN 46385

Call Sign: K9APX
William H Miller
7 W 700 N
Valparaiso IN 46383

Call Sign: KC9AXU
Brian S Getz
259 W 700 N

Valparaiso IN 46385

Call Sign: NY9L
Benjamin L Austin Sr
81 W Division Rd
Valparaiso IN 46385

Call Sign: K1EWA
Raymond P Awe
246 W Division Rd
Valparaiso IN 463859050

Call Sign: W9EWA
Raymond P Awe
246 W Division Rd
Valparaiso IN 463859050

Call Sign: KC9LLY
Terrance G Clemans
421 W Division Rd
Valparaiso IN 46385

Call Sign: KB9YGE
George A Ault
427 W Division Rd
Valparaiso IN 463859014

Call Sign: KB9RHN
Timothy R Hendershott
356 W Midway Dr
Valparaiso IN 463858739

Call Sign: KY9B
Gary V Roy
1 W Ridgeway Dr
Valparaiso IN 46385

Call Sign: N9KHA
Russell J Erwin
10 W Riidgeway Dr
Valparaiso IN 46385

Call Sign: KC9JAM
Matthew D Stermer
406 W Southfield Ln

Valparaiso IN 463859645

Valparaiso IN 46383

Valparaiso IN 46383

Call Sign: KC9MQF
Leroy J Bailey
W US 6
Valparaiso IN 46385

Call Sign: N9WXX
John C Gallagher
12 Williamsburg
Valparaiso IN 46363

Call Sign: WB9VJH
Jan M Riddell
1906 Worthington Dr
Valparaiso IN 463833930

Call Sign: WB9NLZ
Timothy A Stabler
2153 Walker Dr
Valparaiso IN 463857045

Call Sign: KB9HAO
Douglas J Van Wienen
158 Willow St
Valparaiso IN 46383

Call Sign: WD9GCO
Paul A Braun
2102 Yorktowne Dr
Valparaiso IN 46383

Call Sign: N9KDS
Kirby D Slifer
2554 Walker Dr
Valparaiso IN 46385

Call Sign: N9HLX
Jeffrey J Klemczak
204 Willowtree Dr
Valparaiso IN 46383

Call Sign: KA9WFN
Danny R Bickerstaff Sr
2215 Yorktowne Dr
Valparaiso IN 463833921

Call Sign: W9EHE
Kenneth L Stedman
1206 Washington Ave
Valparaiso IN 46383

Call Sign: KC9QYJ
Noelle E Hill
390 Wilshire Ct
Valparaiso IN 46385

Call Sign: N9POL
Jason D Walther
Valparaiso IN 46384

Call Sign: KB6BPI
Kathleen A Bradley
Valparaiso IN 46384

Call Sign: KB9IC
Leonard A Kraft
401 Westchester Ln
Valparaiso IN 46385

Call Sign: KB9F
Dale V Hewitt
135 Wind Whistle Dr
Valparaiso IN 46383

Call Sign: W9MBA
Kathleen A Bradley
Valparaiso IN 46384

Call Sign: KC9MXB
Forrest B Travis
421 Westchester Ln
Valparaiso IN 46385

Call Sign: KB9YGH
Heather L Hewitt
135 Wind Whistle Dr
Valparaiso IN 46383

Call Sign: KA6SGT
Peter W Bradley
Valparaiso IN 46384

Call Sign: KI4BHF
Daniel J Mills
401 Westchester Ln
Valparaiso IN 46385

Call Sign: KC9IHN
Samuel A Tallman
3804 Winter Ln
Valparaiso IN 48385

Call Sign: W9IP
Peter W Bradley
Valparaiso IN 46384

Call Sign: KC9VEH
David L Mallonee
55 Westside Park Ave
Valparaiso IN 46385

Call Sign: AC2E
Dale F Kempf
1953 Woodridge Cir
Valparaiso IN 463836630

Call Sign: KA6SGT
Peter W Bradley
Valparaiso IN 46384

Call Sign: WB9EQI
Philip H Empey Jr
499 Wexford Rd

Call Sign: KB9FFN
Edward C Dixon
251 Worchester Dr

Call Sign: N9HK
Steven J Genovese
Valparaiso IN 46384

Call Sign: KC9QYZ
Coastal Rf Society
Valparaiso IN 46384

Call Sign: K9PC
Porter County ARC
Valparaiso IN 46384

FCC Amateur Radio Licenses in Van Buren

Call Sign: KB9UOS
Brent A Kennedy
3053 N 1100 E
Van Buren IN 46991

Call Sign: KB7WFU
William R Brown
4132 N 600 E
Van Buren IN 46991

Call Sign: N9ICE
William R Brown
4132 N 600 E
Van Buren IN 46991

Call Sign: KA9HDG
Charles R Rodecap
6602 N 900 E
Van Buren IN 46991

FCC Amateur Radio Licenses in Wabash

Call Sign: KB9UCS
David O Summers
100N
Wabash IN 469928650

Call Sign: N9WPS
Chester King
500S
Wabash IN 46992

Call Sign: KB9CVU

Kristine R Solloway
470 Alena St
Wabash IN 46992

Call Sign: KB9TFZ
Brian C Pettit
829 Berkley Dr
Wabash IN 46992

Call Sign: KA9ZJW
Kenneth H Burnworth
545 Bond St
Wabash IN 46992

Call Sign: KB9DYM
Frank W Langford
Box 106C Lot 57
Wabash IN 46992

Call Sign: N9KCV
Ronald D Spencer
24 Broadmoor Dr
Wabash IN 46992

Call Sign: W9CDG
Carlos D Guerrero
1481 Columbus St
Wabash IN 46992

Call Sign: KC9PXB
Pascual D Guerrero
1485 Columbus St
Wabash IN 46992

Call Sign: KA9SBG
James D Black
770 E 250 S
Wabash IN 46992

Call Sign: KB9THE
George A Fairchild
565 E Hill St
Wabash IN 46992

Call Sign: KB9WKP

Denise D Pettit
285 E Main St
Wabash IN 46992

Call Sign: WA9UYR
Kenneth E
Hettmansperger
1 Elmwood Dr
Wabash IN 46992

Call Sign: KC9NKQ
Richard D Lower
530 Fairfield Dr
Wabash IN 46992

Call Sign: WB7ABW
Clark C Shearer
1284 Falls Ave
Wabash IN 46992

Call Sign: N7RIB
Kevin R Dorsey Tyler
1299 Falls Ave
Wabash IN 46992

Call Sign: N9XIH
Steven M Wendt
1500 Florence St
Wabash IN 46992

Call Sign: N9UAX
Keith A Walters
1623 King St
Wabash IN 46992

Call Sign: N9TAB
Larry L Richey
115 Manchester Ave
Wabash IN 46992

Call Sign: N9NYQ
Edward Miller
825 Michigan St
Wabash IN 46992

Call Sign: KA9OPM
Mathew Lucas
1507 Morris
Wabash IN 46992

Call Sign: KA9FCU
John A Brane
4574 S 400 W
Wabash IN 46992

Call Sign: N9MNU
Larry J Watson II
865 Sunset Dr
Wabash IN 46992

Call Sign: KA9FCV
Patrick S Davis
1647 N 100 E
Wabash IN 46992

Call Sign: KB9QAN
Conrad F Driesen
4972 S Bailey Rd
Wabash IN 46992

Call Sign: KA9ZIA
Linda S Mitting
1485 Tanglewood Dr
Wabash IN 46992

Call Sign: KC9AYL
Glenn E Lightner
2514 N 700 W
Wabash IN 46992

Call Sign: KC9HEZ
Richard L Hosier
7513 S Meridian Rd
Wabash IN 46992

Call Sign: NT9O
David O Summers
6984 W 100 N
Wabash IN 469928650

Call Sign: W3TTP
Glenn E Lightner
2514 N 700 W
Wabash IN 46992

Call Sign: W2RLH
Richard L Hosier
7513 S Meridian Rd
Wabash IN 46992

Call Sign: WB9DKH
Robert S Mitting
6969 W 100 S
Wabash IN 46992

Call Sign: KB9PLV
Ralph C Frank
4010 N 700 W
Wabash IN 46992

Call Sign: KC9NKR
Robert D Brown
101 Shady Ln
Wabash IN 46992

Call Sign: WB9YEY
Robert C Greer
423 W 250 S
Wabash IN 46992

Call Sign: N9WVM
John P Netro Jr
477 N Fisher St
Wabash IN 46992

Call Sign: N9BBC
Robert D Brown
101 Shady Ln
Wabash IN 46992

Call Sign: KA9ZJP
Michael J Devore
355 W 500 S
Wabash IN 46992

Call Sign: KC9NKS
Karen A Netro
477 N Fisher St
Wabash IN 46992

Call Sign: W9NPL
Melvin P Thurlow
15 Sherman St
Wabash IN 46992

Call Sign: N9KNN
Paul M Bergman
511 Washington St
Wabash IN 46992

Call Sign: KB9JTM
Robert L Kiefaber
529 N Wabash St
Wabash IN 46992

Call Sign: W9HNO
Donald G Spangler
235 Southwood Dr
Wabash IN 46992

Call Sign: WB9JTF
William E Givens
Wabash IN 46992

Call Sign: KA9ZJS
Kyle M Kerr
Wabash IN 46992

Call Sign: N9VUM
William R Middleton
562 Railroad St
Wabash IN 46992

Call Sign: KB9NSO
John P Netro Jr
495 Stitt St
Wabash IN 46992

Call Sign: K9WCR

Wabash County Ema
ARC
Wabash IN 46992

Call Sign: KC9BUY
Wabash County Ema
ARC
Wabash IN 46992

FCC Amateur Radio Licenses in Wakarusa

Call Sign: KA9RTF
Laura M Rhoades
County Side Est
Wakarusa IN 46573

Call Sign: KB9NZW
Jeff J Mast
63703 CR 1
Wakarusa IN 46573

Call Sign: KG4HOS
Benjamin J Snyder
66831 CR 1
Wakarusa IN 46573

Call Sign: KB9VPN
Charles W Kurk
65103 CR 3
Wakarusa IN 46573

Call Sign: N9UEG
John S Duesler
66773 CR 3
Wakarusa IN 46573

Call Sign: KC9UWH
Timothy C Lechlitner
30797 CR 32
Wakarusa IN 46573

Call Sign: KA9HKZ
Thomas D Tarman
28810 CR 38

Wakarusa IN 465739706

Call Sign: WD9AWU
Max W Doering
28722 CR 38 R 1
Wakarusa IN 465739755

Call Sign: N6RHP
Valerie D Kurk
210 S Elkhart Ave
Wakarusa IN 46573

Call Sign: AE9U
Phillip L Bowers
102 Sunset Ct
Wakarusa IN 465730018

Call Sign: N9SIX
Daniel R Cripe
308 W Harrison St
Wakarusa IN 46573

Call Sign: K9HDH
Elkhart ARC
Wakarusa IN 46573

FCC Amateur Radio Licenses in Walkerton

Call Sign: KA9DVB
Brian D Ramsbey
19662 1C Rd
Walkerton IN 46574

Call Sign: KB9GFZ
Sonny E Pierce
Box 325A
Walkerton IN 46574

Call Sign: KB9GGM
Angel M Pierce
Box 325A
Walkerton IN 46574

Call Sign: N0YWW

Jerome Durham
111 Clover Dr
Walkerton IN 46574

Call Sign: W9BAK
Frank A Noreikis
11033 E Kanney
Walkerton IN 46574

Call Sign: KA9SJQ
Guy N Bridges
11196 E Pottawatomie Tr
N
Walkerton IN 46574

Call Sign: KA9MXL
Bernard J Small
11604 E South Ave
Walkerton IN 46574

Call Sign: KB9MTF
Eugene E Vermilyer
8201 E SR 4
Walkerton IN 46574

Call Sign: N9ICM
David G Kaufman
406 Glenwood Dr
Walkerton IN 46574

Call Sign: KC9HGU
Pamela S Kaufman
406 Glenwood Dr
Walkerton IN 46574

Call Sign: KC9TCH
James R Christie
126 Grissom Dr
Walkerton IN 46574

Call Sign: W9WPD
James R Christie
126 Grissom Dr
Walkerton IN 46574

Call Sign: NW9O
Eugene J Walker
112 Lake St
Walkerton IN 46574

Call Sign: KA9KJV
William H Sherwood
326 Lilac Dr
Walkerton IN 46574

Call Sign: N9USD
Robert L Stafford
826 N Queen Rd
Walkerton IN 46574

Call Sign: N9YBC
Tom L Stafford
826 N Queen Rd
Walkerton IN 46574

Call Sign: N9USN
Thomas E Cotton
17046 North St
Walkerton IN 46574

Call Sign: KB9KE
Joseph M Malec
8195 North St
Walkerton IN 46574

Call Sign: KC9BDO
Terry R Greene
3141 Plymouth La Porte
Trl
Walkerton IN 465748236

Call Sign: W9TRG
Terry R Greene
3141 Plymouth La Porte
Trl
Walkerton IN 465748236

Call Sign: KB8VQS
Wayne L Buckhanan
30818 Rockstroh Rd

Walkerton IN 46574

Call Sign: KC9DZV
Andrew J Baugh
2968 S 800 E
Walkerton IN 46574

Call Sign: KC9TCG
Jeffrey W Waters
10851 Seneca Ln
Walkerton IN 46574

Call Sign: N9ICP
Jeffrey W Waters
10851 Seneca Ln
Walkerton IN 46574

Call Sign: KC9VKC
Scott R Bryant
29868 Smith Rd
Walkerton IN 46574

Call Sign: KC9OCH
Betsy S Pairitz
72099 Spruce Rd
Walkerton IN 46574

Call Sign: KC9GZM
Thaddeus J Pairitz
72099 Spruce Rd
Walkerton IN 46574

Call Sign: WB9T
Jon M Pairitz
72099 Spruce Rd
Walkerton IN 465748708

Call Sign: N9PCN
Nathaniel J Pairitz
72099 Spruce Rd
Walkerton IN 46574

Call Sign: N9PCR
Julius A Erdelyi
467 Sycamore Rd

Walkerton IN 46574

Call Sign: KA9MUZ
Roger F Fry
4437 Tamarack Rd
Walkerton IN 46574

Call Sign: KB9OVA
Jack S Rankert
7641 Topinabee
Walkerton IN 46574

Call Sign: N9ML
Bernard J Small
20350 W 5th Rd
Walkerton IN 46574

Call Sign: KB9ITM
Aaron R Meyer
609 Washington Ave
Walkerton IN 46574

Call Sign: N9QEN
Jon A Meyer
609 Washington St
Walkerton IN 46574

Call Sign: KA9RRZ
Joseph E Walker
103 Willow Dr
Walkerton IN 46574

Call Sign: KC9RPG
Rex A Swift Sr
72864 Willow Tr
Walkerton IN 46574

Call Sign: KC9ACC
Anthony J Dombrowski
101 Wood Creek Dr
Walkerton IN 465749781

**FCC Amateur Radio
Licenses in Walton**

Call Sign: KA7OVR
Muriel J Newburn
Box 37
Walton IN 46994

Call Sign: KA9ASP
Mary C Guy
Box 9
Walton IN 46994

Call Sign: KB9OYX
Robert V Maughmer
5932 Creek Ridge Rd
Walton IN 46994

Call Sign: K9WEK
Daniel H Hopper
10428 E CR 450 S
Walton IN 46994

Call Sign: N9UKR
Homer D Foster
404 E Dutchess
Walton IN 46994

Call Sign: KE9GO
Randall G Newburn
4397 E SR 218
Walton IN 46994

Call Sign: W9GUY
Don J Guy
8677 E SR 218
Walton IN 46994

Call Sign: KA9BZW
Michael J Guy
8677 E SR 218
Walton IN 46994

Call Sign: K9WET
Ralph L Piercy
107 N High St
Walton IN 46994

Call Sign: KA9NIU
Edward D Newburn
700 S 450 E
Walton IN 46994

Call Sign: KB9QKZ
David A French
6171 S 900 E
Walton IN 46994

FCC Amateur Radio Licenses in Wanatah

Call Sign: KB9YML
Chris M Chavis
401 N Illinois St
Wanatah IN 46390

Call Sign: N9OST
Brad A Rocke
14401 S 700 W
Wanatah IN 46390

Call Sign: KA9VSN
Harlan A Siegesmund
8131 S 900 W
Wanatah IN 46390

Call Sign: KC9OHK
David S Watkins
6066 W 1600 S
Wanatah IN 46390

Call Sign: KB9SCJ
Robert F Baum
8602 W 900 S
Wanatah IN 46930

Call Sign: W9RZR
Robert F Baum
8602 W 900S
Wanatah IN 46390

Call Sign: N9VLT
Barbara A Miller

Wanatah IN 46390

Call Sign: N9RKY
Todd E Miller
Wanatah IN 46390

FCC Amateur Radio Licenses in Warren

Call Sign: KB9JDM
Robert A Richardson
4271 E 900 S
Warren IN 46792

Call Sign: W9DNC
Phillip E Young
801 Huntington Ave Ste 100A
Warren IN 46792

Call Sign: WB9CFT
Miriam I Young
801 Huntington Ave Ste 129A
Warren IN 46792

Call Sign: KD9MD
Ralph W Haney
309 N Grover St
Warren IN 46792

Call Sign: KB9GAQ
Earl W Adkins
626 N Wayen St
Warren IN 46792

Call Sign: W9WIX
Shirley E Murray
7327 S 1000 W 90
Warren IN 46792

Call Sign: N5MY
Charles A Murray
7327 S 1000 W 90
Warren IN 46792

Call Sign: N9YWB
Andy E Thompson
10146 S 700 W
Warren IN 46792

Call Sign: KC9HOW
Nichole Zumbrun
207 S Grover Apt 2B
Warren IN 46792

Call Sign: KB9WJN
William A Van Haften
7593 S SR 3 90
Warren IN 46792

Call Sign: KB9YQE
Brian L Zumbrun
3536 W 1000 S
Warren IN 46792

Call Sign: KB9YLS
Jonathan E Zumbrun
3536 W 1000 S
Warren IN 46792

Call Sign: KB9YQJ
David Zumbrun
6889 W 1000 S
Warren IN 46792

Call Sign: KC9HML
M Leroy Scott II
593 W 450 S
Warren IN 46792

Call Sign: KB9WQN
Daniel C Zumbrun
5429 W 500 S 90
Warren IN 46792

Call Sign: KC9SNG
Joe A Compton
2700 W 900 S
Warren IN 46792

Call Sign: KB9YAO
Linda Bowman
3955 W 900 S
Warren IN 46792

Call Sign: KB9WFO
Ted Bowman
3955 W 900 S
Warren IN 46792

Call Sign: KB9YAN
Arthur D Graff
5236 W 900 S
Warren IN 46792

Call Sign: N9QVI
Christopher R Richardson
Warren IN 46792

Call Sign: KC9PQM
Amanda L Reed
Warren IN 46792

Call Sign: K9OTA
Amanda L Reed
Warren IN 46792

Call Sign: KC9PQN
Simeon E Reed
Warren IN 46792

Call Sign: W9SIM
Simeon E Reed
Warren IN 46792

**FCC Amateur Radio
Licenses in Warsaw**

Call Sign: K9LSR
John Piasecki Sr
2128 Blue Water
Warsaw IN 46580

Call Sign: W9OED

James P Berner
5193 Bobwhite Dr
Warsaw IN 46582

Call Sign: KB9DLT
Peggy J Girard
Box 169
Warsaw IN 46580

Call Sign: N9IOJ
Verlin A Young
Box 170B
Warsaw IN 46580

Call Sign: KB9AXJ
Leslie M Estep
Box 353
Warsaw IN 46580

Call Sign: N9CPZ
Paul H Russell
Box 436
Warsaw IN 46580

Call Sign: KC9TRP
Steve K Sausaman
1443 Brookview Ave
Warsaw IN 46580

Call Sign: KC9TRA
Patrick A Briar
2504 Center Dr
Warsaw IN 46580

Call Sign: KB9CTK
Erik D Lindquist
1419 Country Club Dr E
Warsaw IN 46580

Call Sign: N9NJK
Craig W Norrell
1025 Country Club Ln
Warsaw IN 46580

Call Sign: K9GV

George C Van De Water
CR 300W
Warsaw IN 46580

Call Sign: KB9SLS
William K Bergin
3699 CR N 175 E Lot 92
Warsaw IN 46580

Call Sign: NH2W
Daniel A Plett
1215 Duncan Dr
Warsaw IN 46580

Call Sign: KC9RQV
Scott Eddy
6264 E 200 N
Warsaw IN 46582

Call Sign: KC9UBO
Jason R Brown
1692 E 200 N Lot 108
Warsaw IN 46582

Call Sign: KA9ZGC
Michael D Swope
1692 E 200 N Lot 29
Warsaw IN 46580

Call Sign: N9NRX
Rodney A Chiddister
3028 E 250 N
Warsaw IN 46582

Call Sign: K9KTB
James R Abbott
4217 E 300 N
Warsaw IN 46580

Call Sign: KB9SRJ
Dave B McGuire
615 E 300 S
Warsaw IN 46580

Call Sign: KC9TRN

Jeffrey L Puckett
1765 E 300 S
Warsaw IN 46580

Call Sign: KC9UDI
Michelle L Puckett
1765 E 300 S
Warsaw IN 46580

Call Sign: KB9GOZ
Deborah L Stevens
133 E 350 S
Warsaw IN 46580

Call Sign: KB9GPA
William P Stevens Jr
133 E 350 S
Warsaw IN 46580

Call Sign: N6KXD
Philip L Blais
4490 E 450 S
Warsaw IN 46580

Call Sign: KV8KV
Roy E Crosier
800 E Arthur E3
Warsaw IN 46580

Call Sign: WA8TCF
Russell G Wall
940 E Arthur St
Warsaw IN 46580

Call Sign: KA9KHK
Ralph E Hyde
1116 E Center St
Warsaw IN 46580

Call Sign: N9GAF
Richard A Abbott
4217 E CR 300 N
Warsaw IN 465822017

Call Sign: KC9DLR

Karl D Campbell
816 E Fort Wayne St
Warsaw IN 46580

Call Sign: KA9POE
Lee A Lingofelter
504 E Fort Wayne St Apt
2
Warsaw IN 46580

Call Sign: KC9VJU
Bert A Kabana
1321 E Island View Dr
Warsaw IN 46580

Call Sign: KC9PBP
Joe D Armey
1315 E Islandview Dr
Warsaw IN 46580

Call Sign: KC9HUP
Karla J Drudge
2015 E Jefferson St
Warsaw IN 46580

Call Sign: KC9TRE
Kurt A Eberhardt
3370 E Kenway Dr
Warsaw IN 46582

Call Sign: N9MLN
Deona G Moore
518 E Main St
Warsaw IN 46580

Call Sign: KB9DRI
Jay B Moore
518 E Main St
Warsaw IN 46580

Call Sign: KB9JDF
Lauri J Westerhof
1510 E Main St
Warsaw IN 46580

Call Sign: W9JTC
Frederick N Gresso
2201 E Market St
Warsaw IN 46580

Call Sign: N9WLB
Michael J Bonahoom
2590 E Oak Ln
Warsaw IN 46582

Call Sign: N9DTR
John P Burns
1702 E Sheridan
Warsaw IN 46580

Call Sign: KG4KJQ
Michael S Lewis
643 E Wildwood Dr
Warsaw IN 46580

Call Sign: KC9NWL
Mark E Fuller
2692 E Wooster Rd
Warsaw IN 46580

Call Sign: KC8GLA
Philip D Gregg
97 Ems B 36 B 2 La
Warsaw IN 46582

Call Sign: N9USF
Michael P Beaver
46 Ems B36 B2 Ln
Warsaw IN 46580

Call Sign: KC9RRU
Mark A Hazelet
1 Ems B37 Ln 83
Warsaw IN 46582

Call Sign: KA9HMY
William G Freestone
1 Ems B37 Ln Lot 60
Warsaw IN 46582

Call Sign: N9SPH
A Joe Schaefer
38 Ems B51A Ln
Warsaw IN 46580

Call Sign: KA9TUQ
Harold A Dunn
85 Ems C 24 E Ln
Warsaw IN 465827885

Call Sign: KA9YOA
Shirley J Dunn
85 Ems C 24 E Ln
Warsaw IN 465827885

Call Sign: K9OIW
William B Eiler
130 Ems C17 Ln
Warsaw IN 465827904

Call Sign: WB9NAV
Clair L McGuire
6 Ems C27Bi Ln
Warsaw IN 46580

Call Sign: KC9TRI
Devon C Lee
36 Ems C28E 1 Ln
Warsaw IN 46582

Call Sign: KB9OUK
Denton P Williams
94 Ems Ln C 27C
Warsaw IN 46582

Call Sign: WB9RRL
Thomas E Buchan
501 Fruitridge Dr
Warsaw IN 465804916

Call Sign: N9AL
Thomas E Buchan
501 Fruitridge Dr
Warsaw IN 465804916

Call Sign: WX9IWX
National Weather Service
Skywarn
260 Gettysburg Ct
Warsaw IN 465825940

Call Sign: WD8PFB
David B Masterson
309 Herscher
Warsaw IN 46580

Call Sign: W9UO
David B Masterson
309 Herscher
Warsaw IN 465803133

Call Sign: WA9ZYC
David F Mayhew
1901 Ironwood Dr
Warsaw IN 46580

Call Sign: KC9GGQ
Kevin W Kosins
311 Kincaide
Warsaw IN 46580

Call Sign: KC9GGP
Bernadette L Kosins
311 Kincaide St
Warsaw IN 46580

Call Sign: N9BS
Barry L Gold
1121 Lakeshore Dr
Warsaw IN 46580

Call Sign: N9JYS
Bradley D Gold
1121 Lakeshore Dr
Warsaw IN 46580

Call Sign: N9JYR
Valerie M Gold
1121 Lakeshore Dr
Warsaw IN 46580

Call Sign: WB4REH
Paul E Wilyard
Ln 85
Warsaw IN 46580

Call Sign: KC9AAC
Charles L Carr
1284 Mark Ln
Warsaw IN 46580

Call Sign: KC9PBQ
Jack C Lowry
115 Mary MacDr
Warsaw IN 46580

Call Sign: KA9QWV
John C Sparks
1516 Maye St
Warsaw IN 46580

Call Sign: KA9ZFU
Vanessa Sparks
1516 Maye St
Warsaw IN 46580

Call Sign: KA9QFA
Billy J Garner
1406 Meadow Lark
Warsaw IN 46580

Call Sign: KA9QEZ
Mark E Garner
1406 Meadowlark Blvd
Warsaw IN 46580

Call Sign: WA0QZK
Jack W Worth
4180 N 20 E
Warsaw IN 46580

Call Sign: KC9KGO
Harry A Sheetz
313 N 225 E
Warsaw IN 46582

Call Sign: KC9MRD
Andrew D Jeffreys
4335 N 300 W
Warsaw IN 46582

Call Sign: K9CWD
Hoosier Lakes Radio
Club
4391 N 300 W
Warsaw IN 46580

Call Sign: KB9PHO
Hoosier Lakes Radio
Club
4391 N 300 W
Warsaw IN 46580

Call Sign: KB9WJB
Matthew C Foreman
1153 N Arbutus Tr
Warsaw IN 46580

Call Sign: K4MAN
Matthew C Foreman
1153 N Arbutus Tr
Warsaw IN 46580

Call Sign: KC9MAD
American Red Cross Of
Koscivsko County
320 N Buffalo St
Warsaw IN 46580

Call Sign: N9PEP
Thomas R Burdey
1730 N Copeland
Warsaw IN 46580

Call Sign: N9HUH
Jack M Harrell
4121 N Deer Run
Warsaw IN 465826908

Call Sign: KC9DCS

Debbie L Murphy
260 N Gettysburg Ct
Warsaw IN 45682

Call Sign: KB8QEV
Patrick B Murphy
260 N Gettysburg Ct
Warsaw IN 46580

Call Sign: WX9DEB
Debbie L Murphy
260 N Gettysburg Ct
Warsaw IN 465825940

Call Sign: WX9PAT
Patrick B Murphy
260 N Gettysburg Ct
Warsaw IN 465825940

Call Sign: WB9JUV
Thomas C Skaggs Sr
3732 N Greenwood Dr
Warsaw IN 46582

Call Sign: WB9YFZ
Gloria S Skaggs
3732 N Greewood Dr
Warsaw IN 46580

Call Sign: KB9WJA
Gloria S Skaggs
3732 N Greewood Dr
Warsaw IN 46582

Call Sign: WD9IJL
Edwin S Purrington
511 N Harrison St
Warsaw IN 465803127

Call Sign: N2WQM
Joel T Cook
600 N Lake St Apt D
Warsaw IN 46580

Call Sign: K9CWD

James K Landis
1704 N Lakeview Blvd
Warsaw IN 46580

Call Sign: WC9U
John P O Lesek
609 N Lindberg Dr
Warsaw IN 46580

Call Sign: KC9ATK
Mark N McConnell
4330 N Old 15 50Wp
Warsaw IN 46582

Call Sign: KC9MRE
Srinivas R Setty
123 N Orchard Dr Apt 5
Warsaw IN 46580

Call Sign: N9SBH
Darrell E Young
701 N Park Ave
Warsaw IN 46580

Call Sign: KC9TRH
Vaughan H Latham
3984 N Prairie St
Warsaw IN 46582

Call Sign: KC9TQZ
Kent A Briar
1090 N Riverwood Ranch
Rd
Warsaw IN 465808786

Call Sign: KC9QOJ
Christopher W Pollnow
1221 N Riverwood Ranch
Rd
Warsaw IN 46580

Call Sign: WA9WBX
Kenneth A McKeand
507 N Union
Warsaw IN 46580

Call Sign: KC9APU
Marcus A Hygema
1935 N Vicky Ln
Warsaw IN 46582

Call Sign: KB9SBI
Terry W Keim
620 N Zimmer Rd
Warsaw IN 46580

Call Sign: K9LZV
Robert M Hoeppner
506 Nancy St
Warsaw IN 46580

Call Sign: KC9RRY
Laura L Herring
410 Parker St
Warsaw IN 46580

Call Sign: KC9RRP
Ryan A Reed
412 Parker St
Warsaw IN 46580

Call Sign: KC9TRB
Larry E Buckmaster Sr
2702 Patterson Rd
Warsaw IN 46582

Call Sign: KB9MOQ
Eric E Teune
512 Perry St
Warsaw IN 46580

Call Sign: N9SBT
John J Weckler
1200 Ranch Rd
Warsaw IN 46580

Call Sign: N9QVU
Ernest Long II
1406 Ranch Rd
Warsaw IN 46580

Call Sign: N9QVV
Terry L Long
1406 Ranch Rd
Warsaw IN 46580

Call Sign: WD9ECL
Paul E Shafer
1621 Ranch Rd
Warsaw IN 46580

Call Sign: N9IMX
Joseph A Kruger
1407 Rivercrest Dr
Warsaw IN 46580

Call Sign: KC9TRJ
Julia V Kincaid
206 Robb Rd
Warsaw IN 46580

Call Sign: KB9WZG
Gerald D Oswalt
1805 Robin Dr
Warsaw IN 465802340

Call Sign: N9GDO
Gerald D Oswalt
1805 Robin Dr
Warsaw IN 465802340

Call Sign: KB9JWI
Thomas A McGuire
1830 Rosemont Ave
Warsaw IN 46580

Call Sign: N9DOT
Robert G Henderson
1906 Rosemont Ave
Warsaw IN 46580

Call Sign: W5DJW
Donald J Ward
1904 Rosemont Ave
Warsaw IN 46580

Call Sign: N9VKV
Dennis A Alberts
978 S 250 E
Warsaw IN 46580

Call Sign: KF9HW
Daniel L Kreger
6830 S 400 E
Warsaw IN 46580

Call Sign: KB9KUL
Denise A O Bryant
1336 S 775 W
Warsaw IN 46580

Call Sign: N9UZM
Ronald A O Bryant
1336 S 775 W
Warsaw IN 46580

Call Sign: KC9RQM
Matthew D Stevens
3210 S Country Club Rd
Warsaw IN 46580

Call Sign: KB9RZB
Harvey C Badman
2798 S Country Club Rd
Lot 40
Warsaw IN 46580

Call Sign: KC9SQL
David E Halas
435 S County Farm Rd
Warsaw IN 46580

Call Sign: KA9OHV
James P Stevens
3227 S County Farm Rd
Warsaw IN 46580

Call Sign: KC9SUB
Elijah D Halas
4357 S County Farm Rd

Warsaw IN 46580

Call Sign: KC9SQM
Emmaline C Halas
4357 S County Farm Rd
Warsaw IN 46580

Call Sign: KC9RRC
Jessica L Halas
4357 S County Farm Rd
Warsaw IN 46580

Call Sign: K9BXG
James L Townsend
6331 S CR 300E
Warsaw IN 46580

Call Sign: KB9OYY
Mark G Kroll
3914 S Elaine Dr
Warsaw IN 46580

Call Sign: KC9RJL
John V Yingling Jr
150 S Hunters Ridge
Warsaw IN 46582

Call Sign: KC9KUW
Philip G Magner III
407 S Indiana St
Warsaw IN 45680

Call Sign: W9PGM
Philip G Magner III
407 S Indiana St
Warsaw IN 45680

Call Sign: KB9OUP
Bryan C Benjamin
2316 S Lake Sharon Dr
Warsaw IN 46580

Call Sign: KG9JN
Marie Benjamin
2316 S Lake Sharon Rd

Warsaw IN 46580

Call Sign: KC9TRQ
Charles A Sherman
2383 S Lake Sharon Rd
Warsaw IN 465806218

Call Sign: KB9VRO
Thomas H Hobart
322 S Lake St
Warsaw IN 46580

Call Sign: K9MMQ
John W Holden
321 S McKinley St
Warsaw IN 46580

Call Sign: KB9EVL
Judy K Holden
321 S McKinley St
Warsaw IN 46580

Call Sign: KC9LUZ
Randy L Schmucker
2249 S Oak Dr
Warsaw IN 46580

Call Sign: KF4TSB
Belinda G Matero
2262 S Old Ditch Rd
Warsaw IN 46580

Call Sign: KC9HBR
Jody E Blue
2767 S Packerton Rd
Warsaw IN 46580

Call Sign: KC9FKF
Paul D Blue
2767 S Packerton Rd
Warsaw IN 46580

Call Sign: KC9GGO
Christopher A Tague
2821 S Packerton Rd

Warsaw IN 46580

Warsaw IN 46580

Warsaw IN 46580

Call Sign: KC9LUY
Larry E Peppel
2461 S Paxton Dr
Warsaw IN 46580

Call Sign: KC9AYT
Sarah B Wood
3529 W 100 S Lot 19
Warsaw IN 46580

Call Sign: N9SCC
William J Frush
156 W 300 S
Warsaw IN 46580

Call Sign: KA9POB
Lloyd D Bowerman
2634 S Rd 15
Warsaw IN 46580

Call Sign: N9JYU
Larry A Kinsey
3356 W 200 N
Warsaw IN 46580

Call Sign: KA9ZFW
Christopher F Sanburn
226 W 300 S
Warsaw IN 465807421

Call Sign: N9AKY
David A Chamness
1720 S Walnut Dr
Warsaw IN 46580

Call Sign: KB9UQA
Don M Jones
1038 W 200 S
Warsaw IN 465807304

Call Sign: KB9OEI
Craig E Brown
245 W 350 S
Warsaw IN 46580

Call Sign: KB9TUG
Ellis G Hygema
1700 S West Pt Dr
Warsaw IN 46580

Call Sign: WA9PSV
Joseph F Sanburn Jr
1095 W 200 S
Warsaw IN 46580

Call Sign: KB9AXH
Kristi C Brown
245 W 350 S
Warsaw IN 46580

Call Sign: N9EH
Ellis G Hygema
1700 S West Pt Dr
Warsaw IN 46580

Call Sign: KB9OUL
Peter G Kroll
1223 W 200 S
Warsaw IN 46580

Call Sign: KC9JSF
Bruce E Higham
7759 W 400N
Warsaw IN 46582

Call Sign: N9NUY
Karl T Martin
Sand Dollar Dr
Warsaw IN 46580

Call Sign: KC9RTS
Michal Slomczykowski
2609 W 200 S
Warsaw IN 46580

Call Sign: KK5SV
Michael K Carter
2193 W Blackberry Trl
Warsaw IN 46580

Call Sign: KD8UE
Mark S Morrison
1508 Spring Hill Rd
Warsaw IN 46580

Call Sign: KA9ZGQ
Doug A Sanburn
1095 W 200 S
Warsaw IN 46580

Call Sign: K9DGM
Deona G Moore
1621 W Briaridge Rd
Warsaw IN 46580

Call Sign: WB9YST
James P Berner Jr
Suburban Acres Lot 77
Warsaw IN 46580

Call Sign: N9HJG
Mark A Riggle
145 W 300 S
Warsaw IN 46580

Call Sign: W9JBM
Jay B Moore
1621 W Briaridge Rd
Warsaw IN 46580

Call Sign: KC9UDJ
Charles E Mills Jr
6735 W 100 N

Call Sign: KA9ZFV
Audrey J Frush
156 W 300 S

Call Sign: KB9OUJ
Carolyn J Morrison
316 W Center St

Warsaw IN 46580

Call Sign: N9NUE
Orace W Morrison
316 W Center St
Warsaw IN 46580

Call Sign: N9QWF
Dan A Lippincott
416 W Cherry Tree Dr
Warsaw IN 46582

Call Sign: KC9TRG
Mark D Gregory
7605 W Crystal Lake Rd
Warsaw IN 46580

Call Sign: AB9ZA
Mark D Gregory
7605 W Crystal Lake Rd
Warsaw IN 46580

Call Sign: W3MJY
Eugene N Hungerford
1695 W Highland Ct
Warsaw IN 465806402

Call Sign: KC9TRC
Calvin L Couch
320 W Main Retired
Tigers Apt 307
Warsaw IN 46582

Call Sign: KC9TRT
John N Woods
3762 W Old Rd 30 62 E
Warsaw IN 46580

Call Sign: KC9TRR
Diane M Woods
3762 W Old Rd 30 62 E
Warsaw IN 46580

Call Sign: KC9TRS
Joel E Woods

3762 W Old Rd 30 62E
Warsaw IN 46580

Call Sign: KA9TVS
Josef R McGrath
423 W Prairie St
Warsaw IN 46580

Call Sign: NM9Z
Robert McGrath
423 W Prairie St
Warsaw IN 46580

Call Sign: KB9ORT
Timothy M Wendt
7559 W Synder Rd
Warsaw IN 46580

Call Sign: KB9MVR
Ernest W Crettol
409 Westcreek Dr
Warsaw IN 46580

Call Sign: KB9MVQ
Mark W Crettol
409 Westcreek Dr
Warsaw IN 46580

Call Sign: N9TIW
L Dale Neal
Warsaw IN 46581

Call Sign: KC9BSA
George R Glaser
Warsaw IN 46580

Call Sign: KC9RRQ
David E Mcelroy II
Warsaw IN 46581

Call Sign: KC9RRS
Rachel C Mayer
Warsaw IN 46581

Call Sign: KC9OEJ

Raphael G Wolff
Warsaw IN 46581

Call Sign: KC9UUD
Hoosier Lakes Radio
Club
Warsaw IN 46581

Call Sign: N9HUI
Bud Brady
Warsaw IN 465811023

Call Sign: N9LOX
Glenn A Meeks
Warsaw IN 465811782

FCC Amateur Radio Licenses in Waterloo

Call Sign: KD9MG
Robert E Shaffer
3367 CR 10
Waterloo IN 46793

Call Sign: KB9NPD
Michael C Spirek
5242 CR 10
Waterloo IN 46793

Call Sign: KB9QLR
Susan R Spirek
5360 CR 10
Waterloo IN 46793

Call Sign: W9QWI
Howard A Hine
2859 CR 23
Waterloo IN 46793

Call Sign: K9WJH
Maynard D Hine
2859 CR 23
Waterloo IN 46793

Call Sign: KC9KSL

Tyler T Weldon
3244 CR 27
Waterloo IN 46793

Call Sign: KB9MHQ
Michael C Richardson
4516 CR 28
Waterloo IN 46793

Call Sign: KC9LVO
Sheree A Behrendsen
459 CR 39
Waterloo IN 46793

Call Sign: N9LIM
Myron B Ress
318 Knoll Creek Dr
Waterloo IN 46793

Call Sign: KC9BEW
Keith L Lewis
355 N Center St
Waterloo IN 46793

Call Sign: KC2YHX
William S Rundell
380 N Washington St
Waterloo IN 46793

Call Sign: K9FON
Eric A Zerkle
275 Peneton St
Waterloo IN 46793

Call Sign: KC9EDI
Jonathan I Napier
1075 S Center St
Waterloo IN 46793

Call Sign: WA9GNA
Harold W McEntarfer
210 W Maple St
Waterloo IN 467930425

Call Sign: N9NJJ

Curt J Hapner
820 Watermill Ct
Waterloo IN 46793

Call Sign: KC9LOJ
Victor D Sumner
Waterloo IN 46793

FCC Amateur Radio Licenses in Wawaka

Call Sign: N9ICL
Robert G Rice
Box 17
Wawaka IN 46794

Call Sign: K9LBH
Joe K Custer
Box 75
Wawaka IN 46794

Call Sign: WB9AMK
Michael L Smith
6199 N 350 W
Wawaka IN 46794

Call Sign: KB9IBX
Ross M Musselman
7115 N 525 W
Wawaka IN 46794

FCC Amateur Radio Licenses in West Point

Call Sign: KC9UWP
Aaron P Lorton
8225 SR 28 W
Westpoint IN 47992

Call Sign: K9FGX
Nellie A Van Sickle
9929 Turner Rd
West Point IN 47992

Call Sign: W9EJV

Harry R Evans Memorial
Radio Club
9929 Turner Rd
West Point IN 47992

Call Sign: K9KRE
James B Van Sickle
9929 Turner Rd
West Point IN 47992

Call Sign: KB9LLB
Thomas R Melville
8526 W 700 S
West Point IN 479929258

Call Sign: KB9UPM
Billy W Betty
5710 W 800 S
West Point IN 47992

Call Sign: KC9EWG
Hugh N Mcguire
6114 W 800 S
West Point IN 47992

Call Sign: WD9ILD
Patrick A Burgess
6615 W 800 S
West Point IN 47992

FCC Amateur Radio Licenses in Westville

Call Sign: KR9Z
Freddie E Rixie
300S
Westville IN 46391

Call Sign: KC9DJP
Richard D Oberle
604 Alan John Dr
Westville IN 46391

Call Sign: KC9BBE
Nancy L Perkins

208 Ash Pkwy
Westville IN 46391

Call Sign: N9NCY
Nancy L Perkins
208 Ash Pkwy
Westville IN 46391

Call Sign: KD9VB
Eugene L Ward
312 Ash Pkwy
Westville IN 46391

Call Sign: KA9RAL
James B Oursler
335 Birch Pkwy
Westville IN 46391

Call Sign: KC9HQT
Brian A Kehe
580 Cheyenne Ct
Westville IN 46391

Call Sign: WB9QPA
Lee F Dunn
201 Clyborn St Box 755
Westville IN 46391

Call Sign: WD9CNR
Robert L Hall
615 E 900 N
Westville IN 46391

Call Sign: KD9HL
Stephen T Mollman
698 E 900 N
Westville IN 46391

Call Sign: KA5NTB
David H Hawkins
675 E 950 N
Westville IN 46391

Call Sign: KB9TYL
Brett S Zaiko

620 E Hwy 6
Westville IN 46391

Call Sign: KC9KYM
Juergen Nittner II
666 E Hwy 6
Westville IN 46391

Call Sign: N9HPH
Debra M Sax
650 E US 6
Westville IN 46391

Call Sign: N9MXV
Marc J Sax
650 E US 6
Westville IN 46391

Call Sign: KS9L
Marshall A Sax
650 E US 6
Westville IN 46391

Call Sign: N9MQA
Shayna A Sax
650 E US 6
Westville IN 46391

Call Sign: N9RD
Juergen Nittner
666 E US Hwy 6
Westville IN 46391

Call Sign: WB9KTV
Kathy L Nittner
666 E US Hwy 6
Westville IN 46391

Call Sign: N0QGC
Richard S Prochaska IV
611 E Valparaiso St
Westville IN 46391

Call Sign: N0PFC
Melynda K Tipton

812 Elk Ln
Westville IN 46391

Call Sign: KB9KBO
Clifford R Sales
253 Main St
Westville IN 46391

Call Sign: KB9MMV
David F Minnick
573 N 600 E
Westville IN 46391

Call Sign: N9FI
David F Minnick
573 N 600 E
Westville IN 46391

Call Sign: N9PW
Paul D Walker II
599 N 600 E
Westville IN 46391

Call Sign: KC9GBD
Daniel L Canady
661 S Otis Rd
Westville IN 46391

Call Sign: K9OPL
Daniel L Canady
661 S Otis Rd
Westville IN 46391

Call Sign: W9PZR
Edward G Klein
1913 S University Park
Dr 104
Westville IN 46391

Call Sign: KC9FPV
Gregory S Dunlap
914 Sweet Cicely Dr
Westville IN 46391

Call Sign: KB9UA

John W Piper
111 Tulip Dr
Westville IN 46391

Call Sign: WB9SLB
Harry D Walker Sr
10424 W 300 S
Westville IN 46391

Call Sign: KC9CSA
Robert Mannella
11219 W Rt 6
Westville IN 46391

Call Sign: KA9ONS
William A Reid
11199 W SR 2 Lot 4
Westville IN 46391

Call Sign: W9EPF
Donald L Cabe
11199 W SR 2 Lot 4
Westville IN 46391

**FCC Amateur Radio
Licenses in Wheatfield**

Call Sign: N9IUJ
Donald E Mitch
200 W
Wheatfield IN 46392

Call Sign: WD9EBX
Sharon L White
Box 212
Wheatfield IN 46392

Call Sign: KB9HHF
Kenneth R Woolard
Box 329
Wheatfield IN 46392

Call Sign: KB9HHE
Timothy A Woolard
Box 329

Wheatfield IN 46392

Call Sign: KB9CIT
Candy L Evans
Box 386K
Wheatfield IN 46392

Call Sign: N9ISD
Garry L Evans
Box 386K
Wheatfield IN 46392

Call Sign: N9IJD
Garry R Evans
Box 386K
Wheatfield IN 46392

Call Sign: KE9OI
David L Czerniak
694 E 1100 N
Wheatfield IN 46392

Call Sign: KB9VCV
Linda G Burns
927 E 1275 N
Wheatfield IN 463929008

Call Sign: W9ZJJ
Linda G Burns
927 E 1275 N
Wheatfield IN 463929008

Call Sign: N9CEG
William L Burns
927 E 1275 N
Wheatfield IN 463929008

Call Sign: W9OPR
William L Burns
927 E 1275 N
Wheatfield IN 463929008

Call Sign: KB9QZJ
Ron A De Cola
3856 E 1425 N

Wheatfield IN 46392

Call Sign: N9DNO
William S Carter
477 E 950 N
Wheatfield IN 46392

Call Sign: N9PCX
Theodore G Donovsky
3605 Grube Dr
Wheatfield IN 46392

Call Sign: KB9UIP
Jim A Flanigan
4036 Heritage Dr N
Wheatfield IN 46392

Call Sign: KB9VWE
Ronald Johnson
9551 N 100 W
Wheatfield IN 46392

Call Sign: N9YRL
Brett E White
10566 N 200 W
Wheatfield IN 46392

Call Sign: KB9FID
Dorothy E Mitch
10625 N 200 W
Wheatfield IN 46392

Call Sign: KA9EDR
Leo C Crumrine
12096 N 350 W
Wheatfield IN 46392

Call Sign: KC9KGC
David J Kasper
272 N Hilliard St Apt B
Wheatfield IN 46392

Call Sign: N9WGP
Robert J Furman
4181 Patsy Dr

Wheatfield IN 46392

Call Sign: KC9CZF
Dawn M Carlo
45 S Wolf Rd
Wheatfield IN 46392

Call Sign: KC9MAP
Tom L Mcdaniel
11648 Salyer
Wheatfield IN 46392

Call Sign: KF9DO
Daniel E Blaney
1555 W 900 N Box 234
Wheatfield IN 46392

Call Sign: KB9ODN
Michael A Harney
256 W Central
Wheatfield IN 46392

Call Sign: W9YHH
Wayne Van Wienen
4260 W SR 10
Wheatfield IN 46392

Call Sign: KD9SR
Scott M Shelhart
12252 W Stalbaum Ln
Wheatfield IN 46392

Call Sign: KB9ZVU
Dave D Lanari
Wheatfield IN 46392

Call Sign: KB9MZK
David Lanari
Wheatfield IN 46392

Call Sign: K9EVG
James Gourko
Wheatfield IN 46392

Call Sign: KC9EJL

Mark S Carlo
Wheatfield IN 46392

Call Sign: KC9HUS
Jasper County Skywarn
Wheatfield IN 46392

FCC Amateur Radio Licenses in Wheeler

Call Sign: KB9ZVT
Arthur K Tuesburg
404 North St
Wheeler IN 46393

Call Sign: KC9ILE
Alex D W Parry
Wheeler IN 46393

FCC Amateur Radio Licenses in Whiting

Call Sign: K9MZP
Charles F Greskovich
1343 119th
Whiting IN 46394

Call Sign: KB9HSF
Donald T Casillas
1108 121st St
Whiting IN 46394

Call Sign: KA9DBX
John E Saliga
1930 Atchison Ave
Whiting IN 46394

Call Sign: KC9SVZ
Joseph M Miklusak
1617 Caroline Ave
Whiting IN 46394

Call Sign: W3ATP
C J Comstock
1948 Indianapolis Blvd

Whiting IN 46394

Call Sign: N9NET
Mary H Comstock
1948 Indianapolis Blvd
Whiting IN 46394

Call Sign: KC9VKB
Leon R Gamino
1545 Lake Ave
Whiting IN 46394

Call Sign: WA9FHS
Daniel T Pauls Jr
1747 Lake Ave
Whiting IN 46394

Call Sign: KB9ONZ
Robert J Kristek
1336 Lakeview Ave
Whiting IN 46394

Call Sign: WD9HFC
Gregory P Holicky
1325 Lakeview St
Whiting IN 46394

Call Sign: WB9MAS
James Holicky Sr
1332 Lakeview St
Whiting IN 46394

Call Sign: KA9SVR
William R Wajvoda
1801 Laporte Ave
Whiting IN 46394

Call Sign: KB9HER
Nick A Kalwinski
2004 Lincoln Ave
Whiting IN 46394

Call Sign: KB9HSP
Joseph A Blasko Sr
1433 Myrtle Ave

Whiting IN 46394

Call Sign: W9DSJ
Albert F Oprisko
1932 New York Ave
Whiting IN 463942047

Call Sign: W9YU
Gerald A Hall
2400 New York Ave
Whiting IN 46394

Call Sign: WD9HXH
William L Haddad
2603 New York Ave
Whiting IN 463942149

Call Sign: WA9NSL
Nels A Kompier
1547 Ohio Ave
Whiting IN 46394

Call Sign: K9IXO
William Oster
1824 Oliver St
Whiting IN 46394

Call Sign: N9RIY
Richard V Dean
2114 Schrage Ave
Whiting IN 46394

Call Sign: KC9JBJ
Charles E Myers
1830 Sheridan Ave
Whiting IN 46394

Call Sign: KC9UVX
Charles E Myers
1830 Sheridan Ave
Whiting IN 46394

Call Sign: KC9ULW
Brian R Rimkus
1313 Stanton Ave

Whiting IN 46394

Call Sign: KA9PEP
Shawn M O Connor
1530 Warwick Ave
Whiting IN 46394

Call Sign: KC9MAS
Jack M Brink
1945 Warwick Ave
Whiting IN 46394

Call Sign: WA9ZTP
Jack M Brink
1945 Warwick Ave
Whiting IN 46394

Call Sign: KB9IDF
Katherine A Excell Harris
1936 Wespark
Whiting IN 46394

Call Sign: WB9HZC
Daniel M Jakubovie
2027 Wespark Ave
Whiting IN 46394

**FCC Amateur Radio
Licenses in Winamac**

Call Sign: KC9YC
Richard E Werner
400E
Winamac IN 46996

Call Sign: KA9PJK
Mavis J Juniper
50N
Winamac IN 46996

Call Sign: KA9CQE
Wayne T Guthrie
1028 Agnew St
Winamac IN 46996

Call Sign: W9MIC
Wayne T Guthrie
1028 Agnew St
Winamac IN 46996

Call Sign: KA9PMX
Bessie M Bain
Box 132
Winamac IN 46996

Call Sign: KA9QPM
John W Bain
Box 132
Winamac IN 46996

Call Sign: KA9MPS
Robert J Walton
1671 E 250 N
Winamac IN 46996

Call Sign: KC9LCV
Jeanette S Richardson
132 E Rays Rd
Winamac IN 46996

Call Sign: WB9WTA
Richard B Harris
1340 E SR 14
Winamac IN 46996

Call Sign: KC9SKL
Benjamin J Hitchens
3136 N 400 E
Winamac IN 46996

Call Sign: KC9SKK
Jessica L Hitchens
3136 N 400 E
Winamac IN 46996

Call Sign: AB9QN
Lincoln Thormahlen
3587 N 400 W
Winamac IN 46996

Call Sign: N9IN
Lincoln Thormahlen
3587 N 400 W
Winamac IN 46996

Call Sign: KB9CAK
John R Kasten
702 N Hathaway St
Winamac IN 469961016

Call Sign: KA9HOU
Joel E Pence
728 N Market St
Winamac IN 46996

Call Sign: WB9RFV
Martin J Sandhage
401 N Monticello St
Winamac IN 469961327

Call Sign: KC9VBQ
Jonathan L Thompson
783 N US Hwy 35
Winamac IN 46996

Call Sign: WM9P
Daniel L Hoffman
422 S Burson
Winamac IN 469961639

Call Sign: N9IDL
Donald G Dommer
719 S Burson St
Winamac IN 46996

Call Sign: KC9LVB
Brandon J Delorenzo
219 S Franklin St
Winamac IN 46996

Call Sign: WD9BHR
Jack L Felker
531 S Market St
Winamac IN 469961554

Call Sign: W9ESW
Dennis D Dowling
3070 S SR 119
Winamac IN 469968421

Call Sign: KA9FYM
Marshall L Thomas
2578 W 300 S
Winamac IN 46996

Call Sign: KA9FLU
Kenneth E Swayze
1882 W 400 S
Winamac IN 469961016

Call Sign: KC9QAQ
Jerry D Lynch
7375 W 600 N
Winamac IN 46996

Call Sign: N9RTD
Alice M Mooi
130 W Erie St
Winamac IN 46996

Call Sign: N9RTE
Henry Mooi
130 W Erie St
Winamac IN 46996

Call Sign: KB9KGE
Ralph W Braun
Winamac IN 46996

**FCC Amateur Radio
Licenses in Winona
Lake**

Call Sign: KC9RQZ
Kristopher A Reed
112 13th St Apt B
Winona Lake IN 46590

Call Sign: W9WAR
Everett L Shoemaker

111 14th
Winona Lake IN 46590

Call Sign: WB9FIF
John McClements
113 15th St
Winona Lake IN 46590

Call Sign: N9TXQ
Charlotte I Austin
200 6th St
Winona Lake IN 46590

Call Sign: N9KHU
Gordon L Austin
1417 Avalon Ct
Winona Lake IN 46590

Call Sign: N9BAI
Robert T Miller
1419 Avalon Ct
Winona Lake IN 46590

Call Sign: KC9RRE
Gene G Gephart
1208 Biblers Ave
Winona Lake IN 46590

Call Sign: W9AXK
John W Campbell
1406 Camelot Dr
Winona Lake IN 46590

Call Sign: KB9AXI
Eric P McGinness
1400 Chestnut St
Winona Lake IN 46590

Call Sign: W9SMZ
William R Larned
111 Columbia Dr
Winona Lake IN 46590

Call Sign: KA9TTW
William L Walker

1402 E 225 S
Winona Lake IN 46590

Call Sign: W9VCY
Robert E Seitz
Grace Village Box 337
Winona Lake IN 46590

Call Sign: KB9QVF
David L Stephenson
2703 Huffman St
Winona Lake IN 46590

Call Sign: KA9THX
Gloria A Schmid
203 Isle View Dr
Winona Lake IN 46590

Call Sign: WA9DPG
Ramon F Schmid
203 Isle View Dr
Winona Lake IN 46590

Call Sign: W9WGH
Eugene S Bridges
1300 Kings Hwy
Winona Lake IN 46590

Call Sign: KC9MRC
Robert B Harkness
2698 Liberty Dr
Winona Lake IN 46590

Call Sign: WB9MKB
Katharine E Leslie
103 Mineral Springs Ave
Winona Lake IN
465901526

Call Sign: KD2ID
David E Beeson
1700 Park Ave
Winona Lake IN 46590

Call Sign: AB9HG

David E Beeson
1700 Park Ave
Winona Lake IN 46590

Call Sign: KB2SLF
Joy A Beeson
1700 Park Ave
Winona Lake IN 46590

Call Sign: KC9DIZ
Joy A Beeson
1700 Park Ave
Winona Lake IN 46590

Call Sign: KC9TQX
Joy A Beeson
1700 Park Ave
Winona Lake IN 46590

Call Sign: N9ZTV
Anthony D Jagger
700 Robson Rd
Winona Lake IN 46590

Call Sign: KC9RRW
Jeff A Holladay
808 Sharon St
Winona Lake IN 46590

Call Sign: KA9PPD
Thomas C Skaggs Jr
101 Southfield Rd
Winona Lake IN 46590

Call Sign: AA9WX
Robert M Horne
812 W Canal St
Winona Lake IN 46590

Call Sign: KC9CN
Richard E Lindquist
2511 Westwood Rd
Winona Lake IN
465901702

Call Sign: N9WSK
Steven R Hill
3008 Widaman St
Winona Lake IN 46590

Call Sign: N7GVV
James E Raisler
1438 Winchester Ct
Winona Lake IN 46590

Call Sign: N9USG
Lamar W Peugh
401 Wood St
Winona Lake IN 46590

Call Sign: KB7IRT
Ryan D Peugh
401 Wood St
Winona Lake IN 46590

Call Sign: W9JAC
Roger D Peugh
401 Wood St
Winona Lake IN
465901217

Call Sign: KB9ORY
Kimberly A Stout
1401 Wooster Rd
Winona Lake IN 46590

Call Sign: KX2F
Abel David Jr
1415 Wooster Rd
Winona Lake IN 46590

Call Sign: KA9YAL
Christia S Campbell
Winona Lake IN 46590

Call Sign: KA9QND
Daniel B Green
Winona Lake IN 46590

Call Sign: KA9YAM

Ivan Campbell
Winona Lake IN 46590

Call Sign: KD9OV
John B Campbell
Winona Lake IN 46590

Call Sign: KC9RQY
William E Darr
Winona Lake IN 46590

Call Sign: K9JOD
William E Darr
Winona Lake IN 46590

FCC Amateur Radio Licenses in Wolcott

Call Sign: KA9SGI
Carl L Moore
307 N Range St
Wolcott IN 47995

Call Sign: N9ITC
Larry L Dill
7732 W 100 N
Wolcott IN 47995

Call Sign: KC9PTM
Andrew L Allie
507 W North St
Wolcott IN 47995

Call Sign: WA9RAY
Raymond W Allie II
511 W North St
Wolcott IN 479950036

Call Sign: KB9ZAS
Raymond W Allie II
Wolcott IN 479950036

FCC Amateur Radio Licenses in Wolcottville

Call Sign: WE9I
Paul R Hohenstein
635S
Wolcottville IN 46795

Call Sign: N9LOT
Roy D Sutton
Adams Lake
Wolcottville IN 46795

Call Sign: KB9BRA
Carol S Hohenstein
Box 445H
Wolcottville IN 46795

Call Sign: KC9TJA
Douglas W Lancaster
510 E 485 S
Wolcottville IN 46795

Call Sign: KC9DBL
Douglas W Lancaster
510 E 485 S
Wolcottville IN 46795

Call Sign: W9WRH
James M Gust
2560 E 500 S
Wolcottville IN 46795

Call Sign: N9FUY
Karen S Maple
2680 E 500 S
Wolcottville IN 46795

Call Sign: KC9GQY
Anton J Lutz
5036 E 620 S
Wolcottville IN 46795

Call Sign: N9UZI
Robert Bruce
5056 E 620 S
Wolcottville IN 46795

Call Sign: KB9HMJ
Rex D Whetzel
1455 E 650S
Wolcottville IN 46795

Call Sign: KC9DOZ
Andrew M Yensco Jr
6890 E 700 S
Wolcottville IN 46795

Call Sign: KA9YNM
John A Wainwright Jr
R 1
Wolcottville IN 46795

Call Sign: N9UDZ
Ross A Miller
5595 S 030 W
Wolcottville IN 46795

Call Sign: KC9TLU
Jeffrey S Poyser
6220 S 125 E
Wolcottville IN 46795

Call Sign: KC9MTB
Barry J Borucki
5465 S 550 E
Wolcottville IN 46795

Call Sign: KC9RAA
Jack Dold
4460 S 930 E
Wolcottville IN 46795

Call Sign: WB9ZEZ
Kurt A Cripe
5614 S 980 E
Wolcottville IN
467958722

Call Sign: KB9FOX
Gary A Phillips
Wolcottville IN 46795

FCC Amateur Radio Licenses in Woodburn

Call Sign: KB9FSB
Gregory E Garrison
22112 Ash St
Woodburn IN 46797

Call Sign: KG9QY
Gregory E Garrison
22112 Ash St
Woodburn IN 46797

Call Sign: KC9HOB
Ryan J Chandler
9303 Bull Rapids Rd
Woodburn IN 46797

Call Sign: WA9NMQ
Raymond C Valentine
4102 Carl St Box 131
Woodburn IN 46797

Call Sign: KB9GOB
Roger D Flood
5102 Clovedale Dr
Woodburn IN 46797

Call Sign: N9ANF
Thomas L Hall
18610 Doty Rd
Woodburn IN 46797

Call Sign: KD9SV
Gary R Nichols
4121 Fahlsing Rd
Woodburn IN 46797

Call Sign: K9KGY
Herbert L Beattie
4718 Homestead Trl
Woodburn IN 46797

Call Sign: KC9BYC
John R Yunker

22506 Maumee Center
Rd
Woodburn IN 46797

Call Sign: KC9CGN
Gerald M Woodbury
3813 N Roussey Rd
Woodburn IN 46797

Call Sign: N9CKN
Peter E Thompson
21722 N SR 101
Woodburn IN 467979555

Call Sign: KC9QVR
Daniel L Cummins
20329 Notestine Rd
Woodburn IN 46797

Call Sign: W8UZ
Donald P Jordan
22725 Overrmeyer St
Woodburn IN 46797

Call Sign: K9GXI
Robert E Zimmerman
22536 Stenger St Box 9
Woodburn IN 46797

Call Sign: N9YNL
Steven J Ash
Woodburn Rd
Woodburn IN 46797

Call Sign: KB9RTB
Max A Foust
Woodburn IN 46797

FCC Amateur Radio Licenses in Yeoman

Call Sign: WG1I
Michael S Cooney
190 N Parsonage St
Yeoman IN 47997

FCC Amateur Radio Licenses in Yoder

Call Sign: KC9TRD
David D Ditton
9002 Hamilton Rd
Yoder IN 46798

Call Sign: N9JYP
Joseph C Hathaway
34 Red Birch Dr
Yoder IN 467989420

Call Sign: KB9OXO
Scott W Crouch
4102 S County Line Rd
Yoder IN 46798

FCC Amateur Radio Licenses in Young America

Call Sign: N9ZMW
Charlene A Henderson
Young America IN 46998

FCC Amateur Radio Licenses in Zanesville

Call Sign: KA9SBD
Jerry R Stephenson
Zanesville IN 46799